Museum

Design Museum Ghent **FRIDAY, 1 SE**

SECRET SECOND MUS

"How come I didn't know about it before?"

This stately brick building may look old, but the dusty exterior gives way to wide hallways of white marble and a collection of oil paintings dating back to the 15th century. Located behind the Design Museum, this unnamed museum is the secret of a few people who can navigate their way through the surrounding laneways. A routine stop in the cultural landscape for those who know how to find it, the old building is news to most people, including many who consider themselves insiders. "It's amazing, but how come I didn't know about it before?" Say frustrated cultural workers, "their collection of Italian and Flemish paintings is very important".

The building is an odd combination of a Flemish Renaissance exterior and Greek Revival interior housing a historical collection featuring marble statues and Italian and Flemish painting. The museum also holds a mysterious programme of events and talks often held in the very early hours of the morning. Finding the museum on your own can be a recipe for disorientation. Located west of the Design Museum through a seemingly impossible sequence of laneways, the museum's hours are subject to fluctuation. Approach with caution if entering not by invitation.

Alvar Aalto & Émile Gallé smashed in

Dead Textile Tycoon with sense of humour

Dreams

TEMBER 2017

EUM SURFACES

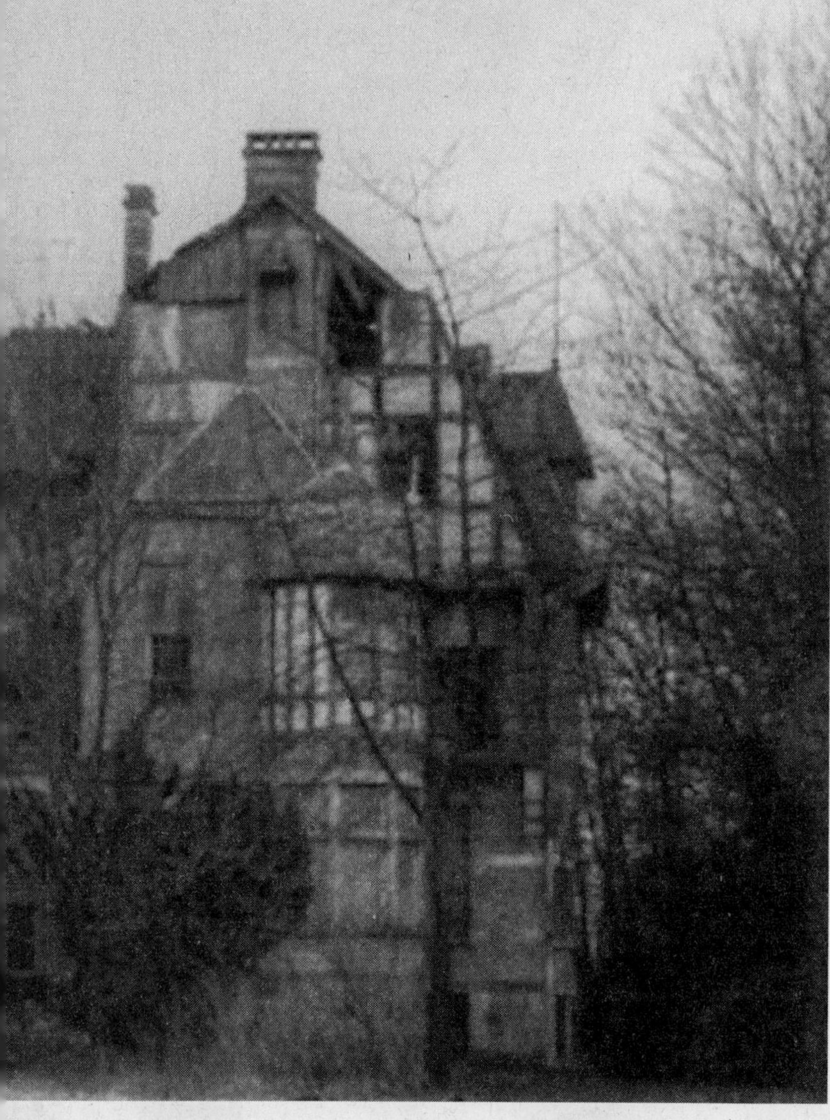

Collection hidden under football stadium seats

Around 20,000 works in the collection of the Design Museum are being stored under the seats of an undisclosed football stadium. Special atmospheric temperature and light levels create conditions under which the invaluable collection will not degrade. There are plans for future developments that include the installation of a glass ceiling/floor, so that fans can look down at the collection from their seats during boring games. It is all part of a move by the museum to get more varied crowds interested in the museum.

Crowds, crowds, crowds, crowds and more crowds!

The museum is packed solid with people, most of them drunk, and the group leaders are starting to blame each other. A tour of carpentry students interested in joinery have taken apart a chair, the guards cannot reach them, the leader of a group of retirees has picked up a curved steel leg dropped by the students and is fencing them out of the building shouting it's booked. The crowd is so dense that no one can move and the guards can't even see the works anymore and can only assess the damage by means of the smashing, cracking and tearing noises. They shout, but everyone is already shouting and no one can hear anyone.

Works turned around to reveal beautiful backsides

Ingenuity draws visitors

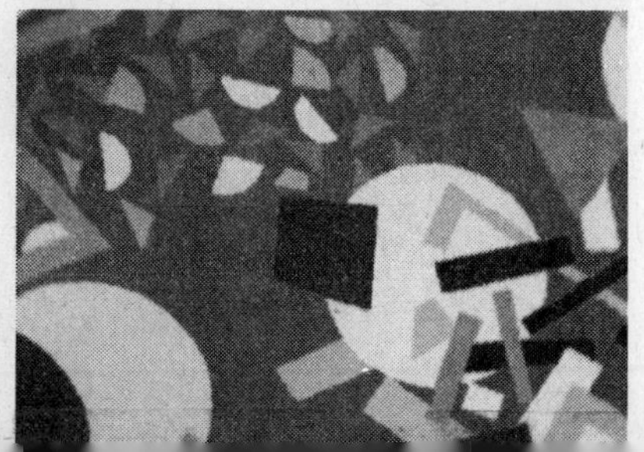

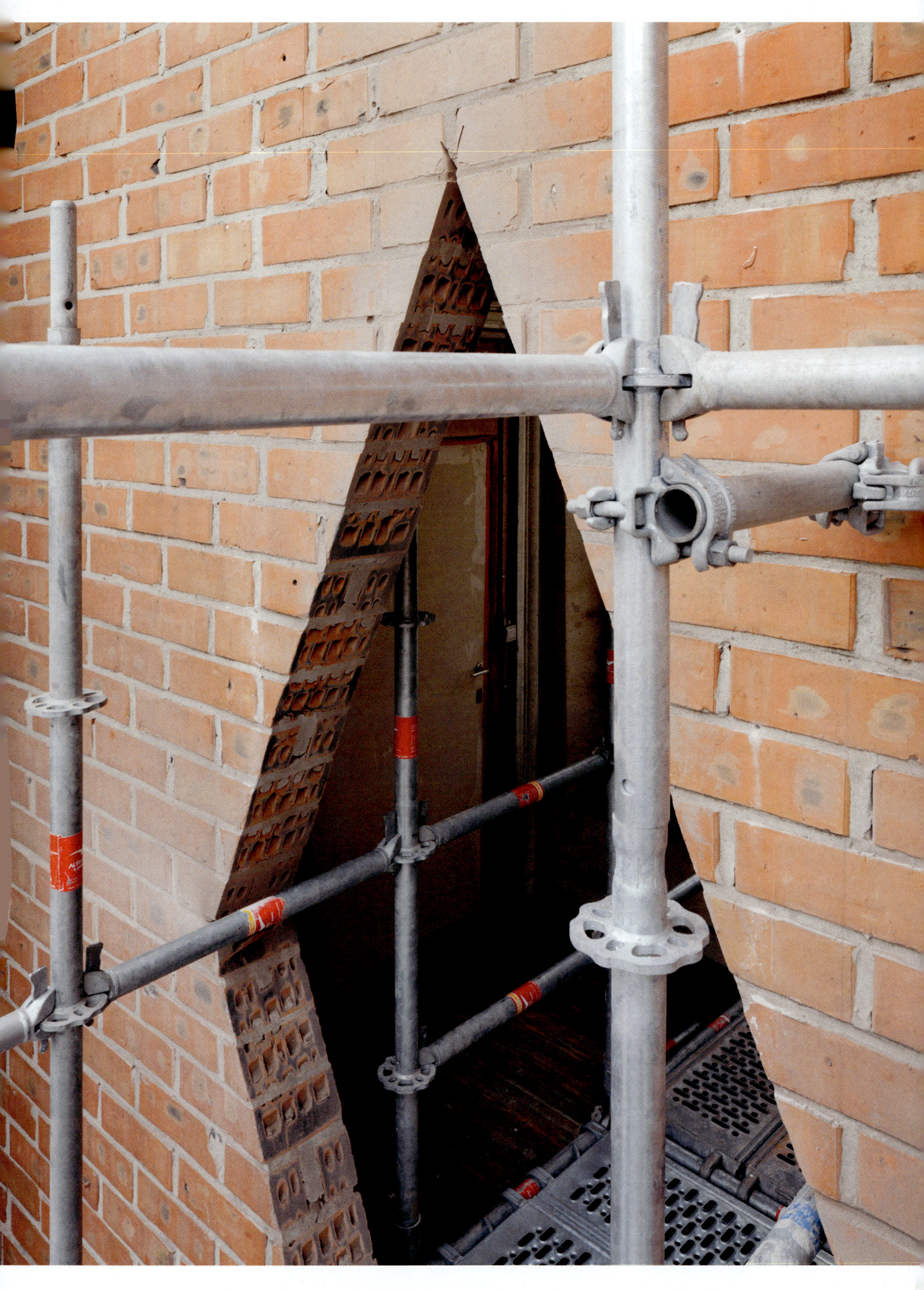

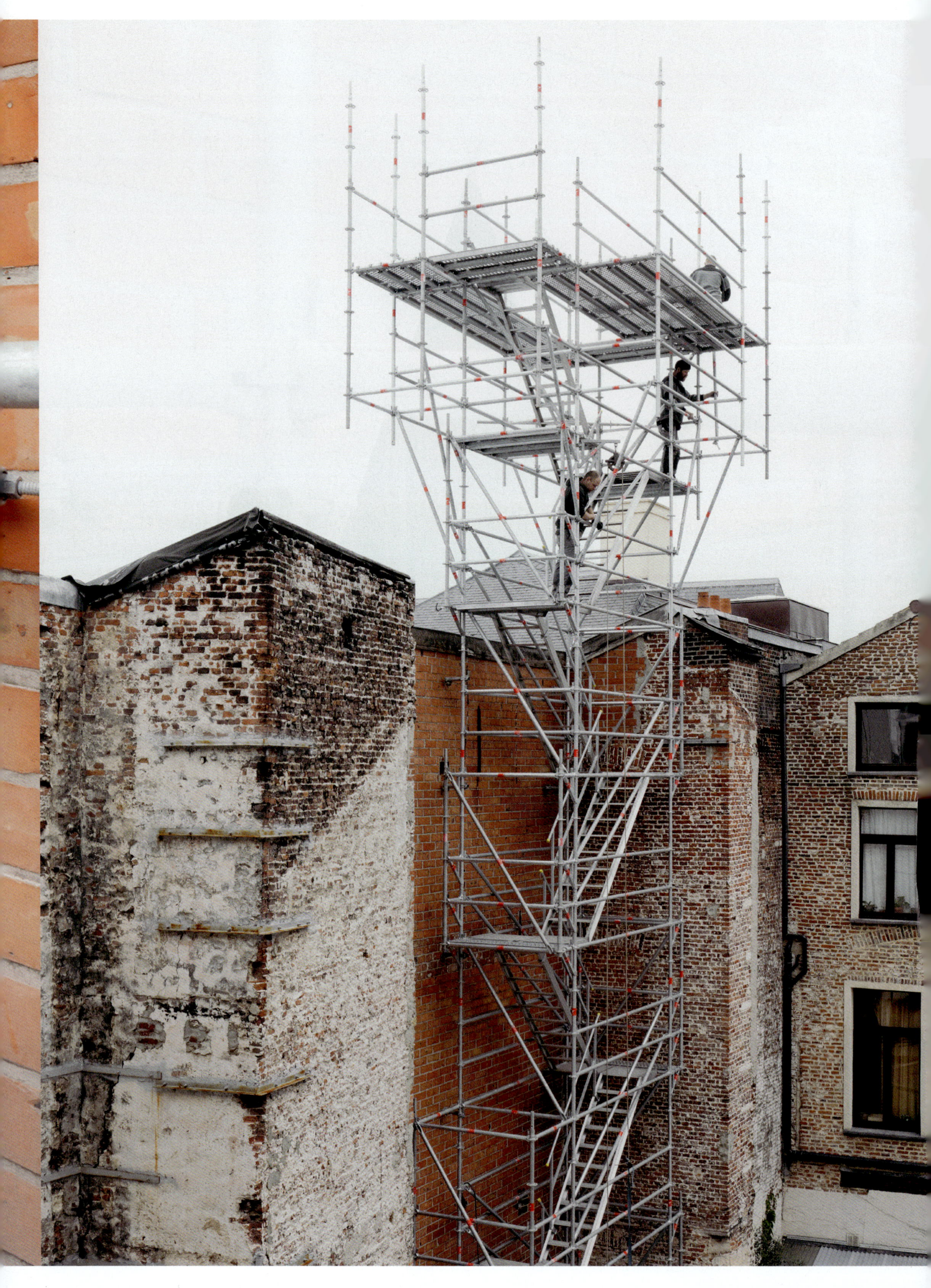

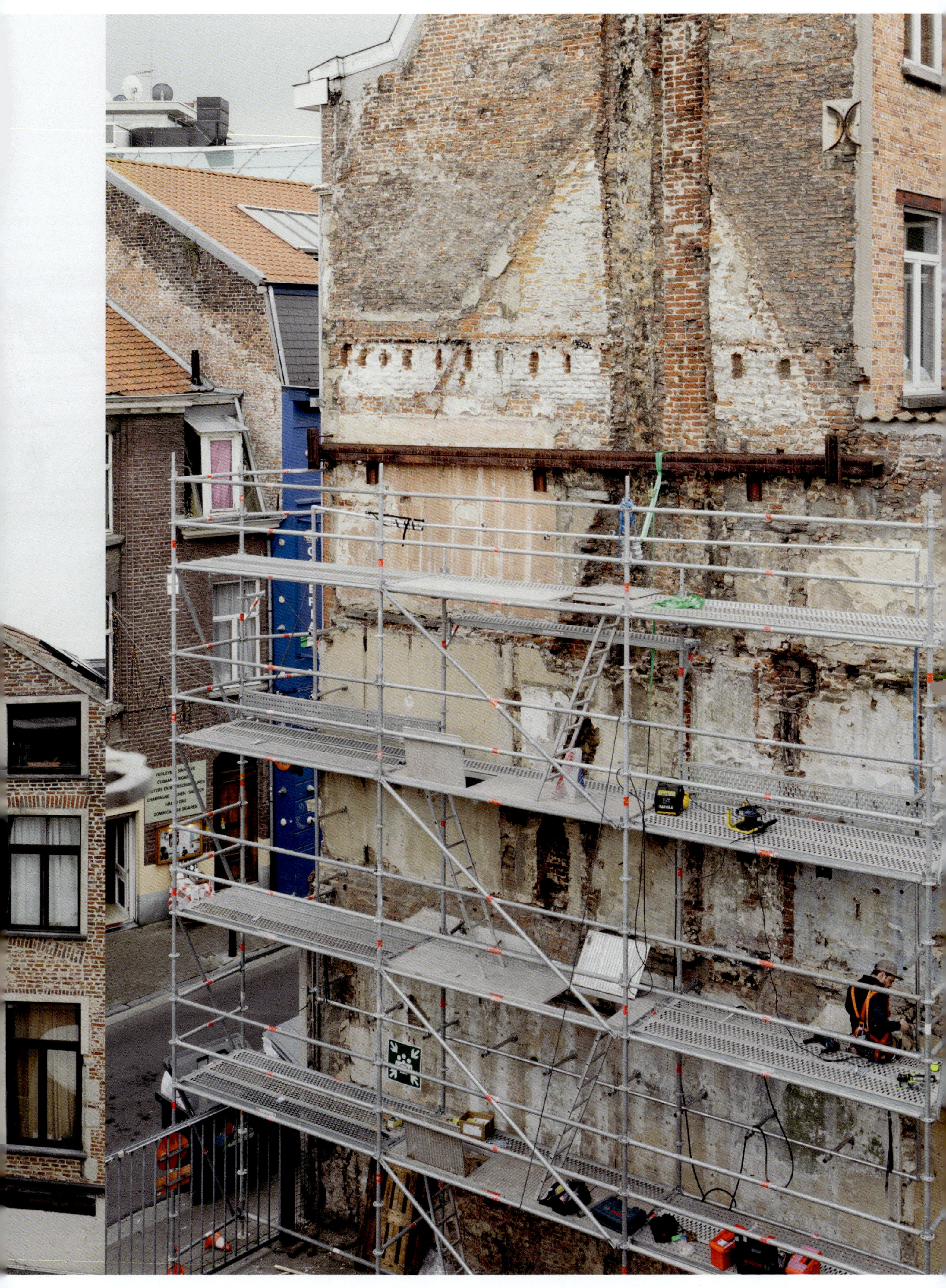

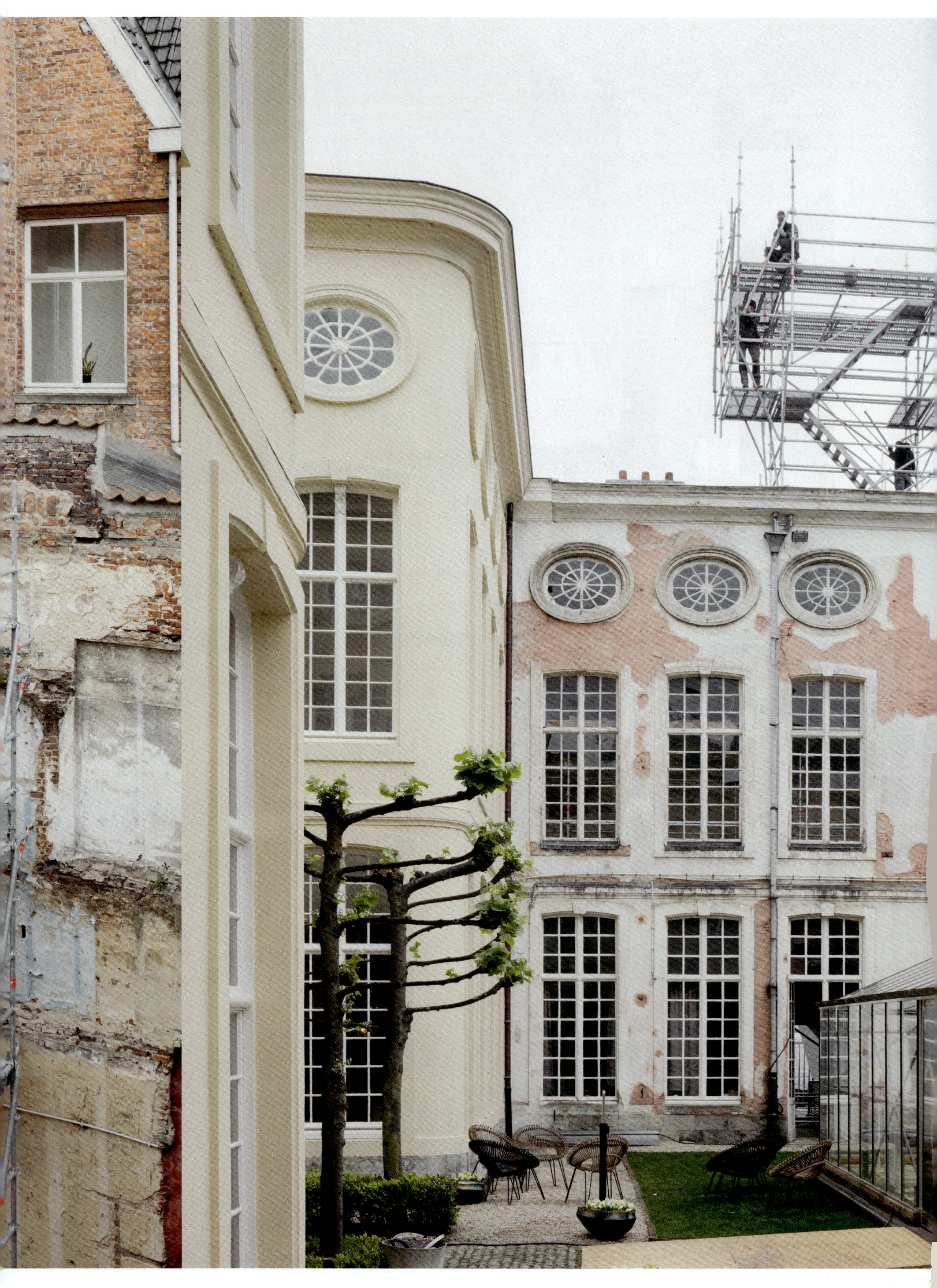

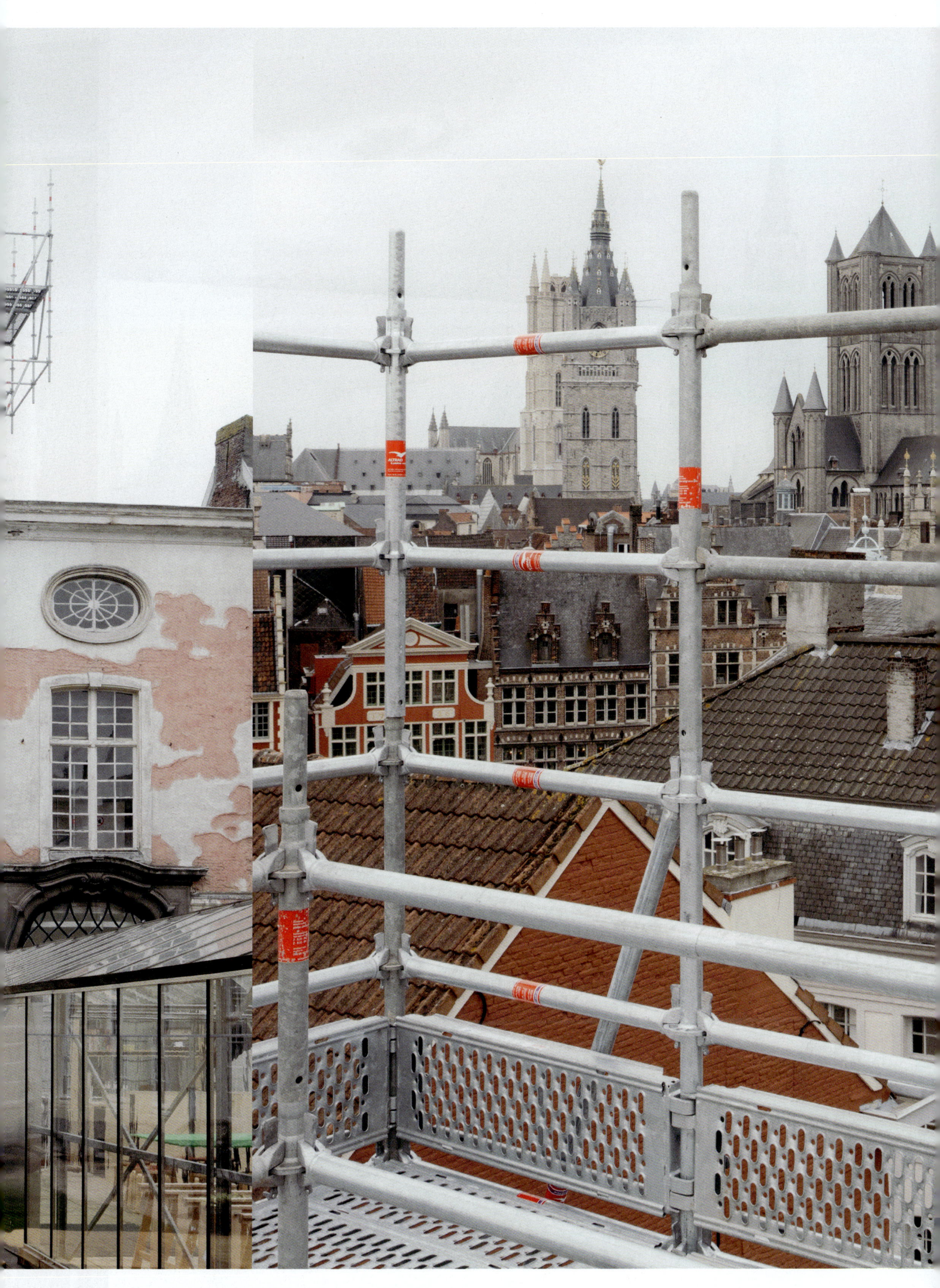

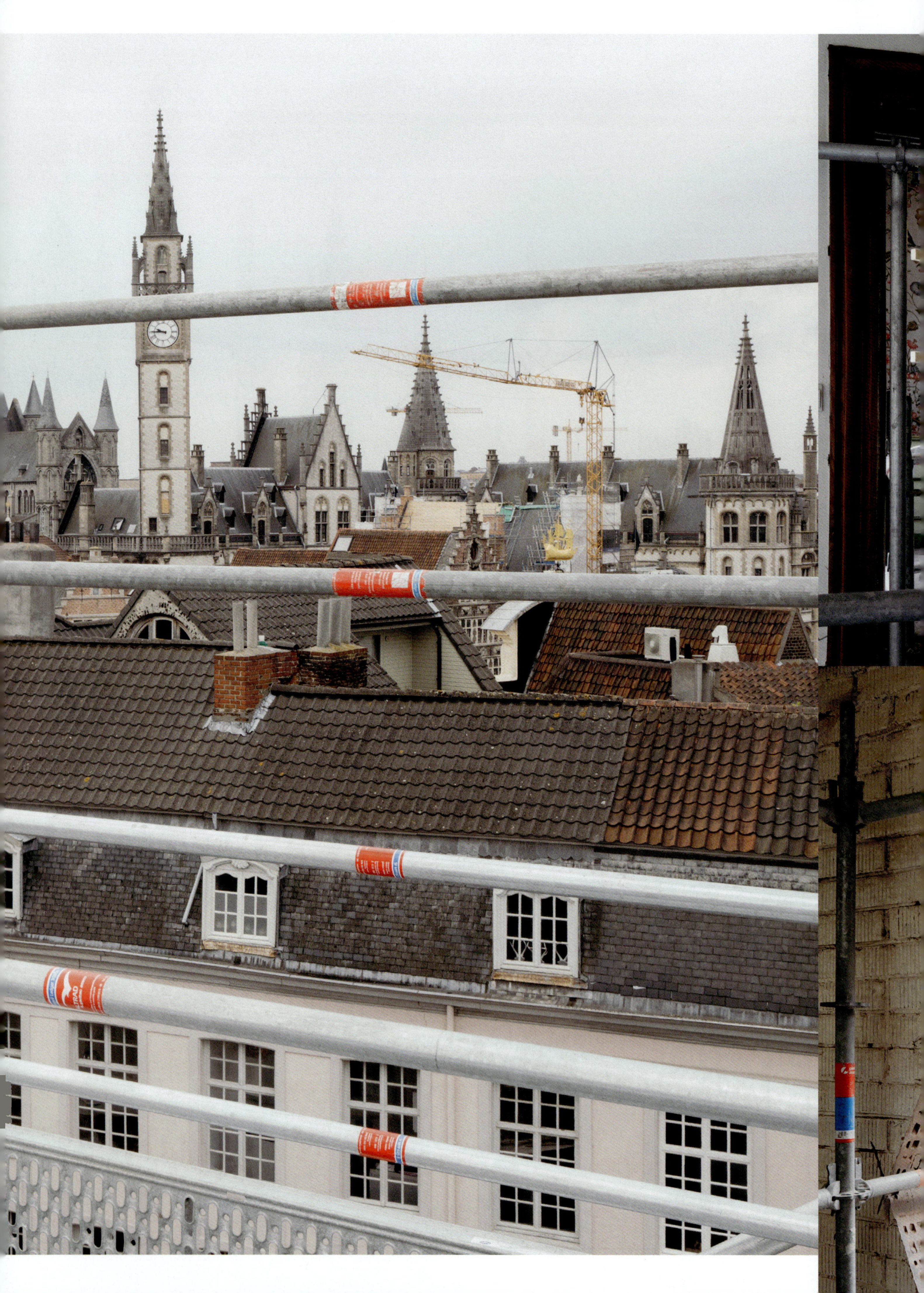

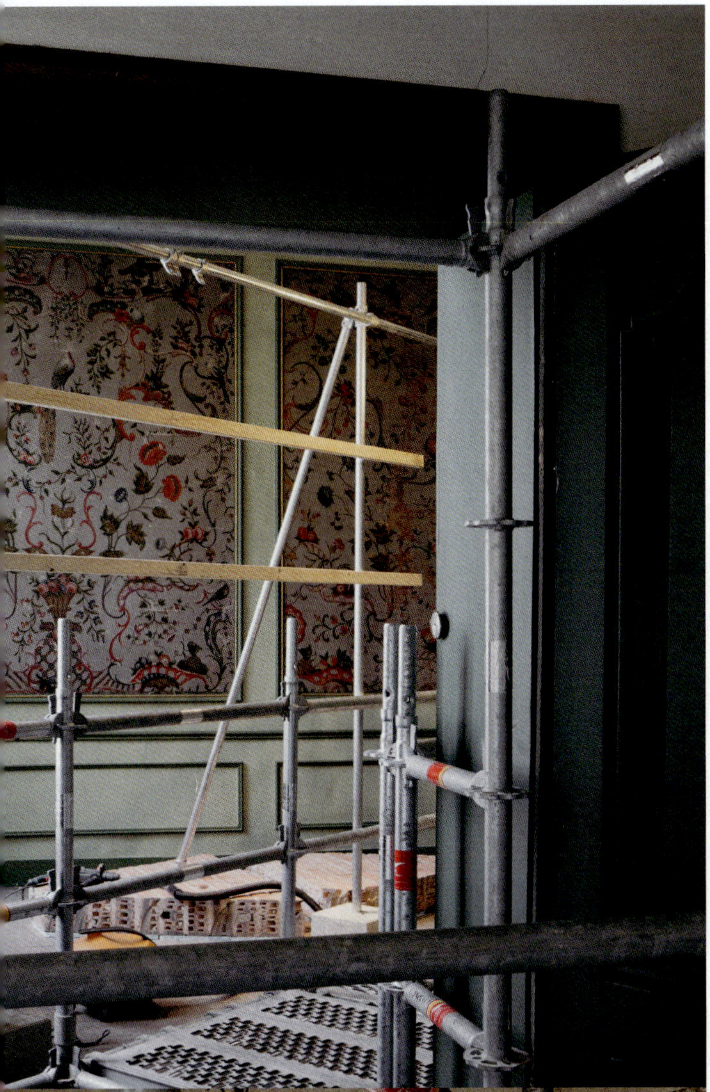

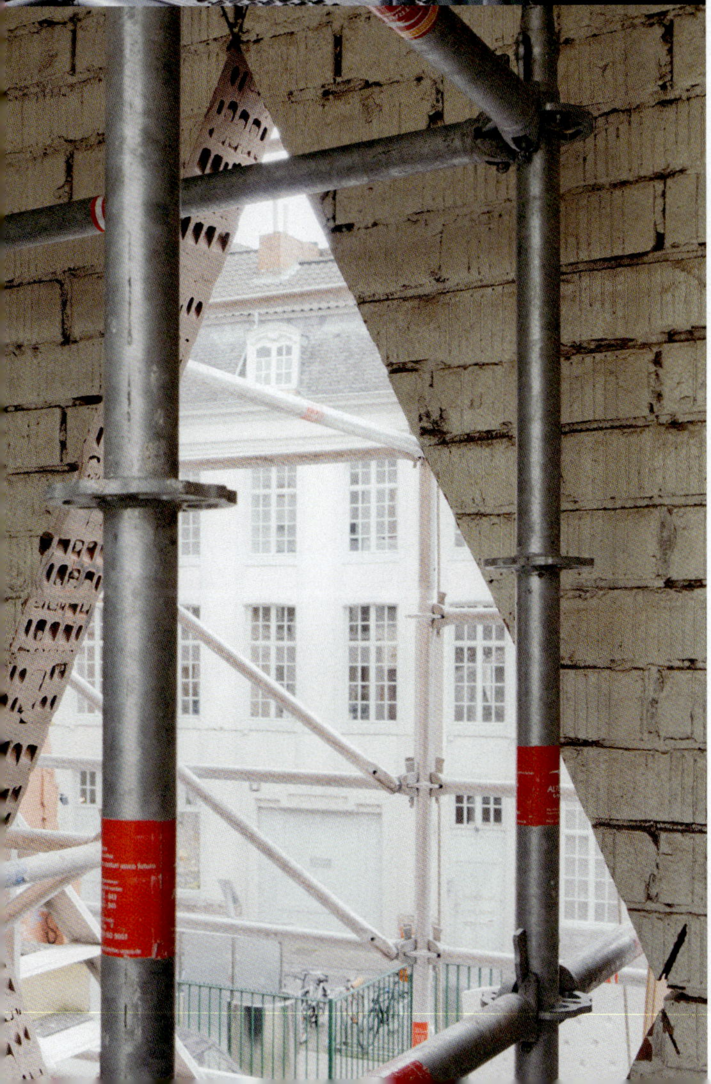

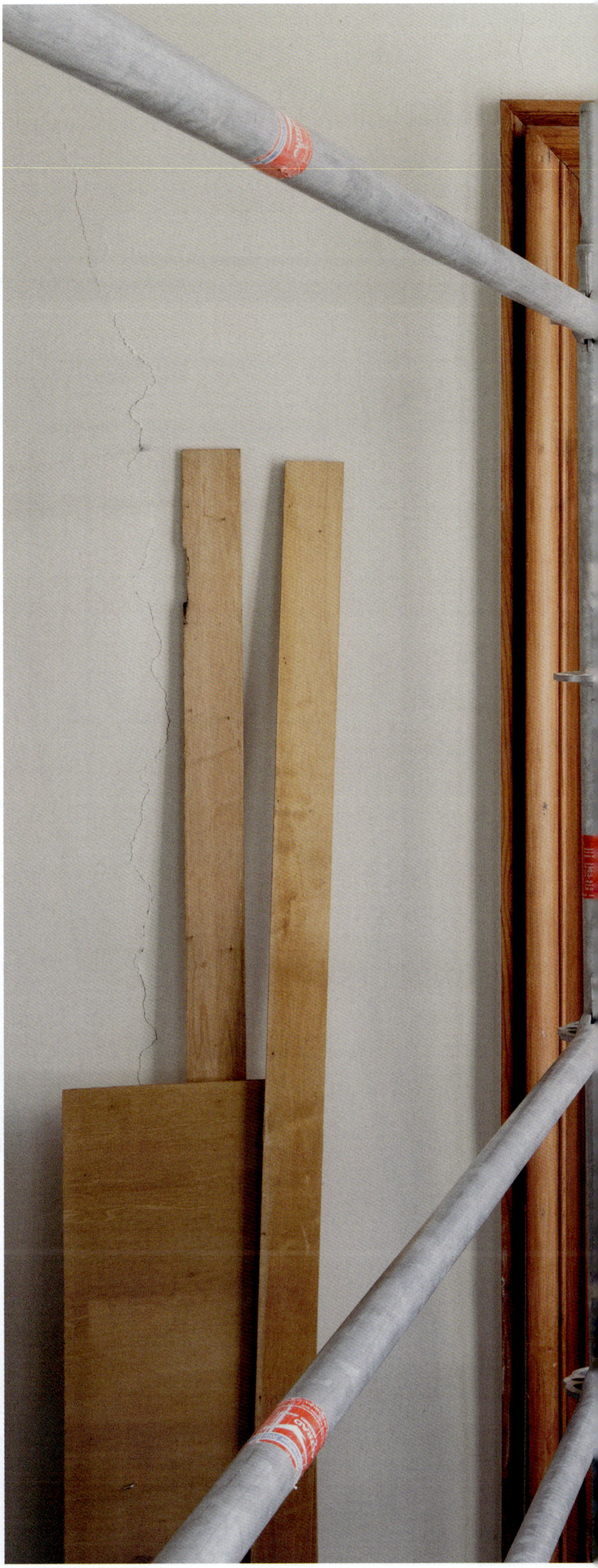

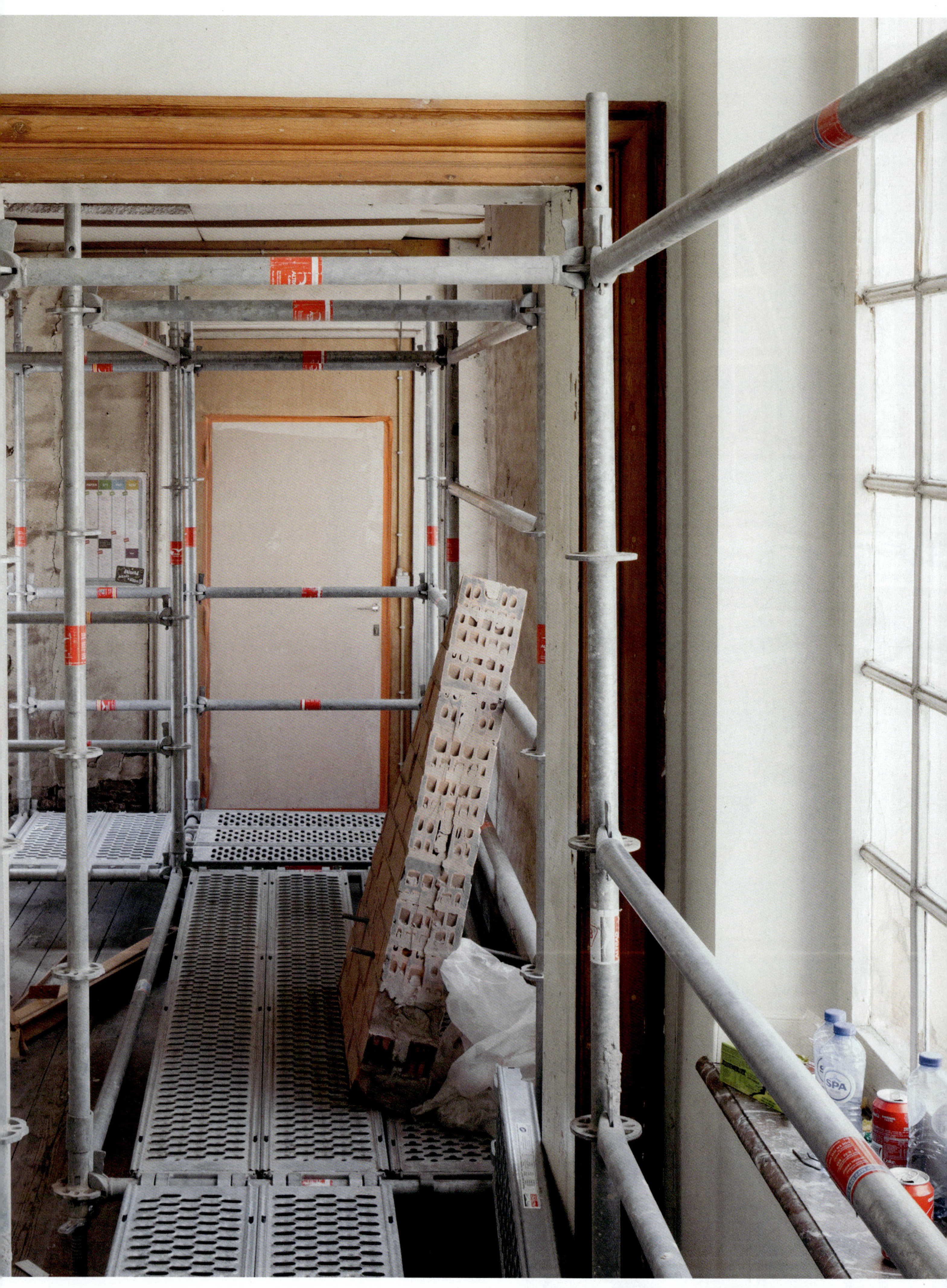
SPA

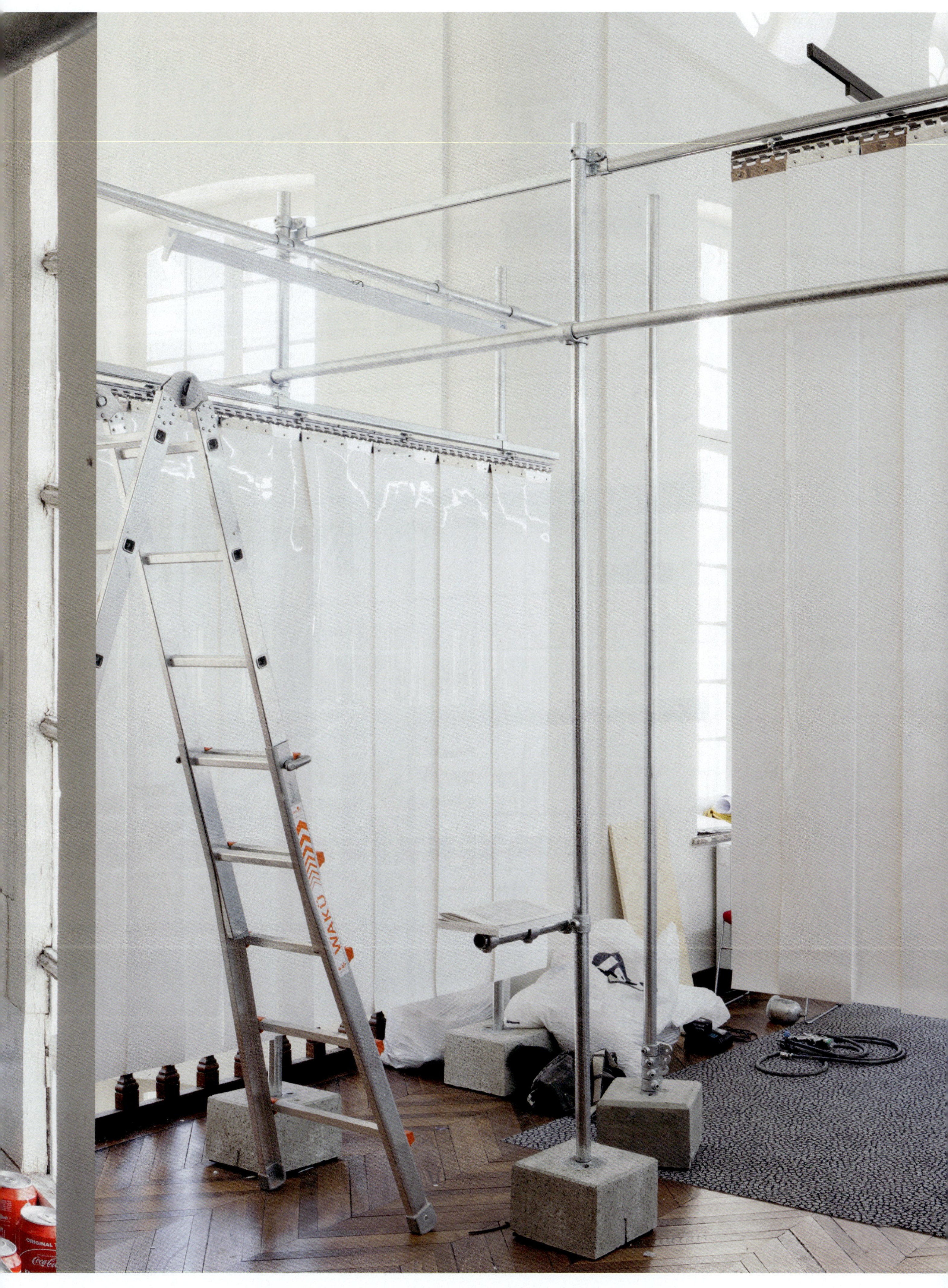
WAKO

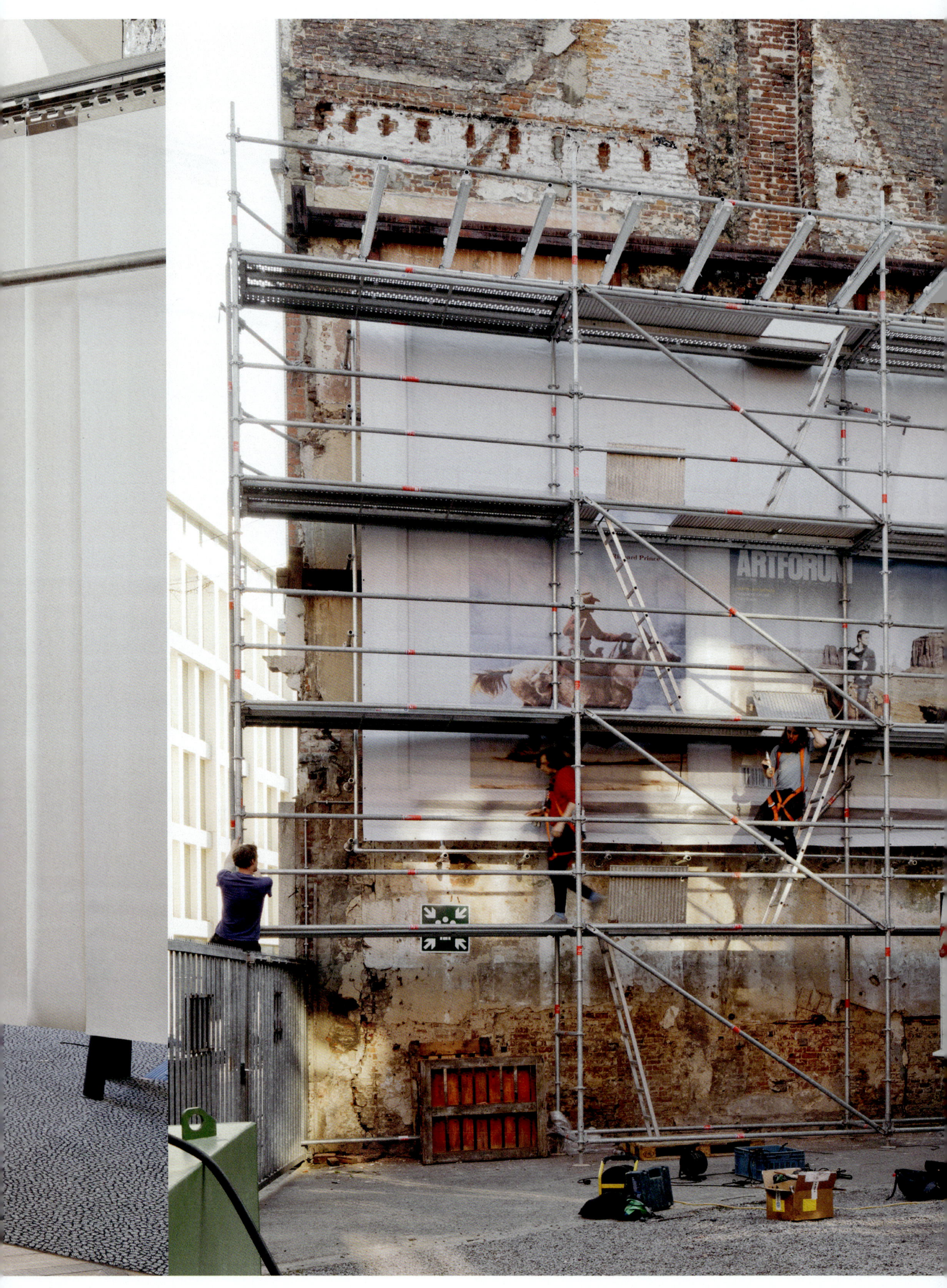

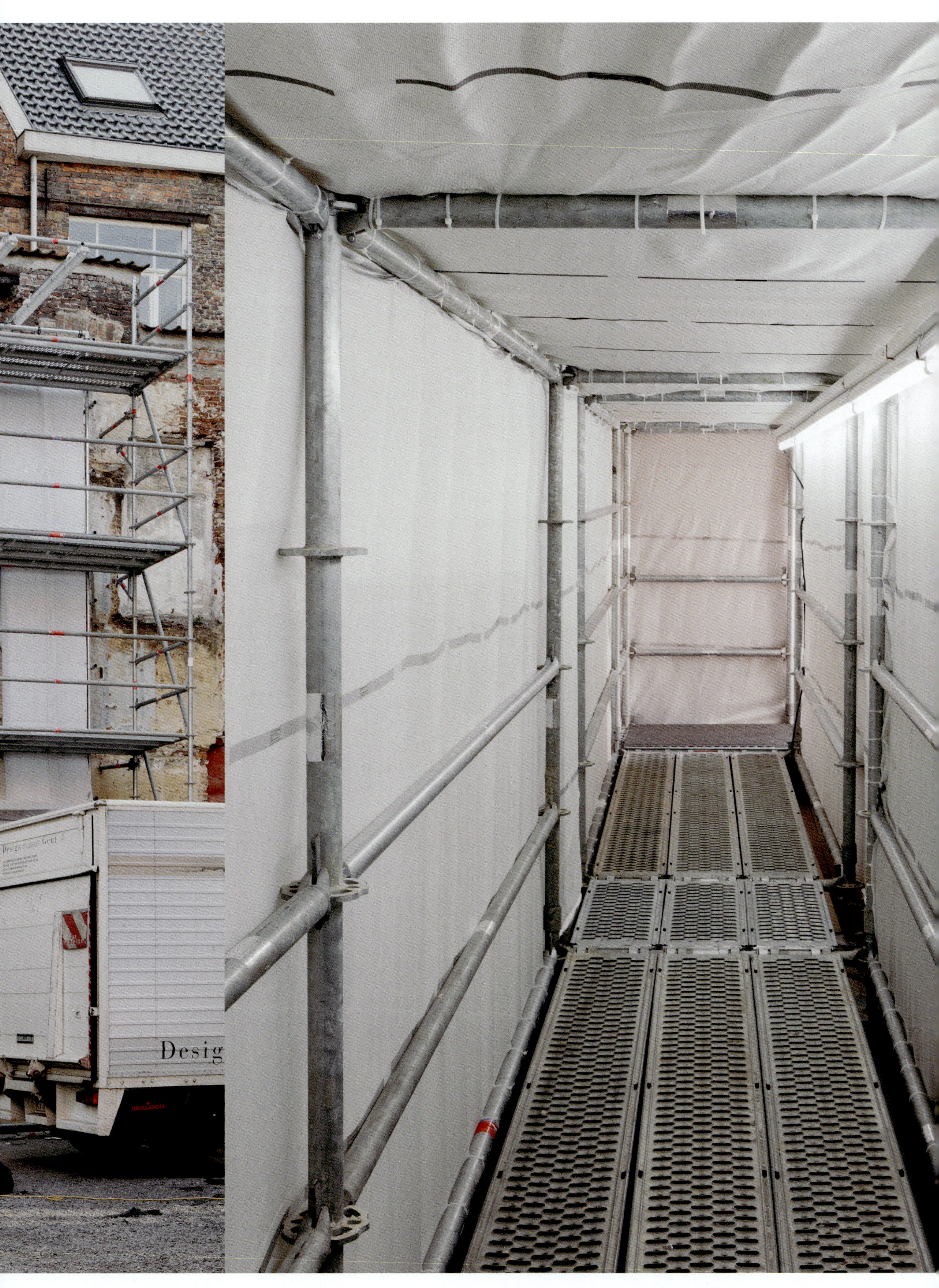
Design museum Gent
Desig
DHOLLANDIA

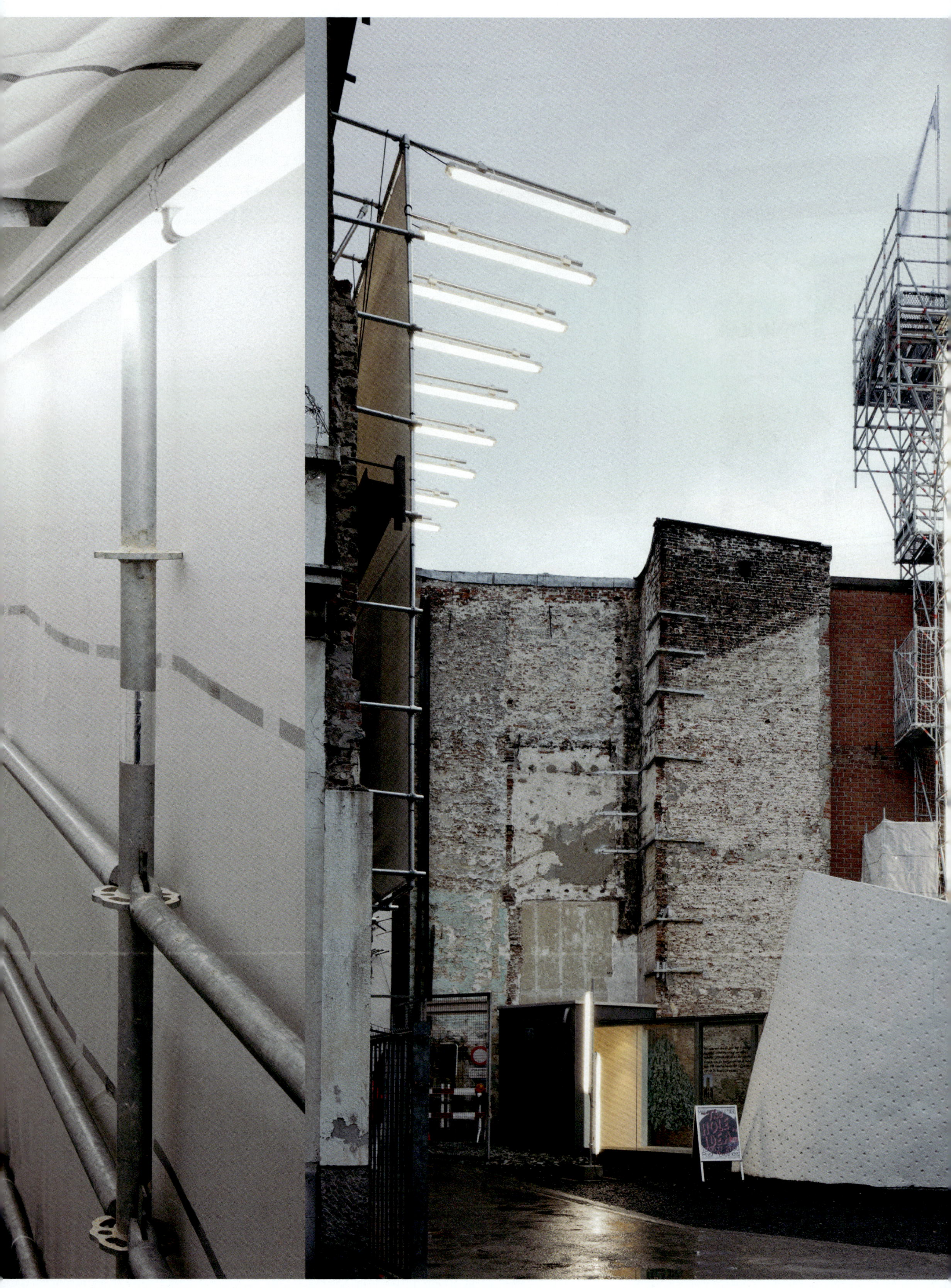

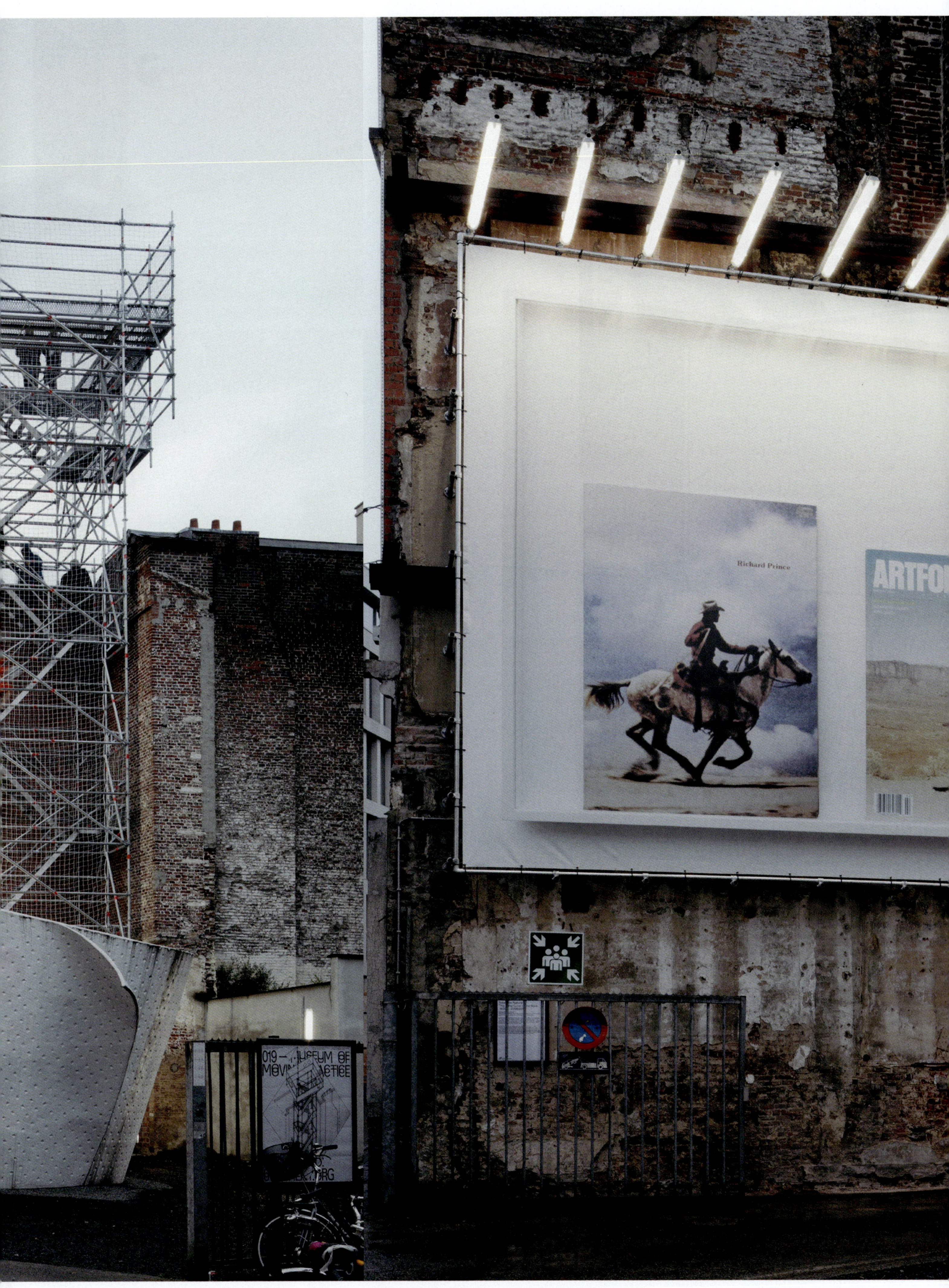

MORITZ KÜNG, *Selección Natural - This is the Cover of the Book, Richard Prince / Martin Kippenberg*, May 2017

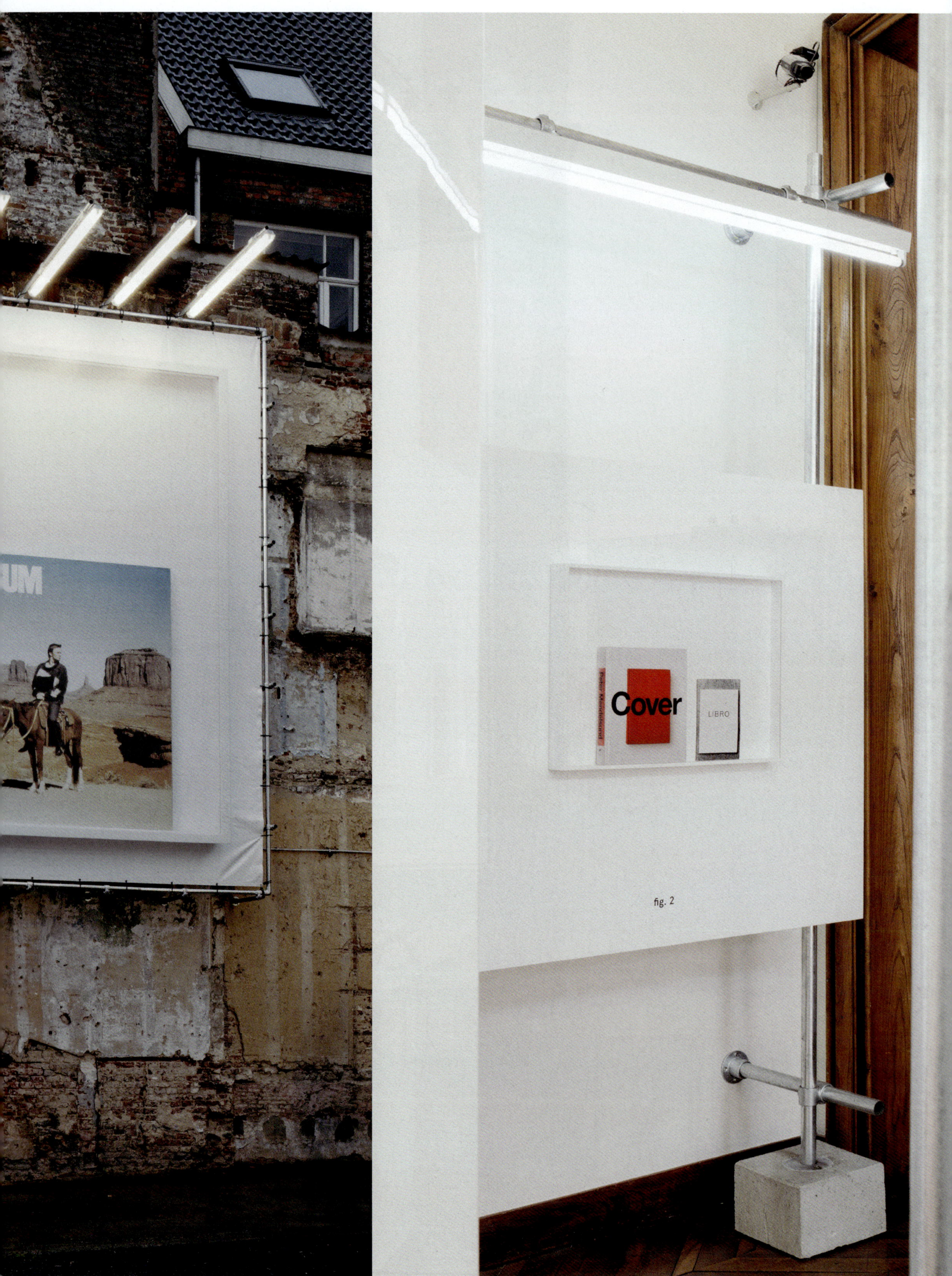

MORITZ KÜNG, *Selección Natural - This is the Cover of the Book*, May 2017

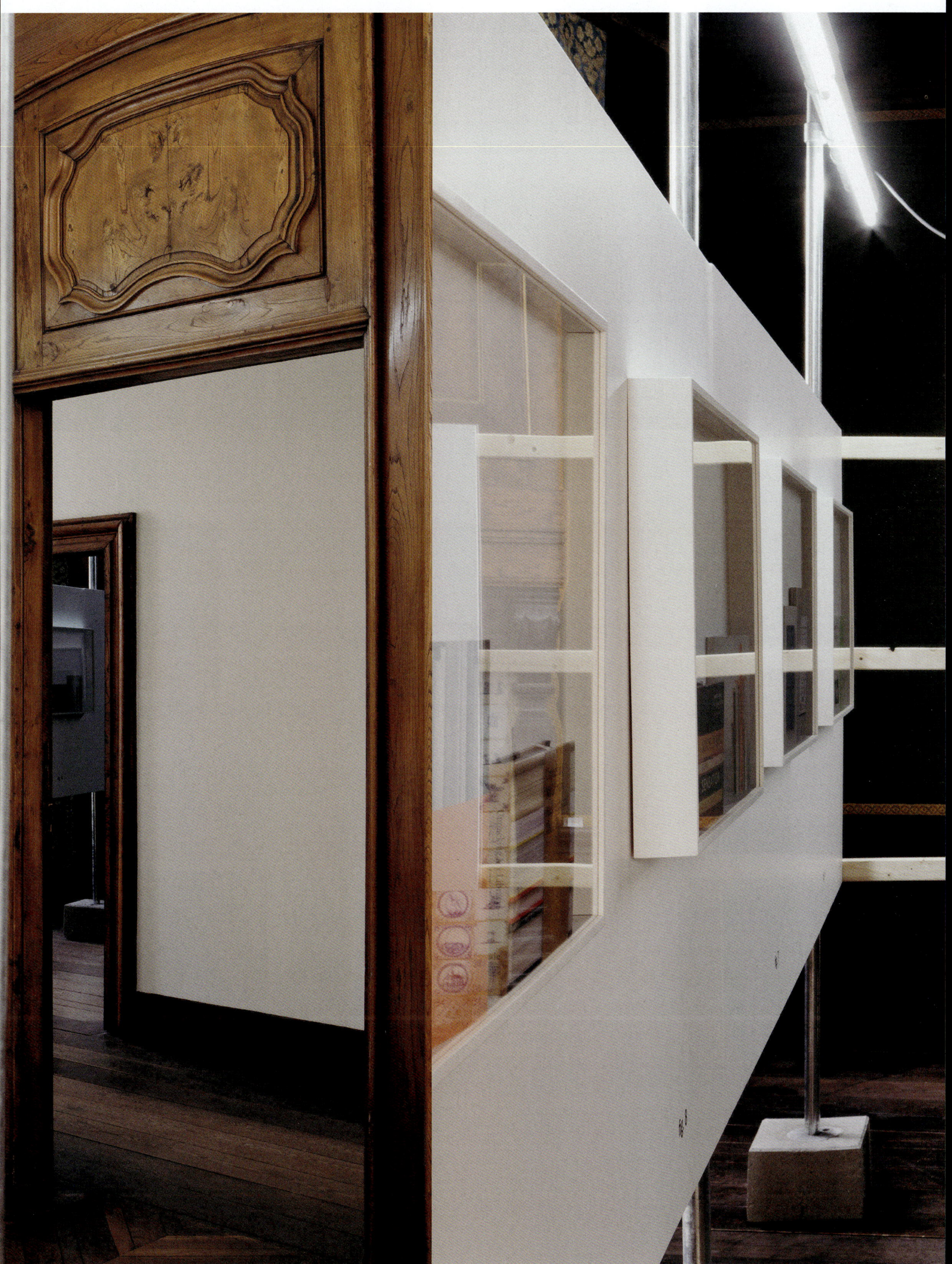

MORITZ KÜNG, *Selección Natural - This is the Cover of the Book*, May 2017

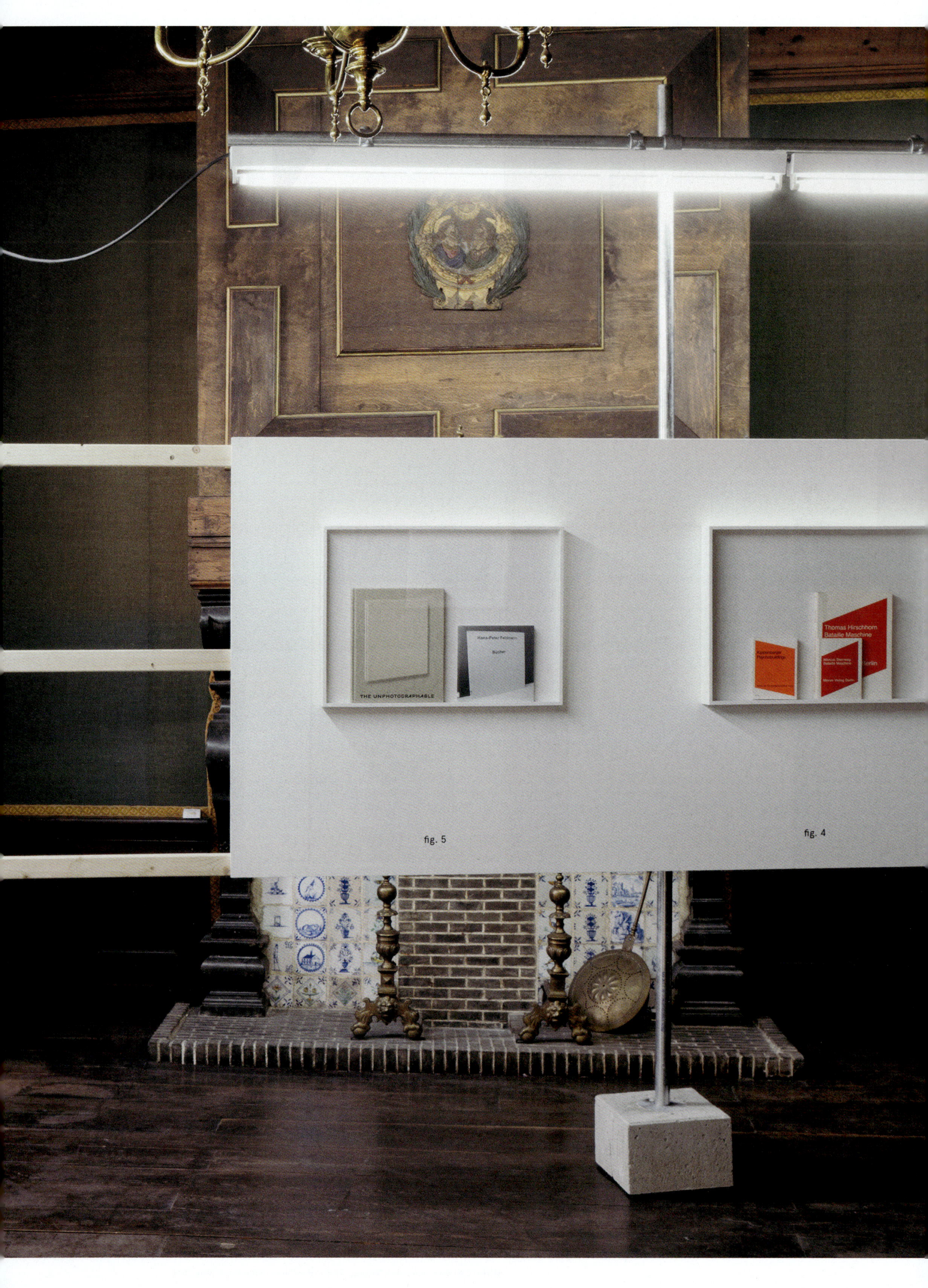
THE UNPHOTOGRAPHABLE
Hans-Peter Feldmann
Bücher
Thomas Hirschhorn
Bataille Maschine
Merve Verlag Berlin
fig. 5
fig. 4

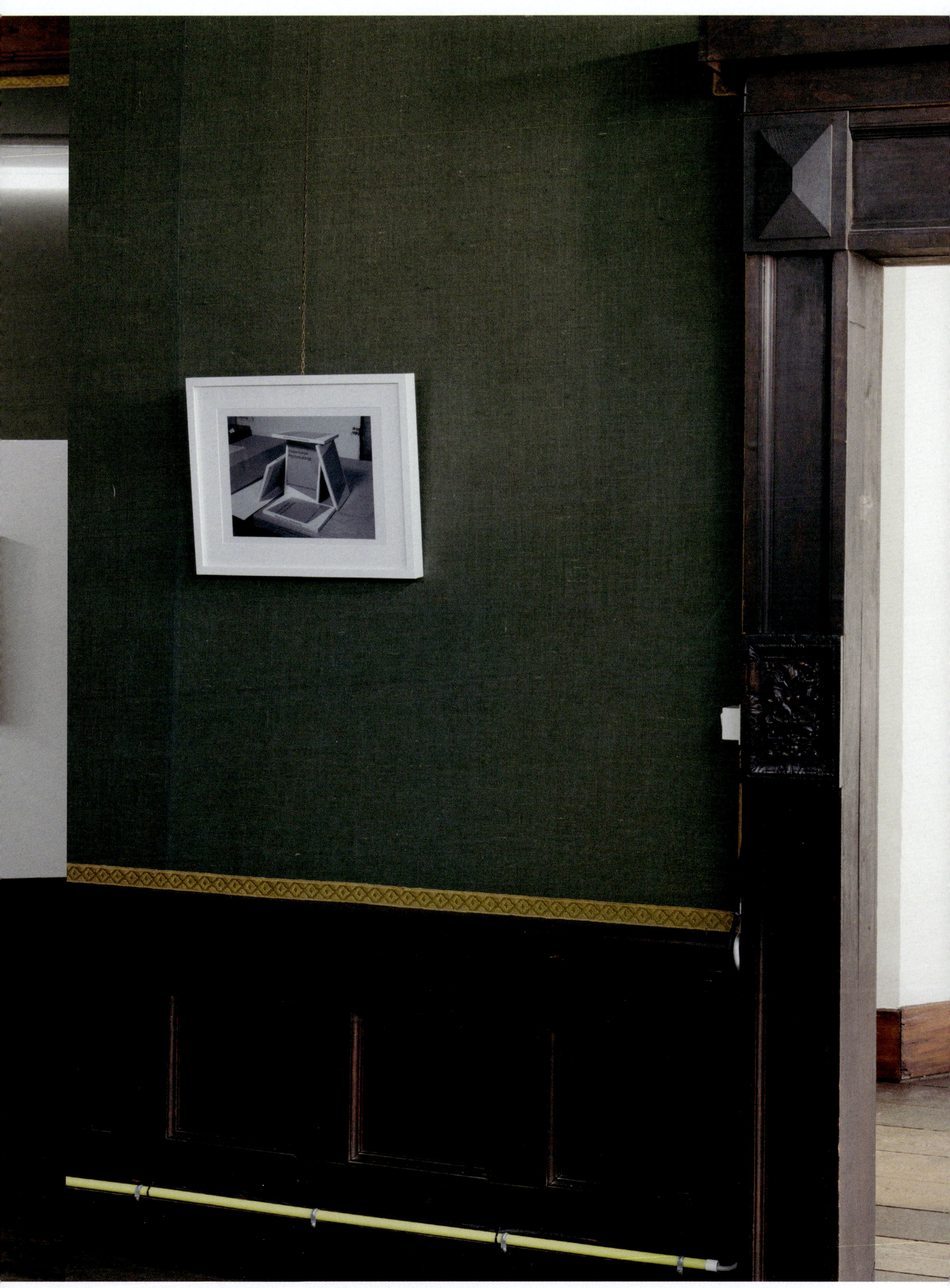

DEREK SULLIVAN, *Persistent Huts*, in collaboration with *Tatjana Pieters Gallery*, June 2017

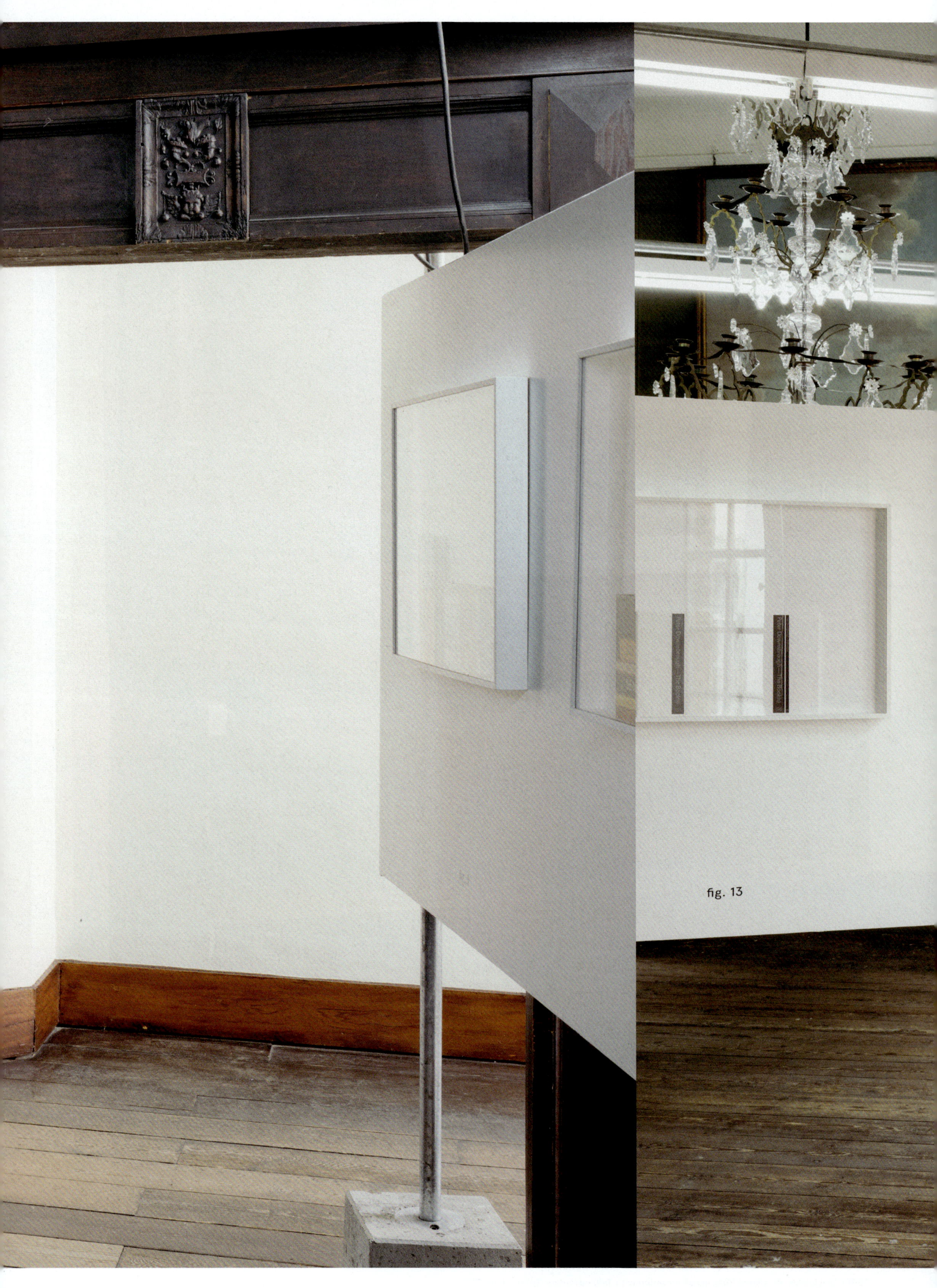

fig. 13

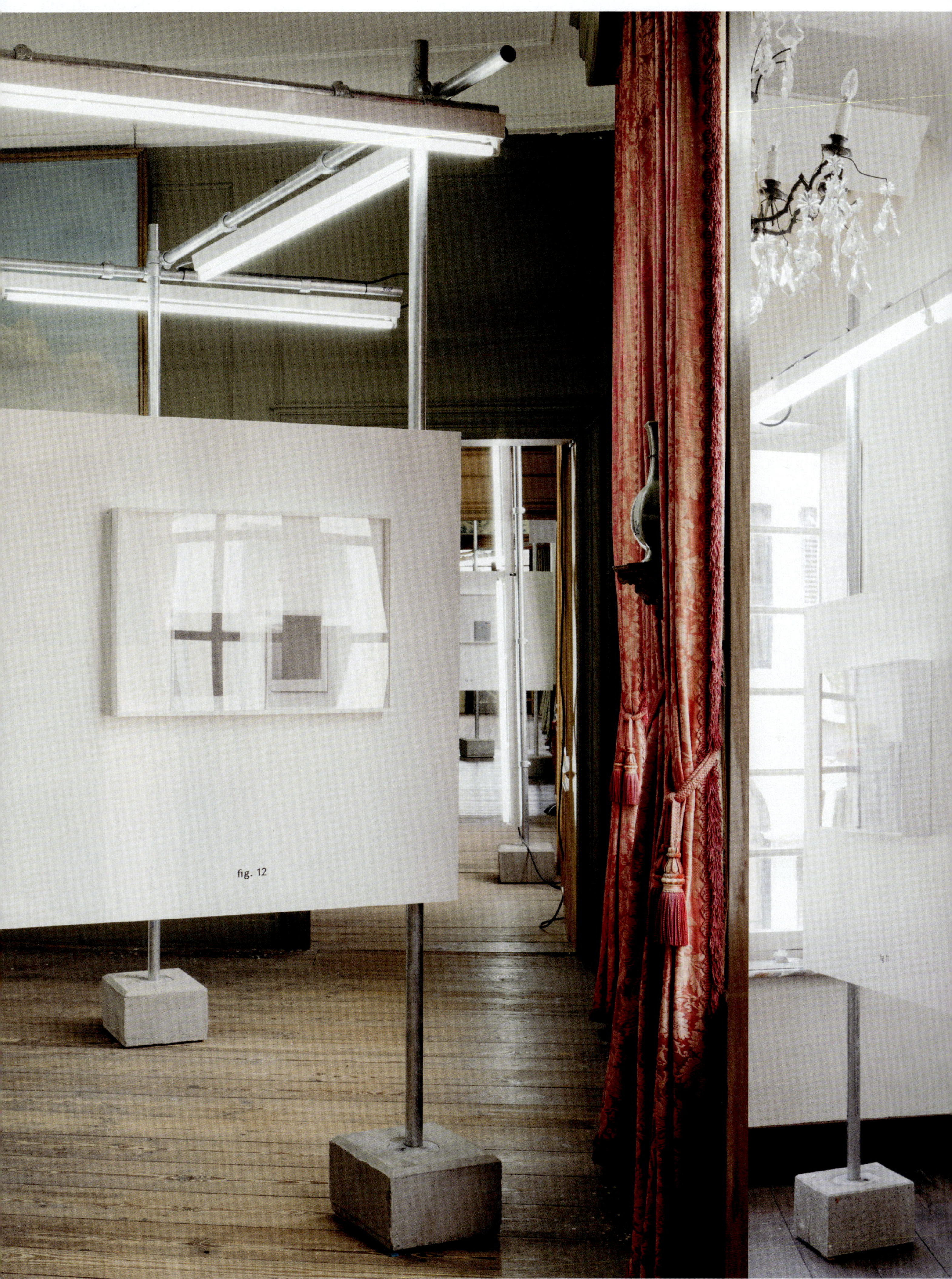

MORITZ KÜNG, *Selección Natural - This is the Cover of the Book*, May 2017

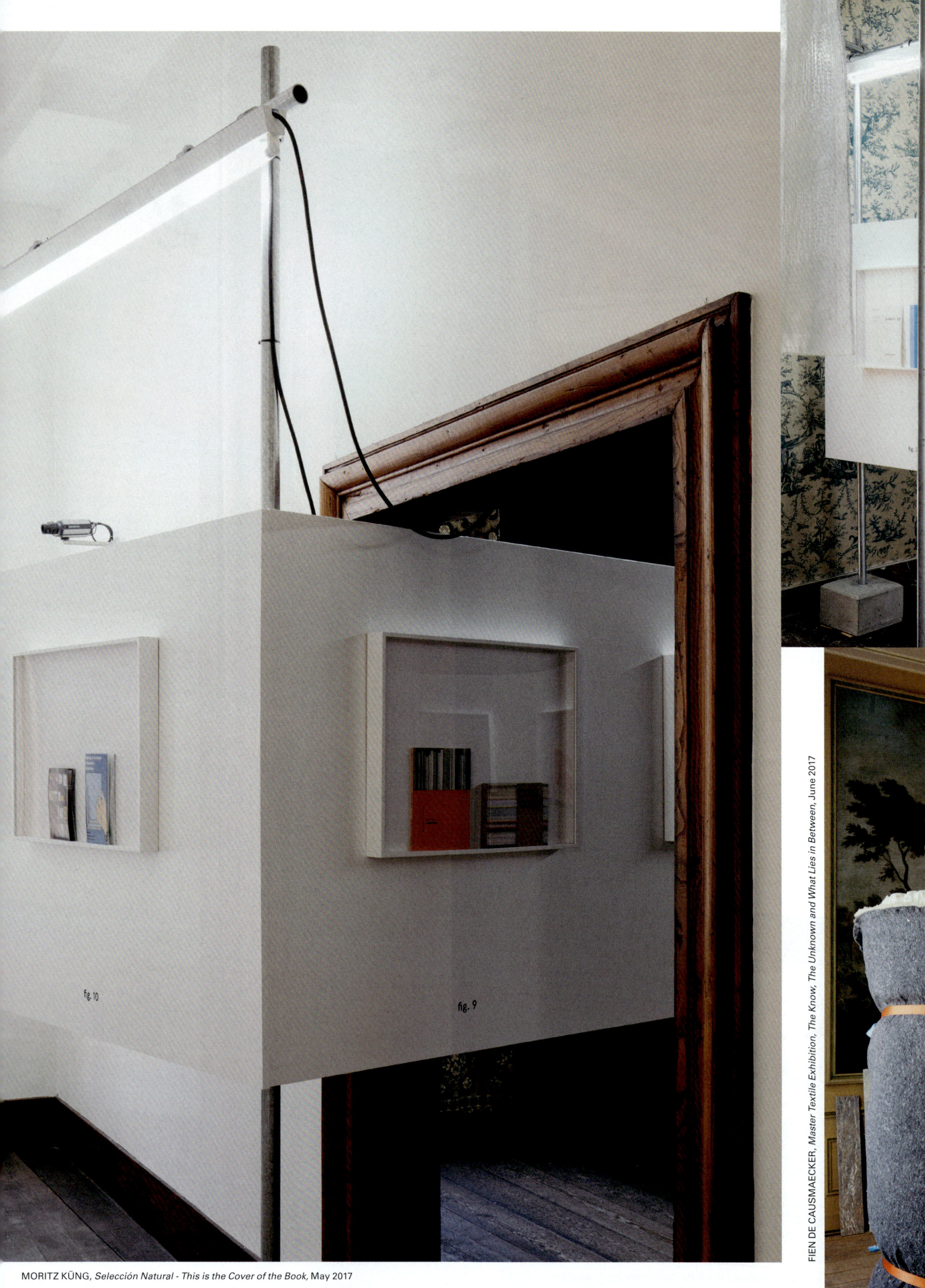

FIEN DE CAUSMAECKER, *Master Textile Exhibition, The Know, The Unknown and What Lies in Between*, June 2017

MORITZ KÜNG, *Selección Natural - This is the Cover of the Book*, May 2017

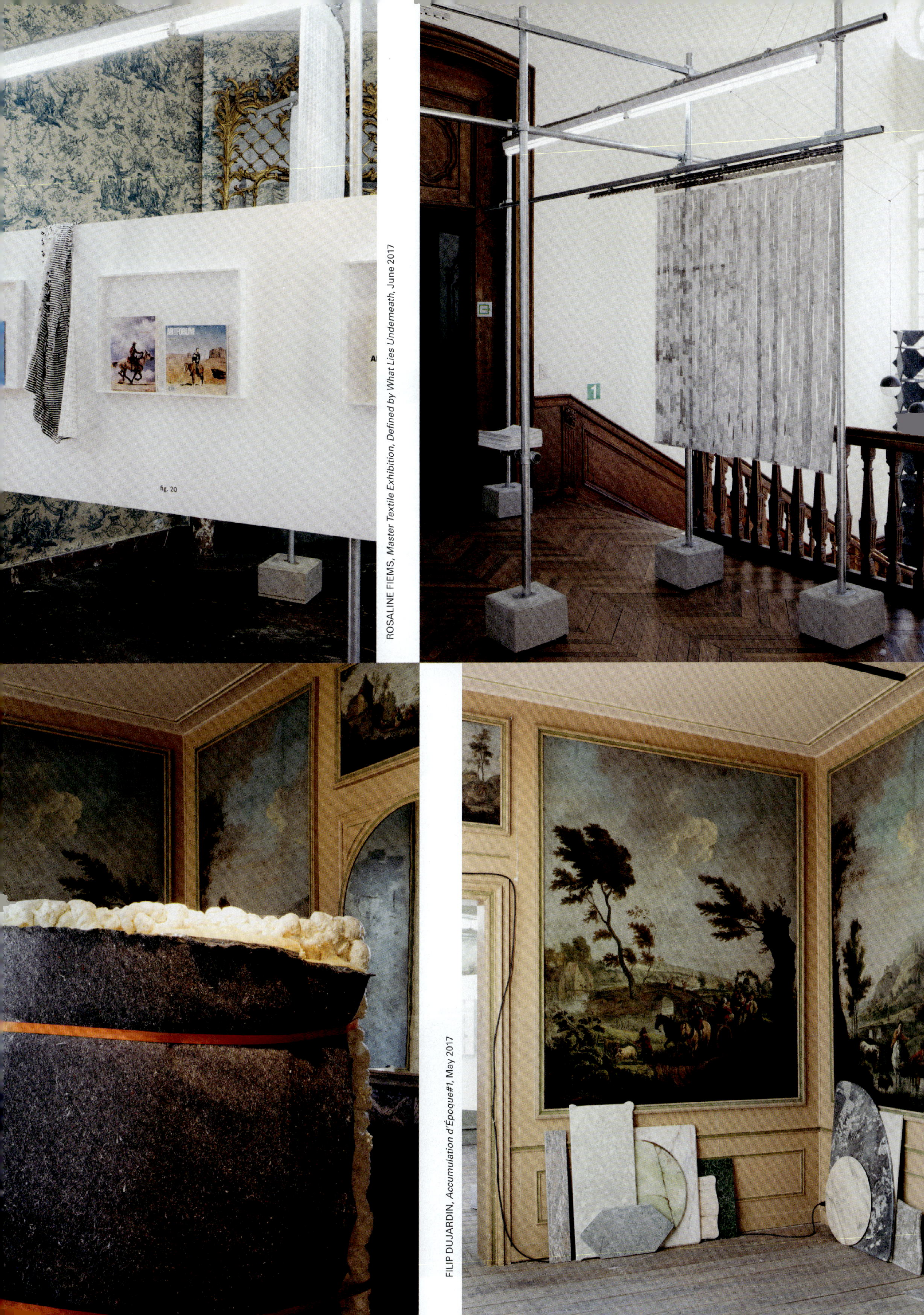

ROSALINE FIEMS, *Master Textile Exhibition, Defined by What Lies Underneath*, June 2017

FILIP DUJARDIN, *Accumulation d'Époque#1*, May 2017

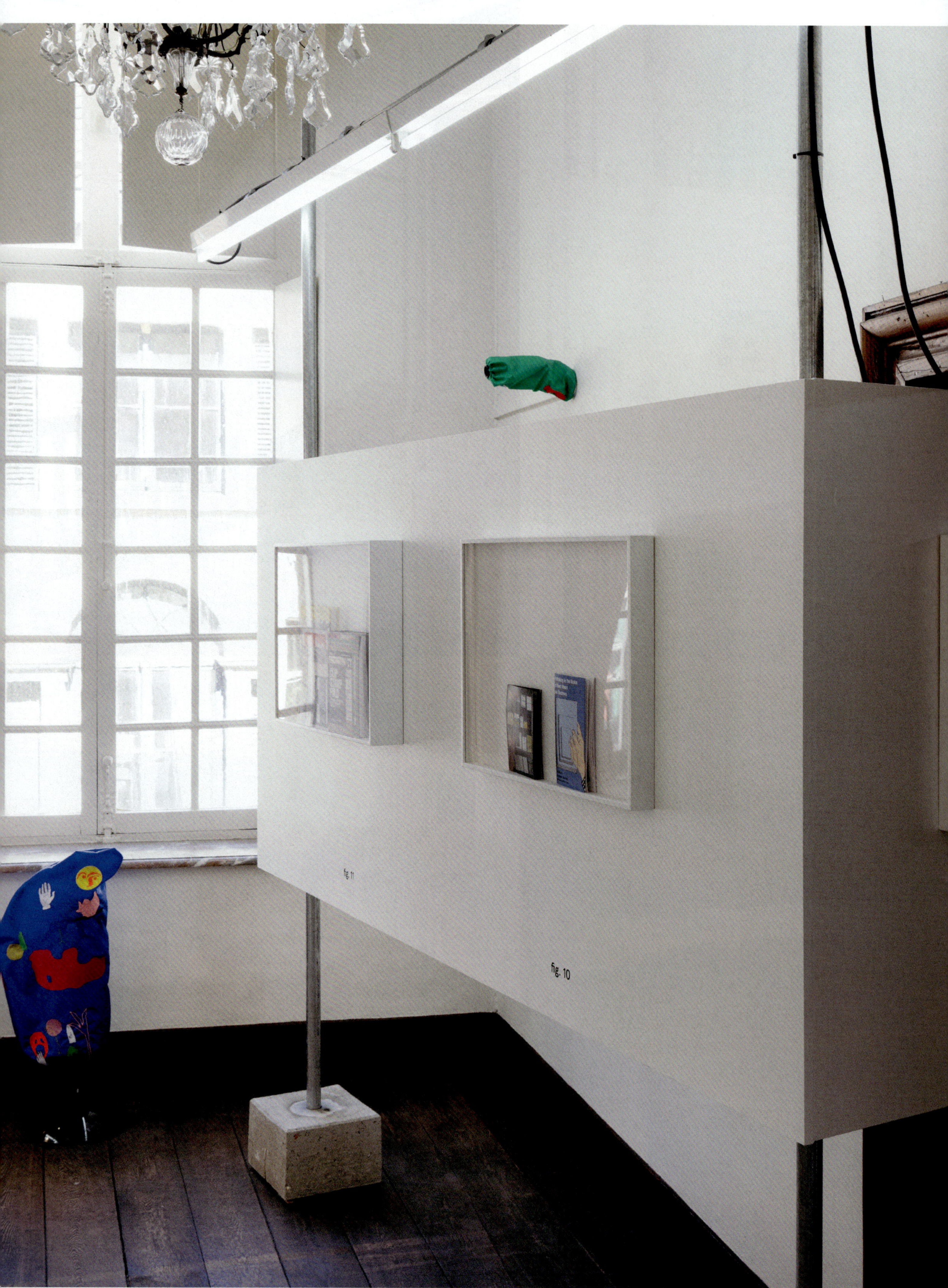

CHARLOTTE STUBY, *Master Textile Exhibition, Camera (cover), Fire Extinguisher (cover)*, June 2017

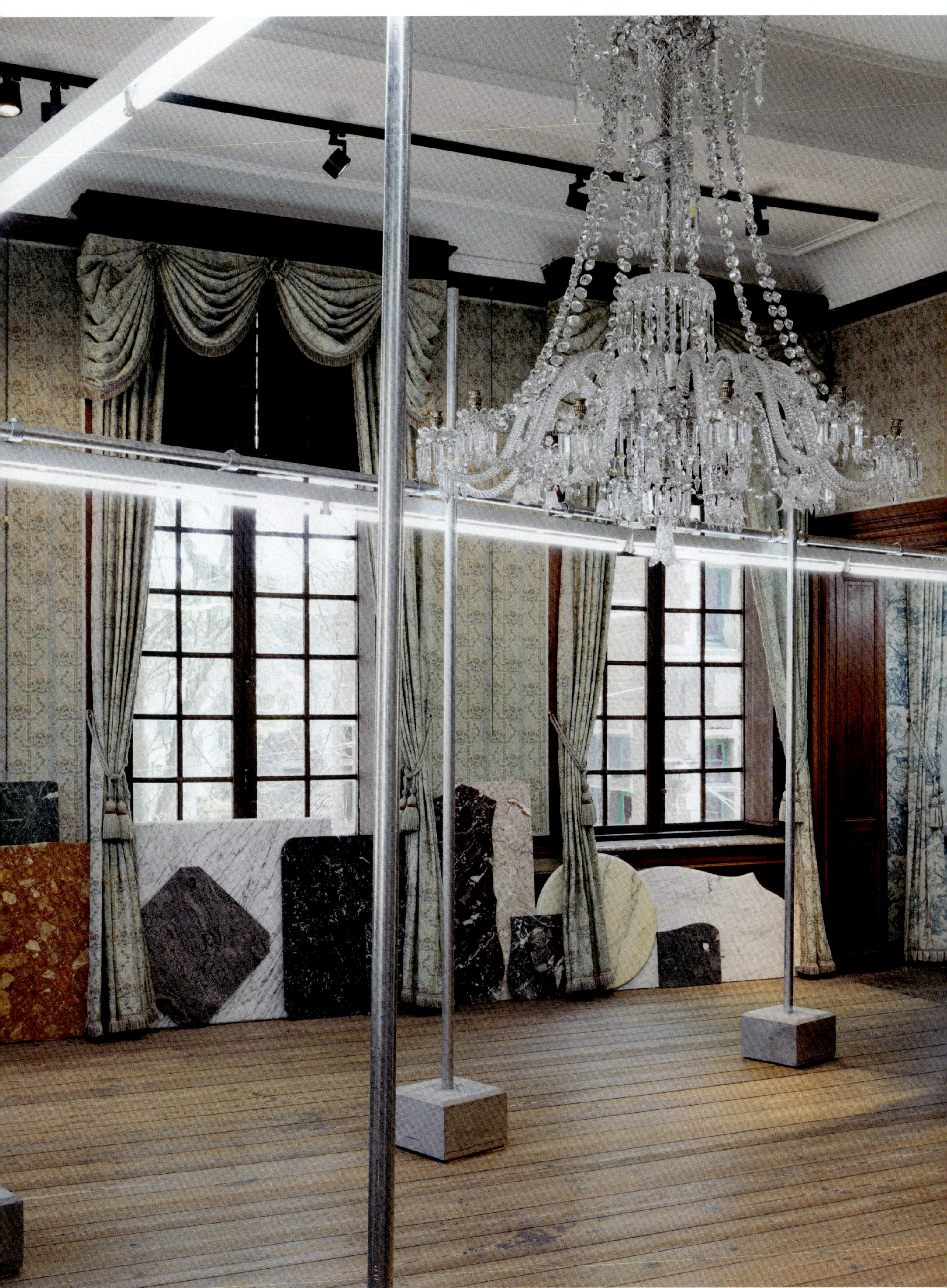

FILIP DUJARDIN, *Accumulation d'Époque#1*, May 2017

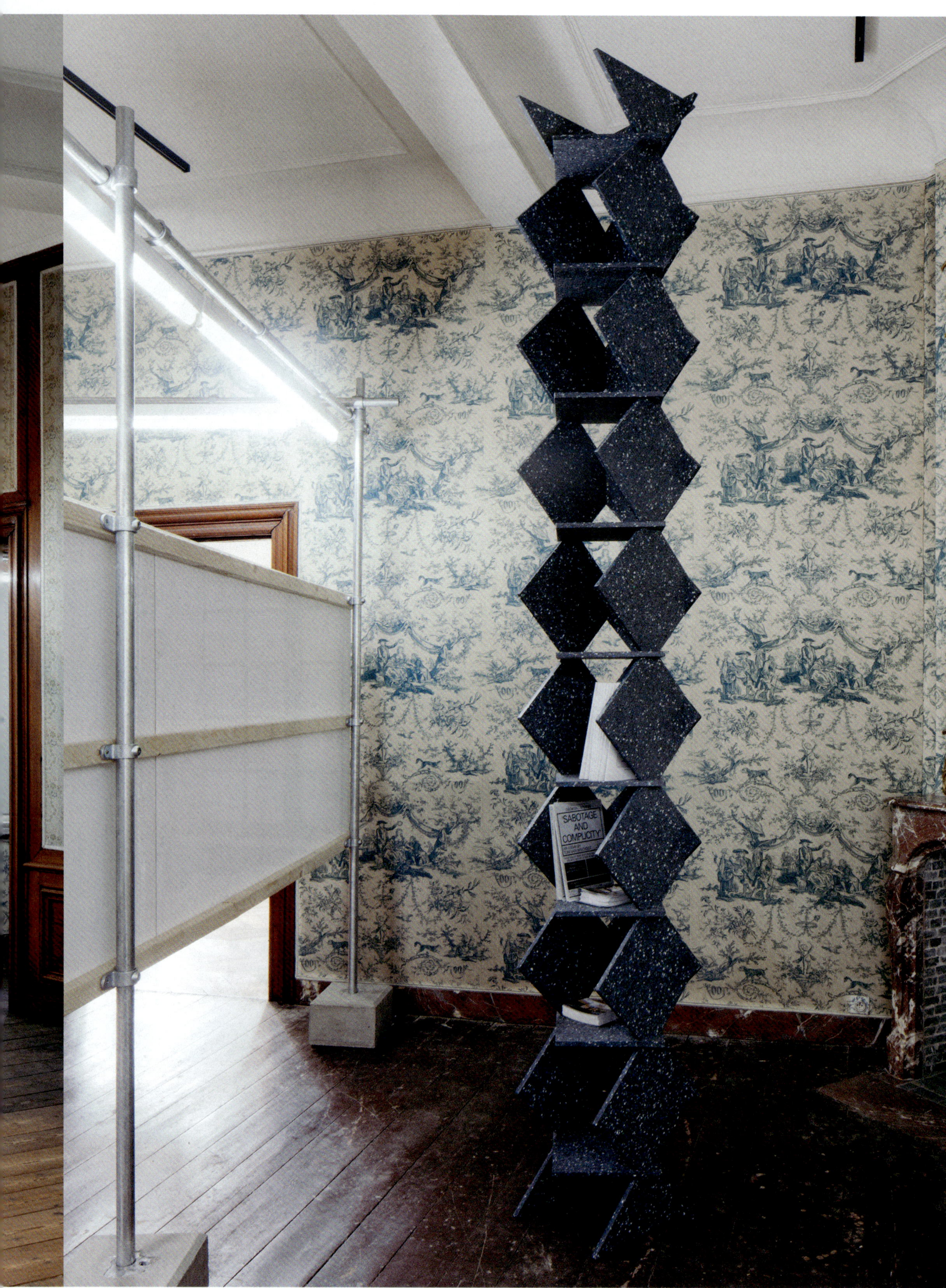

THEO DE MEYER / ARTHUR DEKKER, *Setting Up A Cabinet*, June 2017

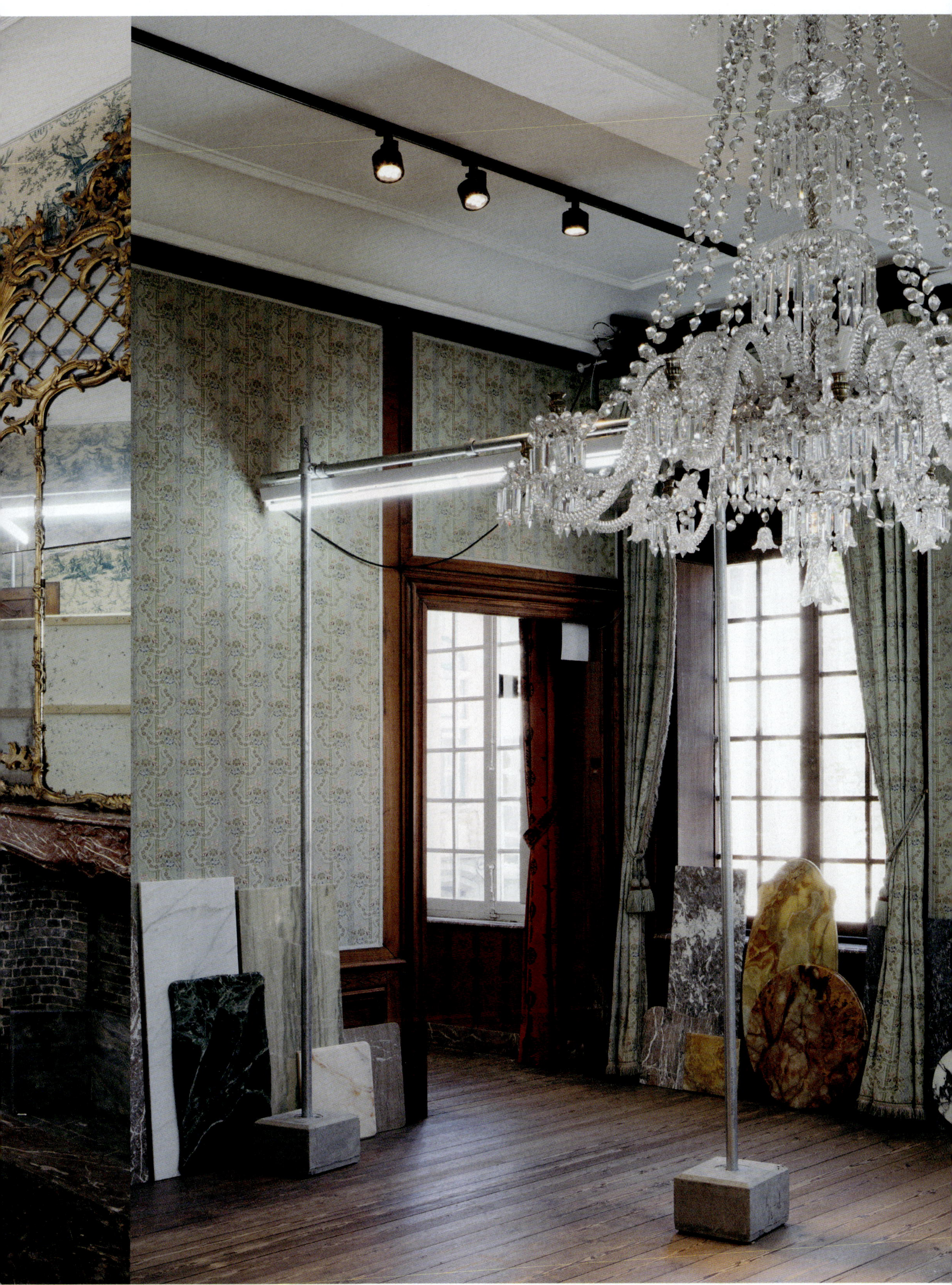

FILIP DUJARDIN, *Accumulation d'Époque#1*, May 2017

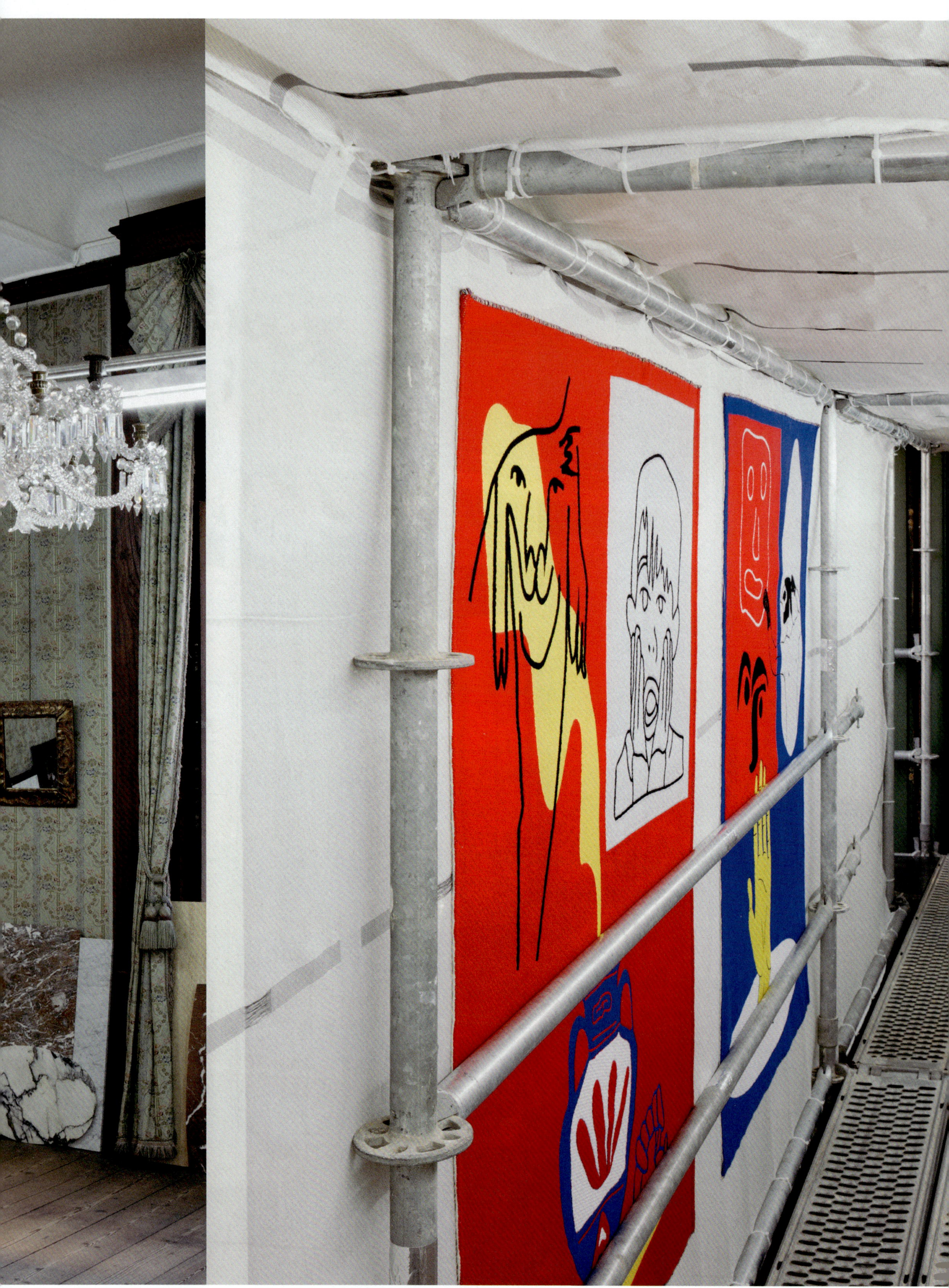

CHARLOTTE STUBY, *Master Textile Exhibition, Joro and Ali, Diptich*, June 2017

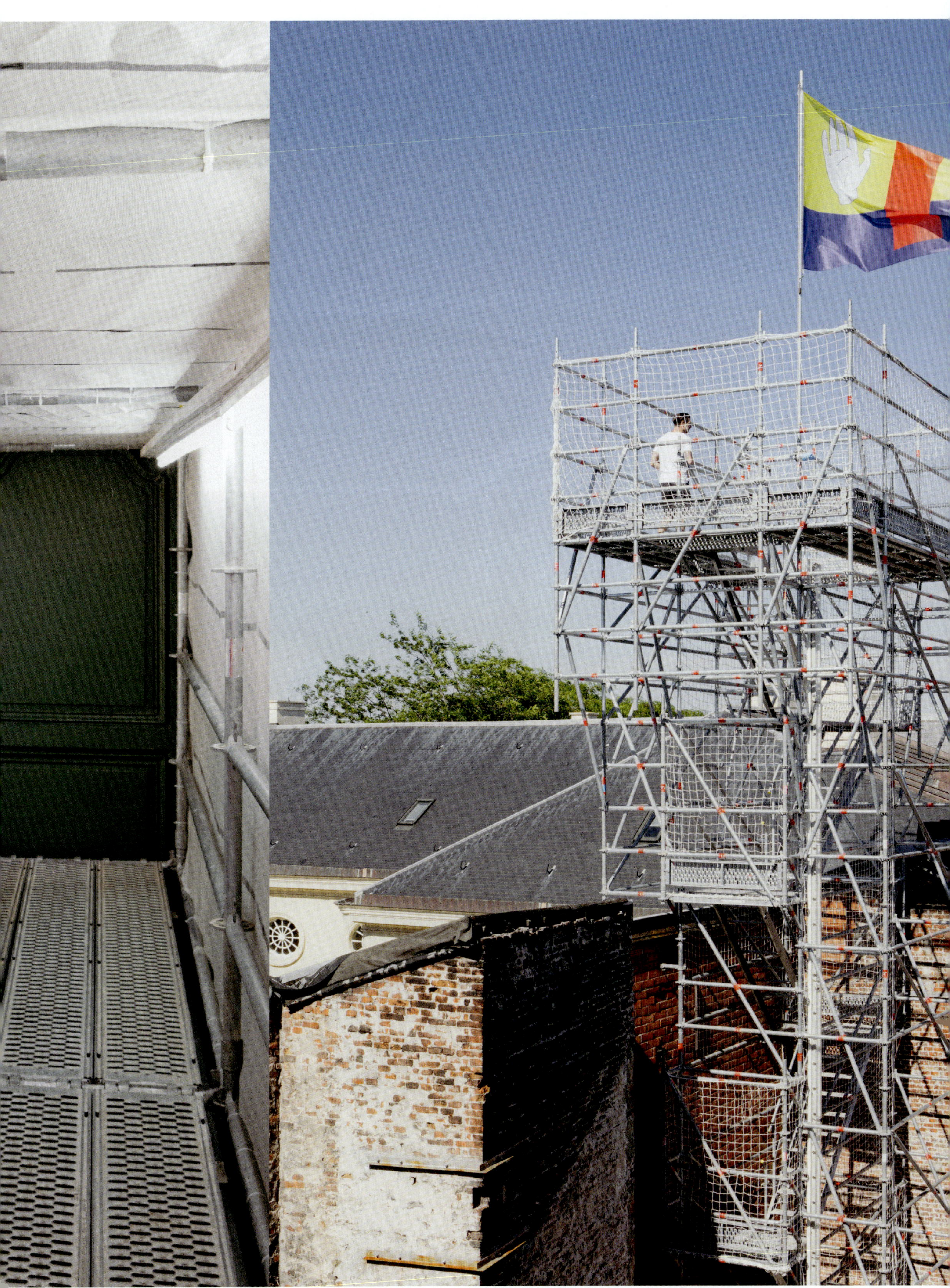

CHARLOTTE STUBY, *Master Textile Exhibition, Flag*, June 2017

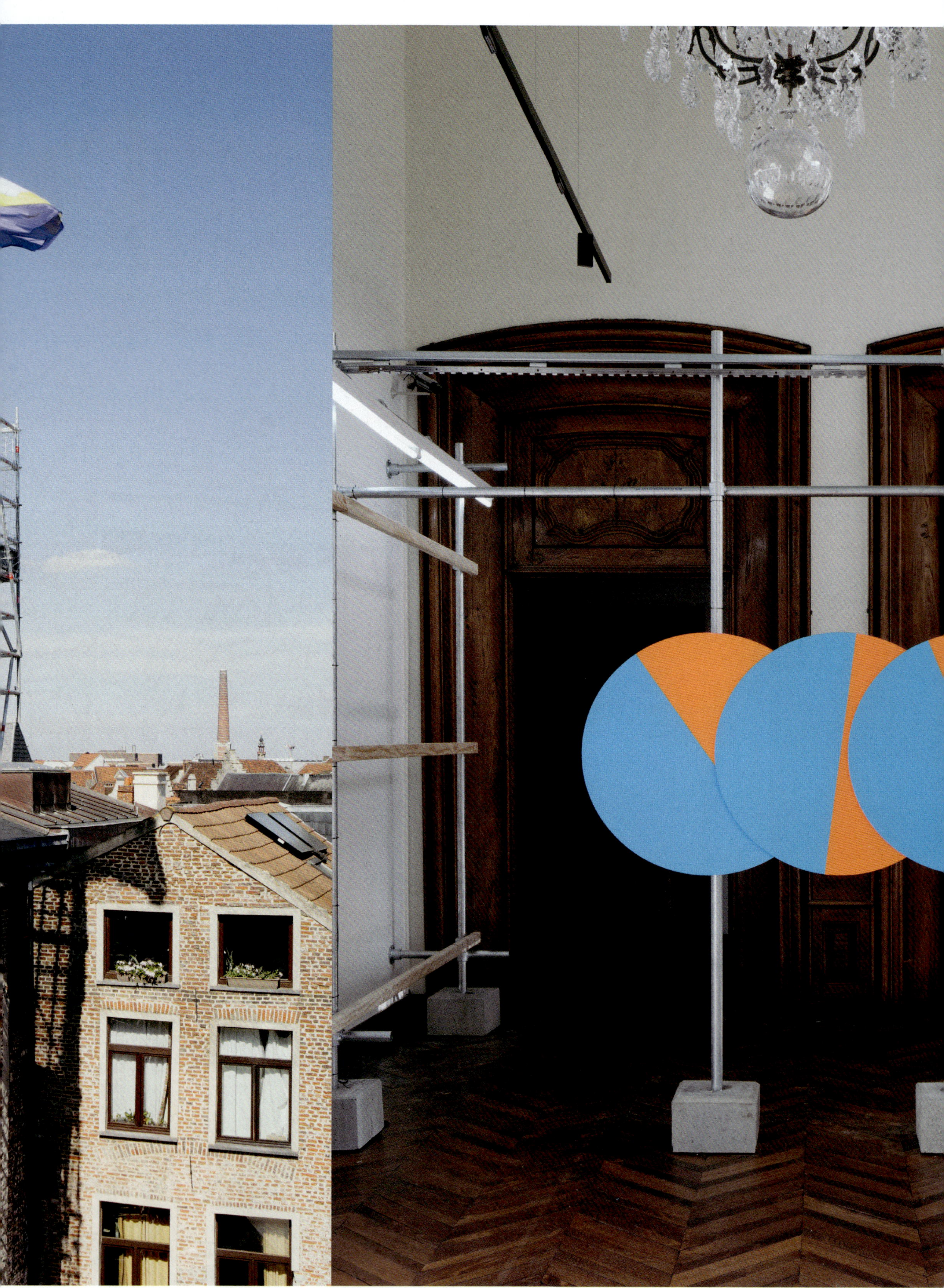

KAREL MARTENS, *Motion, Three Times (in Blue and Orange)*, July 2017

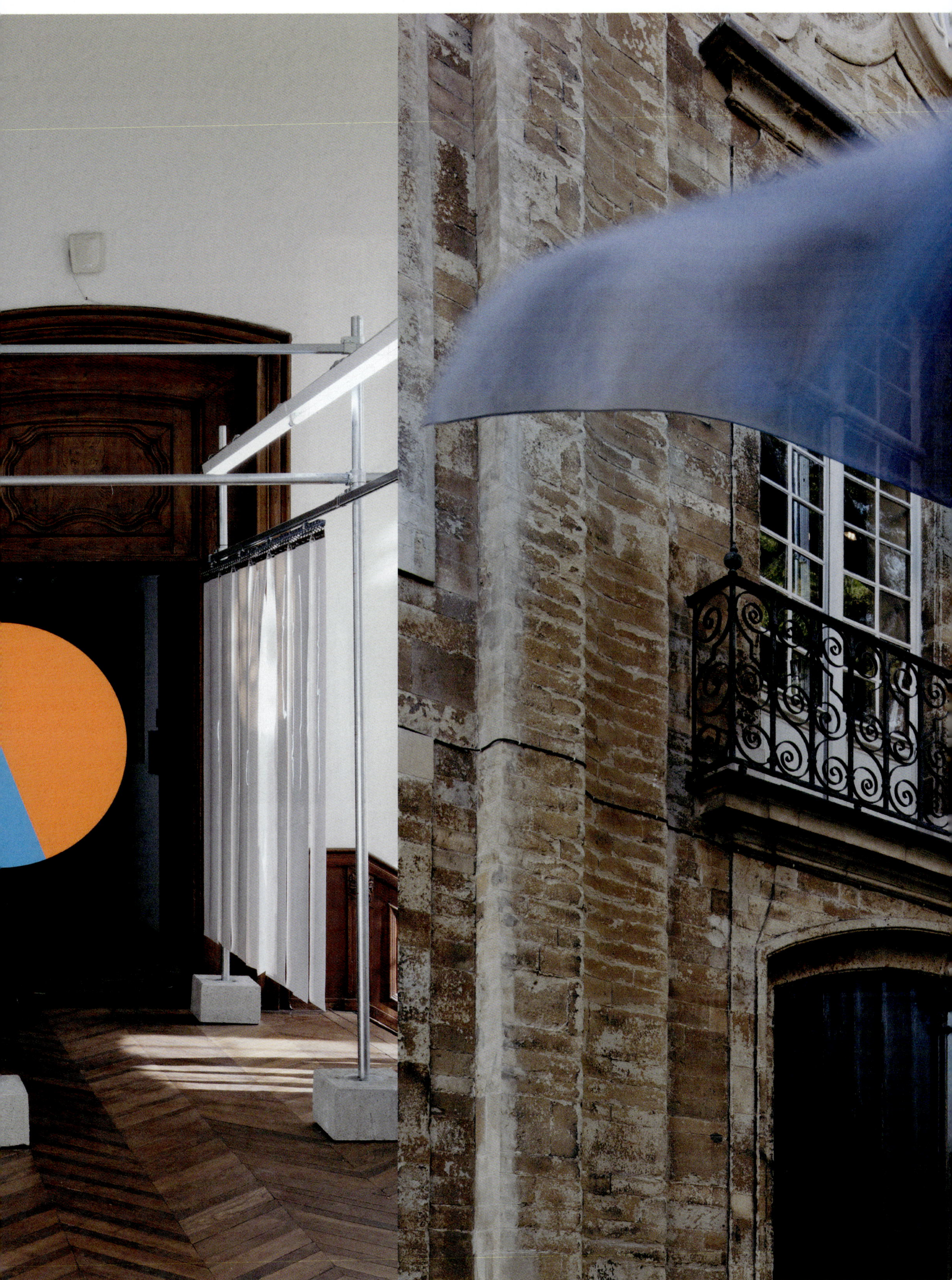

STIJN COLE, *New Colors / Sunrise 8/6/2017*, July 2017

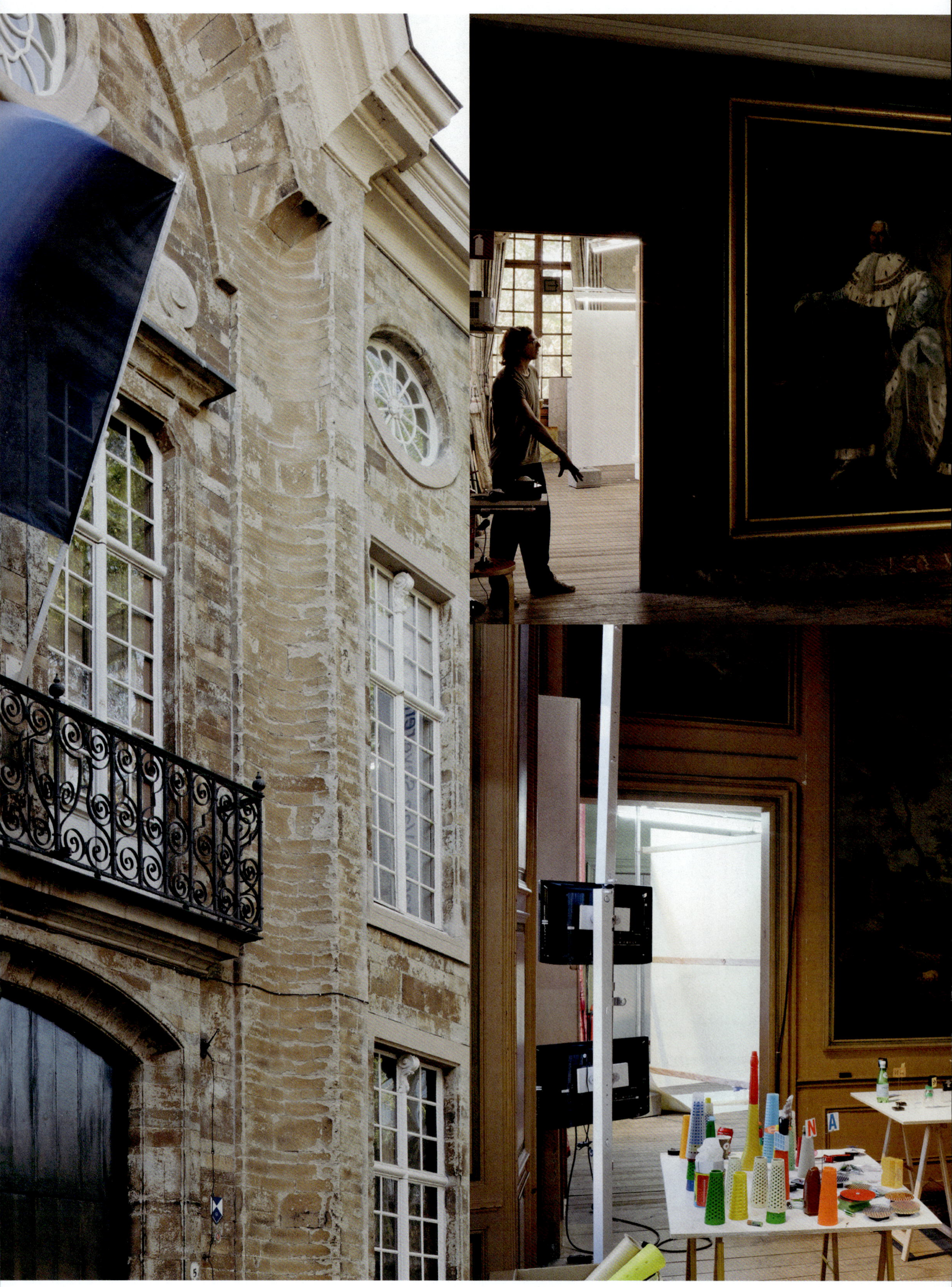

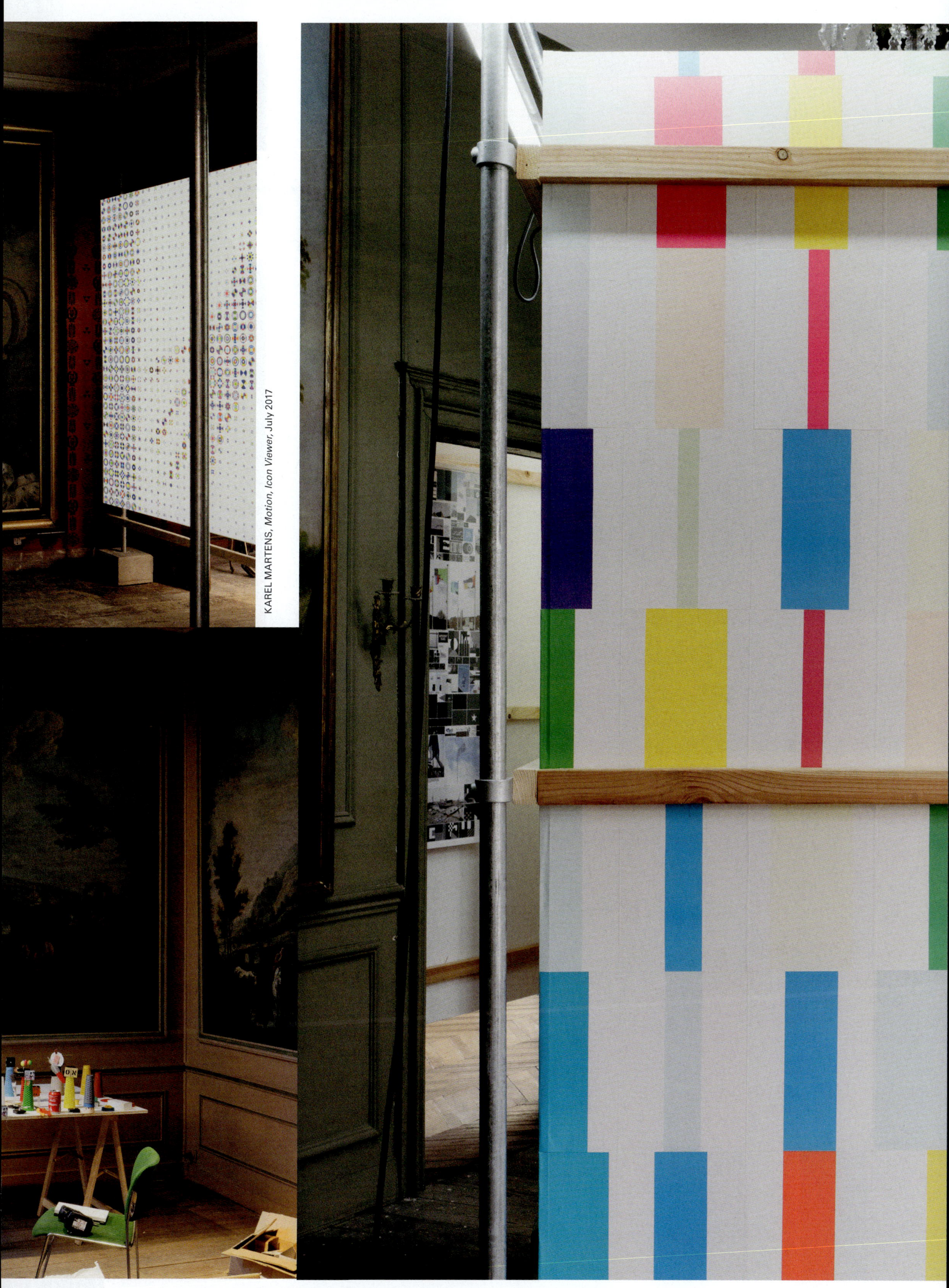

KAREL MARTENS, *Motion, Icon Viewer*, July 2017

KAREL MARTENS, *Motion, A4 Wallpaper*, July 2017

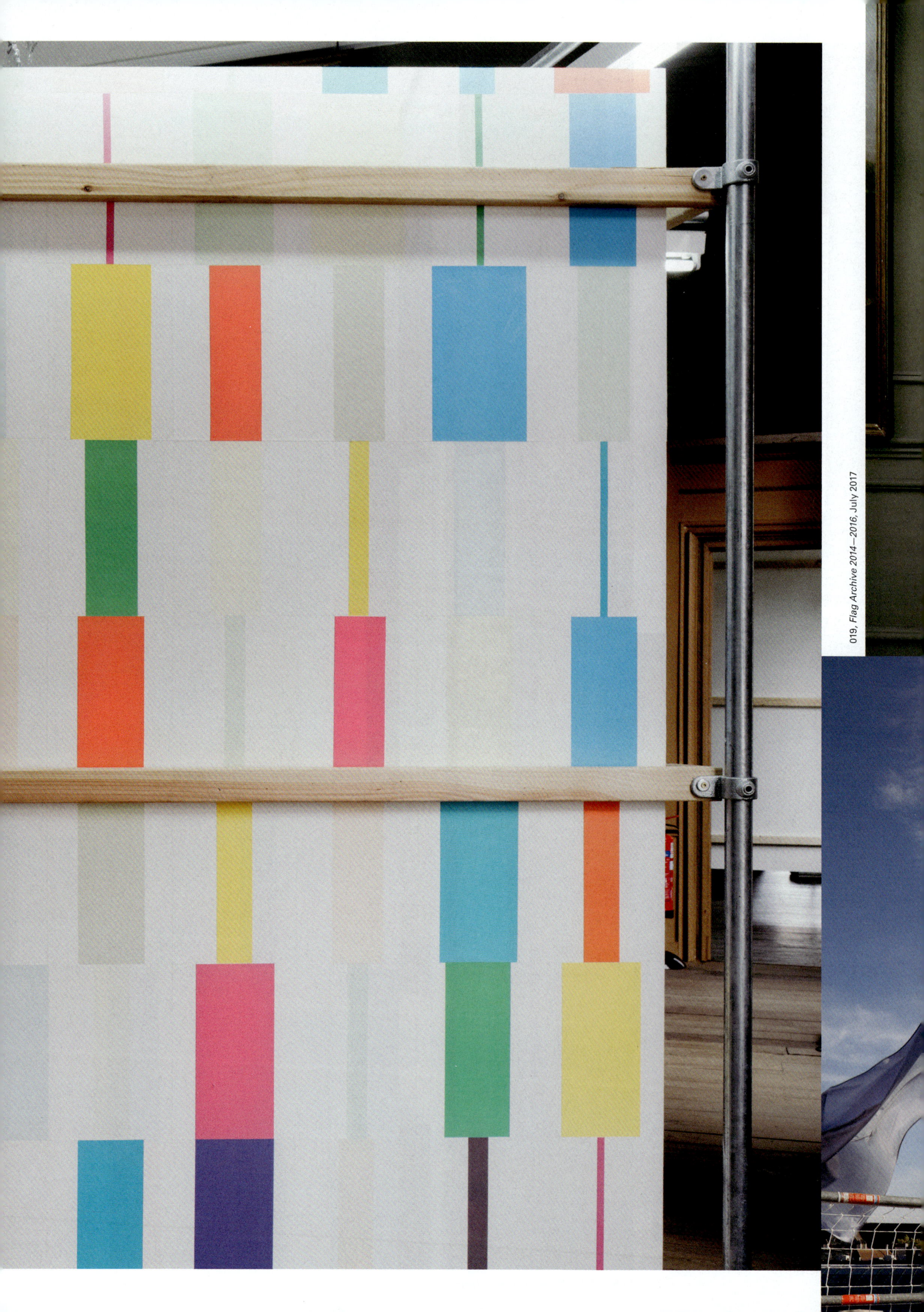

019, *Flag Archive 2014—2016*, July 2017

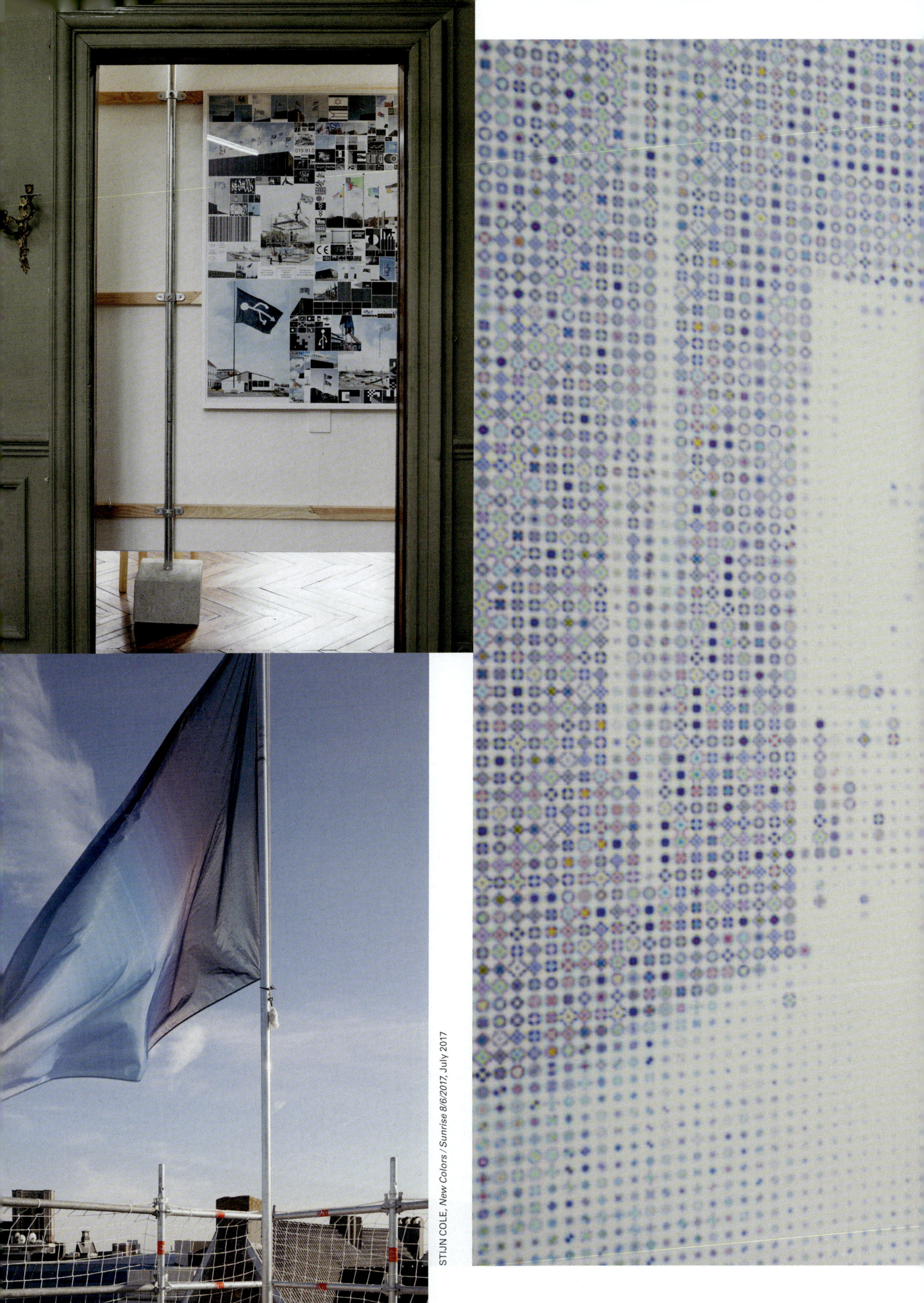

STIJN COLE, *New Colors / Sunrise 8/6/2017*, July 2017

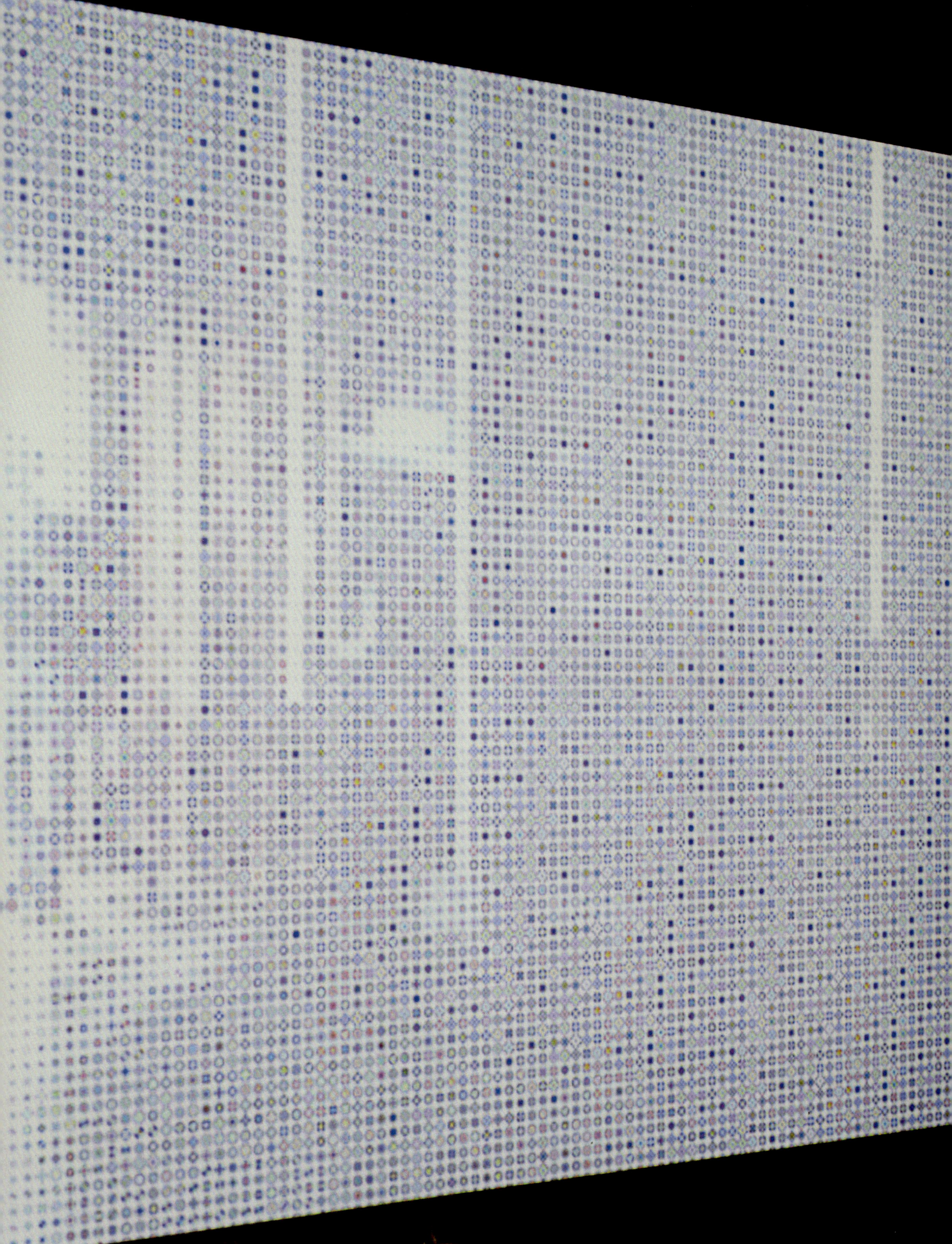

KAREL MARTENS, *Motion, Icon Viewer*, July 2017

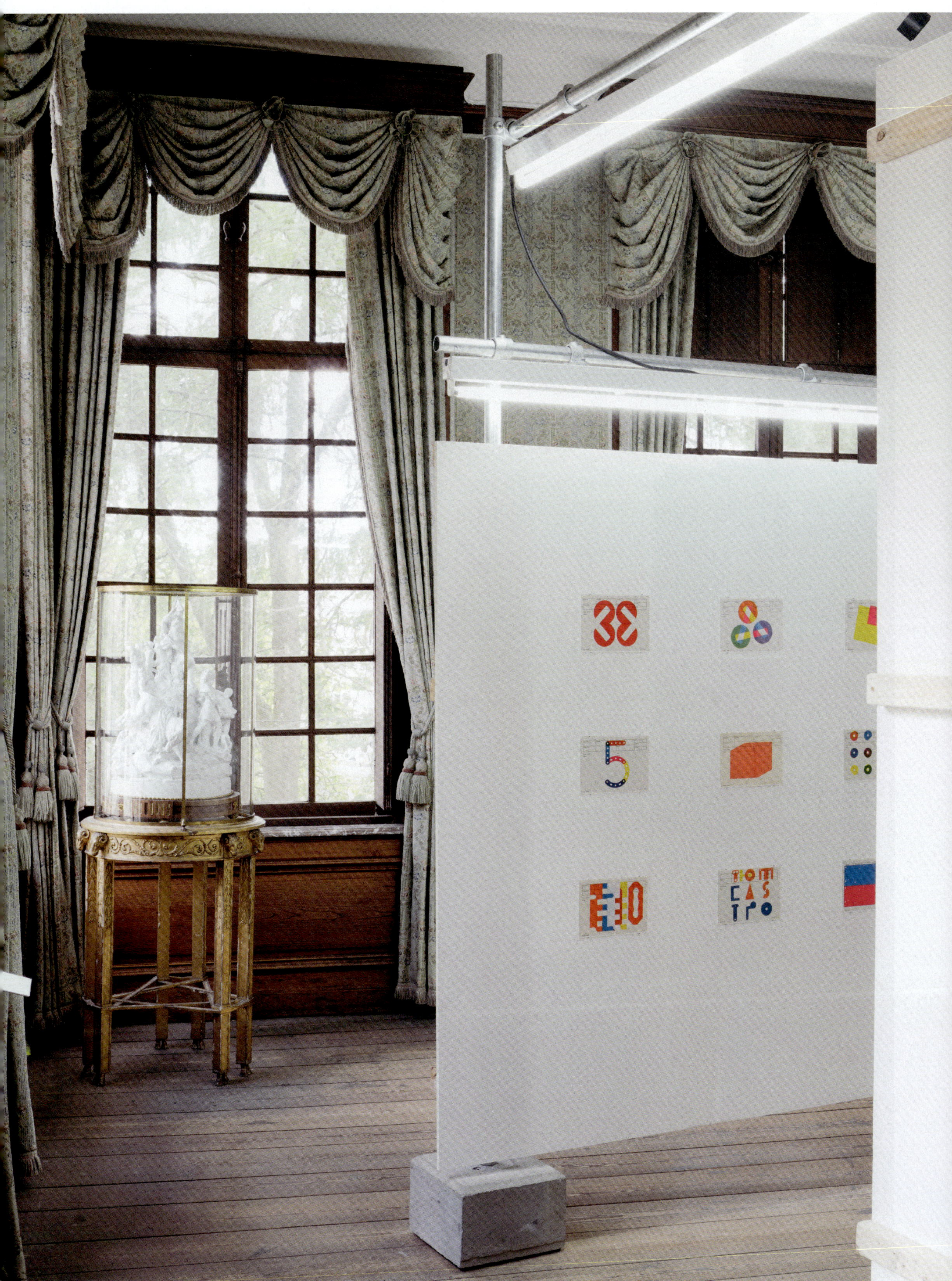

KAREL MARTENS, *Motion, Untitled (1990–2016)*, July 2017

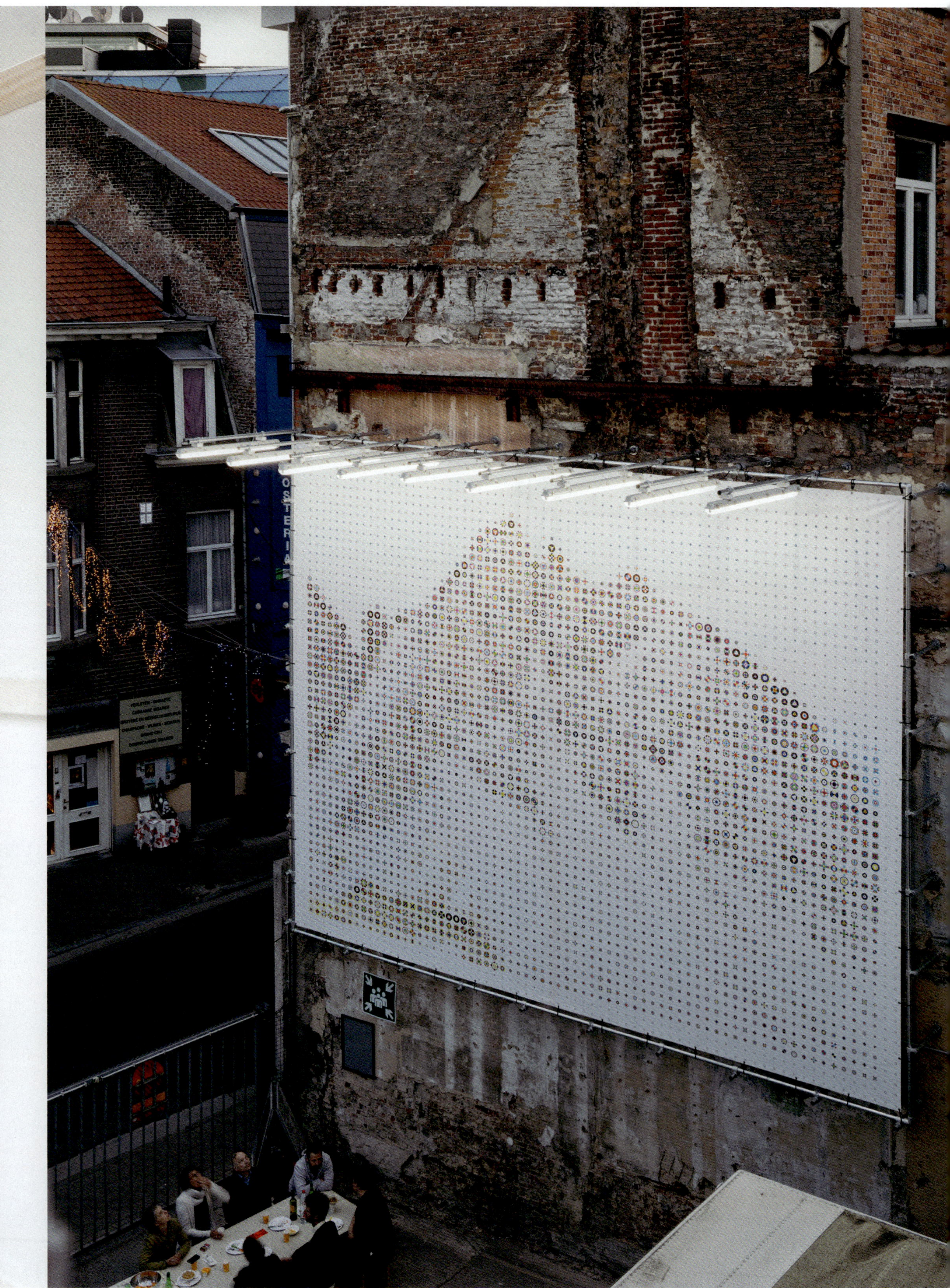

KAREL MARTENS, *Motion, Mountain Wall*, July 2017

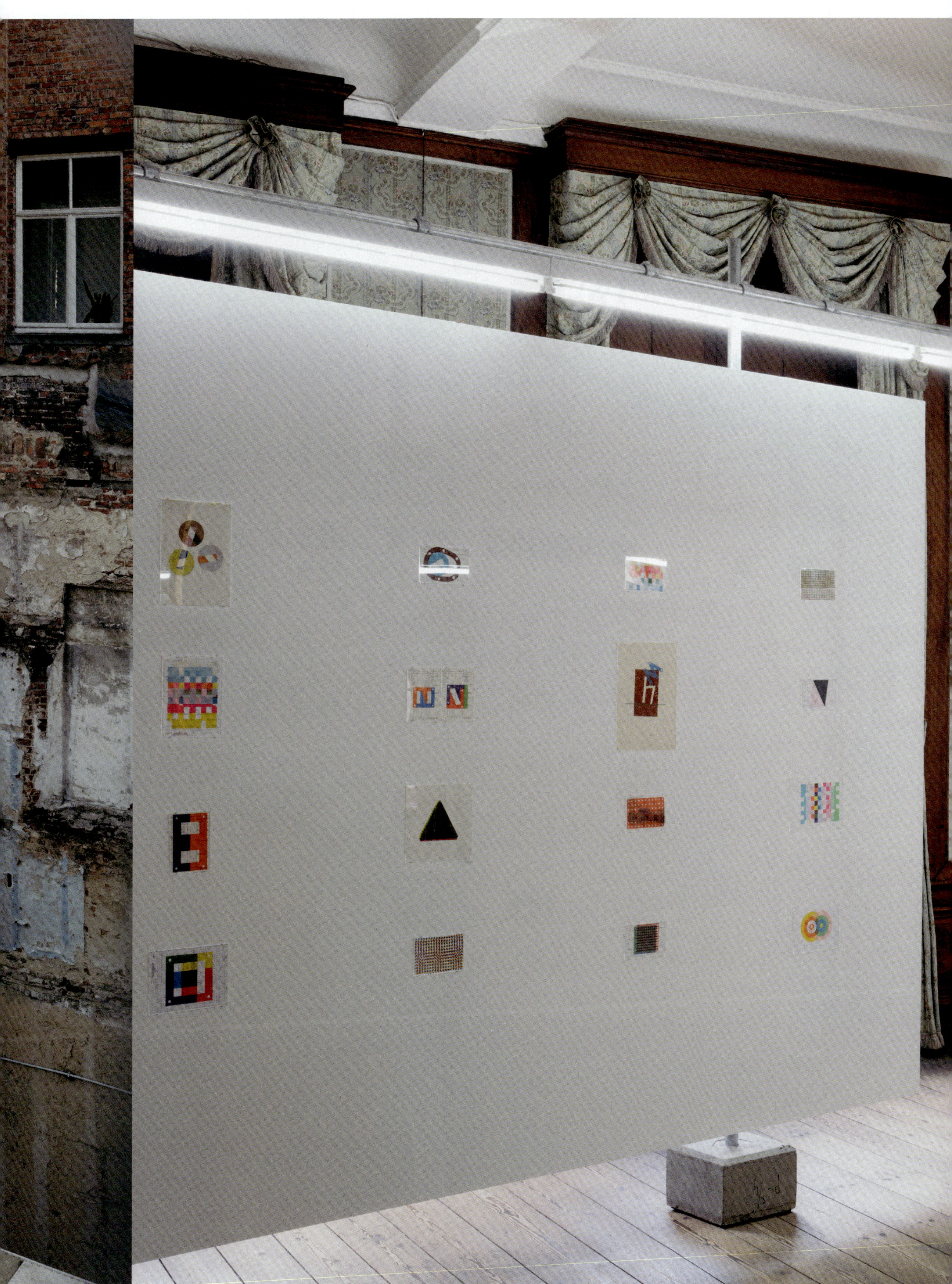

KAREL MARTENS, *Motion, Untitled (1990–2016)*, July 2017

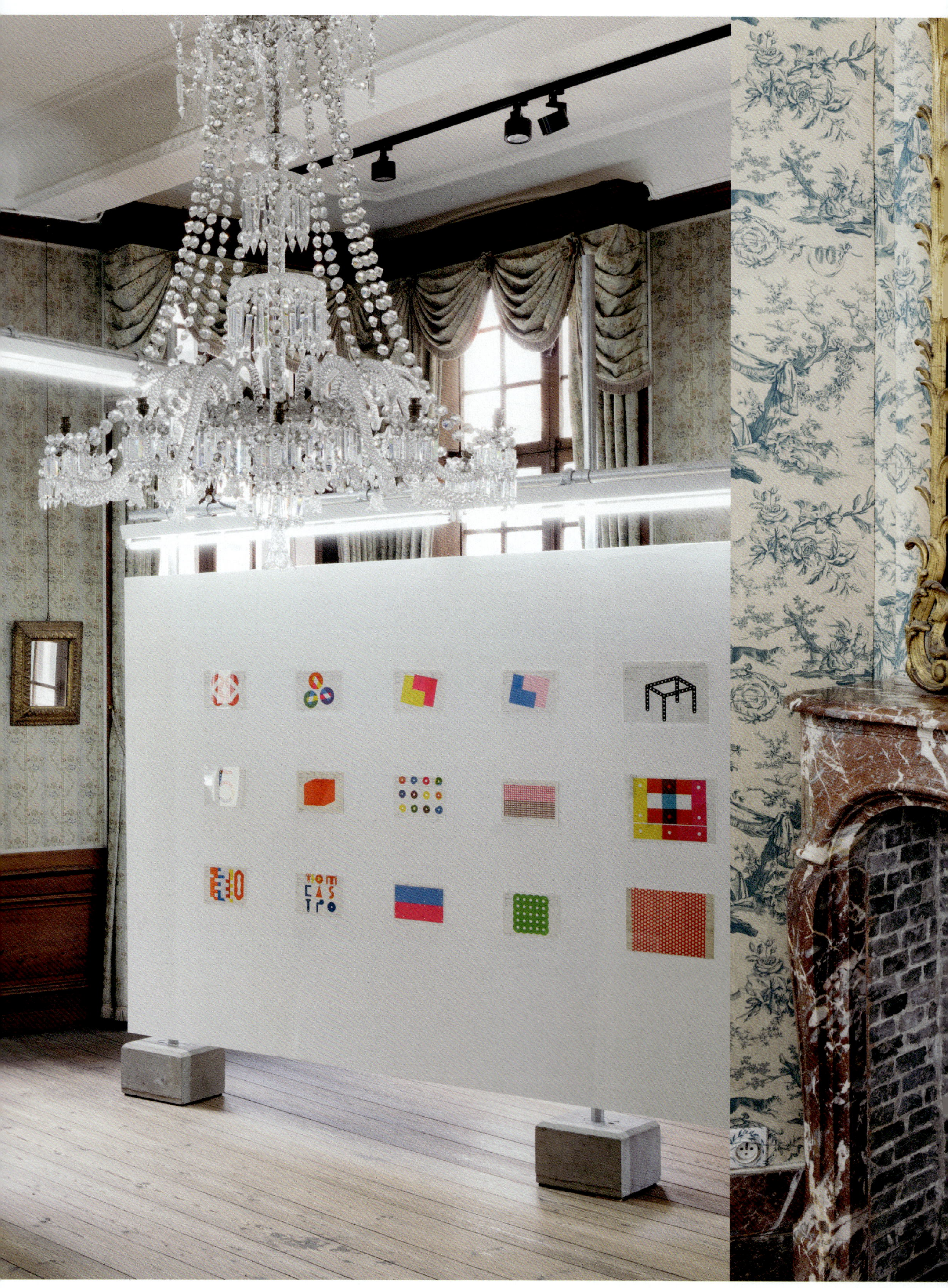
tom
CAS
TRO

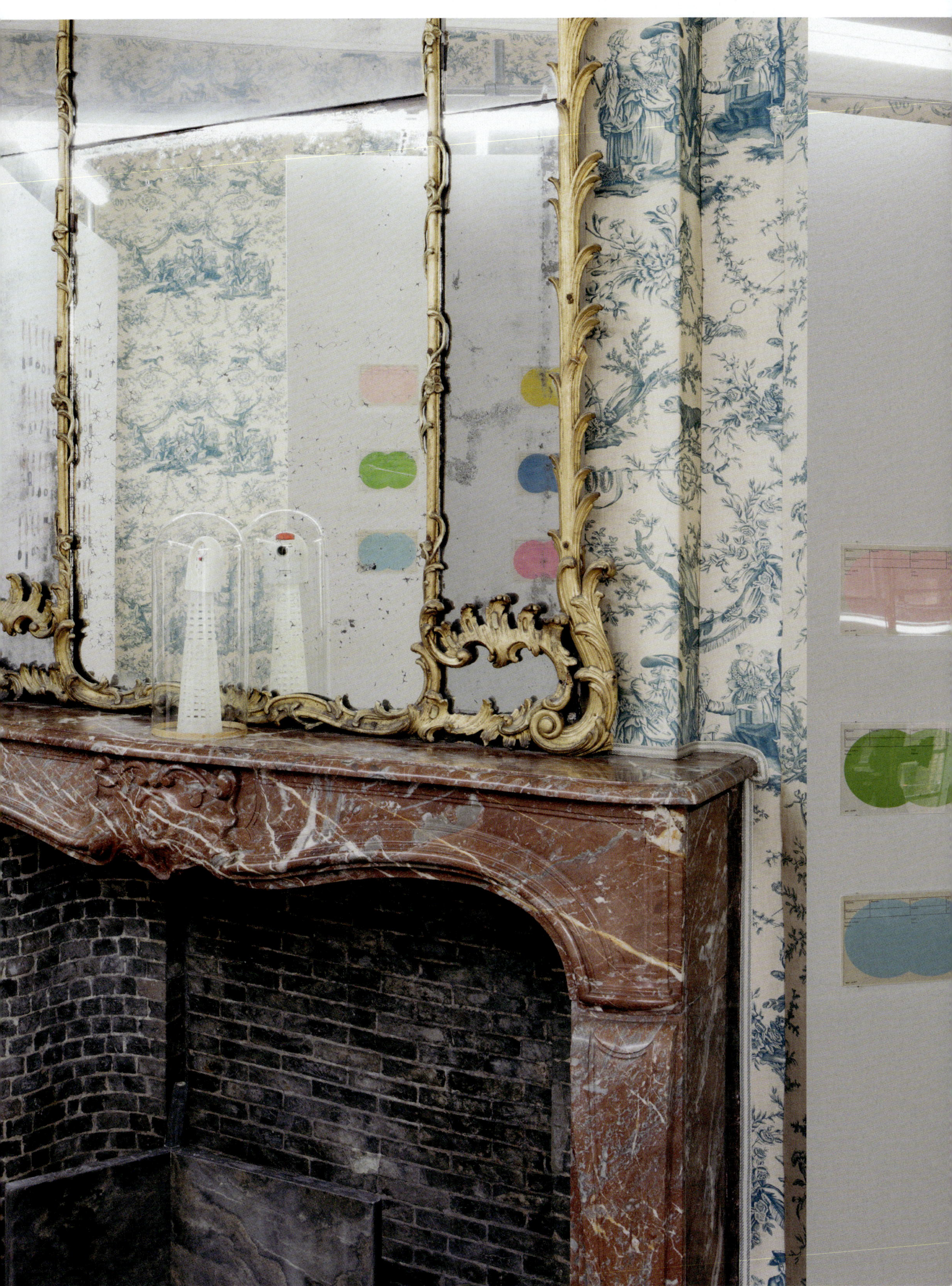

KAREL MARTENS, *Motion*, *Clockworks*, July 2017

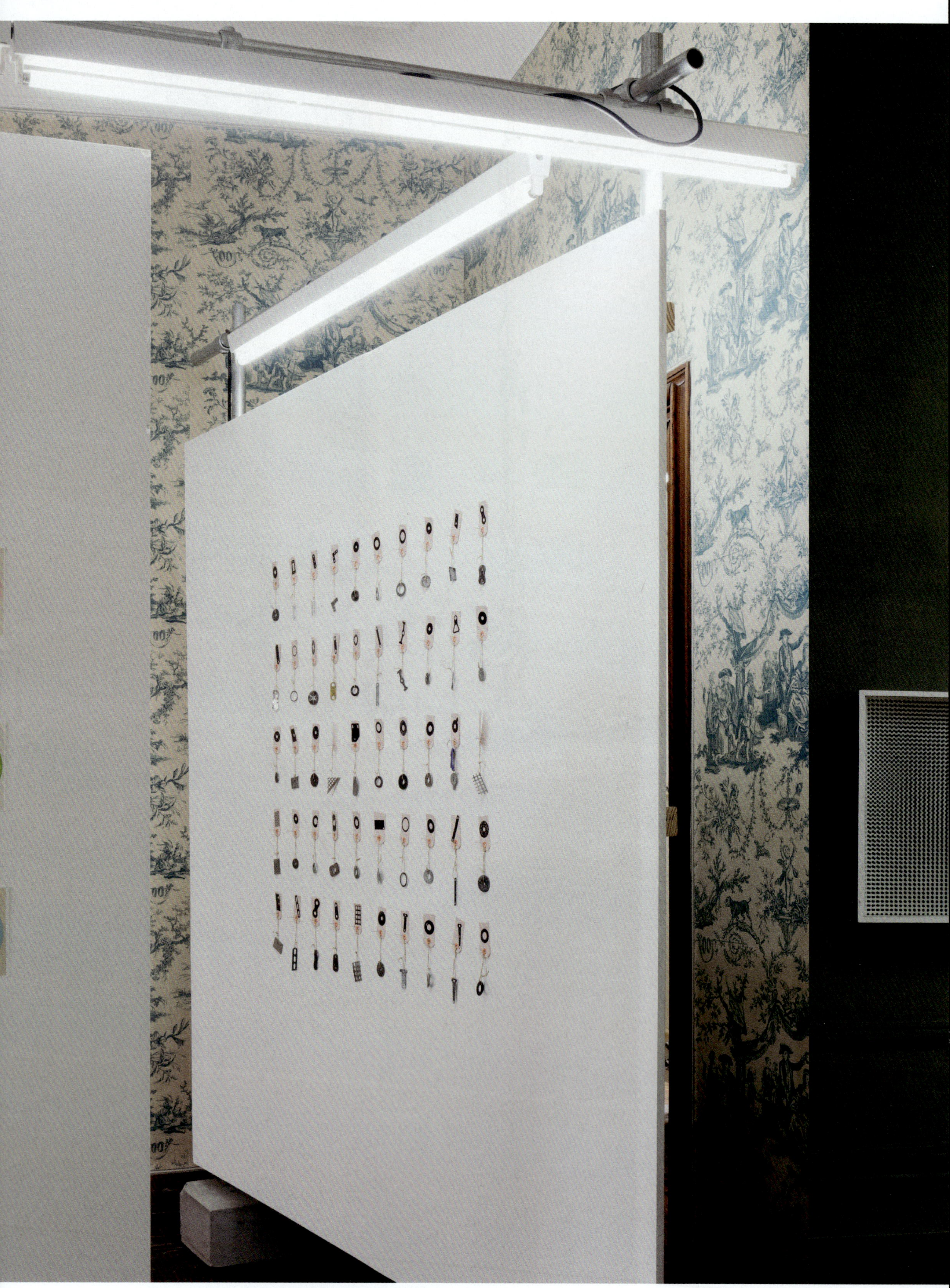

KAREL MARTENS, *Motion, 50 Labels with found objects (2000)*, July 2017

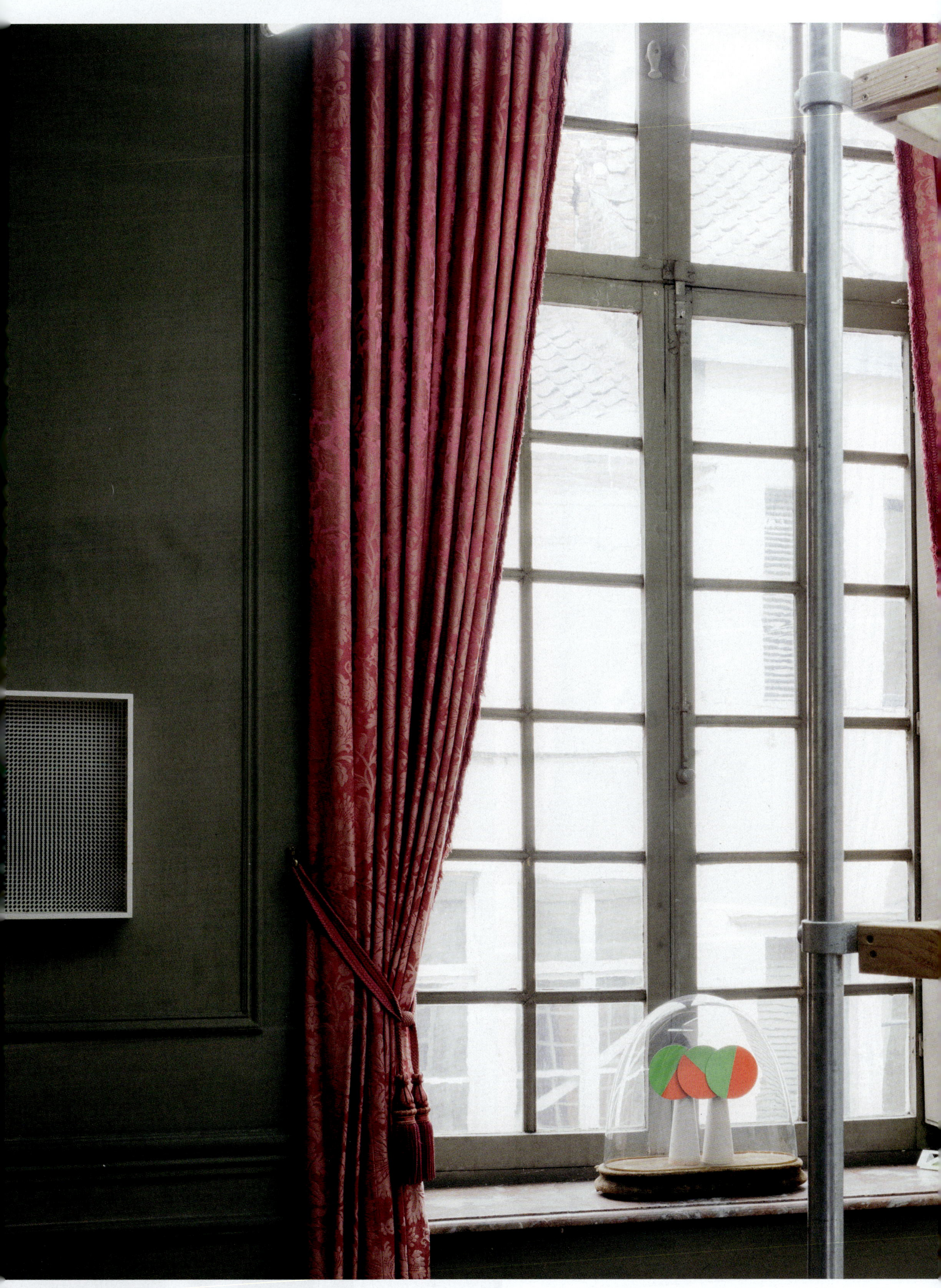

KAREL MARTENS, *Motion, Untitled (1964) & Clockworks*, July 2017

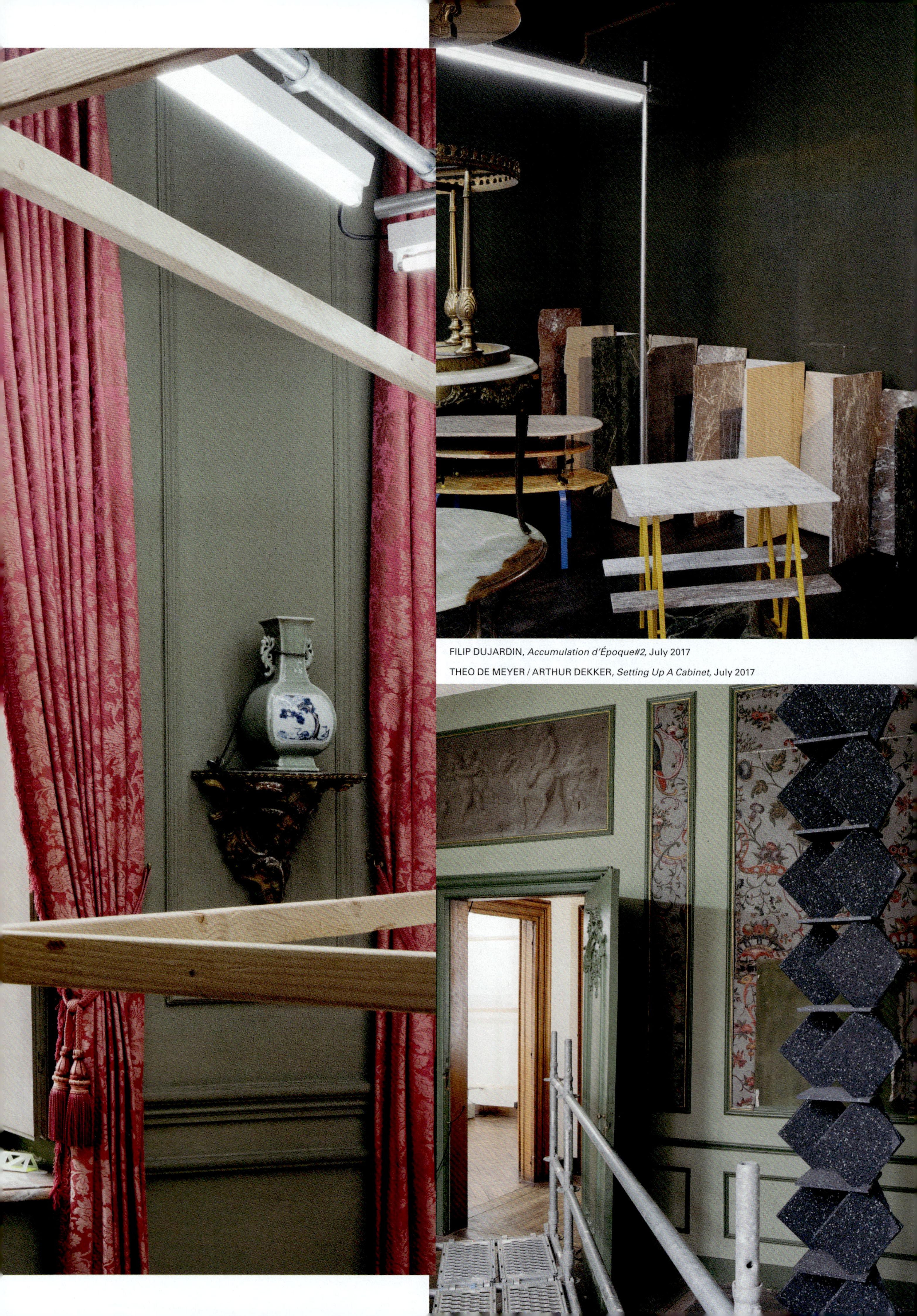

FILIP DUJARDIN, *Accumulation d'Époque#2*, July 2017

THEO DE MEYER / ARTHUR DEKKER, *Setting Up A Cabinet*, July 2017

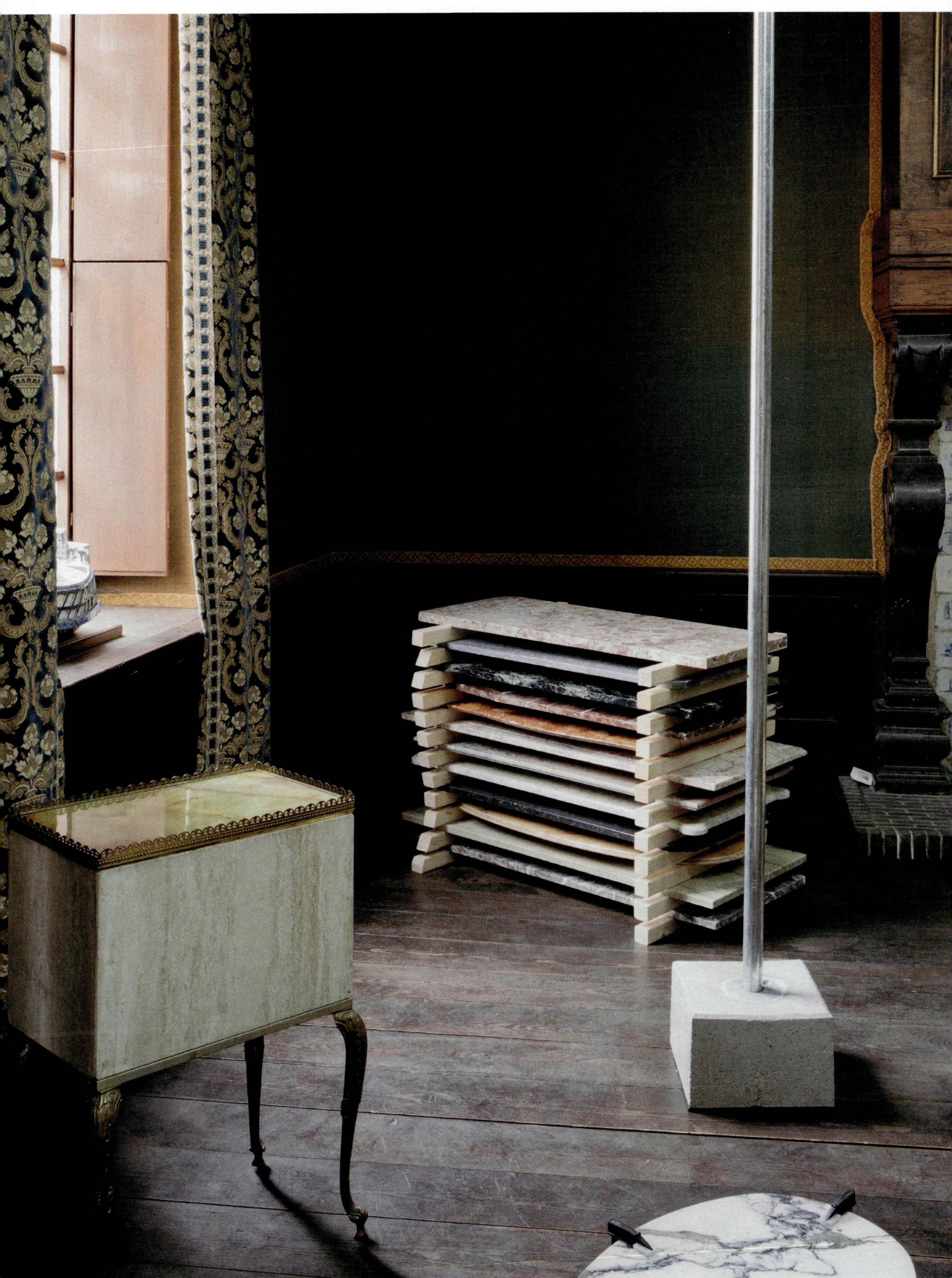

FILIP DUJARDIN, *Accumulation d'Époque#2*, July 2017

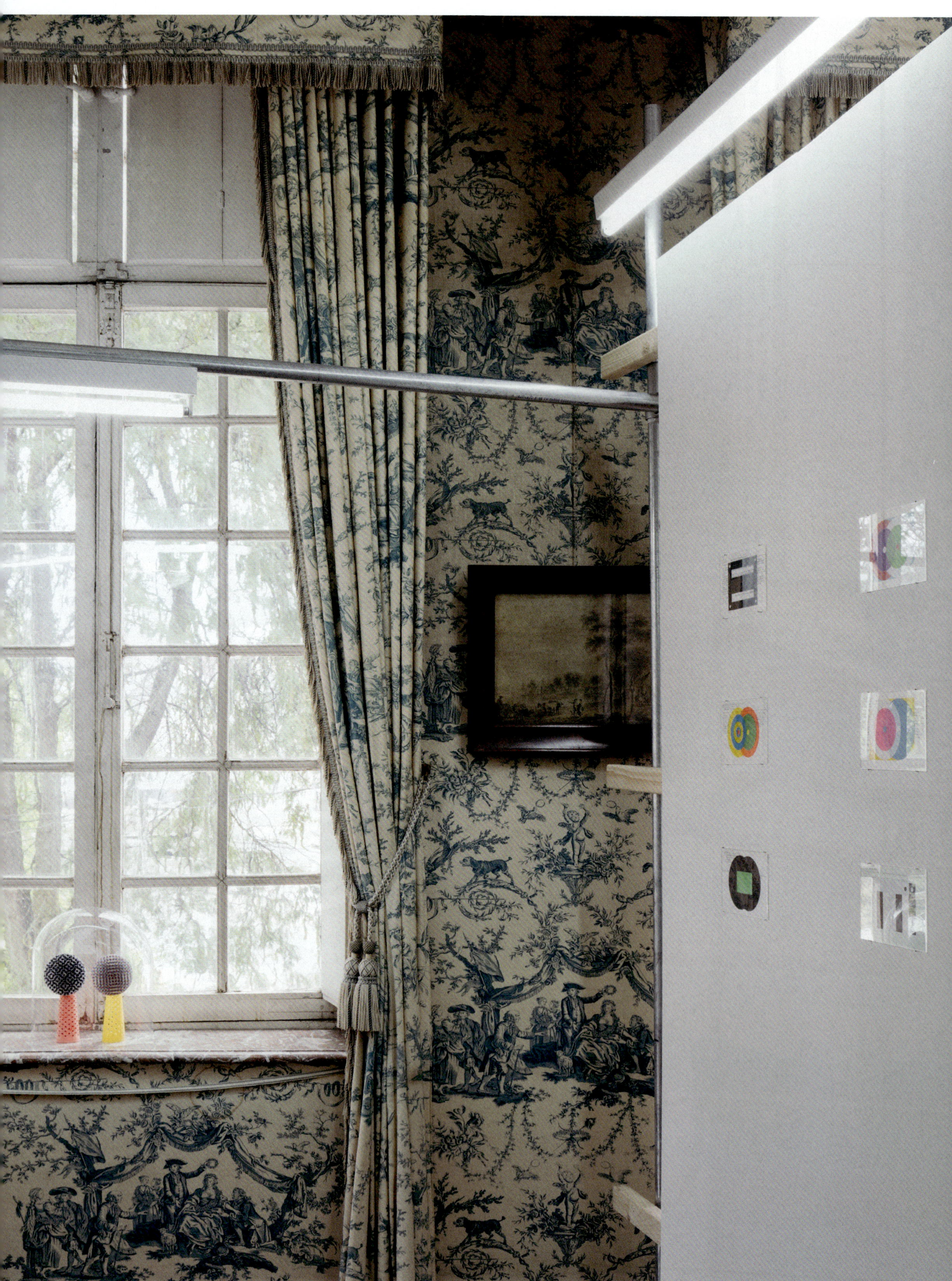

KAREL MARTENS, *Motion, Untitled (1990–2016)* & *Clockworks*, July 2017

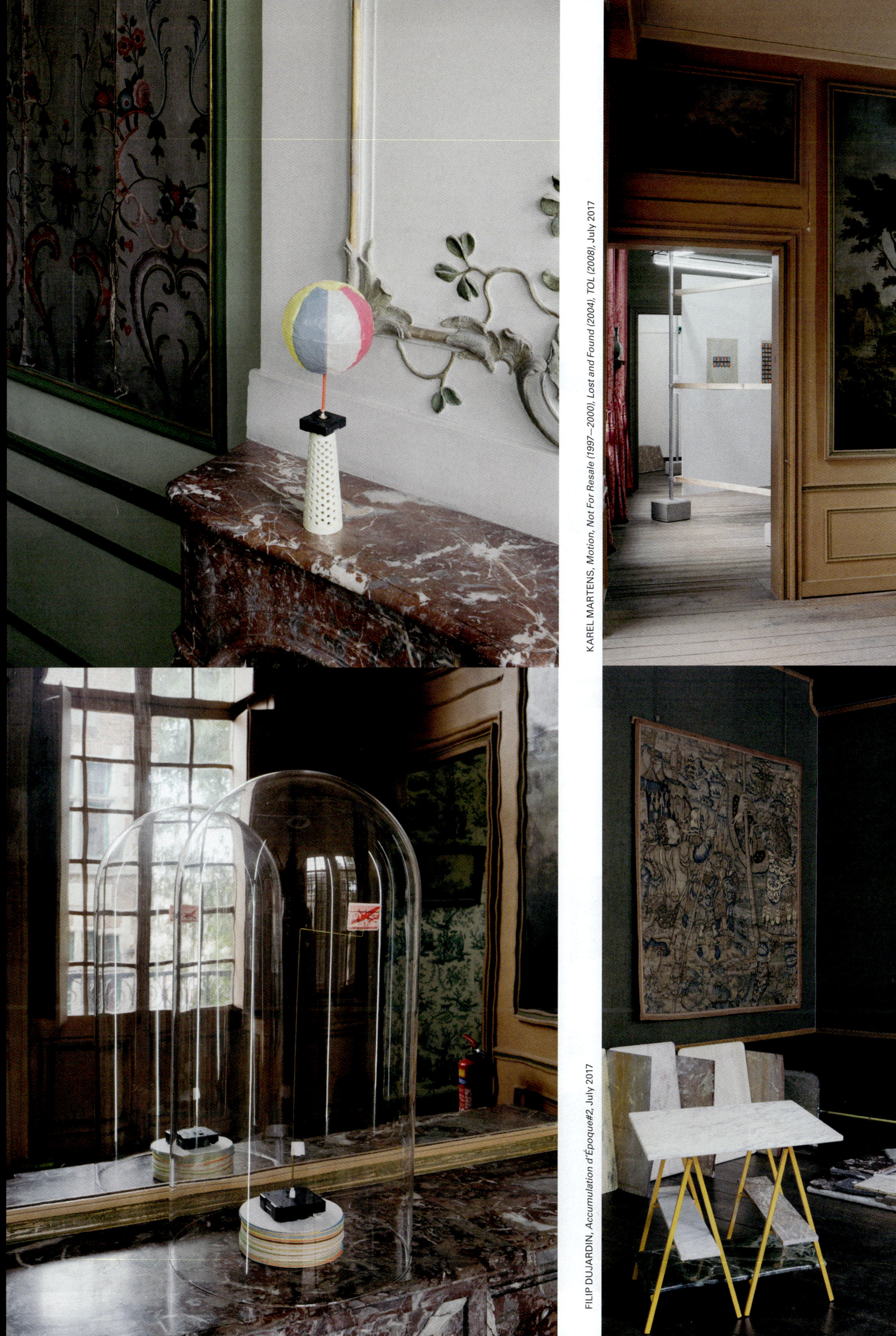

KAREL MARTENS, *Motion*, *Not For Resale* (1997—2000), *Lost and Found* (2004), *TOL* (2008), July 2017

FILIP DUJARDIN, *Accumulation d'Époque#2*, July 2017

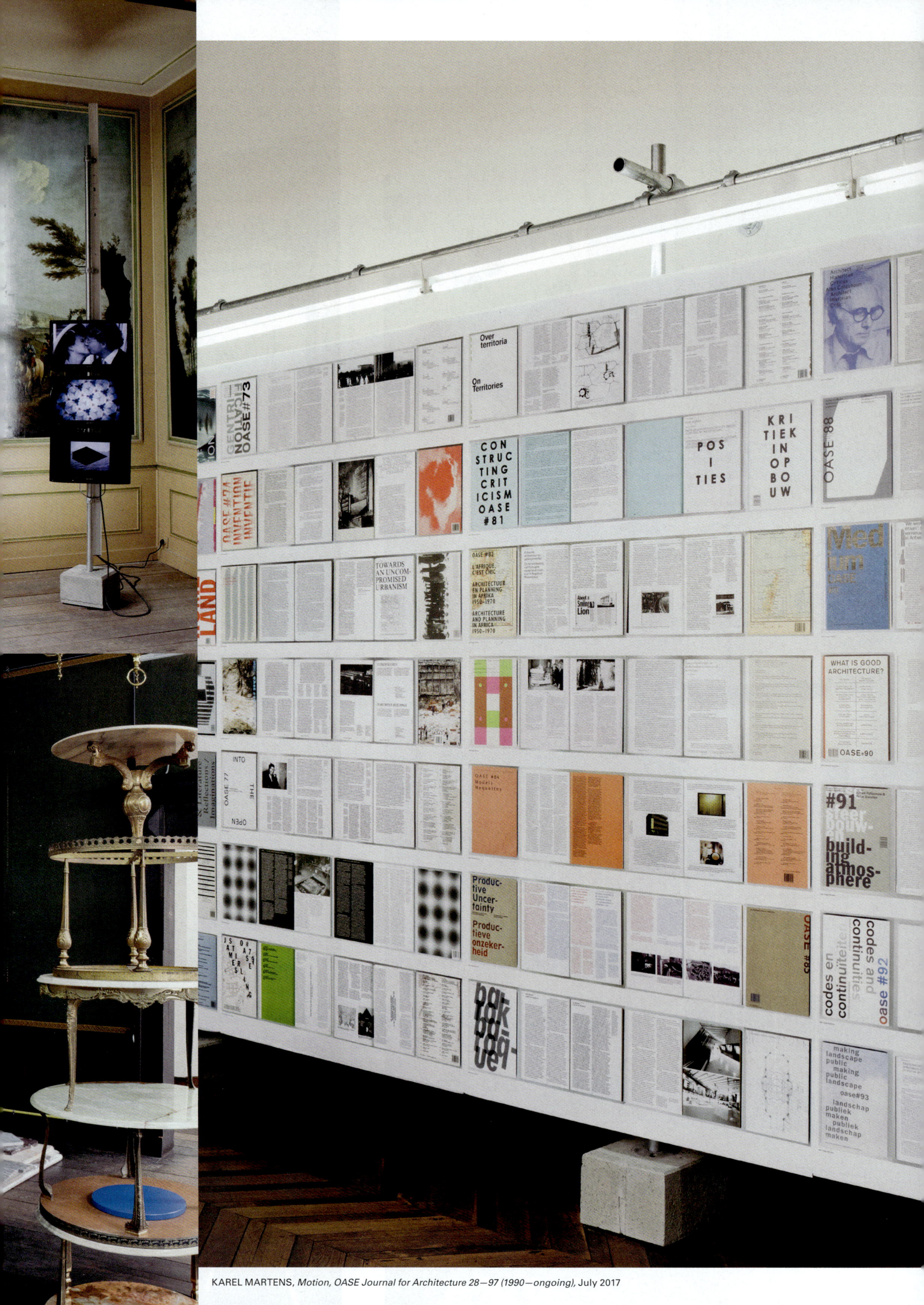

KAREL MARTENS, *Motion, OASE Journal for Architecture 28—97 (1990—ongoing)*, July 2017

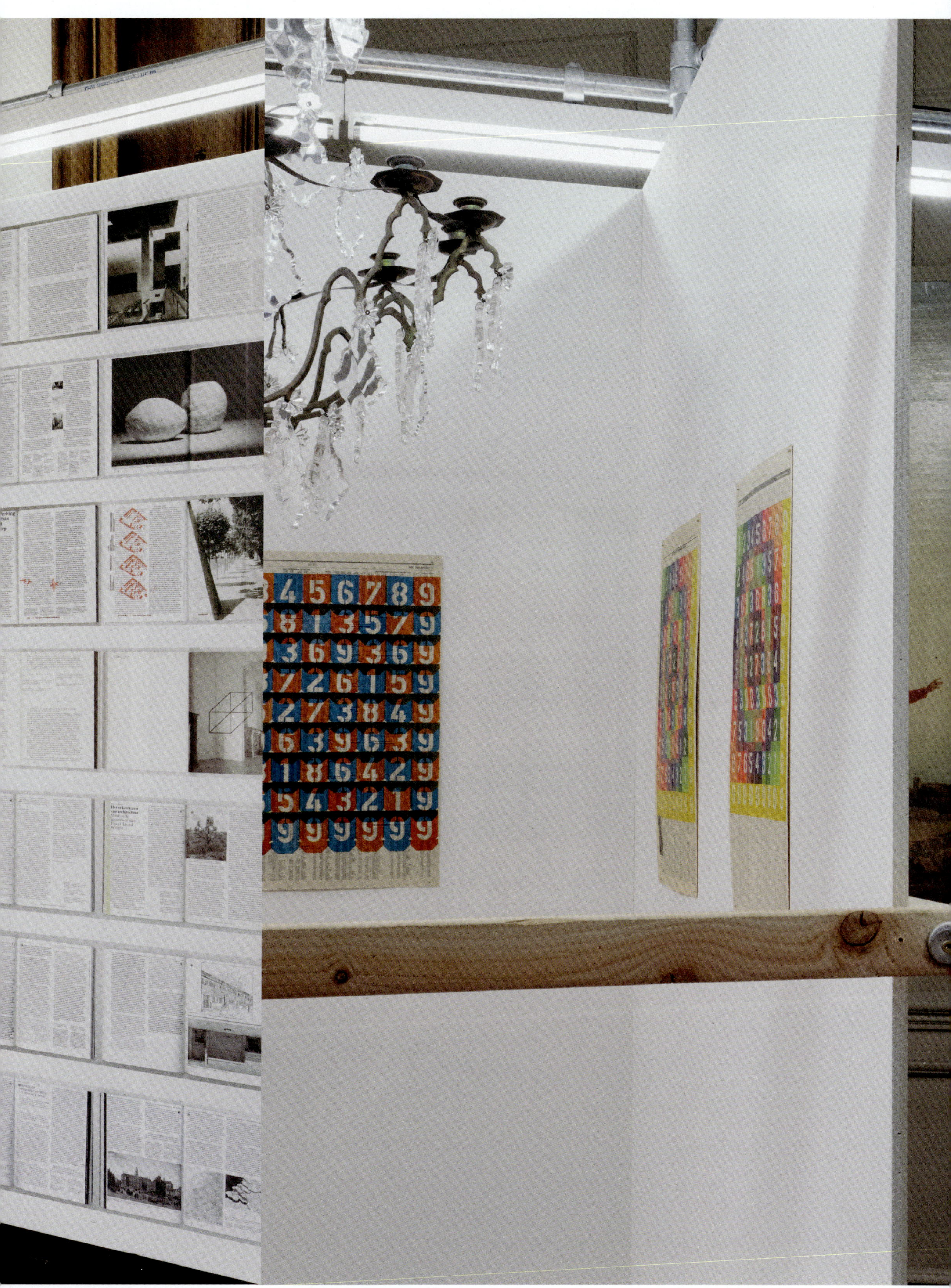

KAREL MARTENS, *Motion, Stencilled Numbers (1992 / 2011)*, July 2017

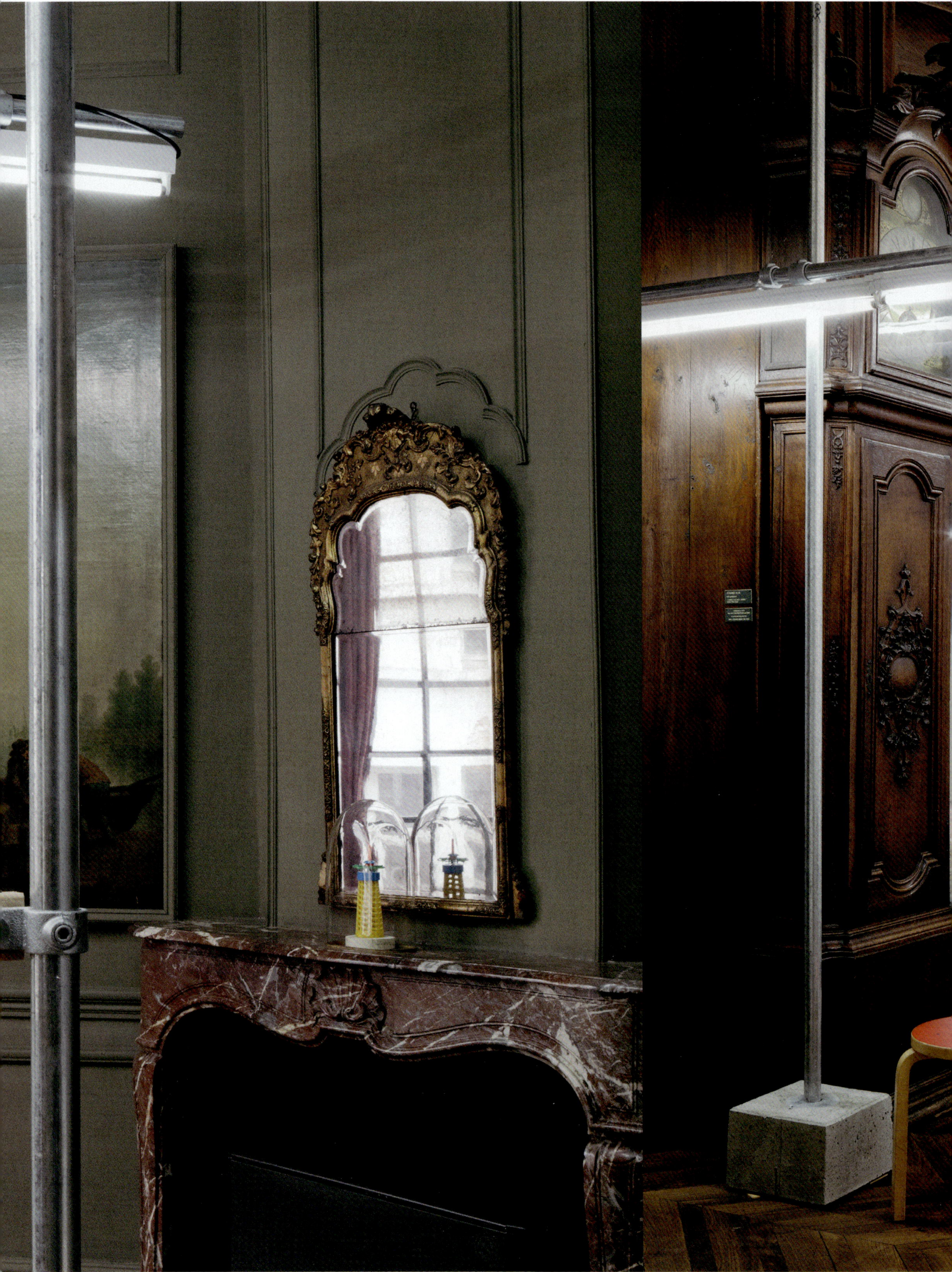

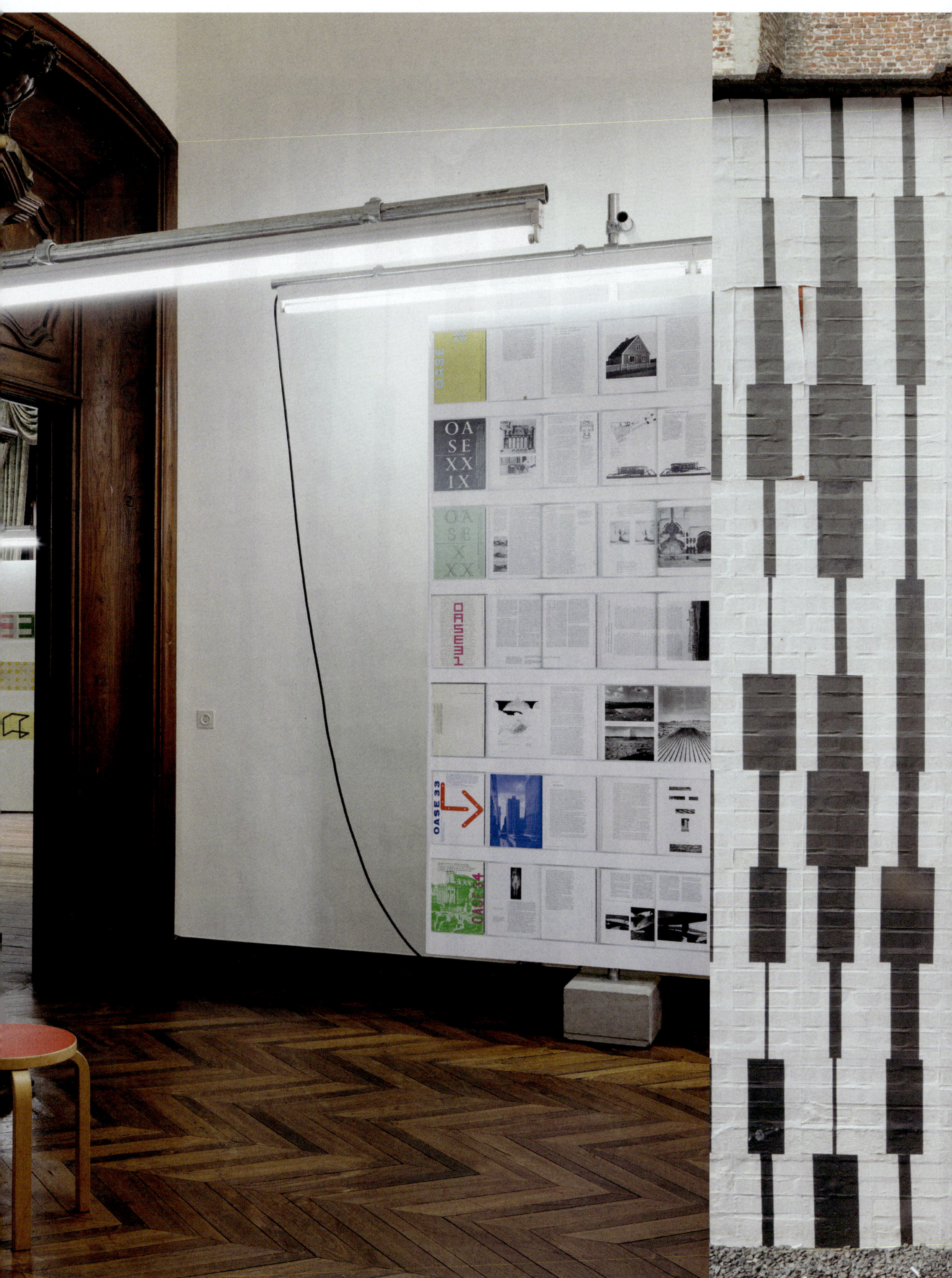

KAREL MARTENS, *Motion, OASE Journal for Architecture 28—97 (1990—ongoing)*, July 2017

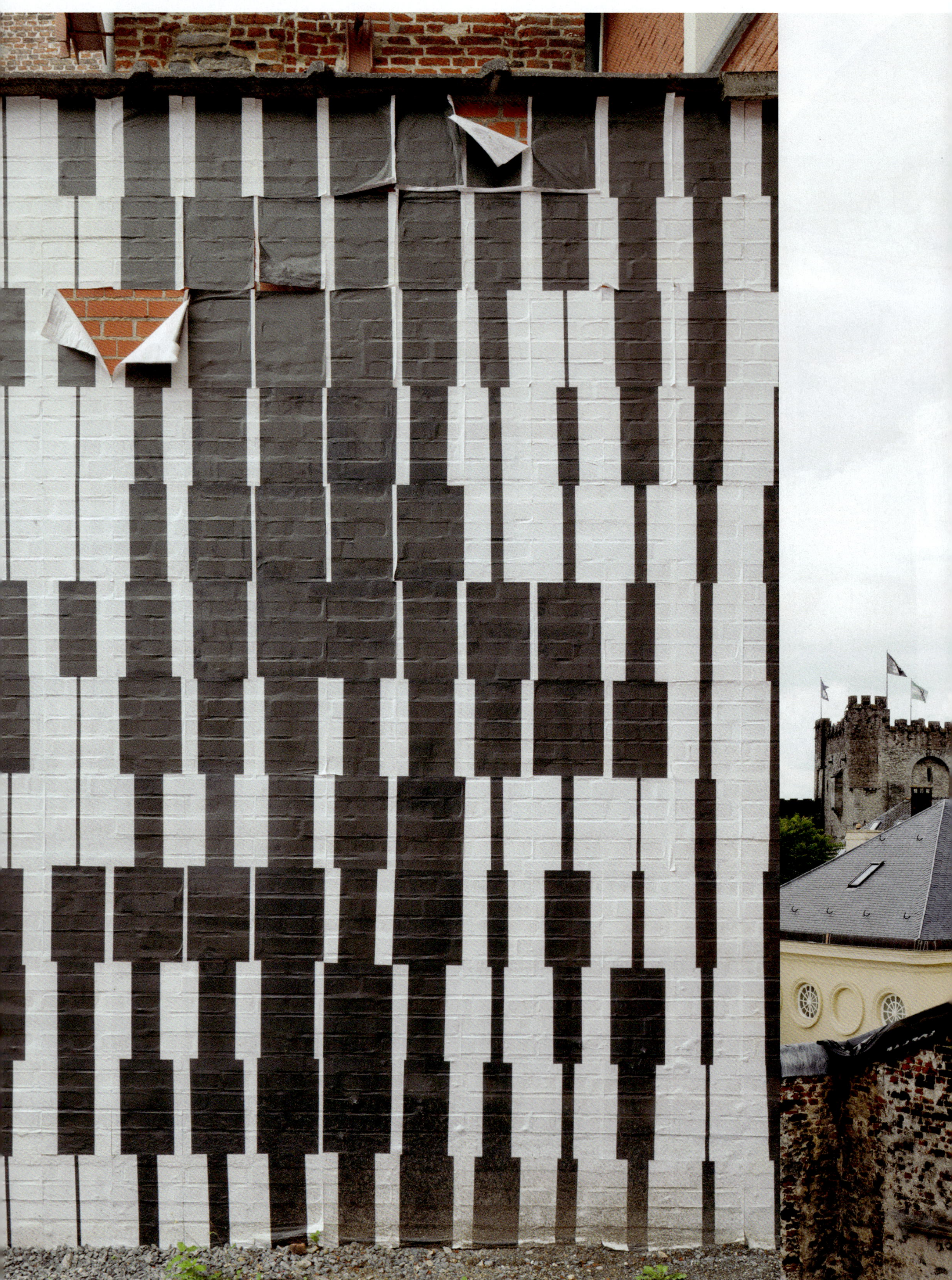

KAREL MARTENS, *Motion, A4 wallpaper*, July 2017

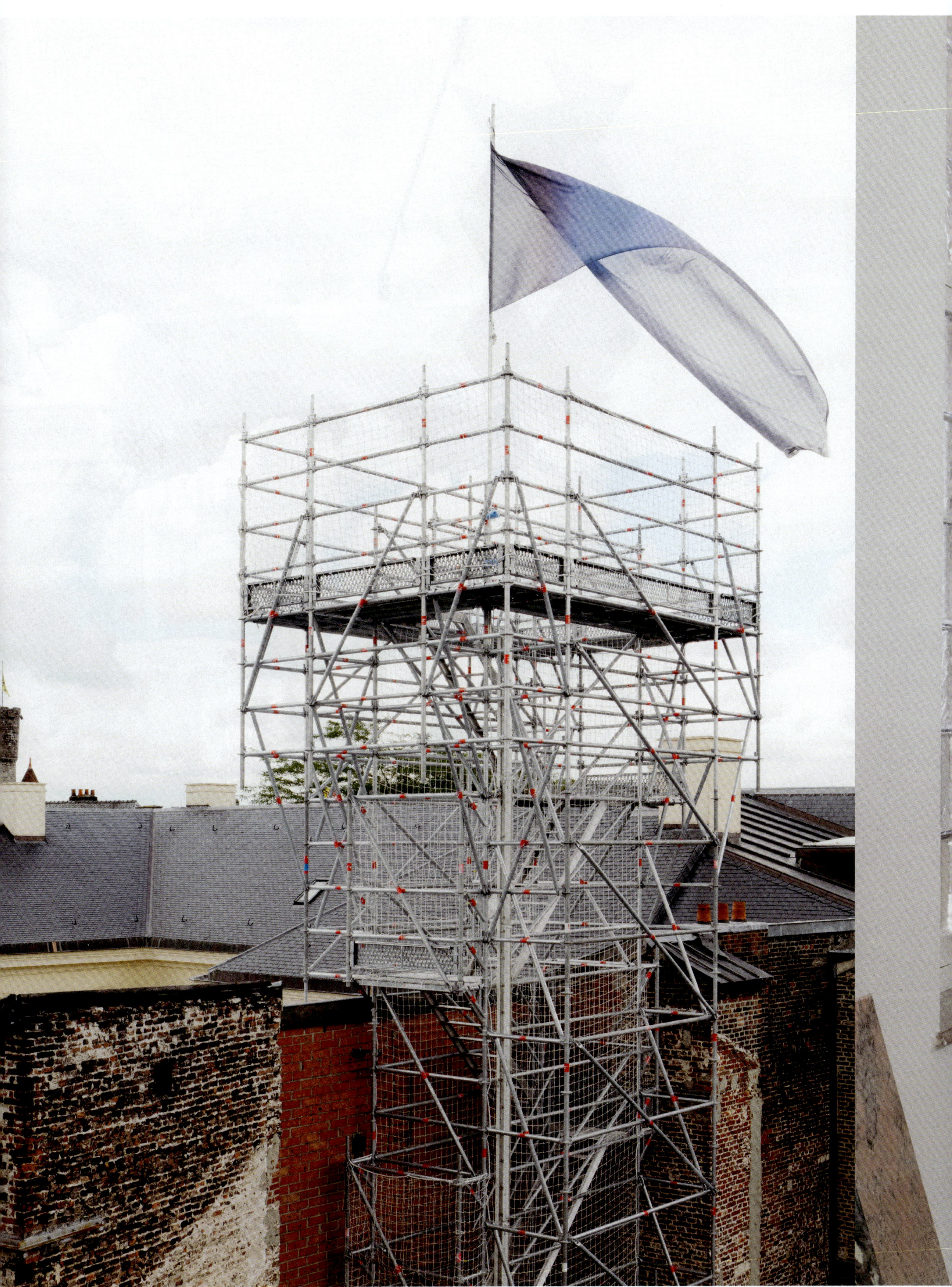

STIJN COLE, *New Colors / Sunrise 8/6/2017*, July 2017

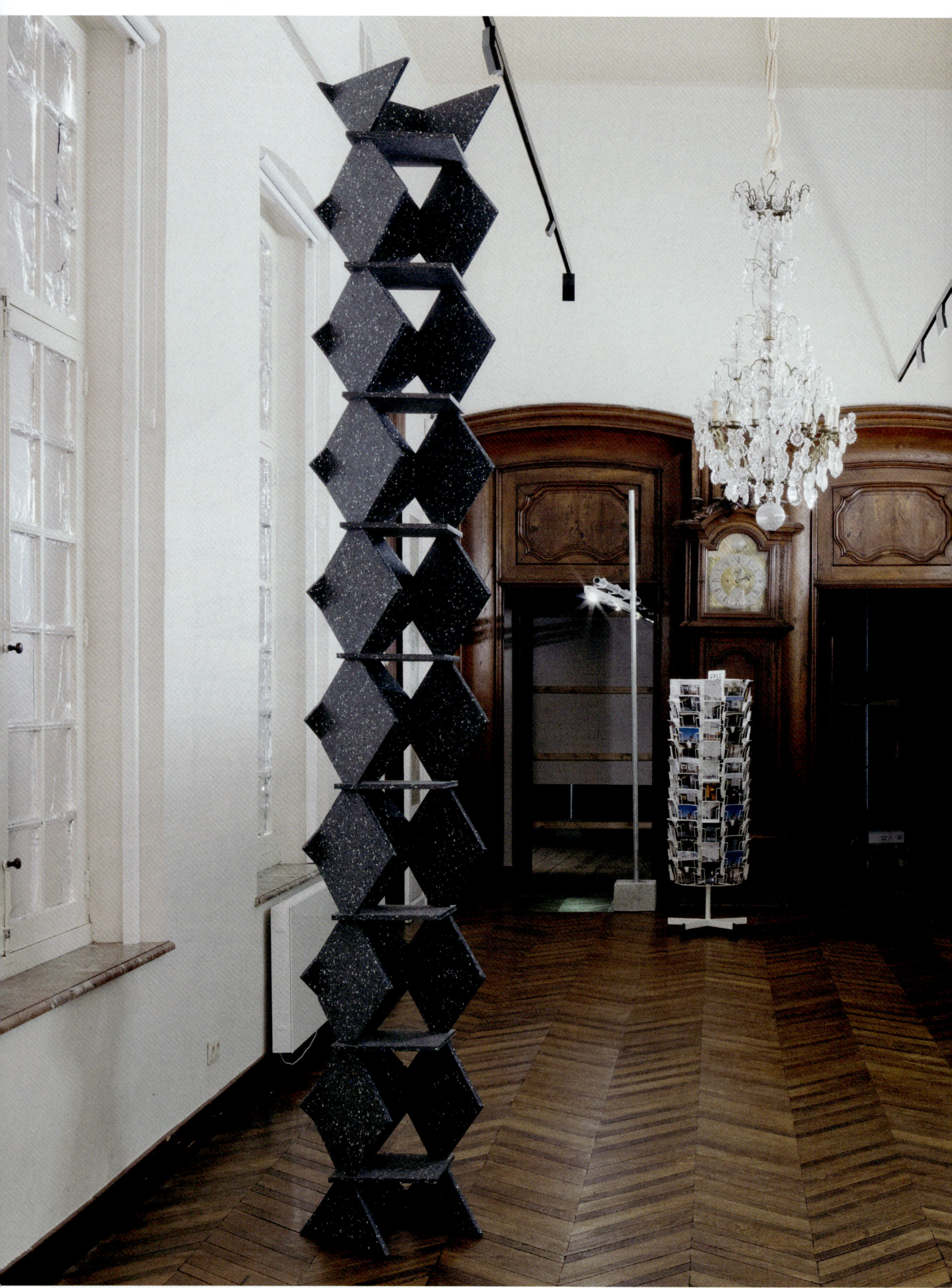

THEO DE MEYER / ARTHUR DEKKER, *Setting Up A Cabinet*, August 2017
MANOR GRUNEWALD, *External Hard Disk (E.H.D.)*, August 2017

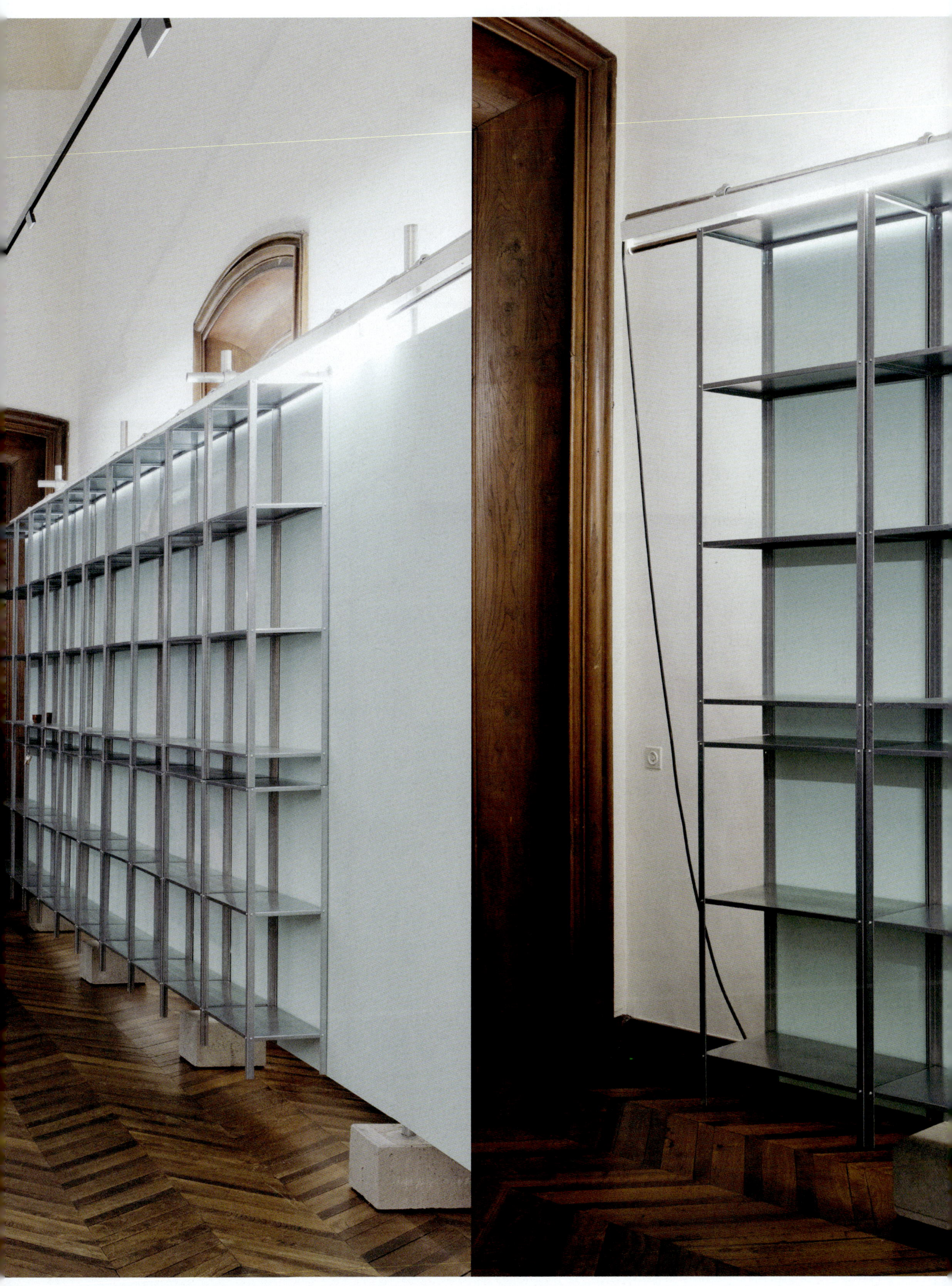

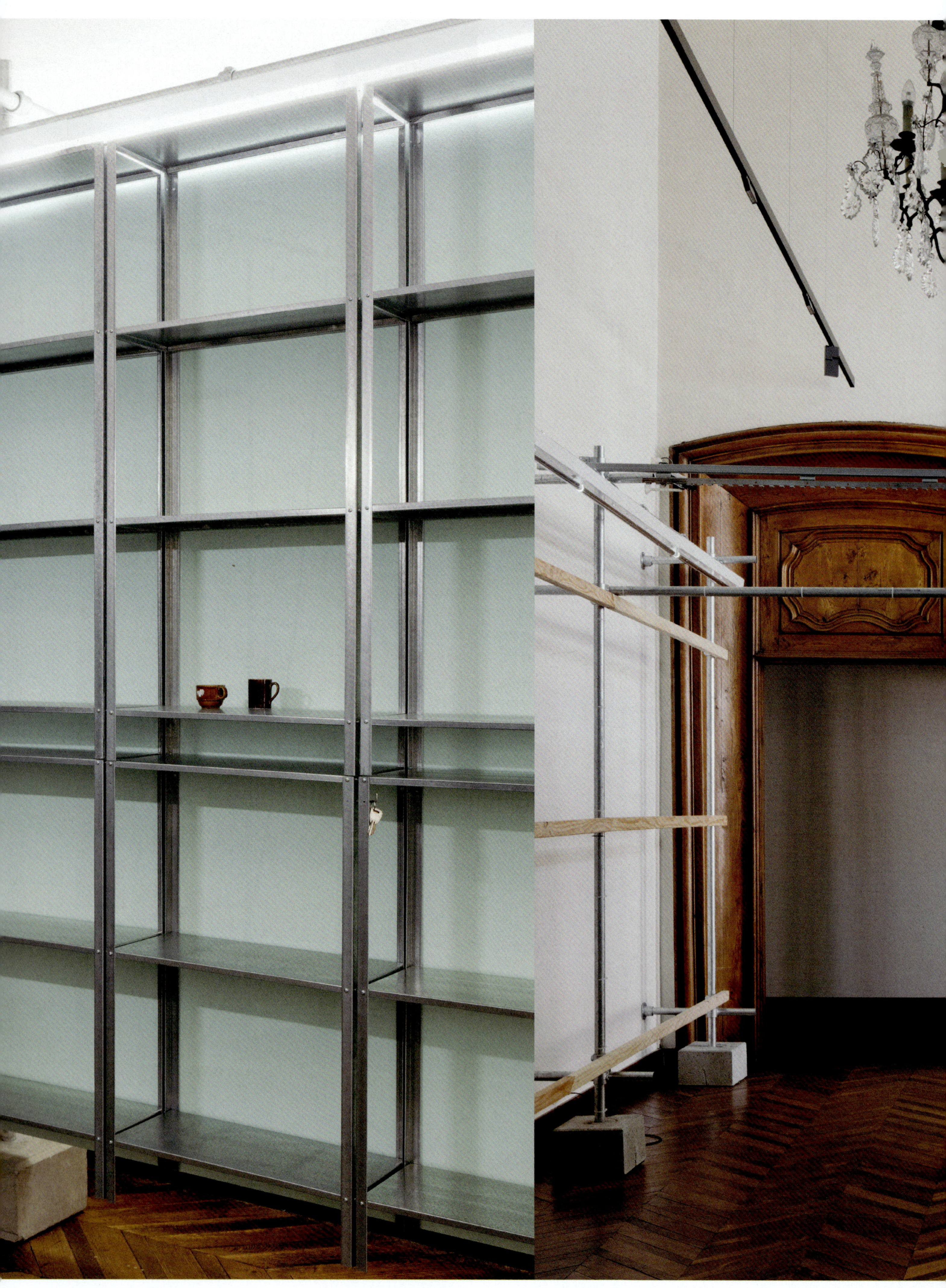

LYDIA DEBEER, *Absence Makes The Heart Grow Fonder, The View (2014)*, August 2017

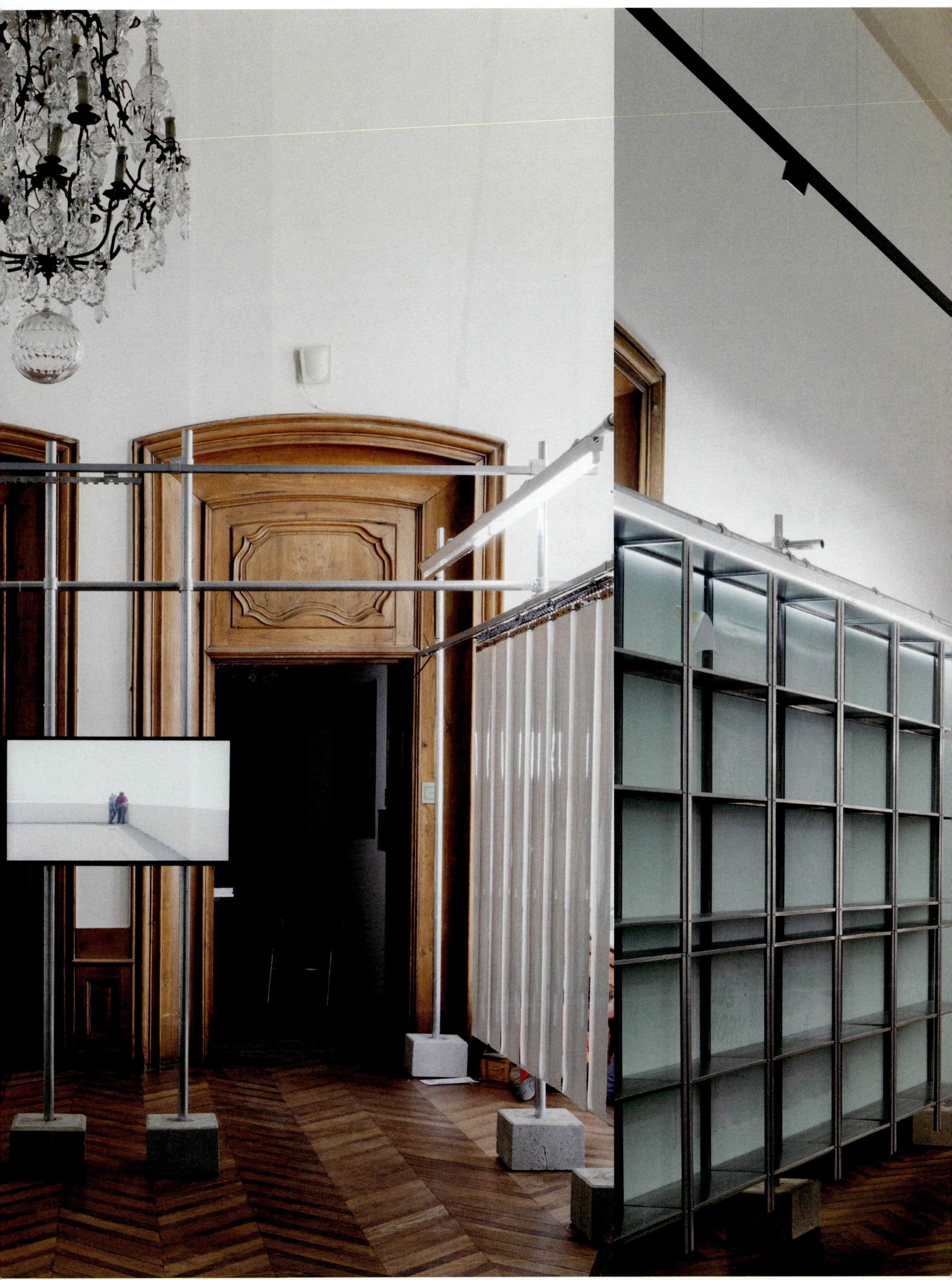

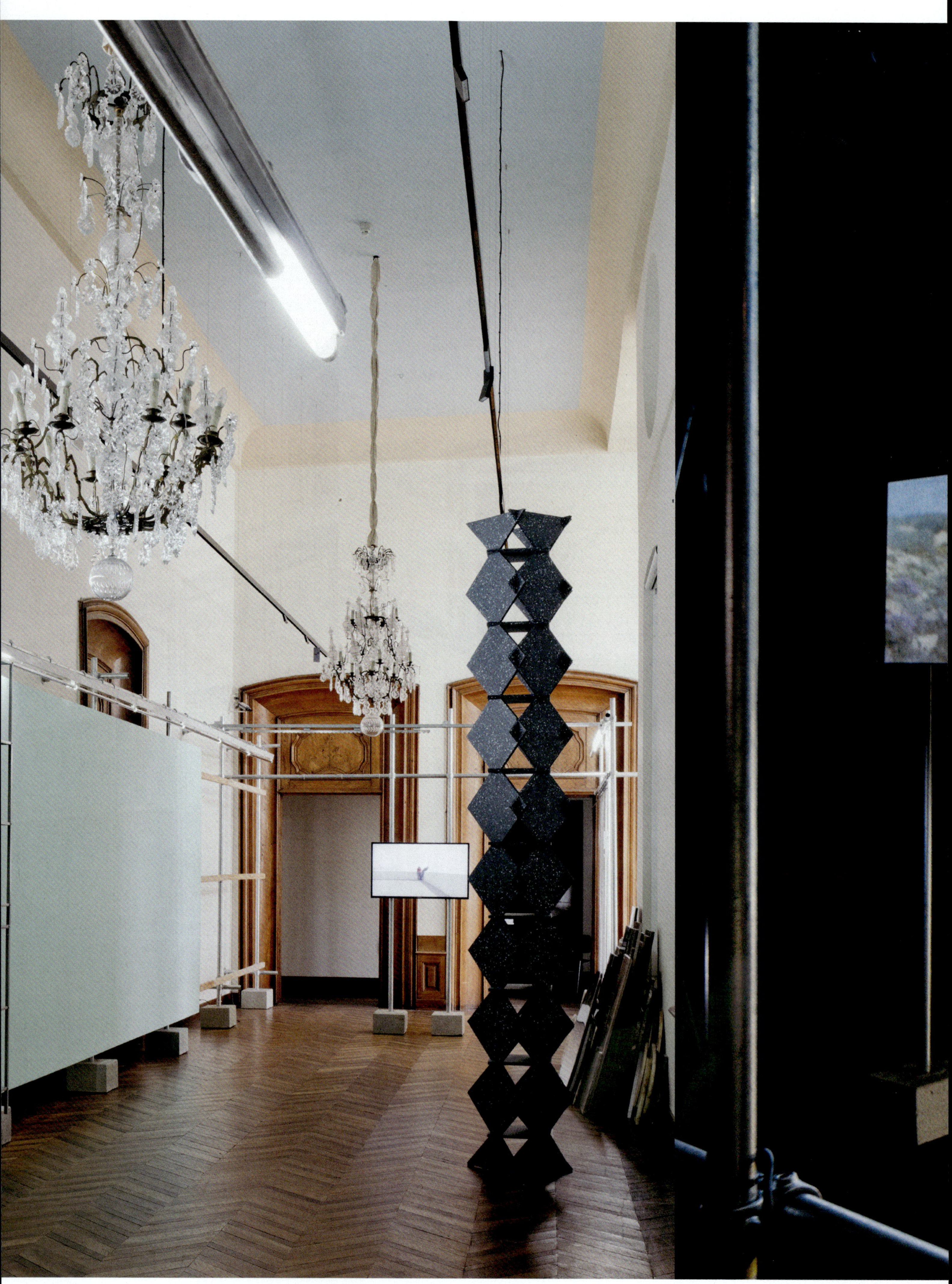

THEO DE MEYER / ARTHUR DEKKER, *Setting Up A Cabinet*, August 2017
MANOR GRUNEWALD, *External Hard Disk (E.H.D.)*, August 2017

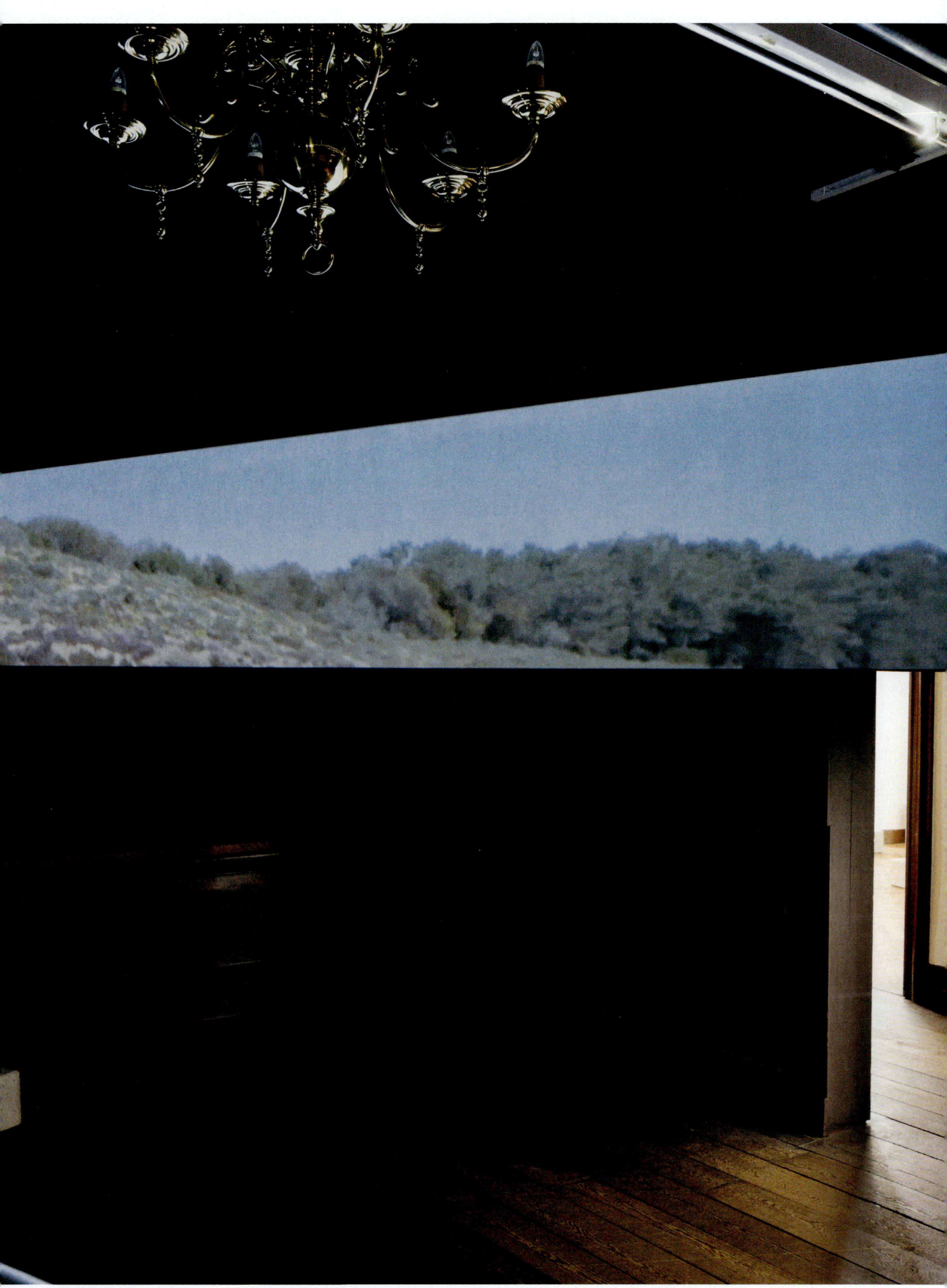

LYDIA DEBEER, *Absence Makes The Heart Grow Fonder, Offing (2016)*, August 2017

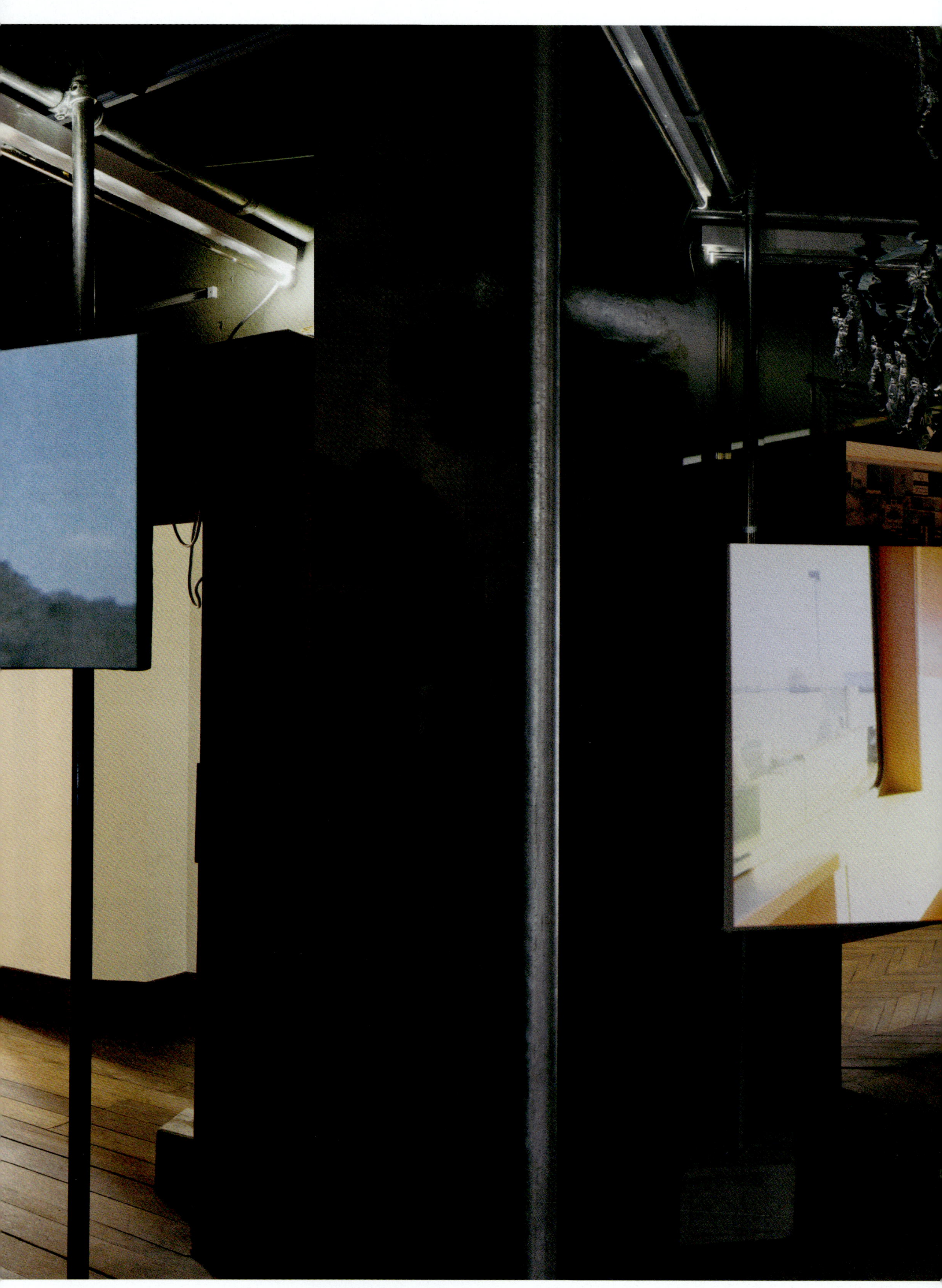

LYDIA DEBEER, *Absence Makes The Heart Grow Fonder, In Languor, I merely wait (2016)*, August 2017

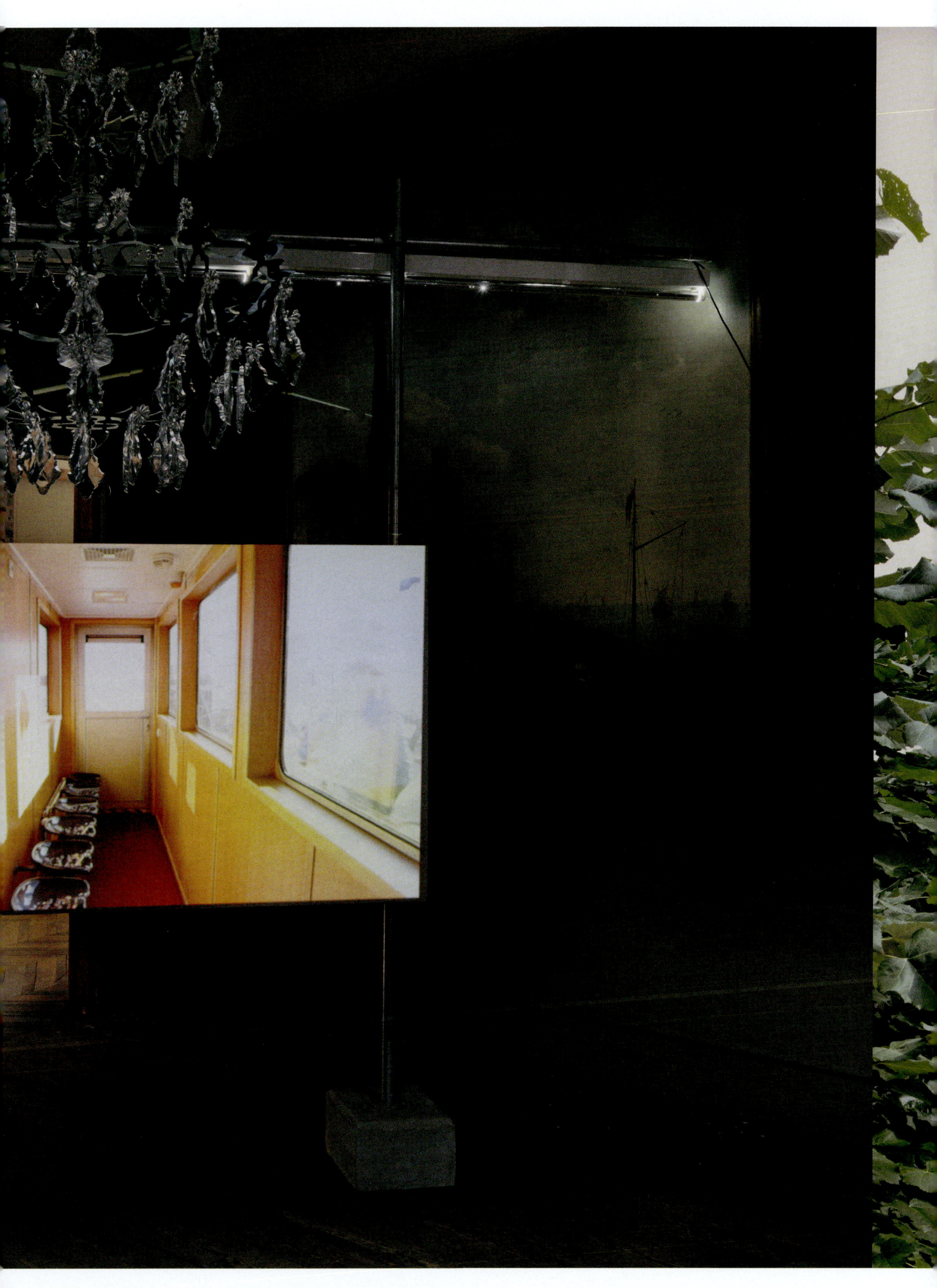

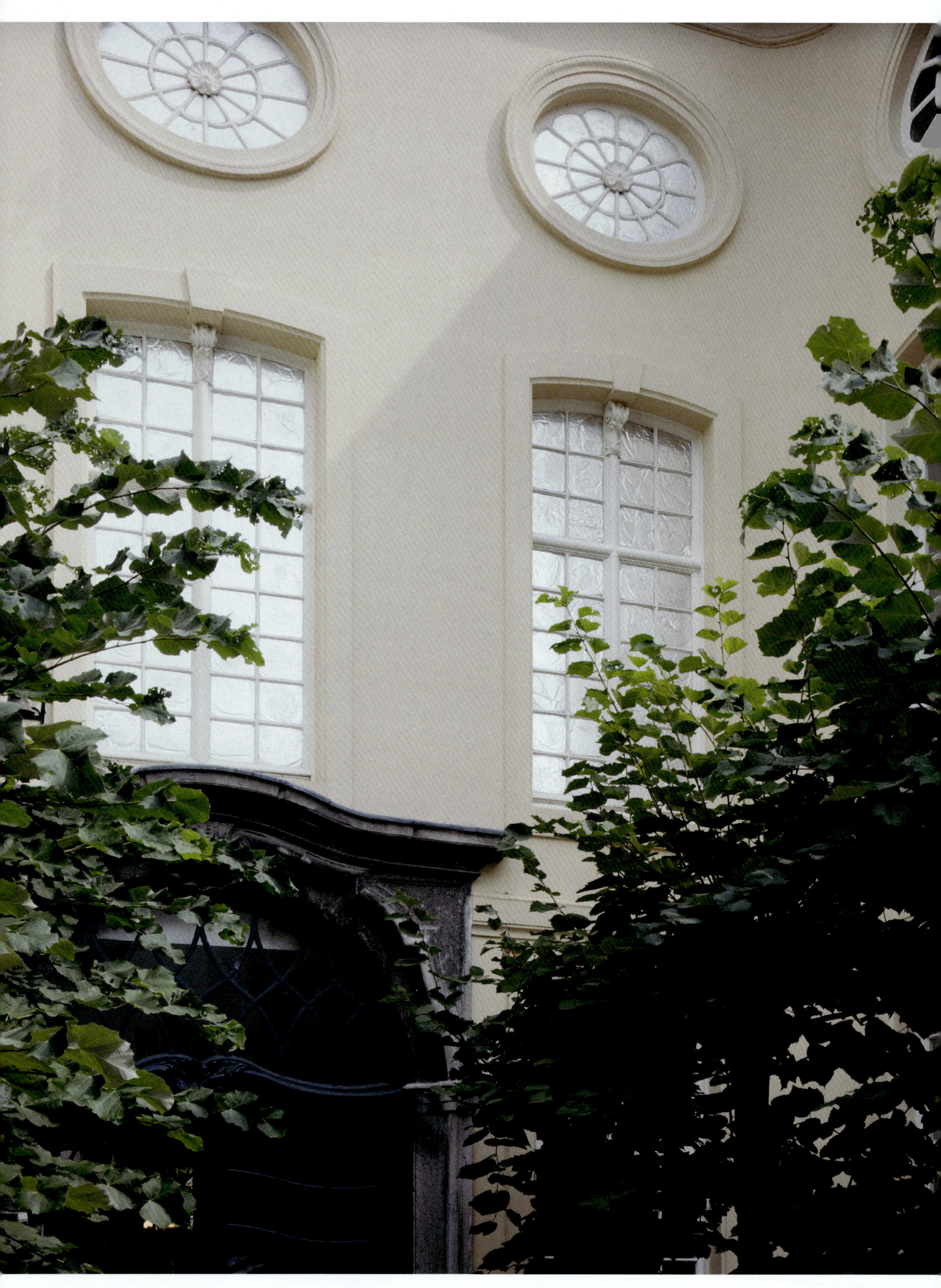

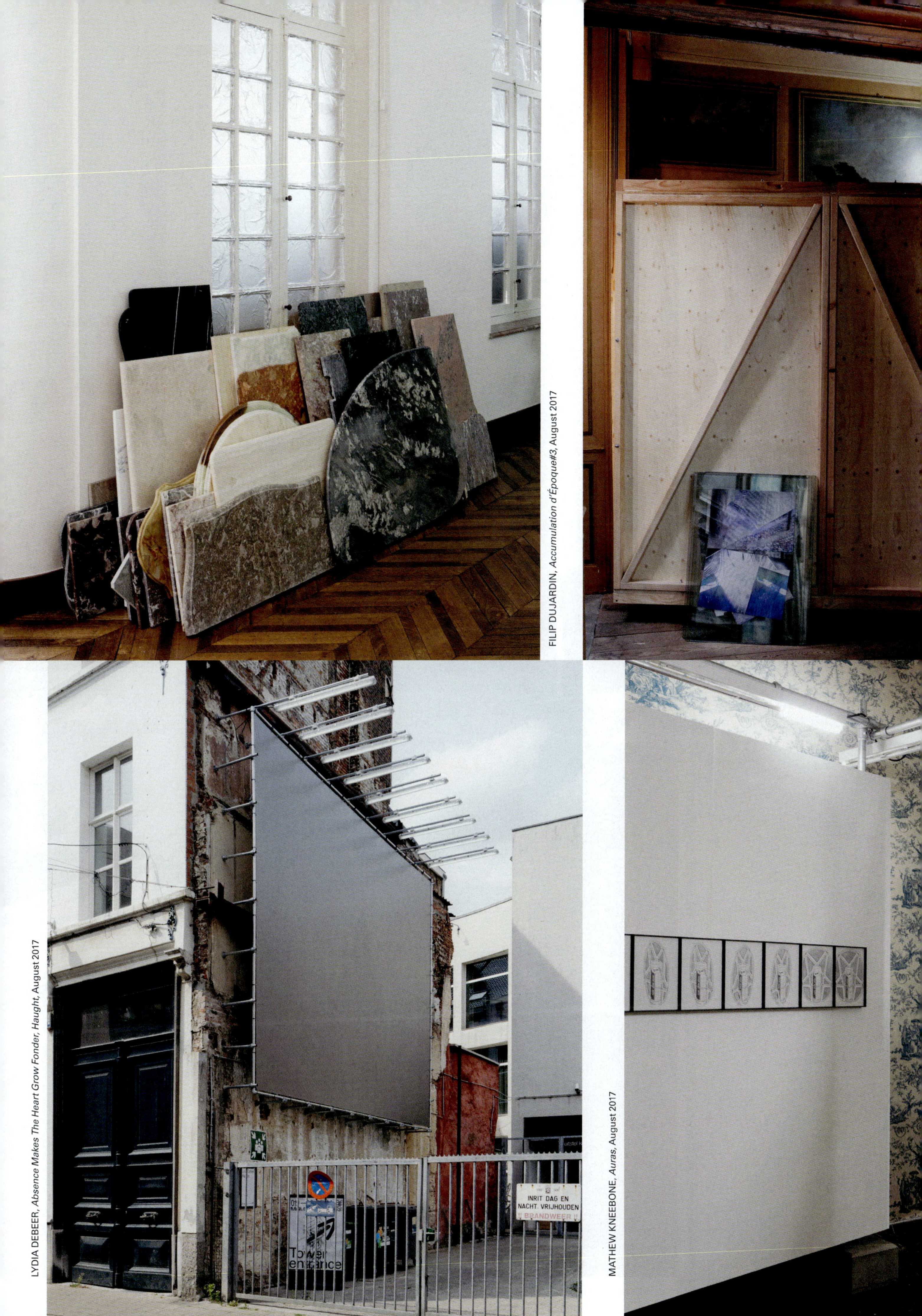

FILIP DUJARDIN, *Accumulation d'Époque#3*, August 2017

LYDIA DEBEER, *Absence Makes The Heart Grow Fonder, Haught*, August 2017

MATHEW KNEEBONE, *Auras*, August 2017

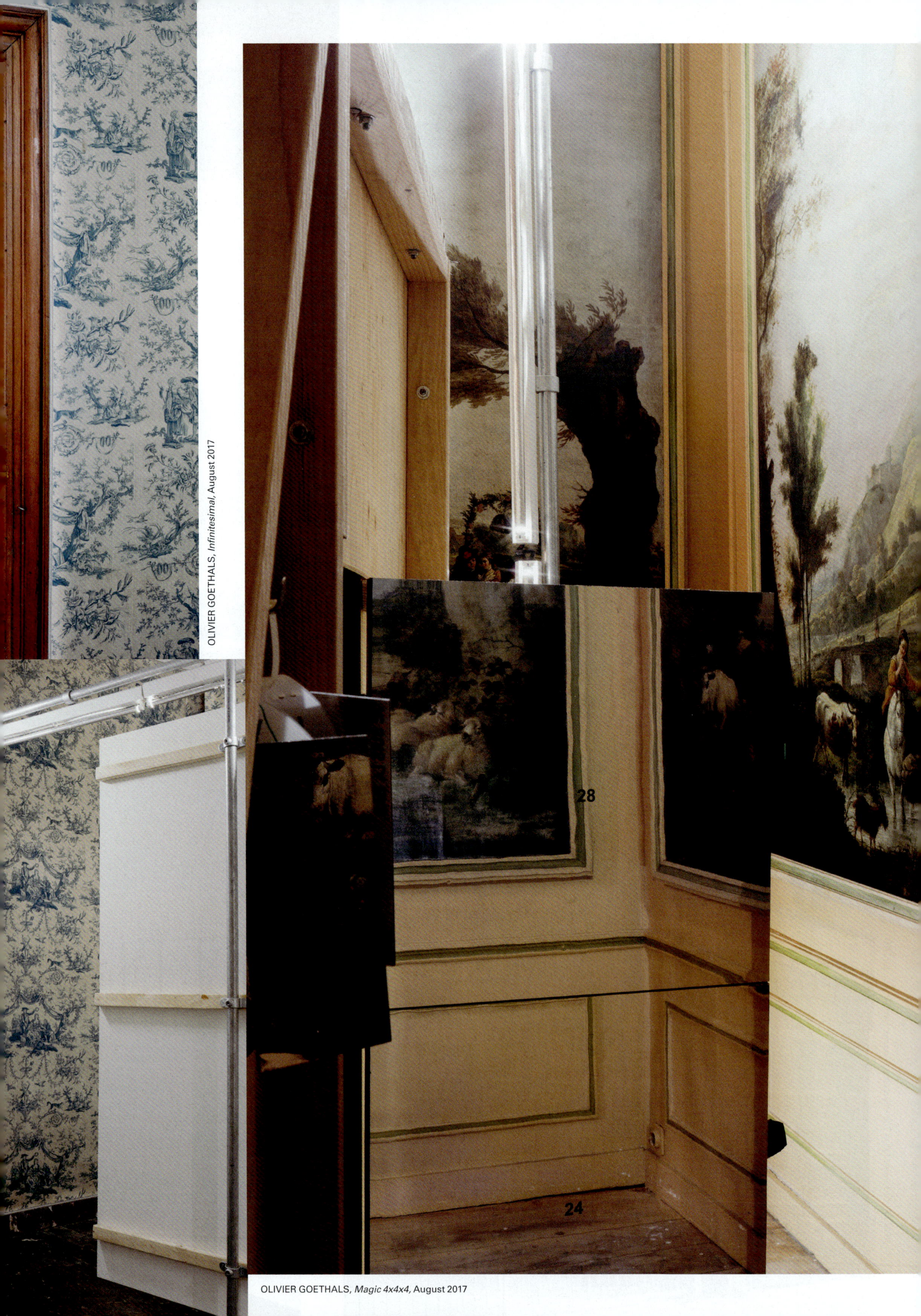

OLIVIER GOETHALS, *Infinitesimal*, August 2017

OLIVIER GOETHALS, *Magic 4x4x4*, August 2017

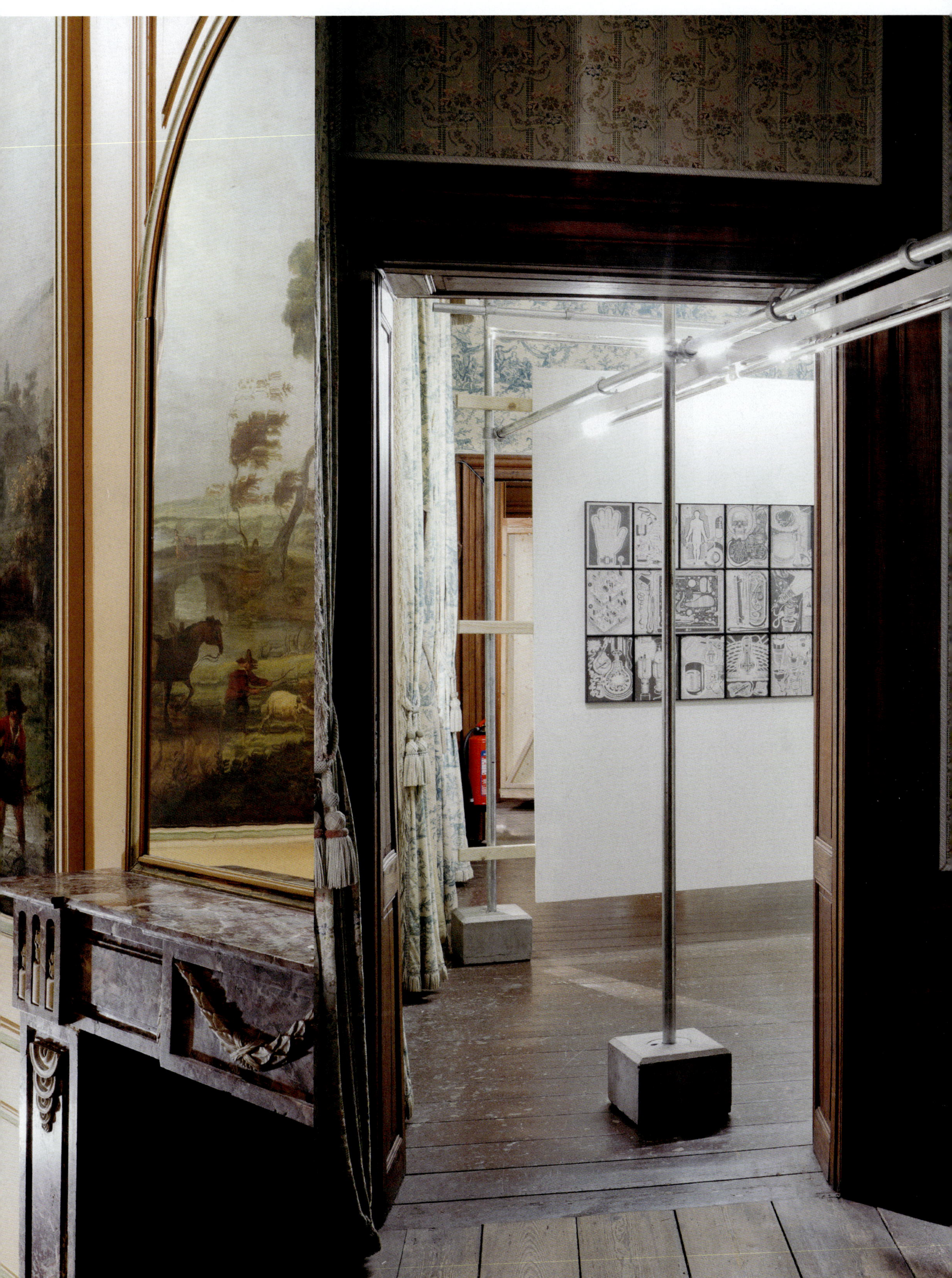

MATHEW KNEEBONE, *Auras*, August 2017

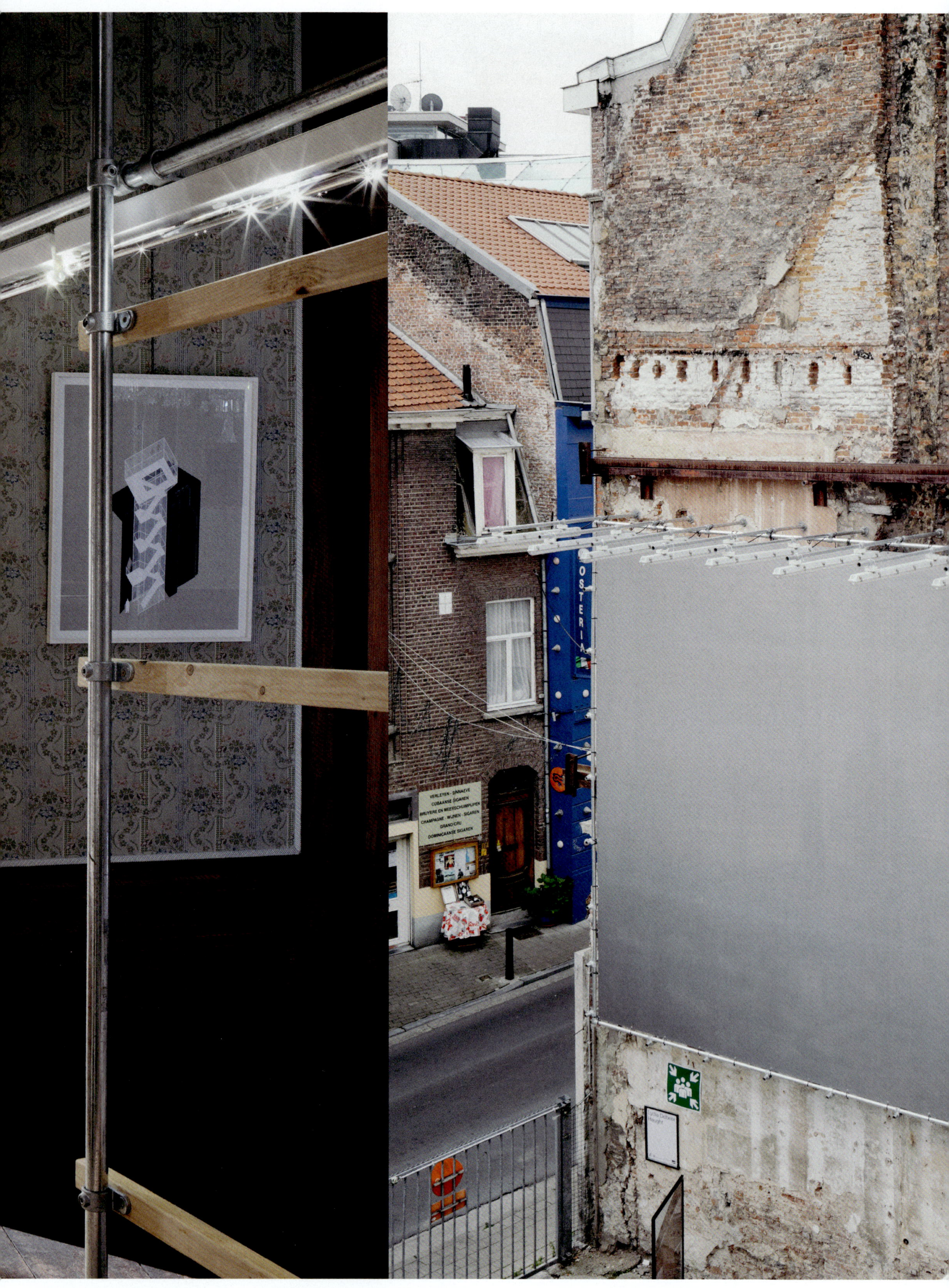

OLIVIER GOETHALS, *Museum Of Moving Practice*, August 2017

LYDIA DEBEER, *Absence Makes The Heart Grow Fonder, Haught*, August 2017

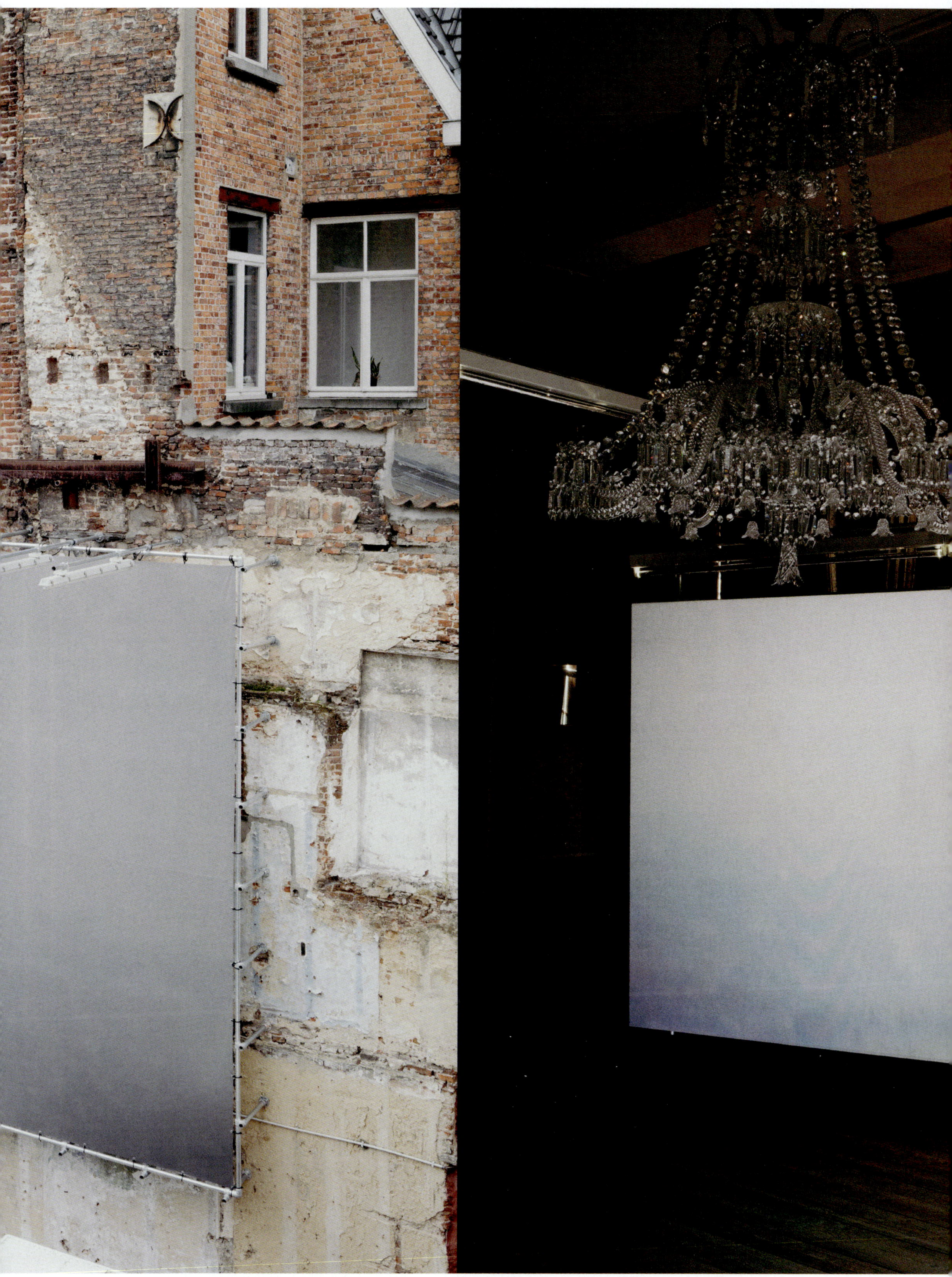

LYDIA DEBEER, *Absence Makes The Heart Grow Fonder, 25,* August 2017

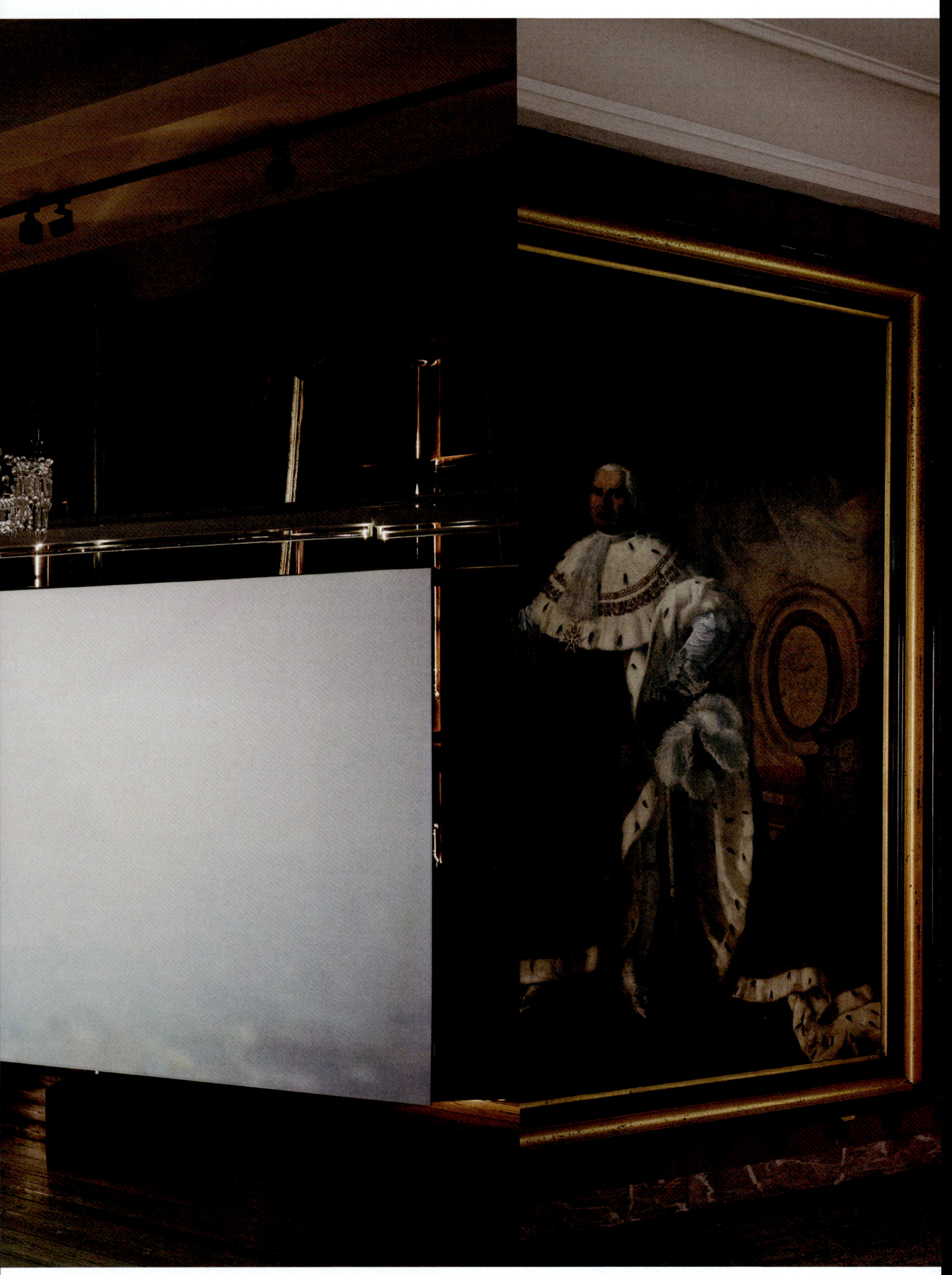

BEN THORP BROWN, *Toymakers*, August 2017

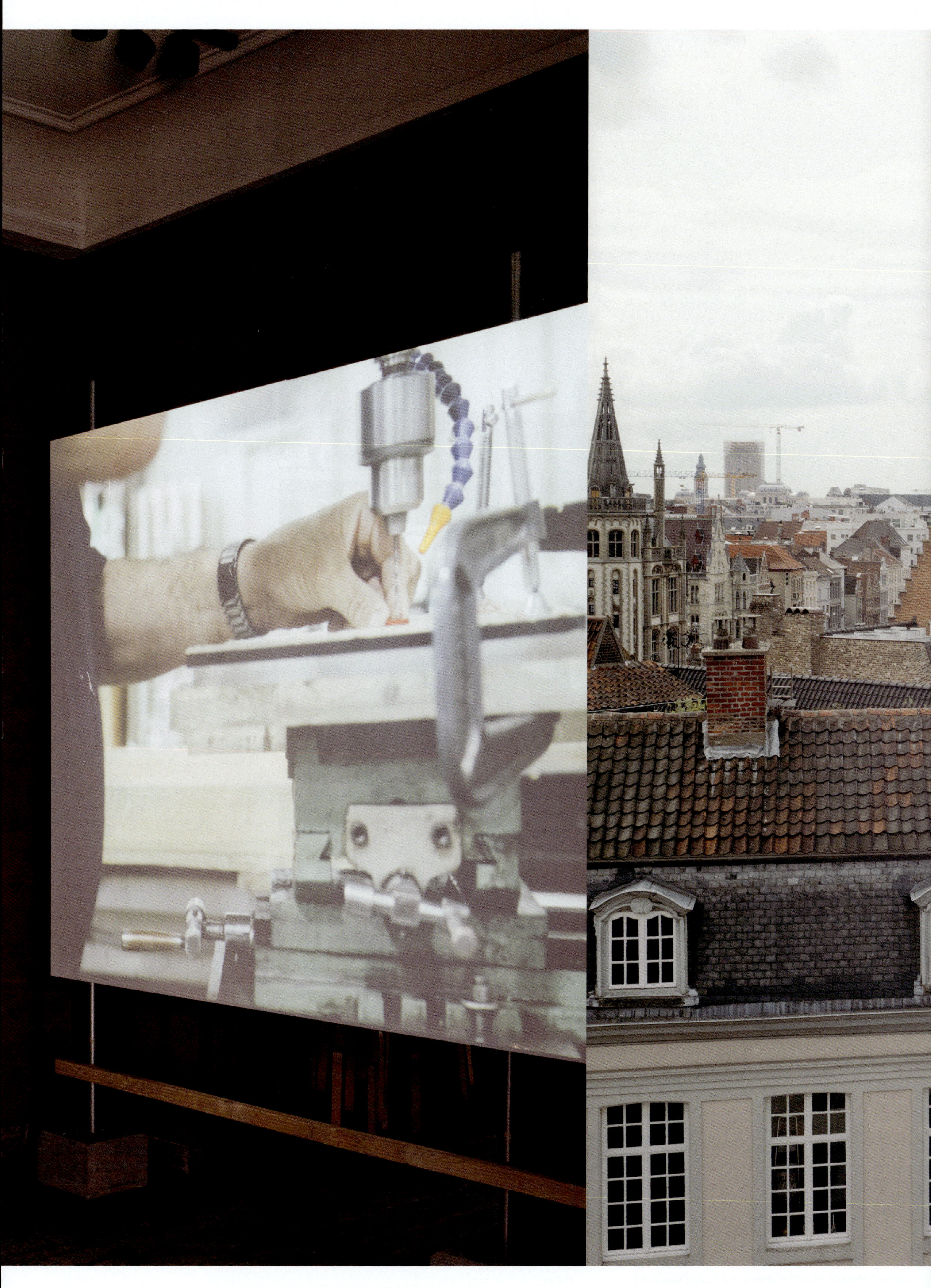

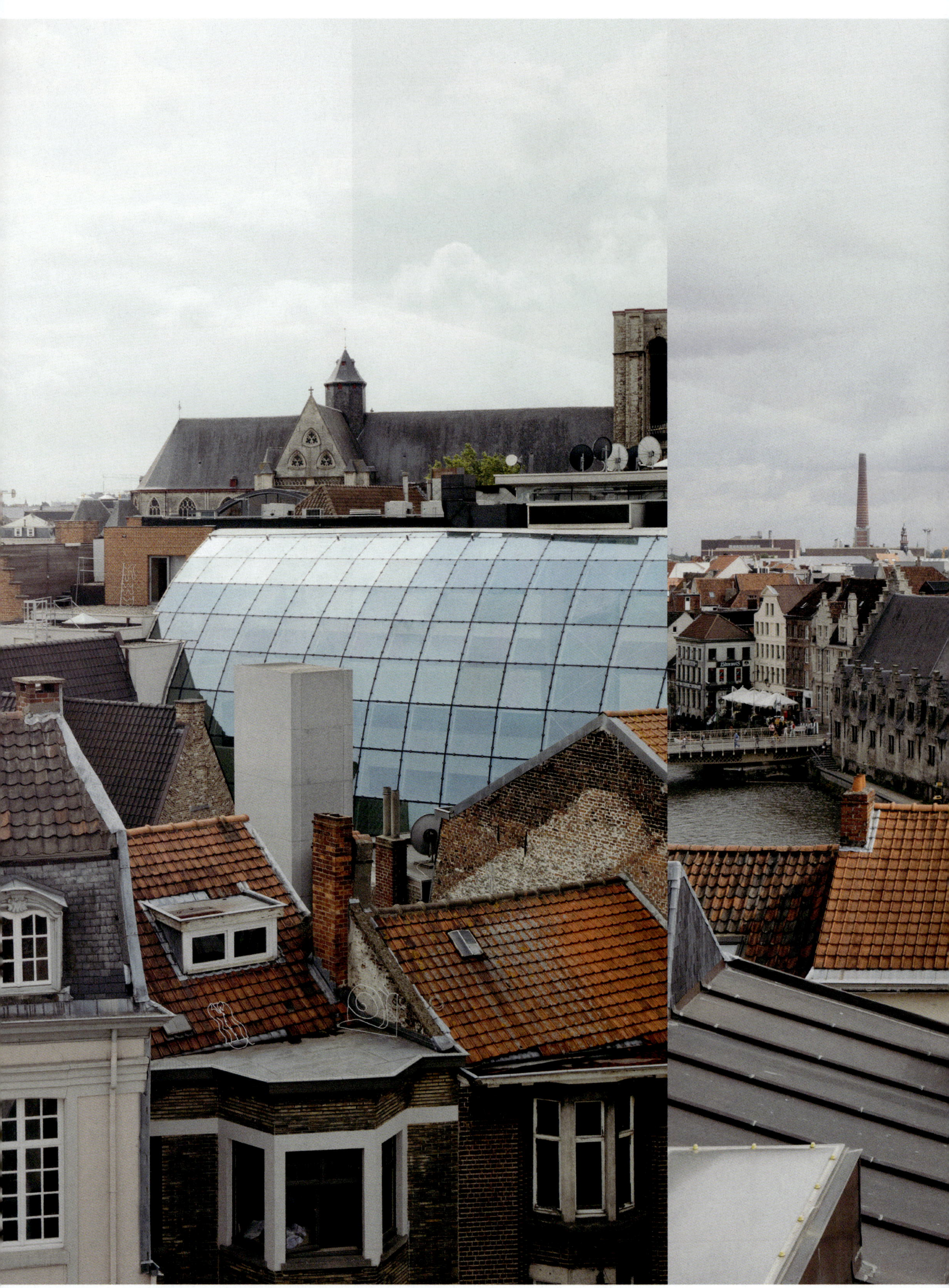

QUENTON MILLER, *Here I Am, Writing You A Letter*, August 2017

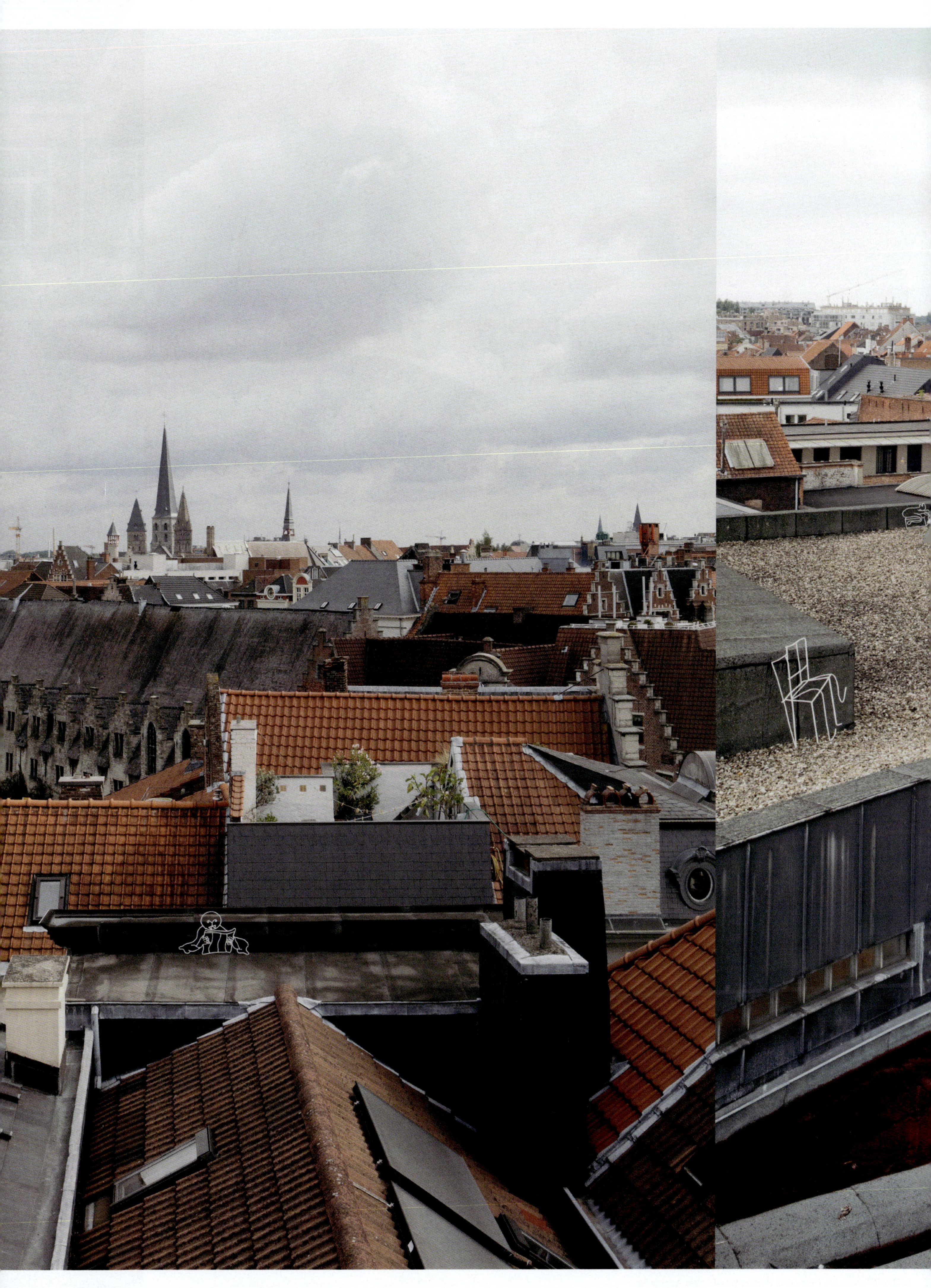

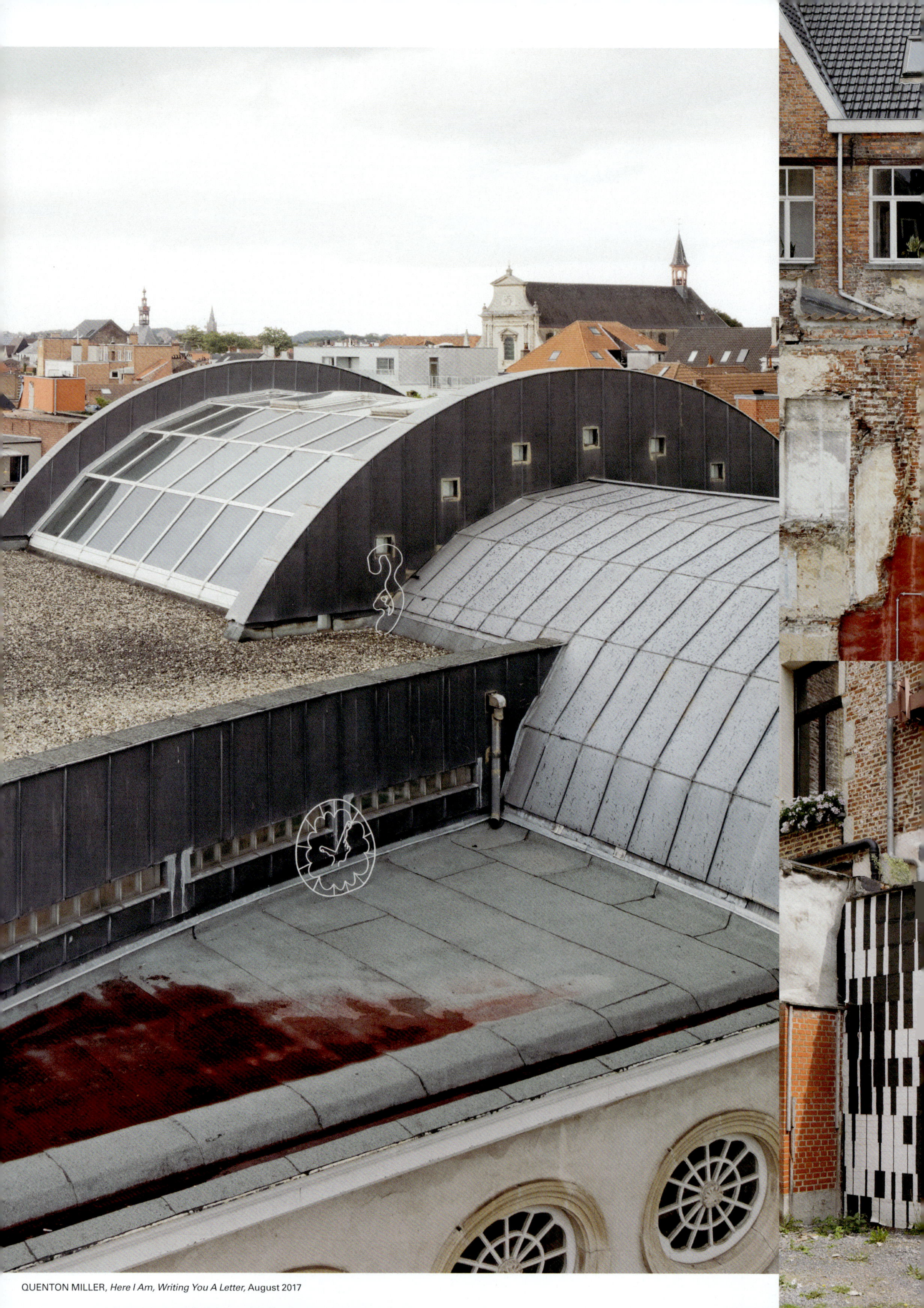

QUENTON MILLER, *Here I Am, Writing You A Letter*, August 2017

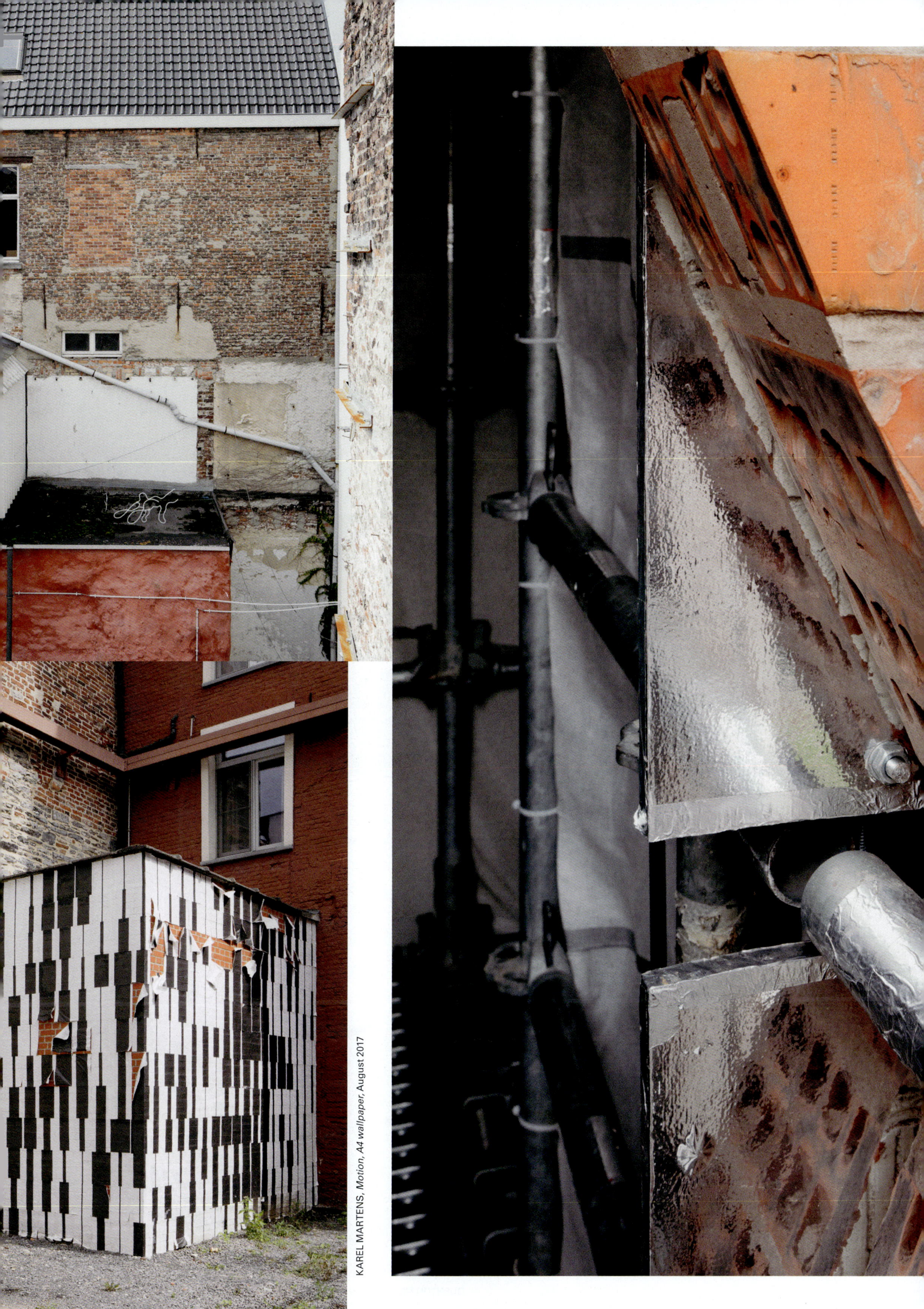

KAREL MARTENS, *Motion, A4 wallpaper*, August 2017

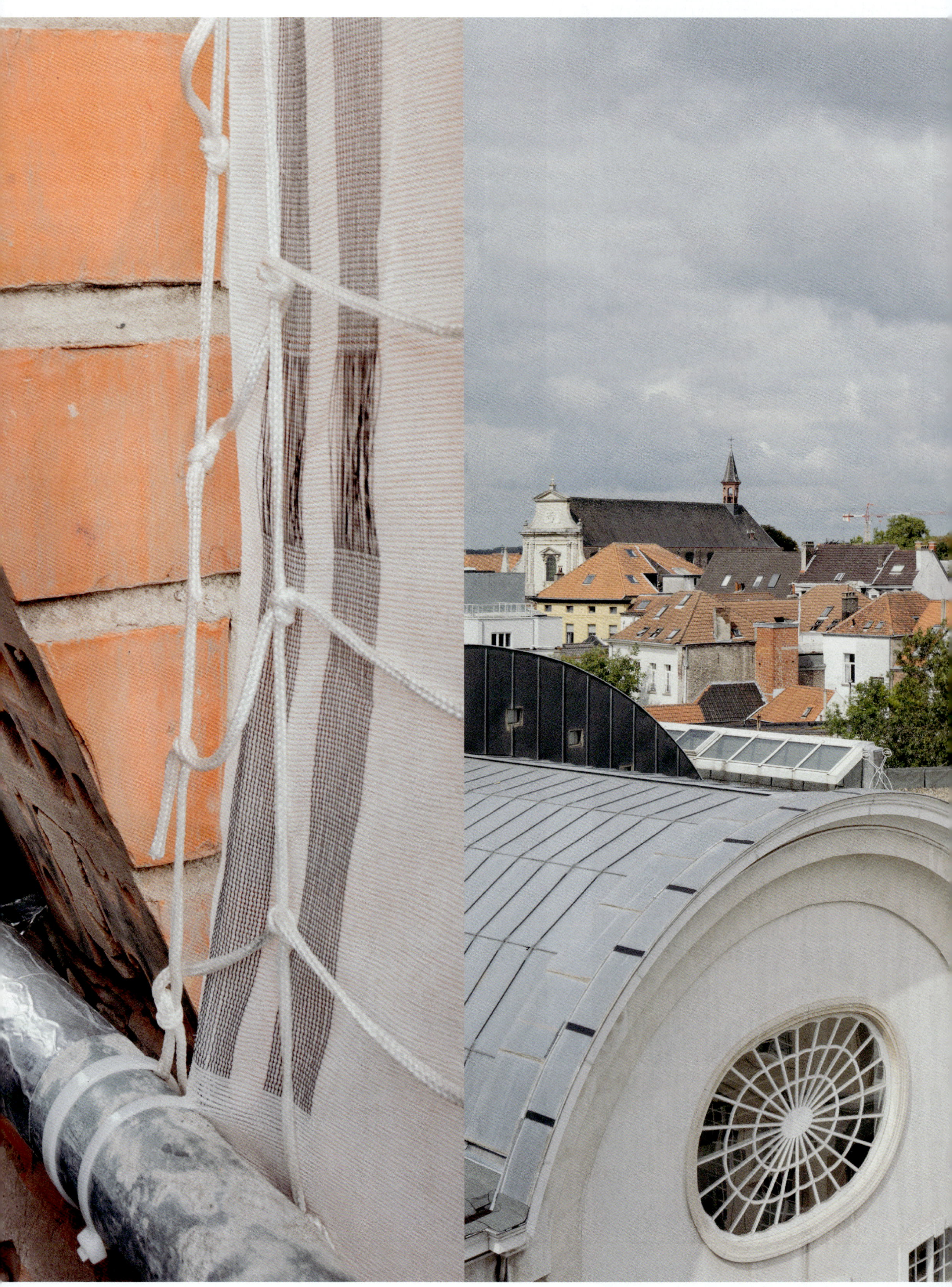

QUENTON MILLER, *Here I Am, Writing You A Letter*, August 2017

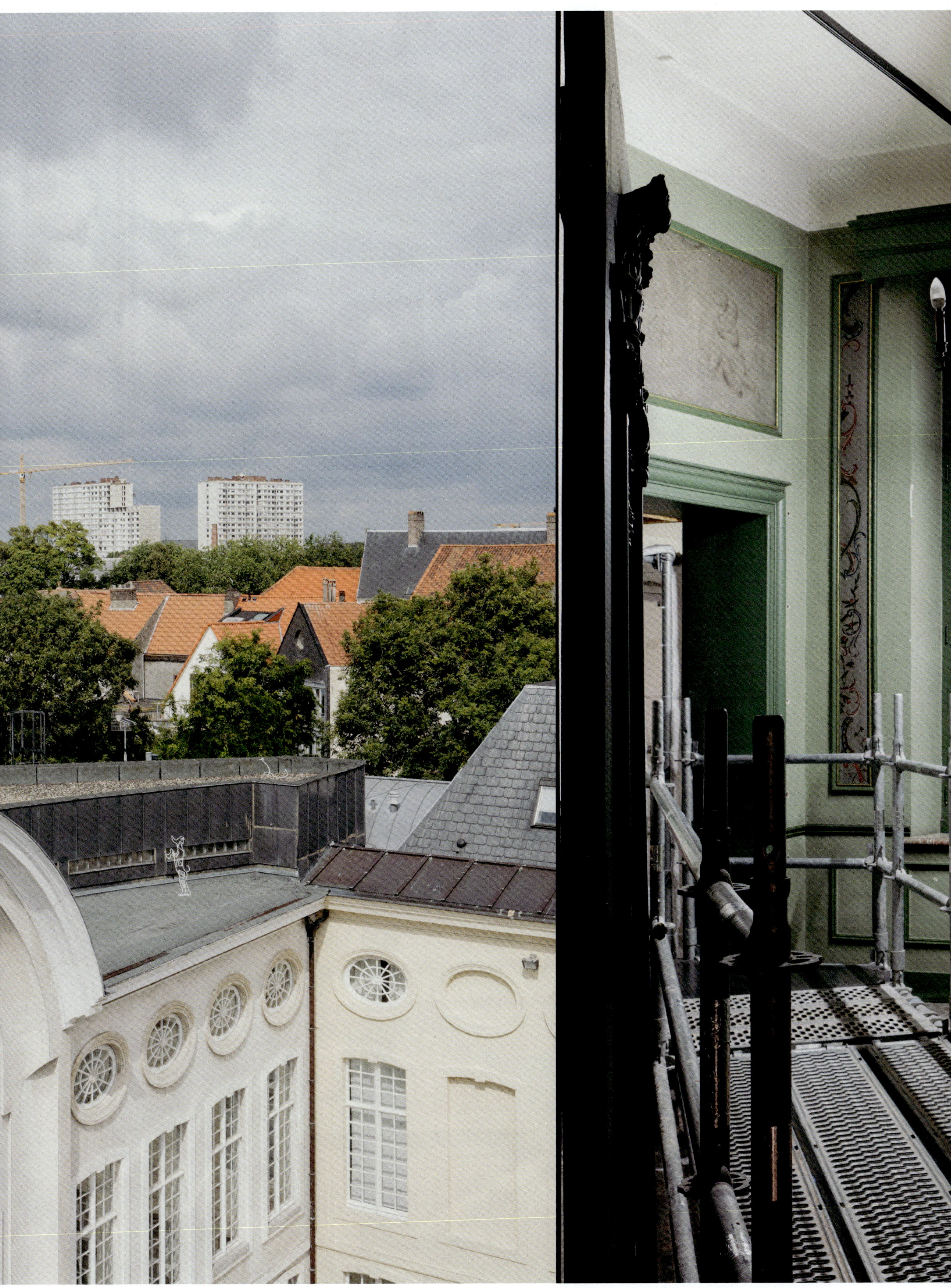

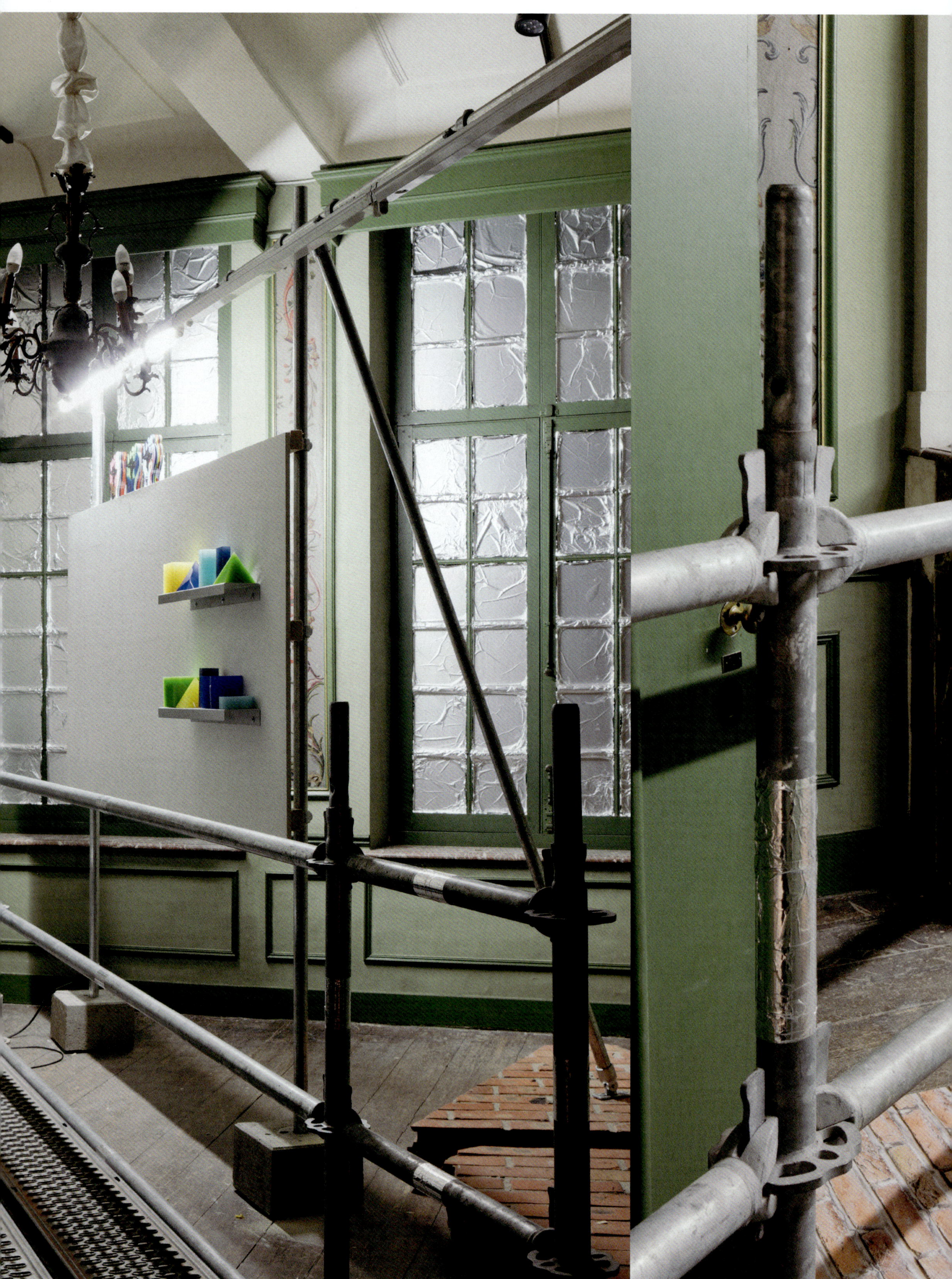

BEN THORP BROWN, *Toymakers*, August 2017

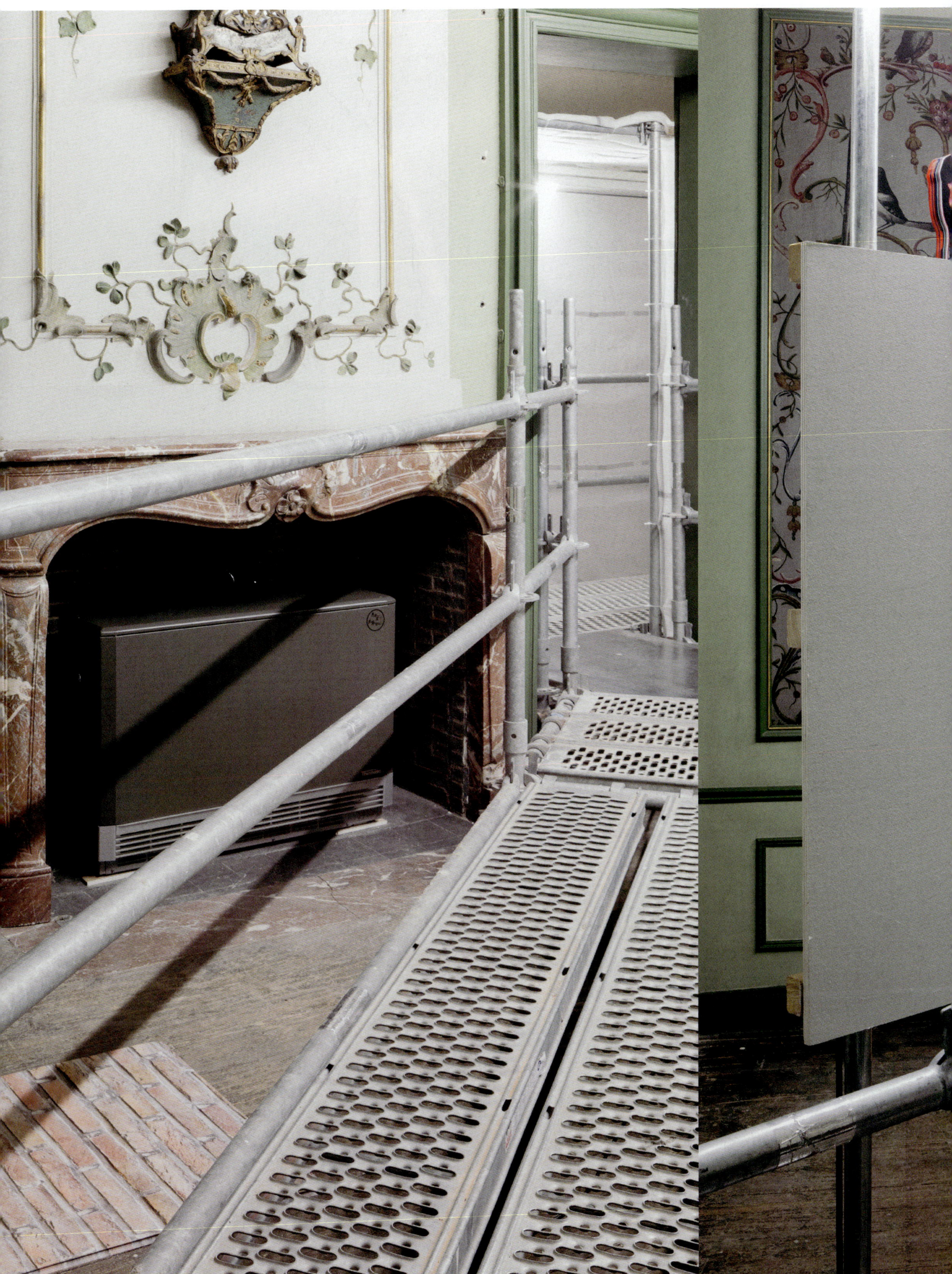

INE MEGANCK, *The Secret Portal*, August 2017

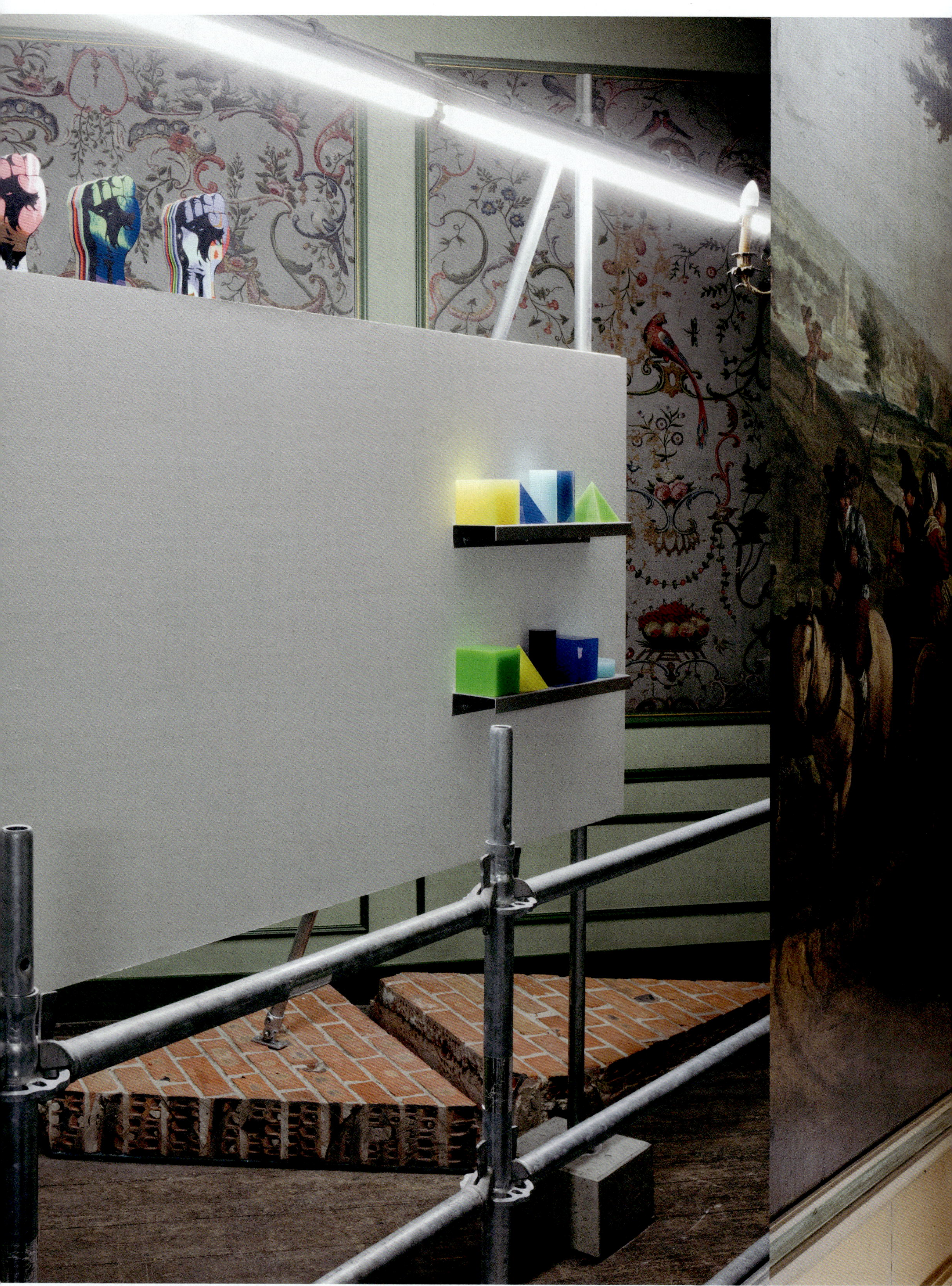

BEN THORP BROWN, *Toymakers*, August 2017

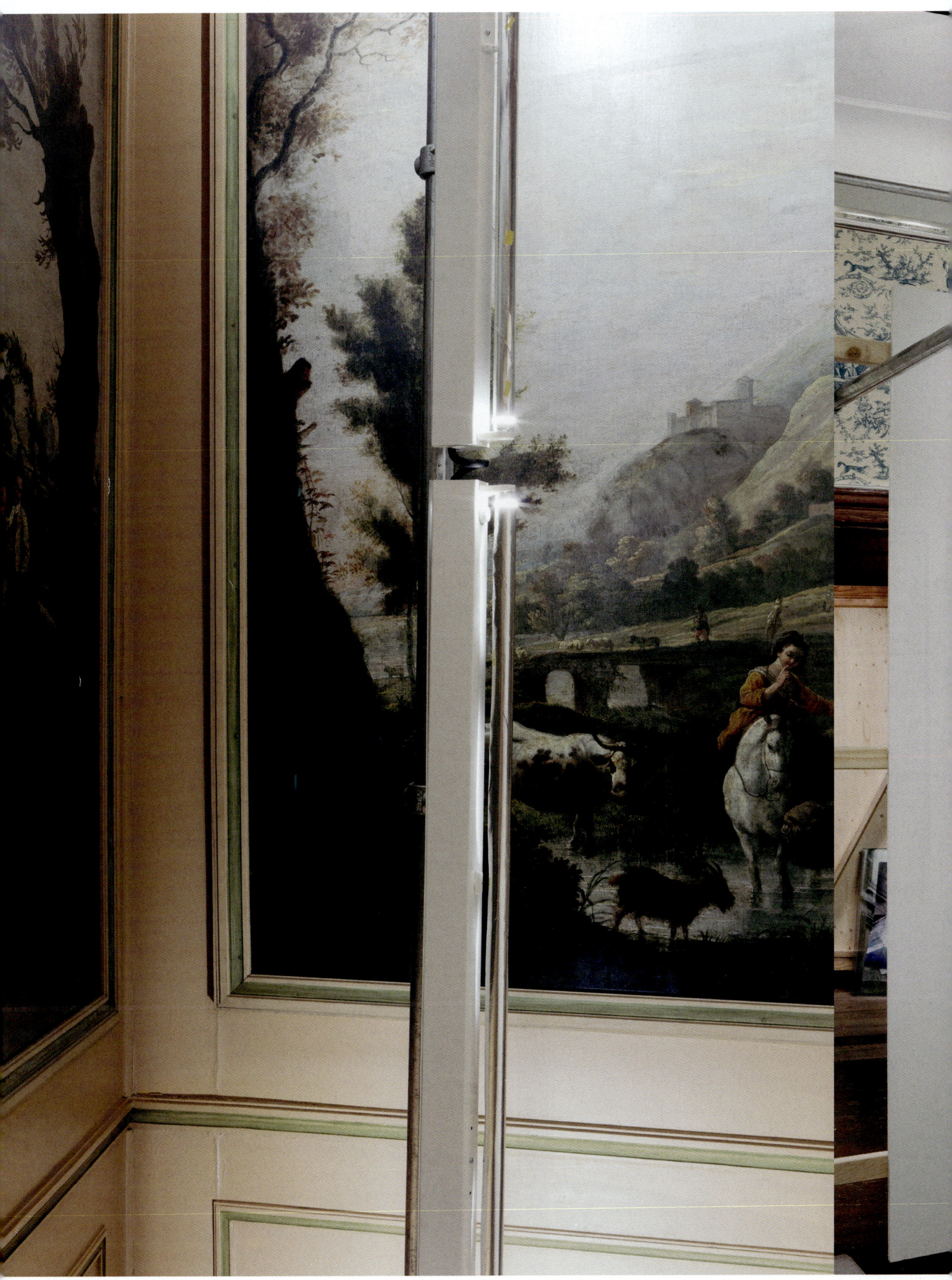

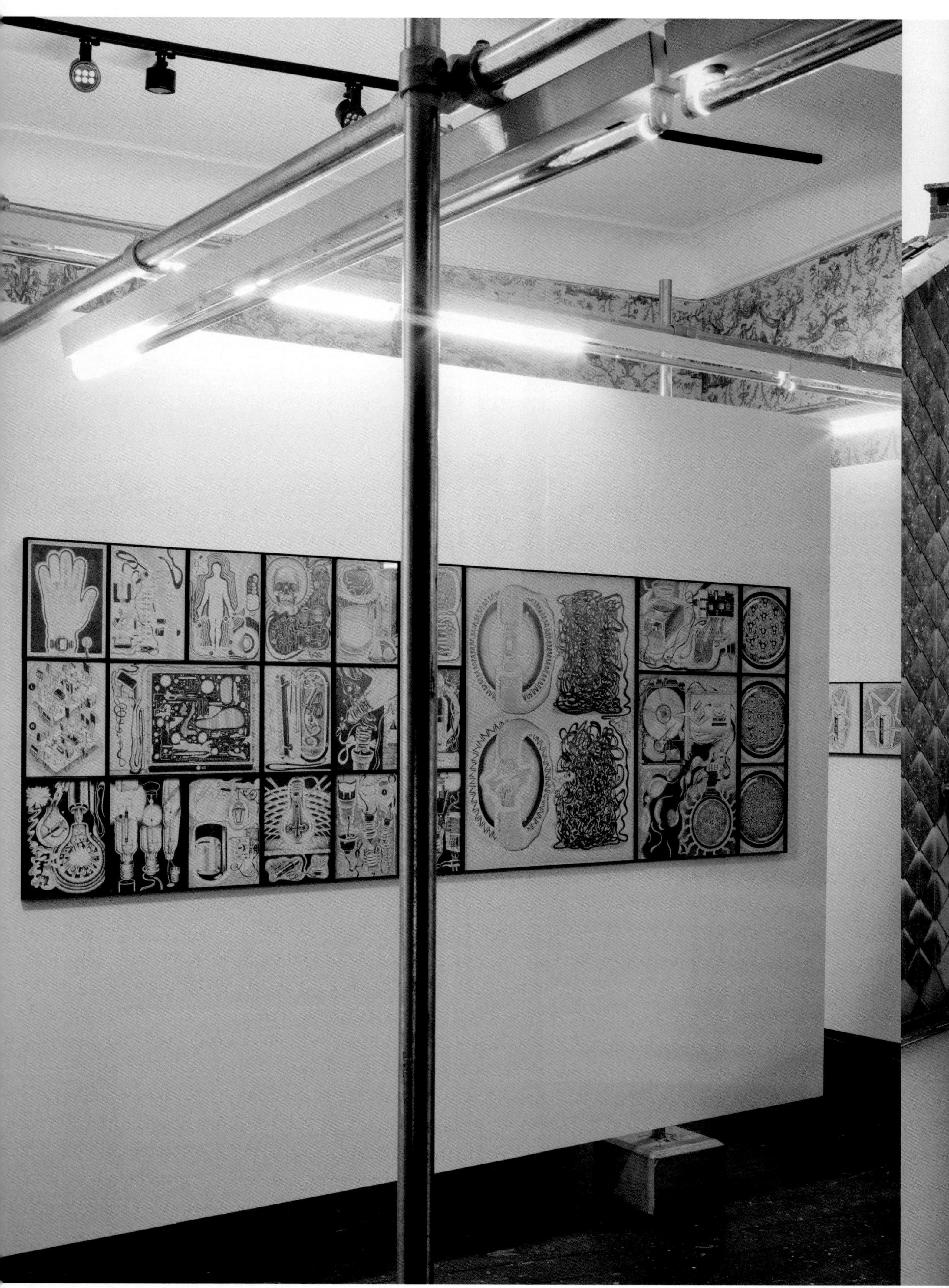

MATHEW KNEEBONE, *Auras*, August 2017

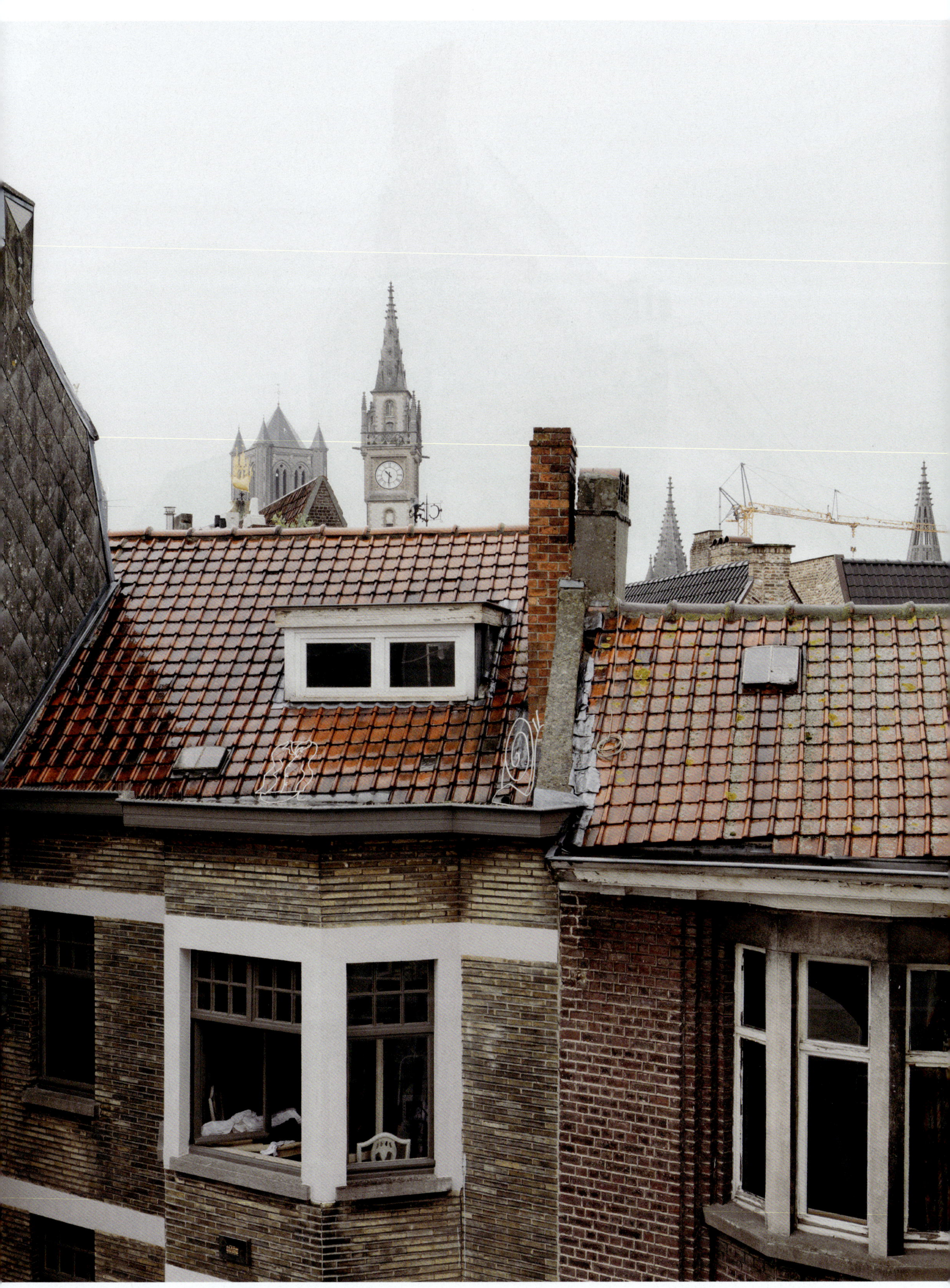

QUENTON MILLER, *Here I Am, Writing You A Letter,* August 2017

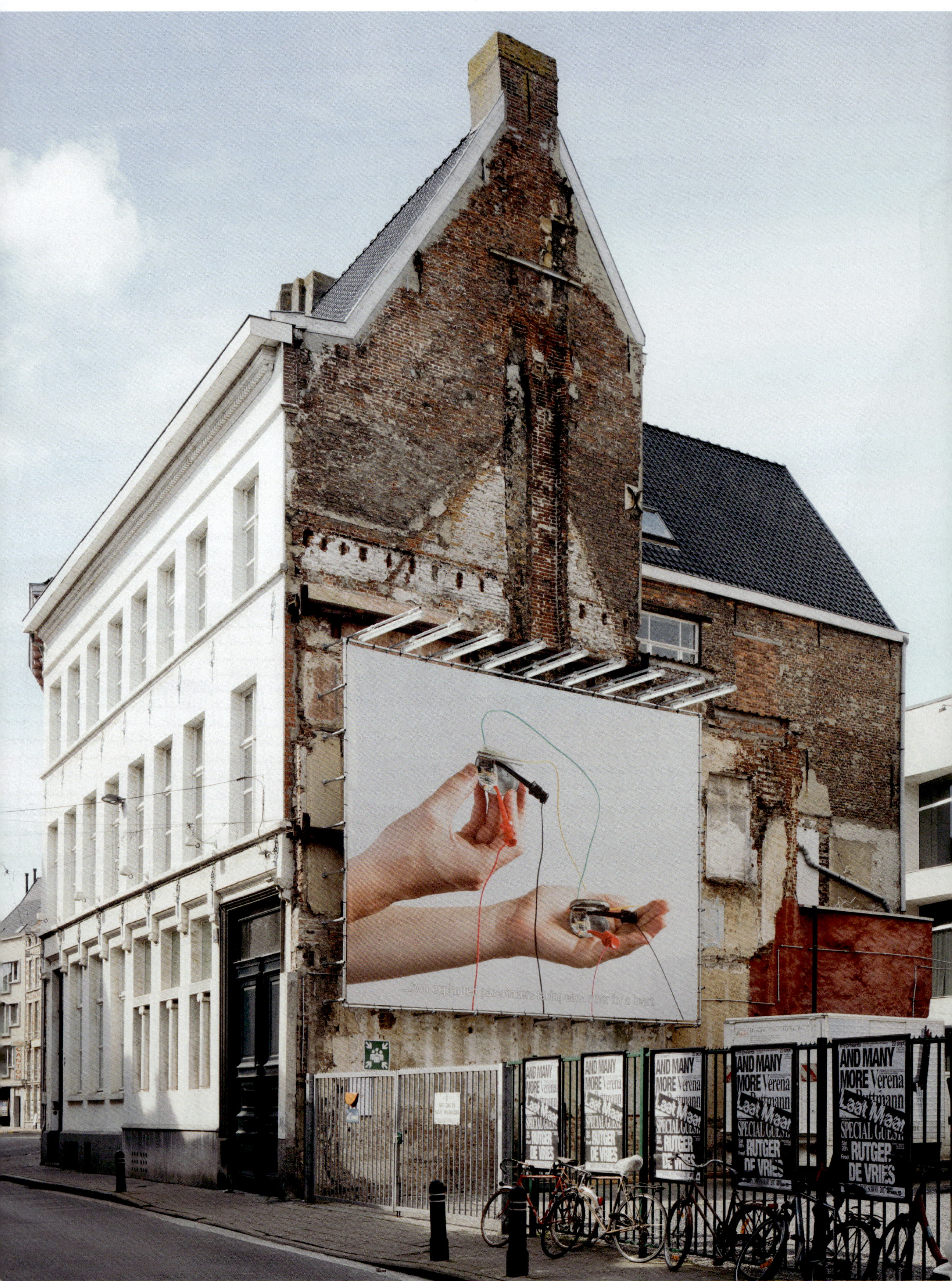

MICHIEL DE CLEENE, *Transitory Nature, Two Explanted Pacemakers Taking Each Other For A Heart*, September 2017

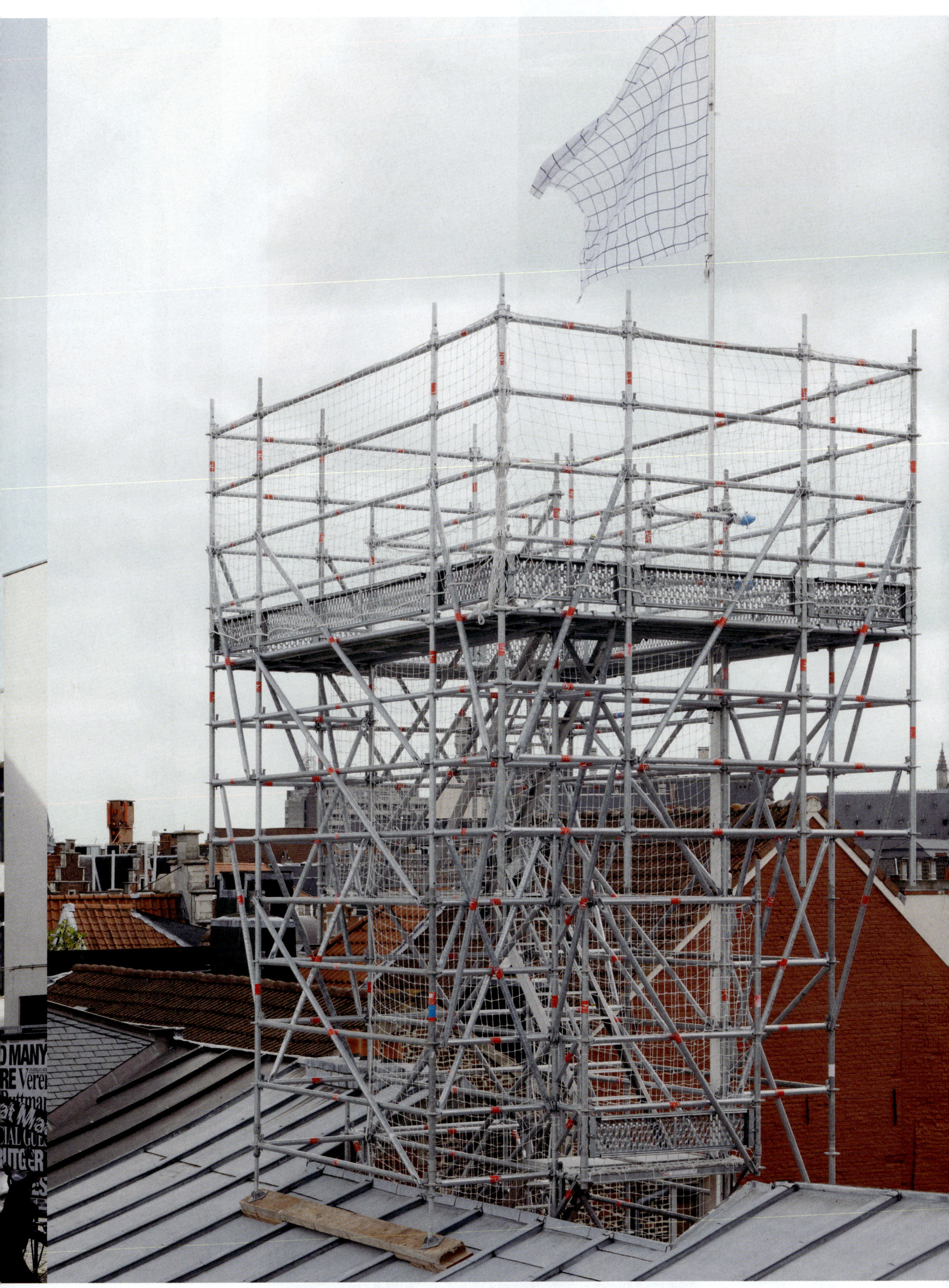

DE CLEENE DE CLEENE, *F#1-13*, September 2017

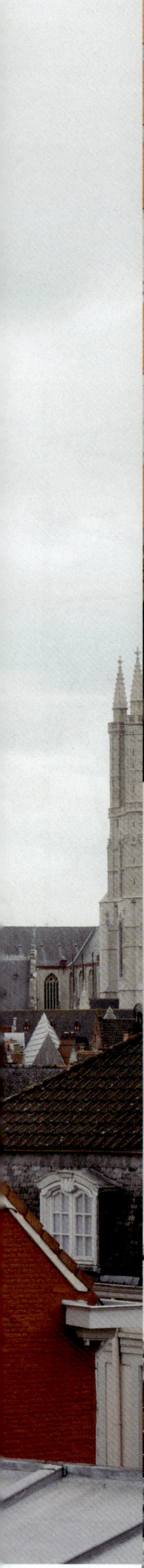

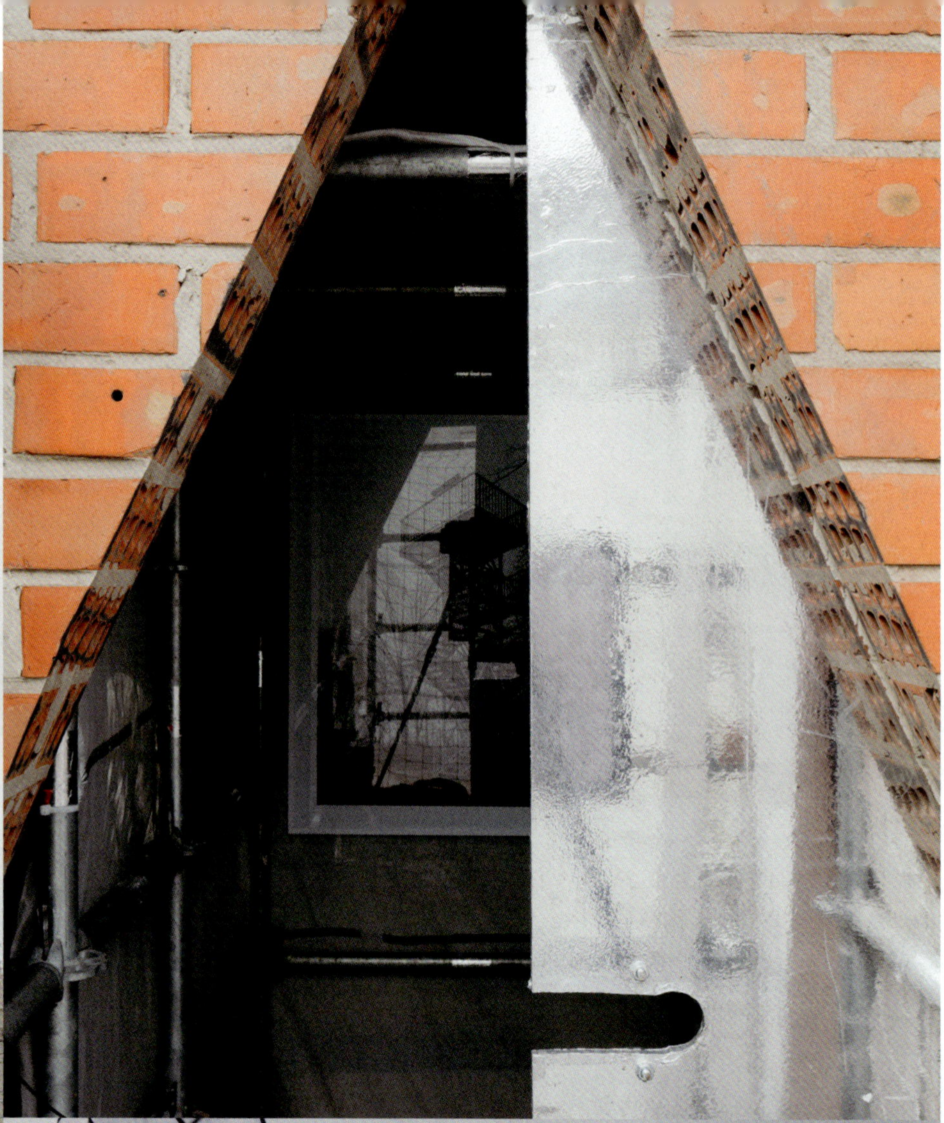

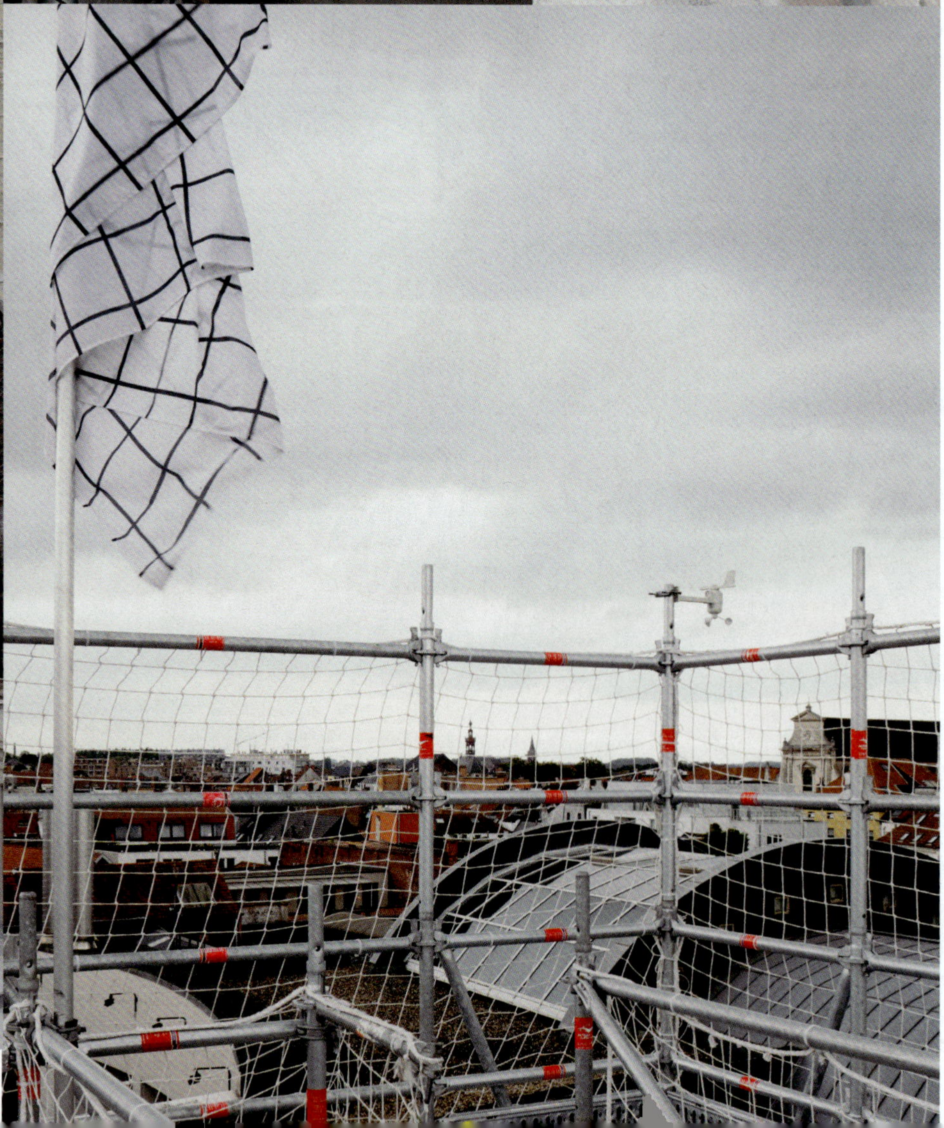

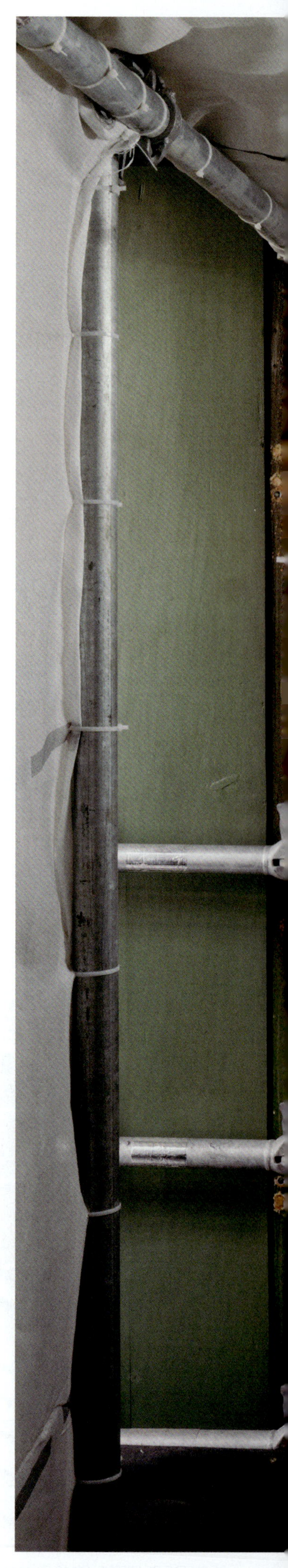

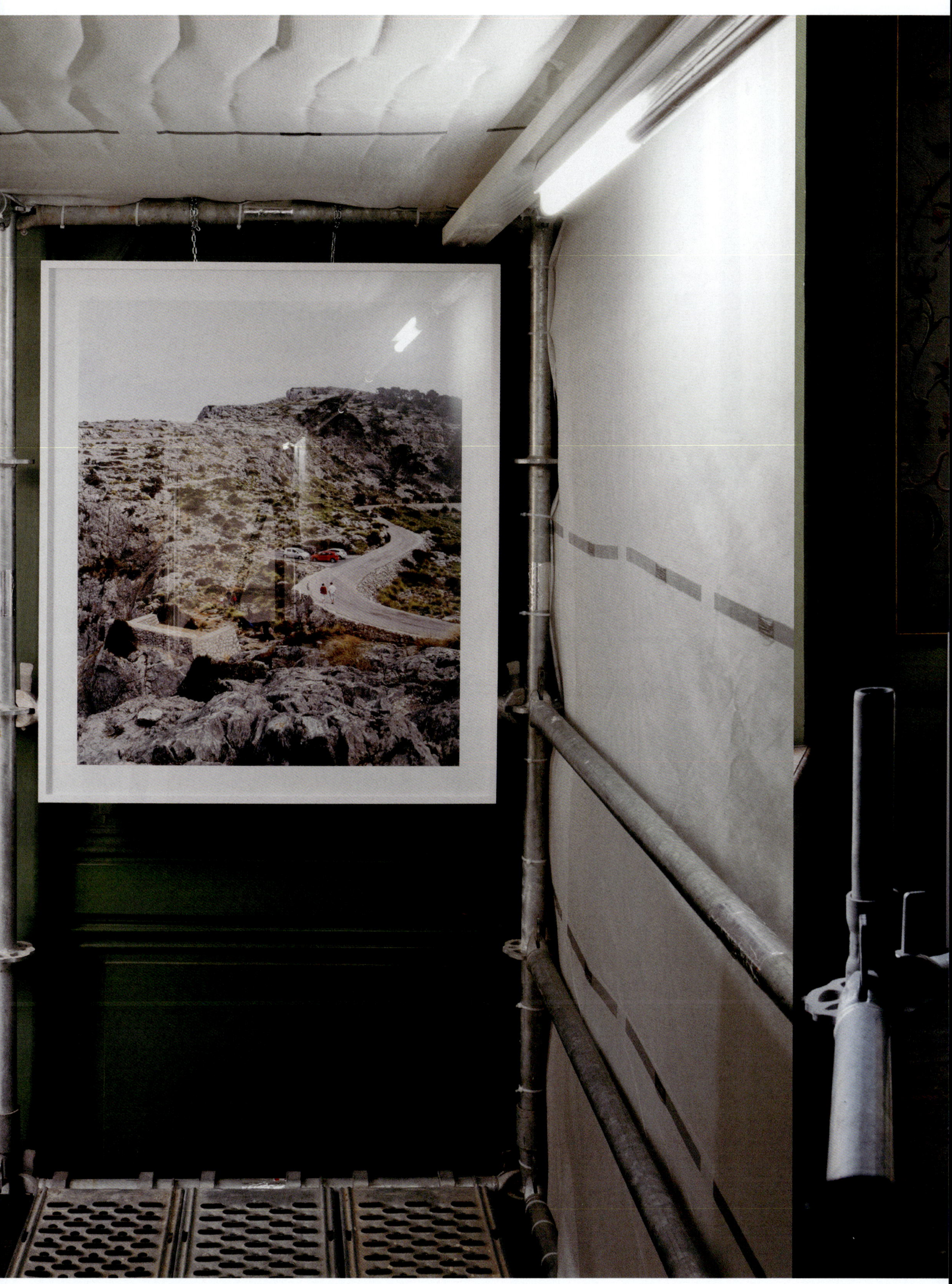

MICHIEL DE CLEENE, *-scope (2015)*, September 2017

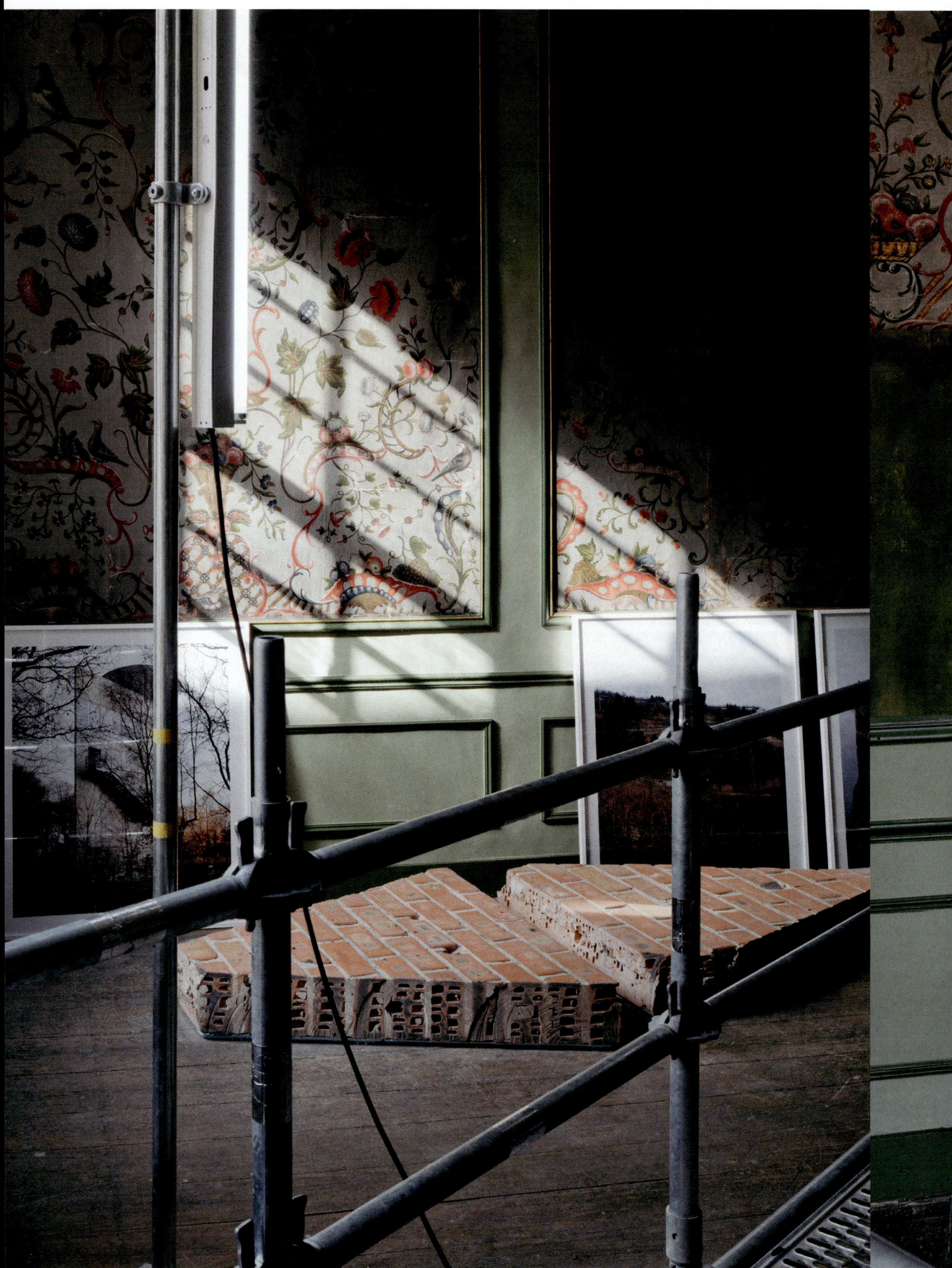

MICHIEL DE CLEENE, *-scope (2015)*, September 2017

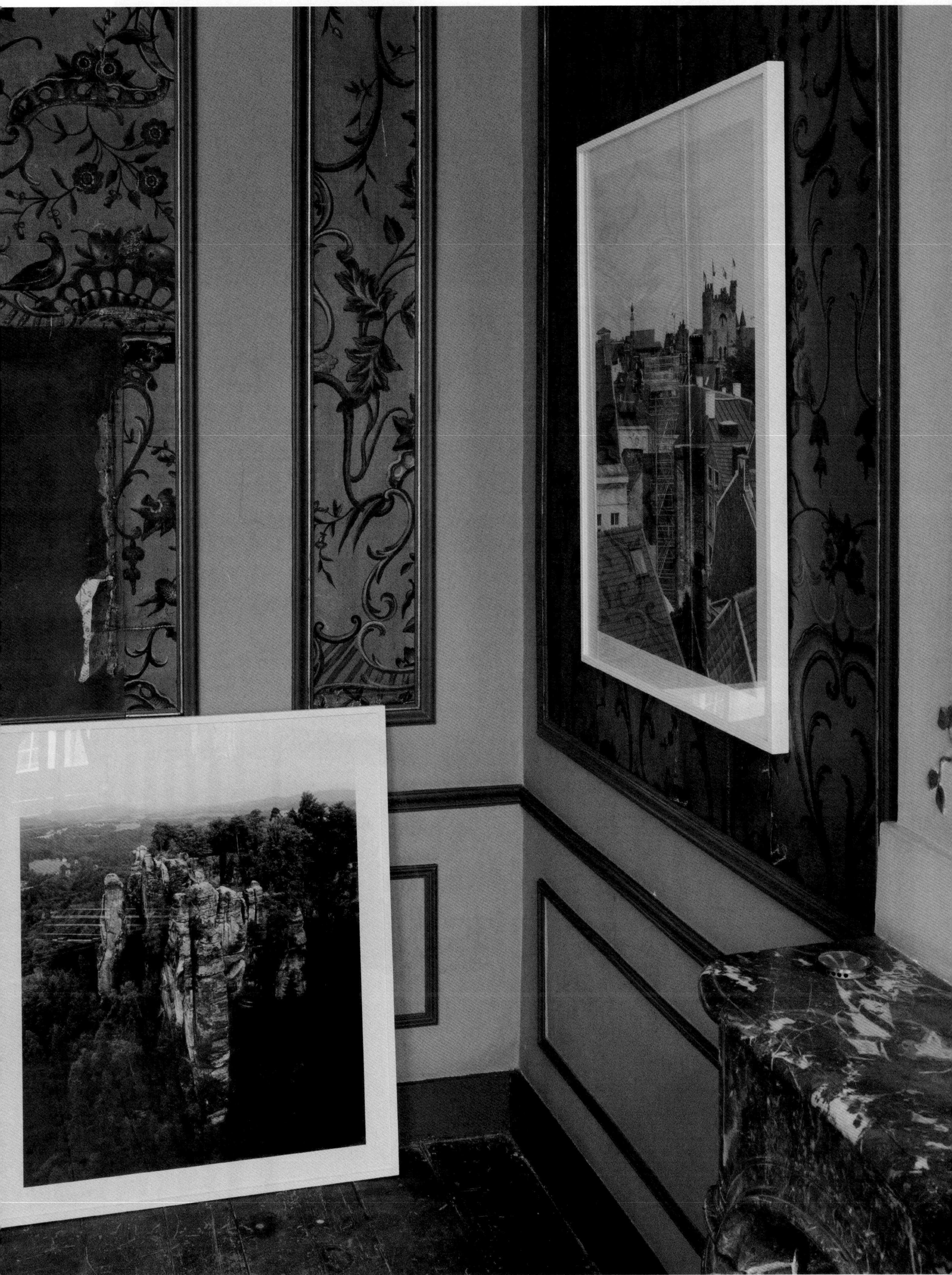

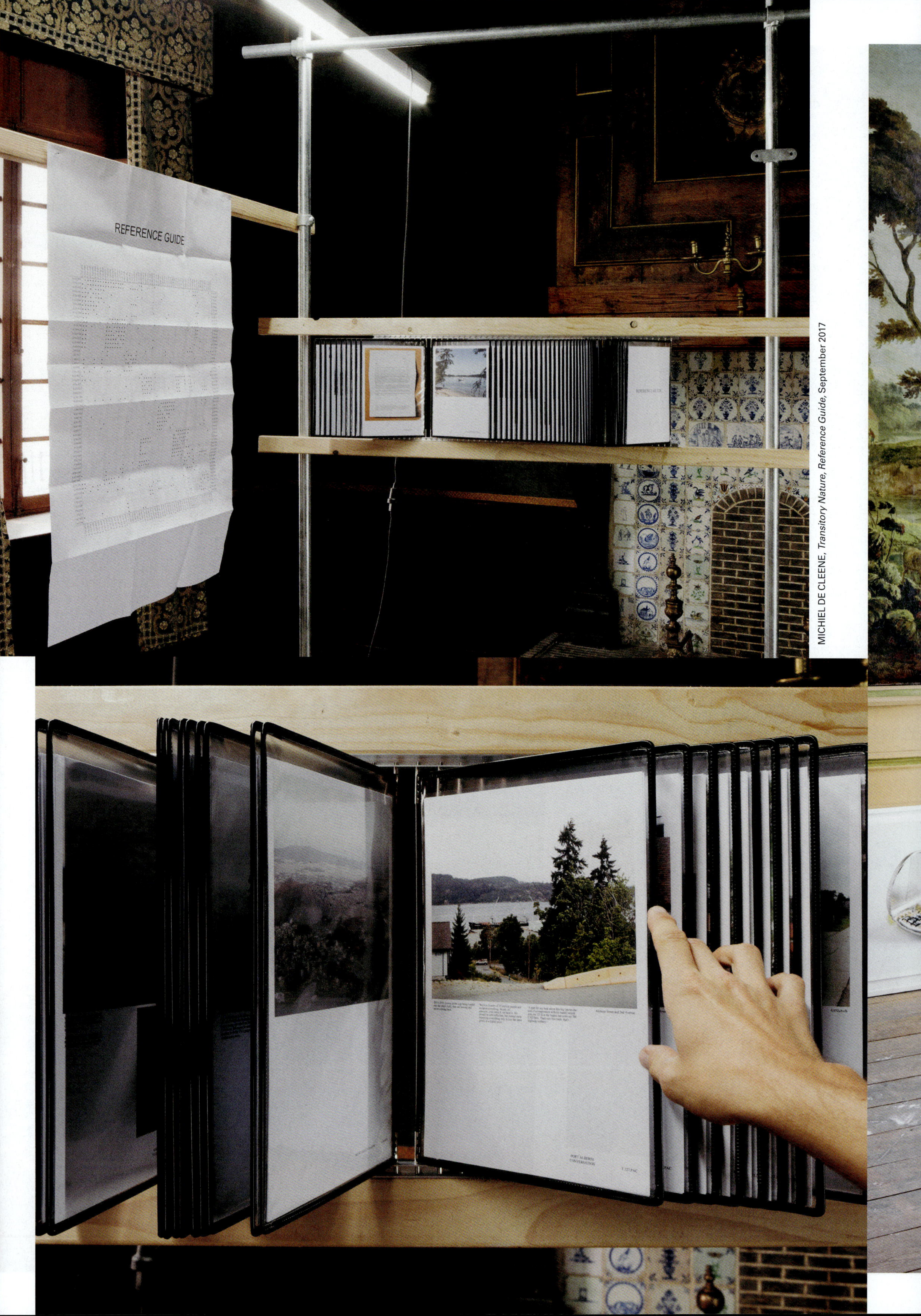

MICHIEL DE CLEENE, *Transitory Nature, Reference Guide*, September 2017

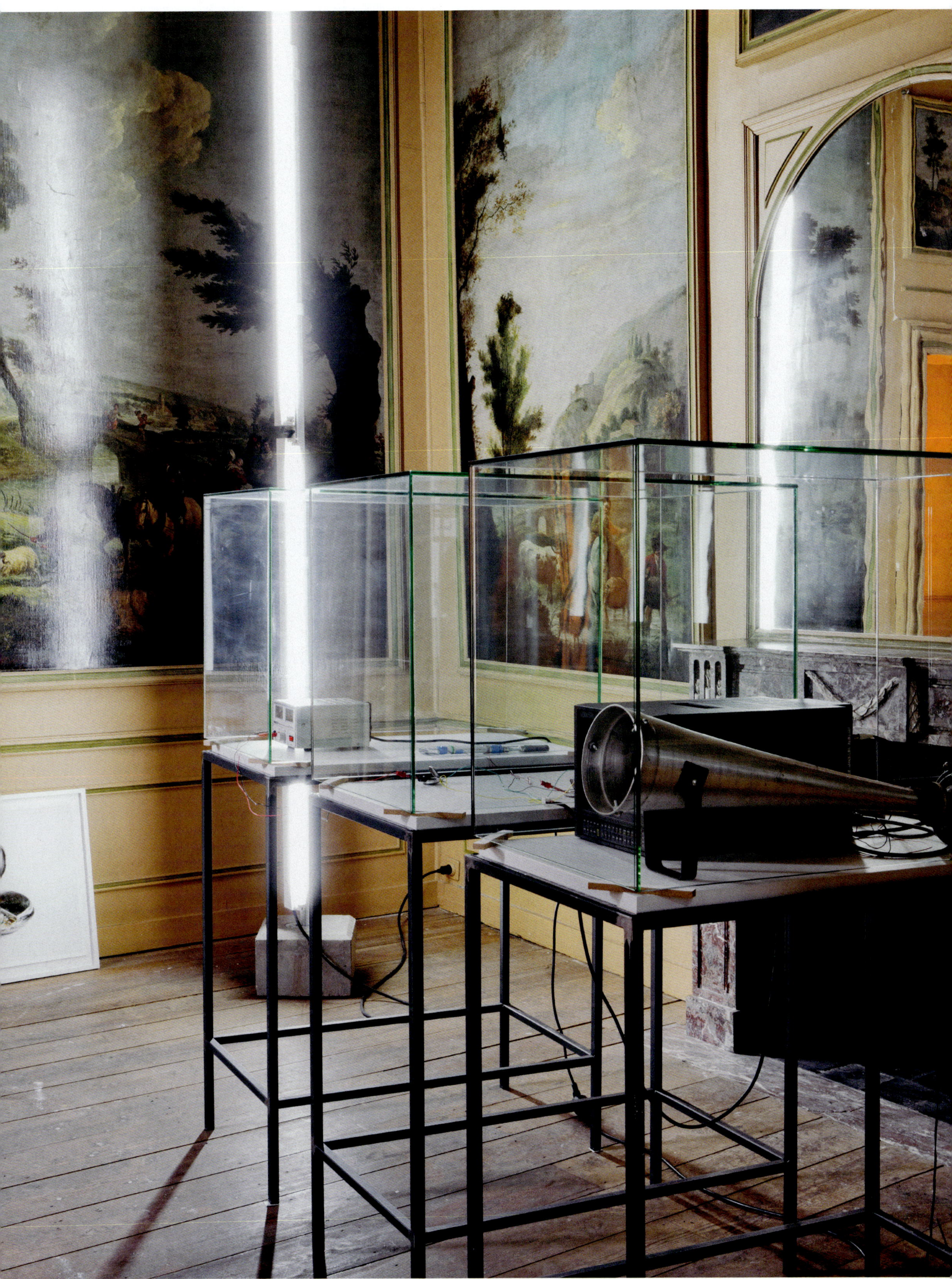

MICHIEL DE CLEENE, *Transitory Nature, Two Explanted Pacemakers Taking Each Other For A Heart*, September 2017

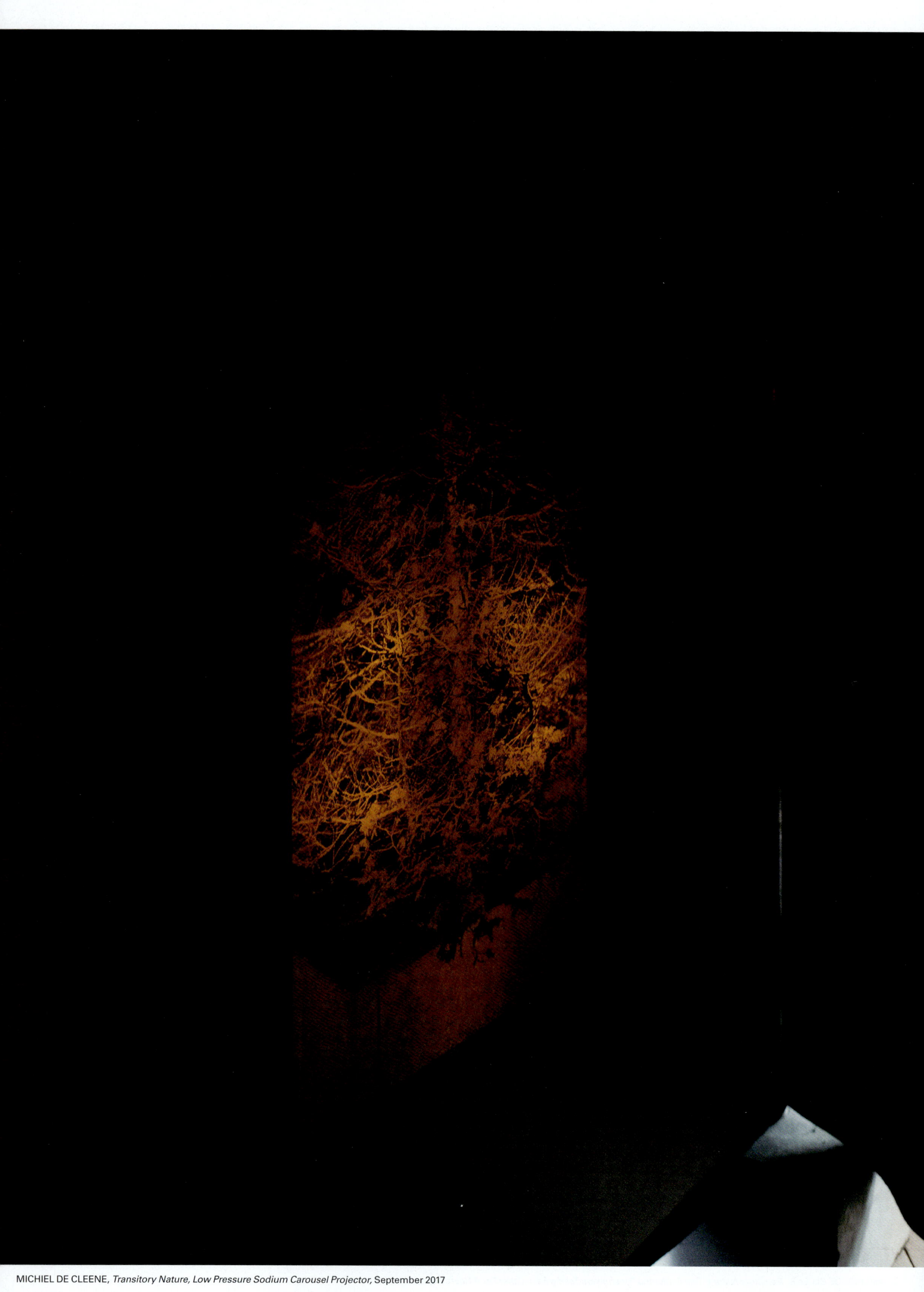

MICHIEL DE CLEENE, *Transitory Nature, Low Pressure Sodium Carousel Projector,* September 2017

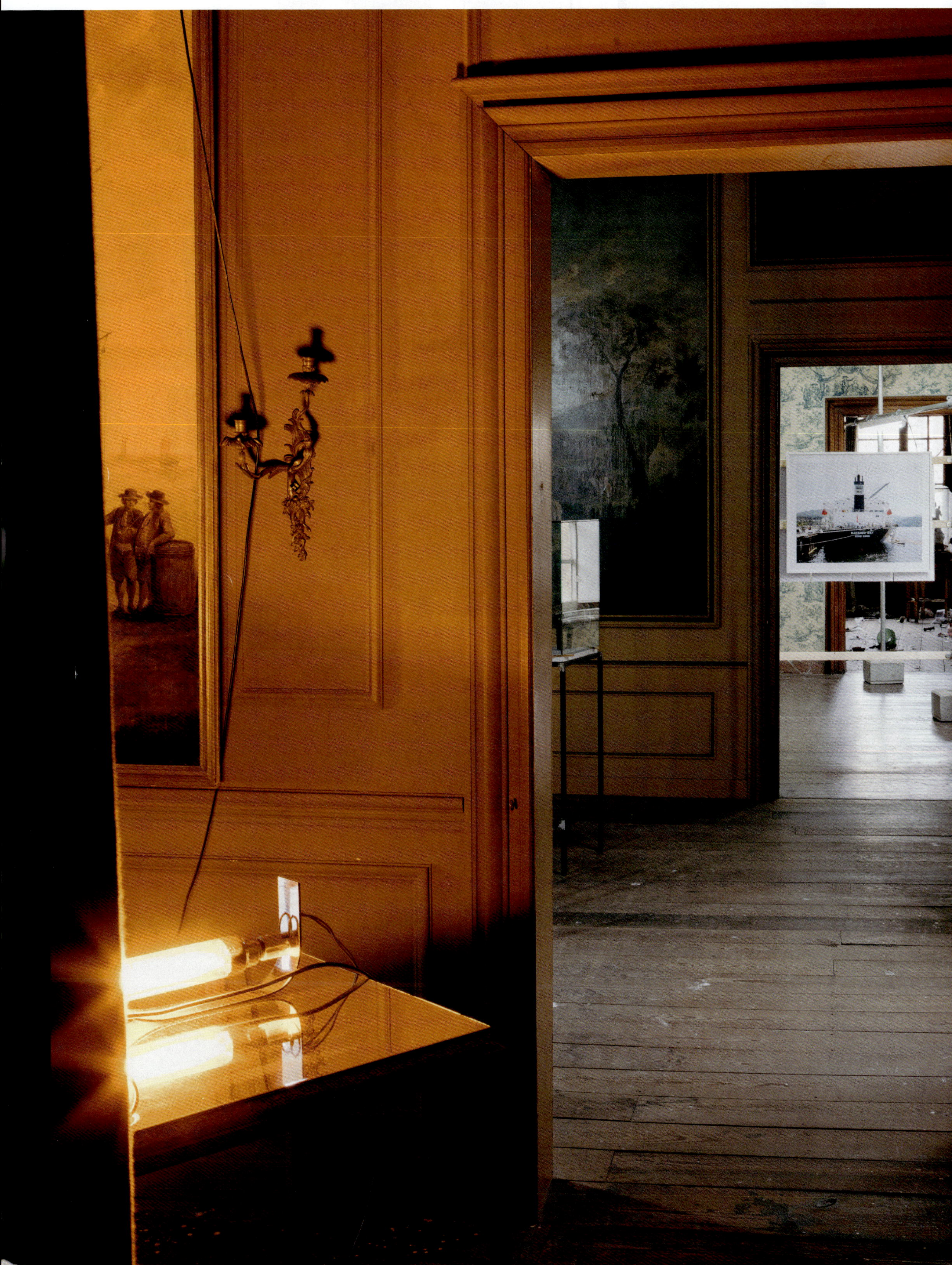

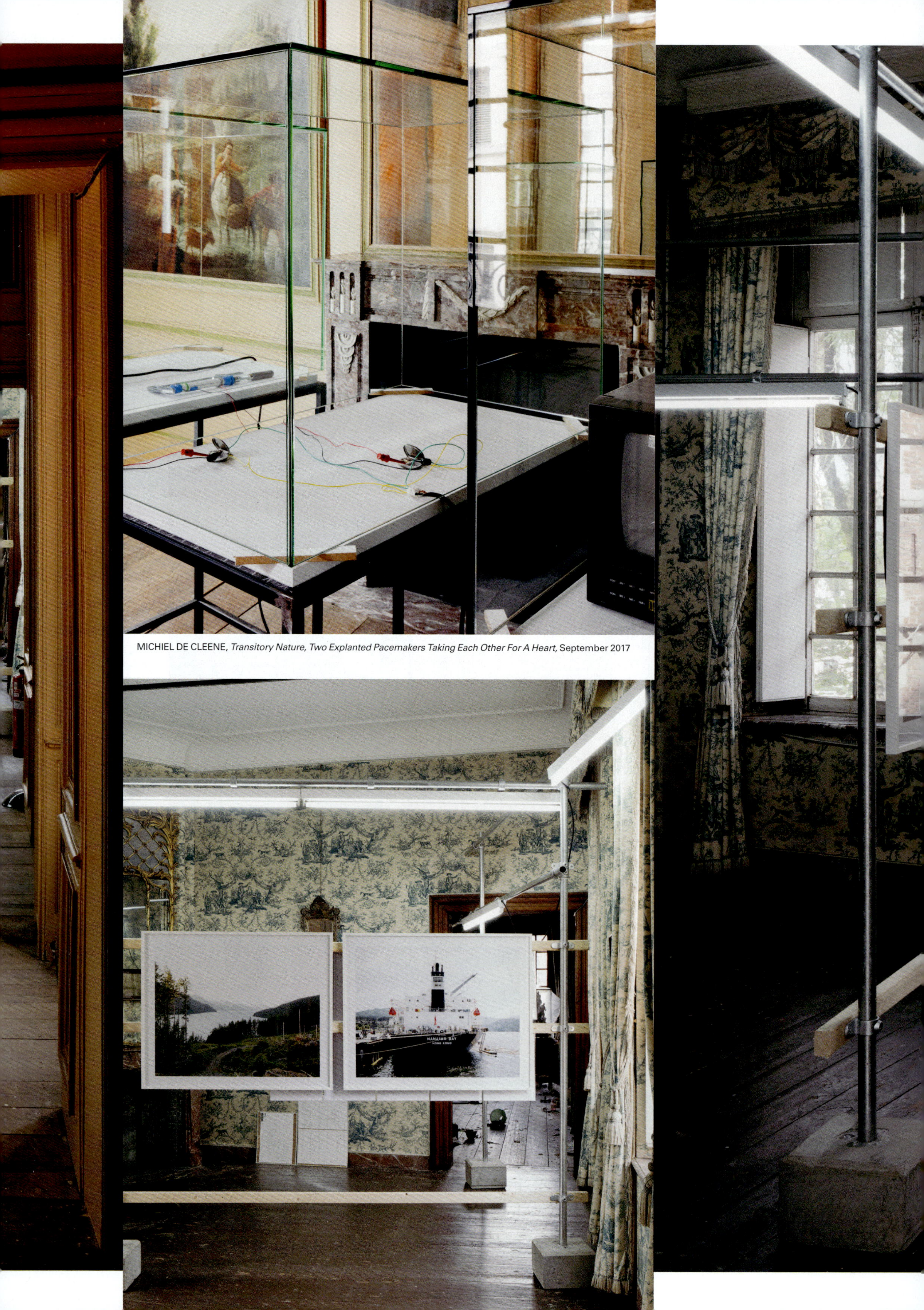

MICHIEL DE CLEENE, *Transitory Nature, Two Explanted Pacemakers Taking Each Other For A Heart,* September 2017

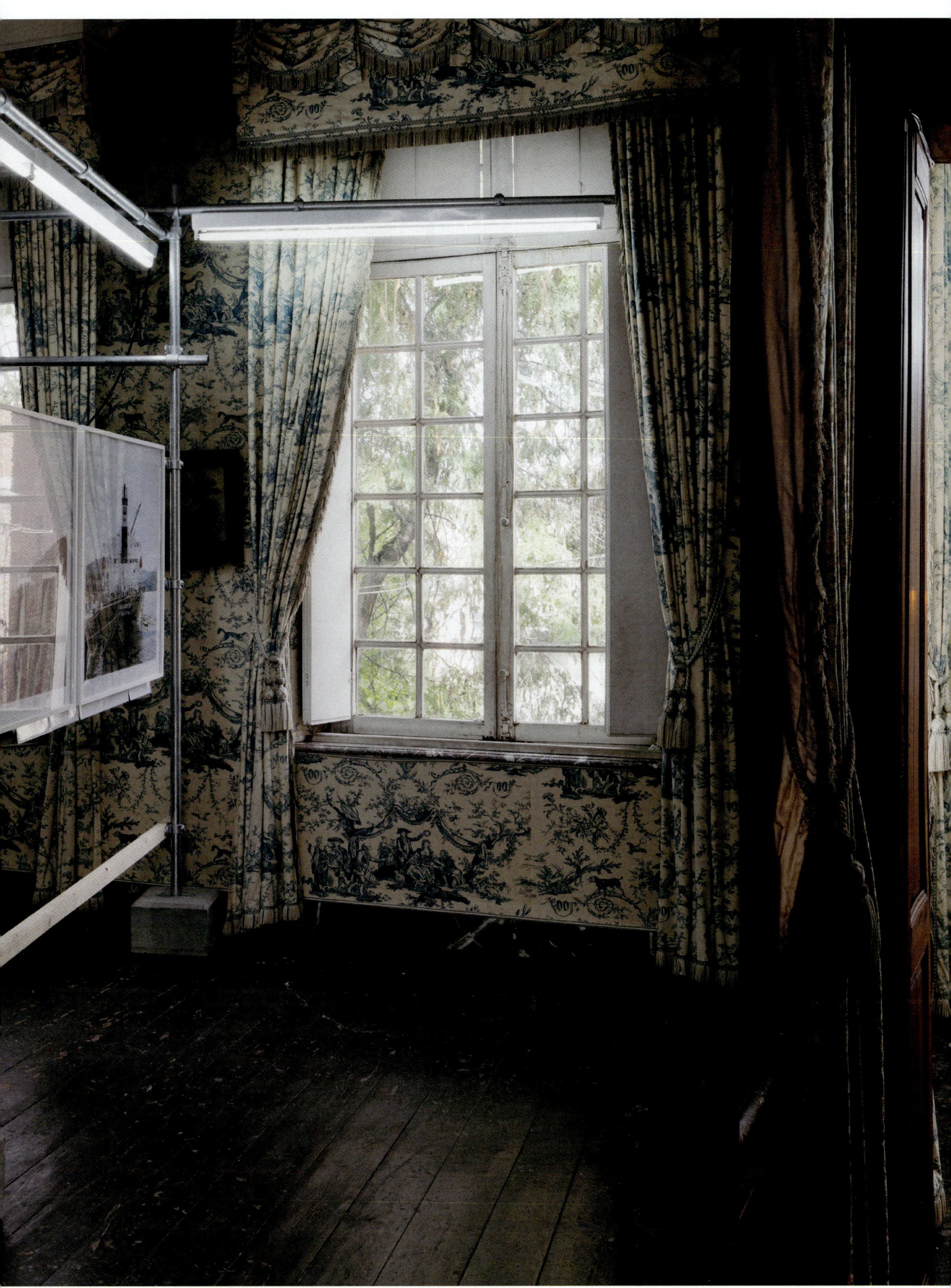

MICHIEL DE CLEENE, *Transitory Nature, The Restored Masts Of The Sant Juan Bautista*, September 2017

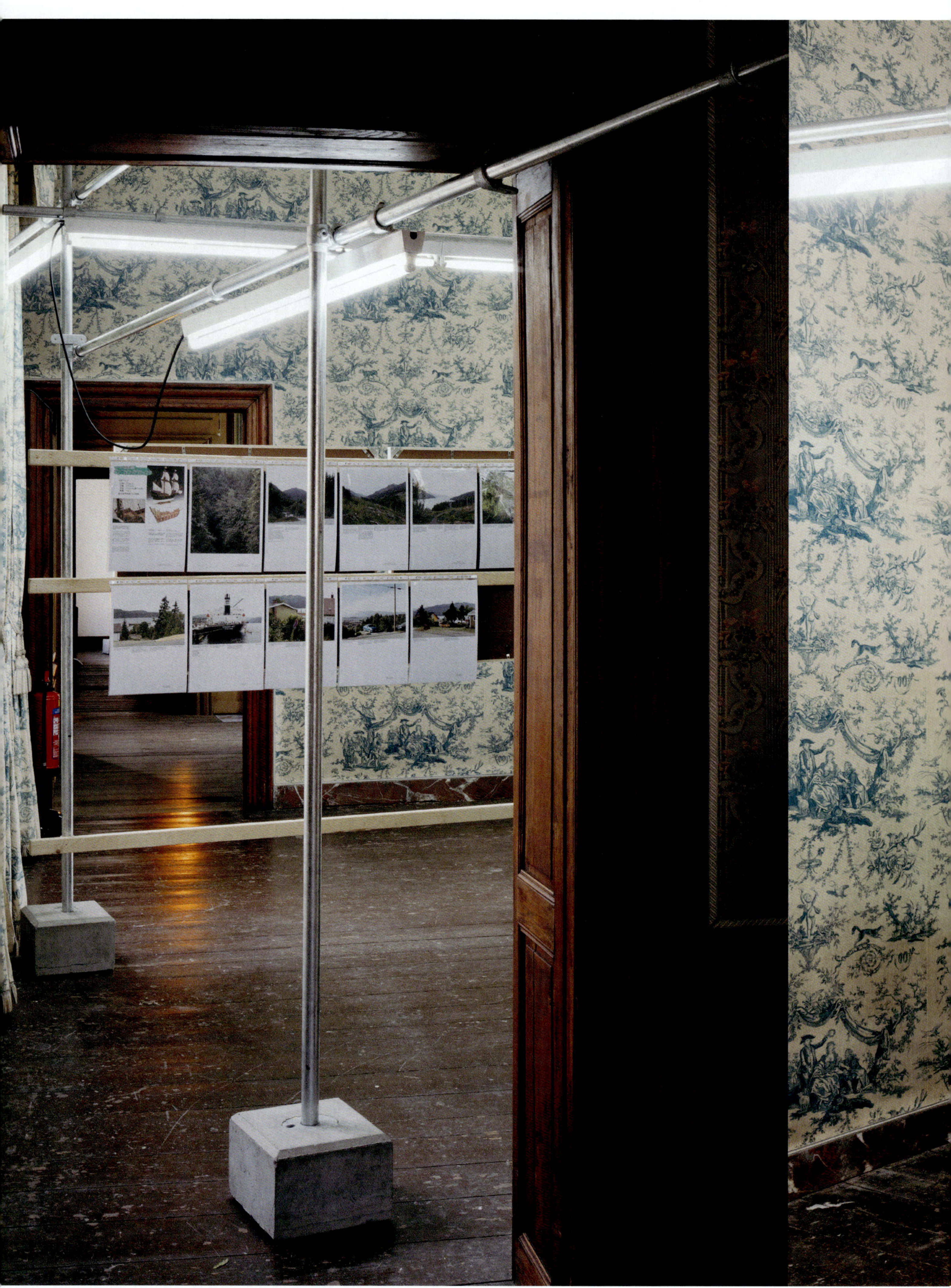

MICHIEL DE CLEENE, *Transitory Nature, The Restored Masts Of The Sant Juan Bautista*, September 2017

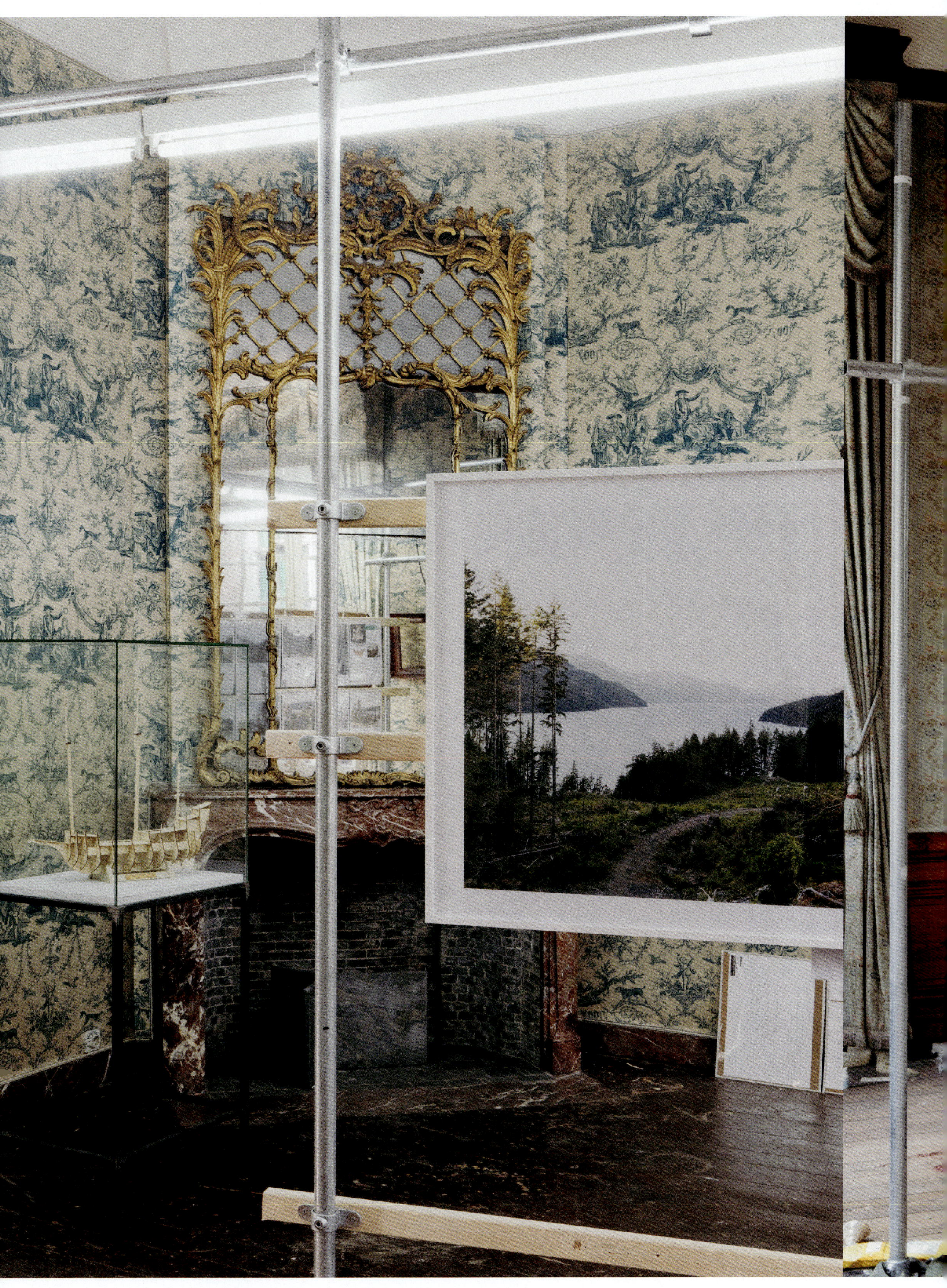

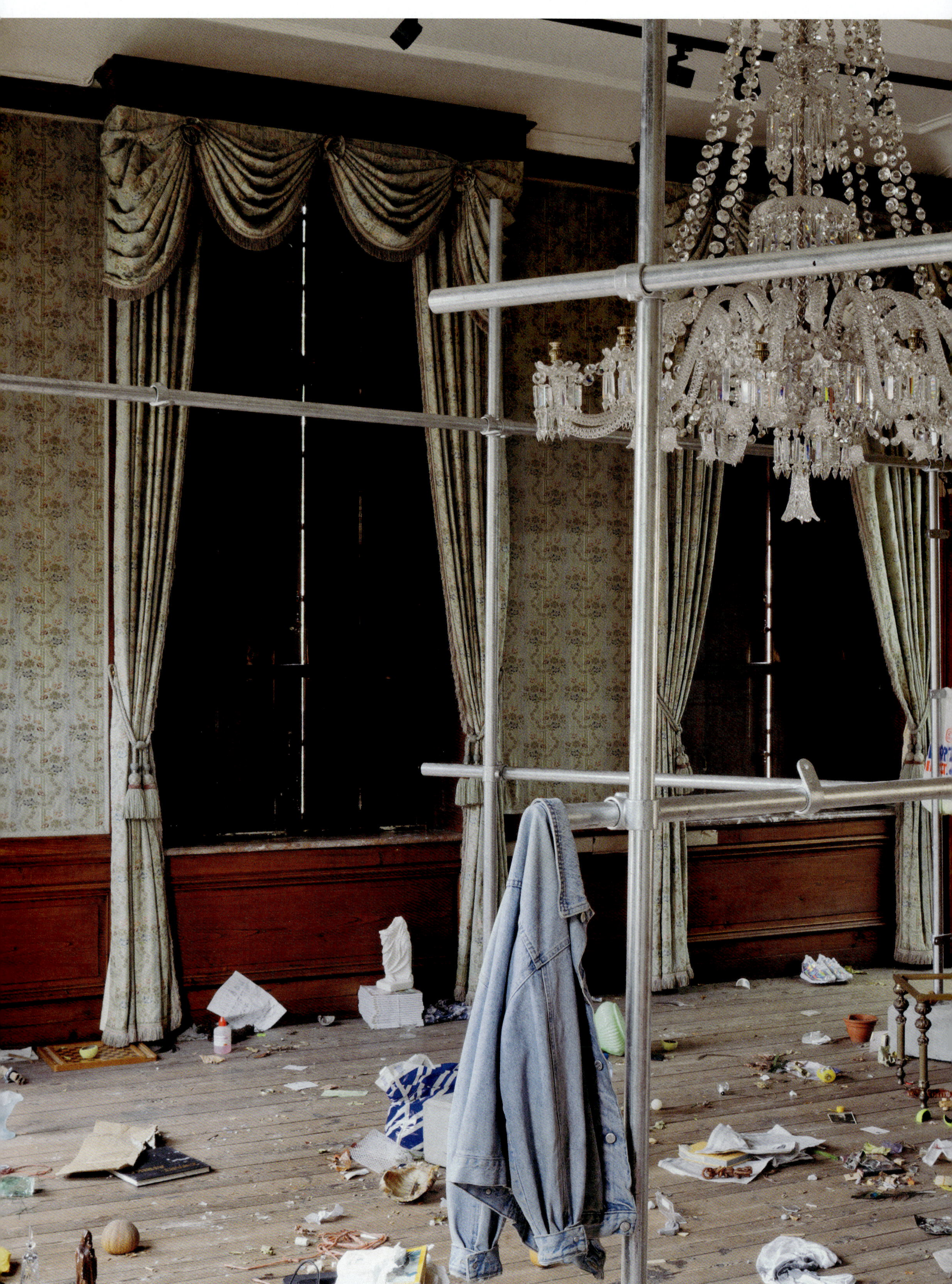

NICOLÁS LAMAS, *Before Disappearing*, September 2017

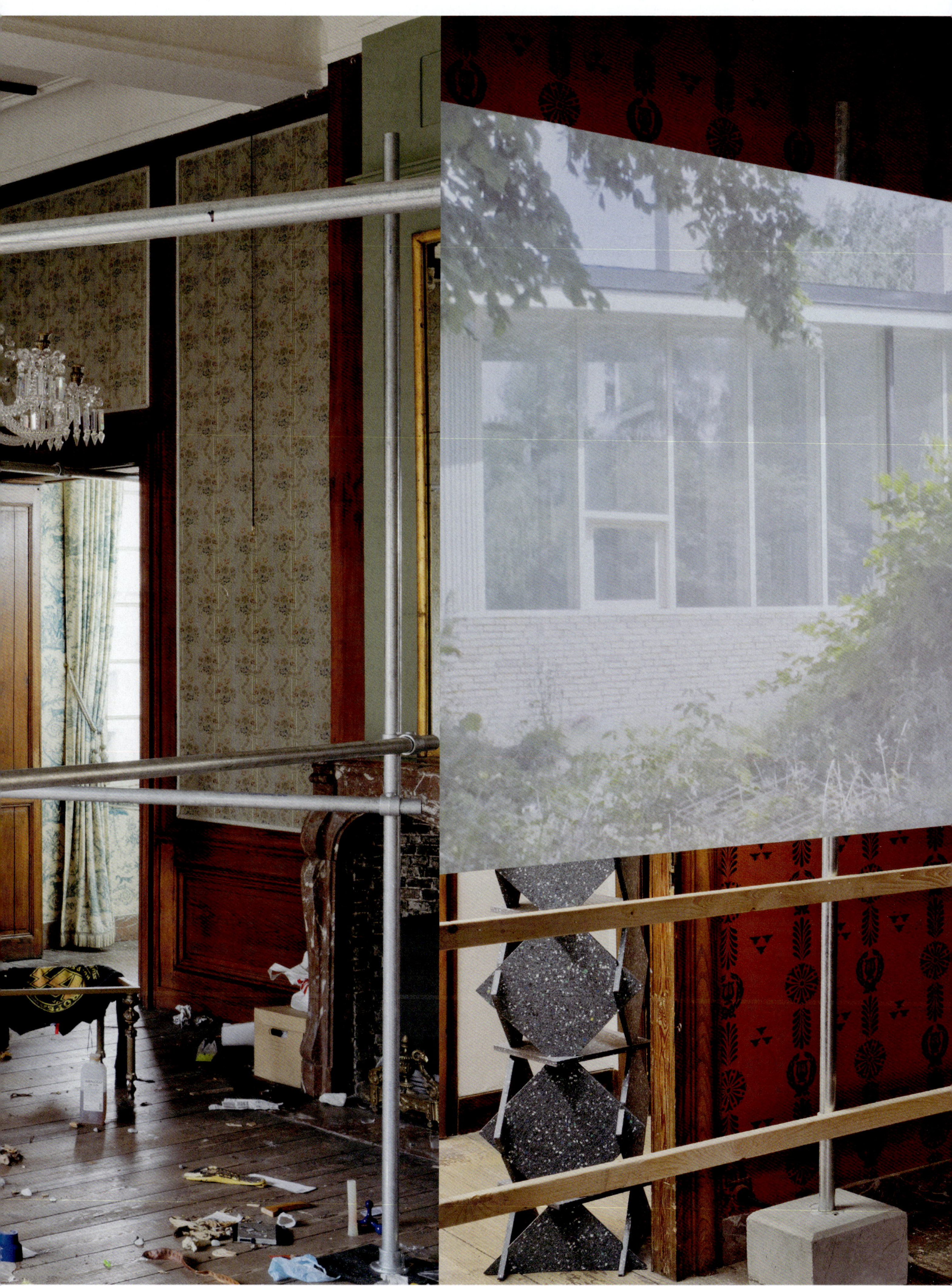

JULIE PFLEIDERER / MIRIAM ROHDE, *Actual Size Real Time#1, Partial Views*, September 2017
THEO DE MEYER / ARTHUR DEKKER, *Setting Up A Cabinet*, September 2017

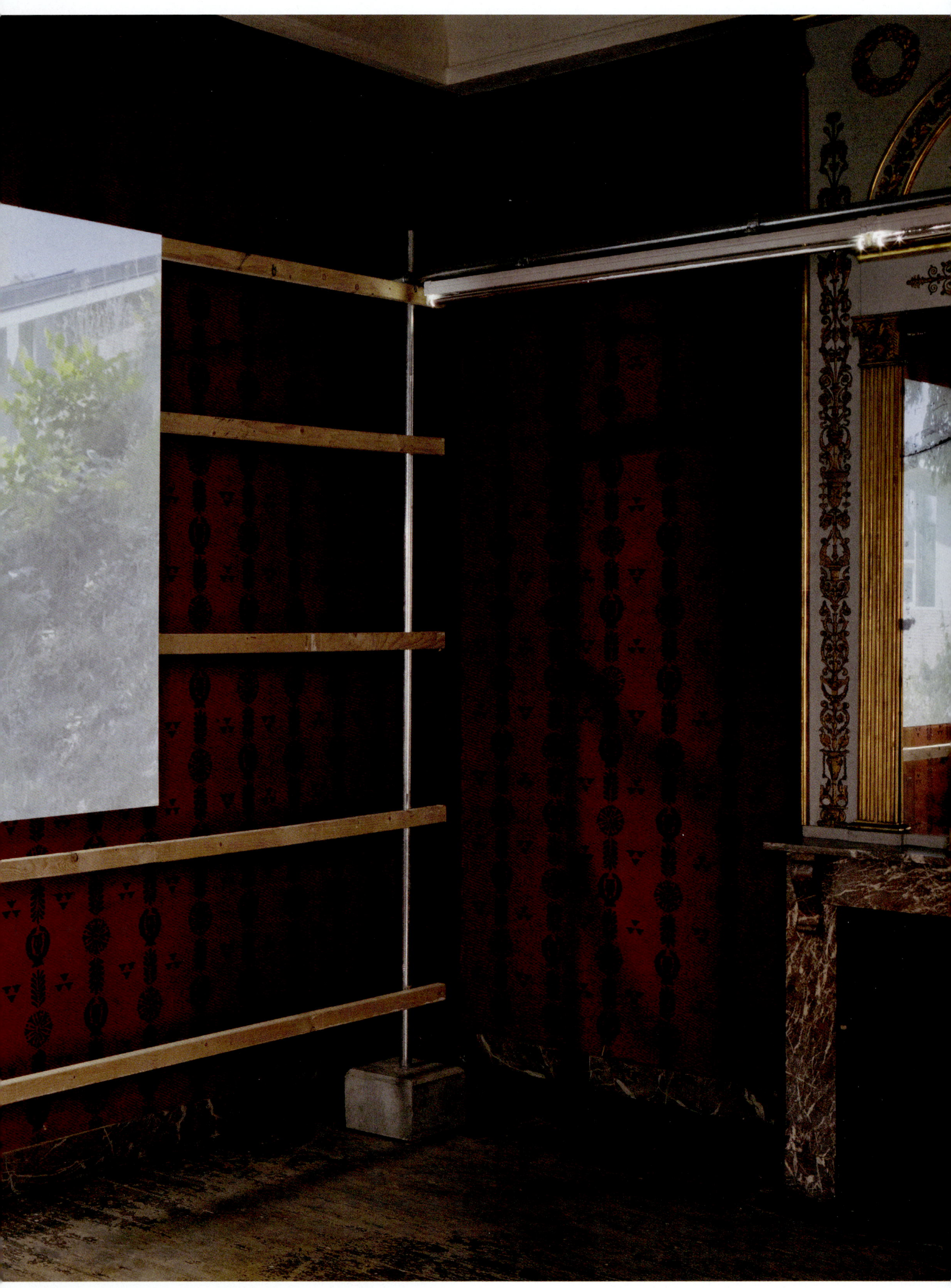

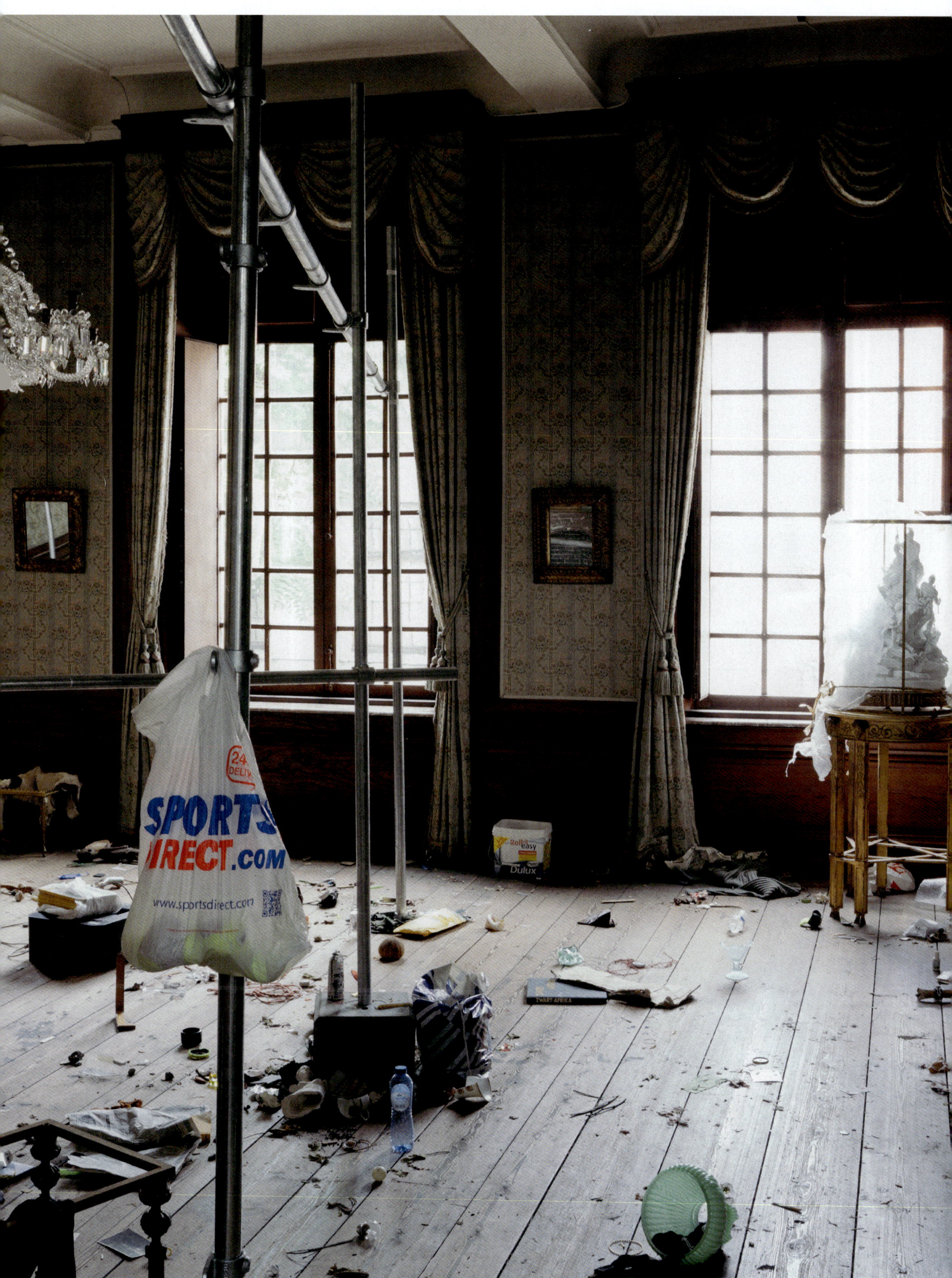

NICOLÁS LAMAS, *Before Disappearing*, September 2017

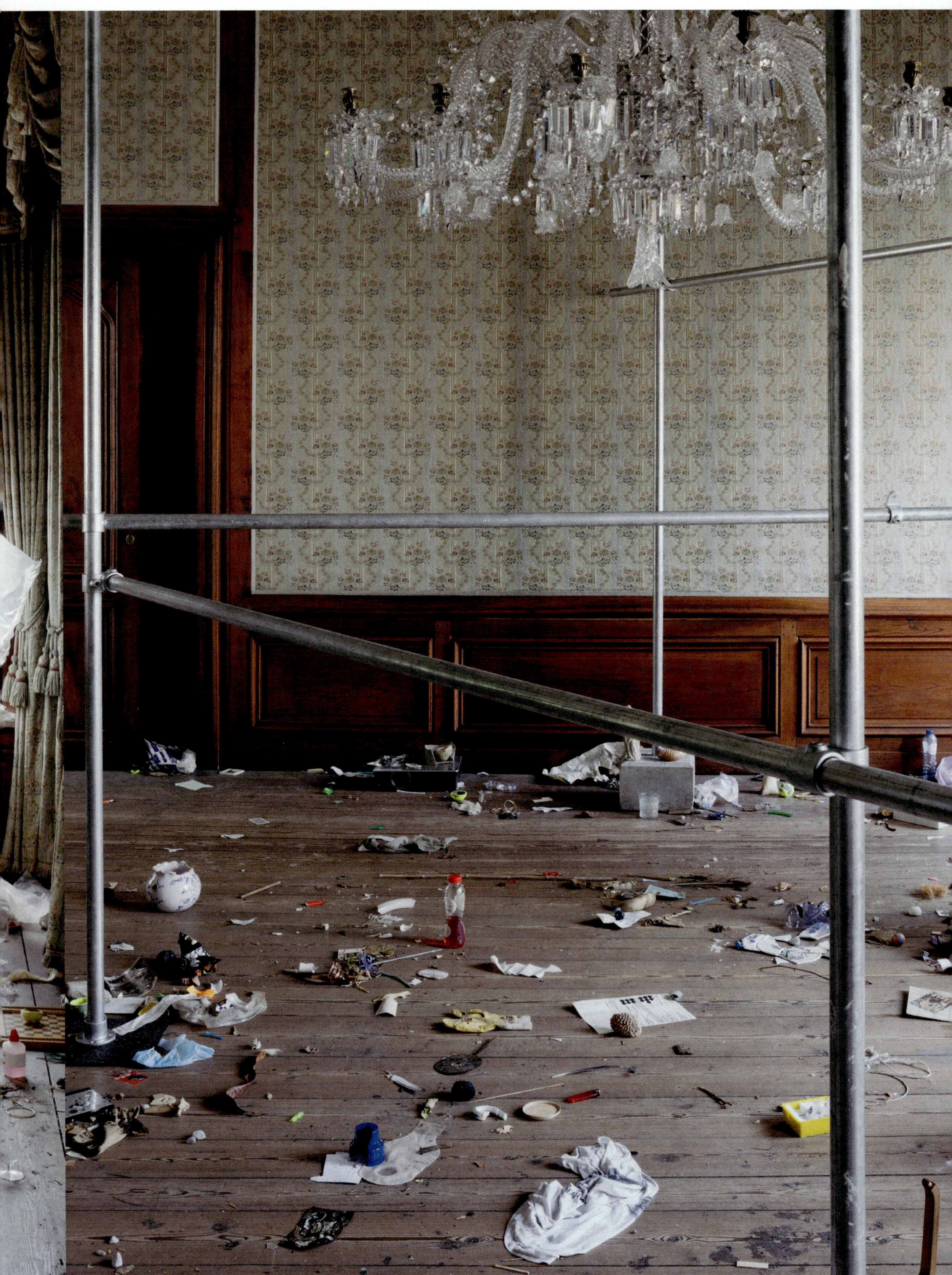

NICOLÁS LAMAS, *Before Disappearing*, September 2017

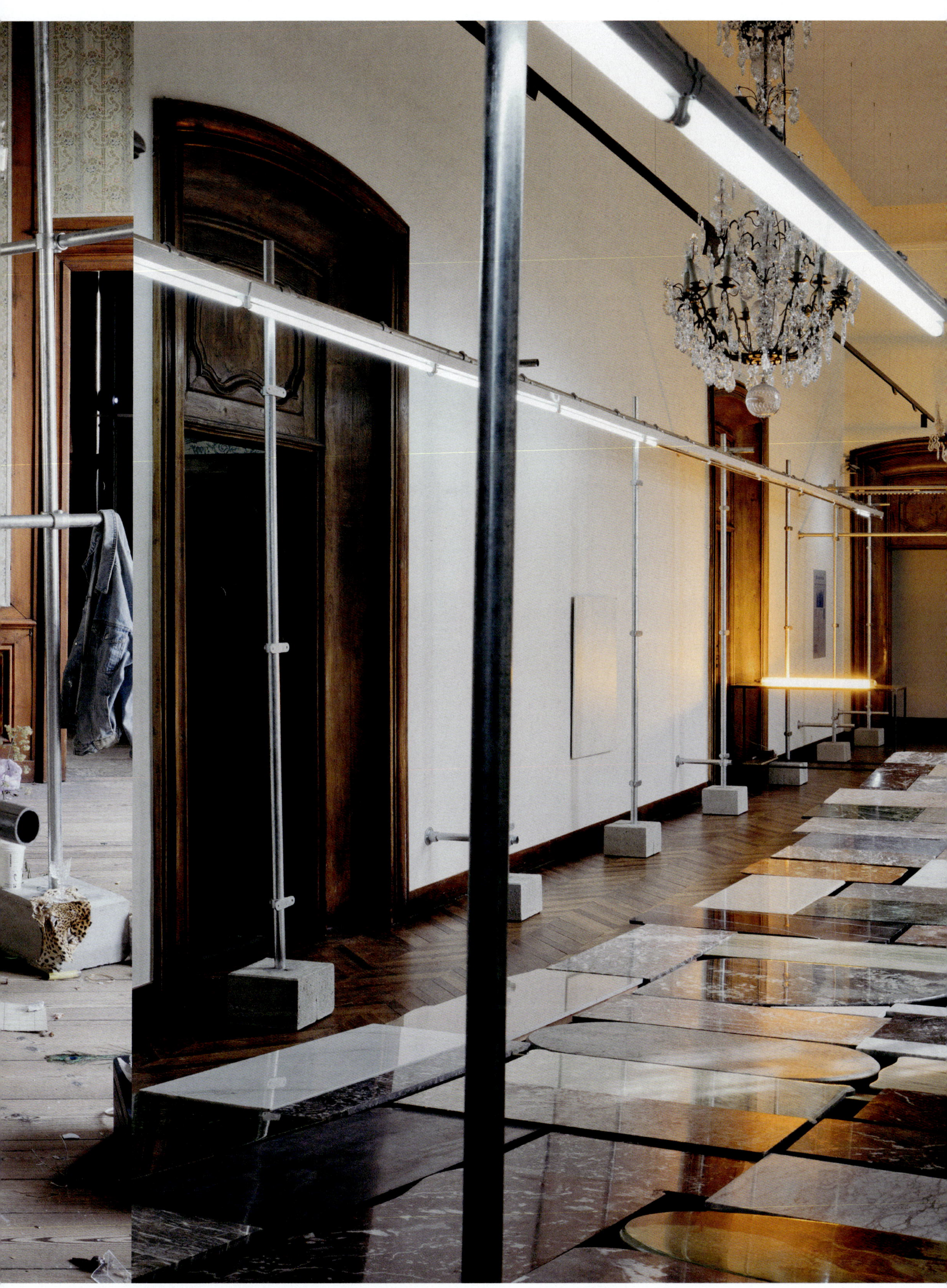

FILIP DUJARDIN, *Accumulation d'Époque#4*, September 2017
MICHIEL DE CLEENE, *Transitory Nature, Low Pressure Sodium Light*, September 2017

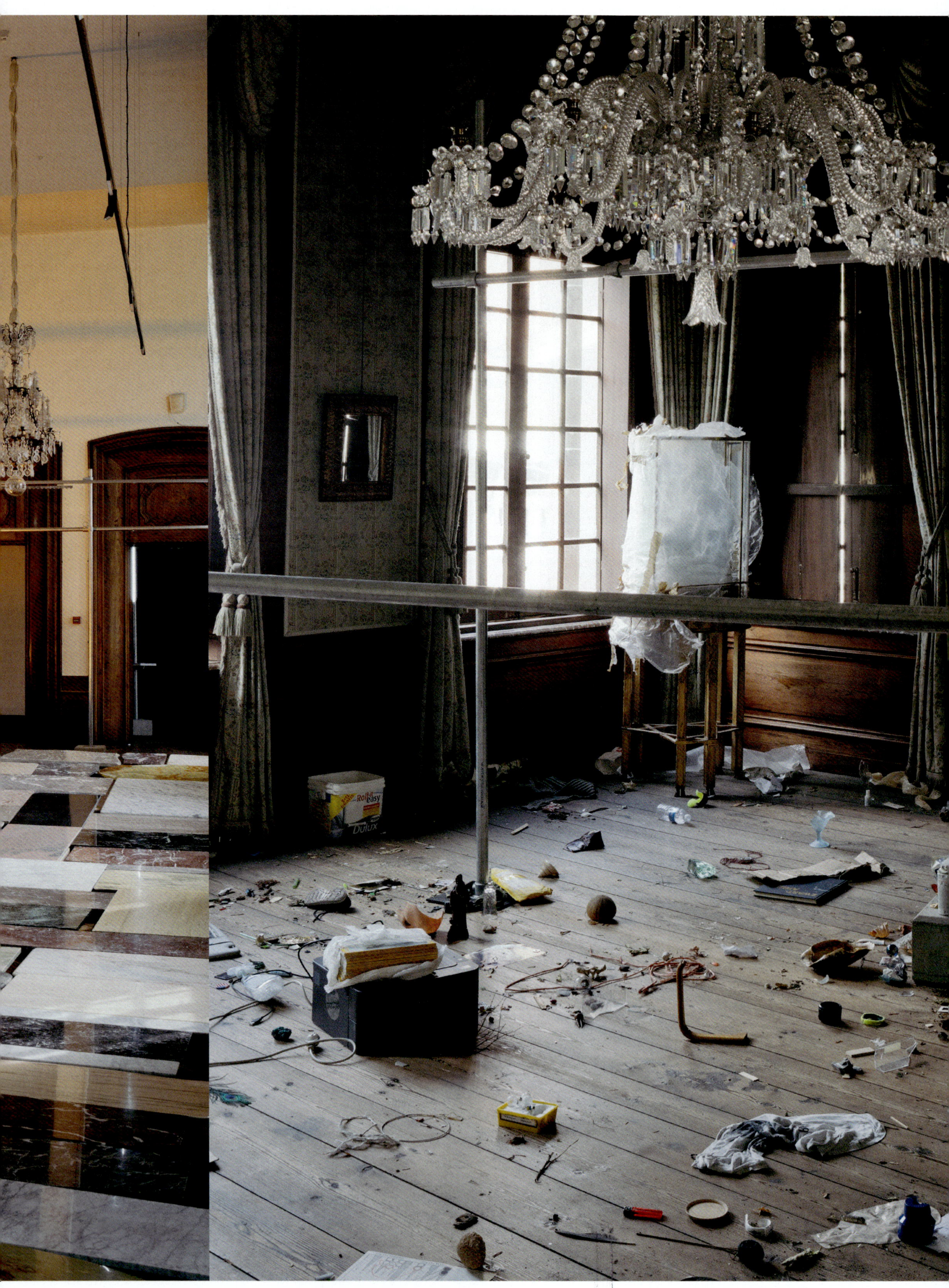

NICOLÁS LAMAS, *Before Disappearing*, September 2017

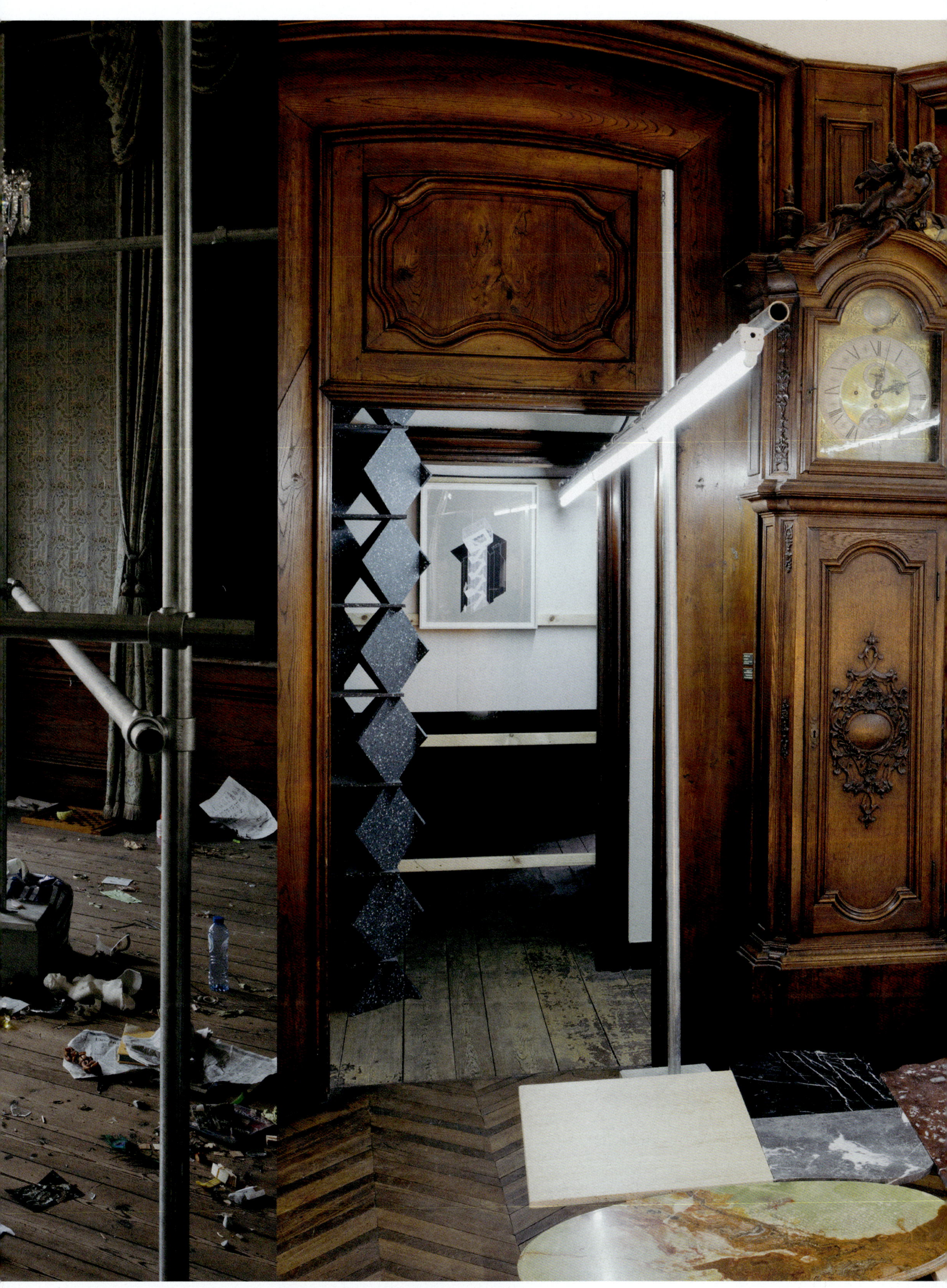

THEO DE MEYER / ARTHUR DEKKER, *Setting Up A Cabinet*, September 2017
OLIVIER GOETHALS, *Museum Of Moving Practice*, September 2017

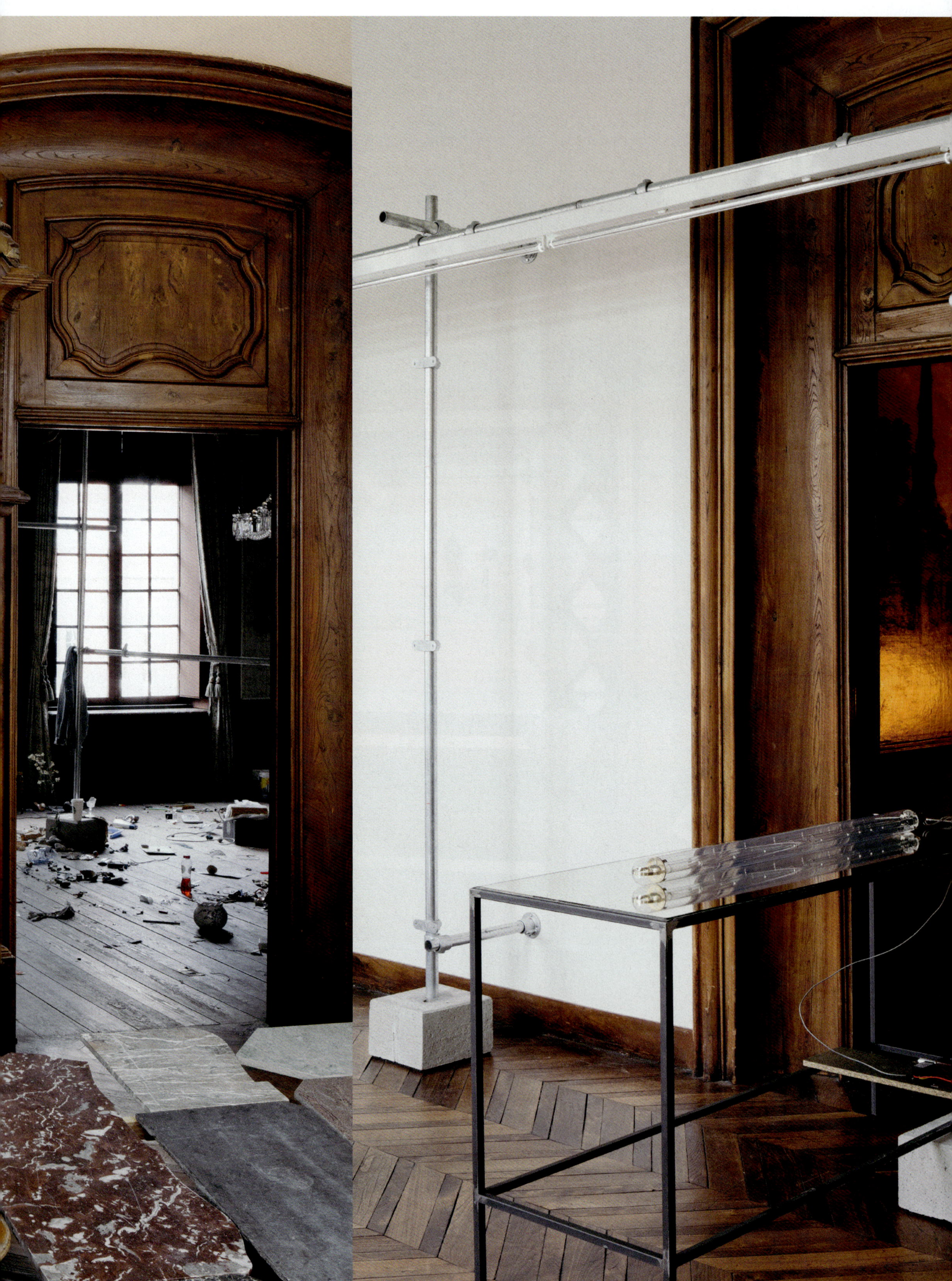

MICHIEL DE CLEENE, *Transitory Nature, Low Pressure Sodium Light,* September 2017

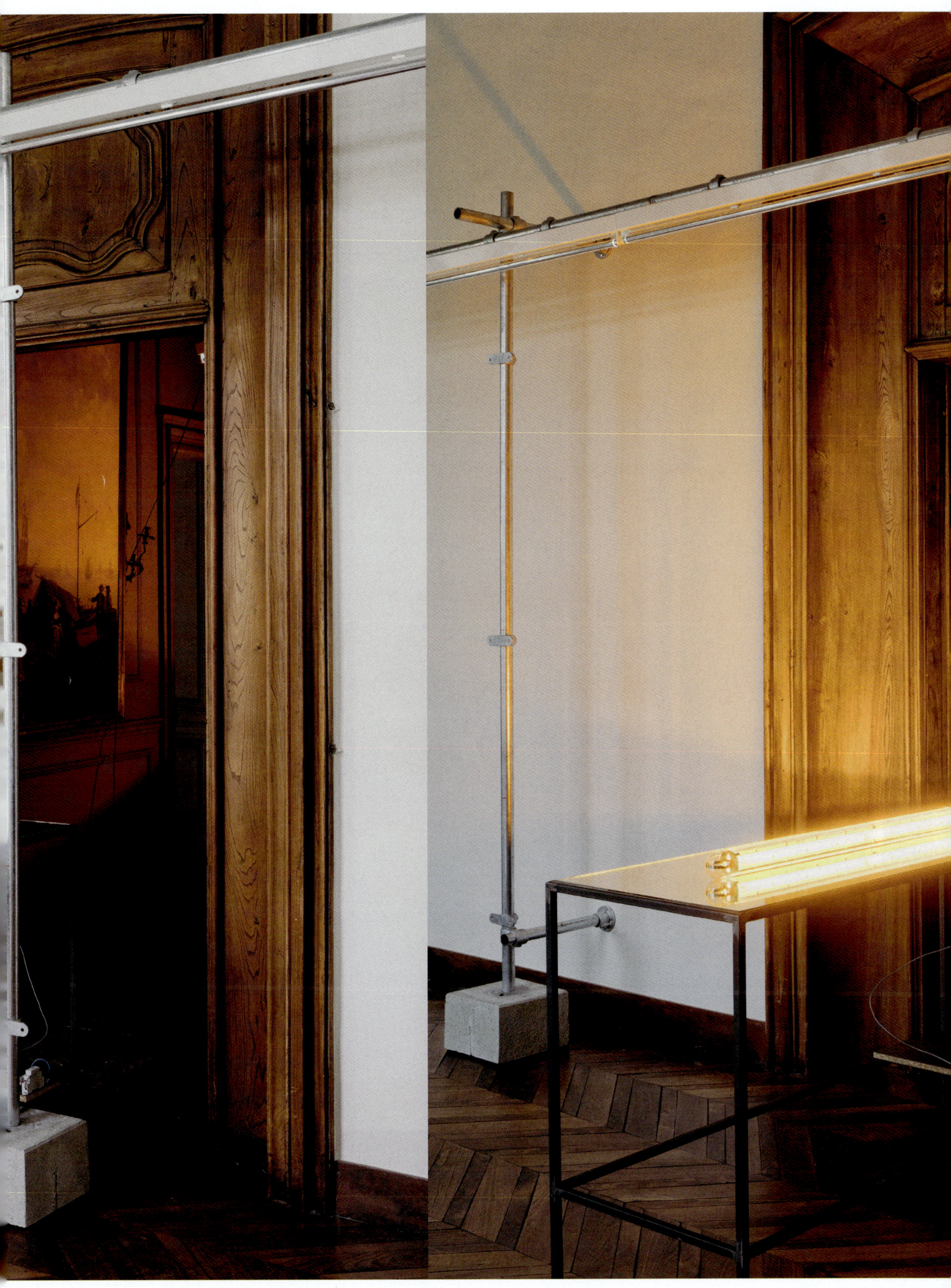

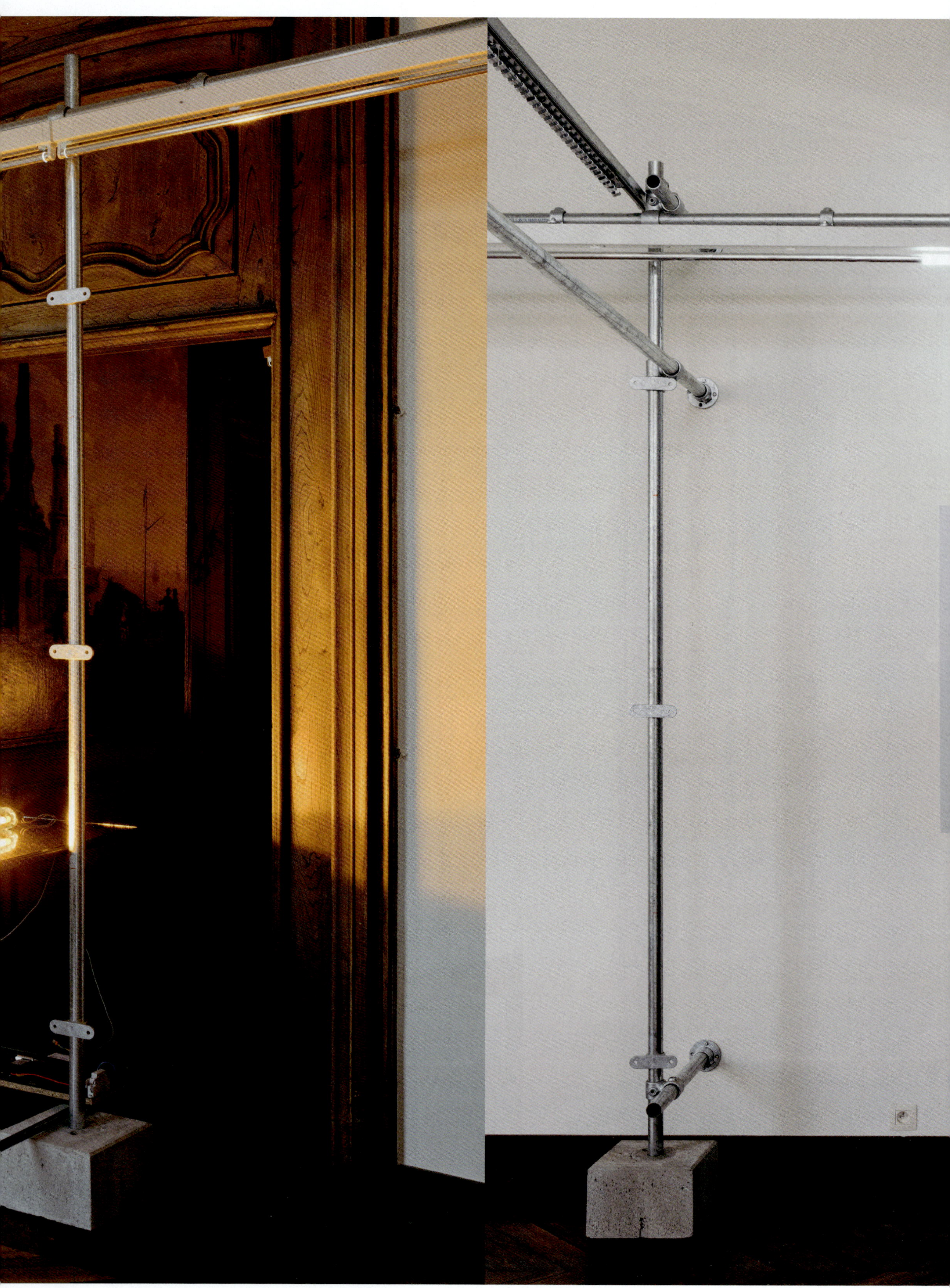

ACTION, *Museum Dreams*, September 2017

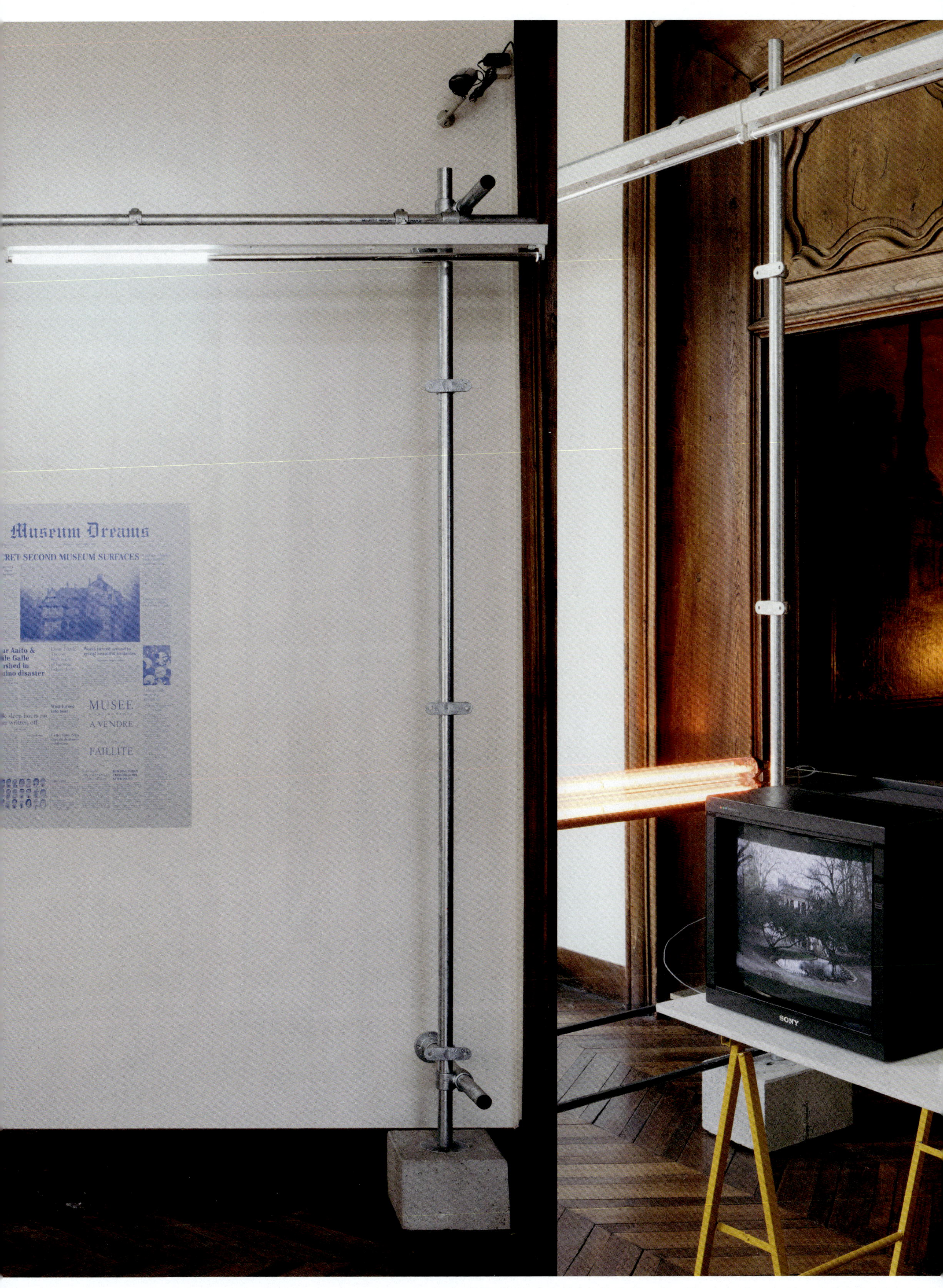
Museum Dreams
SECOND MUSEUM SURFACES
Works turned around to reveal beautiful backsides
MUSEE
A VENDRE
FAILLITE
SONY

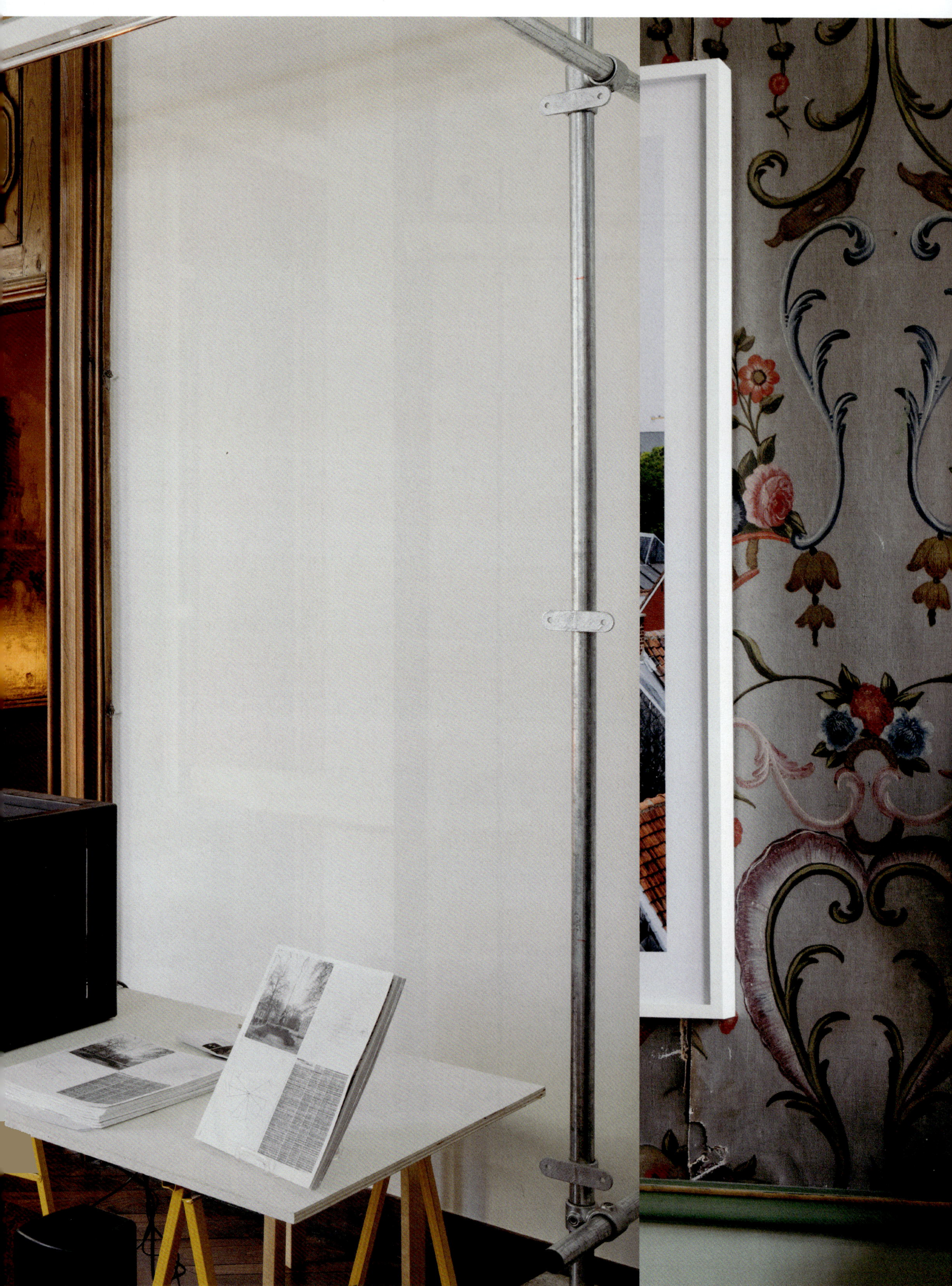

DE CLEENE DE CLEENE, *F#1-13, Booklaunch*, in collaboration with *Art Paper Editions*, September 2017

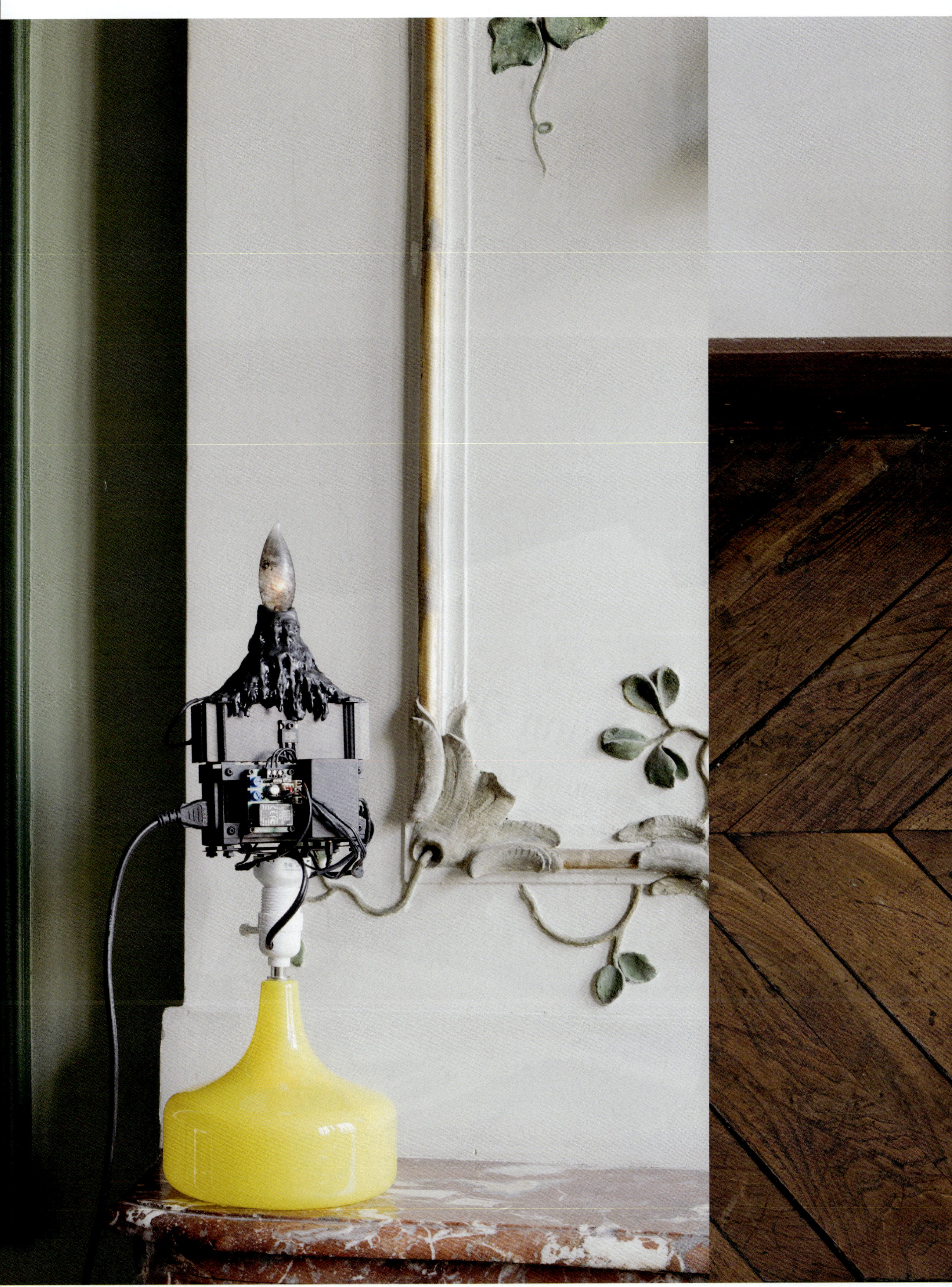

MATHEW KNEEBONE, *Singing Light*, September 2017

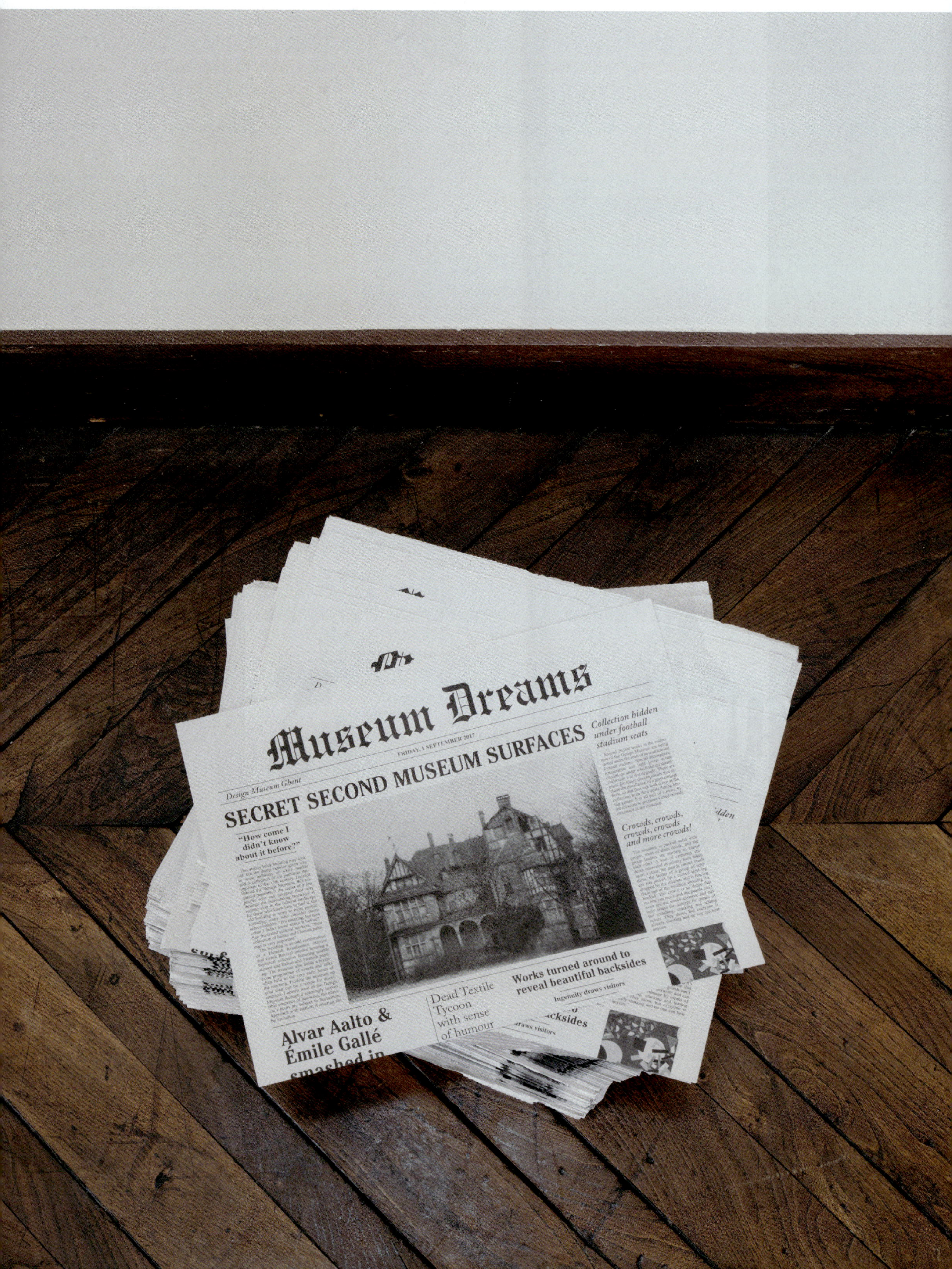

ACTION, *Museum Dreams*, September 2017

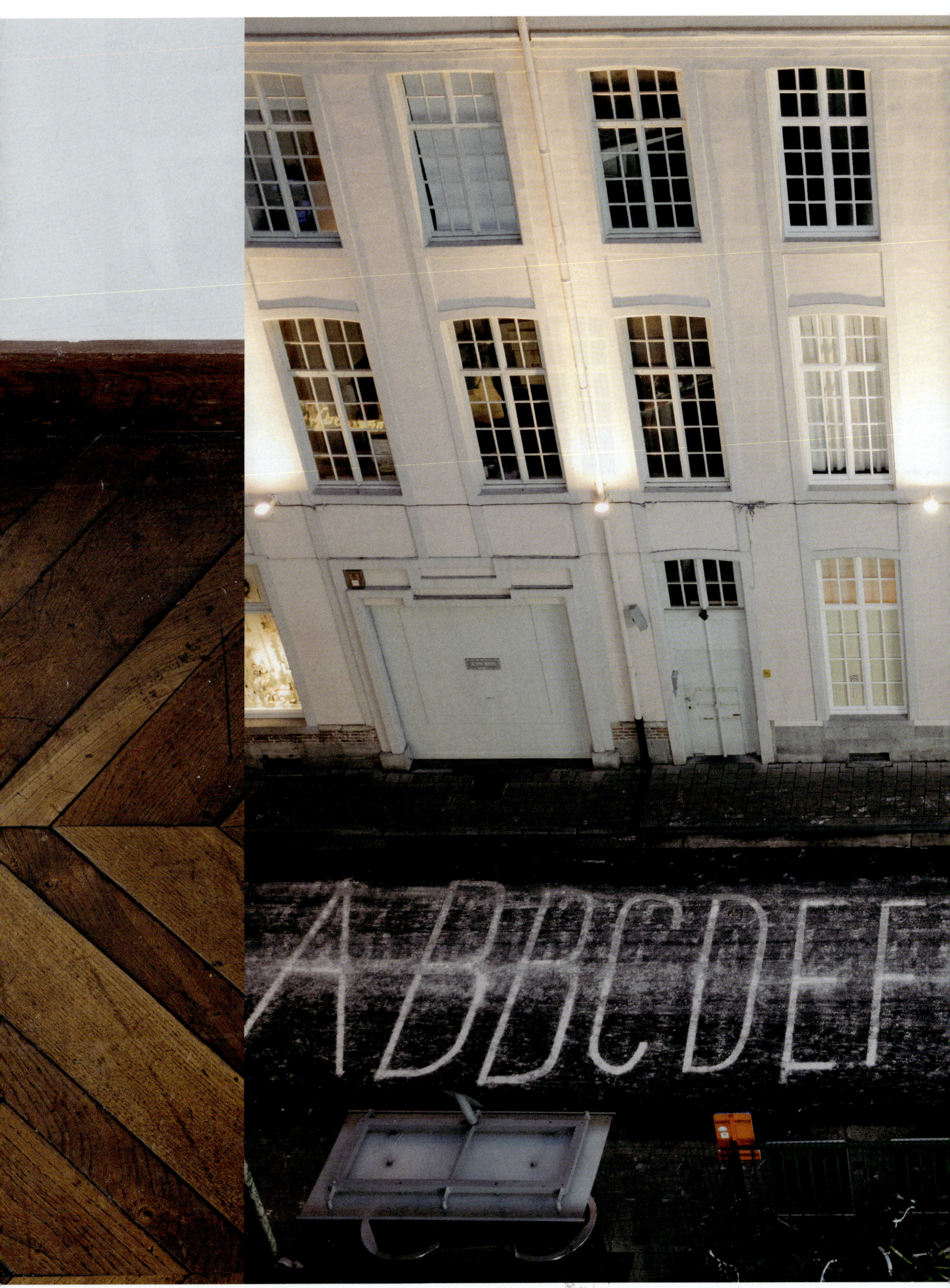

ILKE GERS, *ABCs*, September 2017

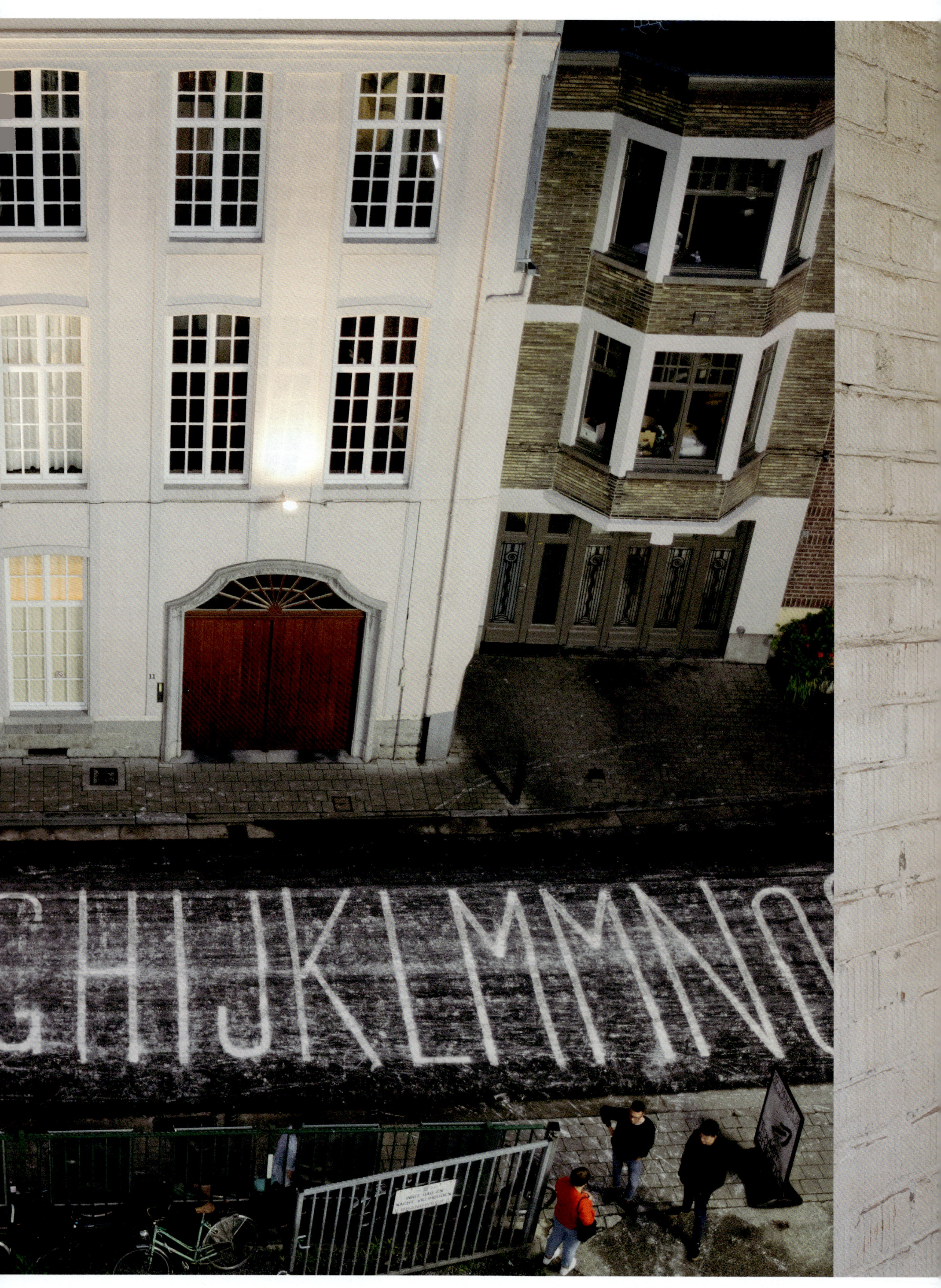
HIJKLMMN

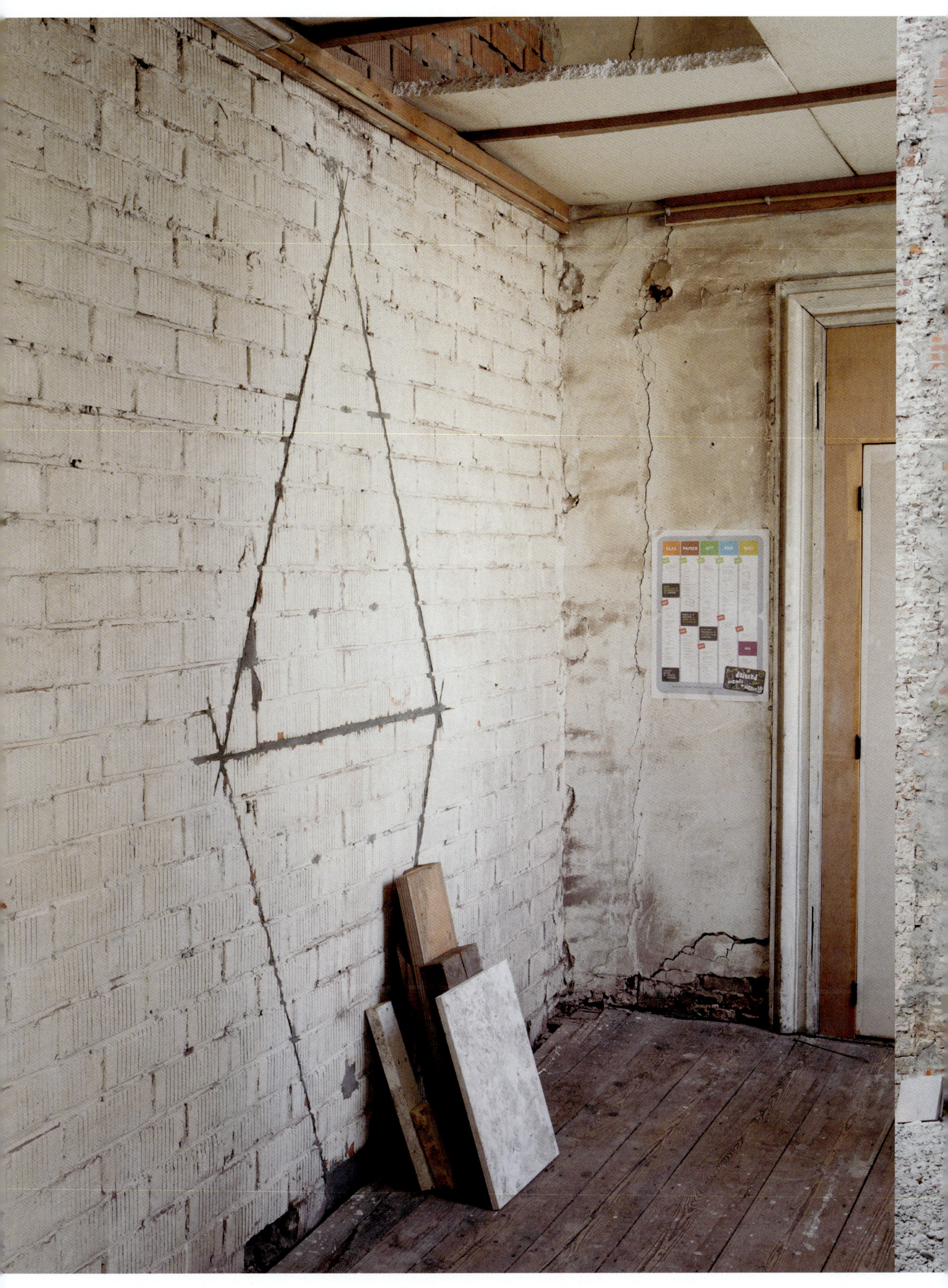
GLAS
PAPIER
GFT
duizend

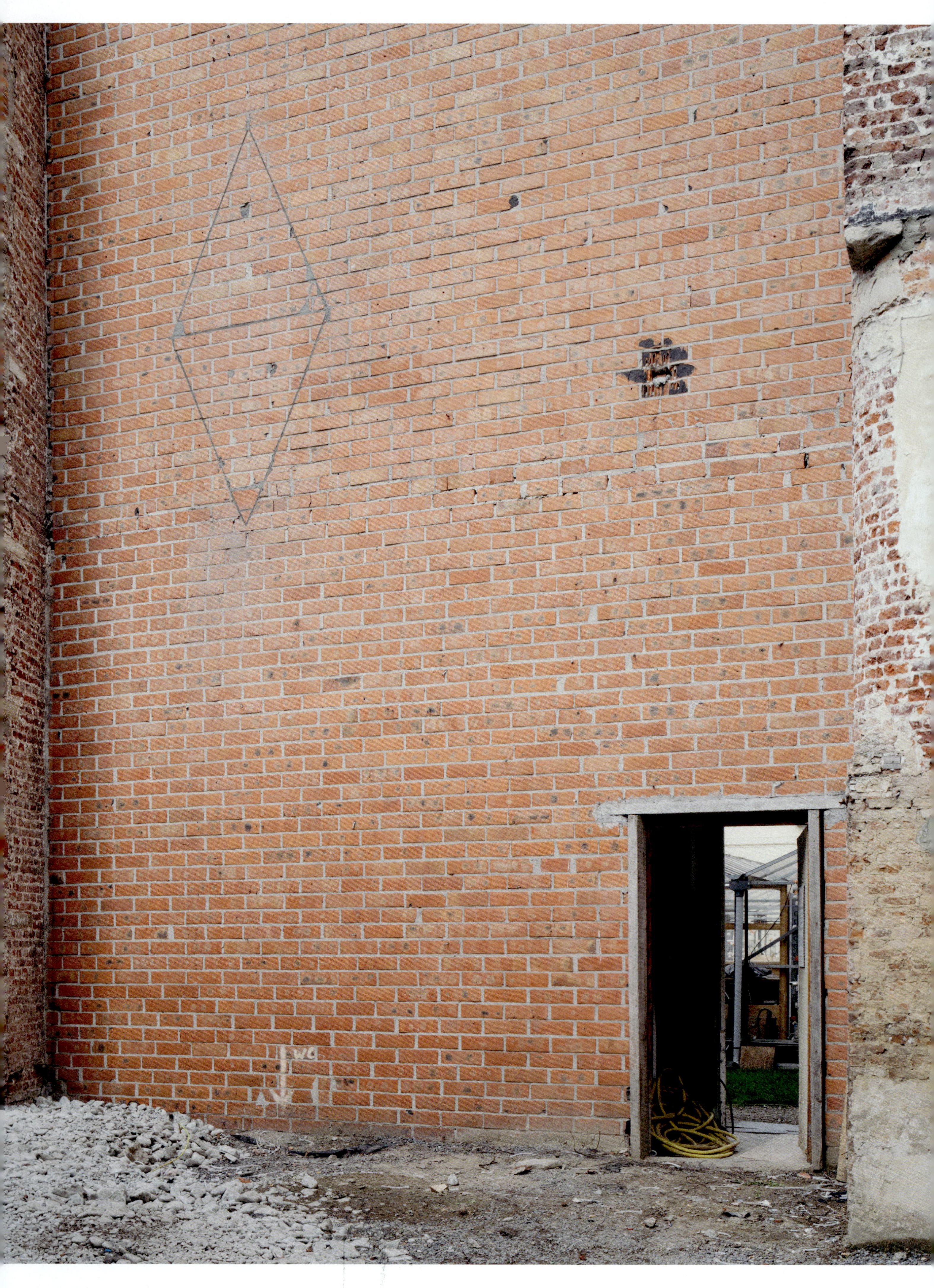
WC

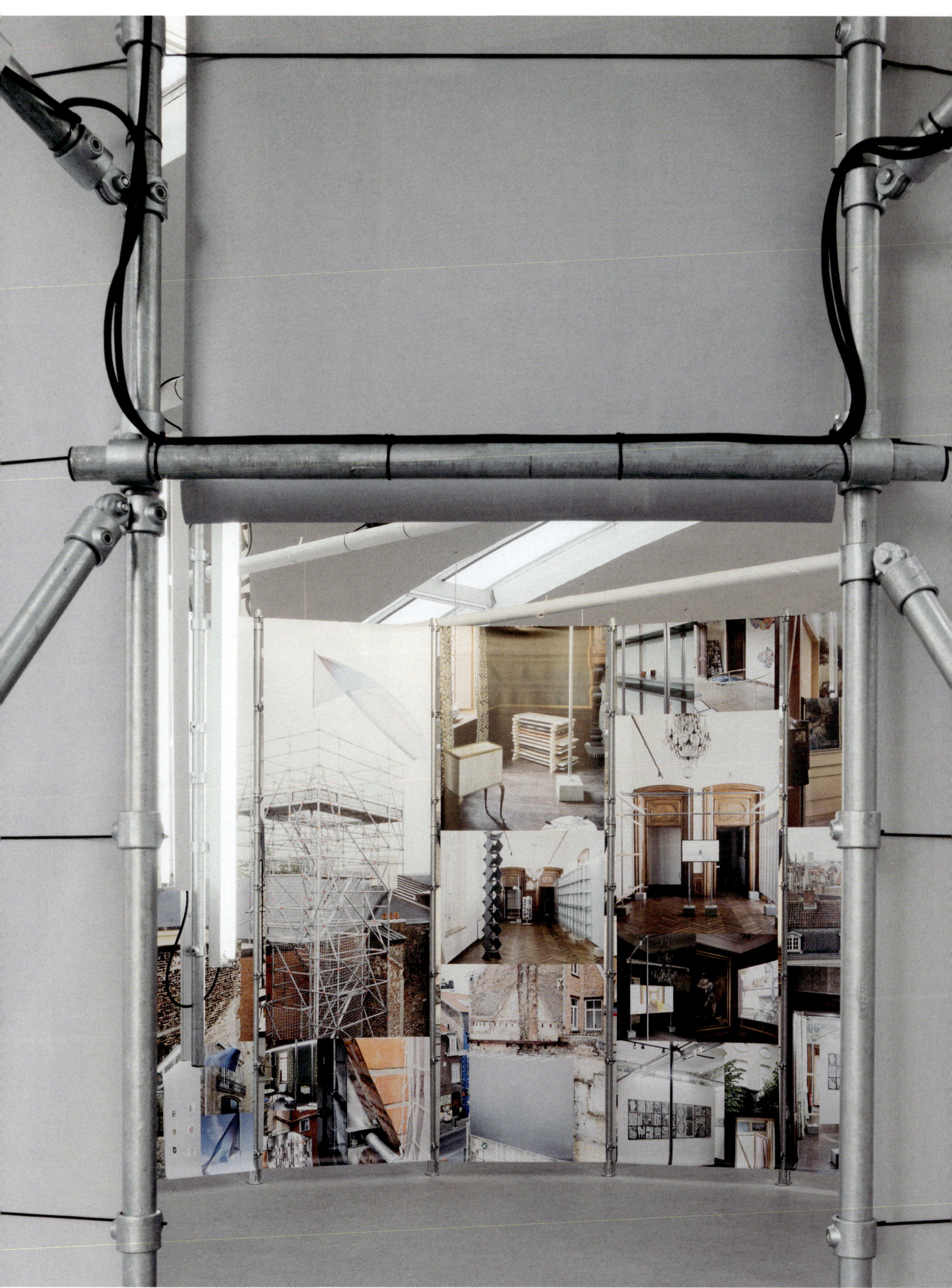

019, RE-EXHIBITING MUSEUM OF MOVING PRACTICE, De Fabriek Eindhoven, in collaboration with *LUCA School Of Arts Ghent*, October 2017

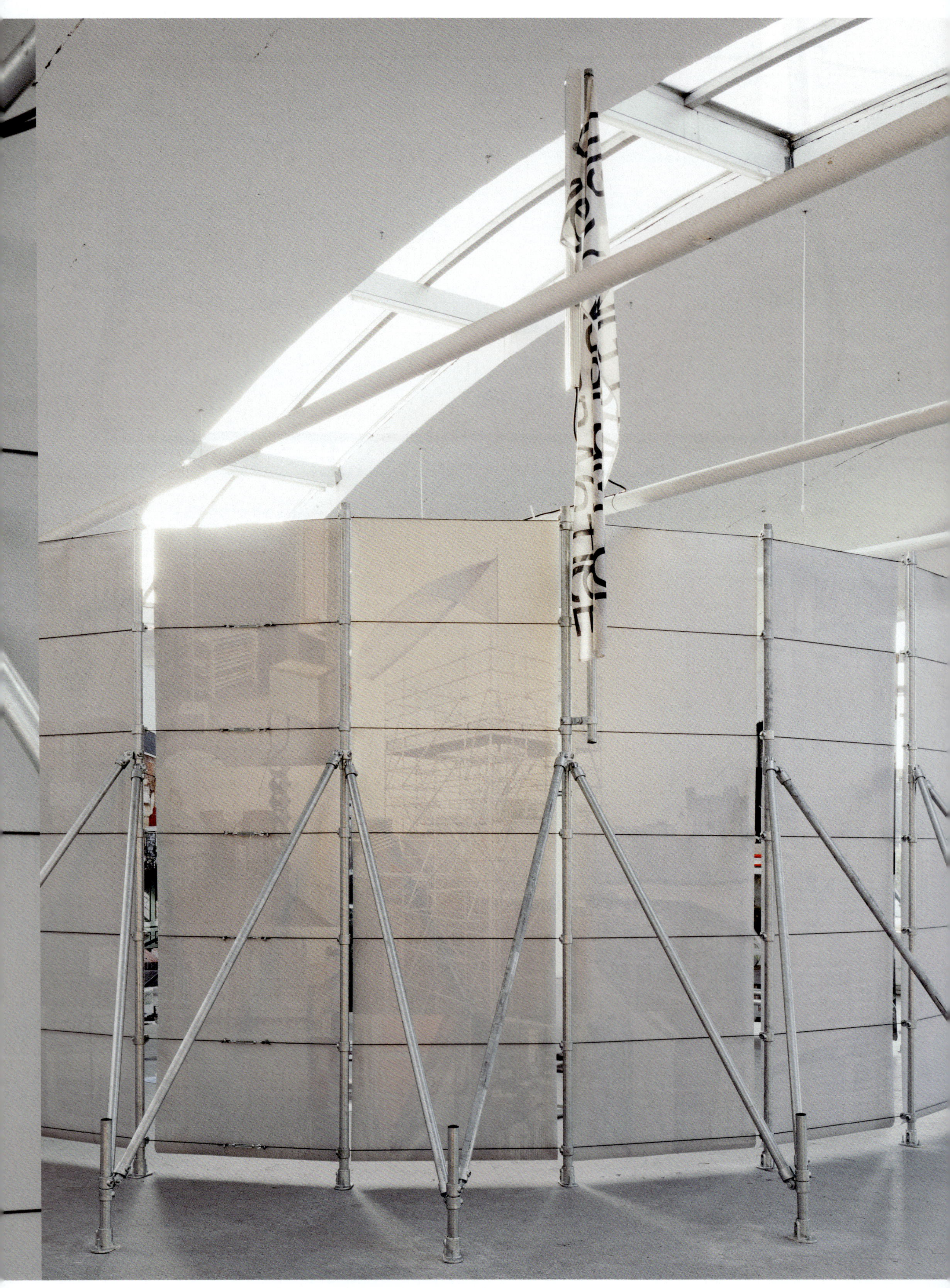

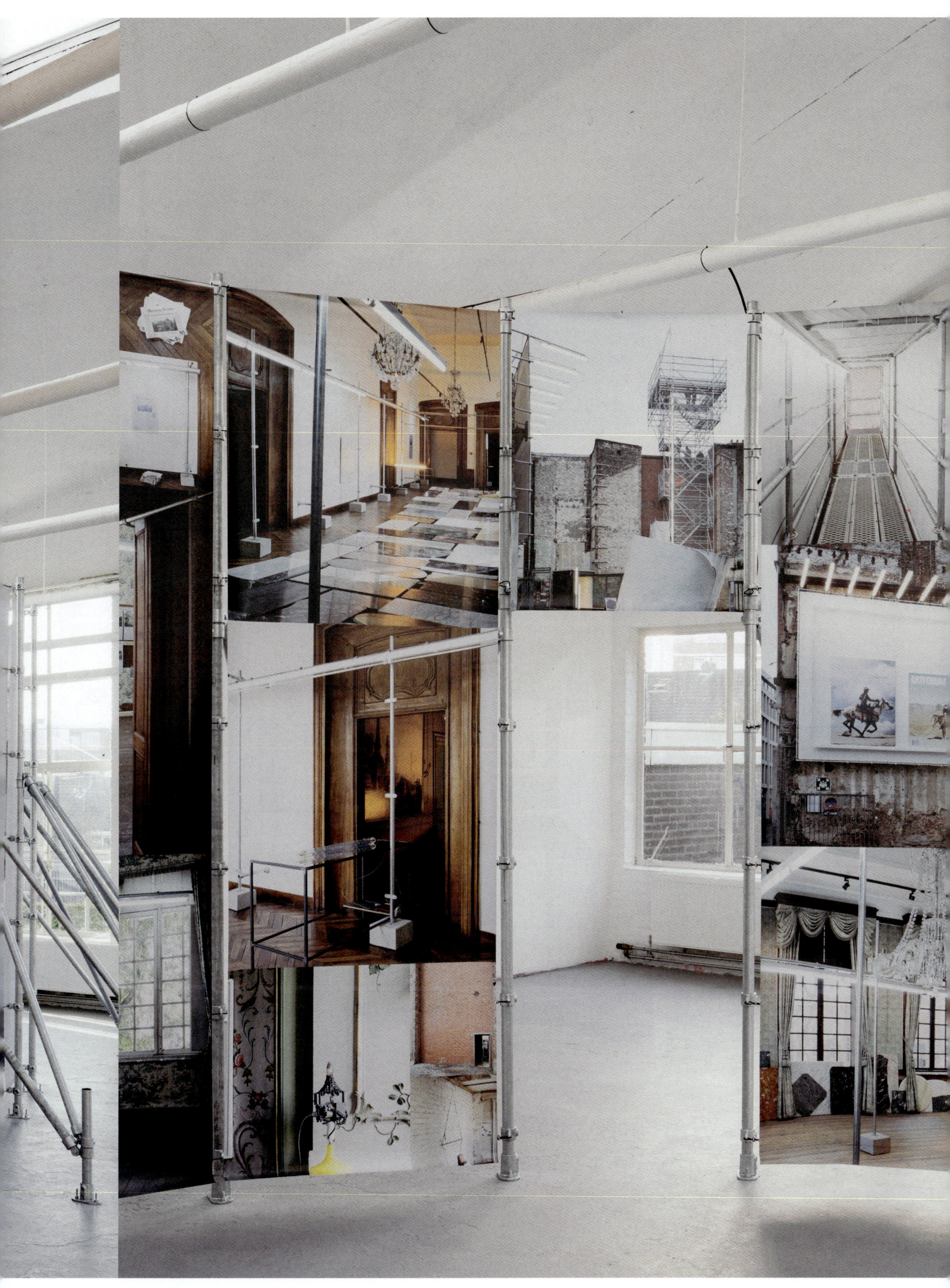

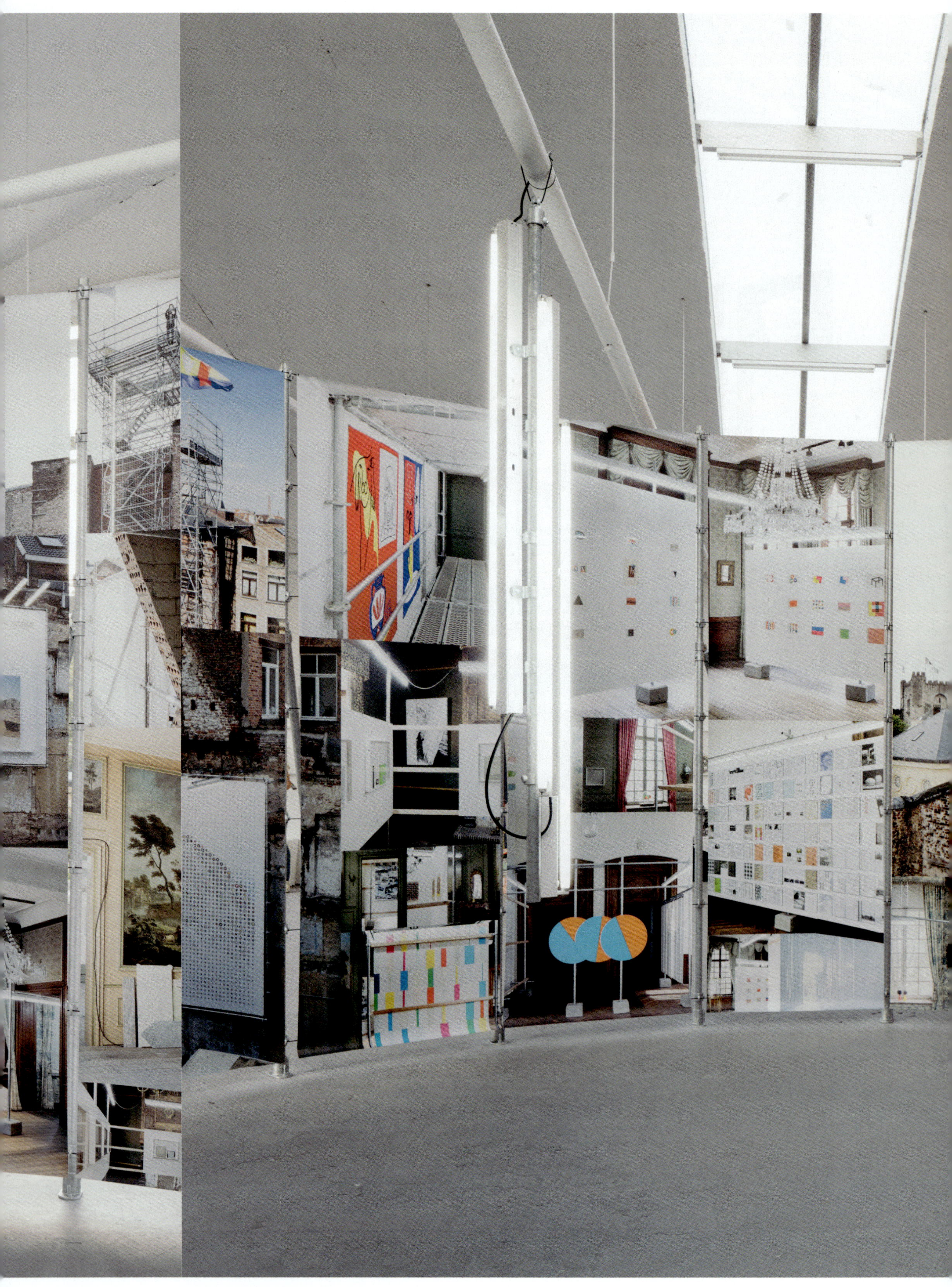

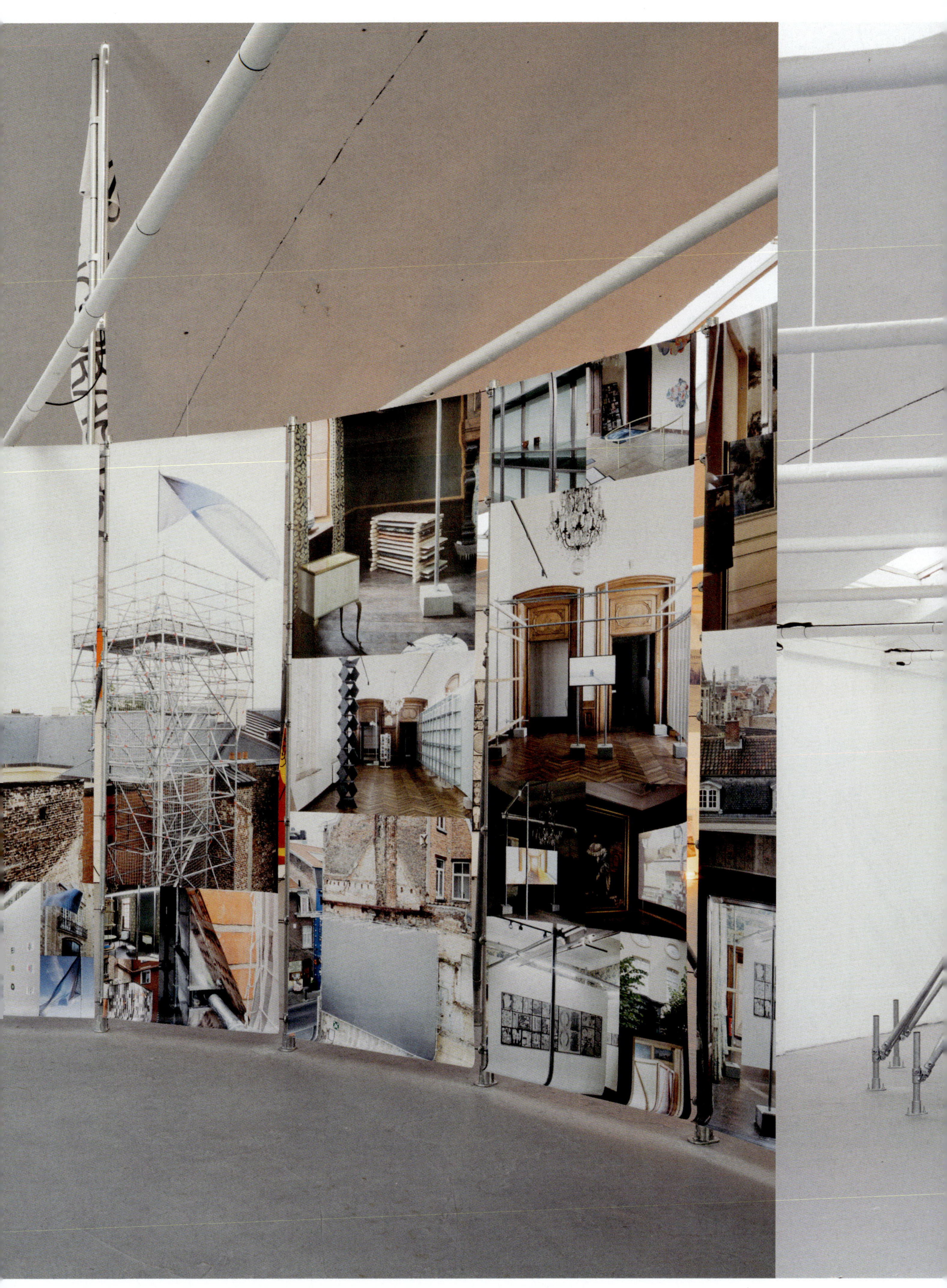

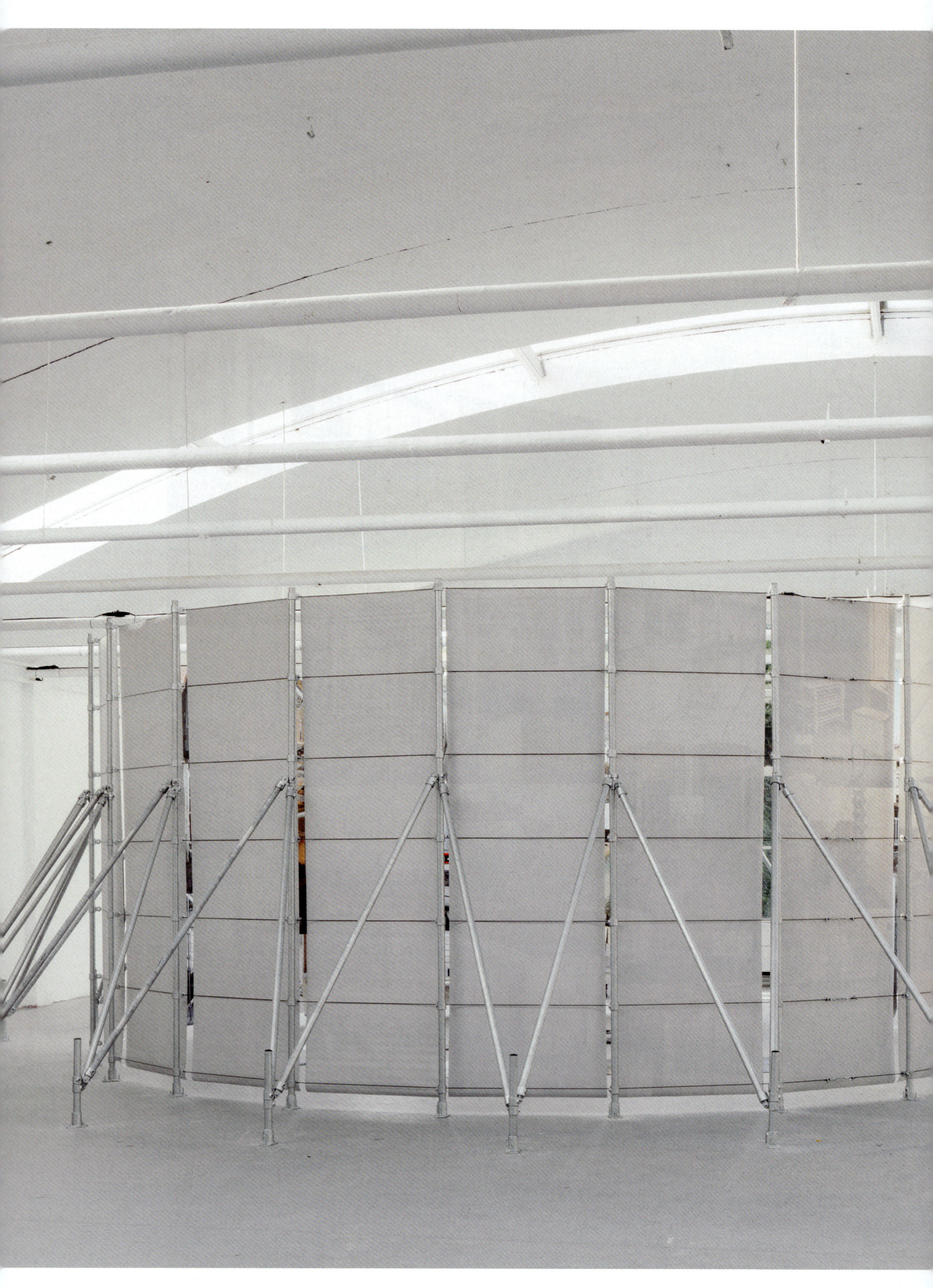

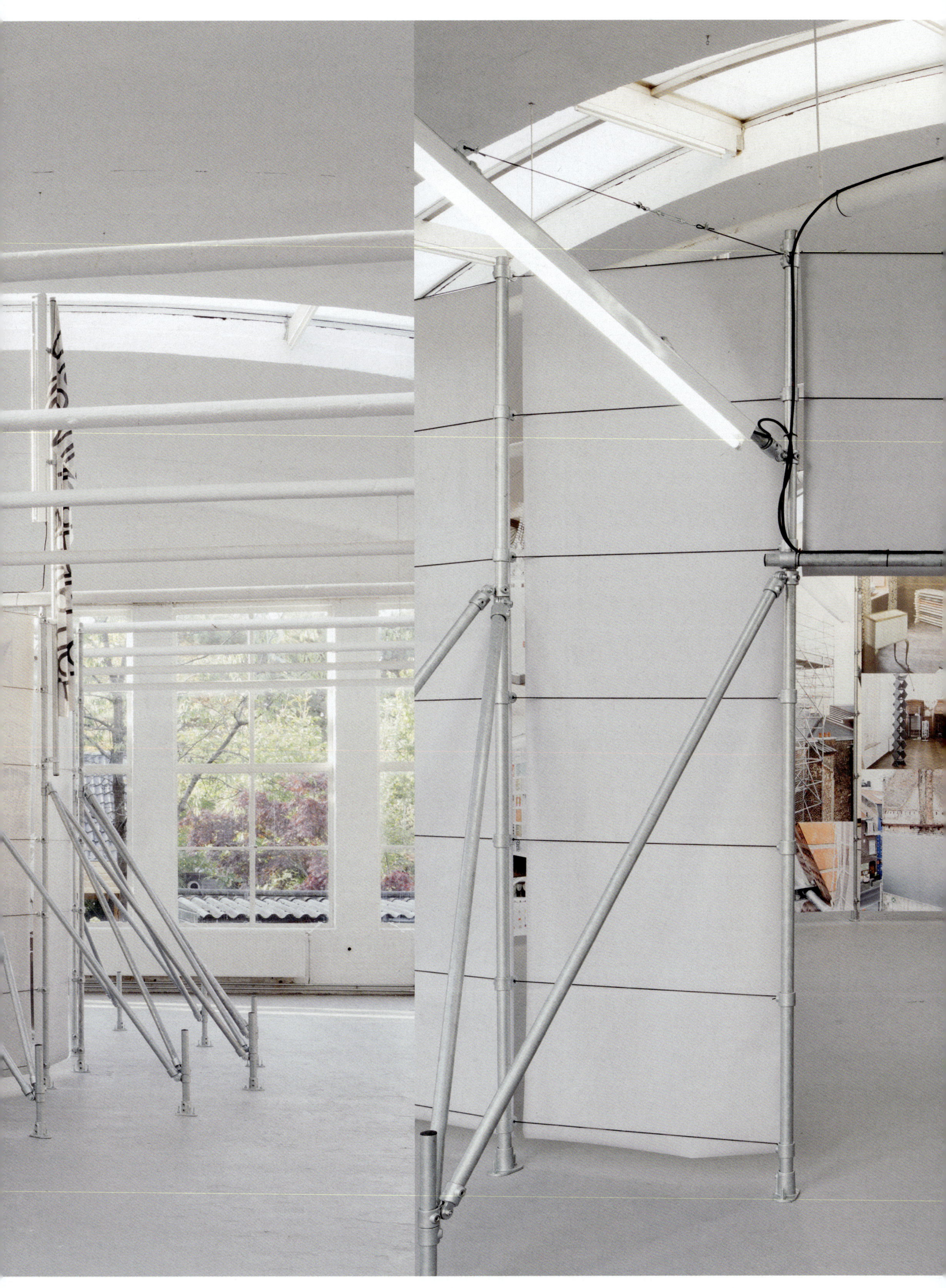

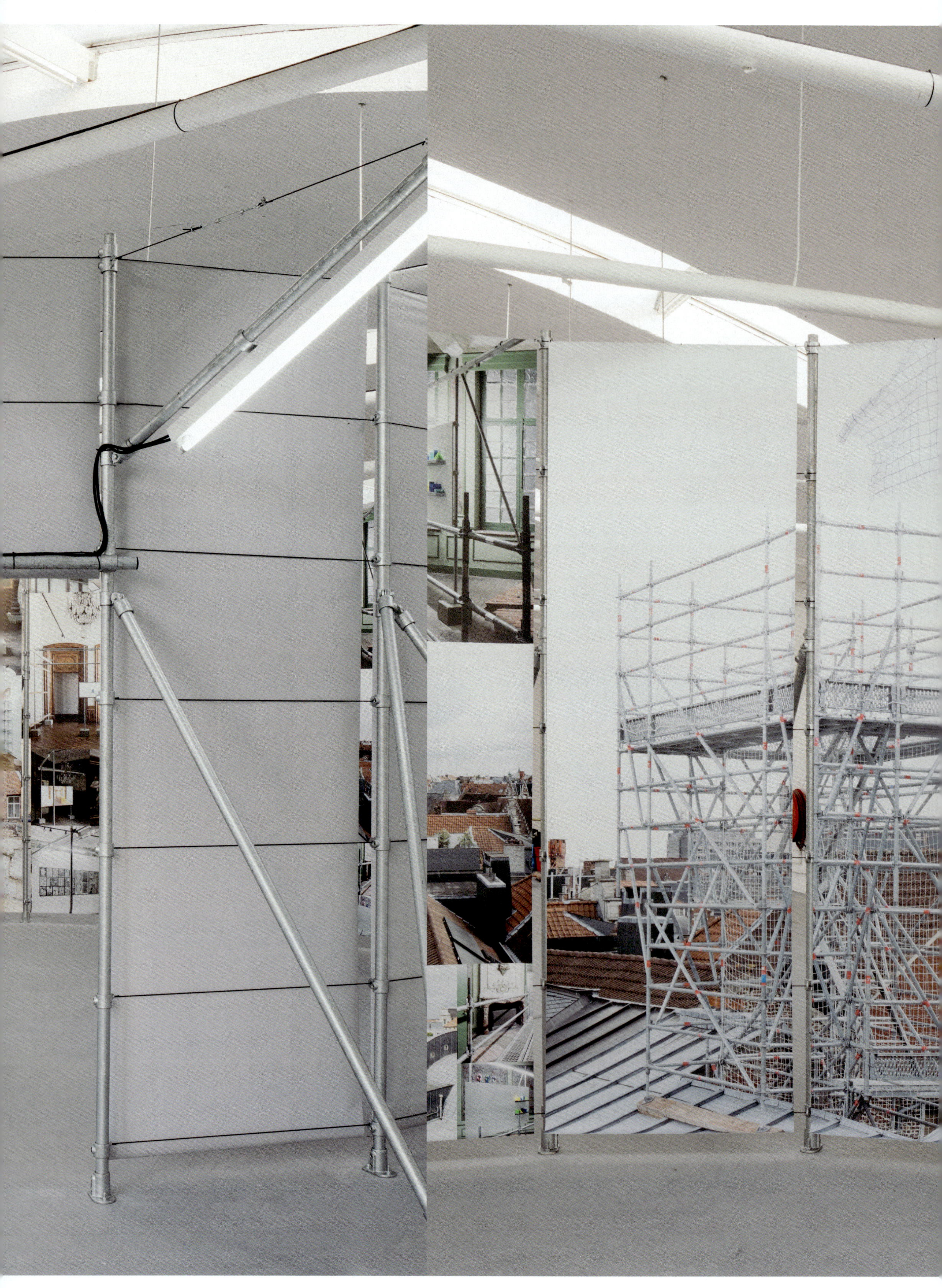

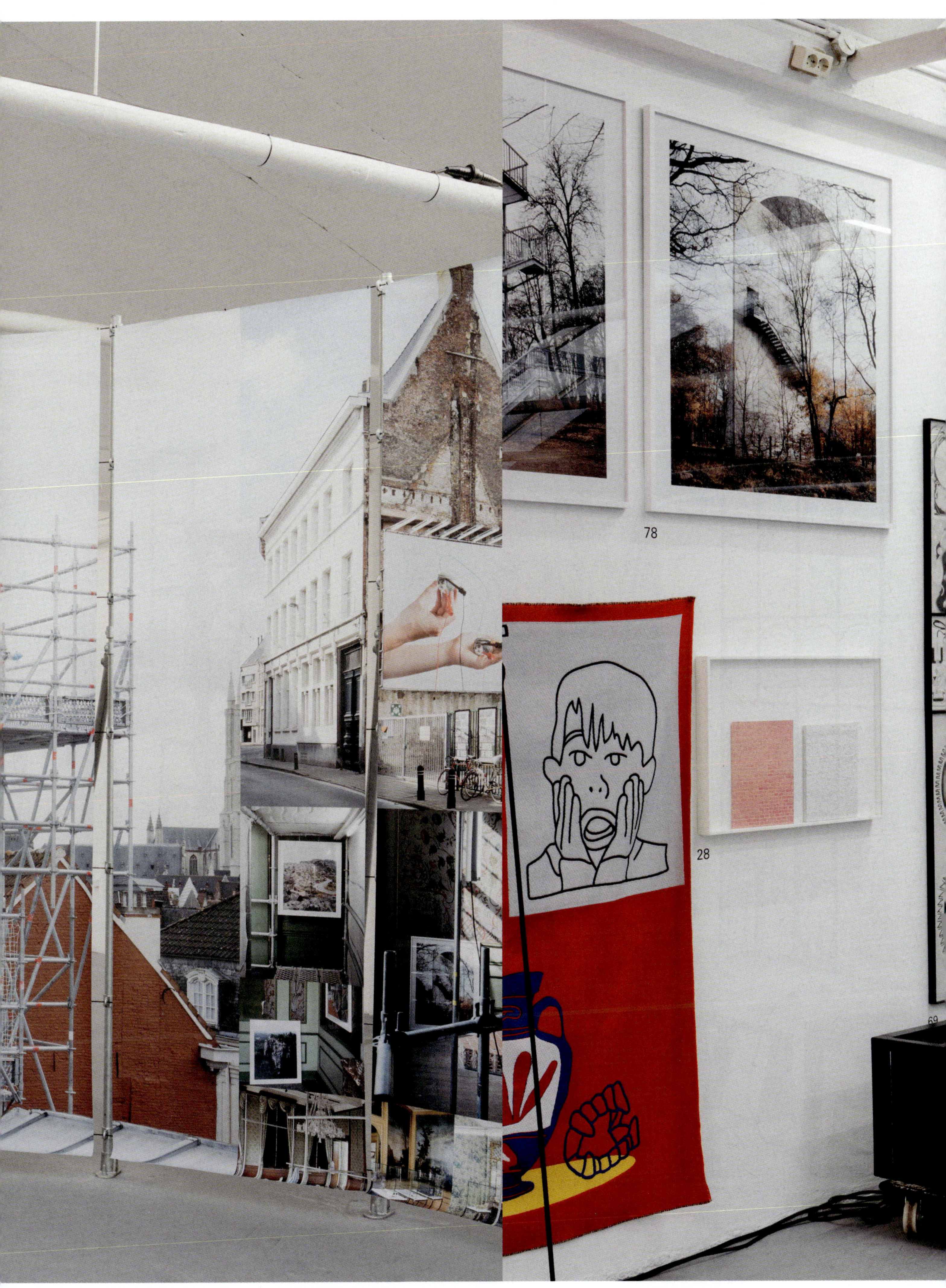

76—79. MICHIEL DE CLEENE, *-scope*, October 2017
28. MORITZ KÜNG, *Selección Natural - This is the Cover of the Book*, October 2017

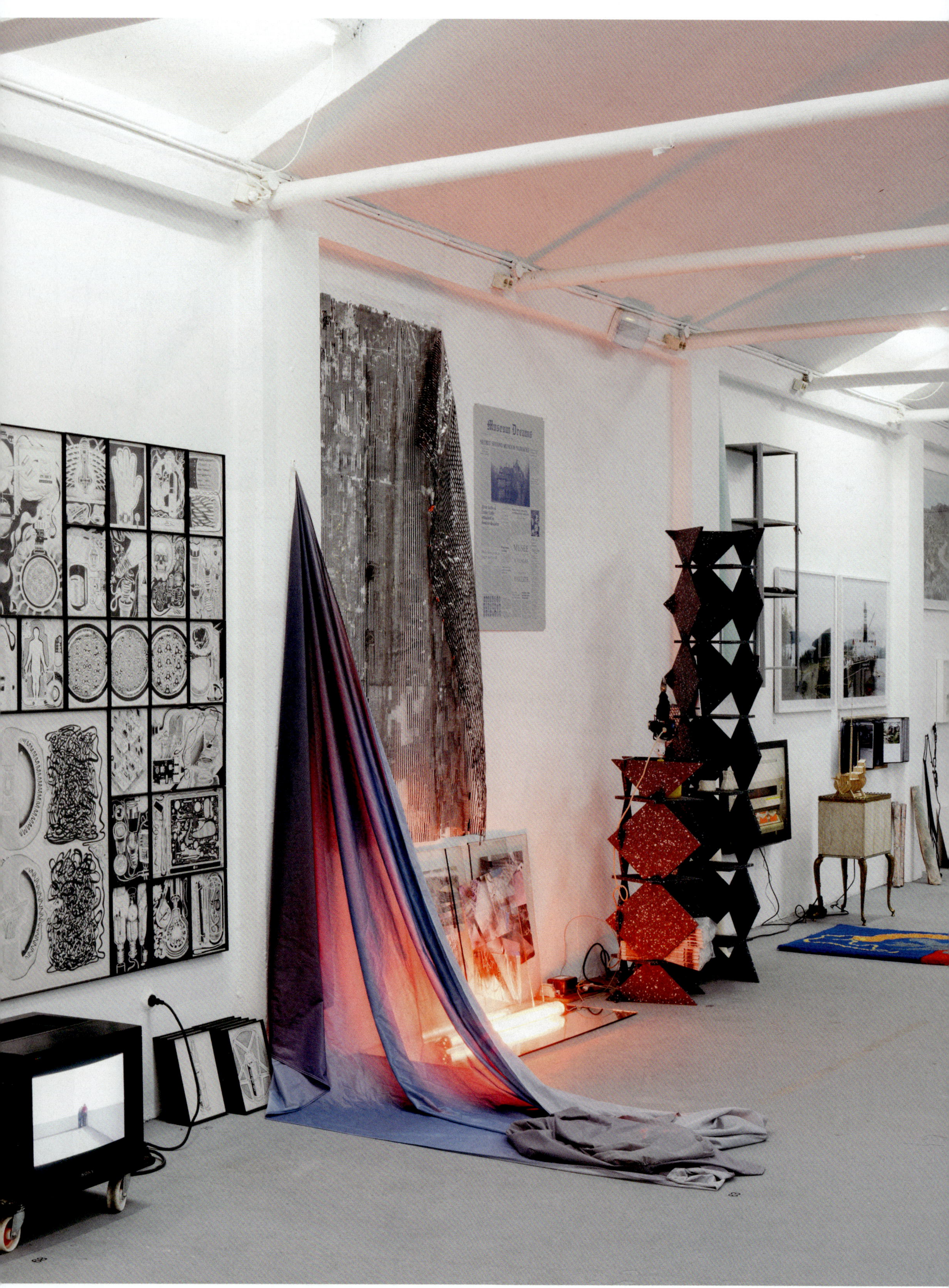

68. LYDIA DEBEER, *The View*, October 2017
70. MATHEW KNEEBONE, *Auras*, October 2017

63. STIJN COLE, *New Colors / Sunrise 8/6/2017*, October 2017

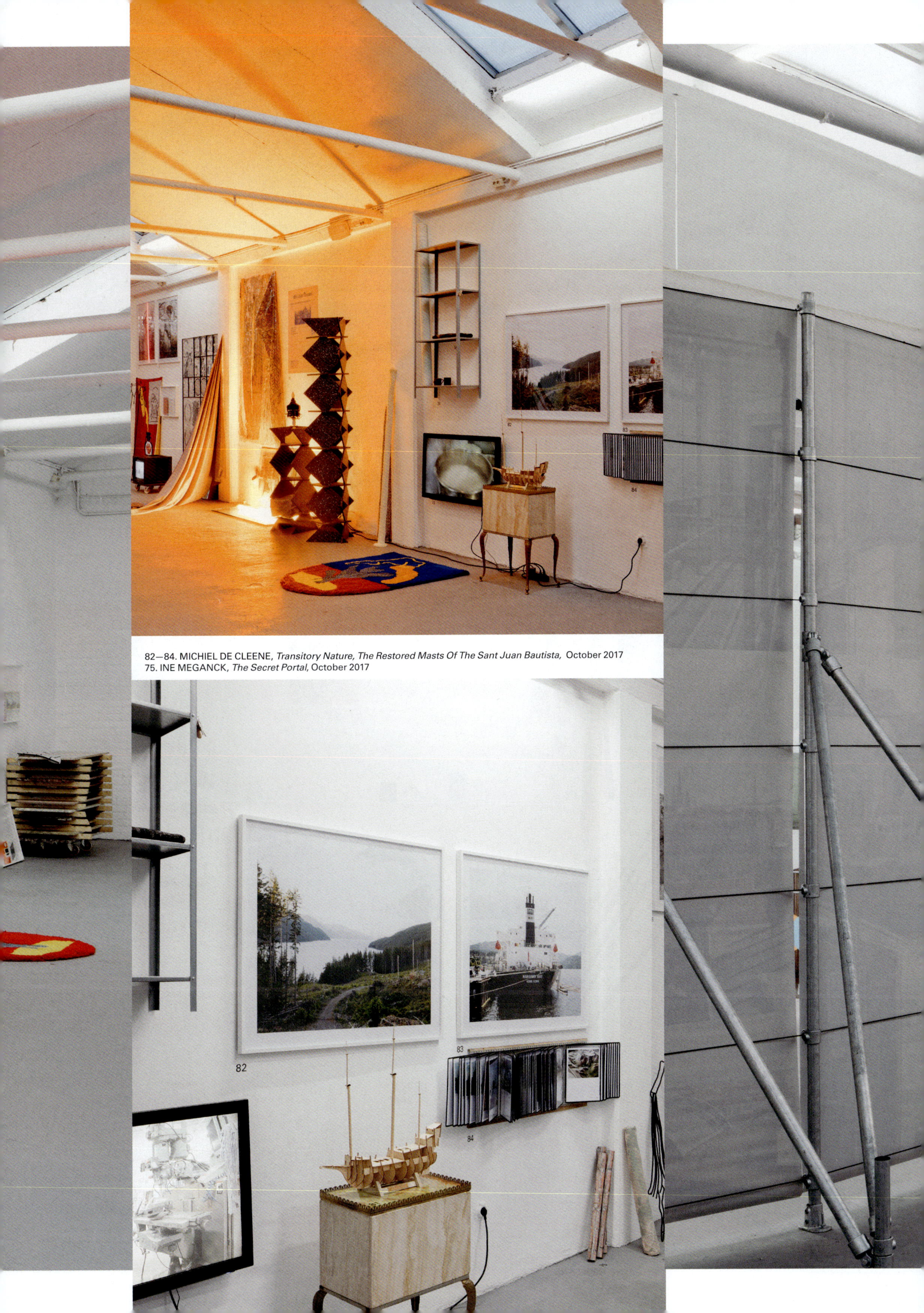

82—84. MICHIEL DE CLEENE, *Transitory Nature, The Restored Masts Of The Sant Juan Bautista,* October 2017
75. INE MEGANCK, *The Secret Portal*, October 2017

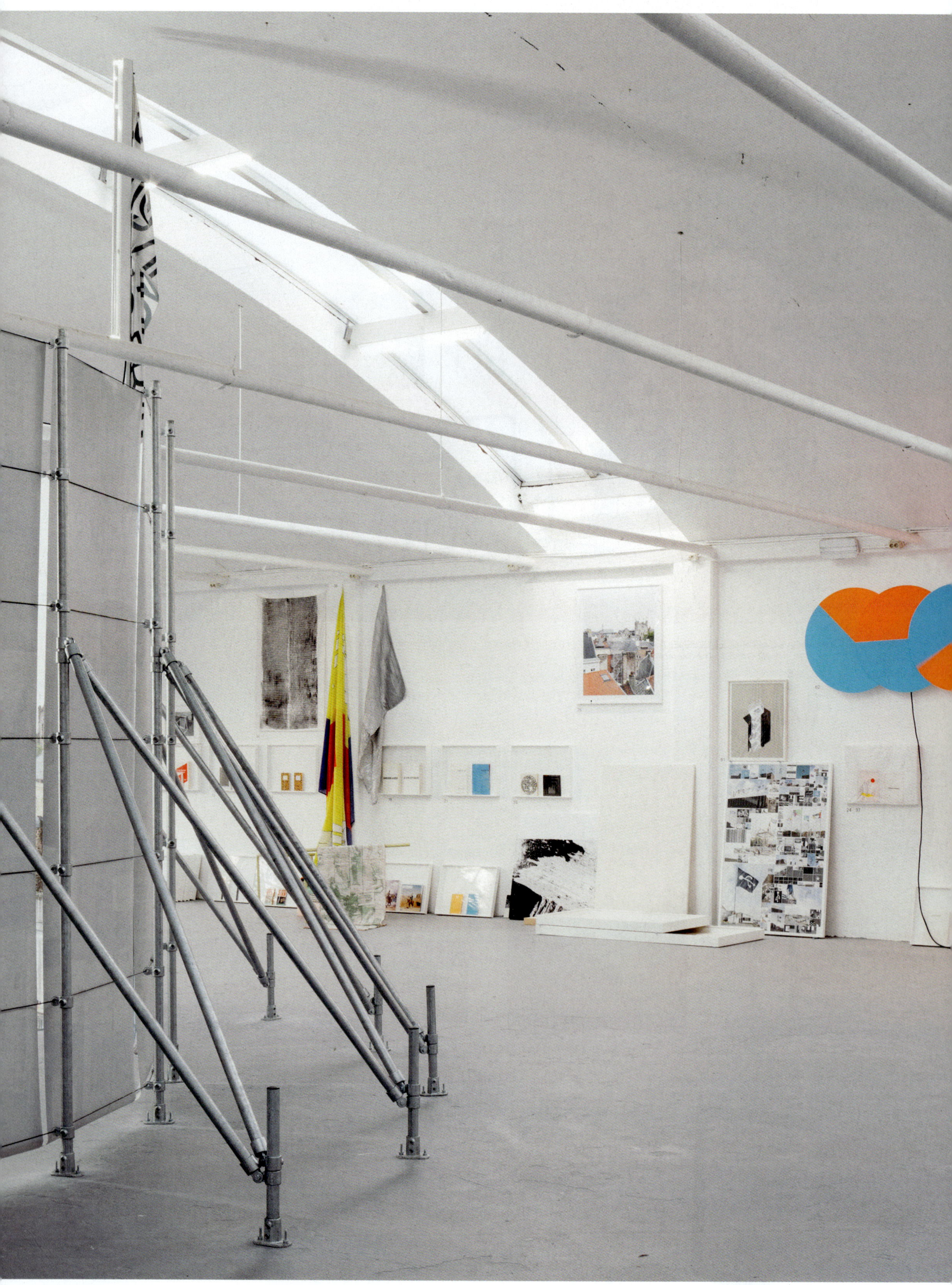

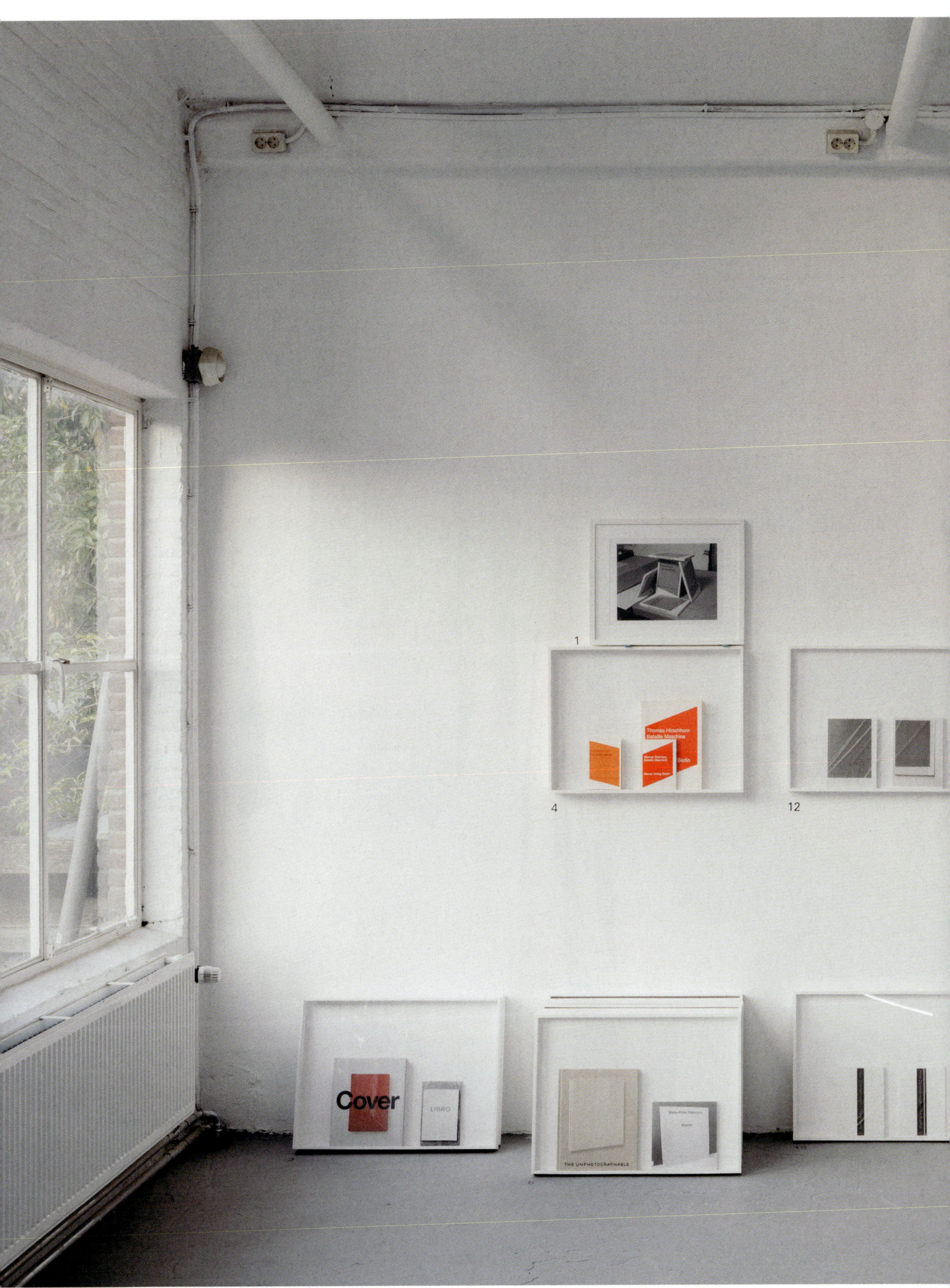

2—33. MORITZ KÜNG, *Selección Natural - This is the Cover of the Book*, October 2017

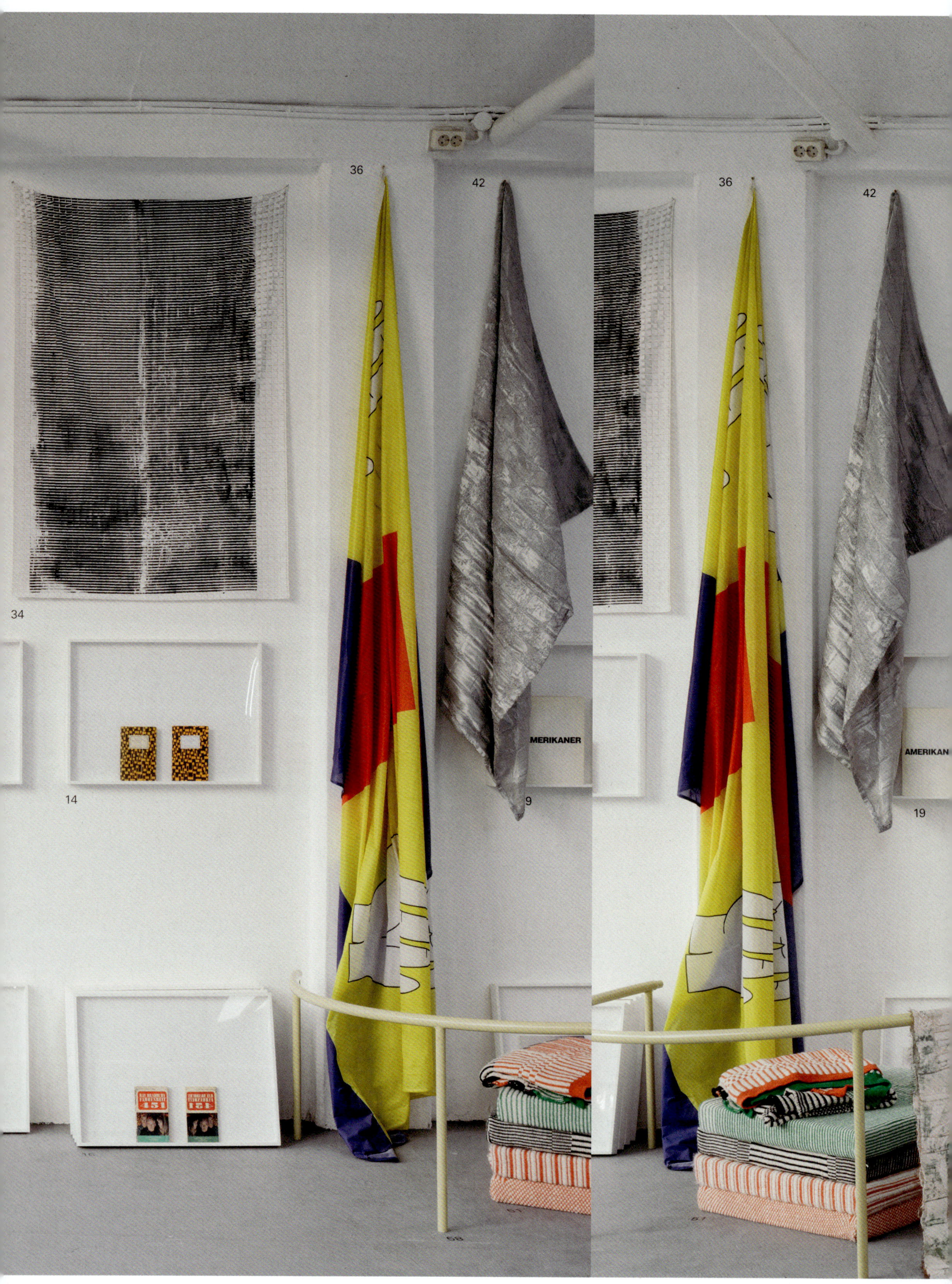

34. ROSALINE FIEMS, *Defined By What Lies Underneath*, October 2017
58. COMMON ROOM, *Ring* October 2017

36—41. CHARLOTTE STUBY, October 2017
42—44. FIEN DE CAUSMAECKER, October 2017

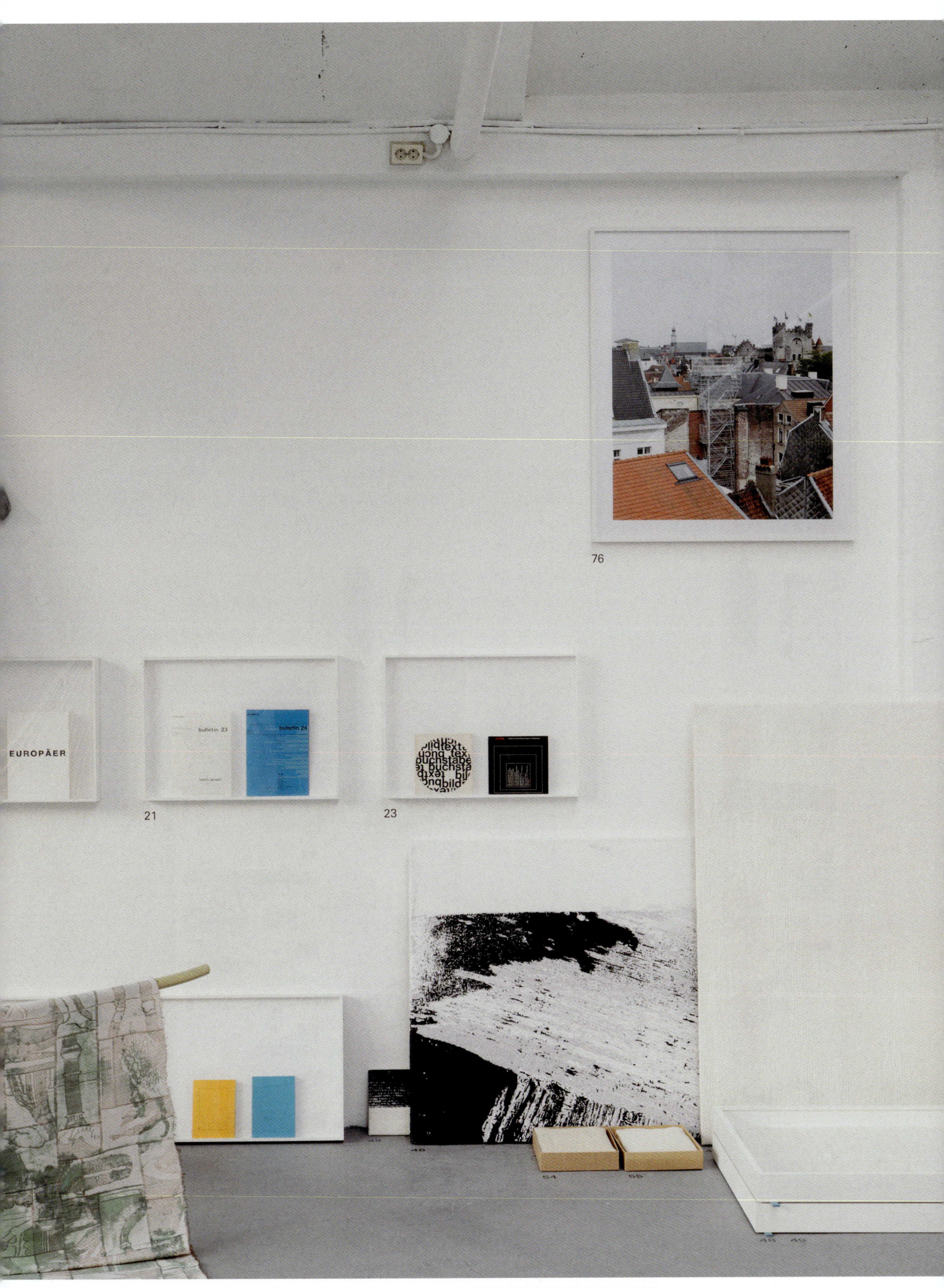

41. FIE MALEM, *(T)Huis*, October 2017
44. FIEN DE CAUSMAECKER, October 2017

45—50. DAPHNE MULDER, October 2017
54—57. LISA BAERSCHNEIDER, October 2017

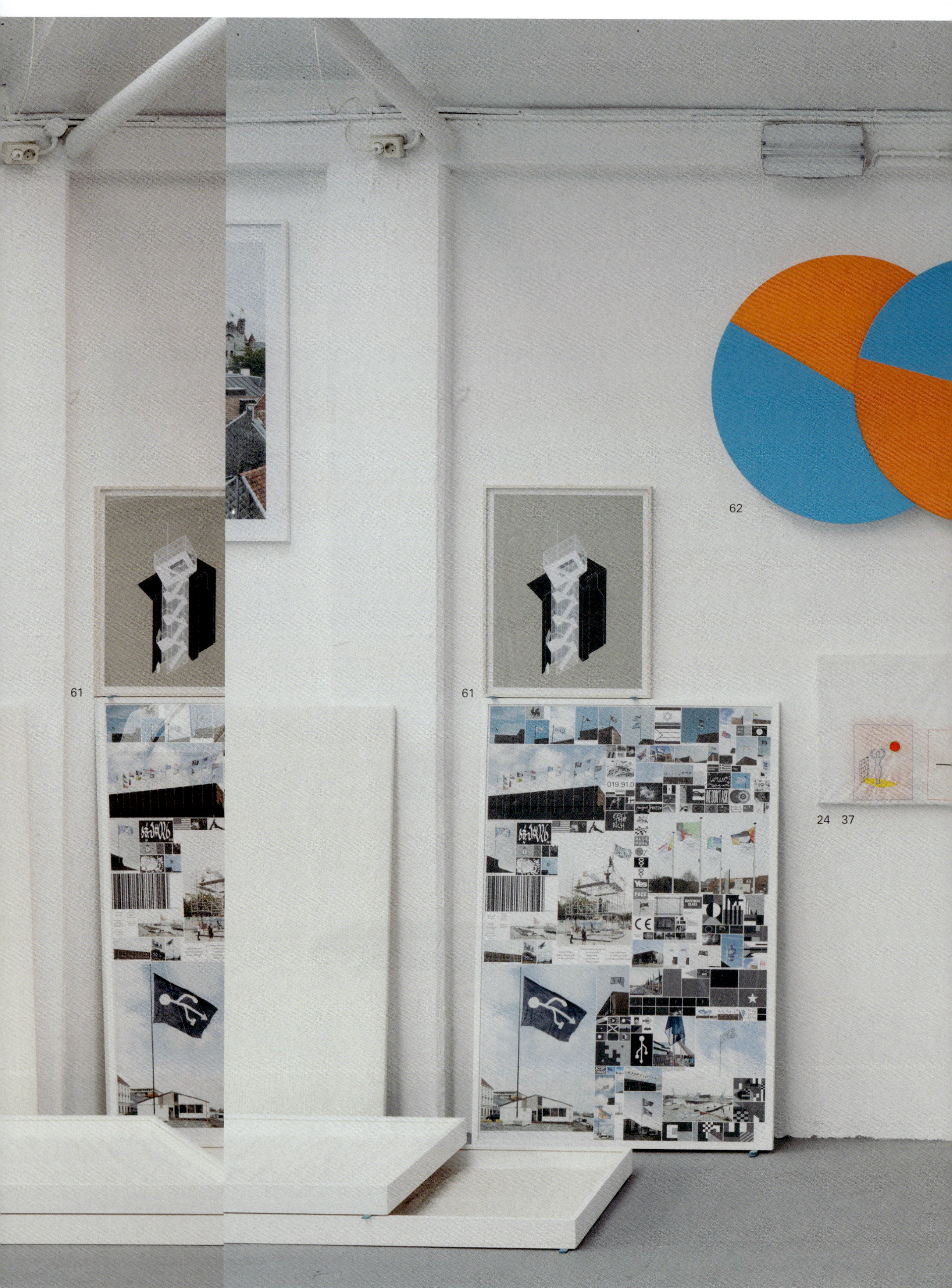

61. 019 / OLIVIER GOETHALS, *Museum Of Moving Practice & Flag Archive (2014—2016)*, October 2017
62. KAREL MARTENS, *Three Times (In Blue And Orange)*, October 2017

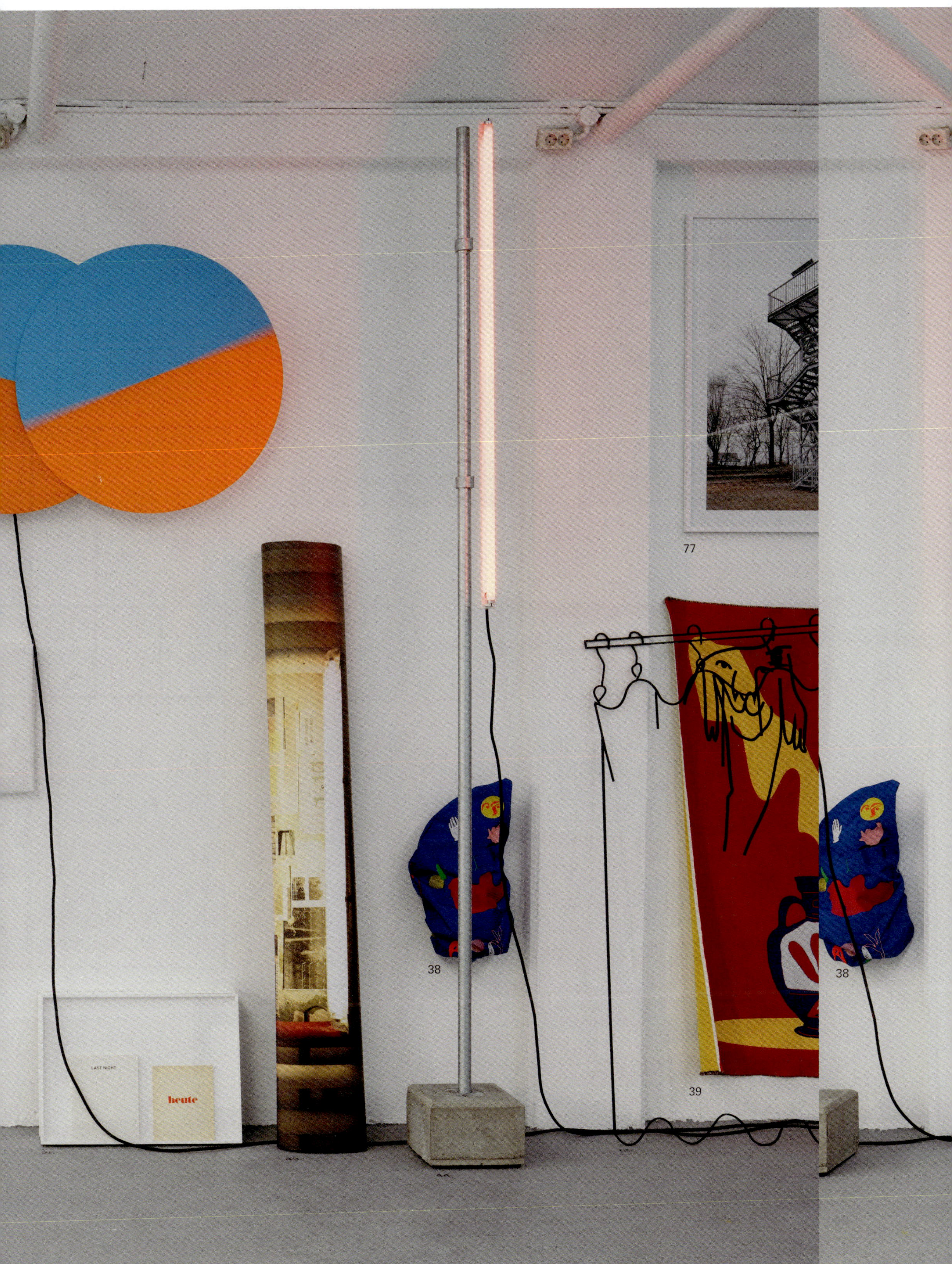
77
LAST NIGHT
heute
38
38
39

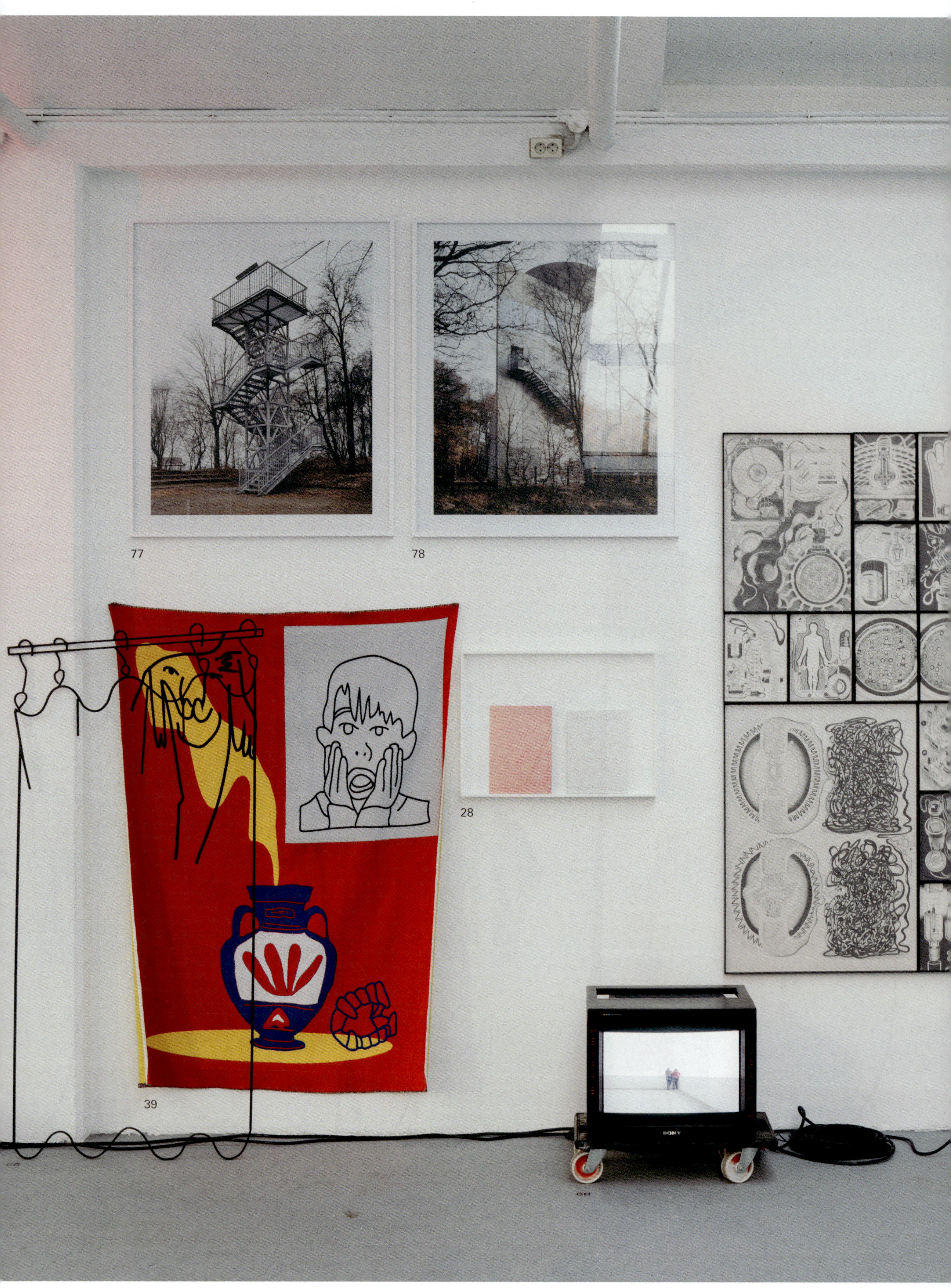

66. QUENTON MILLER, *Here I Am, Writing You A Letter,* October 2017

68. LYDIA DEBEER, *The View,* October 2017
70. MATHEW KNEEBONE, *Auras,* October 2017

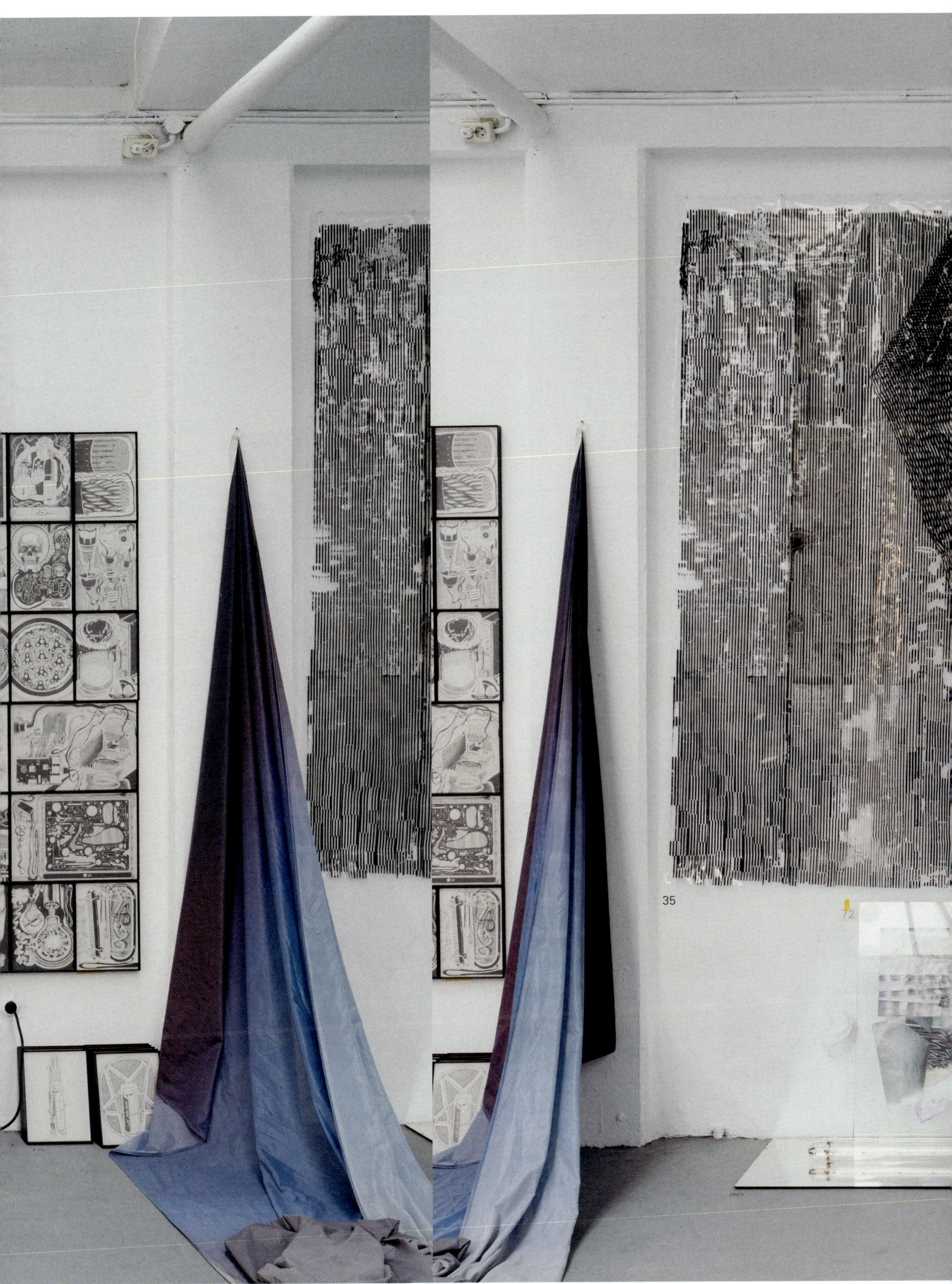

35. ROSALINE FIEMS, *Defined By What Lies Underneath*, October 2017
72. OLIVIER GOETHALS, *Infinitesimal*, October 2017

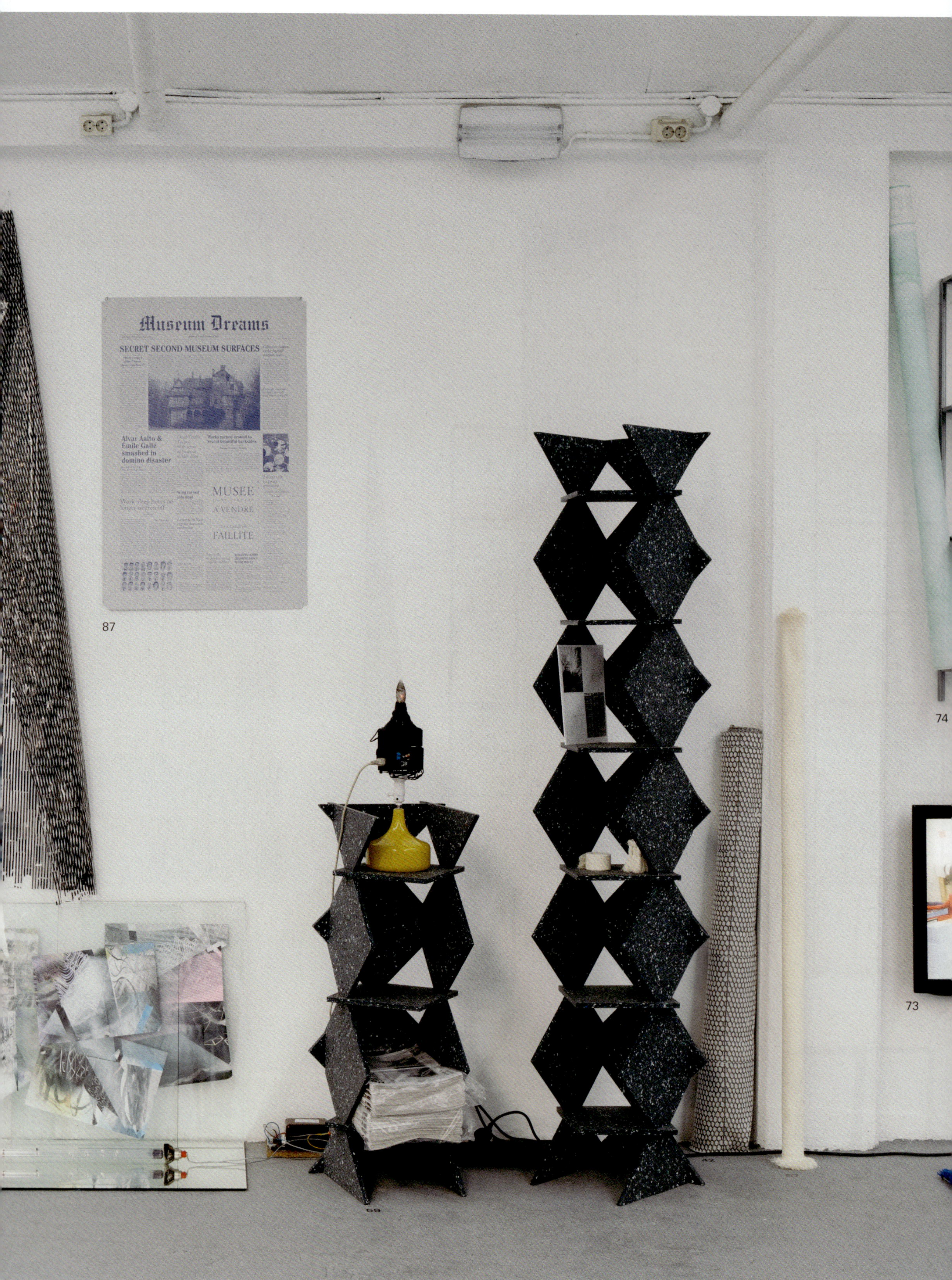

87. ACTION, *Museum Dreams*, October 2017
59. THEO DE MEYER & ARTHUR DEKKER, *Setting Up A Cabinet*, October 2017

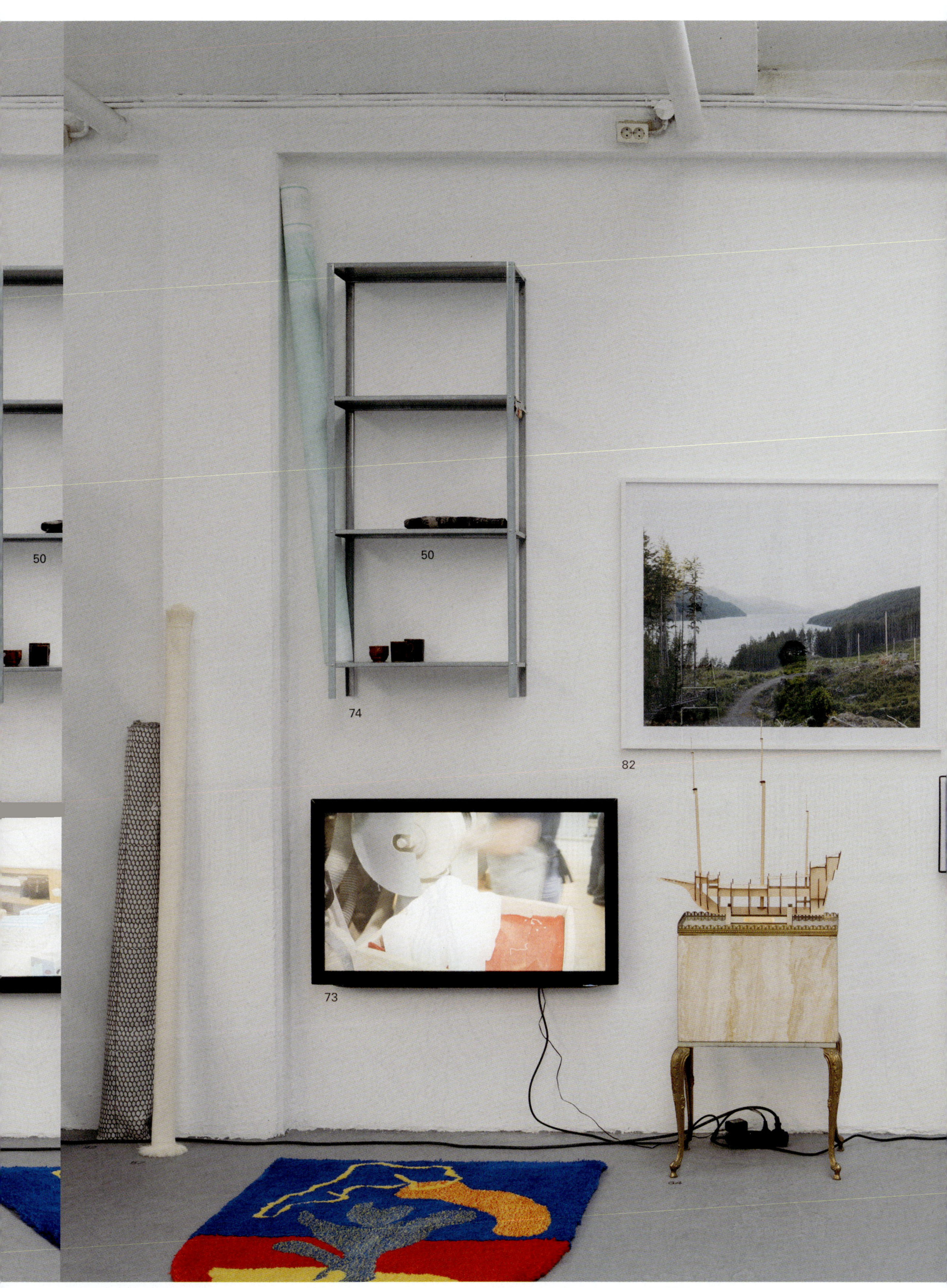

50. DAPHNE MULDER, October 2017
74. MANOR GRUNEWALD, *External Hard Disk (E.H.D.)*, October 2017
73. BEN THORP BROWN, *Dealtoys*, October 2017
64. FILIP DUJARDIN, *Accumulation d'Époque#2*, October 2017

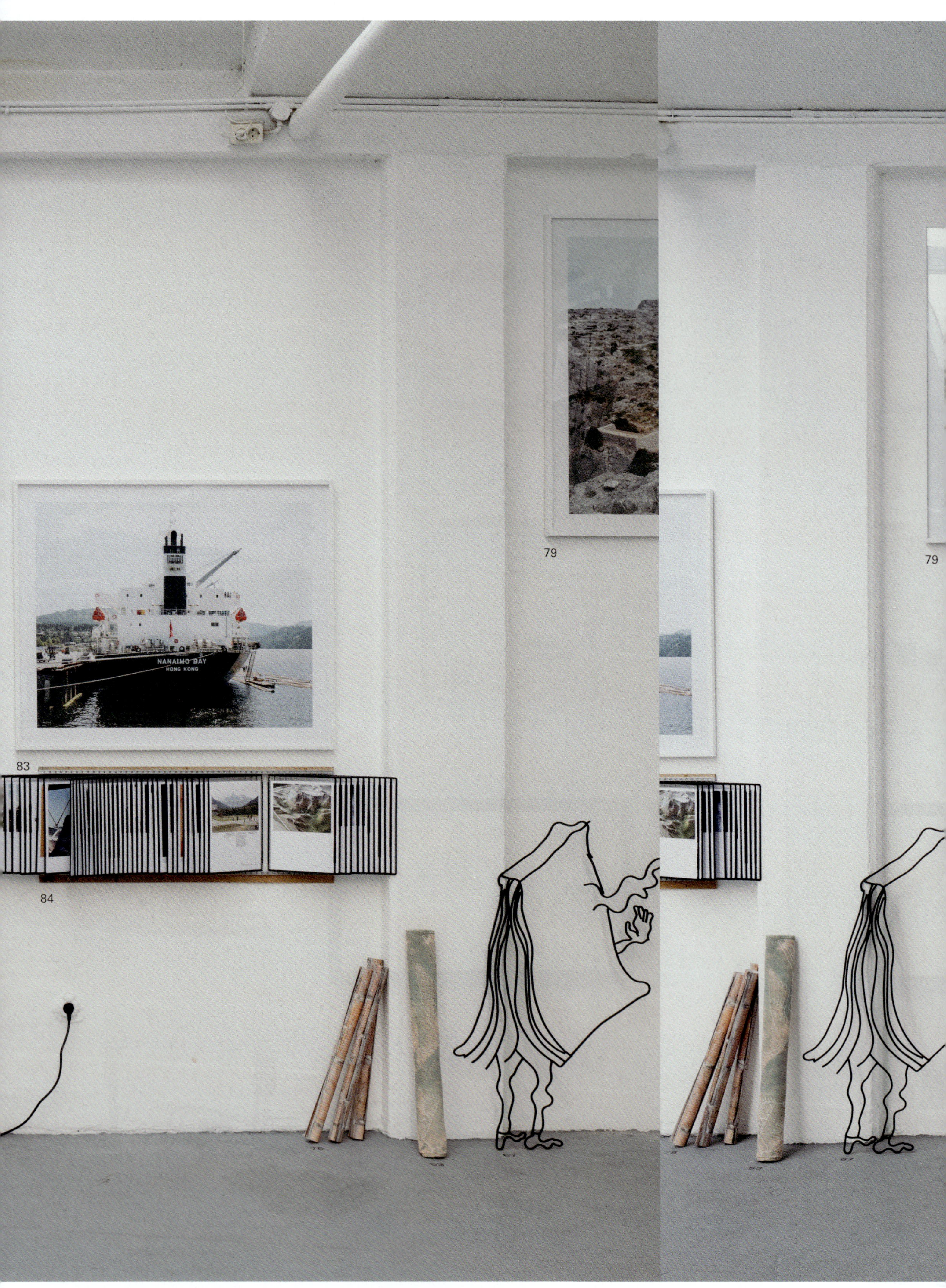

76—86. MICHIEL DE CLEENE, October 2017
75. INE MEGANCK, *The Secret Portal*, October 2017

53. LAURA VAN BIERVLIET, *A Fragmented Reality*, October 2017
67. QUENTON MILLER, *Here I Am, Writing You A Letter*, October 2017

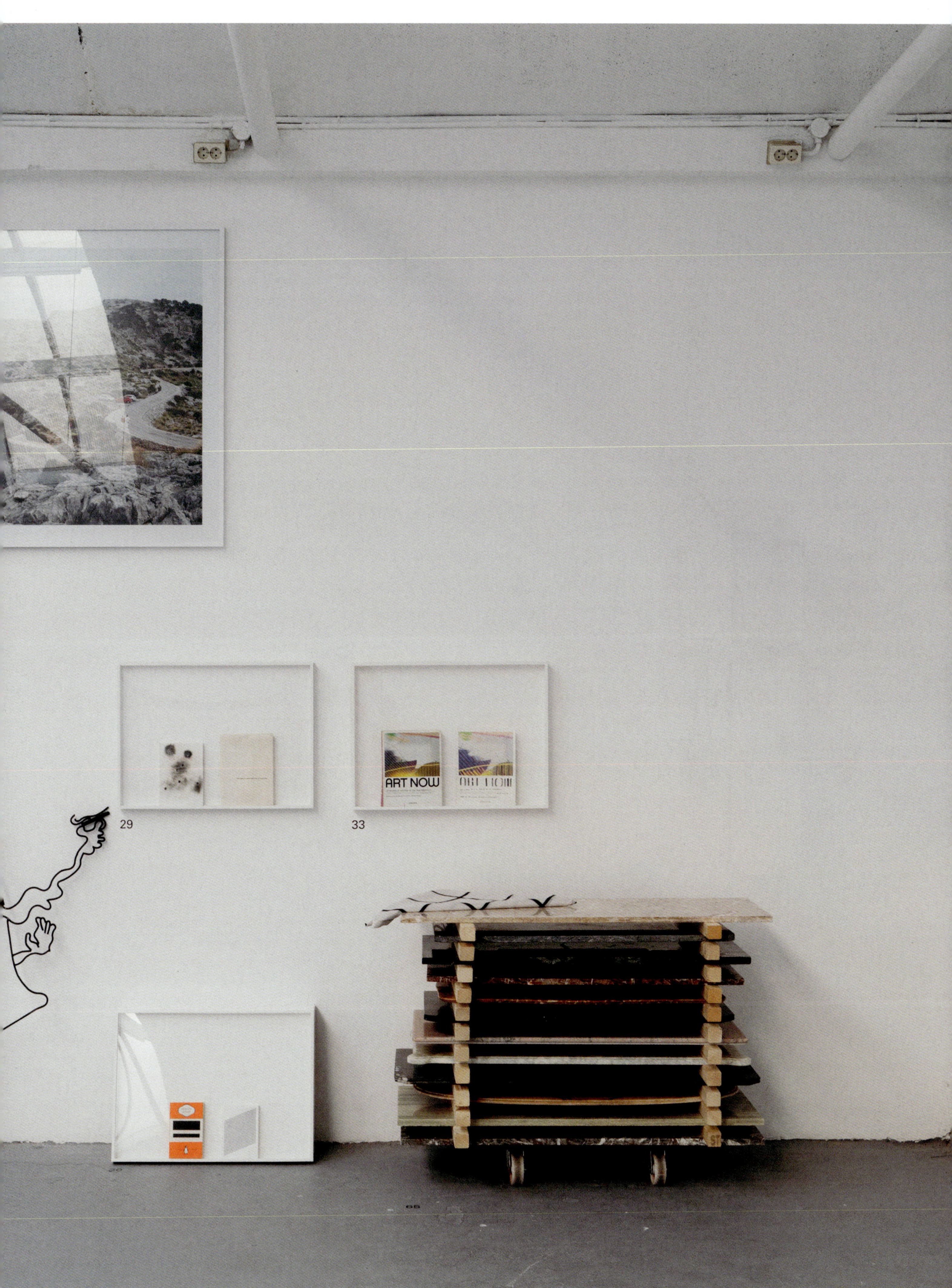

2—33. MORITZ KÜNG, *Selección Natural - This is the Cover of the Book*, October 2017
65. FILIP DUJARDIN, *Accumulation d'Époque#2*, October 2017

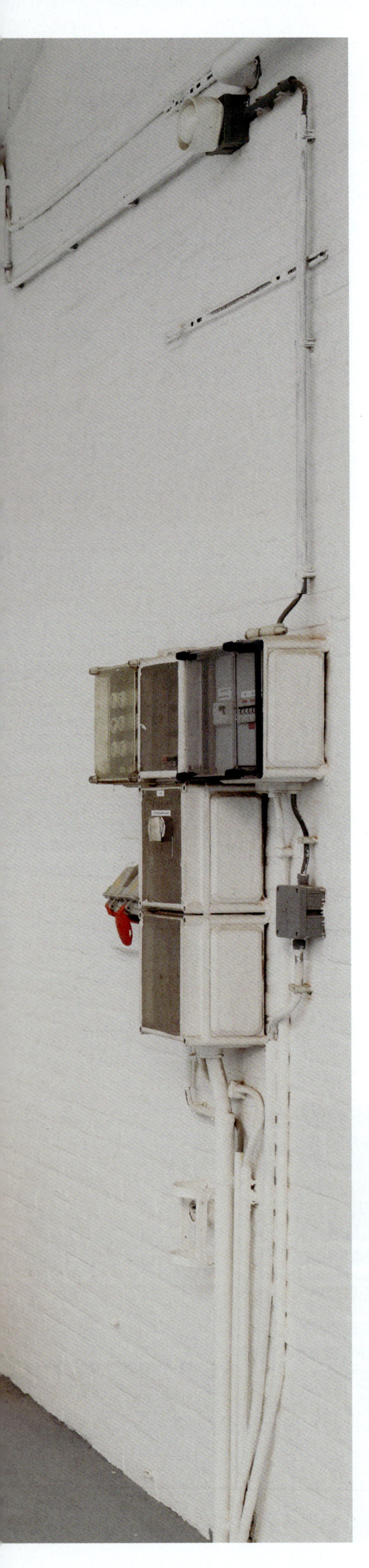

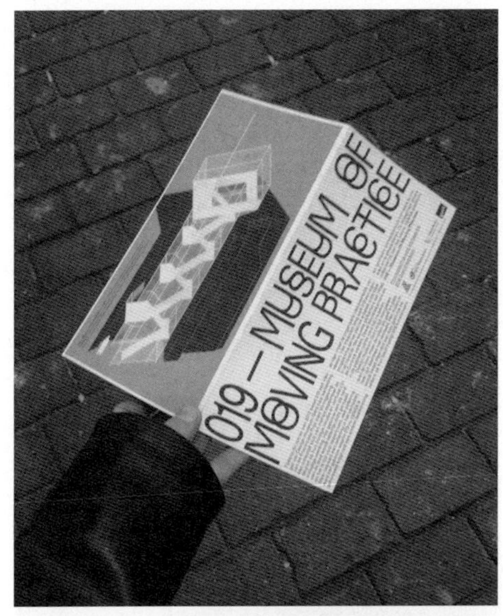

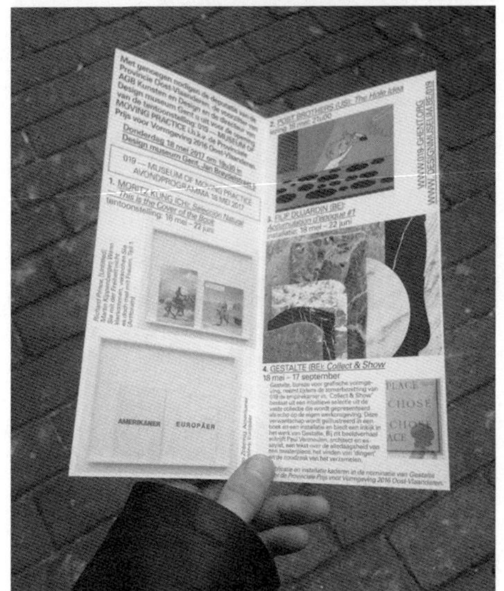

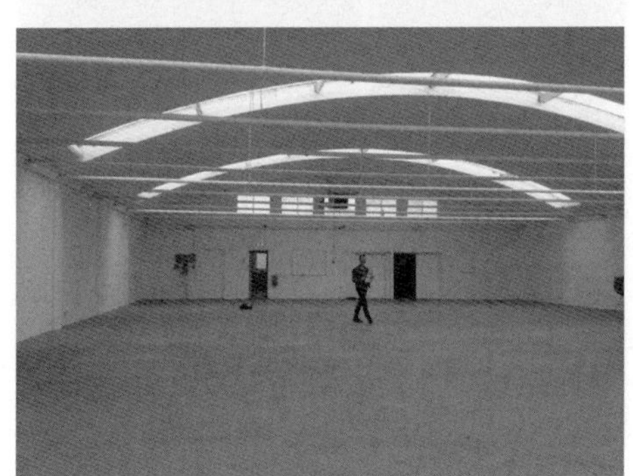

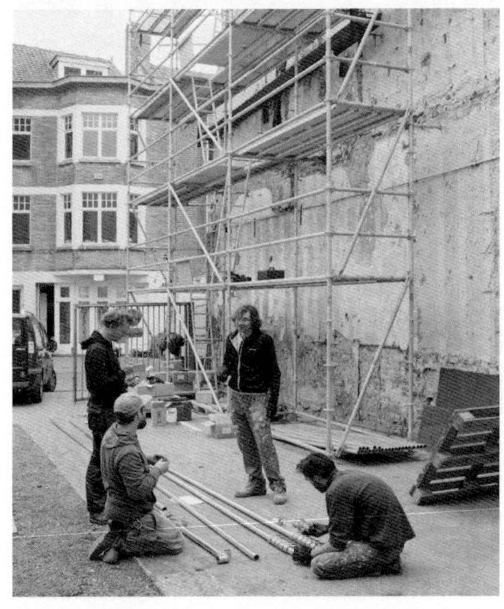

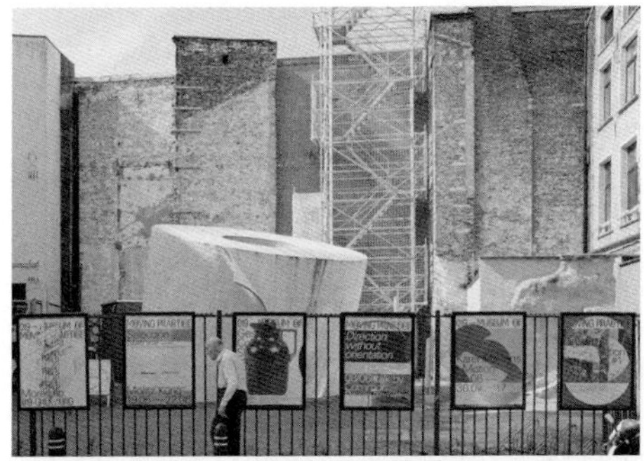

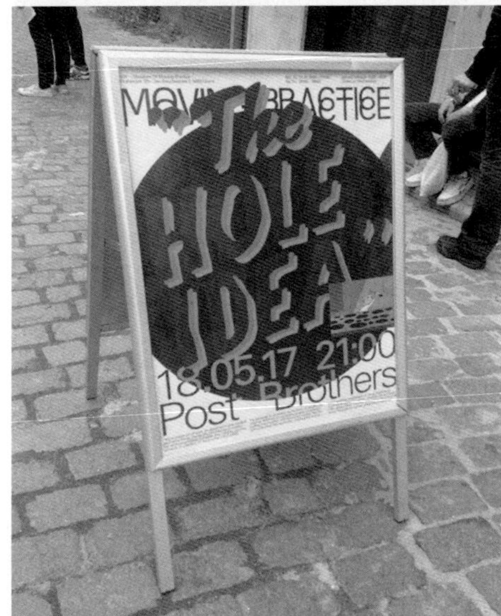

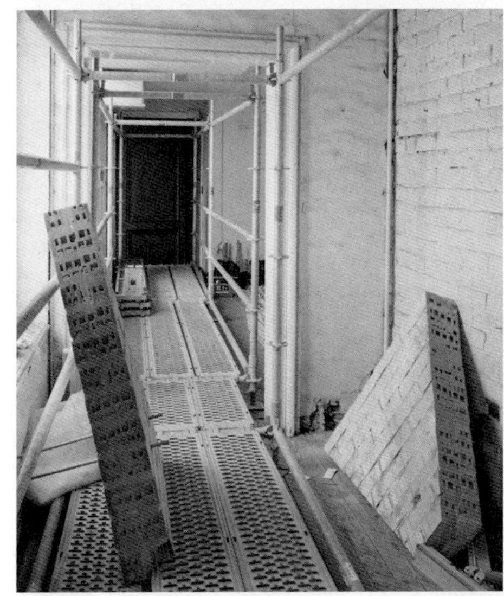

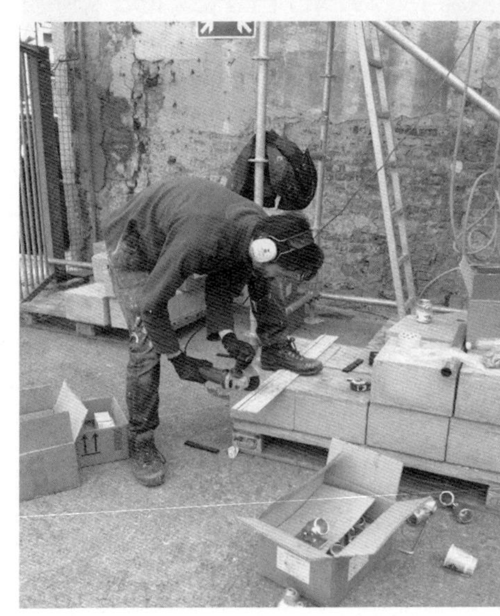

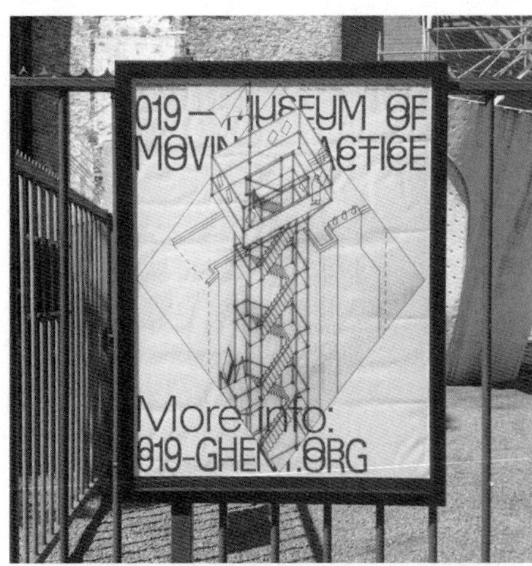

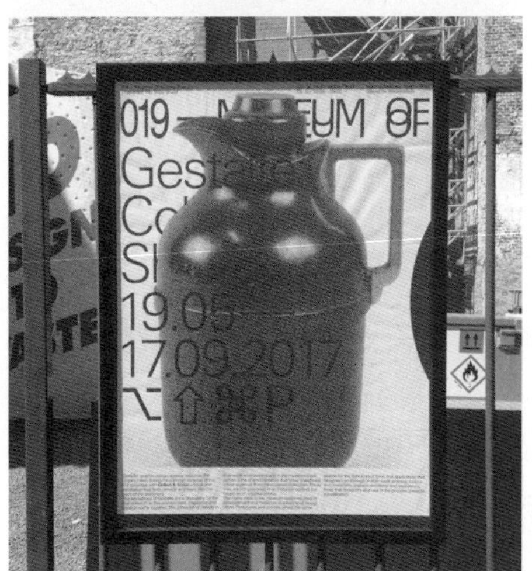

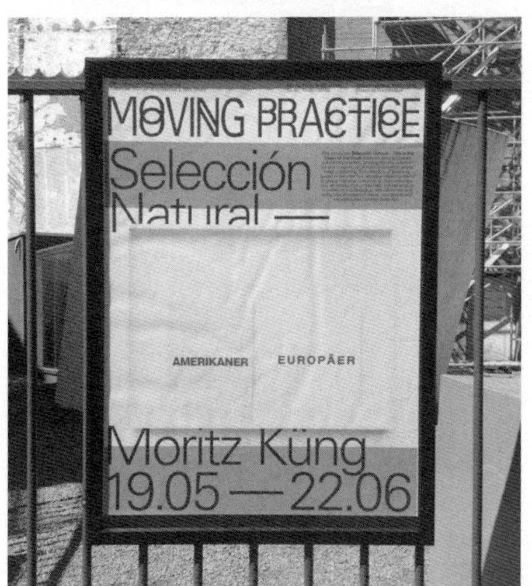

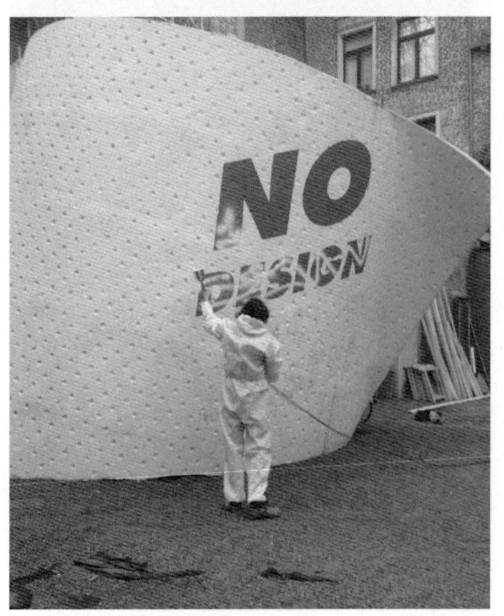

Selection of (cell phone) images, May—October 2017, © Bieke Criel, Michiel De Cleene, Olivier & Valentijn Goethals

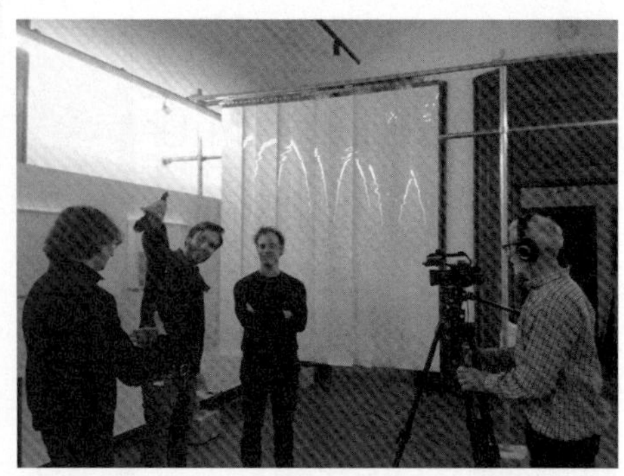

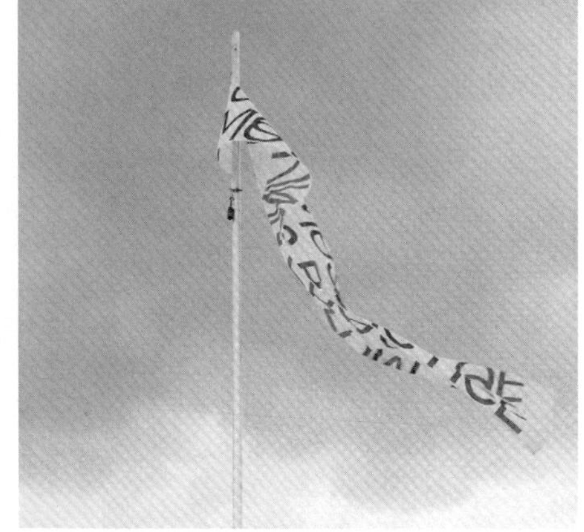

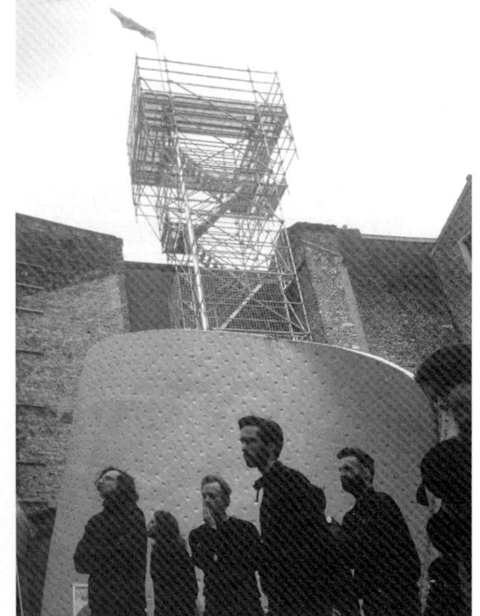

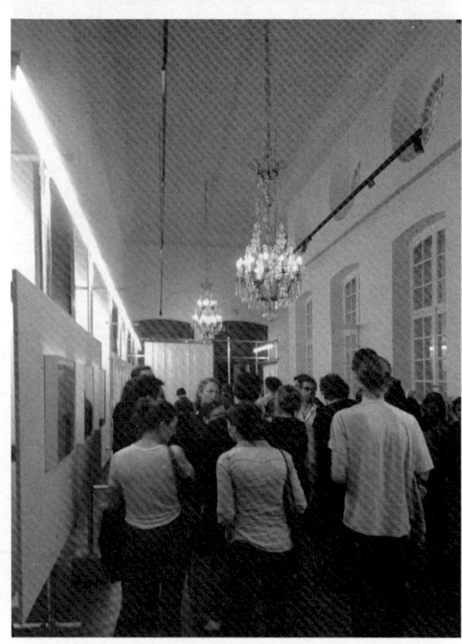

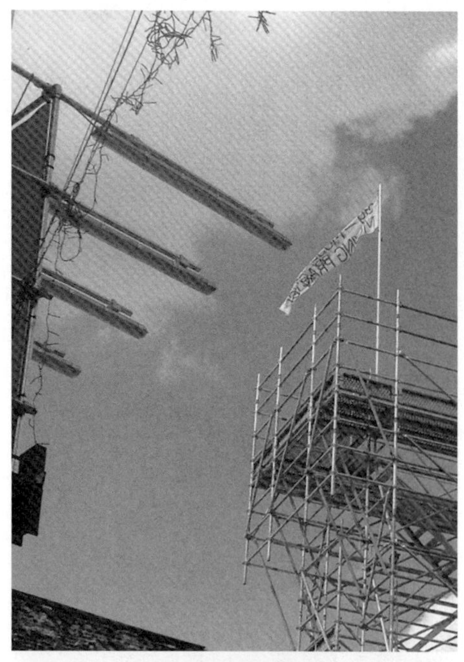

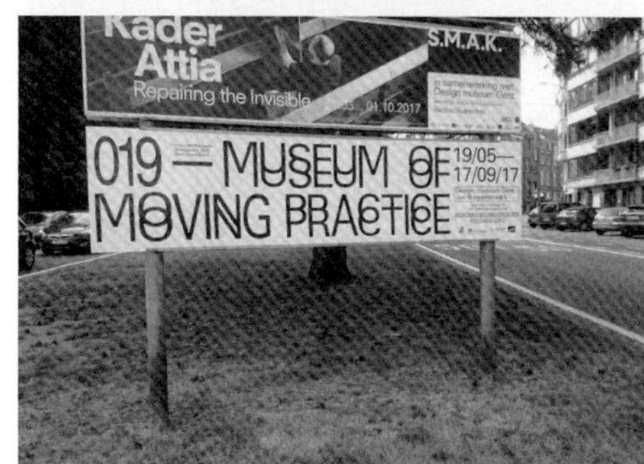
Kader
Attia
Repairing the Invisible
S.M.A.K.
019 — MUSEUM OF
MOVING PRACTICE
19/05—
17/09/17

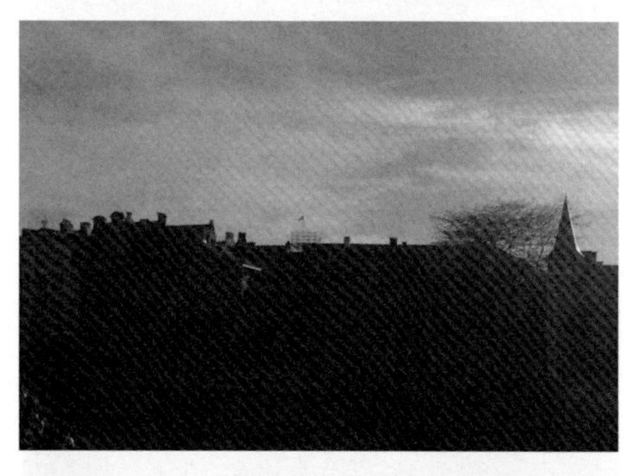

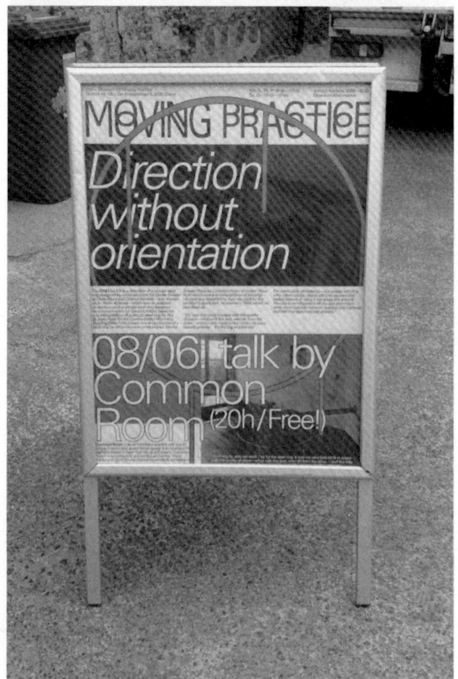
MOVING PRACTICE
Direction
without
orientation
08/06: talk by
Common
Room (20h/Free!)

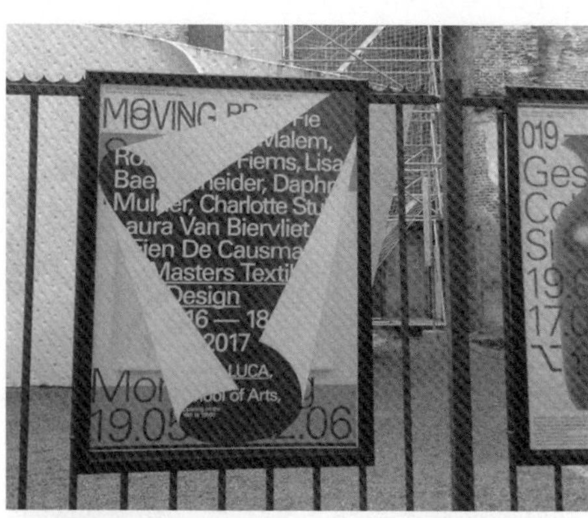
MOVING PRACTICE
Masters Textile
Design
2017
19.05
019

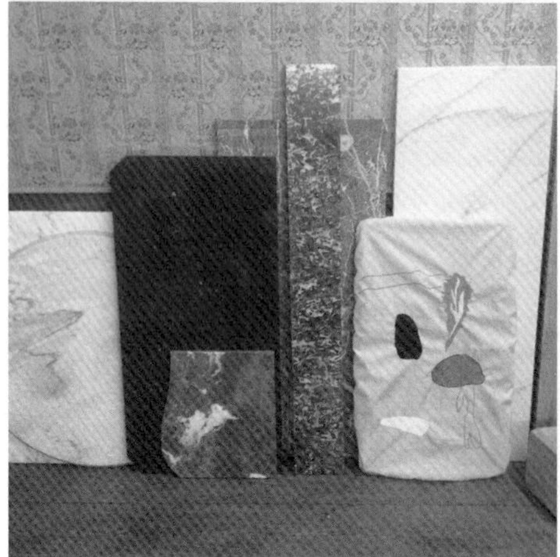

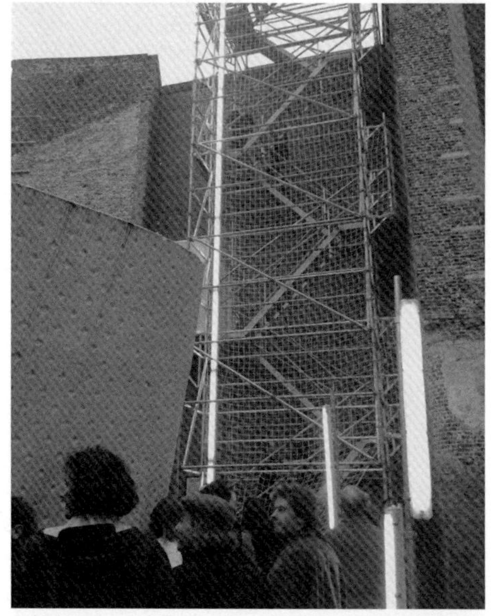

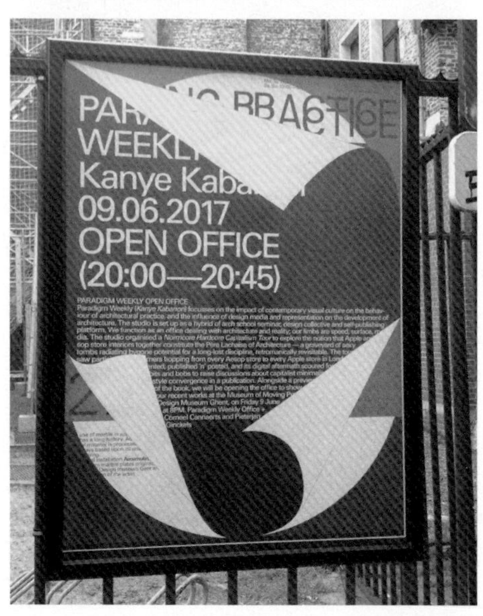
PARA
WEEKL
Kanye Kaba
09.06.2017
OPEN OFFICE
(20:00—20:45)
PARADIGM WEEKLY OPEN OFFICE

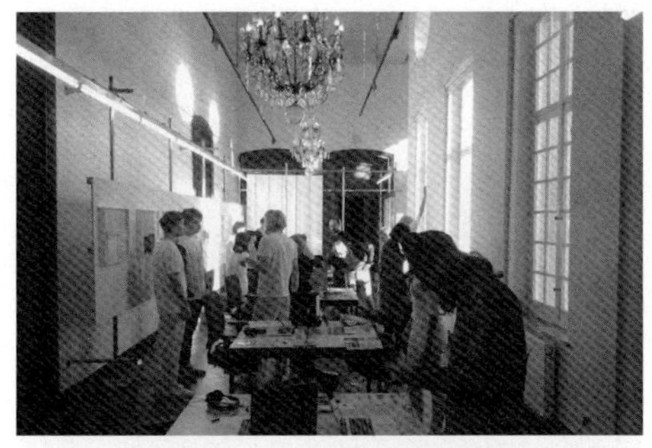

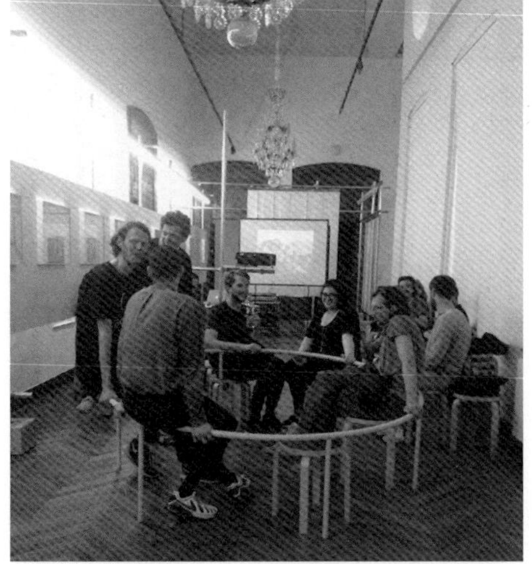

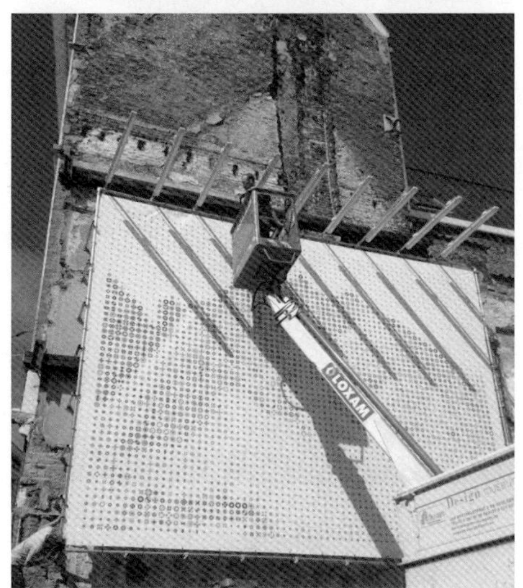
LOXAM

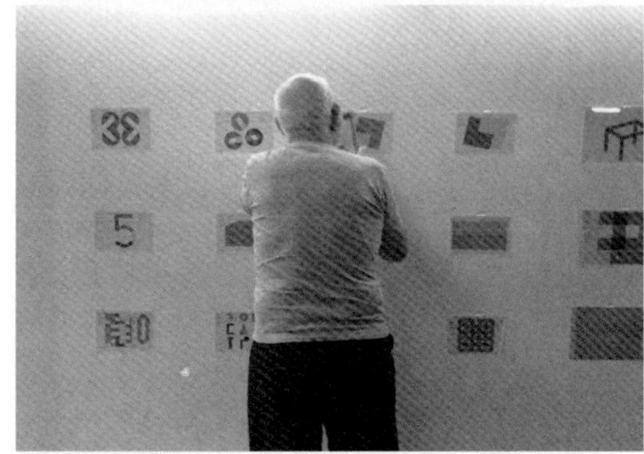

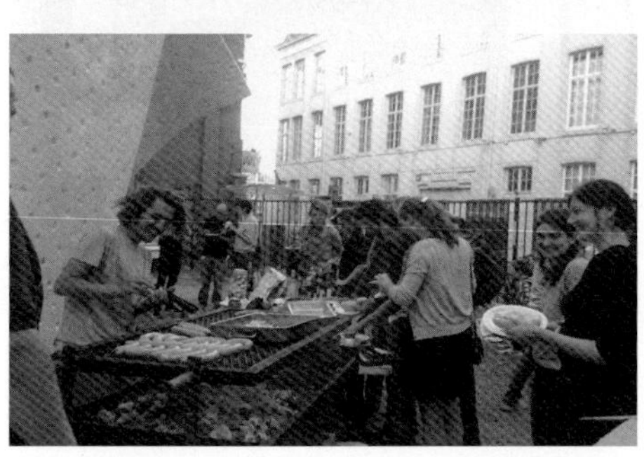

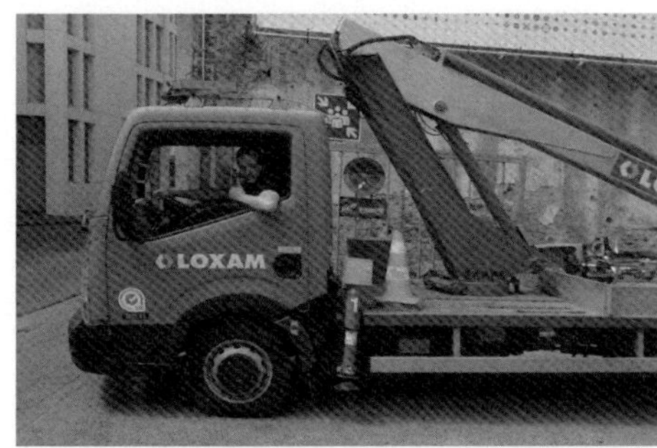
LOXAM

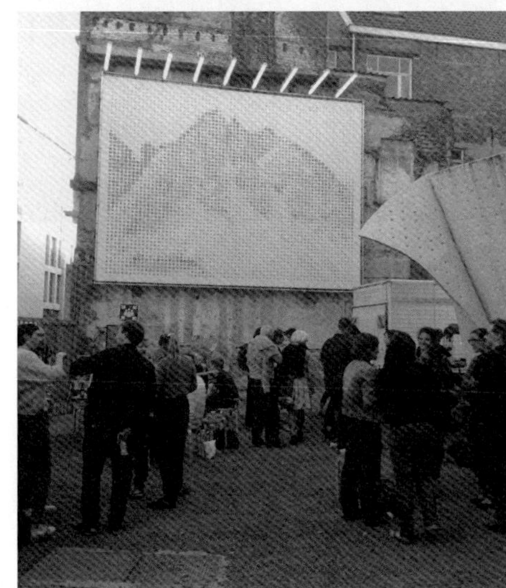

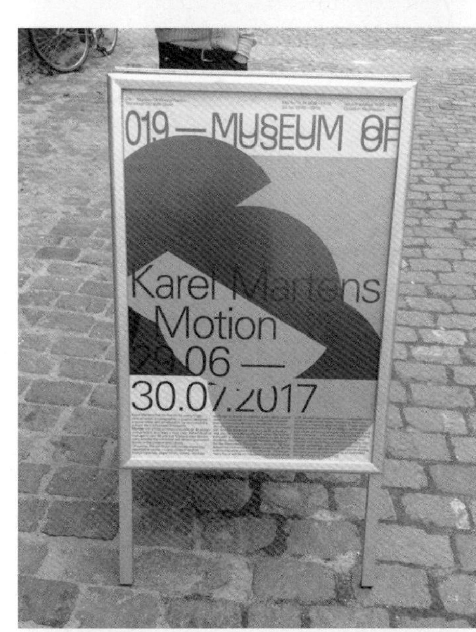
019 — MUSEUM OF
Karel Martens
Motion
29.06 —
30.07.2017

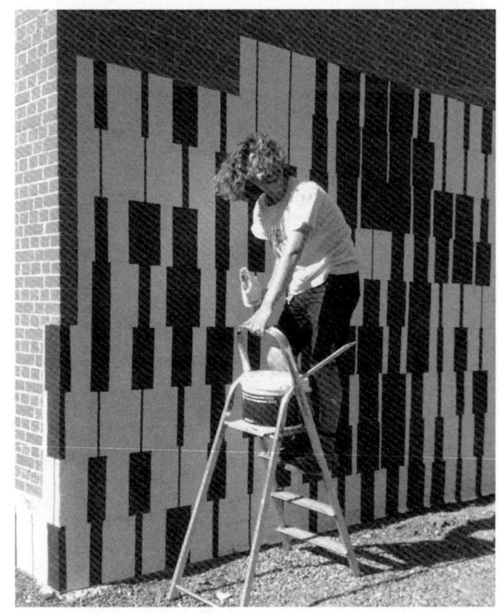

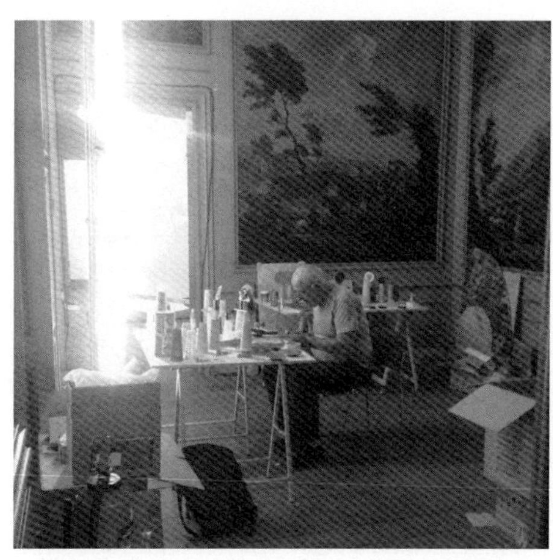

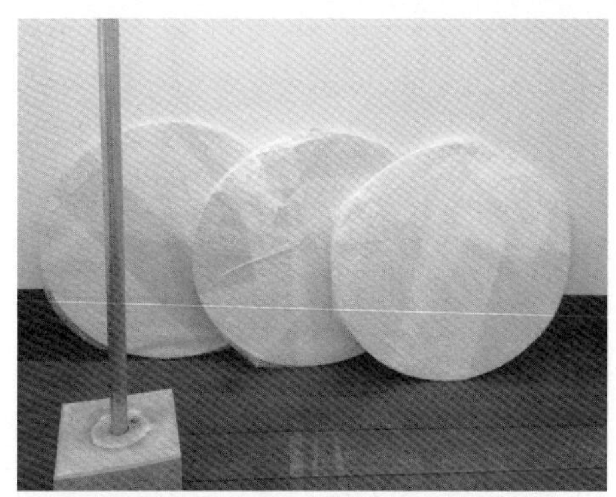

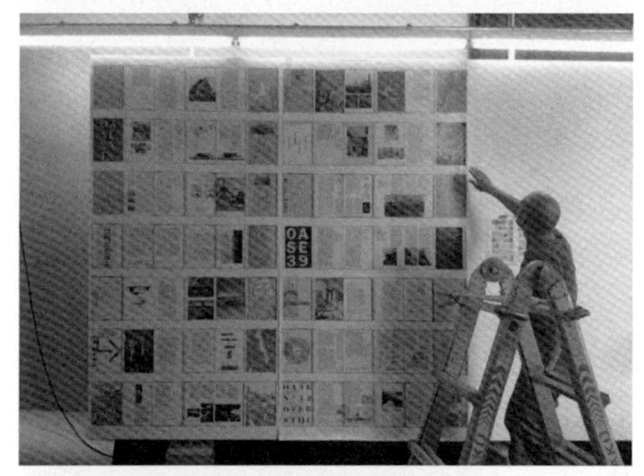

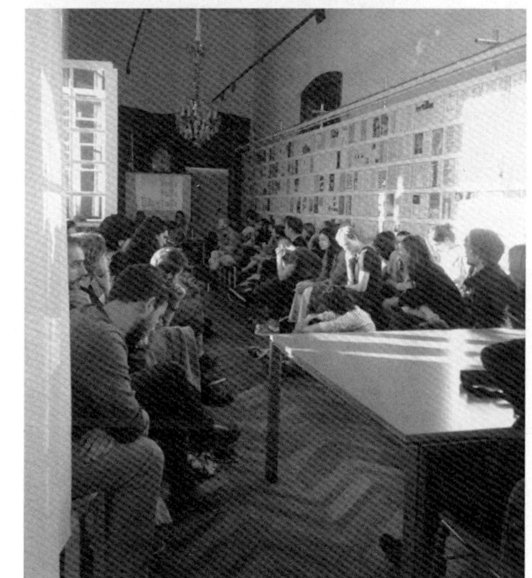

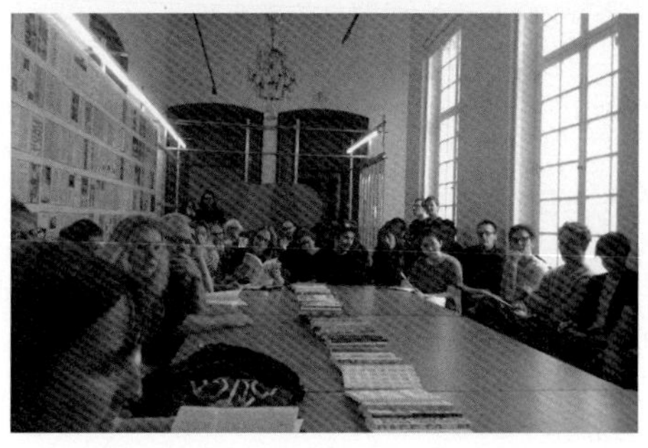

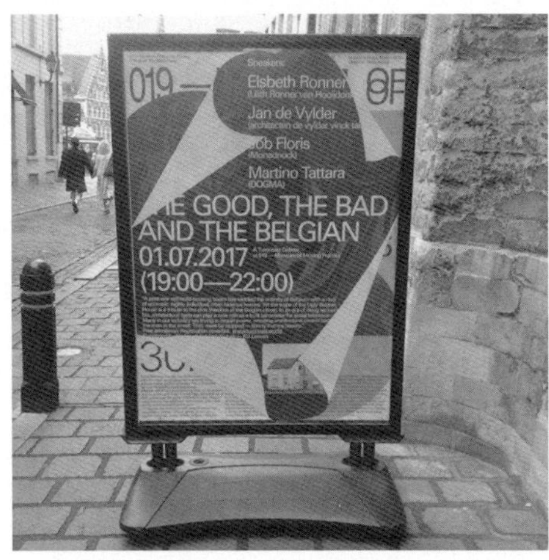
Elsbeth Ronner
Jan de Vylder
Job Floris
Martino Tattara
AND THE BELGIAN
01.07.2017
(19:00—22:00)

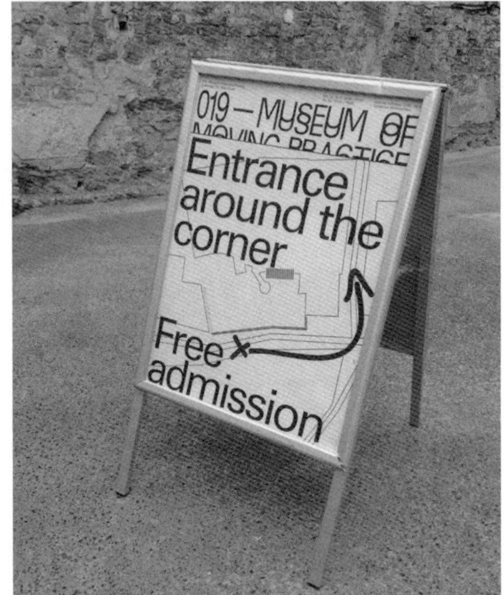
019—MUSEUM OF
Entrance around the corner
Free admission

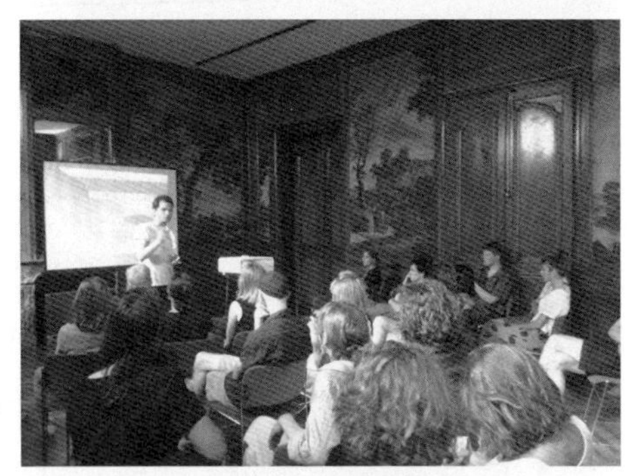

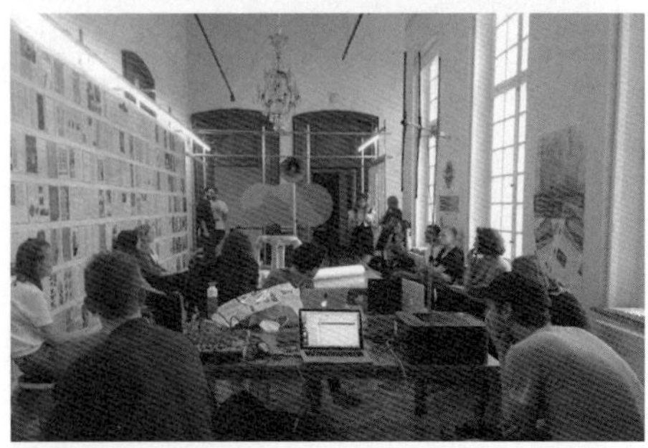

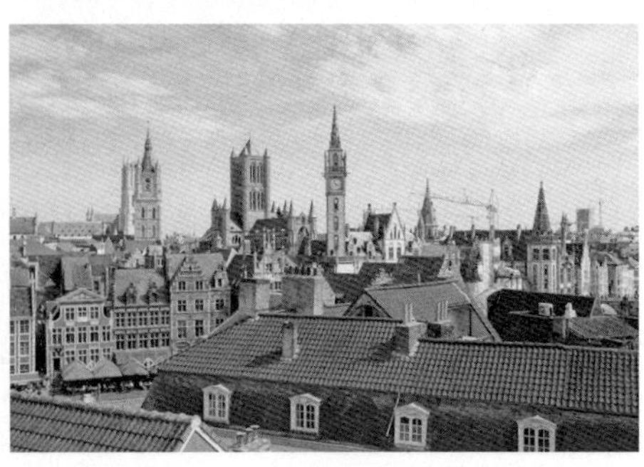

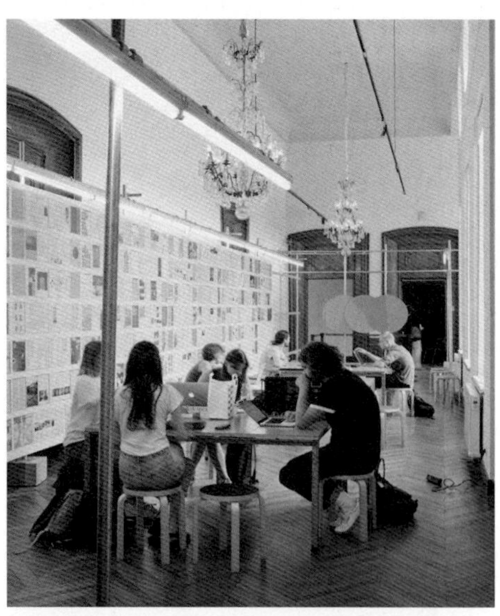

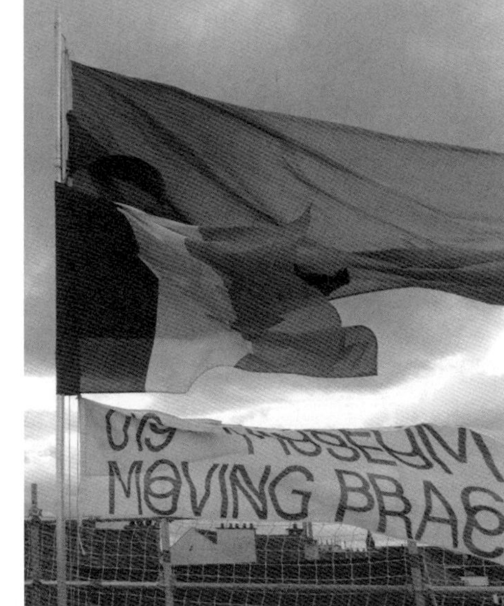
MOVING PRAC

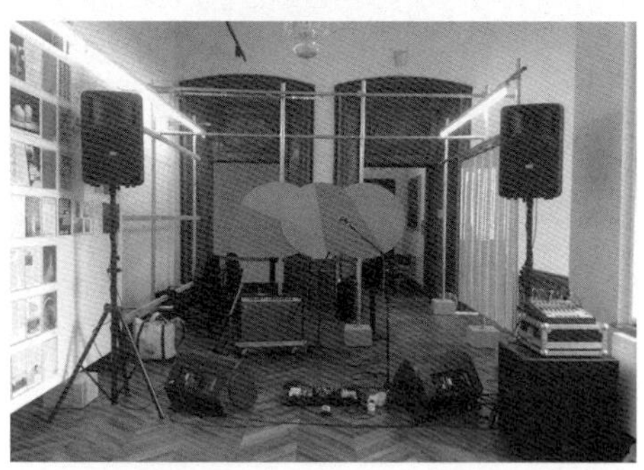

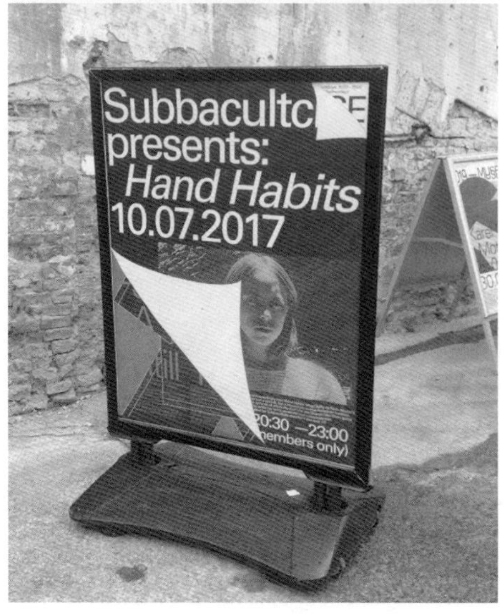
Subbacultc
presents:
Hand Habits
10.07.2017
20:30 —23:00

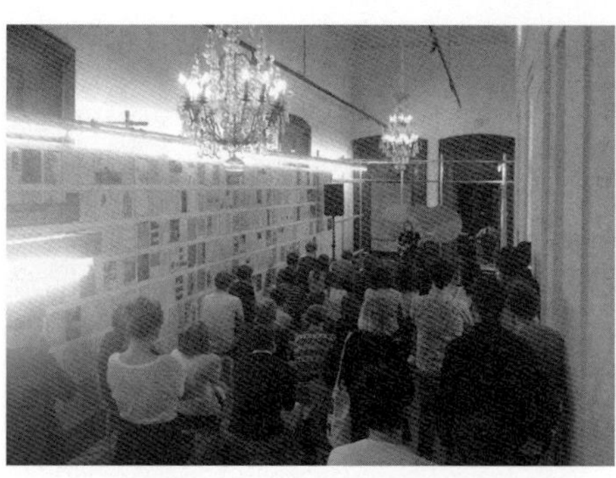

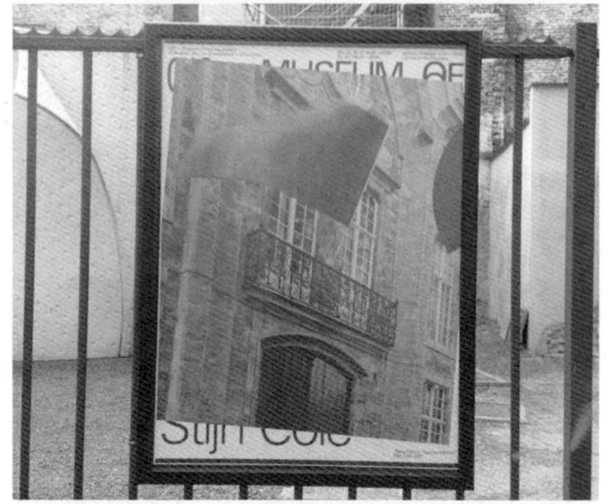
MUSEUM OF

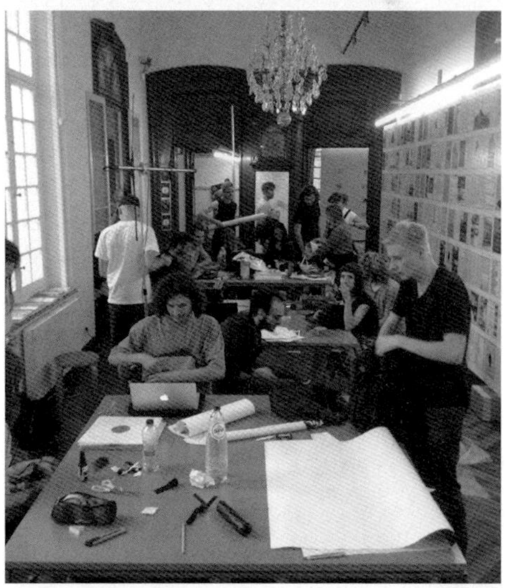

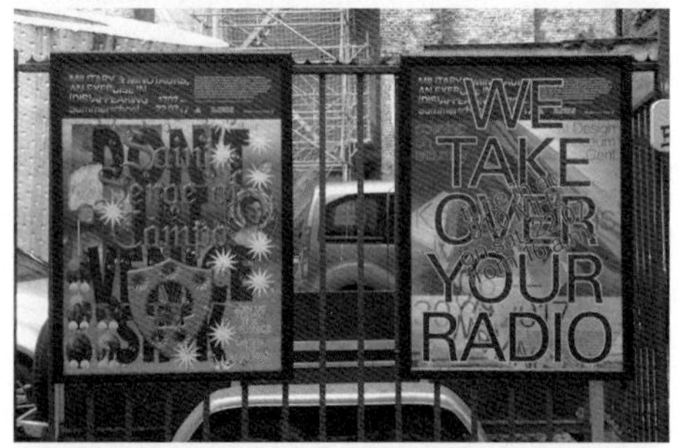
WE TAKE OVER YOUR RADIO

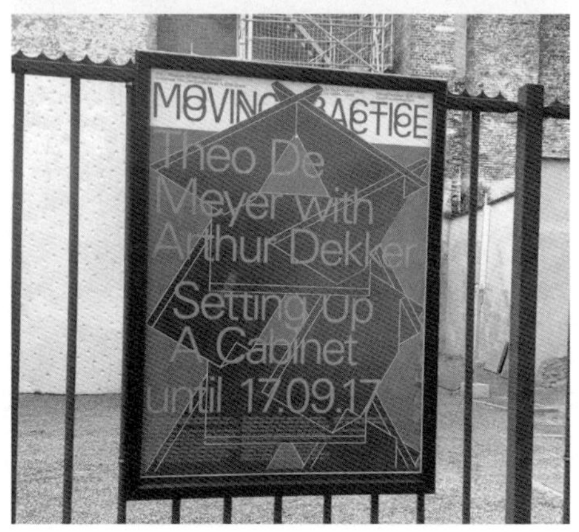
Theo De Meyer with Arthur Dekker
Setting up A Cabinet
until 17.09.17

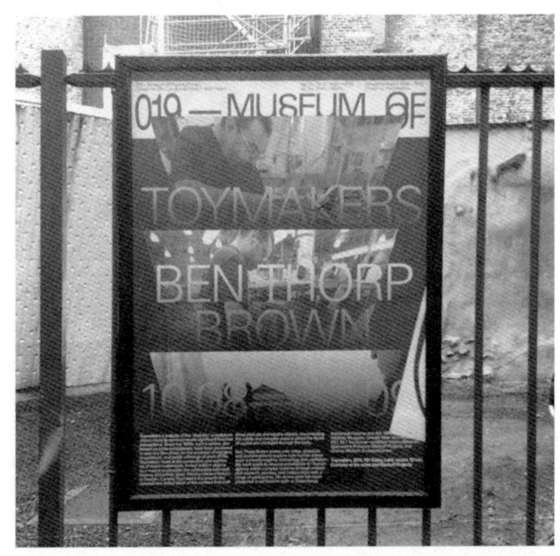
019 — MUSEUM OF
TOYMAKERS
BEN THORP

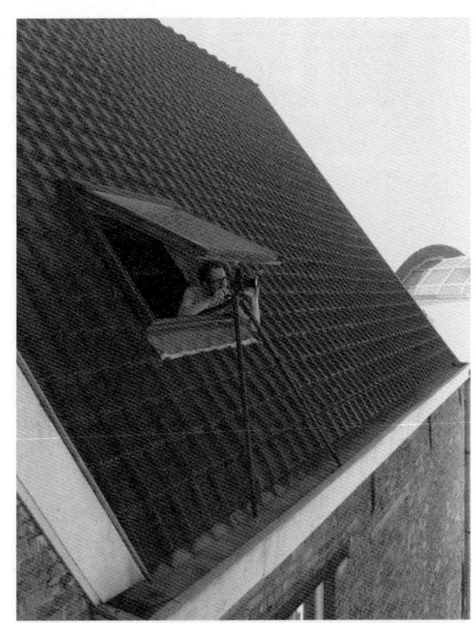

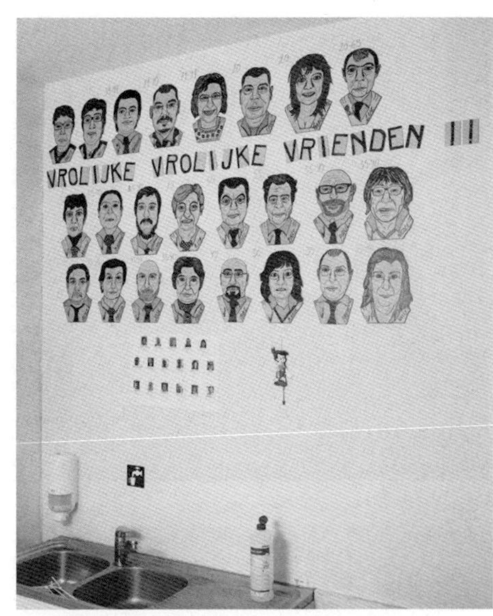
VROLIJKE VROLIJKE VRIENDEN

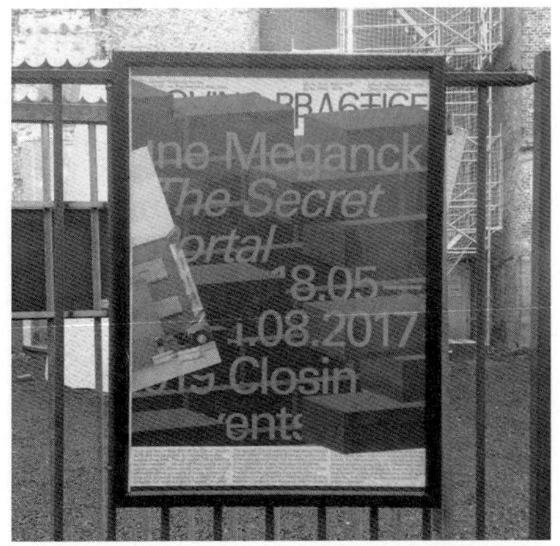
The Secret

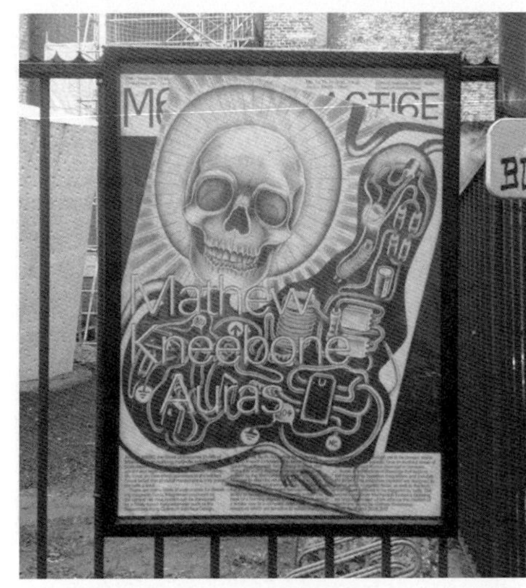
Auras

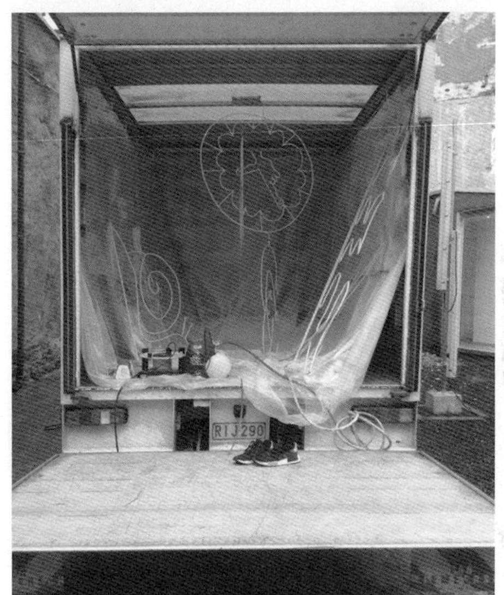
RIJ290

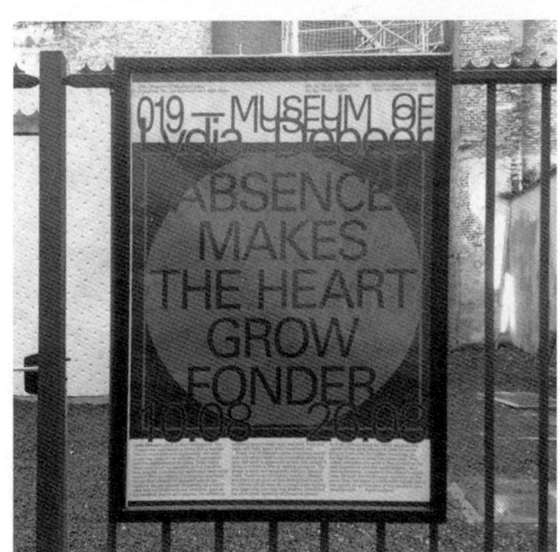
019 — MUSEUM OF
ABSENCE
MAKES
THE HEART
GROW
FONDER

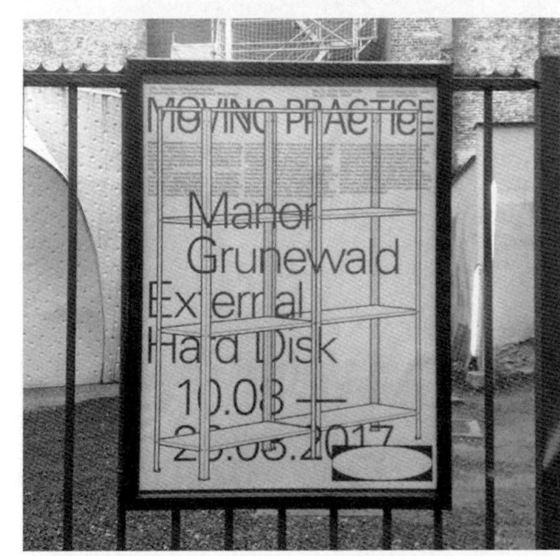
MOVING PRACTICE
Manor
Grunewald
10.08 —

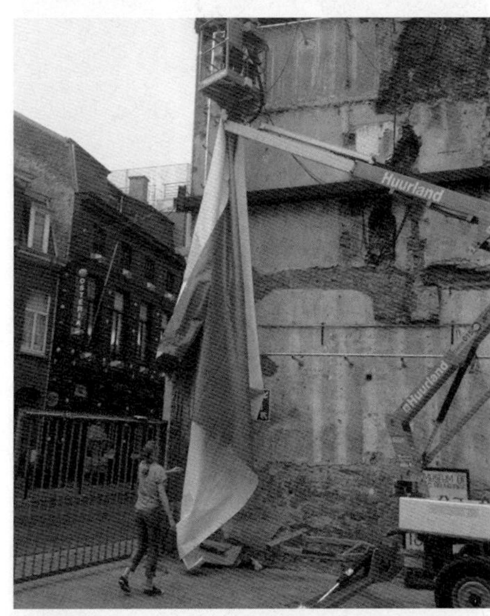
Huurland

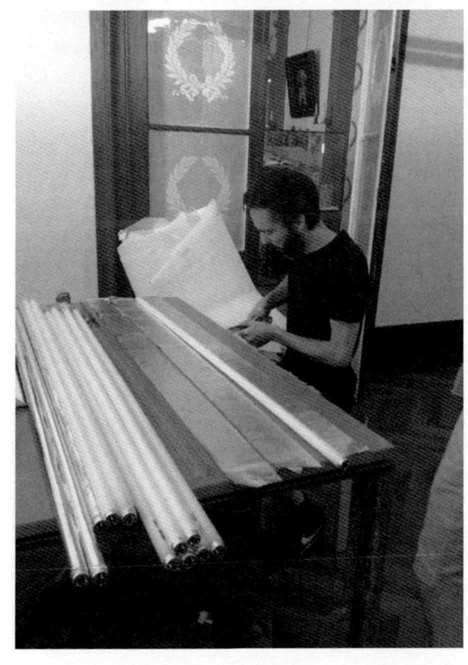

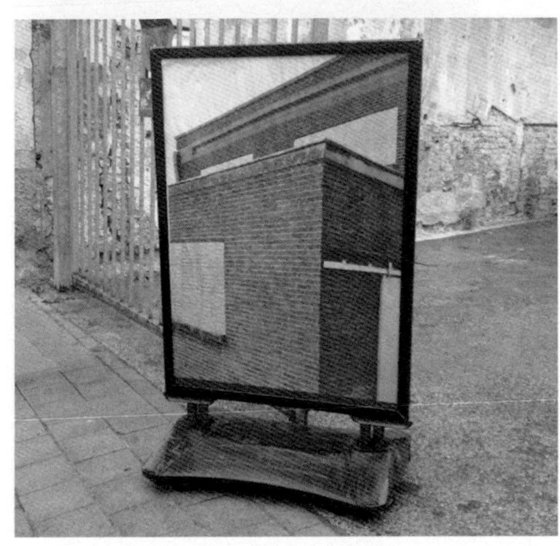

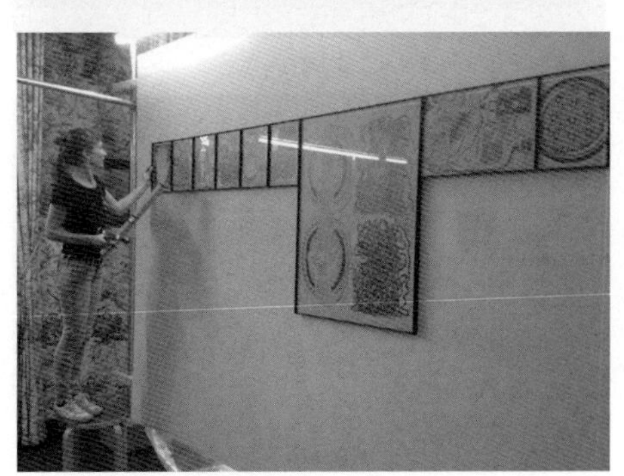

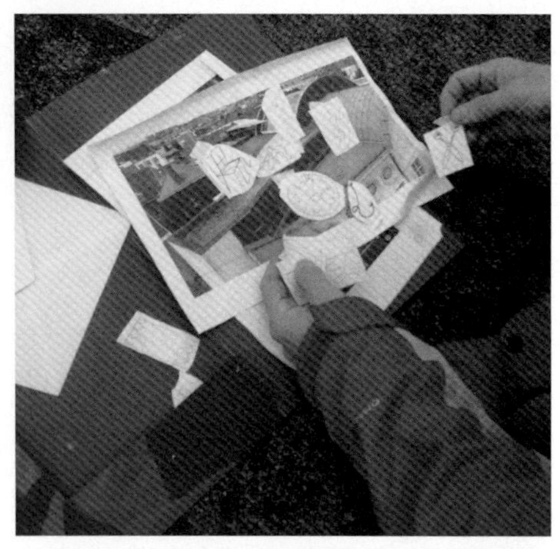

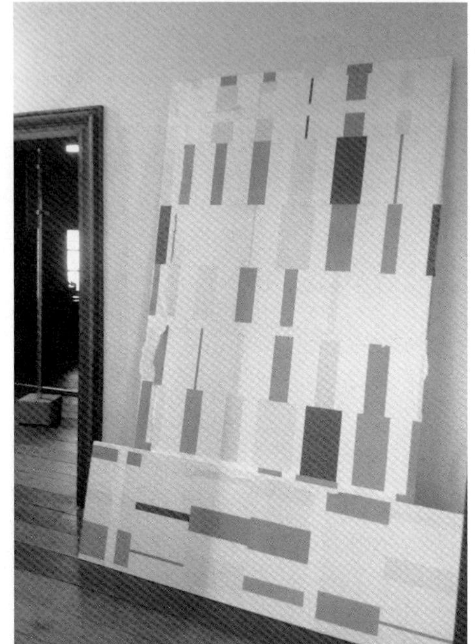

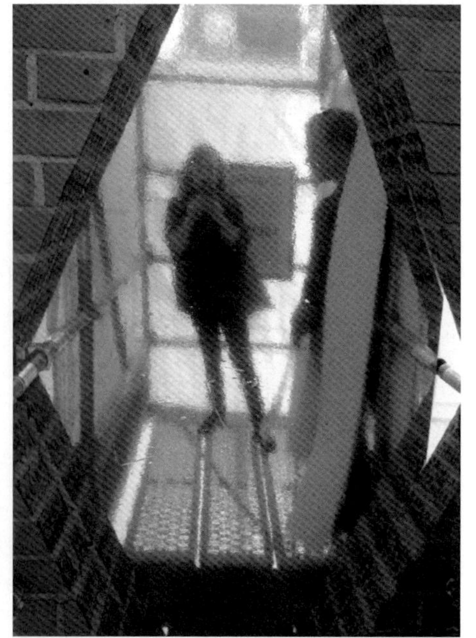

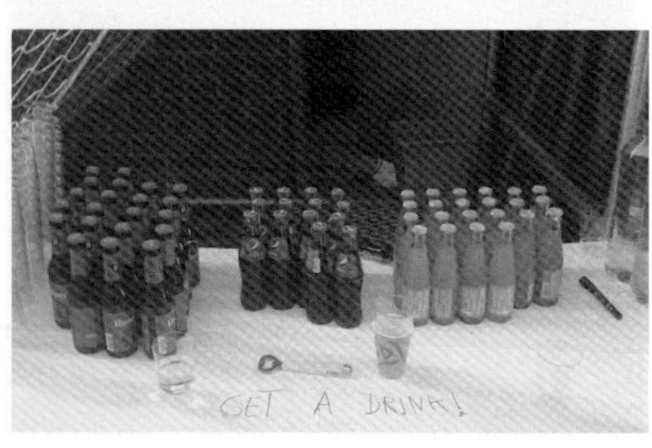
GET A DRINK!

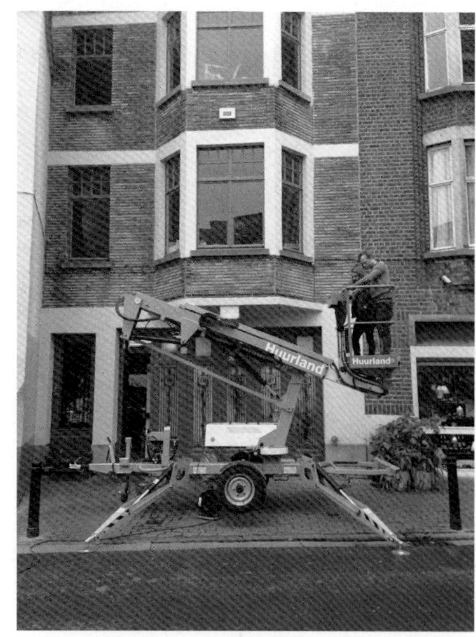
Huurland
Huurland

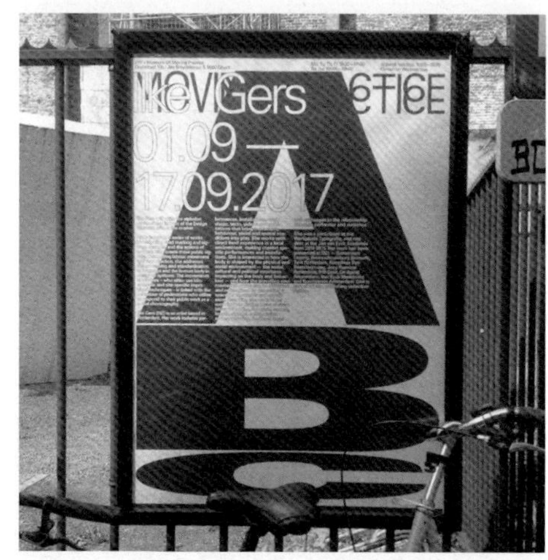
01.09 —
17.09.2017

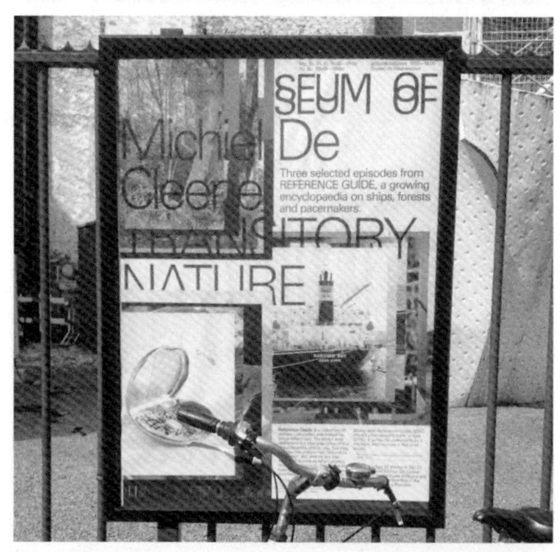
SEUM OF
Michiel De
Cleene
Three selected episodes from REFERENCE GUIDE, a growing encyclopaedia on ships, forests and pacemakers.
NATURE

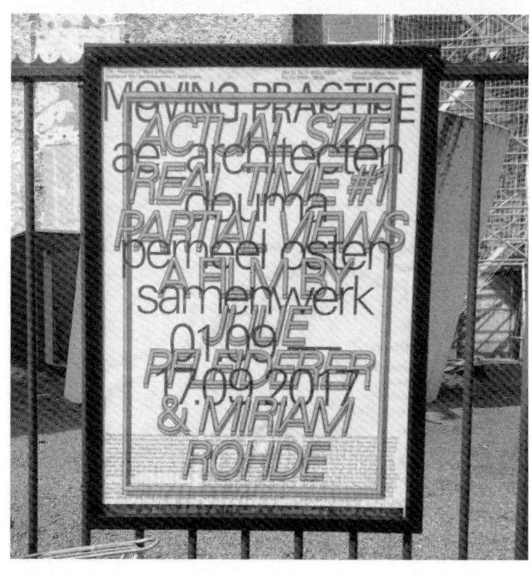
MOVING PRACTICE
ACTUAL SIZE
ae architecten
REAL TIME #1
PARTIAL VIEWS
A FILM BY
samenwerk
JULIE
PFLEIDERER
17.09.2017
& MIRIAM
ROHDE

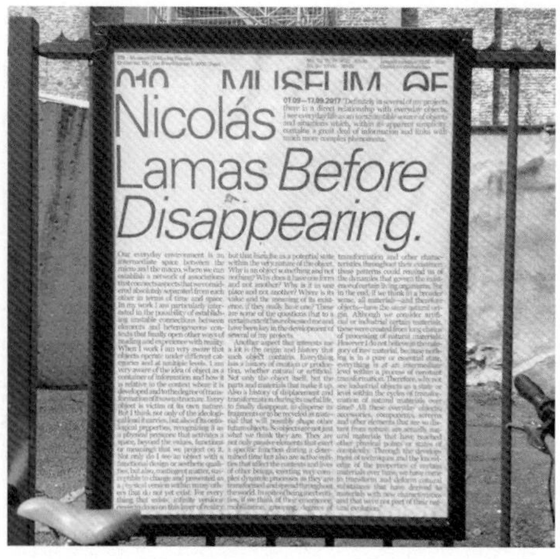
Nicolás
Lamas Before
Disappearing.

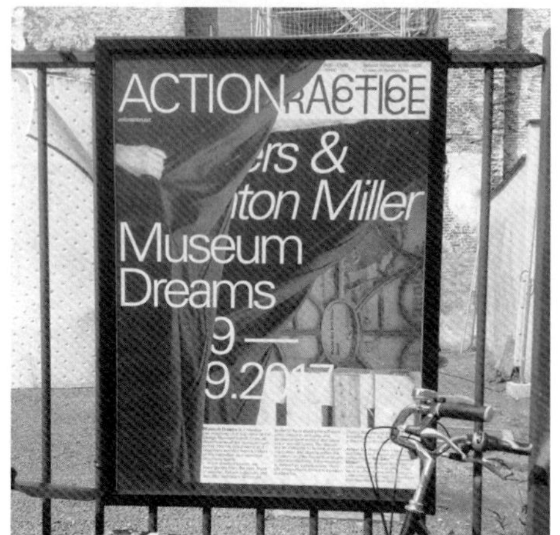
ACTION
Museum
Dreams

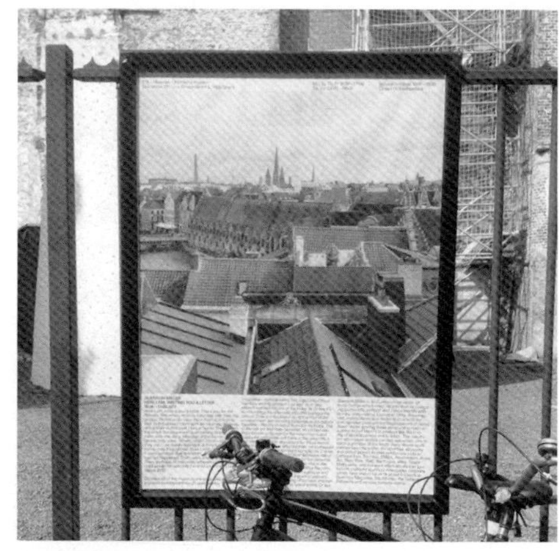

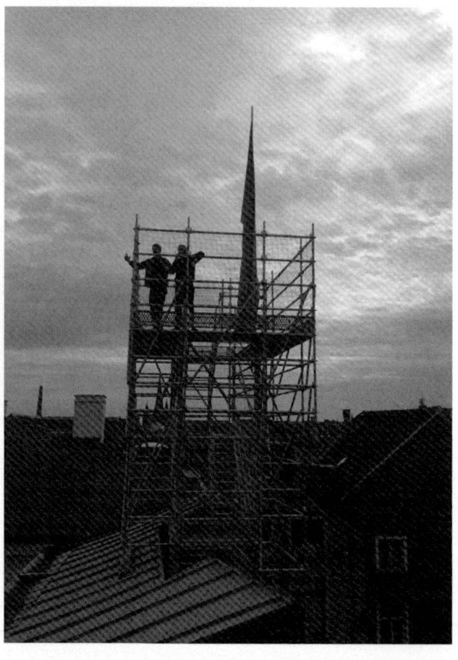

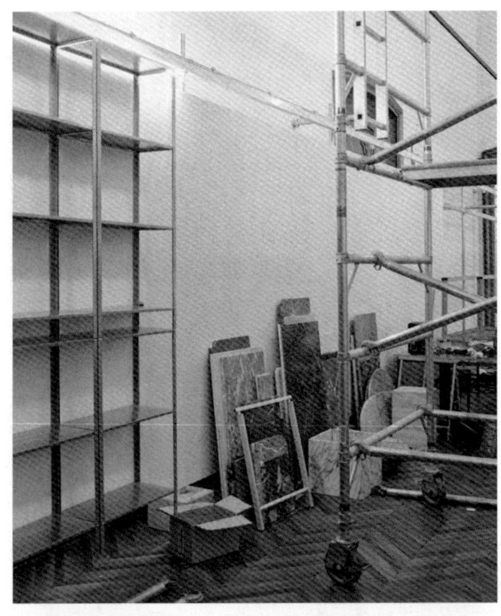
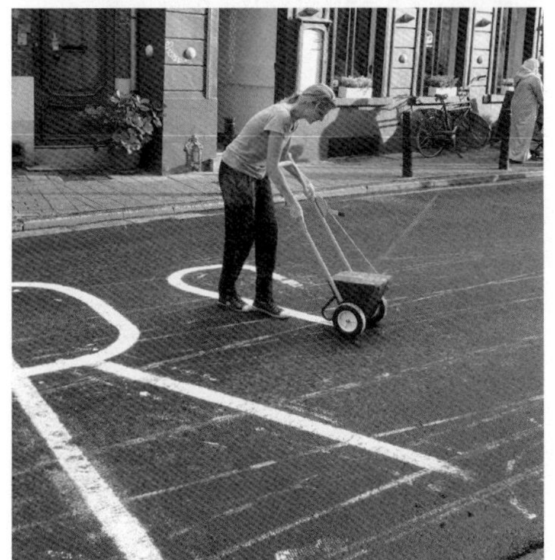
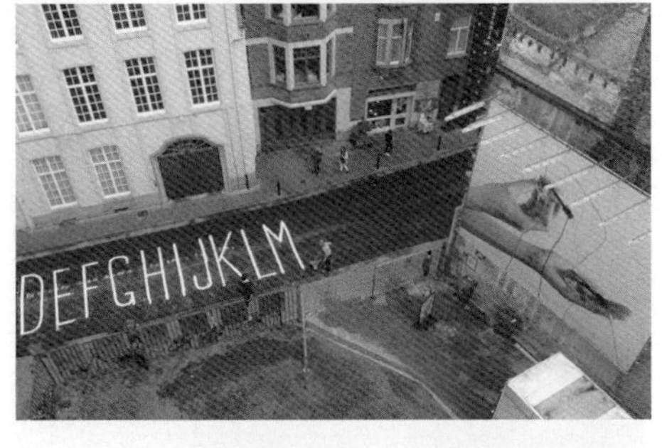
DEFGHIJKLM
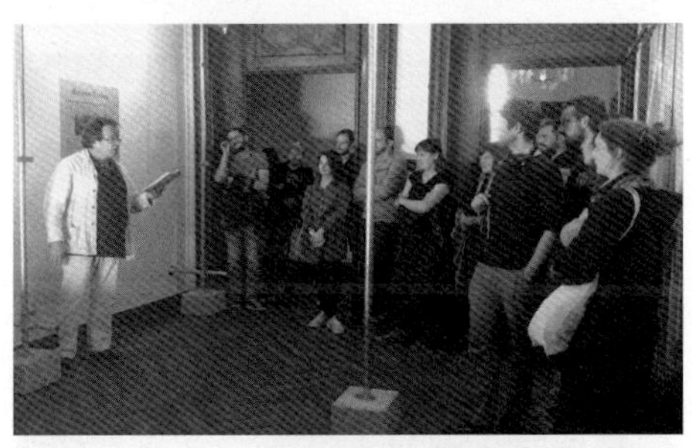
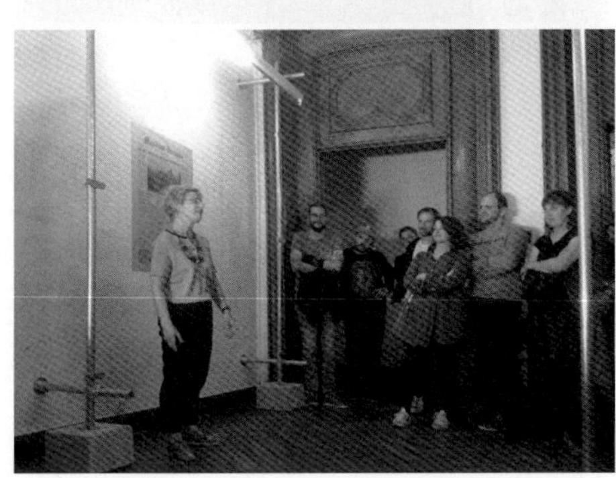
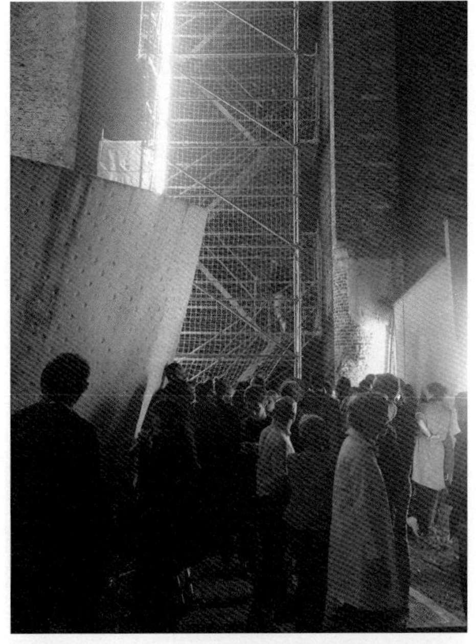
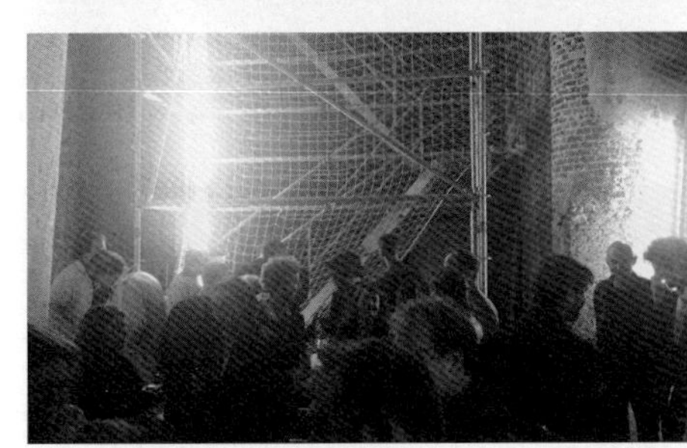
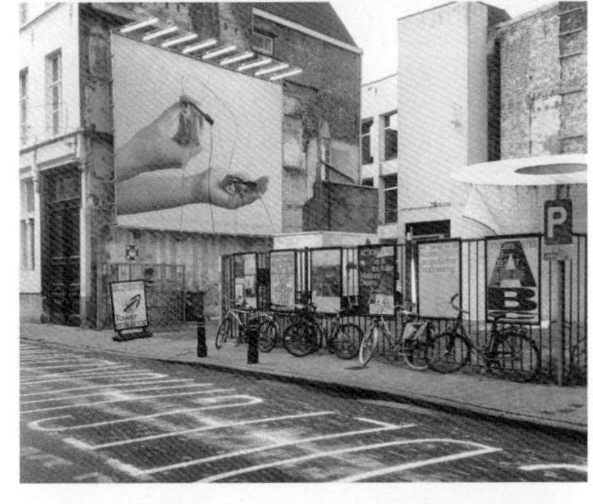
P
A
B
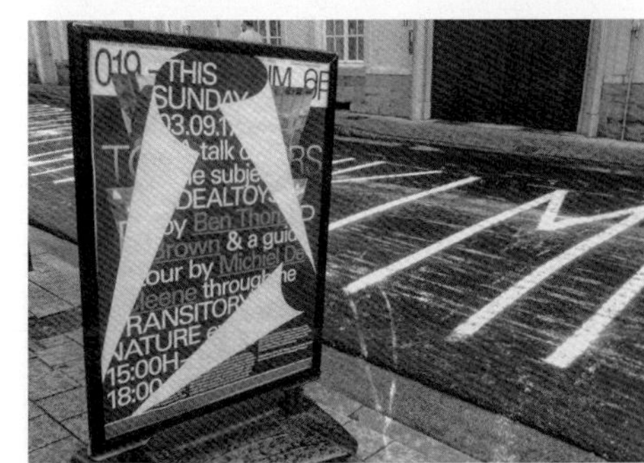
THIS
SUNDAY
talk
DEALTOYS
& a
tour by
through
15:00H
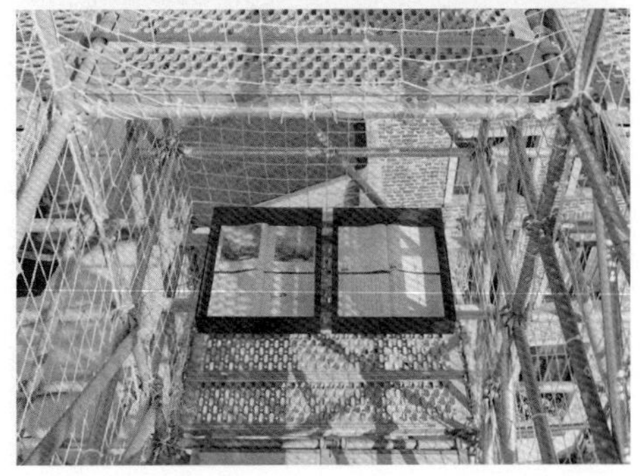
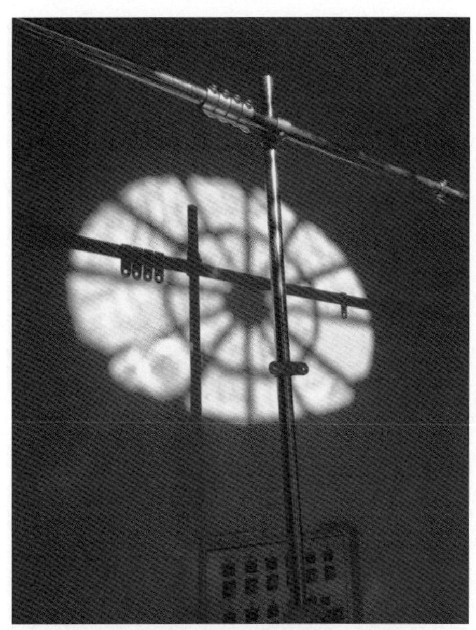
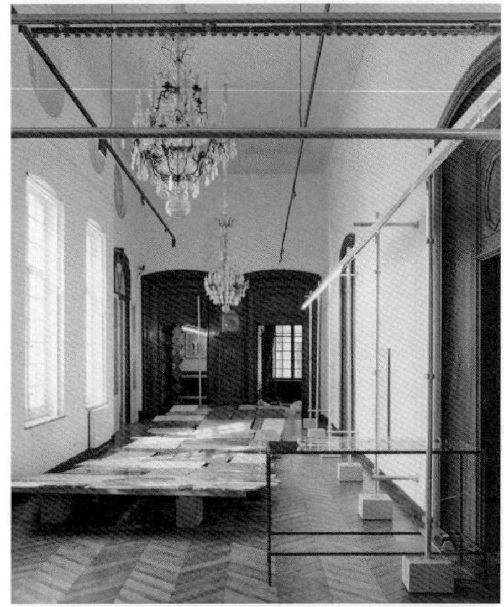
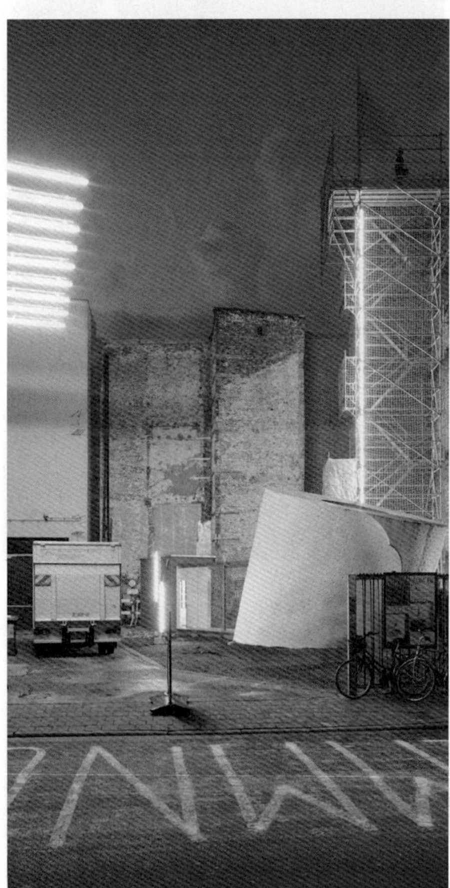

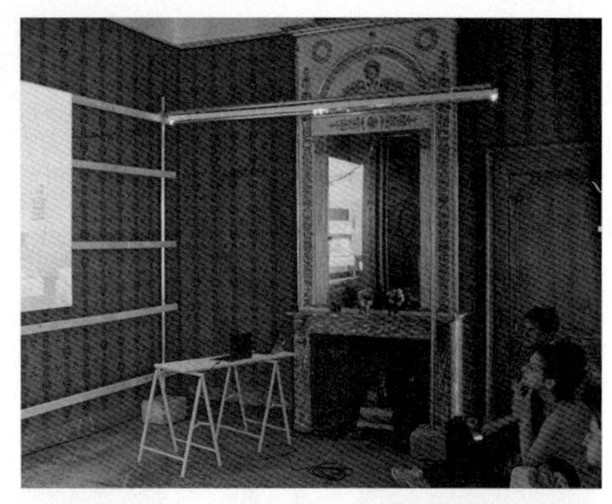

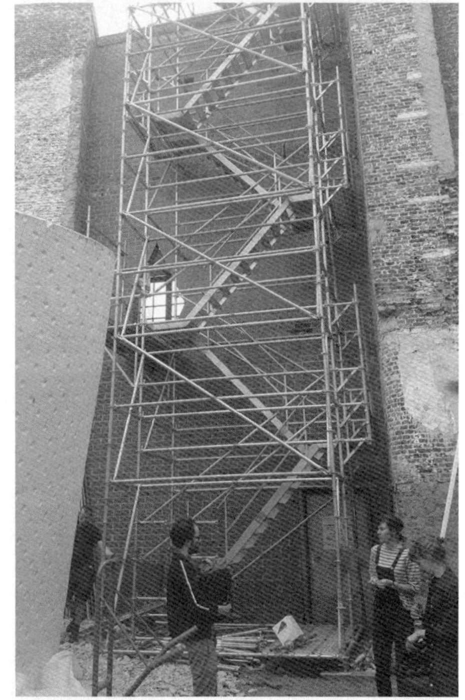

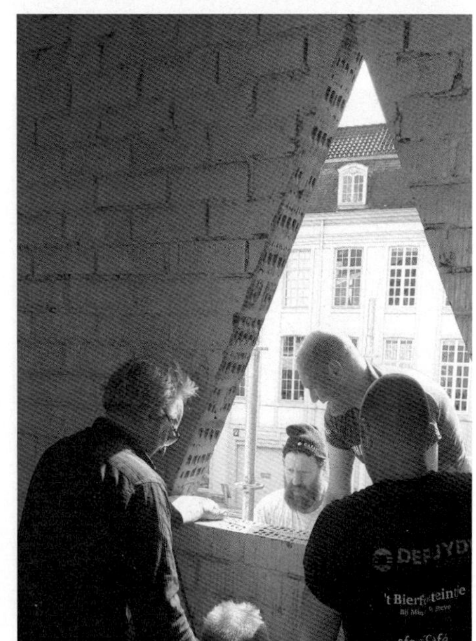

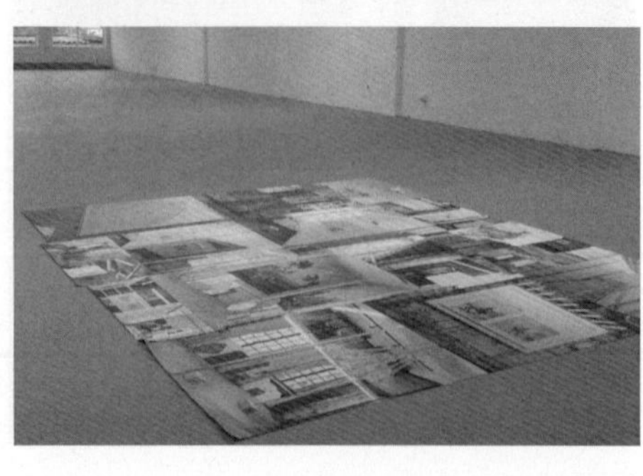

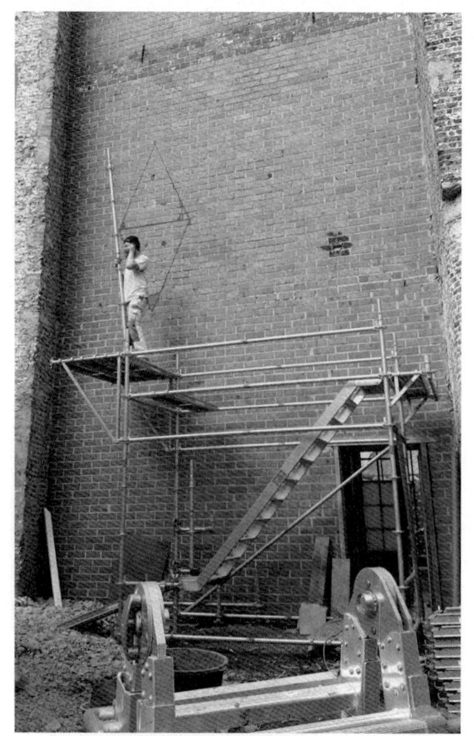

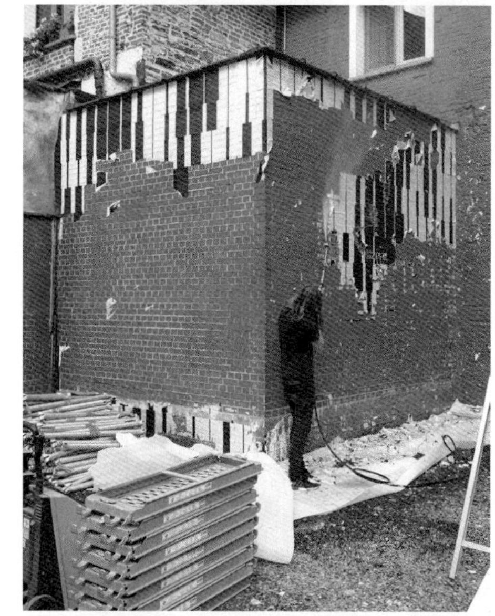

RE—
EXHIBITING
/MUSEUM
OF
MOVING
PRACTICE
CONVERSATIONS — RESEARCH PROJECTS MASTERS TEXTILE DESIGN LUCA SCHOOL OF ARTS

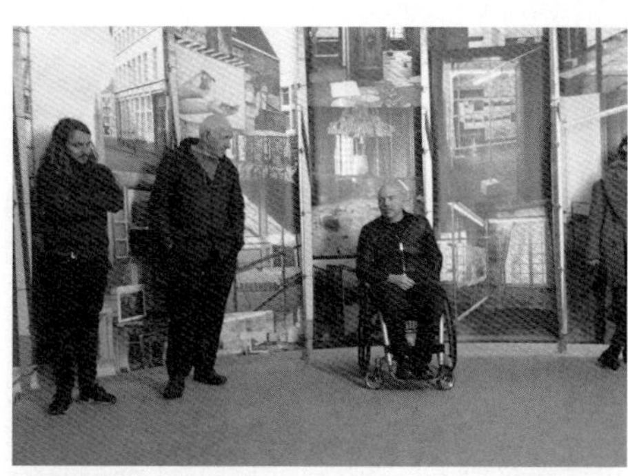

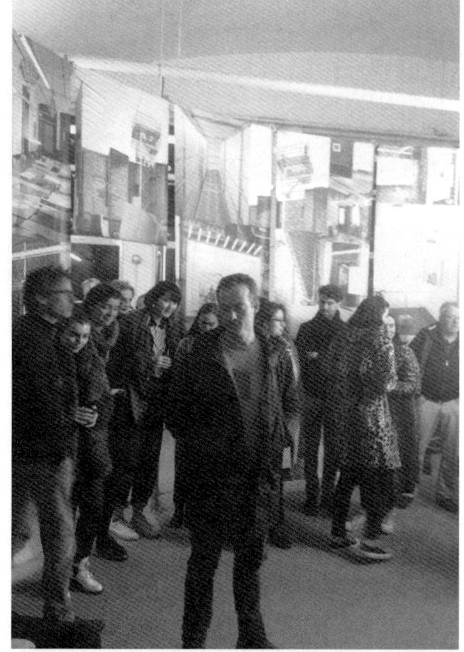

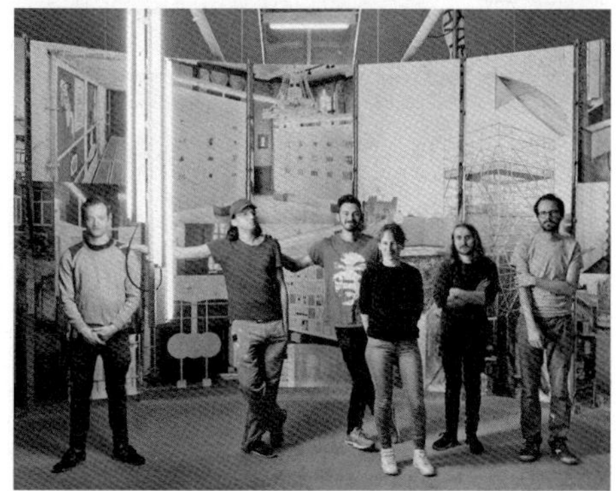

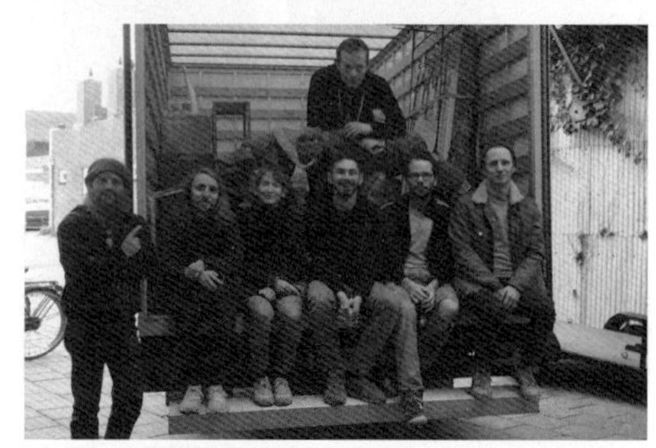

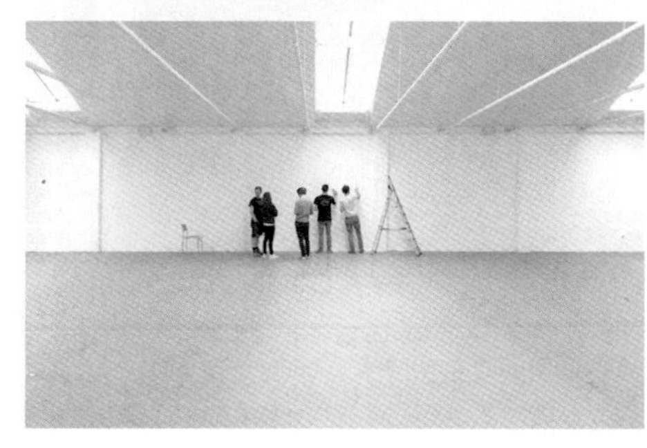

PARALLEL PROJECTIONS
PREM KRISHNAMURTHY

P!, 2012–2017

This "unconventional vest-pocket space"[1] is a "weird wormhole"[2] — "not your usual art-world entity."[3] "More ecosystem than exhibition"[4] venue, it's "a space to watch,"[5] "prodding the fraught marriage of form and the social"[6] by remaining "irresistibly complex and colorful, if a little hard to decipher."[7] With a "notably self-reflexive sense of humor,"[8] it takes a "concise"[9] approach that's a "contradictory patchwork"[10] of "artist-writer-curators and assorted polymaths"[11] while avoiding the "drearily arcane."[12] P! is a "place for speculative reason,"[13] "a physical environment"[14] with "prankish synergy"[15] that "indicates how a gallery space is anything but neutral"[16] and never exists "purely as financial speculation."[17] Its "quick-fire exhibitions addressing contemporary value systems"[18] use "sleight of hand"[19] to "blur the boundaries of art and design,"[20] while pointing "toward timely issues."[21] These "games and puzzles"[22] — "intensely pleasurable, gorgeously sensual,"[23] yet "witty"[24] — are "vehicles of self-portraiture,"[25] an "experimental travelogue"[26] "through the dire and bifurcated political landscape"[27] by an "inexhaustible brainiac."[28] "A certain amount of this must be taken as tongue-in-cheek, but like the readymade, a certain amount of it is deadly serious."[29] "Claiming nothing, it claims everything."[30]

BIBLIOGRAPHY

1. "Marc Handelman / Arthur Ou / Peter Rostovsky." *The New Yorker*, 20 May 2013.
2. Andrew Russeth, "Hitting It Off." *The New York Observer*, 10 February 2014.
3. Nancy MacDonell, "Open Agenda: P! In Chinatown." *New York Times T Magazine*, 18 September 2012.
4. Rachel Ellis Neyra, "Critics' Pick: The Stand." *Artforum.com*, 10 February 2017.
5. Will Brand and Corinna Kirsch, "Project Projects Co-Founder Opens a 'Mom-and-Pop-Kunsthalle' in Chinatown." *ArtFCity*, 31 August 2012.
6. Annie Godfrey Larmon, "Critics' Pick: Céline Condorelli." *Artforum.com*, 5 May 2017.
7. "Céline Condorelli." *The New Yorker*, 15 May 2017.
8. Kaelen Wilson-Goldie, "Critics' Pick: Process 01: Joy." *Artforum.com*, 16 October 2012.
9. Nova Benway, "Permutation 03.2: Re-Place." *Modern Painters*, July/August 2013.
10. David Markus, "Rainbows to No Place: Société Réaliste and the Ayn Rand Apocalypse." *Hyperallergic*, 12 October 2013.
11. Karen Rosenberg, "Brian O'Doherty: Connecting the ...." *The New York Times*, 28 March 2014.
12. Peter Plagens, "Lyrical Forms, Social Commentary and Handiwork." *The Wall Street Journal*, 12 October 2013.
13. Rhett Jones, "Yams Collective Brings Ferguson Themed Installation to the LES." *AnimalNewYork.com*, 12 September 2014.
14. David Frankel, "Brian O'Doherty." *Artforum*, June 2014.
15. Johanna Fateman, "Critics' Pick: Post-Speculation." *Artforum.com*, October 2014.
16. Gemma Tipton, "Critics' Pick: Brian O'Doherty." *Artforum.com*, 28 March 2014.
17. Jason Farago, "Around Town: New York, USA", *Frieze*, May 2015.
18. Iona Whittaker, "Michal Helfman." *Art in America*, September 2015.
19. Zachary Sachs, "Critics' Pick: Klaus Wittkugel and Anton Stankowski." *Artforum.com*, 6 February 2016.
20. Martha Schwendener, "Blurring the Boundary Between Art and Design." *The New York Times*, 28 August 2015.
21. Karen Schiff, "Maryam Jafri." *Art in America*, June/July 2016.
22. "Brian O'Doherty." *The New Yorker*, 14 April 2014.
23. Nick Currie, "The Office and the Orgasm: The Monoprints of Karel Martens." *Mousse*, Issue 57, Feb-March 2017.
24. Blake Gopnik, "Daily Pic (#1395: i)," *blakegopnik.com*, 22 September 2015.
25. Holland Cotter, "Brian O'Doherty." *The New York Times*, 10 February 2017.
26. Mimi Wong, "Futures Again: Wong Kit Yi", *ArtAsiaPacific.com*, 4 April 2017.
27. Rachael Rakes, "The Stand." *Village Voice*, 22 February 2017.
28. "Real Flow." *ArtinAmerica.com*, 6 March 2015.
29. Jonathan T.D. Neil, "Derivative Work." *ArtReview Asia*, Summer 2015.
30. Will Heinrich, "Controlled Experiments." *The New York Observer*, 22 October 2012.

How can you tell the story of a space? There are the less and more obvious modes: an oral history with its participants, an exhibition of archival documentation and ephemeral materials, a printed catalogue listing all programs, a hagiographic text focused on the major highlights, etc. Each form has its value, particularly from the perspective of institutionalization—seeking to legitimize a certain kind of practice, trying to *rewrite* history to make it seem smoother, more narrative, more strategic. For, from the perspective of later audiences (including but not limited to: funding bodies; future employers; other, larger institutions; professional colleagues; family members who just don't understand; children and other descendents), this kind of coherence and forethought may seem essential. For them, the past was never anything apart from *intentional*. Today, in the eyes of many would-be exhibition-makers, designers, and artists (or even just folks messing around with forms), spaces in between, where things cannot be explained in a neat and tidy way, simply do not exist.

This text exists, necessarily, in fragments. It's neither a history of my own space, P! (which operated on Broome Street in New York City from 2012–2017), nor an account of the ostensible subject of this text, 019 (which was founded in Ghent in 2014 and still exists). Yet at the same time, it is perhaps both of these things. I'd like to think that, much in the spirit of both of these endeavors, it's an attempt to work through a set of questions in the open and perhaps formulate some new questions along the way. Let's see if it works.

With a tip of my hat to my dear friend and colleague Martin Beck, I'll start by self-reflexively introducing the invitation, my initial (mis)understanding of it, subsequent developments, and then its eventual realignment.

It all begins with an email: 019's invitation to write a text for their upcoming book. My immediate sense of both pleasure and dread. I appreciate 019 and their "Museum of Moving Practice" project very much, but how can I possibily fit in a thoughtful, properly-researched essay about their work with all of the commitments I already have, including moving to Berlin and opening a new exhibition space, amidst other curatorial and design deadlines? I ask them how much they can pay me, which is, unsurprisingly, modest. The calculus ends with me rejecting the project, following my self-imposed promise to say "no" to more things in the coming year.

Which is followed by the insistence of Valentijn, one of 019's co-founders, his flexibility to try to make the text possible, his openness to my first suggestion of changing the format (into an interview with him and other co-founders of the space, which seems easier and more straightforward), to changing the timing (i.e., giving me more of it!). My reconsideration of my initial refusal, and also the sense that I can learn something from talking with 019.

A Skype interview is planned, performed, and recorded with Valentijn and Tomas. It's somewhat brusque, functional. I am constrained by many time commitments. I try to be journalistic and accomplish the interview efficiently.

The transcript comes back and it doesn't seem of great value to them, or really, to anyone. They write that they think it's mostly on the surface, and that, to be more interesting and worthy of publishing, it might need another interview for depth. Still exceptionally busy, and now in the midst of professional and personal life changes, I sit on the email for several weeks.

Valentijn nudges several times, knowing that the initial (extended) deadline draws near. I hesitate, delay, procrastinate, and then finally read the interview again—and recognize that they're right, it's not very good. I failed to ask even basic questions to get the facts straight, e.g., who founded it, when, where, etc. We would have to conduct at least another interview over email, if not several rounds, to create an interesting and readable text.

I start to have an inkling that perhaps I should write something more speculative: a piece about why I first agreed to do the piece, and what I have projected from my own practice with P! onto their space. That this might be more compelling, and that I might actually learn more from it. And also, since the publication has a more limited and specific distribution than I'm sometimes used to, I might have the opportunity to experiment more.

I start to take notes for this direction in a flurry. I propose to 019 that I could either conduct another email interview, as previously discussed, or, as an alternative, pursue a more exploratory, fragmentary piece. I also tell them that, even though I am personally more excited about the second direction, I don't know if it's a good idea because of the time constraints and work involved. I propose that we skype.

Valentijn writes back that they are interested in the second direction. We skype very briefly. He tells me they always thought of this text more as a "commission," an opportunity for me to write something interesting to me, rather than just as a way to describe and memorialize their practice (as I had initially assumed). He also says that they might even be able to potentially extend the deadline yet again, that having a good piece is more important than the timing. All very encouraging words, and I start to get excited.

After less than 20 minutes of chatting, I have to leave for another meeting. But the decision seems to have made itself. Before I even step into the Berlin S-Bahn, I've already started to type into a new Google doc. The text starts with, "How can you tell the story of a space?"

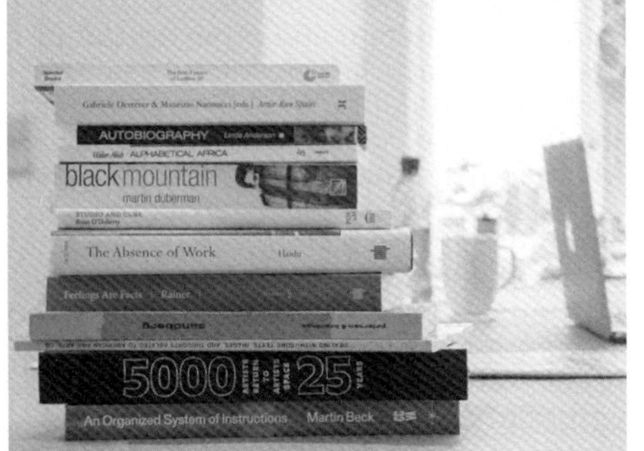

There's a set of books on my new desk in Berlin. Some of them are reminders of other spaces—experimental venues for art or culture that no longer exist, or that now live on in another form entirely. None of these art spaces were meant to enjoy old age, necessarily, and many never intended to become authoritative. And yet here these objects are: records of how a program may eventually become history.

Each book has its own approach, organization, and design. I had originally intended to write a brief synopsis and critique of each, as a way to move forward with my own thoughts about publishing a history of P!, but that seems less urgent now. Perhaps I'll return to the topic later.

There's another book, anyways, that I far prefer to any of these: *SONSBEEK 93*, from the public exhibition curated by Valerie Smith in the Dutch town of Arnhem in 1993. Although it appears to be a catalogue, it's not actually about a space or project that's past, but rather one that (within the temporality of the book's production) is *still to come*. Normal, you might say smugly, for an exhibition catalogue, which is usually published before the exhibition has taken place. And yet this one's organized not as a mere projection or encapsulation (which all of those other books are, just looking in the opposite direction), but rather as a living document: a kind of sketchbook for an exhibition-yet-to-come, it includes all of the curator's field notes of meetings with artists, commissions in progress, her (sometimes withering) curatorial critique and feedback to artists, their proposals, writings, and more. So, although it's a past collection of future-facing documents, it feels *vital*. The design, by Wigger Bierma (who later co-founded the Werkplaats Typografie, also in Arnhem, NL—which is, coincidentally, also the space that connects me to 019), is cool, calm, conceptual—but also masterful in using a minimum of means to describe different textual voices and modes of engagement. It's plainspoken yet adaptive.

In its curatorial, editorial, and design approach, this book is not about a finished project, it's about how things emerge. It's tight in the right places, while also loose (and candid) enough to let you in. To employ a word that editor Sina Najafi (my new office-mate in Berlin, who is also connected to Valerie Smith, as she herself is to my new space) used when describing a recent event I organized: the book is "porous"—open enough to allow for feedback and dialogue. If I'm ever writing a history of my work or life, or projecting my notes forward, I'd wish for the same.

It's February 24, three days after starting this piece. I'm on a plane back to New York City and have to choose a first song to listen to while writing. 2018's writing needs a new vibe, so I start with Tony Williams Lifetime's "Joy Filled Summer"—a bombastic jazz-fusion track. Allan Holdsworth's guitar solo shredding through a bridge is motivating.

Last year's writing music was different. It was marked by a single album on repeat: *Dysnomia* by Dawn of Midi, a nearly hour-long masterwork of polyrhythmic acoustic music. It's something like a profound piece of minimal techno produced only by bass, drums, and prepared piano. I was lucky to witness its genesis and development over the course of several years, in live concerts and private performances that culminated in the album. Three musicians of the highest calibre, working together to develop a seamless, enveloping, continuous work of aural choreography.

For more a year, I listened to the album on endless repeat while writing. Even though I may eventually have tired of it, I realized that it became a datum in my periapatetic working-writing life: a constant regardless of whether I was writing at my desk, in a foreign hotel, in my second (now first) home in Berlin, on a plane, train, or automobile. The music became my audio working environment, particularly for the composition of *P!DF*.

If I understand correctly, the three musicians who made Dysnomia are barely friends anymore. Constructing a complex, collaborative masterwork together takes its toll.

Let's start a table of my initial impressions around the similarities and differences between 019 and P!:

019	P!
Spontaneous	Strategic
Improvisatory	Presentational
Youthful	Historically-grounded
Fast 'n' loose	Overly precise
Cheap	Expensive
Light	Weighty
Fun	Serious
Extensible	Bounded

The list could go on, but the gist is obvious: I project onto 019 everything that I wish P! had been, I treat 019 as the corrective to P!'s imagined failures. Of course, in reality, both 019 and P! probably contain aspects of both columns. It's just that later, you remember something differently, once it's over and you've decided to move in another direction.

Which is why I decided to write this piece in the first place: because my first encounter with 019 and their project "Museum of Moving Practice" was so interesting: odd, unresolved, and overlapping, yet still authorial. It seemed so related to where I might hope to continue with my own future practice, that I thought I should think more about them in order to understand myself.

I've always thought that it's better to let a space expire before it becomes a zombie. Or at least let it change its name, acknowledging that it's now a new entity. The argument against this, of course, is that organizations, like people, grow and change, even to the point of being unrecognizable to themselves later—but it's still the same flesh, the same person. Others would say the opposite: each moment of consciousness represents an entirely different person, the narrative frame that creates a sense of "self" is false and misleading. This unresolved tension is why some people keep notebooks or conduct what's known as "feedback analysis" (writing self-reflectively about key life decisions as you make them): to be able to look back later and compare what you originally set out to do with where things ended up.

In September 2016, I was invited to take part in a special forum at the 9th Gwangju Biennial called "To All the Contributing Factors," organized by Binna Choi and Maria Lind. The event included representatives of some 100 small- to medium-scale arts organizations. I was asked to facilitate a workshop with several organizations from Australia, New Zealand, Korea, and Japan. It became a kind of intensive group-therapy session about why our organizations were founded and continued to exist. Based on our day-long discussion, I authored a text and speculative proposal for an "institutional graveyard" for independent art spaces. Emerging out of our conversations, it was a free pass for exhausted spaces to shut their doors, yet still sleep well, knowing that their legacy would be preserved.

Since it seems unlikely at this point that the planned second volume of the Biennial catalogue will ever be published, I'll reproduce part of the text here:

Every small- or medium-scale art institution must die sometime. This inevitable end paves the way for others to emerge in an increasingly overcrowded, underfunded, and over-producing field. But with each disappearing artist-run or alternative space, each mini-collapse or silent goodbye, the discourse of exhibition-making loses another set of unique memories and practices—even though they were most likely insufficiently received and appreciated in their own time, given the glut of contemporary arts programming coupled with a relative dearth of attentive publics.

To combat this ongoing forgetting, we propose the Archives of Institutional Memory (AIM), a graveyard for small- to medium-sized cultural spaces, which will contain digital and physical archives including correspondence and program documentation. At the same time, this graveyard functions as a forward-looking seed bank, containing in its material remnants exhaustive fodder for future generations of experimental exhibition-makers.

AIM is located in Brisbane, Queensland, Australia. Since the publication of Nevil Shute's 1957 novel, *On the Beach*, Australia has occupied a particular place in the popular imagination as one of the last areas that could survive a global apocalypse of nuclear, military, or environmental nature. Australia's relative geographic isolation has already contributed to the evolution of unique species of animal life and the mutation of digital memes through natural selection. For AIM, this isolation serves a second purpose: it ensures protection, safety, longevity, and remove, which are essential for future contemplation and study.

Housed in the museum-grade, climate-controlled building at the Institute of Modern Art (IMA), the Archives of Institutional Memory (AIM) offers expiring small- to medium-scale spaces a physical depository for their objects and archives. Spaces of different sizes can be leased for an affordable fee over a long term. These fees help contribute to the IMA's operating budget and ensure its ability to preserve its peers' memories in the long term.

AIM also offers named donor opportunities for funding these archival plots. This is the perfect way for larger-scale and better-funded global institutions, organizations, and individuals to acknowledge and help repay the debt they owe to smaller spaces. By taking risks, investing sweat equity, and embracing precariousness, these spaces are essential for supporting artistic research, nurturing nascent discourses and markets, and greasing the wheels of contemporary art—even after they close.

The text was fun to write, a mock institutional tone for a modest proposal. It was also a tongue-in-cheek swan song, since I had already planned and announced the final year of P! by that point. I remember dreaming, hoping that someone might take P!'s archive off my hands and allow me to no longer worry about annoying and costly questions of preservation. Closing one thing cleanly allows you to move on to the next.

Even though AIM never actually existed, maybe this very text can be a seed: someone else might read it and make it real.

What's the famous quote about a famous band? That there were only 10 people at their first concert, but every one of them started their own band? I don't remember who it was exactly, and writing from a plane without internet, I don't care to fact check it either.

This fragmentary "essay" has become an opportunity to take a journey through my old, unpublished, unpublishable writing. Perhaps this is another kind of graveyard.

2016 in particular was a year when I resolved to write more—lot of texts, fragments, and attempts. I said yes to nearly every invitation to write, however small. Not all of the writing made it into the world (probably for the better), but it was a productive period, something like a year of intensive, craft-building practice. The year culminated with a one-week residency in December at the Villa Empain in Brussels, at the invitation of artist Asad Raza and Foundation Boghussian. I planned to work on one particular text: a fictionalized history of P!, written from the perspective of its floor.

Even though I considered that residency a bit of a failure, in that I didn't finish the text I set out for myself, I see now in retrospect that it was very generative. I've heard it said that a good residency is an opportunity to test new things out, a chance to fail. Perhaps the origins of me thinking of myself as a "writer" in a more serious sense start there: that week, alone with myself in a blank room in Belgium, trying to write.

I worked towards a modest routine. Every morning I would wake up out of my dreams and, without checking email or consuming anything, I would write blindly into a document for approximately an hour. I would try my best not to edit. This process was a lesson from my last sustained stint of writing in 2014, while penning an academic article on East German designer Klaus Wittkugel. What came out the residency this time was open, probing, sometimes diaristic, perhaps overly self-conscious. Occasionally I would nod off at the the computer. Eventually I would get up, make coffee and breakfast, perhaps write a bit more, maybe nap; then shower and begin to work on other pressing projects. By afternoon, I'd be back on New York City time and responding to client and studio emails. I would try to see one person in the evening for dinner or drink, and then return home to sleep early and begin the next day again.

The week was not a success from the standpoint of producing usable writing. But I promised myself to judge neither my writing nor process harshly. The minor discipline of the days gave me a bit of confidence. So, despite the week's potential failures, I reproduce here an excerpt, my final attempt, raw, unedited, of how I tried to tell the story of a space from the perspective of its floor:

The things I've seen. No one else would know them. Maybe the walls, but even they, they care less about the things I do.

When this house was first built, I was installed, sturdy and wooden, into the ground. They leveled me out and made sure I was solid. And for my first years, as a shopfront, I stayed silent and watched. People would scurry across me, vermin as well, and all was the same. I slumbered, snored sometimes, felt my early years as a time of quiet.

Eventually the office came and it was different. Less people, but more hectic. People shouted from office to office. People on the phone. Chairs rolled around on me, creased my skin, wore me down. I tingled sometime from the cold of the winter and the heat of the summer, there were seasons and I watched them shift.

And now this, something new but not so different. A gallery. Yet mainly the difference is the people, their color, their language. Also how long they spend here. And that it's public. No longer an office, no longer for people working, now it's for people looking. Looking is the new work. Everyone does it. Even me.

How do I see things? I have no eyes, I have only a membrane that is my entire surface. Do I have a depth, or am I just a surface? Where do I end, where do I begin?

Now that they're nearly gone, I can consider more deeply what it was they did, to me and the rest of the space.

Colleagues of mine tell me it's unusual for them to change so much. That usually someone moves in, if it's a gallery then they pour a concrete floor, and, *voila!*, that's it and how it will ever be.

Not here, though. In this case, they seemed to treat what was below as a crucial part of the whole. Why. Who knows, maybe a kind of perversity.

As I've said, first I was covered in red, then parts of me in green. Then matte black, then gray. And then covered in cork.

I remember the night that everyone came to celebrate the cork. It was wet out, they arrived, bringing water and snow on their shoes. Of course it filled up, put down a layer of sodden mess. I felt it penetrate, felt it ooze into my seams, start to unloose everything. The first effect was a pop, and then the computer there, sitting on a desk, hissed and let out smoke and shut itself down. An ominous sign. Eventually the water dried, the sockets worked again, and the show continued. But it was a strange way to start.

That cork stayed for longer than even I expected. It was routed into, the tip bit into my skin, which by then felt less like a jacket and more like a hirsute layer. And in that final moment, the one on the floor, he came and cut out a piece of my hair, cut through the cork and bit into my real skin just a little bit, to take out a section and take it with him. And after that, the whole cork was stripped away, leaving me naked again. Which is how I am now.

I know that I'll be stripped back even more, trimmed to fit soon. They tell me that they will take off the vinyl tiles, store them away, so that they bring them somewhere else. For an *exhibition*. What does that mean. I don't know yet, will it feel like me, somewhere else. Or will it just feel like I am reborn again, when some other they comes to pour concrete over me and smooth me out.

An imagined scene in Ghent, one morning. Liberties taken with facts and timing, etc. Written very quickly.

Wake up. Get out of bed. Run a comb across my head.

Just kidding. Start with a cliche, I always say. Gets people to slam the cover closed.

Truth is, there's no single pattern. I don't always wake up first. Sometimes the order's a bit different. Who would've thought.

It's not a big context, Ghent. But it's also not small. There are enough unexpected variables to keep you occupied. So every day unfolds on its own.

Take last Thursday. Karel's show opening the next day at the Design Museum. The works shipped from Munich. And Karel coming.

Then the clock breaks, it stops working. What do you do then? Try to repair it? Or let it stay broken?

I've been known to say, an artwork is always changing. Right in front of your eyes. Consider a stained glass window: the glass is *flowing* like a liquid, just over a long timeframe.

For Brahma, the Hindu god of creation, the entire duration of the universe is a single day of his life. So he would see the colored pigments of the window suspended in a moving surface. It just depends on your reference.

So what does it matter that the clock is broken? This exhibition is only up for three weeks. It's a blip.

What does matter though is the people. And their friendships. Even 80, 90, 100 years is a blip. But at least an elongated Blip, rounded on the sides but extended. That's a timeframe where things start to be more important.

So the short term exists not for the long-term, but it's part of it. And it makes it even possible.

Now that I'm about to have a child, maybe timeframes change again. It starts to be about days, then weeks, months, decades. When is your child going to go to college? And how hot will the winters be by then?

Let's see what happens. I'm optimistic. We've made it this far, and the plan was light-weight. Who's to say it won't continue?

I wonder if I'll actually show 019 or anyone else this writing, these fragments. Will I have a proper editor there? Do I even want one?

I used to be so insecure about my writing, I would only ever submit a text for publication once it was extremely polished. For example: although my 2014 text about Klaus Wittkugel for *The Exhibitionist* underwent extensive revisions with a meticulous editor, Julian Szupinska-Myers, what I sent him as a first draft was as tightly put-together as my then-self could manage. Or my essay for the Art Institute of Chicago's *As Seen* catalogue: also submitted in a quite coherent and well-edited form. They told me it was so clean that the only changes needed were in the punctuation.

Truth be told, this comes from a place of fear and worry. I don't want people to see the things in me that are incoherent, unfinished, uncertain. I am already so unsure about my position and status as a creative person, let alone a *writer*, that I don't want to let them in on that at all.

I still remember reading first drafts by staff writers when I freelanced at the *New York Times Magazine* in 2003. These were real *drafts*, fragments of gobblygook that would need heavy, heavy revision to ever be publishable. At the time, I was mortified: was this how professional writers worked? How lazy! Now, in retrospect, it starts to make more sense. Perhaps as staff writers, they already had the confidence to know that they could produce something polished (and also the support from editors and copy editors along the way). So instead of focusing on the details, they could explore top-level questions of research, investigative work, structure, and other concepts. And worry about the details later, when it's time to worry.

Maybe this is already present in the mode of *K,,* the space I recently opened in Berlin after P!: to have enough confidence in its own track-record to let others see how it develops. To believe that people will understand and appreciate it, even in its awkward, ungainly phases, or perhaps not to care.

I suppose that's the mode of this text as well. What if it's not quite finished, not quite as spick-and-span as usual? What if I let others into the development of the piece, its writing and editing, before I decide to apply my standard level of finish? What more would / could come out of the writing, not only as a product, but as a process?

We all know by now the story of Raymond Carver's editor whats-his-name, who chopped down Carver's sentences to create the style we now know. The editor's role, invisible for so many years (like that of the designer, the curator?), is what creates the inimitable voice of the author and its value.

That being said, I've never read Carver.

In P!*DF*, my auto-monograph and speculative memoir, I begin the section on P! so:

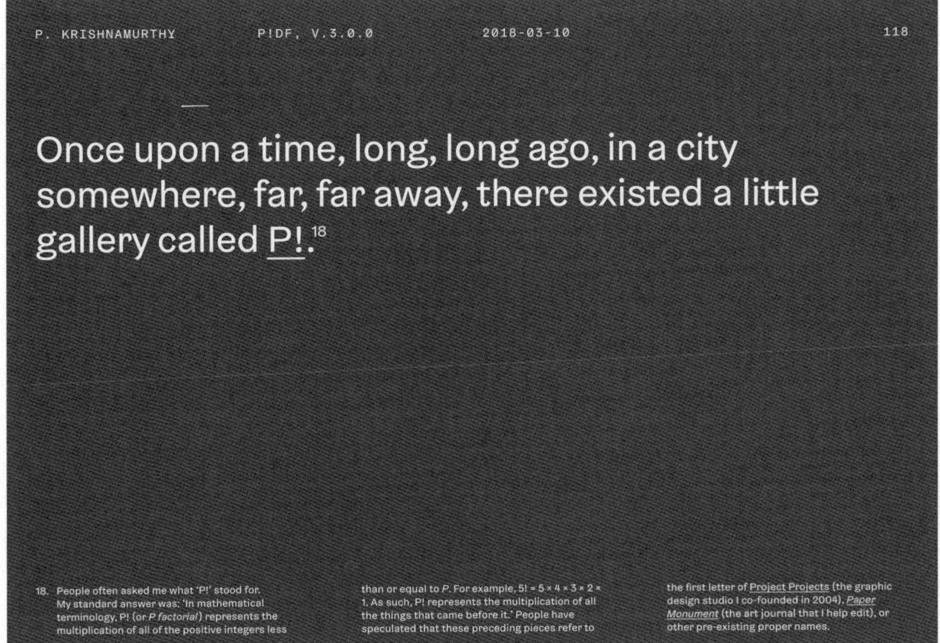

As suggested by my fairy-tale framing, P! was a bit of a fiction. Albeit one, perhaps like those para-fictions that Carrie Lambert-Beatty writes about, that starts in the real world, then moves into literature, and then perhaps back into the real world, influencing both along the way.

I always thought about P! as a *sequence*, like in a musical piece. It was built along principles of contrast, and its program had a form that could become legible to those who looked closely enough.

But its role as a *fiction* was made apparent to me by someone else, through their blunt critique and lack of appreciation. In April 2015, I had recently changed the name of P! to "K." for a fast-paced, six-month cycle of shows. Invited to read for three-minutes at an event celebrating the launch of curator Jens Hoffmann's book, *A–Z of Curating*, I decided on a short performance. Here's a copy of the text for the letter "K" that I declaimed rapidly, only a couple of hours after having emerged from a transatlantic flight:

I.

K: a powerful, punchy character. It evokes Kafka, the KLF, King Kong, Kabbalah, Ketamine—as well as "kainotophobia," the fear of change.

It seems we're hard wired to think that the sun will rise tomorrow just because it did today. But quoting Heraklitus, the pre-Socratic philosopher: "You cannot step twice in the same river, for it's not the same river and you are not the same person"—a statement that evokes a world in flux and mirrors Buddhist notions of the continuously transforming "self" sans fixed essence.

Both design and curating are obsessed with "programs": the legible ordering of things over time. What if change itself were pursued as a program?

II.

K. [K-period] is the name of a gallery on Broome Street, which used to be called P! [P-exclamation]. P! was "a multidisciplinary exhibition space in Chinatown" experimenting with contemporary and historical questions of display. K. occupies the same storefront, yet dubs itself "a new gallery on the Lower East Side." It focuses on economic systems and their construction.

K. has a fixed lifespan: it began in March and expires in August. In this brief moment, it stages a year's program of solo and duo exhibitions, performing the accelerated *Bildungsroman* of a New York gallery. Part of its proposition is ideological: how can such a space function critically from within the market? Part of it is iterative: what happens when ideas must emerge with speed? Part of it is deeply personal: how can risk take one outside of the comfortable and known?

The current exhibition is "North Pole Futures" by Wong Kit Yi. For her, fluctuation and the transparent inadequacies of systems are themselves artistic material. At the center of the show is a mathematical formula for the valuation of future works, which she will create in the Arctic Circle on commission. It's an ephemeral set of artworks priced according to an uncertain future. In these times of speculation and collapse, enumerated variables may appear as relatively stable ground upon which to stand.

III.

K. is for Karaoke

[Performed]

NEW YORK MINUTE (Don Henley)
2:22
Lying here in the darkness
I hear the sirens wail
Somebody going to emergency
Somebody's going to jail
If you find somebody to love in this world
You better hang on tooth and nail
The wolf is always at the door
In a New York minute
Everything can change
In a New York minute
Things can get a little strange
In a New York minute
Everything can change
In a New York minute

During the karaoke bit (which I performed to music), I dramatically pulled my blazer off and threw it into the crowd. Perhaps seventy or eighty people saw it. There exists a video of it by a friend on my computer and probably that's all.

Now, its afterlife is perhaps more interesting to me. Later that week at a museum opening, I ran into one of the event participants, a well-known academic historian of 1960s and 70s alternative spaces in New York. She expressed how much she enjoyed my performance, and how she appreciated my speculative "fiction" about a fast-paced gallery on the Lower East Side.

I had to explain that, in truth, the short-lived gallery I described *actually existed* and that it was *my gallery*. I had renamed my gallery from one letter with punctuation to another letter with punctuation for six months to run an accelerated series of two-week shows playing with economic structures.

She appeared extremely disappointed, even shocked. So it was all just an advertisment for your own gallery? she asked. She had expected that people were presenting three-minute pieces of *substance*, not simply selling themselves. She walked away from the conversation somewhat rudely.

She was right. It was a pitch, an advertisement. But also a fiction. A construction of a space, a space and its program as a story that lives on beyond its time—not necessarily because of what it was, but rather because of what it might be able to be remembered as.

I later had assistance in finding a way to express this both more succinctly and with more complexity. While speaking on a panel with Chris Sharp, the curator-critic co-founder of Lulu, an independent art space in Mexico City that I admire, Chris called Lulu's program of exhibitions a "novel." I thought this was a great description, and took it to heart. Since I was a child, I've always wanted to be a writer, so why couldn't an exhibition space be my novel, my own form of fiction?

The closest I've come to a novel, thus far, is *P!DF*: the interactive book that I have been composing from November 2016 until today.

P!DF didn't start as a book and wasn't originally intended to be published. It began as a semi-straightforward form of self-presentation: an application for an experimental German design prize. A portfolio, a pitch.

Several weeks before my 39th birthday, I was nominated for the prize. Running through options for what to send them, I realized that it would be hard to encapsulate my hybrid practice (between design, curating, researching, writing, teaching, and more) with a FedExed box of printed materials. So instead, I thought I might work in a mode that I've grown to know well over the past 15-odd years: presenting past work to clients and students in a PDF presentation. Working for efficiency, I created a Keynote document that could explain my work to the jury from afar. It was structured like a portfolio, but with a running narrative text and a streak of self-reflexivity, as well as footnotes and comments. Speaking in the second person, it addressed the reader directly: a letter to an assumed public.

The first several weeks of work were a feverish blur. I continued my usual design work in the studio, but every night I'd head home to work all hours, writing and editing the document. I slept less and less, and felt more and more euphoric about the shape things were taking. From the start, I shared the document with those close to me—my partner Emily Smith, for example, who helped me think about how to approach the presentation and selection of projects. Or my mother, who commented that she finally understood what I do as a designer and curator. Or artist Martin Beck, who encouraged me, over Mexican food and beers, to continue with the more abstract and open-ended aspects of the writing. So I edited and revised it continuously until the submission was due, a week before my birthday. That night, I sent a PDF off to Germany; the next day, out of extreme exhaustion and elation, I pursued one of the most wantonly Bacchanalean and self-destructive evenings since my youth—one with negative repercussions and followed by regret, but that still marked a moment.

A week later, Donald Trump was elected as the next President of the United States of America. In the wake of this unimaginable historical moment, the presentation began to shift and morph. While its first version was mostly descriptive, a portfolio, the next version began to consider what design and curating's role could be in times of political trouble, and how the document itself could demonstrate ideas and help to teach others.

The presentation, by now called "Letter to the Jury," continued to change, almost of its own volition. I would edit it obsessively, working on its structure, design, writing, and images in tandem. At De Appel in Amsterdam, I turned it into a performance in which I clicked through each of its slides silently, reading only its footnotes aloud. After that presentation, designer Karel Martens gave me solid critique: it was a good way to present my work, but that it was too "slick" and too obvious. Look again *The Medium is the Massage*, he suggested. How associative its texts and images are in their relationships. A useful prompt.

So it began to develop further, growing in visual and structural complexity. Multiple typographies emerged to differentiate each section, an obsessive micro-level of captioning blossomed, and the document took on more interactivity. Modeled on "Choose Your Own Adventure" books, books for young adults in which the reader can control the narrative flow by choosing specific paths, the presentation expanded to include multiple pathways and internal hyperlinks.

Over the past fifteen years, I've been invited to speak at many art schools and universities about my work as a designer and curator. Typically, I create a new lecture for every such talk. This appeals both to my sense of context-specificity—even as basic as focusing on design work for design students, curating for curatorial students, and such—as well as to a desire to continuously reflect upon the work I've done to date anew through such presentations. Yet the flawed economy of spending days working on a single, poorly-compensated talk always frustrated me. I started to realize that this "Letter" could be a partial answer to the problem: a way to allow the work of writing talks to be *cumulative* rather than *successive*, while also helping me to define myself.

So over the next nine months, whenever asked to present my work in an educational context, I would say yes, and use it as an opportunity to premiere and workshop a new version of the PDF. I would arrive at a lecture with an update to the "Letter"—often completed minutes beforehand on a train or in a taxi cab. Except for that initial appearance at De Appel, I never again read from it; instead, I would invert the structure of these events to focus on the participants. Often this involved giving them a link to download the PDF document, grouping them into working pairs, and asking them to spend 45 minutes (the length of a typical visiting artist talk or screening) together to read and critique the document. I would ask participants to write down their questions, and then would leave for a coffee. Upon my return, the Q&A often started with confusion about the unexpected lecture format, but then expanded into discussions of the relationship of design and curating, questions of structure and typography, organizational and presentational strategies, methods of publishing, details of particular projects, and whatever was on the mind of *those specific students*. The open-ended format allowed them to drive the conversation (rather than me pre-selecting projects or a specific focus for them), and also seemed more productive than a frontal monologue. In any case, their questions were far more considered: since I had explicitly asked them for critique, they seemed more apt to point out failings or concerns directly, rather reproducing the situation in which a presenter's charisma makes attendees feel insecure about challenging them. These workshops became little experiments in public.

For the first half of 2017, this continued with students in art, design, and curating programs at the undergraduate and graduate level. And still the document was altering itself, every week or two, whenever these talks arrived. The next shift arrived with the closing of P! in May 2017.

That Saturday, after our final public program, I visited the graduating MFA graphic design show at Yale with curator and historian Robert Wiesenberger. This developed into a late night conversation on the train back to New York about overlaps in design and art education. The next day, P! had its final Sunday, with friends and colleagues coming by the space spontaneously—

bearing gifts of alcohol, art, and more—to say goodbye. As on other nights, we ordered pizza or dumplings (or maybe both), drank whatever alcohol we had left, and headed to a bar (Beverly's) to finish up the night with a drink. While talking with Jonathan Bruce Williams, a young artist whose work I admire and had shown before, about his personal and professional life, I realized (perhaps with several drinks under my belt) that I did not want to be involved only in producing exhibitions or programs, as in a gallery or museum. As I began to formulate for myself, I wanted to be involved in producing *people*.

And so, over the next weeks and months, the document began another substantial detour, growing to encompass an entirely new narrative strand, written in collaboration with my now-wife, designer and professor Emily Smith. It's composed in her voice, projected years into the future, about our experiments with interdisciplinary pedagogy over during the late 2000s and 2010s. This "red thread" culminates with a manifesto for a school that we "started" in April 2019. So the PDF is the ultimate Choose Your Own Adventure: a document that envisions and lays the groundwork for a specific, speculative future.

The presentation only became *P!DF* a bit later, following the advice of David Reinfurt of O-R-G. He decided to publish this ever-changing document properly, giving it a home and a distribution mechanism apart from my informal ones. He also proposed the name "P!DF", which seemed entirely appropriate. And so, in its current iteration, as an ever-evolving e-book, it encapsulates the story of a space, as well as the history of a practice in the midst of its own formation.

As of the time of this writing, a final section of *P!DF* was added for version 3.0, released on 10 March 2018. It's a kind of "Koda" covering my current context and preoccupation: a one-year residency and fellowship from KW Institute for Contemporary Art, which has made it possible for me to relocate to Berlin and take time for reflection.

In February, I opened *K,* [K-Komma], a space in Berlin-Schöneberg that dubs itself a "workshop for exhibition-making." It's been in the planning for several years and conceives of itself as a single year-long exhibition that changes over time. After I first spoke with 019, I realized that this structure bears much in common with the "Museum of Moving Practice," which was one of the primary reasons why I thought it'd be interesting to contribute a text in this context.

Rather than focusing simply on presentation, *K,* is about production and perhaps even play: a space between "studio and cube" that can constantly change and adapt and move, without worrying too much about what people think of it. Open to the public only for certain slivers of time, it both creates a private space for developing ideas, as well as a public space for collaboration. This means that I invite artists, designers,

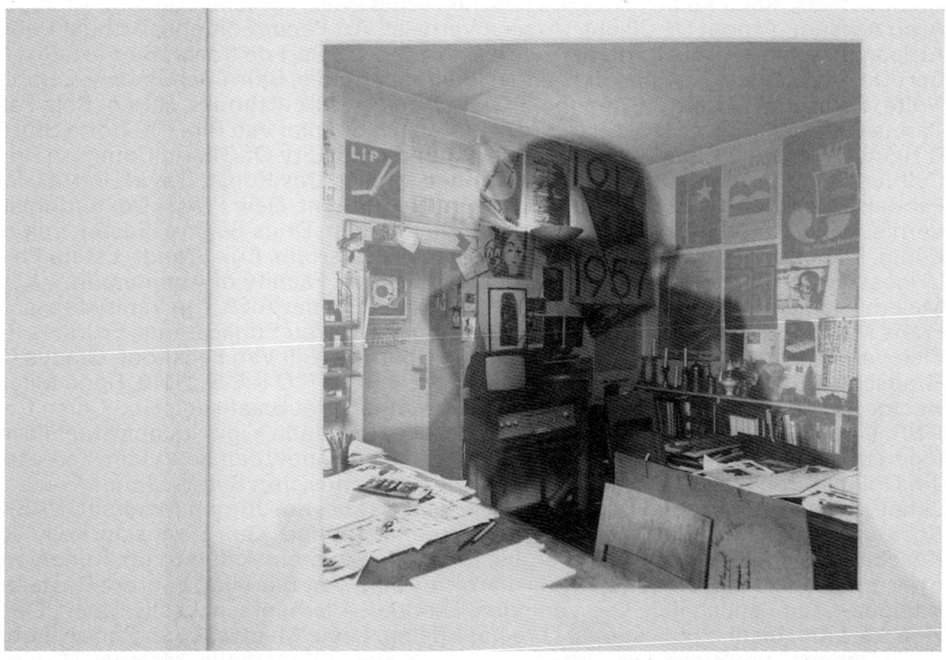

curators, and others into the space to think with me about projects, which then manifest themselves visibly, in one form or another. But there's no necessity that these activities assume a specific form, such as a six-week exhibition or similar. They can emerge and take shape over time.

Balancing this amorphous self-definition, *K,* is a space that also believes in constraints. One such system: everyone who is part of the 2018 program must have a name (or pseudonym) that starts with the letter "K." Hence, the year started with a presentation of East German graphic designer **K**laus Wittkugel, whom I've been researching for a decade (and who happens to share initials with **K**W, who are supporting the project), coupled with a conversation with design historian Jeremy '**K**ai' Aynsley (who took on his nephew's name as a pseodonym), continuing with collaborations with Emily **K**ing, Christopher **K**ulendran Thomas, Annika **K**uhlmann, Na **K**im, **K**onrad Renner & Christoph **K**noth (together with their students from the **K**lasse Digitale Grafik), and so on. This arbitrary approach gives us a formal frame, a specific space, in which to operate, as well as the freedom to move outside of our typical comfort zones.

Another related, yet not entirely anticipated aspect of the project: I've started to write alliterative texts for *K,* in both German and English. It's a form that I had played with in the past, but never quite trusted for its absurdist tack. But for now I've embraced it entirely, trying to work minor language games into every ephemeral event text. Many of these are probably lost on the audience, but some are more obvious. Here's one such fragment, from the end of KW's "official" brochure on the project. I reproduce it in English (though I actually prefer the German version for its snappy K's):

> From this cold-weather kickoff with the classic communism of Klaus Wittkugel, *K,* careens forward on a seemingly-chaotic yet calmly-calibrated course. Over the calendar year, the space compounds collaborators, commingling their individual conceptions of exhibition-making. Rather than crystallizing completely from the start, this cast catalyzes a cycle of crescendoing experimentation with contrasting formats and approaches. Comprising both calculated and casual additions, subtractions, and multiplications—of artworks, objects, ideas, and displays—the presentation accumulates. And so *K,* constructs itself, one komma-delimited character at a time.

Who knows what will happen with this year of *K,*. It's already challenged me and tweaked my thinking: I had been so focused on finished products for the past fifteen years, that I had nearly forgotten what it means to put something unfinished, uncertain, into the world. I'm starting to suspect that to do so—as 019 also embody in their project —is a genuine mixture of selfishness and generosity. On the one hand, you are openly putting into public a thing made primarily for yourself and that you'd like to look at, but this very rawness (in just the right quantity) might allow others to enter in, in those fragile moments before everything's sanded down to a smooth, supple, beautiful form. In this way, an unfinished space—or a piece of unfinished, in-progress writing—might ideally act as a gift.

Which brings me back to the commission of this essay itself: a residency within a publication, a treasured gift of paper-pulp column-inches and airplane-bounded time-spans. A chance to experiment with a text, to try to compose in a different way. To capture what I have tried to do with P!, and what might link it to the important work that 019 continues to accomplish. To live within words, as in spaces, rather than dying in them.

P. Krishnamurthy
New York—Berlin, 21 February—21 March 2018

S&D:024 are: 4478 Zine, 8 Ball Zines, a/b Books, Accattone, Action, Adolfo, Ae_architecten, Alberto García del Castillo, Aline Bouvy, All Things Contemporary, Alles Kan, Alma Matters, a+m bookstore edizioni, Amina Saâdi, And Many More, Animal Press, Anna Kulachek, Anna Puschel, Anne Wies, Annelien Snyers, Archipel, Arctic Paper Benelux, Arne Wastyn, Arno Amandt, Arnout De Cleene, Arseen Verhelst, Art Paper Editions, Artbeat Publishers, Arthur Dekker, Arthur Haegeman, Artlead, Asa Moto, atelier arnederuyte, Bandiz Studio, Bart de Baets, Be-Part, Bea1991, Ben Thorp Brown, Bernard Villers, Bert De Backer, Bert Huyghe, Bieke Criel, Billboard Series, Björn Schumacher, Bobby Dekker, Bom Dia Boa Tarde Boa Noite, Boomtown, Bram De Jonghe, Bráulio Amado, Bulk artbooks, Buren, Béla Pablo Janssen, CQMT, Camiel Diels, Carina Diepens, Carton 123, Chambre Autmatique, Chantal van Rijt, Charlotte Stuby, Charlotte Thomas, Chiba, Chloé D'Hauwe, Christine Denamur, Christopher Hamamoto, City Of Ghent, Common Room, Corneel Cannaerts, Corné Bloed, Cultuur Gent, DOUMA, Daniel Eatock, Daphne Mulder, Das Kunst, David Horvitz, David Kalata, De Cleene De Cleene, De Fabriek Eindhoven, Derek Sullivan, Design museum Gent, Dew Press, Dexter Sinister, Diagonal Press, Dienst Stedelijke Vernieuwing en Gebiedsgerichte Werking, Do the Print, Dries Segers, Easter, Editions Menard, Edizione Multicolore, Eike König, Elsbeth Ronner, Emi Kodama, Emmanuelle Quertain, Erik Brandt, Estate Philippe Vandenberg, Esther Venrooy, Eva L'Hoest, Experimental Jetset, FAK Feminist Collective, Faculty of Architecture – KU Leuven, Febe Man, Ferre Marnef, Fie Malem, Fien De Causmaecker, Filip Dujardin, Fiona Banner AKA The Vanity Press, Flandres Gouvernement, Florance Giroud, Frans Masereel Centrum, Frederik Sutter, From Me To You Publications, Fruzsina Pintér, Fw: Books, Féros magazine, Für dich Verlag, Gagarin, Gaika, Gestalte, Gianni Goethals, Gill Van Eeckhout, Gladys Dumez, Gloria Glitzer, Goedele Dewilde, Grafische Cel, Guang Yu, Gustave Demoen, H E 4 R T B R O K E N, H110, Hana Miletic, Hand Habits, Hannelore van Dijck, Hector Devriendt, Helmut Smits, Hermine Cooreman, Het Balanseer, Hou Chien Cheng, Humboldt Books, IF Publications, IFBR, INFABORE (former I.F.B.R), Il Palestino, Ilke Gers, Inan Yigit, Inconsistant Face-Body Relationship, Ine Meganck, Inge Ketelers, Jade Kerremans, Jan & Randoald, Jan Panev, Jan de Vylder, Jan van Eyck Academie, Jens Wijnendaele, Jiri Oplatek, Job Floris, Joep Van Baast, Jolien Wallenus, Jon Sueda, Jonas Von Lenthe, Jordi Rondeel, Joëlle Tuerlinckx, Juhee, Julia Gersten, Julie Pfleiderer, Julie Vankerckhoven, Jurgen Maelfeyt, KASK, School of Arts, Karel Martens, Kasper Bosmans, Kasper De Vos, Katrien Doms, Katrien Lagrange, Kedr Livanskiy, Kelly Vermeiren, Ken Garland & Associates, Kitschic Ediciones, Kobe Vandenberghe, Kraak, Kunstverein Amsterdam, Kunstverein München, Kåre Frang, LUCA, School of Arts, La Houle, Laat Maar, Lara Gasparotto, Laura Van Biervliet, Laurent Bosteels, Laurent Dupont, Le Bal, Le1f, LeMegot Editions, Leen Vantichelen, Leo Verlinden, Leontien Allemeersch, Leslie Steen, Lieselot Hoedt, Lisa Baerschneider, Lisa Van Hoecke, Little bit ill. Publications, Lore Vanuffelen, Louie Mauws, Loup Sarion, Lubok Verlag, Lucas Devriendt, Lugemik, Lydia Debeer, Lyre Press, Lysandre Begijn, MER. Paper Kunsthalle, Malenki, Manor Grunewald, Manuel Padding, Marc Nagtzaam, Marching Church, Margot Vanhassel, Marie Van den Broucke, Marijs Kempynck, Marion, Beaupere, Mark Goethals, Marketa de Borggraef, Marlena Rether, Martin Belou, Martino Tattara, Mathew Kneebone, Mathieu Serruys, Matière Primaire, Matteo Paris, Max Kesteloot, Max Pinckers, Mayke Vandenweyer, Mert Sen, Mevis & Van Deursen, Micha Hulsmans, Micha Zweifel, Michaël Bussaer, Michaël van den Abeele, Michiel De Cleene, Milan W., Miriam Rohde, Moritz Kung, Murmuur, Nana Esi, Nedyalko Balev, Nel Aerts, Nick Coenen, Nicolás Lamas, Niek Pladet, Nina Canell, Nucleo, Nástio Mosquito, OASE / NAI010, OK-RM, Occasional Papers, Olivier Goethals, Onomatopee, Oriol Vilanova, Orrorin Daydream, PERNEEL OSTEN, POV Books, Pantofle Books, Paul Barsch, Paula Stoffijn, Paulien Wellens, Pauwel De Buck, Peter Lenaerts, Pieter Paul Pothoven, Pieter Vermeersch, Pieterjan Ginckels, Post Brothers, Posture Editions, Prem Krishnamurthy, Provincie Oost-Vlaanderen, Provincie West-Vlaanderen, Pruikduif, Publication Studio Rotterdam, Quenton Miller, RIOT, Ramsdam Books, Remorqueur, Reninca Van Den Broeck, Rikako Nagashima, Robbe Nachtergaele, Robbert Liekens, Robin Watkins, Roel Kerkhofs, Roma Publications, Ronny Duquenne, Roosje Klap, Rosaline Fiems, Royal Academy of Fine Arts Antwerp, Rutger De Vries, SAMENWERK, SMAK, SMIB, SO Gent San Rocco magazine, Sanam Khatibi, Sanne Janssens, Santiago Taccetti, Sascha Lobe, Sheniqua World Tour, Shim Daeki, Shim Hyojun, Silke Vandekerckhove, Silvio Ebner, Sleeperhold Publications, Sofie Gagelmans, Sophie Nys, Sophie Verhulst, Sorry, Not Sorry, Spector Books, Stan D'Haene, Stedelijke Jeugddienst, Steve Slingeneyer, Steven Van Raan, Stijn Cole, Studio Joost Grootens, Stéphanie Saadé, Subbacultcha, Syracuse, TSAR Editions, Tatjana Pieters, Tauba Auerbach, Telma Lannoo, Terrain Vague, The Eriskay Connection, The Future Publishing and Printing, Theo De Meyer, Thomas Caron, Thomas Desmet, Thomas Min, Thomas Zipp, Théophile's Papers, Tim Bryon, Tjobo Kho, Tom Bruin Slot, Tom Van Imschoot, Tomas Lootens, Turncoats, Two Books, VAI / Vlaams Architectuurinstituut, Valentijn Goethals, Valiz, Van Eeghem BVBA, Verena Buttmann, Victor Sirot, Victor Vanwassenhove, Vincent Maillard, Volcano The Bear, Vooruit, Ward Heirwegh, Waxy, We Became Aware, Werkplaats Typografie, Willem Boel, Will Holder, Willem Boel, Wim Lambrecht, Witte de With, Wouter Vannes, Xavier Mary, Yana Foqué, YellowPress, Yin Yin Wong, Ynne Dewever, múltiplos, éditions Menard,...

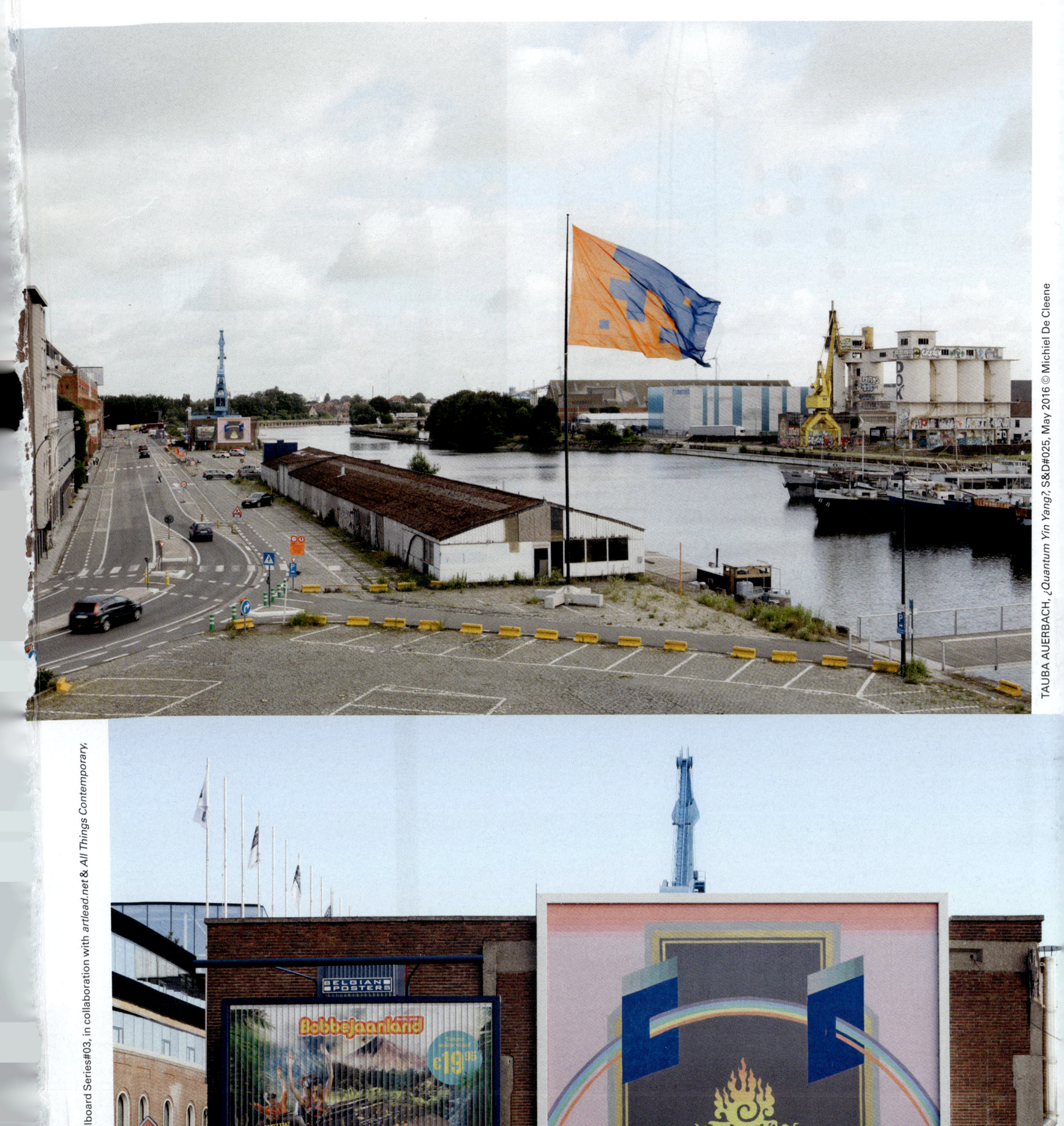

TAUBA AUERBACH, *¿Quantum Yin Yang?*, S&D#025, May 2016 © Michiel De Cleene

KASPER BOSMANS, *Smalt (Cobalt Filter and Cream*, Billboard Series#03, in collaboration with *artlead.net* & *All Things Contemporary*, May 2016 © Michiel De Cleene

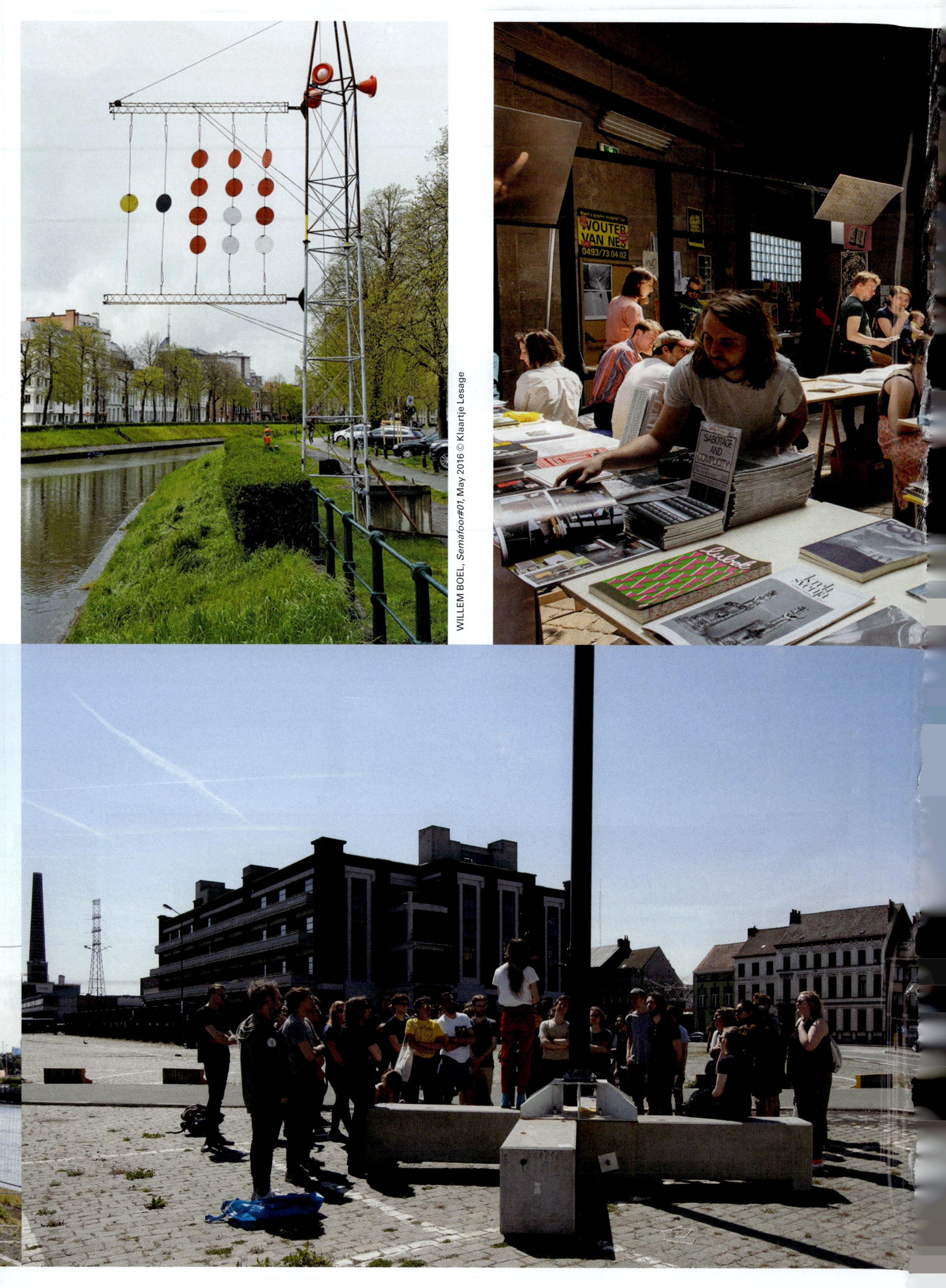

WILLEM BOEL, *Semafoor#01*, May 2016 © Klaartje Lesage

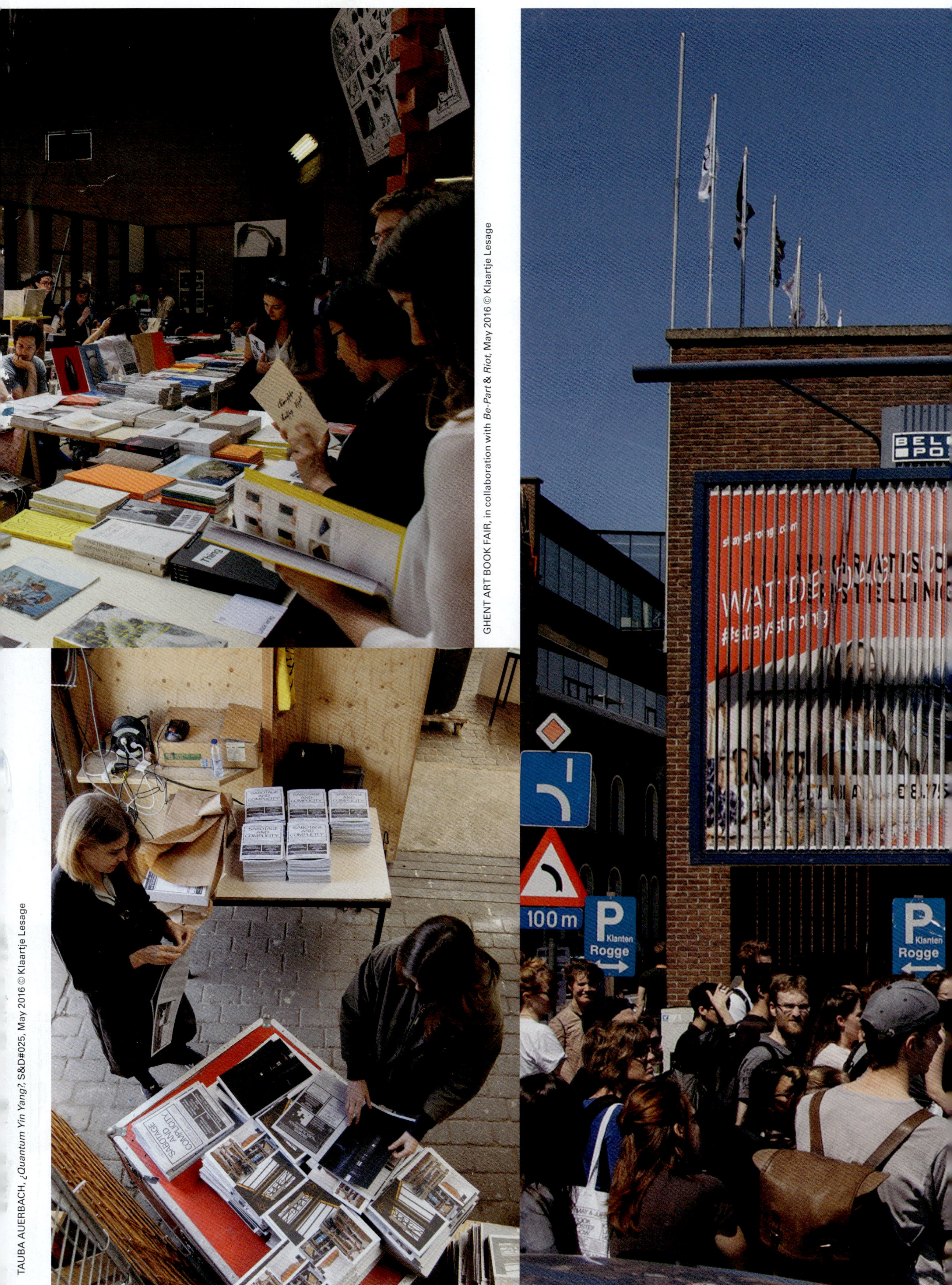

GHENT ART BOOK FAIR, in collaboration with *Be-Part* & *Riot*, May 2016 © Klaartje Lesage

TAUBA AUERBACH, *¿Quantum Yin Yang?*, S&D#025, May 2016 © Klaartje Lesage

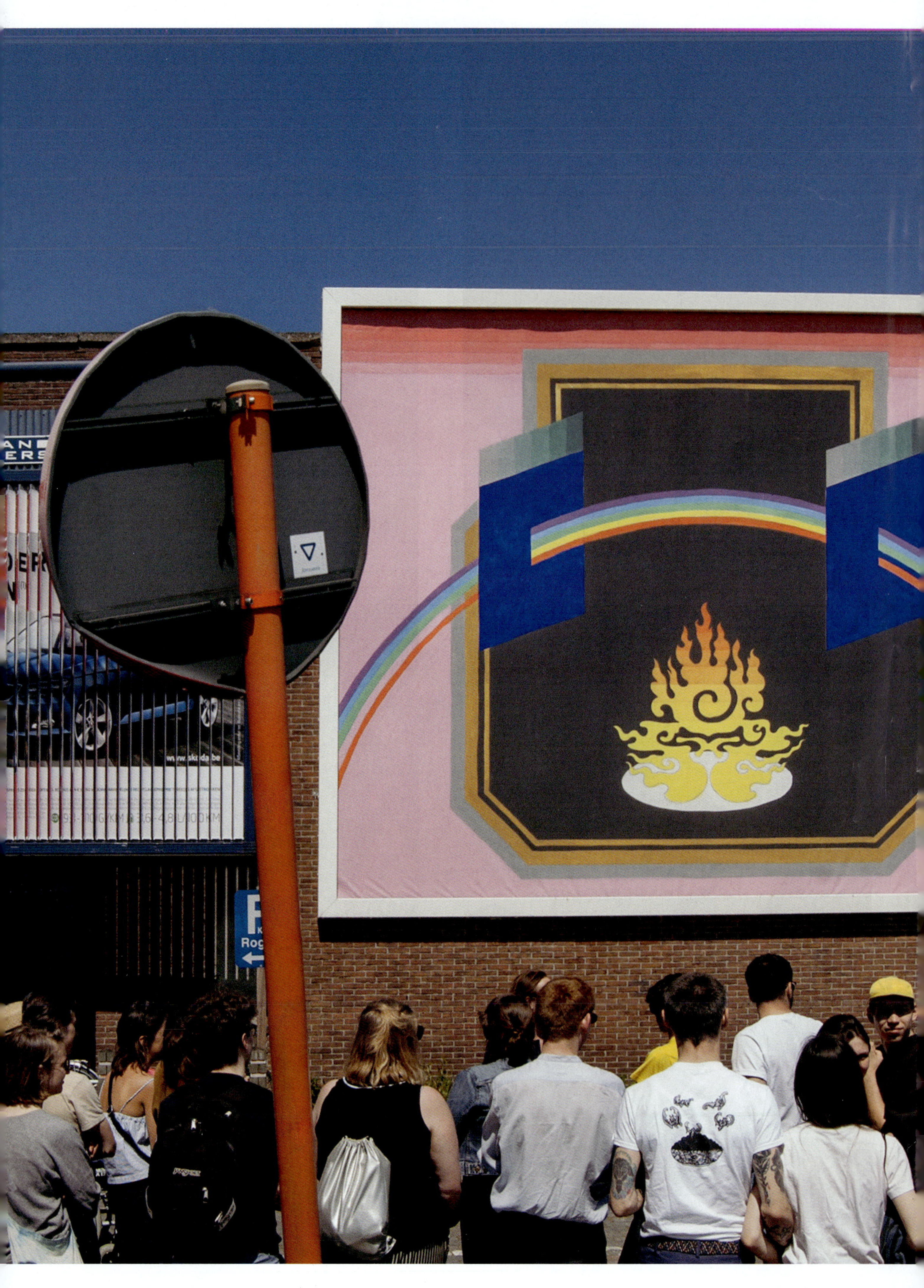
www.skoda.be
P

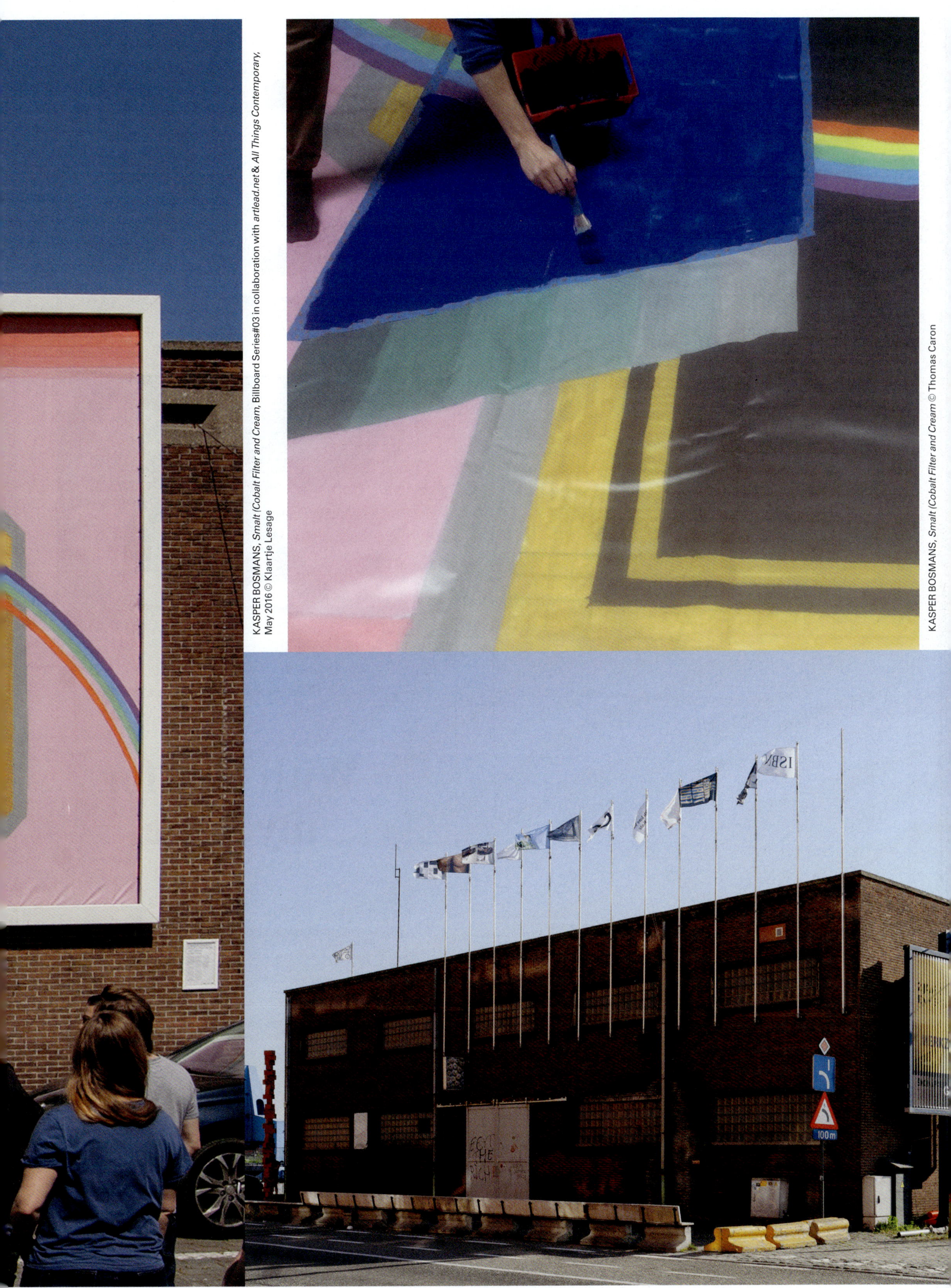

KASPER BOSMANS, *Smalt (Cobalt Filter and Cream*, Billboard Series#03 in collaboration with *artlead.net* & *All Things Contemporary*, May 2016 © Klaartje Lesage

KASPER BOSMANS, *Smalt (Cobalt Filter and Cream* © Thomas Caron

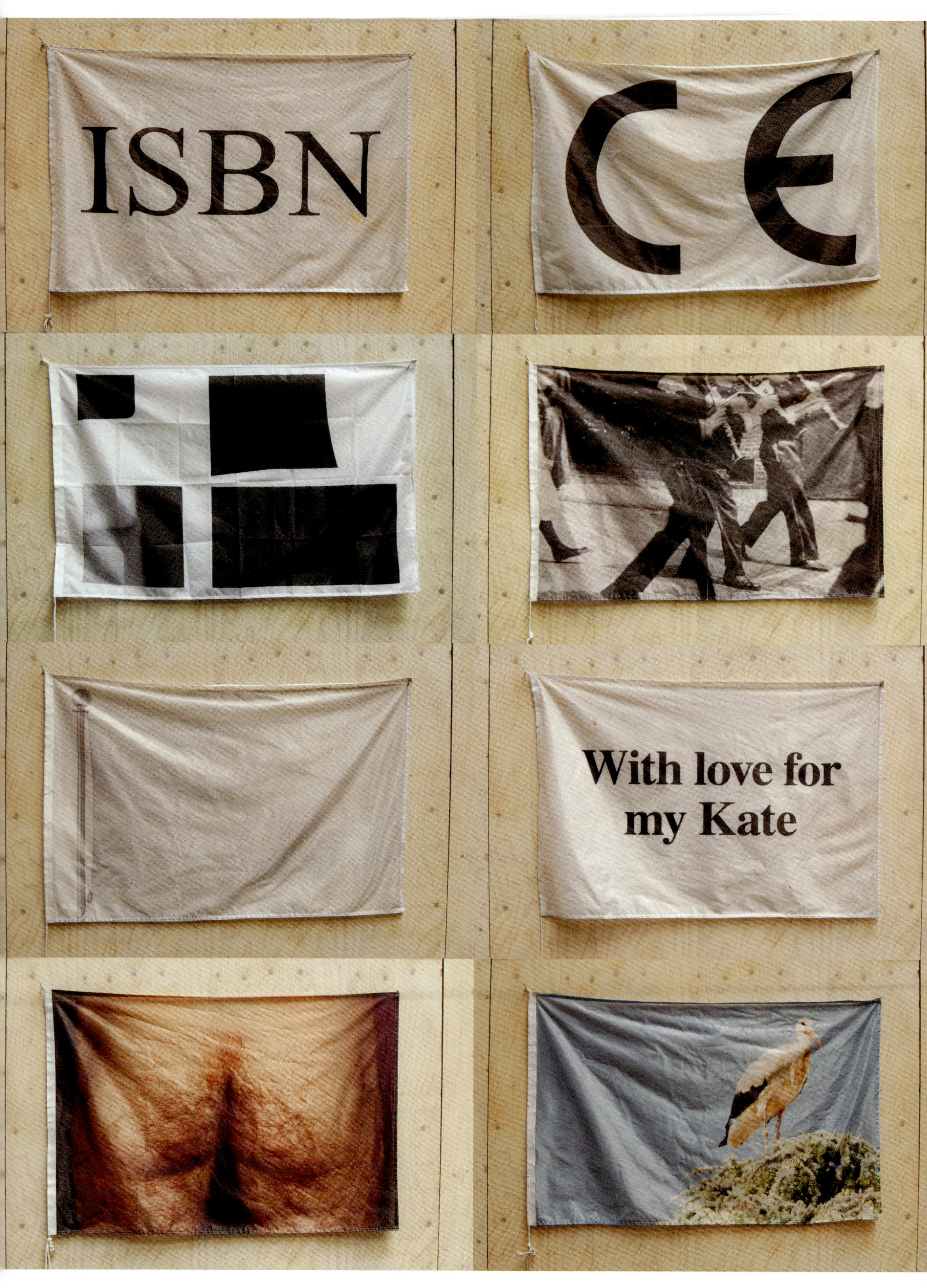
ISBN
CE
With love for
my Kate

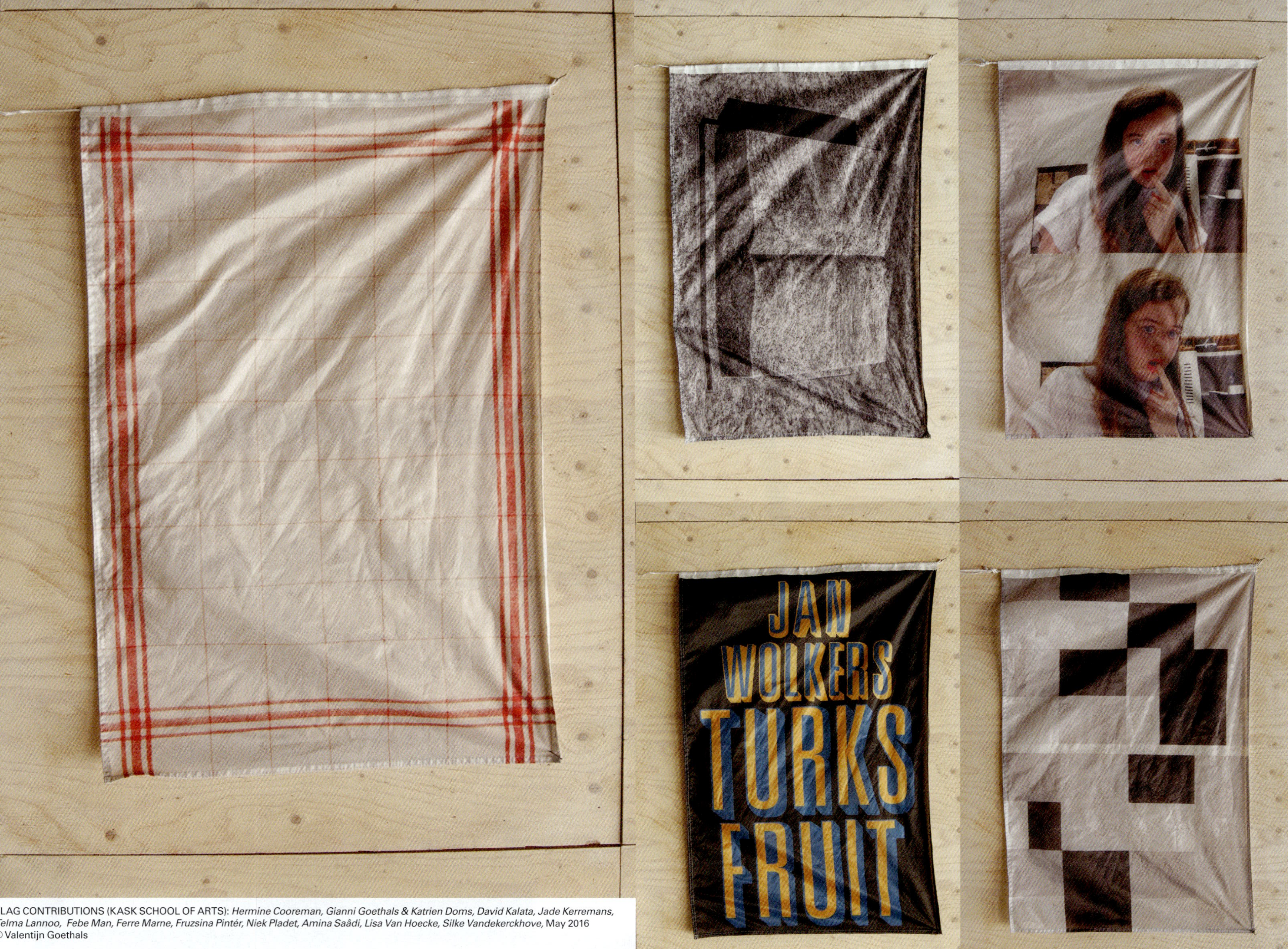

FLAG CONTRIBUTIONS (KASK SCHOOL OF ARTS): *Hermine Cooreman, Gianni Goethals & Katrien Doms, David Kalata, Jade Kerremans, Telma Lannoo, Febe Man, Ferre Marne, Fruzsina Pintér, Niek Pladet, Amina Saâdi, Lisa Van Hoecke, Silke Vandekerckhove,* May 2016
© Valentijn Goethals

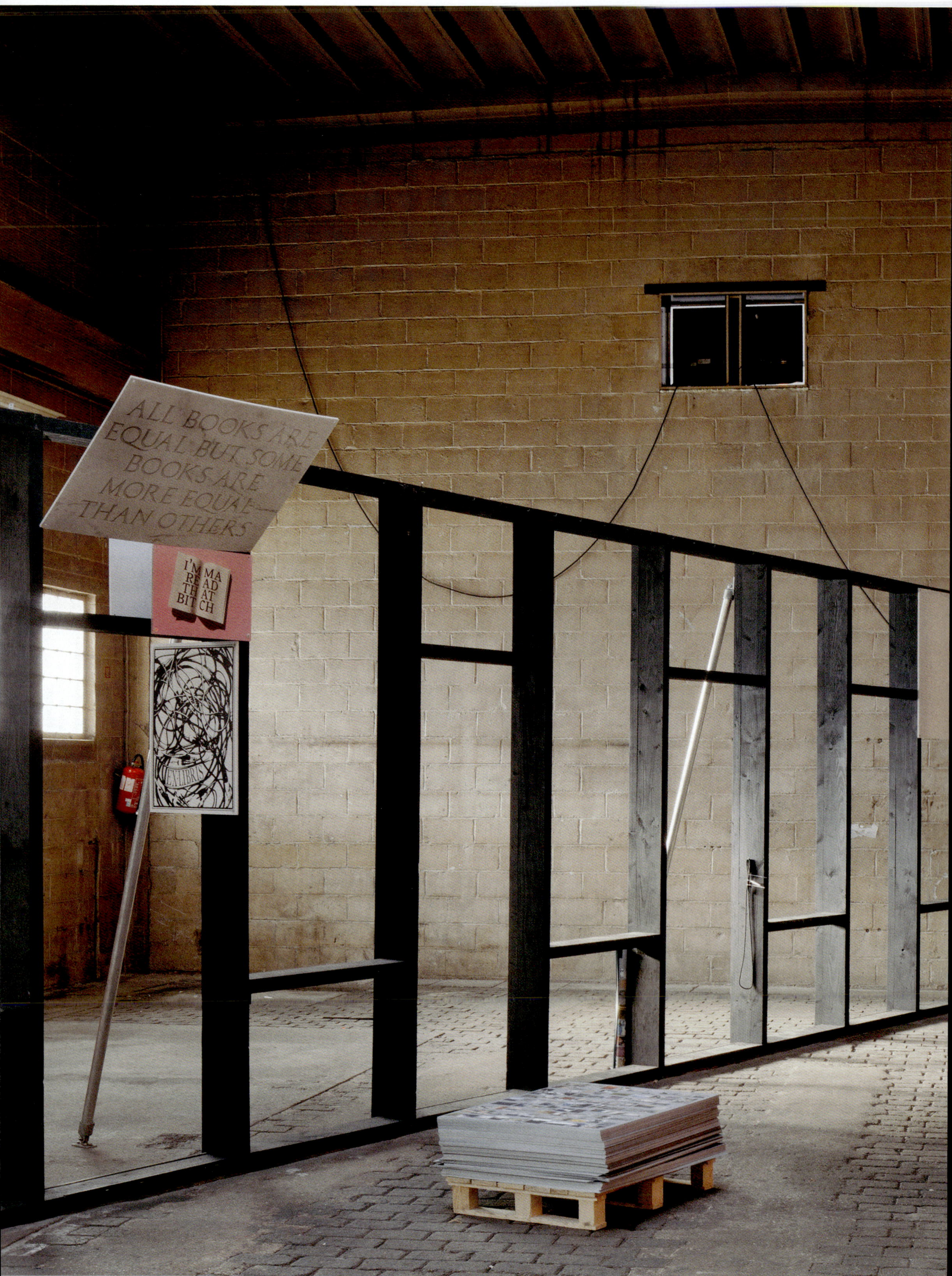
ALL BOOKS ARE
EQUAL BUT SOME
BOOKS ARE
MORE EQUAL
THAN OTHERS
I'M READ THAT BITCH
MA AD AT CH
EX LIBRIS

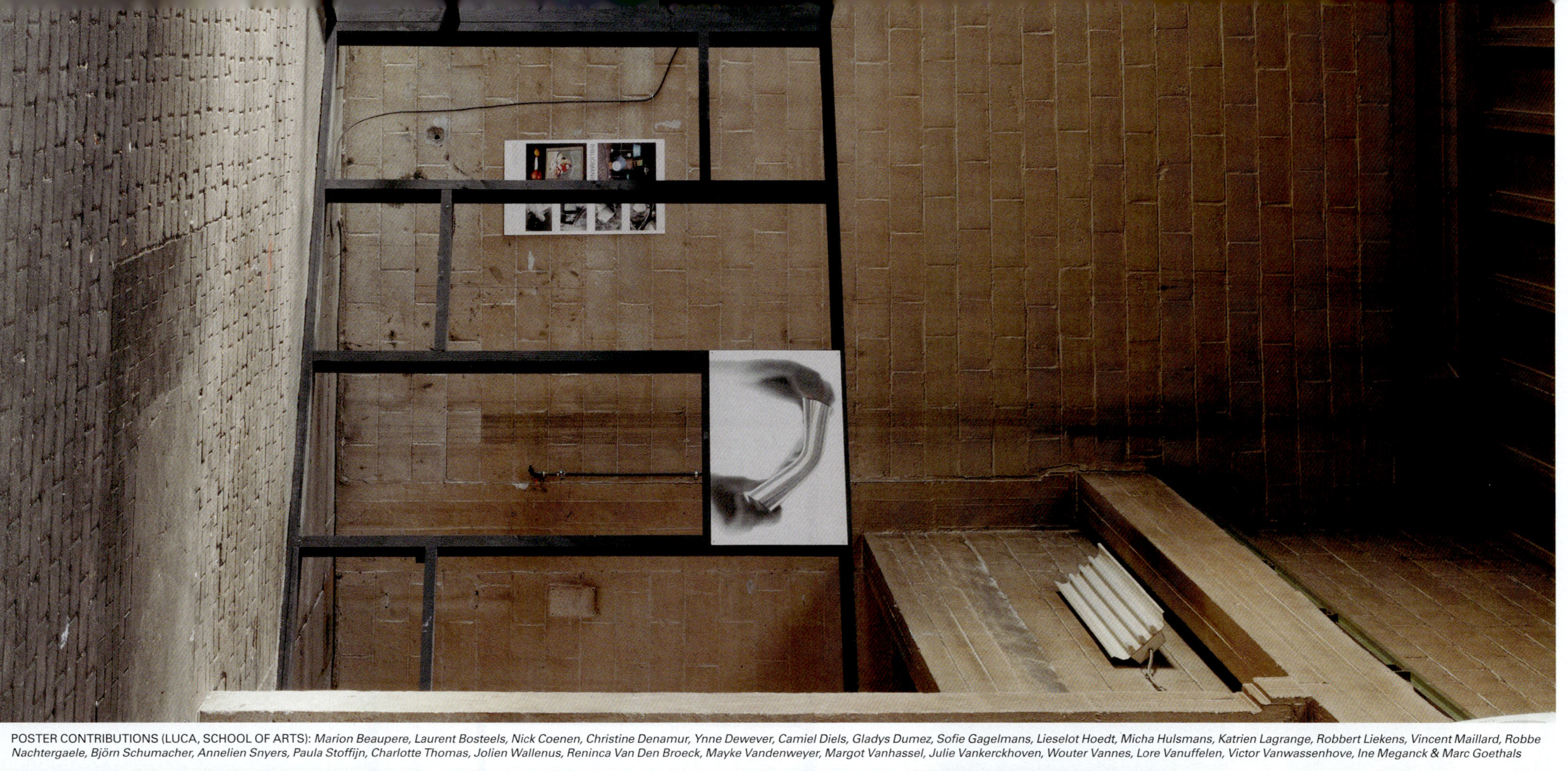

POSTER CONTRIBUTIONS (LUCA, SCHOOL OF ARTS): *Marion Beaupere, Laurent Bosteels, Nick Coenen, Christine Denamur, Ynne Dewever, Camiel Diels, Gladys Dumez, Sofie Gagelmans, Lieselot Hoedt, Micha Hulsmans, Katrien Lagrange, Robbert Liekens, Vincent Maillard, Robbe Nachtergaele, Björn Schumacher, Annelien Snyers, Paula Stoffijn, Charlotte Thomas, Jolien Wallenus, Reninca Van Den Broeck, Mayke Vandenweyer, Margot Vanhassel, Julie Vankerckhoven, Wouter Vannes, Lore Vanuffelen, Victor Vanwassenhove, Ine Meganck & Marc Goethals*

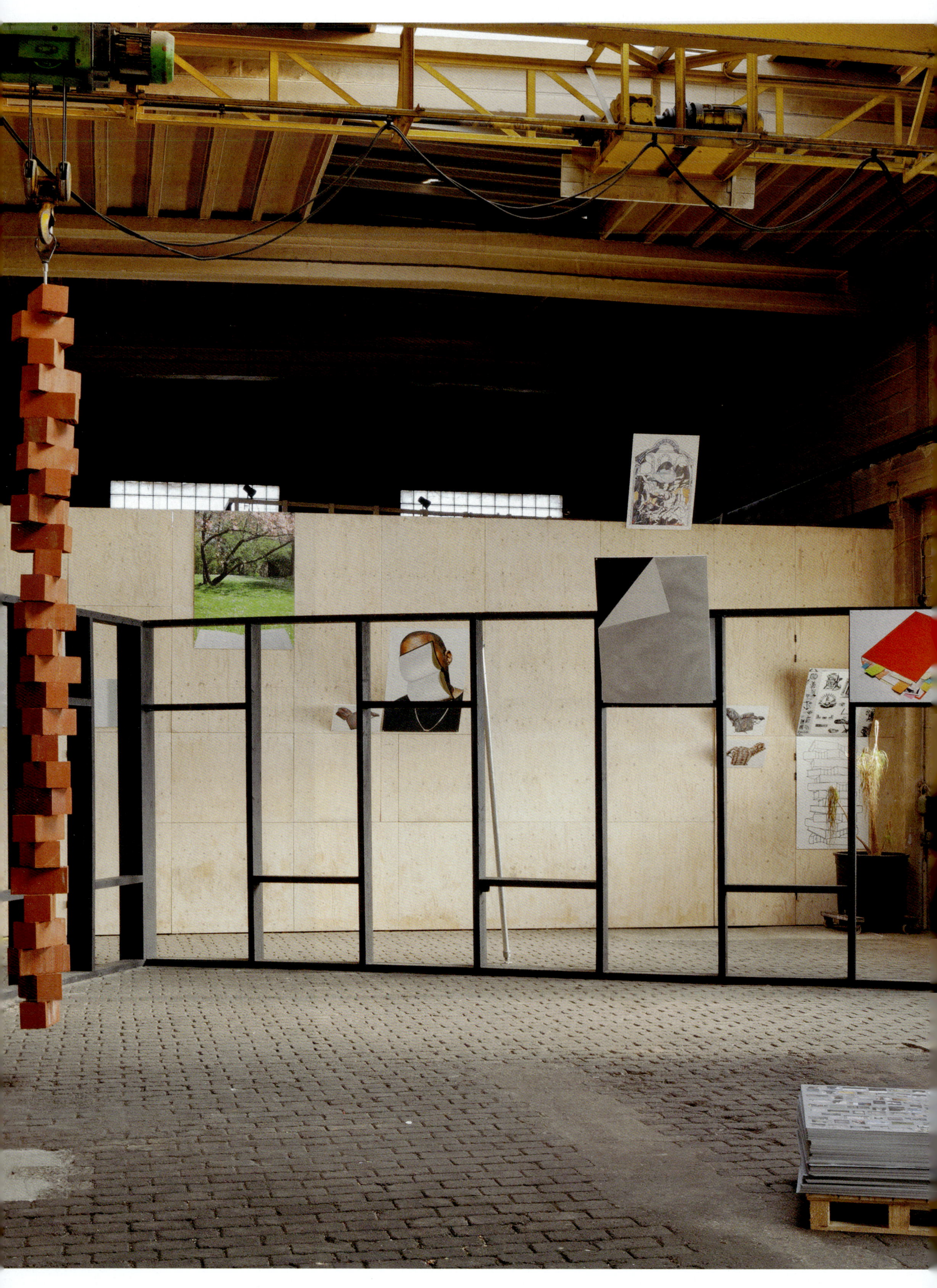

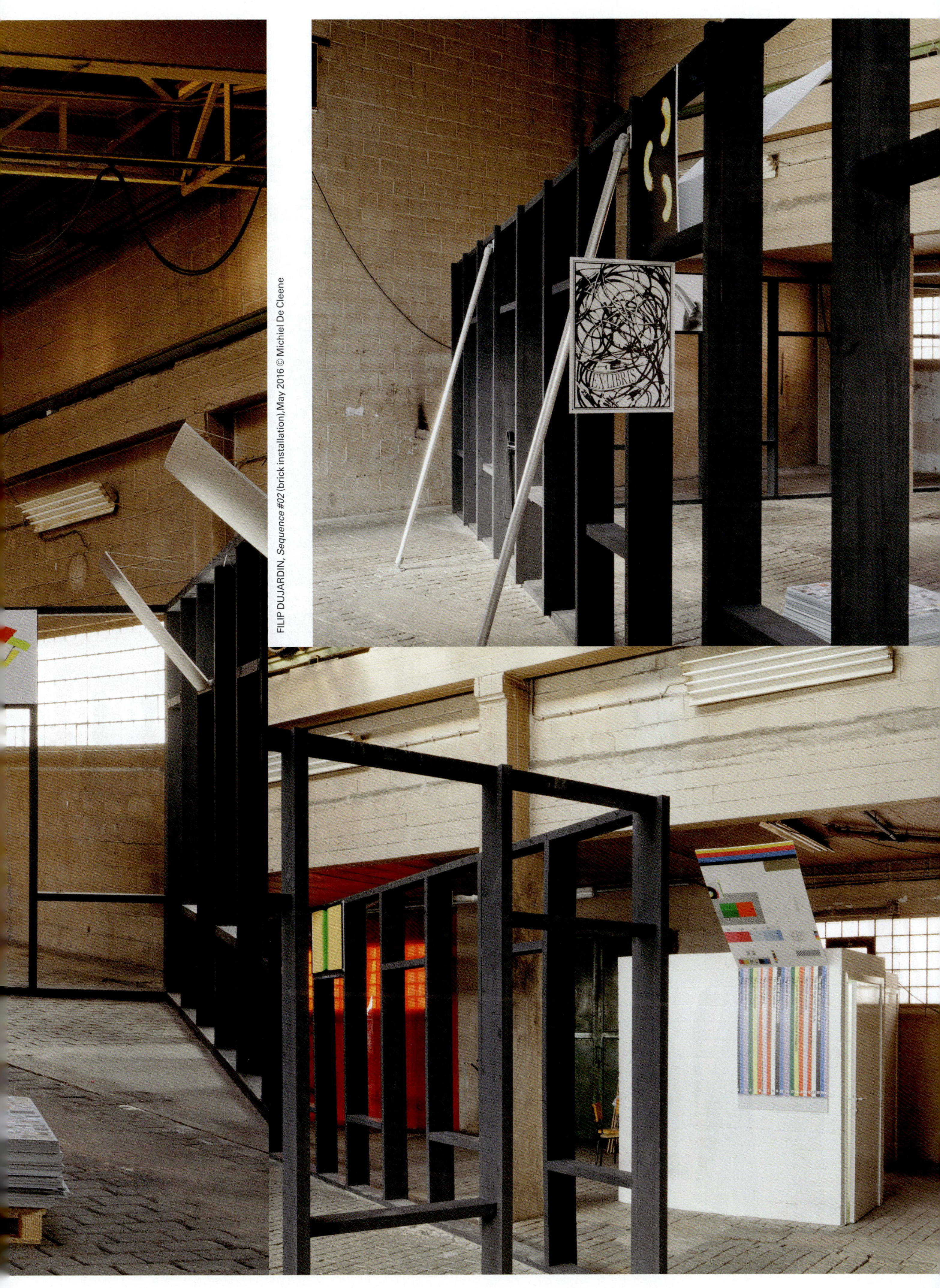

FILIP DUJARDIN, *Sequence #02* (brick installation), May 2016 © Michiel De Cleene

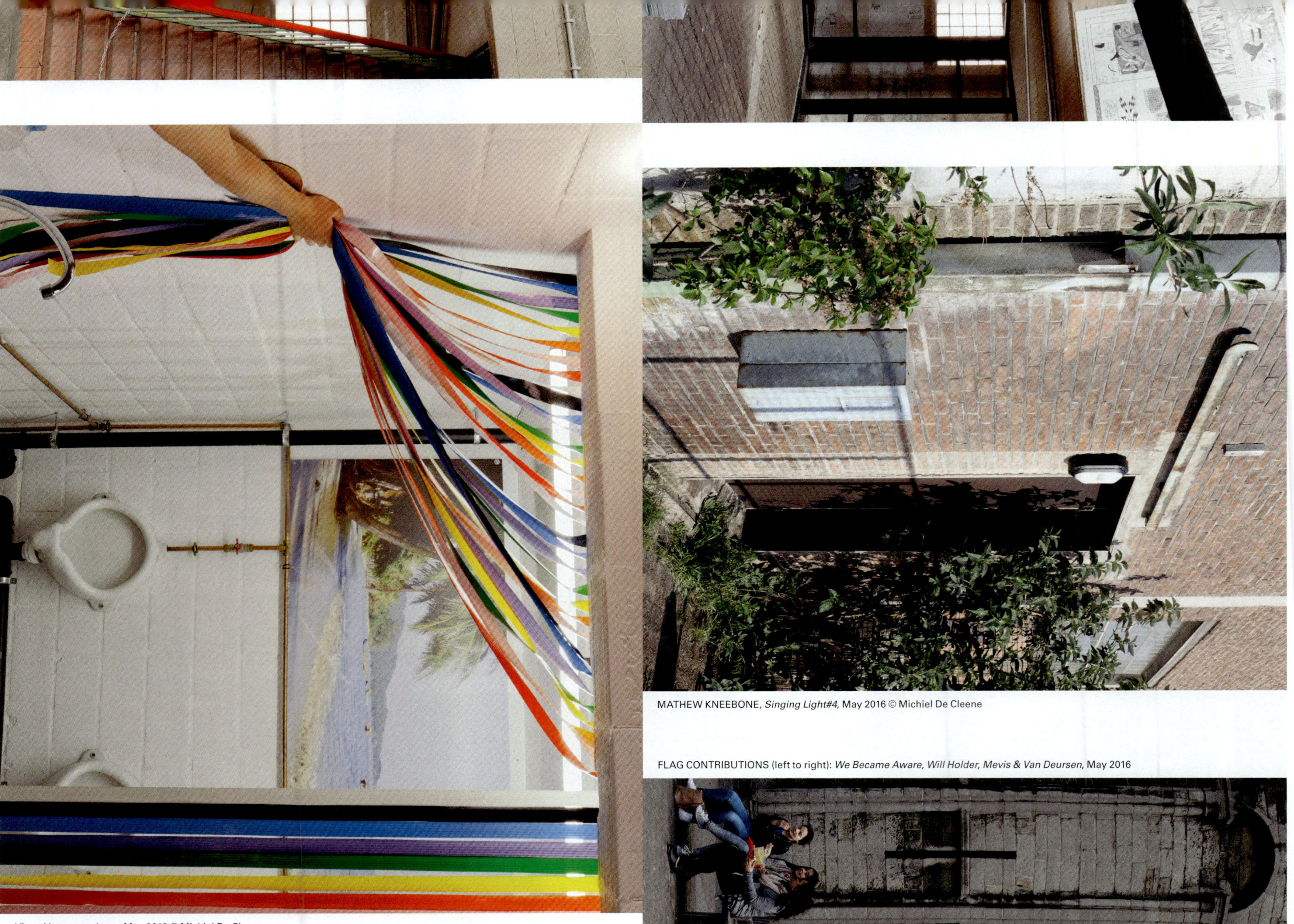

Victor Vanwassenhove, May 2019 © Michiel De Cleene

MATHEW KNEEBONE, *Singing Light#4*, May 2016 © Michiel De Cleene

FLAG CONTRIBUTIONS (left to right): *We Became Aware, Will Holder, Mevis & Van Deursen*, May 2016

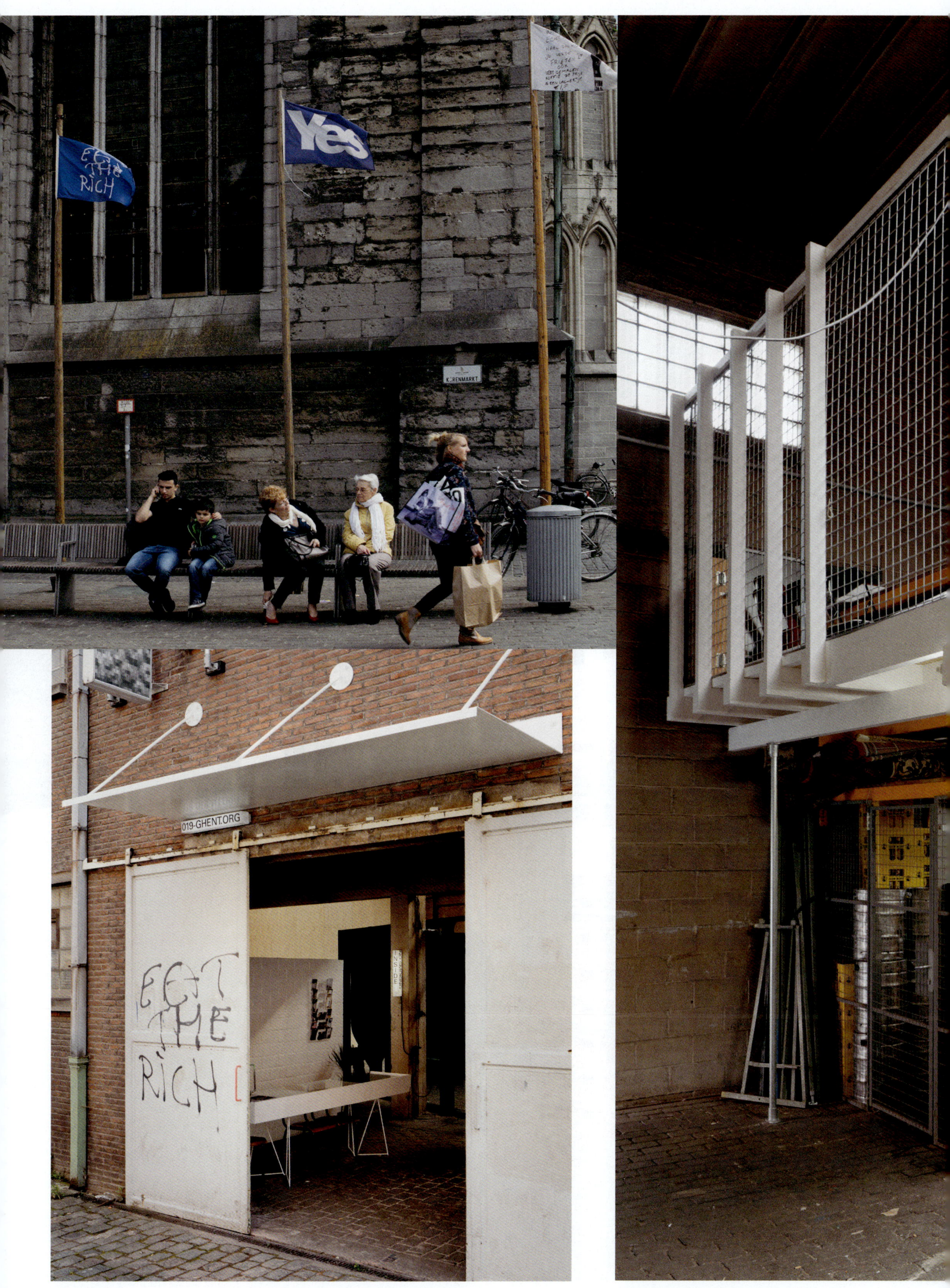
Yes
KORENMARKT
019-GHENT.ORG

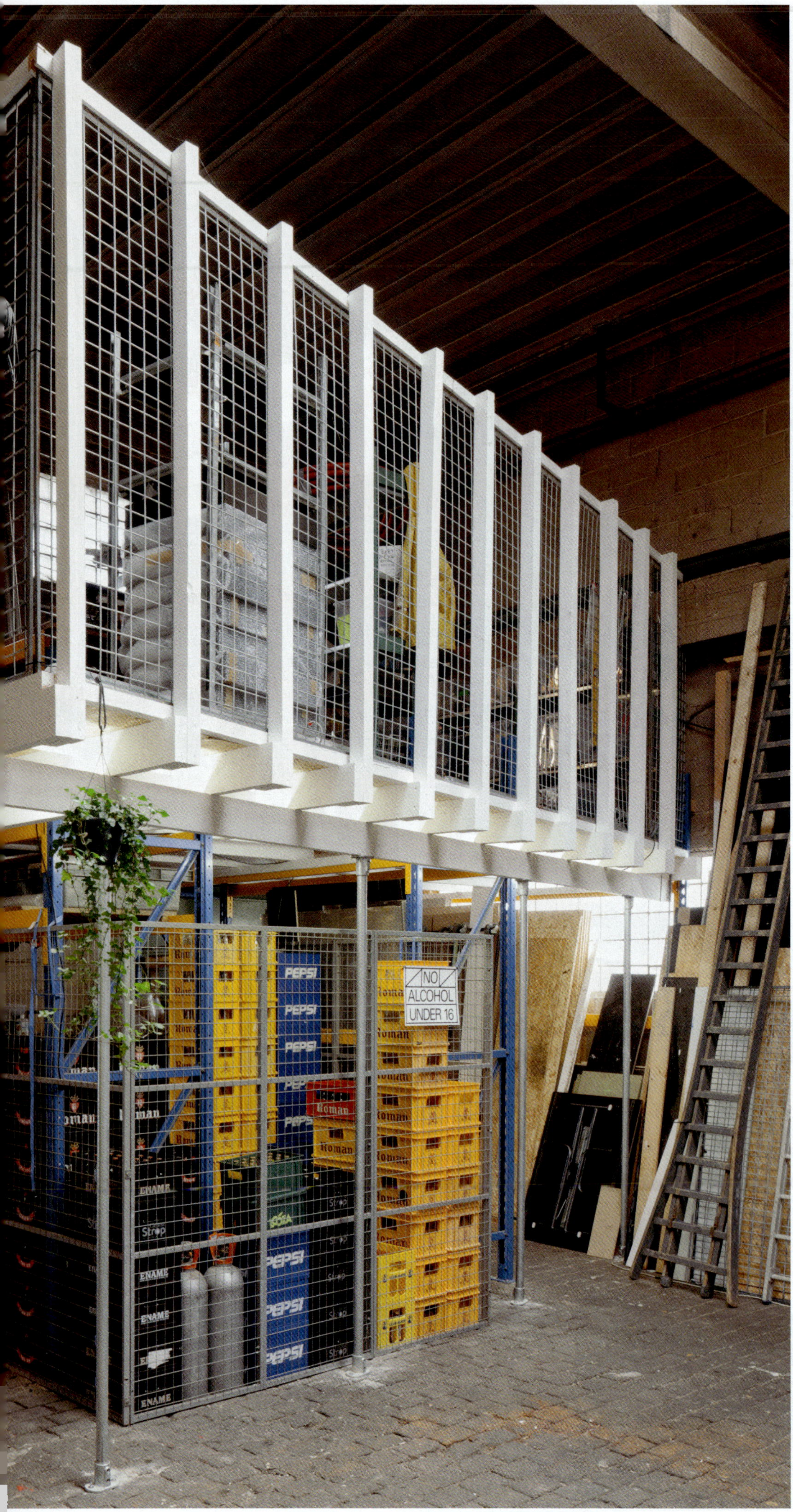

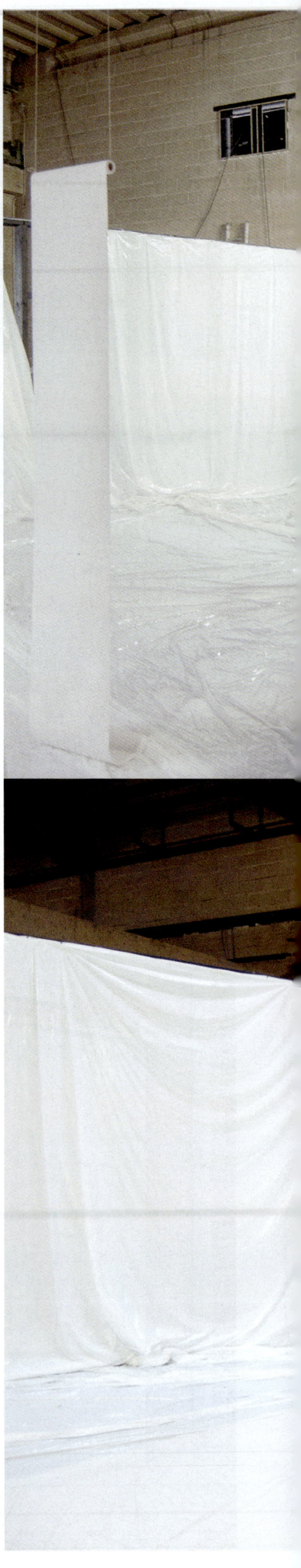

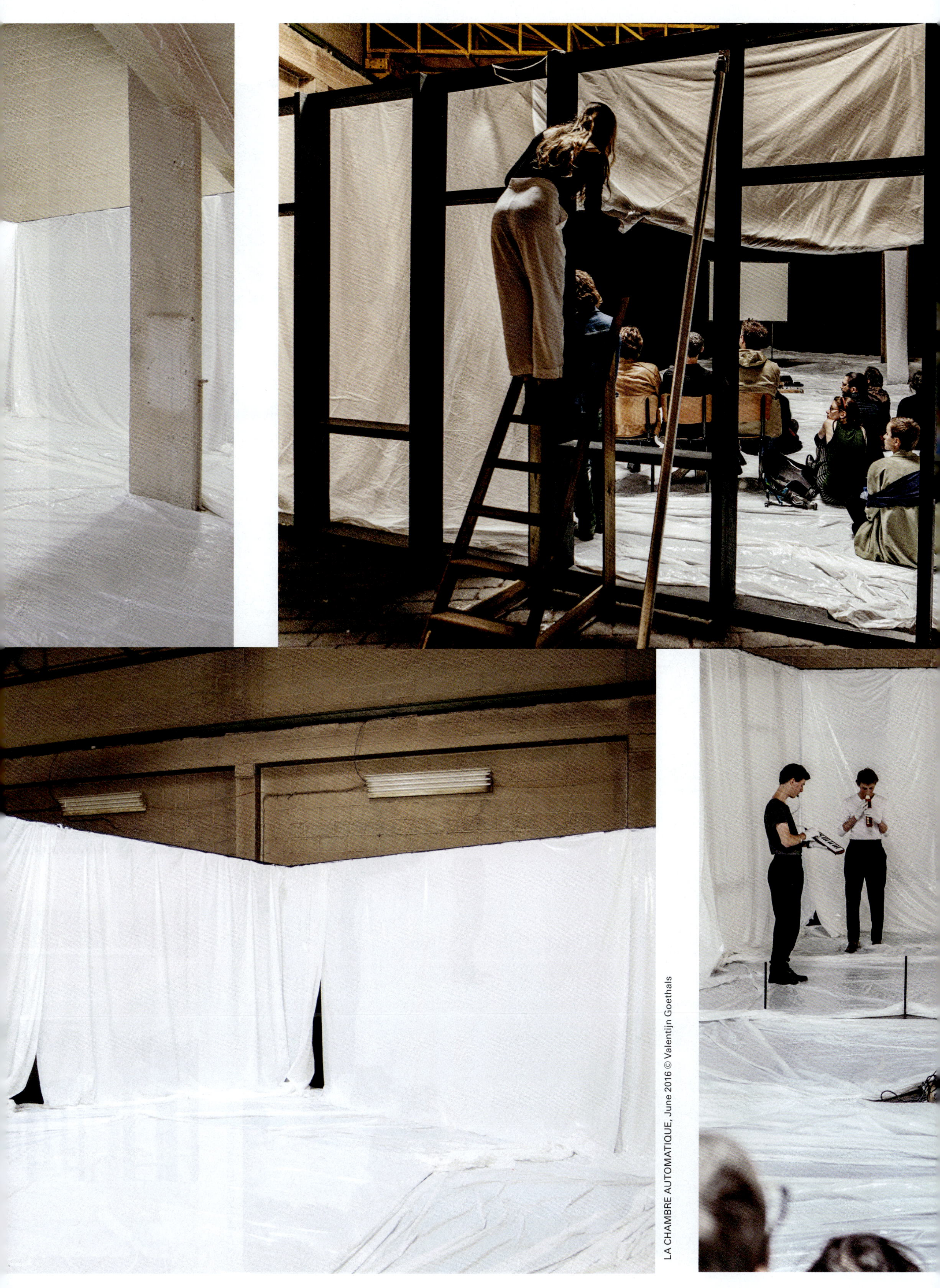

LA CHAMBRE AUTOMATIQUE, June 2016 © Valentijn Goethals

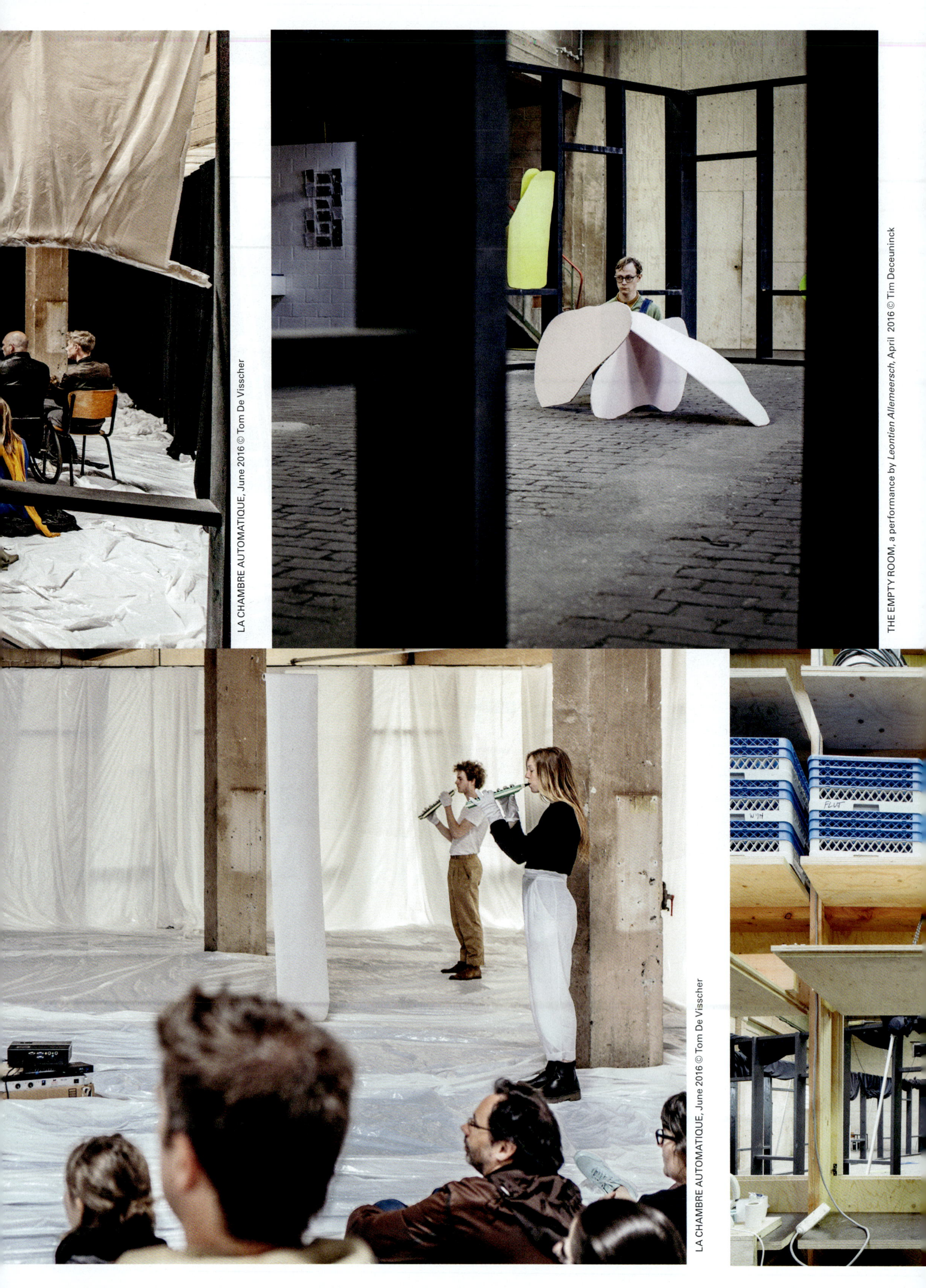

LA CHAMBRE AUTOMATIQUE, June 2016 © Tom De Visscher

THE EMPTY ROOM, a performance by *Leontien Allemeersch*, April 2016 © Tim Deceuninck

LA CHAMBRE AUTOMATIQUE, June 2016 © Tom De Visscher

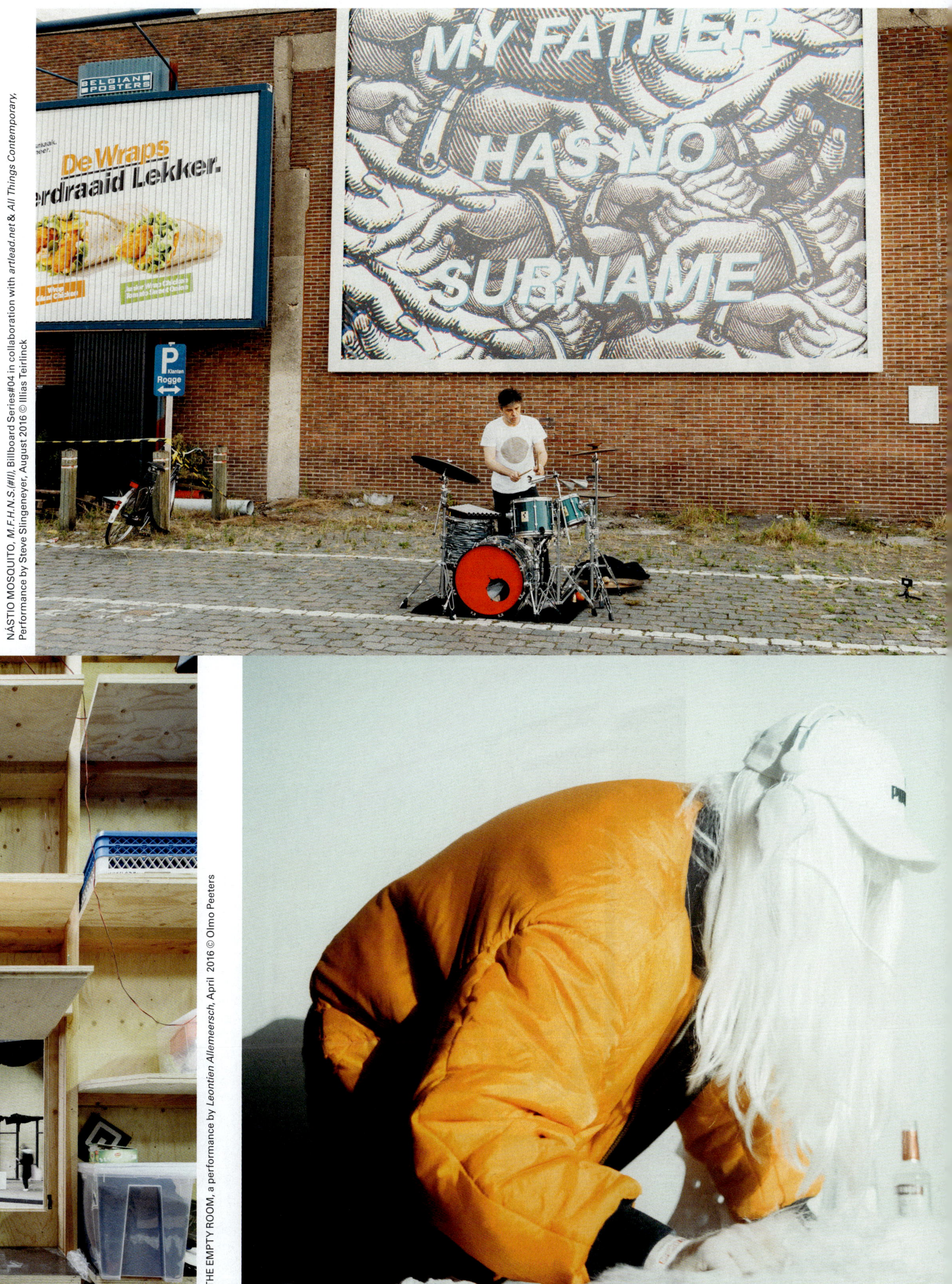

NÁSTIO MOSQUITO, *M.F.H.N.S.(#II)*, Billboard Series#04 in collaboration with *artlead.net* & *All Things Contemporary*, Performance by Steve Slingeneyer, August 2016 © Illias Teirlinck

THE EMPTY ROOM, a performance by *Leontien Allemeersch*, April 2016 © Olmo Peeters

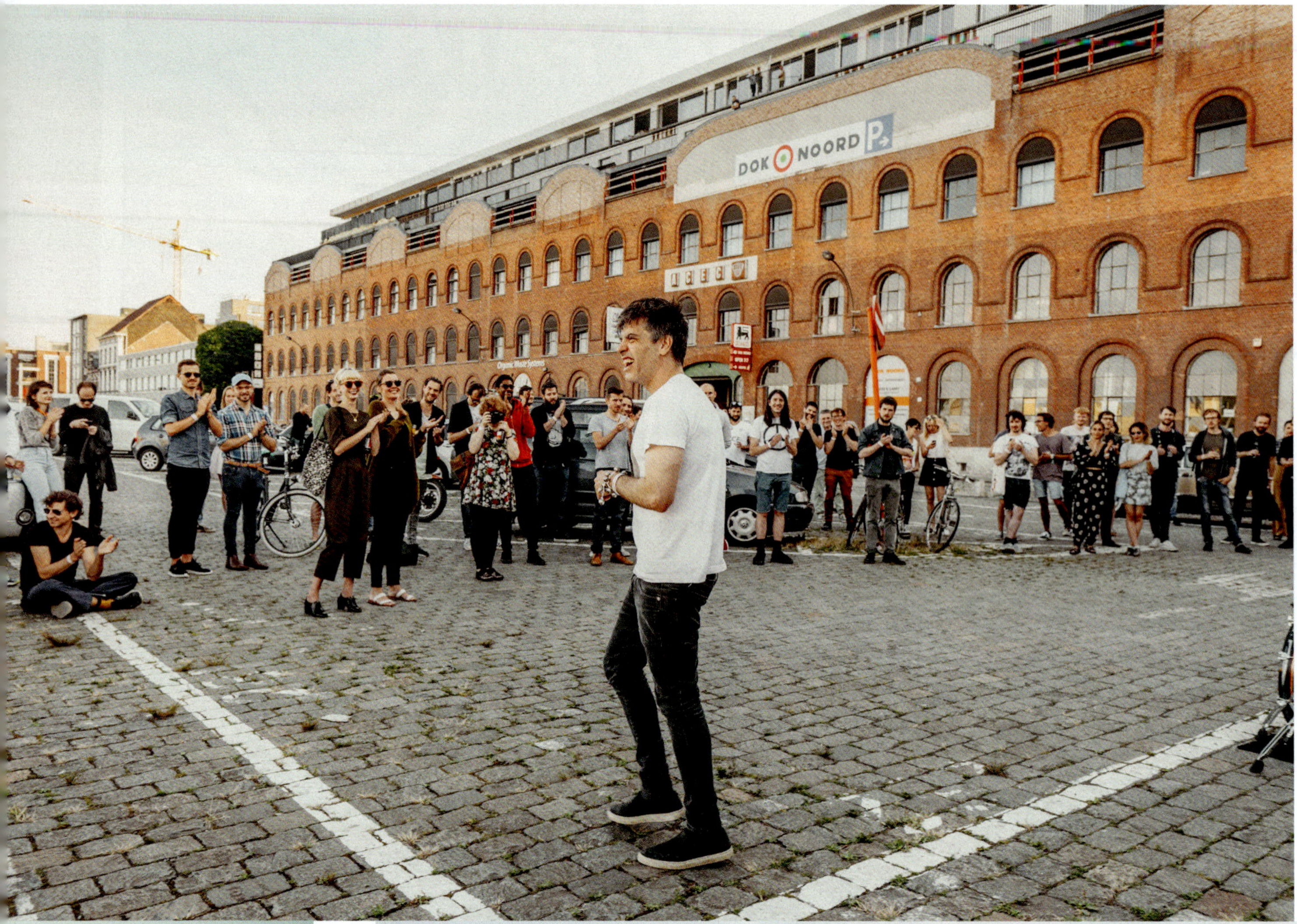

STEVE SLINGENEYER Performance in front of Nástio Mosquito, *M.F.H.N.S.(#II)*, Billboard Series#04 in collaboration with *artlead.net* & *All Things Contemporary*, August 2016 © Illias Teirlinck

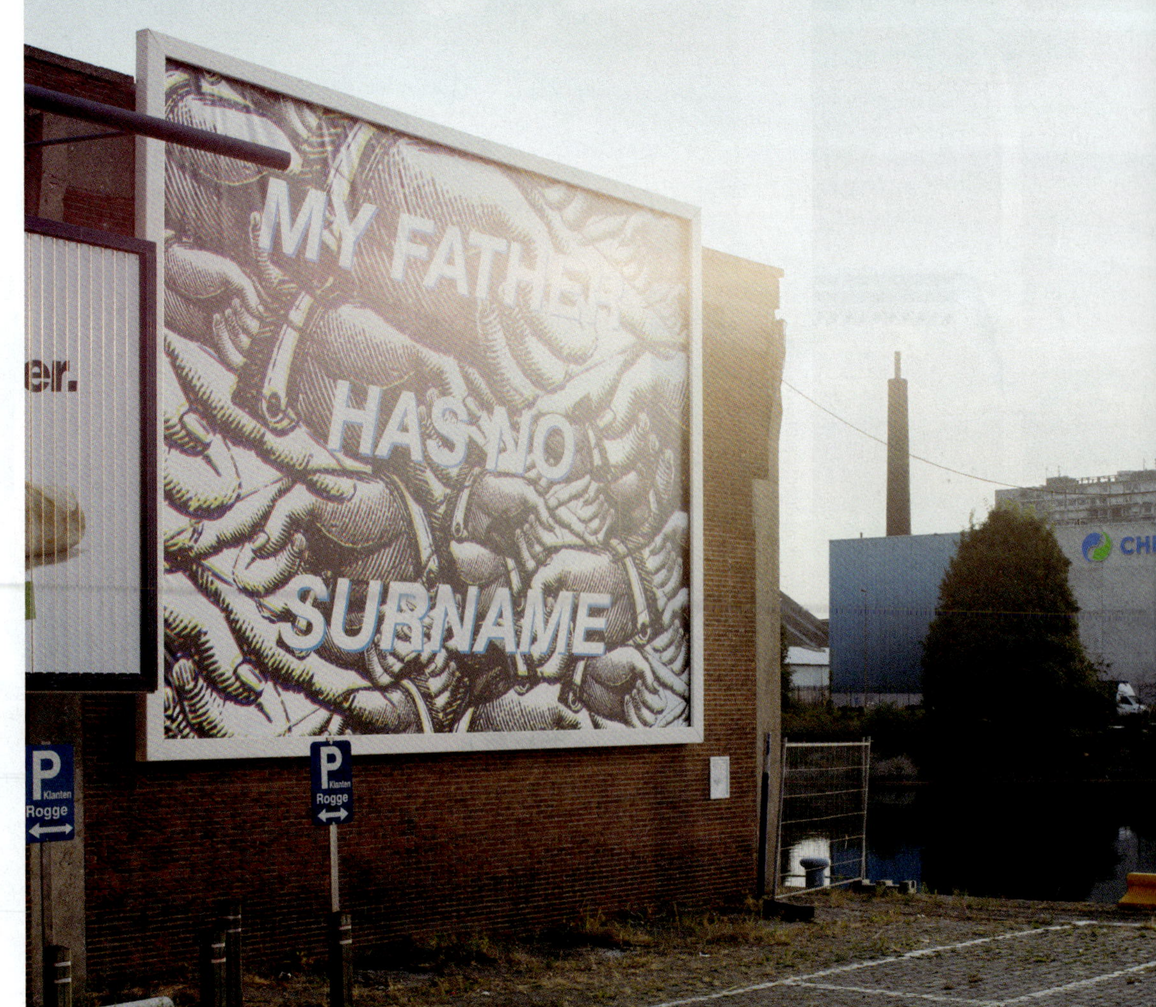

SHENIQUA WORLD TOUR at DIFFERENT CLASS, in collaboration with *Subbacultcha*, August 2016 © Illias Teirlinck

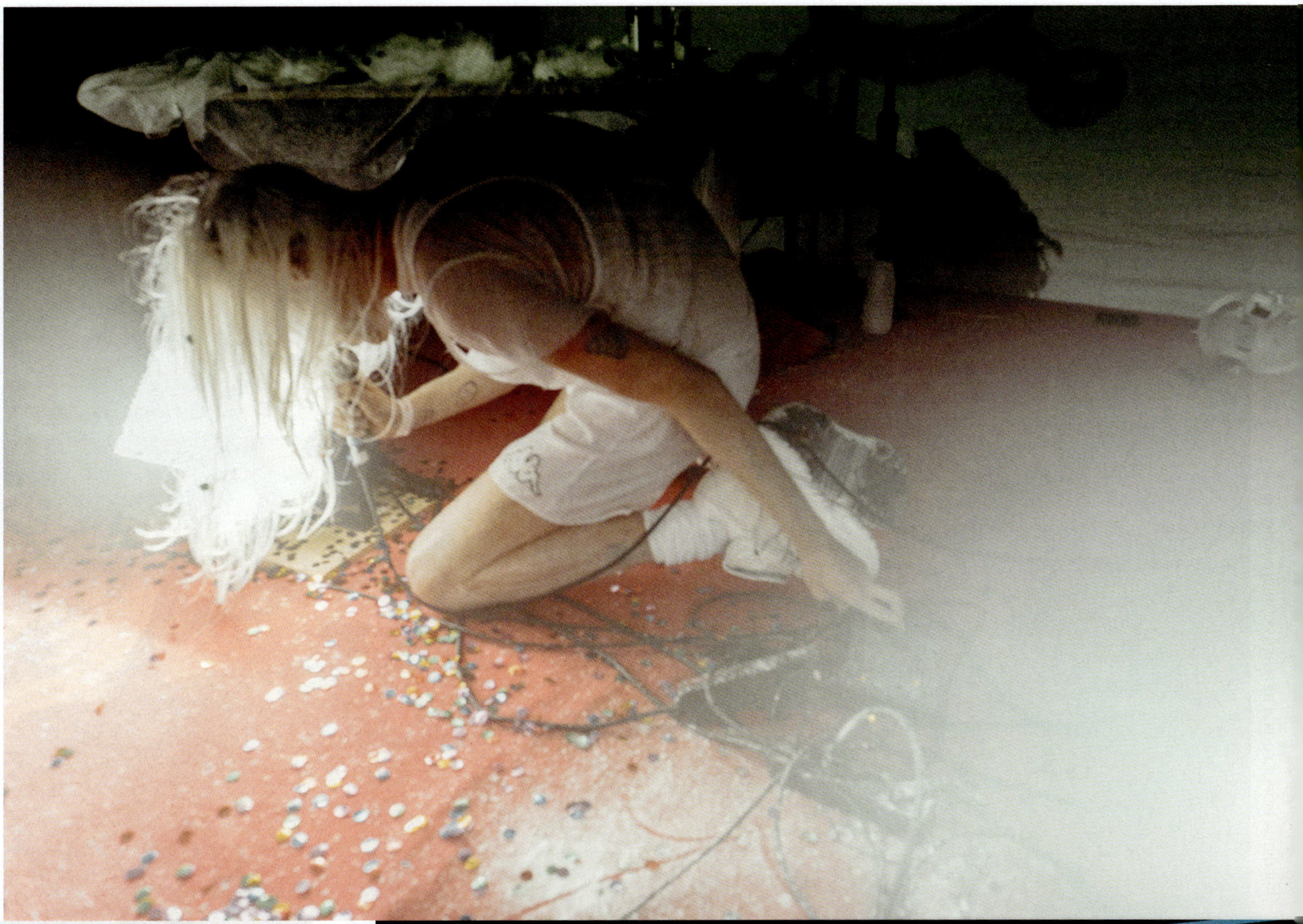

SHENIQUA WORLD TOUR at DIFFERENT CLASS, in collaboration with *Subbacultcha*, August 2016 © Illias Teirlinck

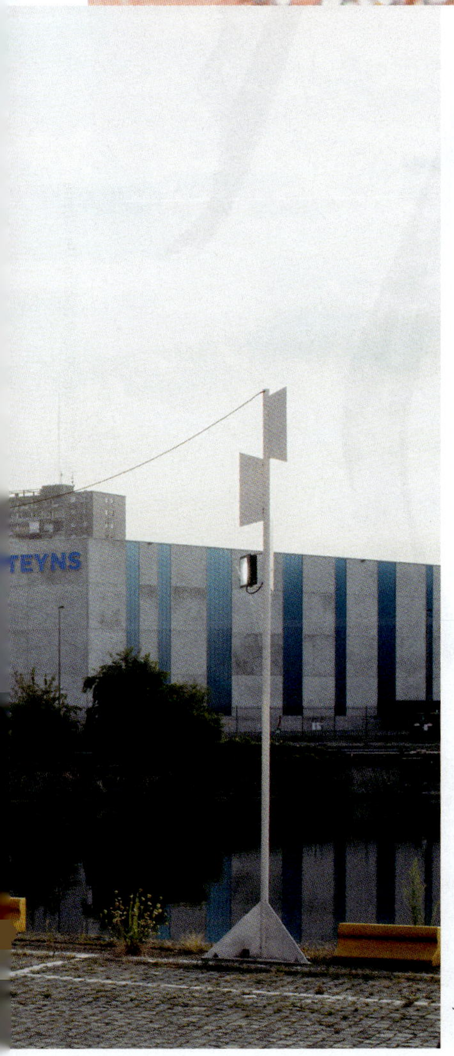

NÁSTIO MOSQUITO, *M.F.H.N.S.(#II)*, Billboard Series#04 in collaboration with *artlead.net* & *All Things Contemporary* © Michiel De Cleene

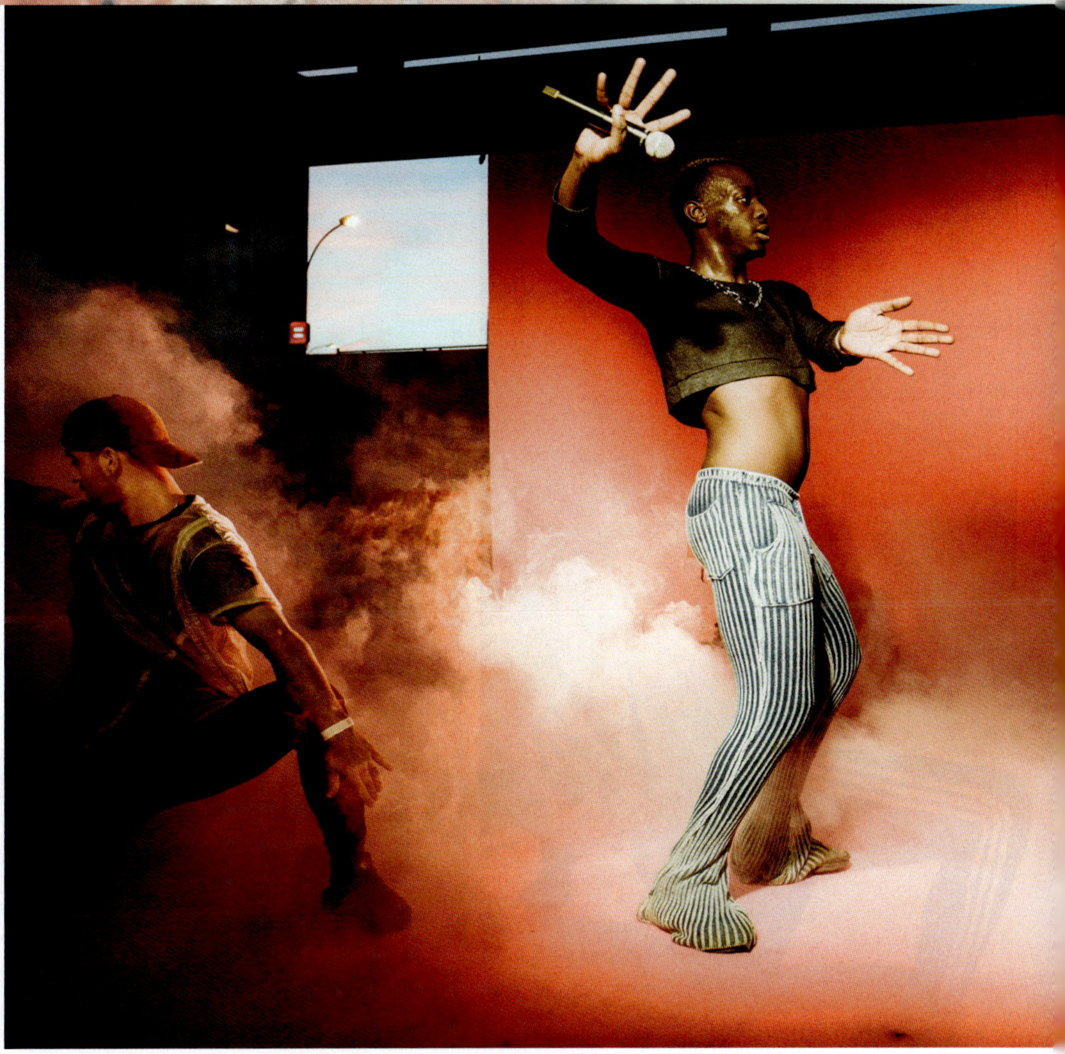

LE1F at DIFFERENT CLASS, in collaboration with *Subbacultcha*, August 2016 © Illias Teirlinck

WE BECAME AWARE, *We Know, They Don't, But They'll Soon Find Out*, S&D#025, July 2016 © Michiel De Cleene

SHENIQUA WORLD TOUR at DIFFERENT CLASS, in collaboration with *Subbacultcha*, August 2016 © Illias Teirlinck

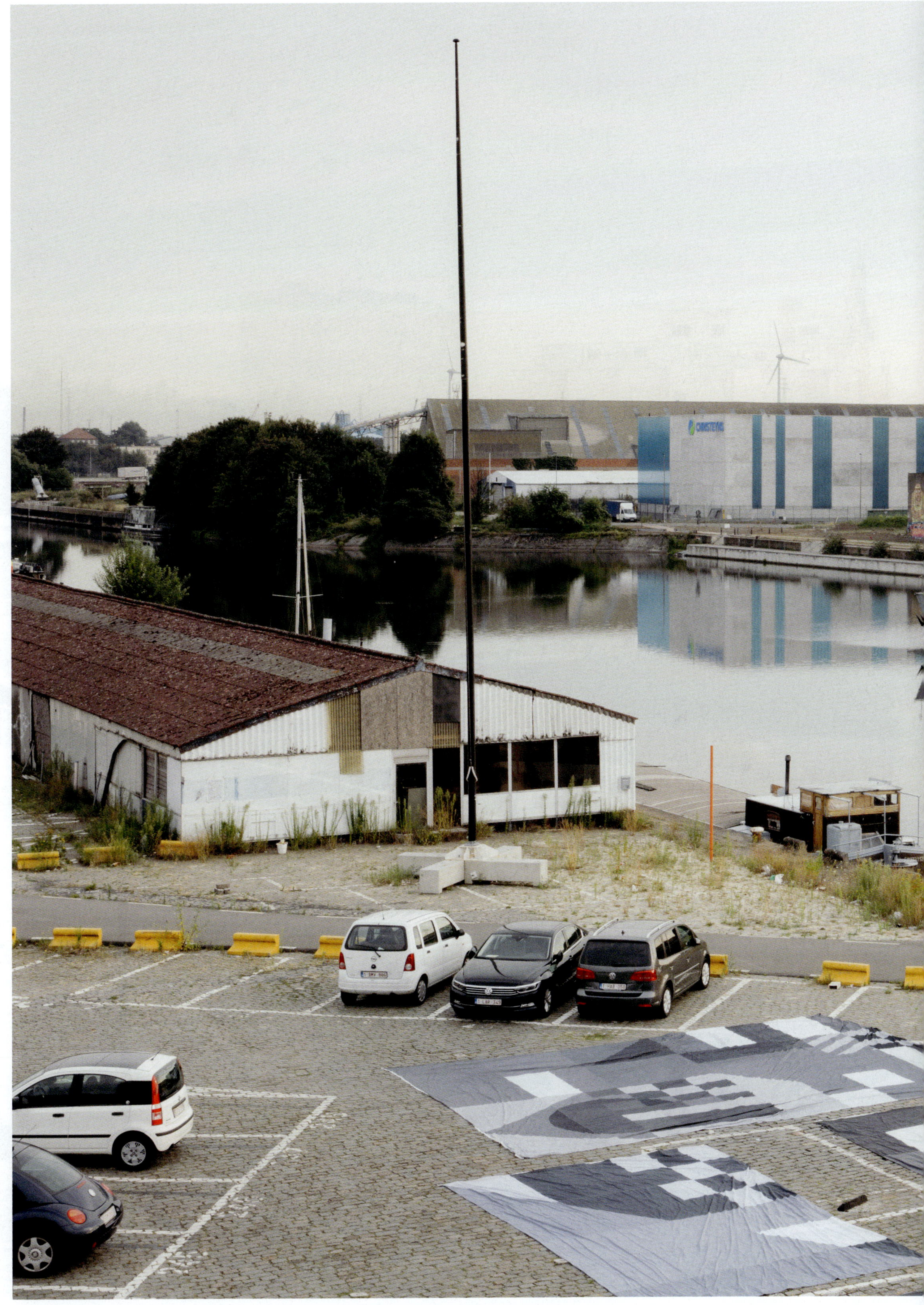

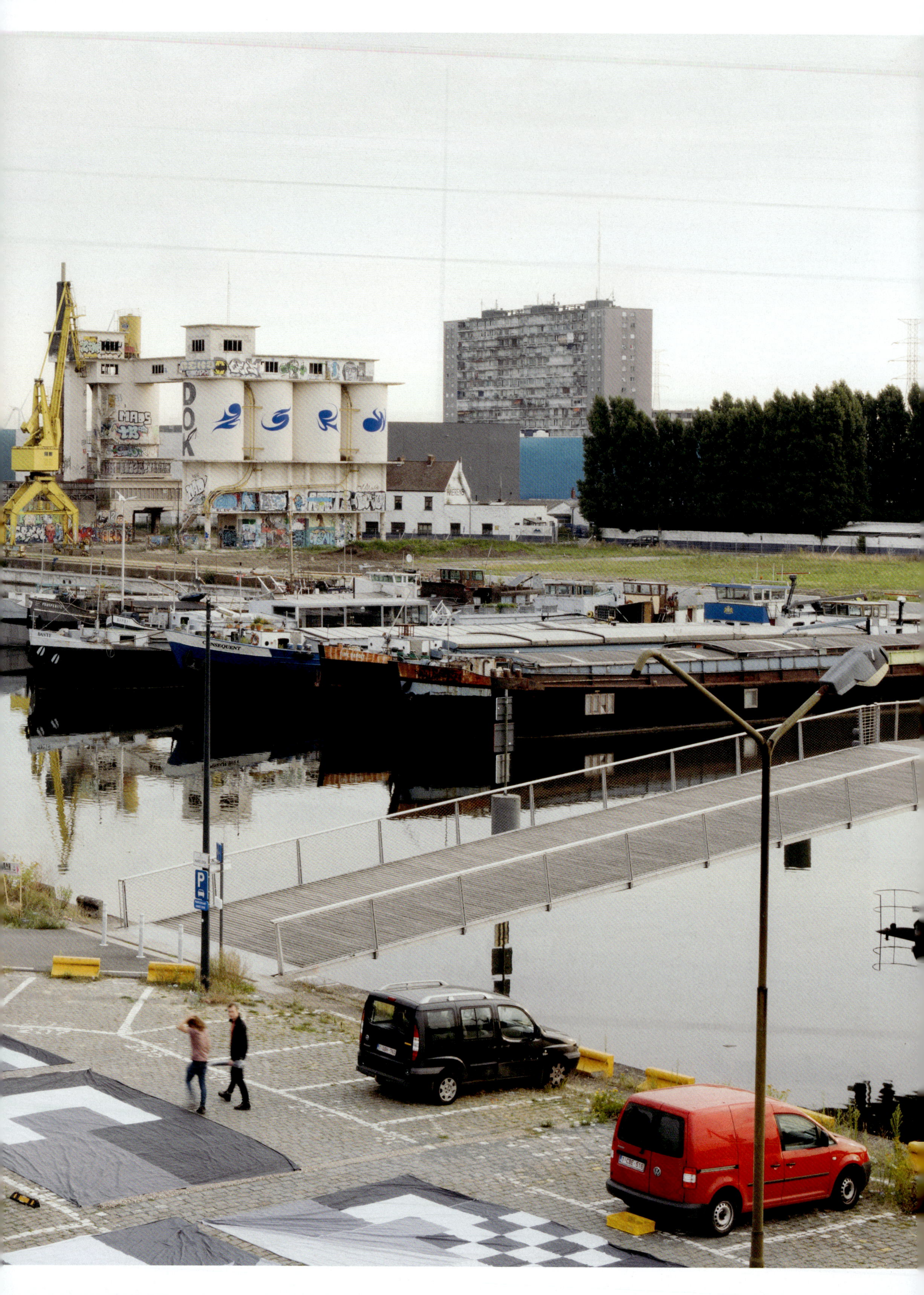
DOK

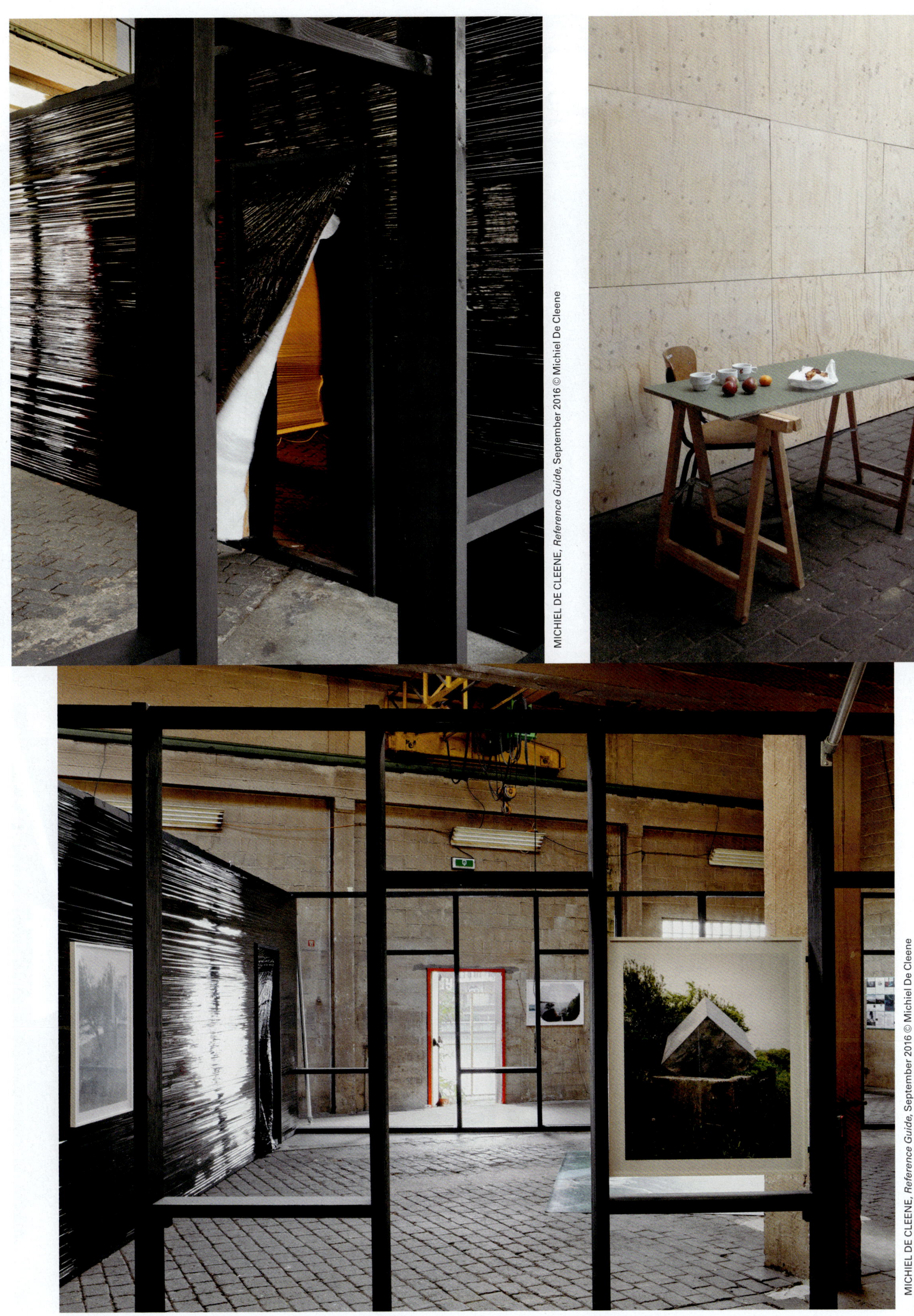
MICHIEL DE CLEENE, *Reference Guide*, September 2016 © Michiel De Cleene

MICHIEL DE CLEENE, *Reference Guide*, September 2016 © Michiel De Cleene

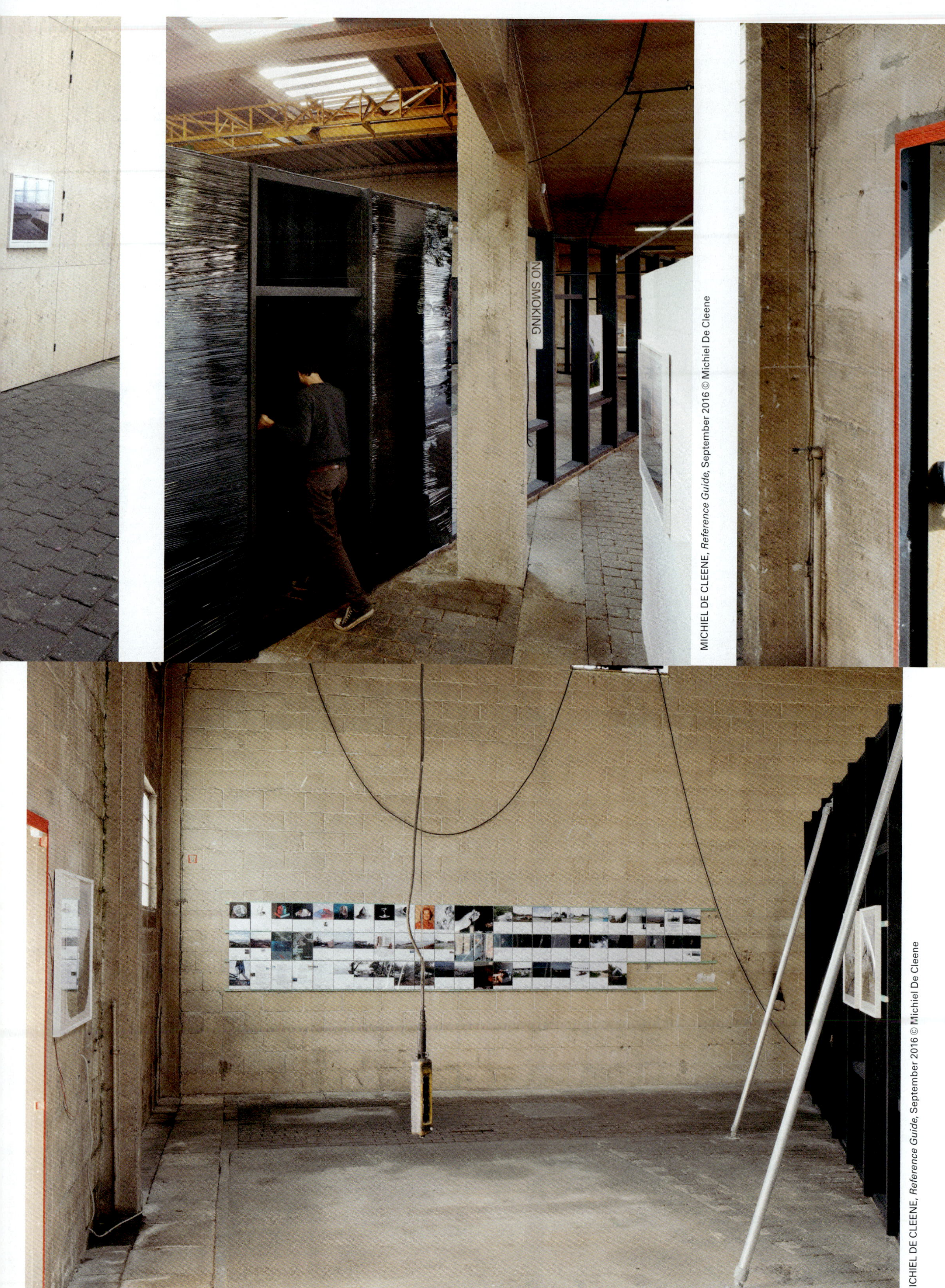

MICHIEL DE CLEENE, *Reference Guide*, September 2016 © Michiel De Cleene

MICHIEL DE CLEENE, *Reference Guide*, September 2016 © Michiel De Cleene

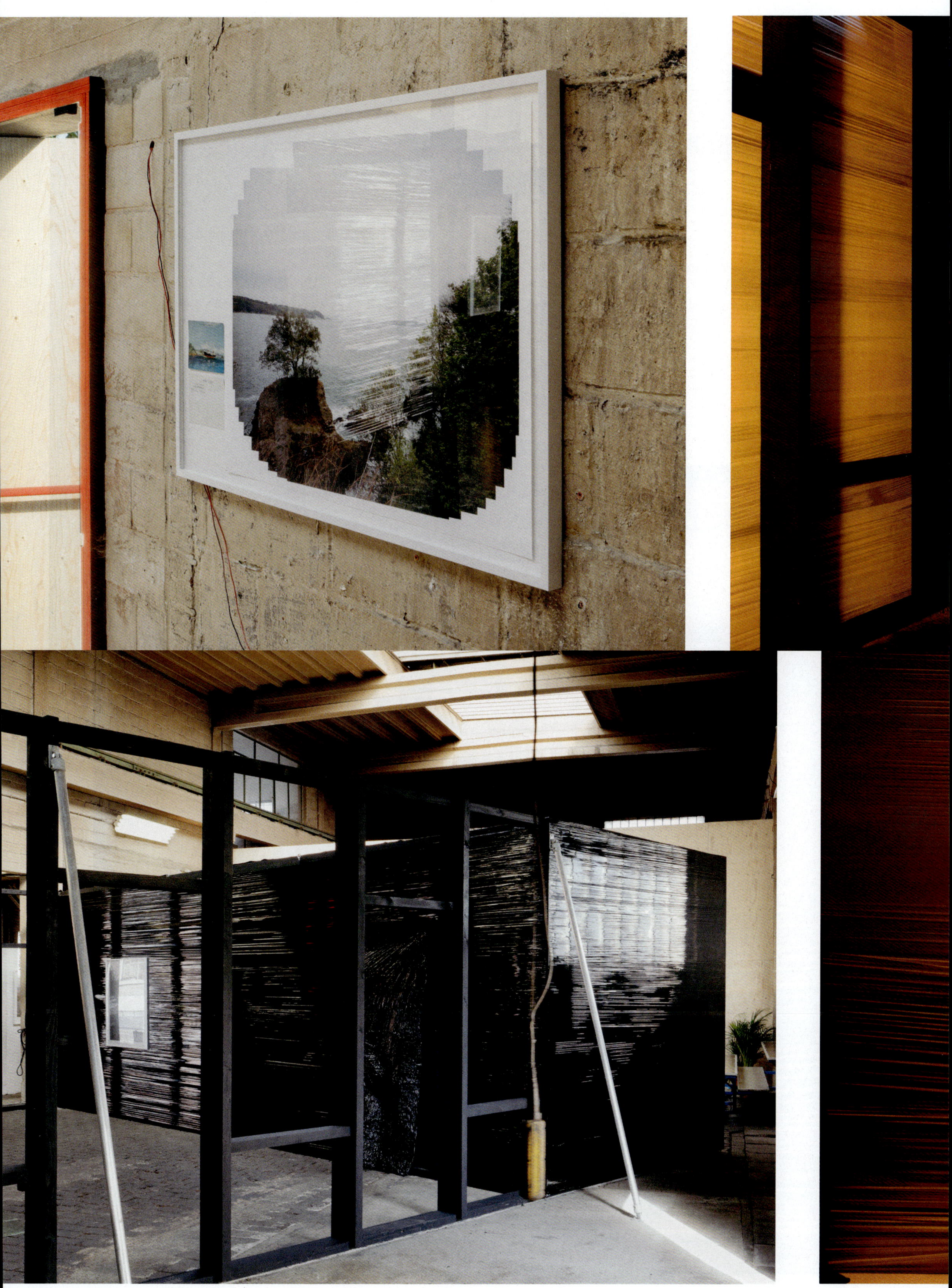

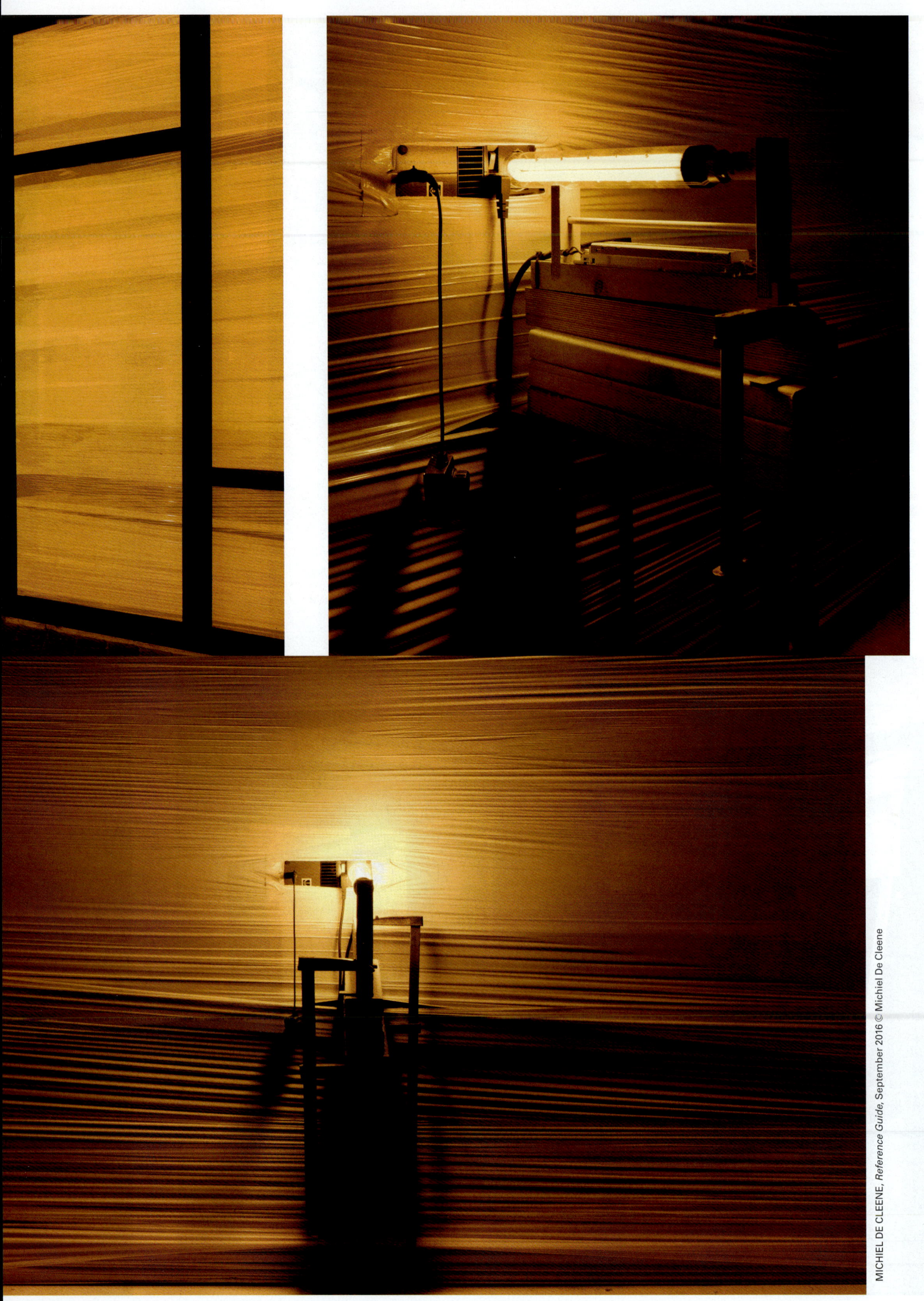

MICHIEL DE CLEENE, *Reference Guide*, September 2016 © Michiel De Cleene

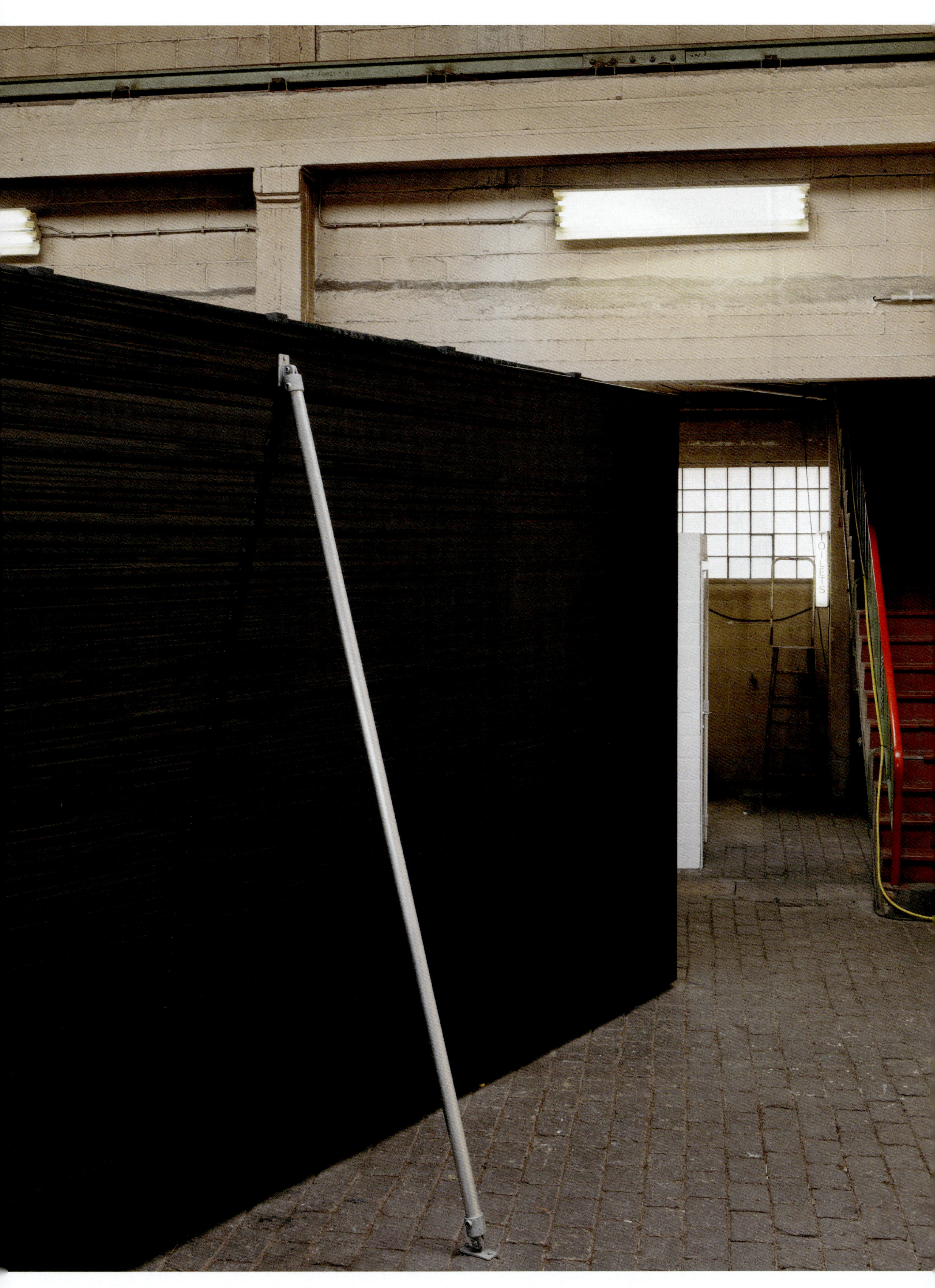
TOILETS

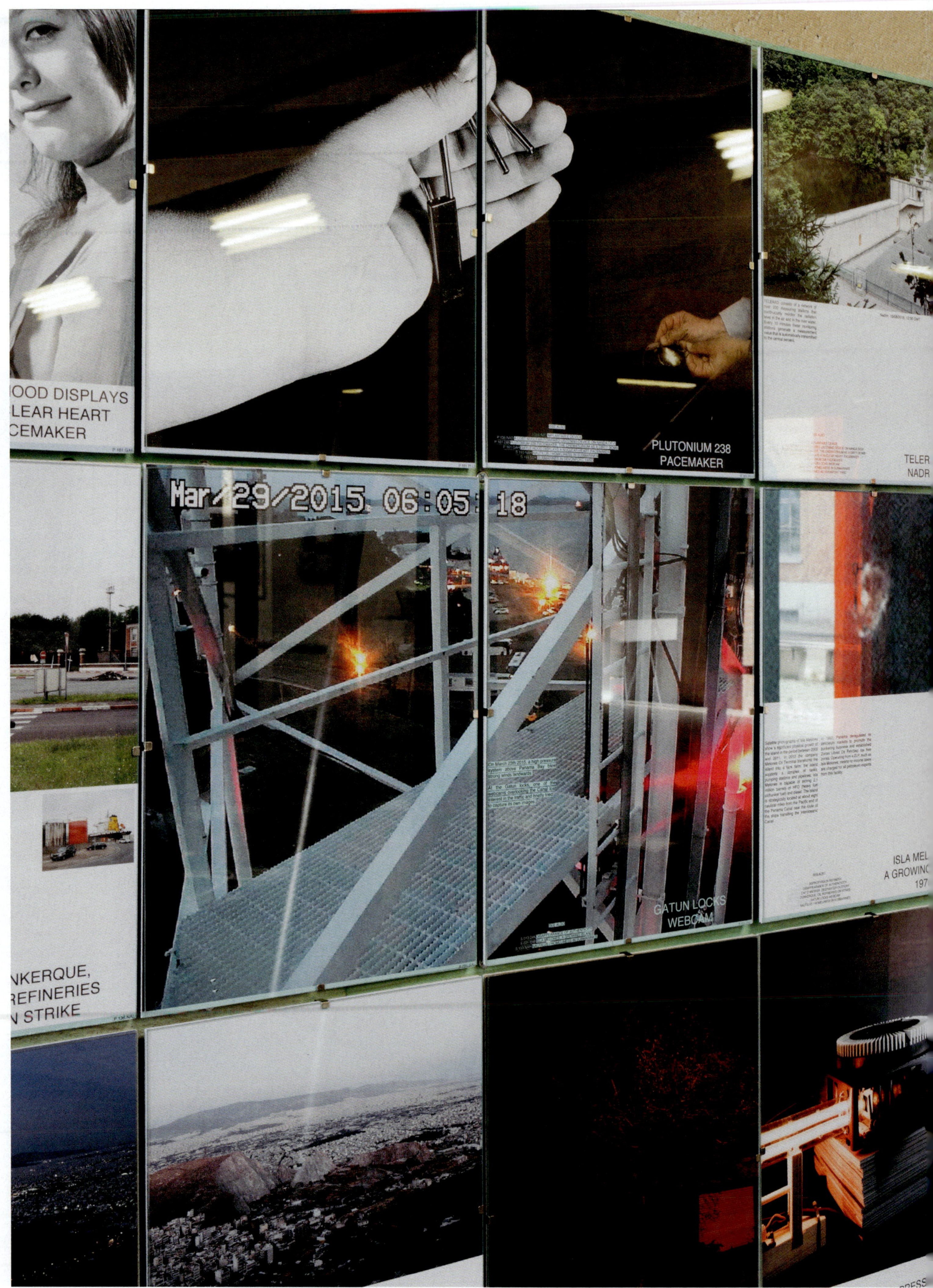

OOD DISPLAYS
LEAR HEART
CEMAKER
PLUTONIUM 238
PACEMAKER
TELER
NADR
Mar/29/2015 06:05:18
GATUN LOCKS
WEBCAM
ISLA MEL
A GROWING
197
NKERQUE,
REFINERIES
N STRIKE

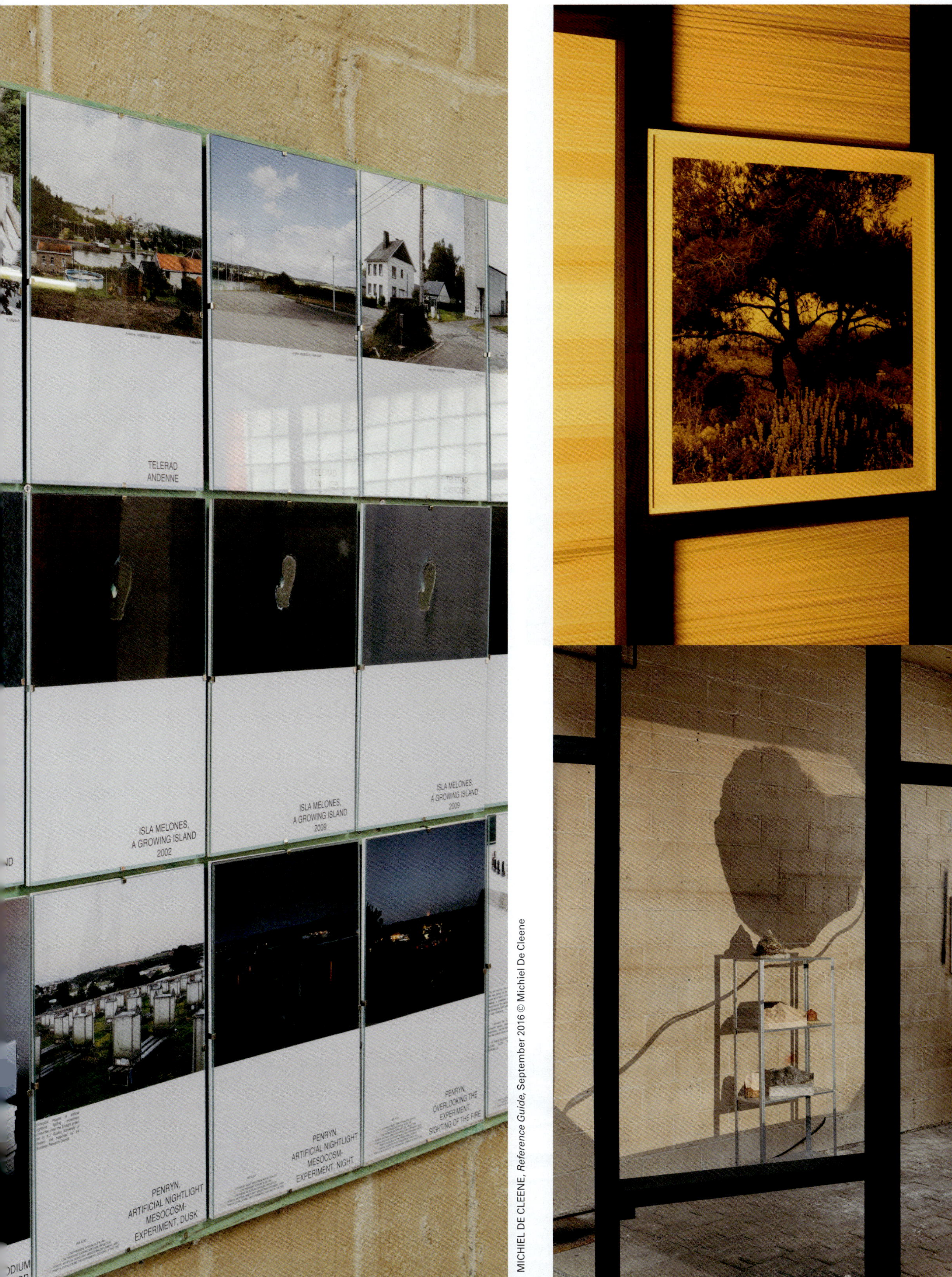

MICHIEL DE CLEENE, *Reference Guide*, September 2016 © Michiel De Cleene

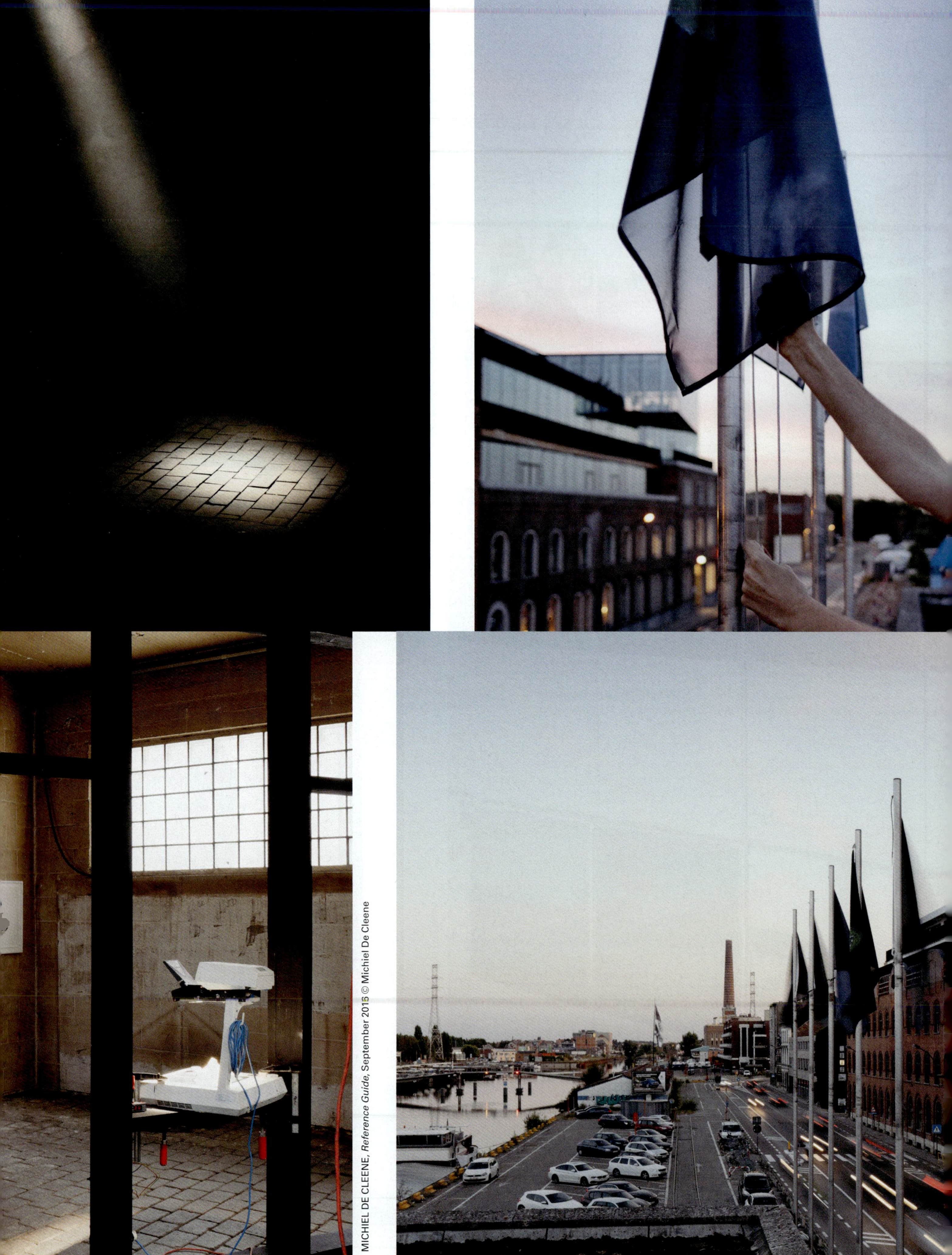

MICHIEL DE CLEENE, *Reference Guide*, September 2015 © Michiel De Cleene

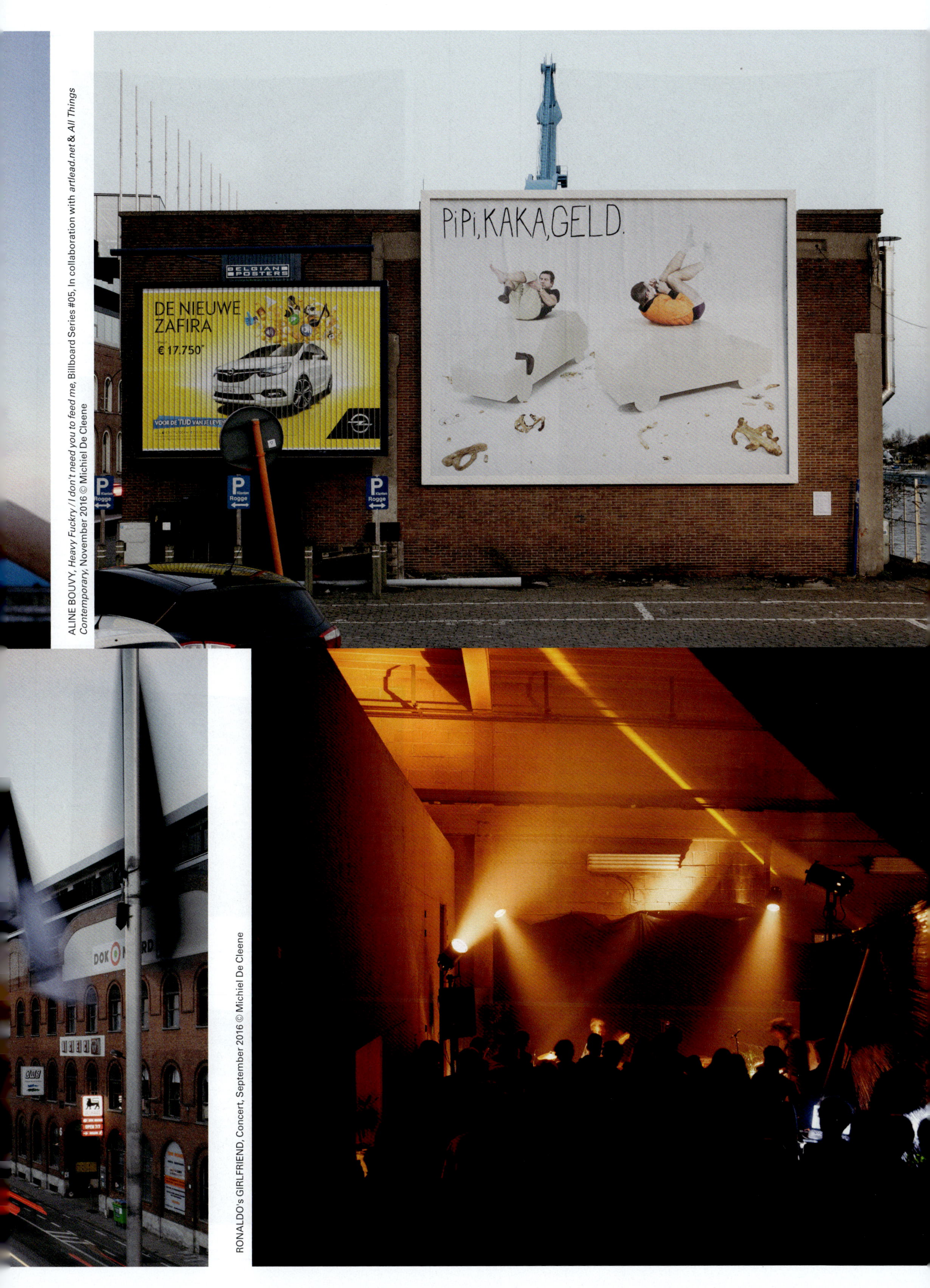

ALINE BOUVY, *Heavy Fuckry / I don't need you to feed me*, Billboard Series #05, In collaboration with *artlead.net* & *All Things Contemporary*, November 2016 © Michiel De Cleene

RONALDO's GIRLFRIEND, Concert, September 2016 © Michiel De Cleene

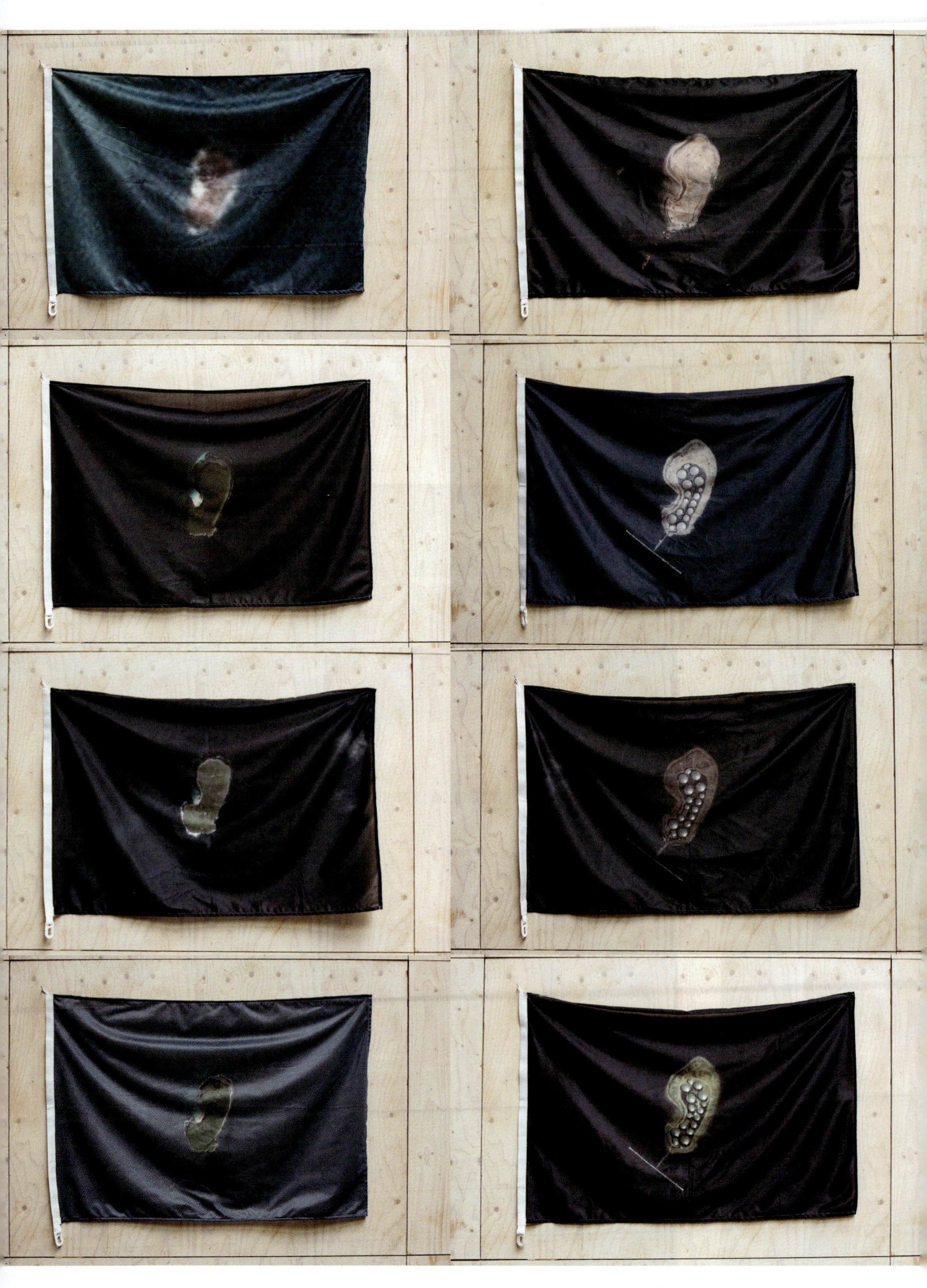

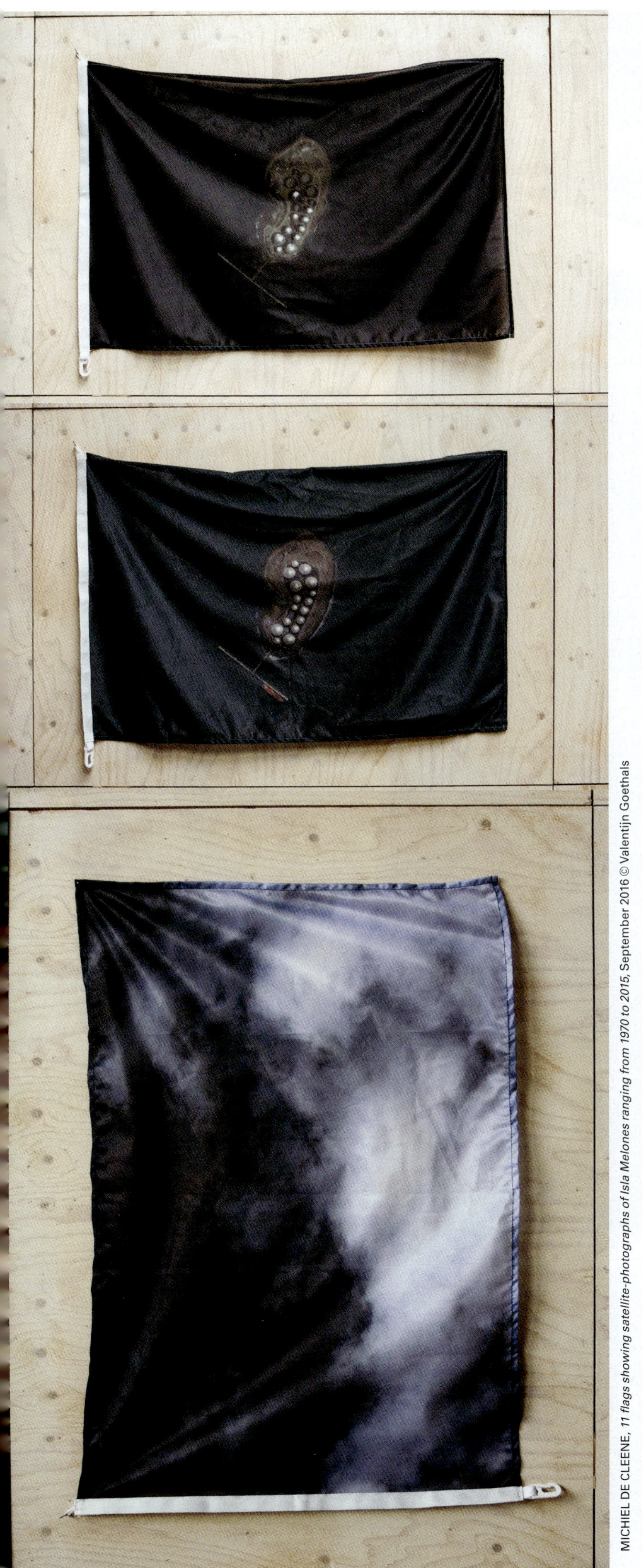

MICHIEL DE CLEENE, *11 flags showing satellite-photographs of Isla Melones ranging from 1970 to 2015*, September 2016 © Valentijn Goethals

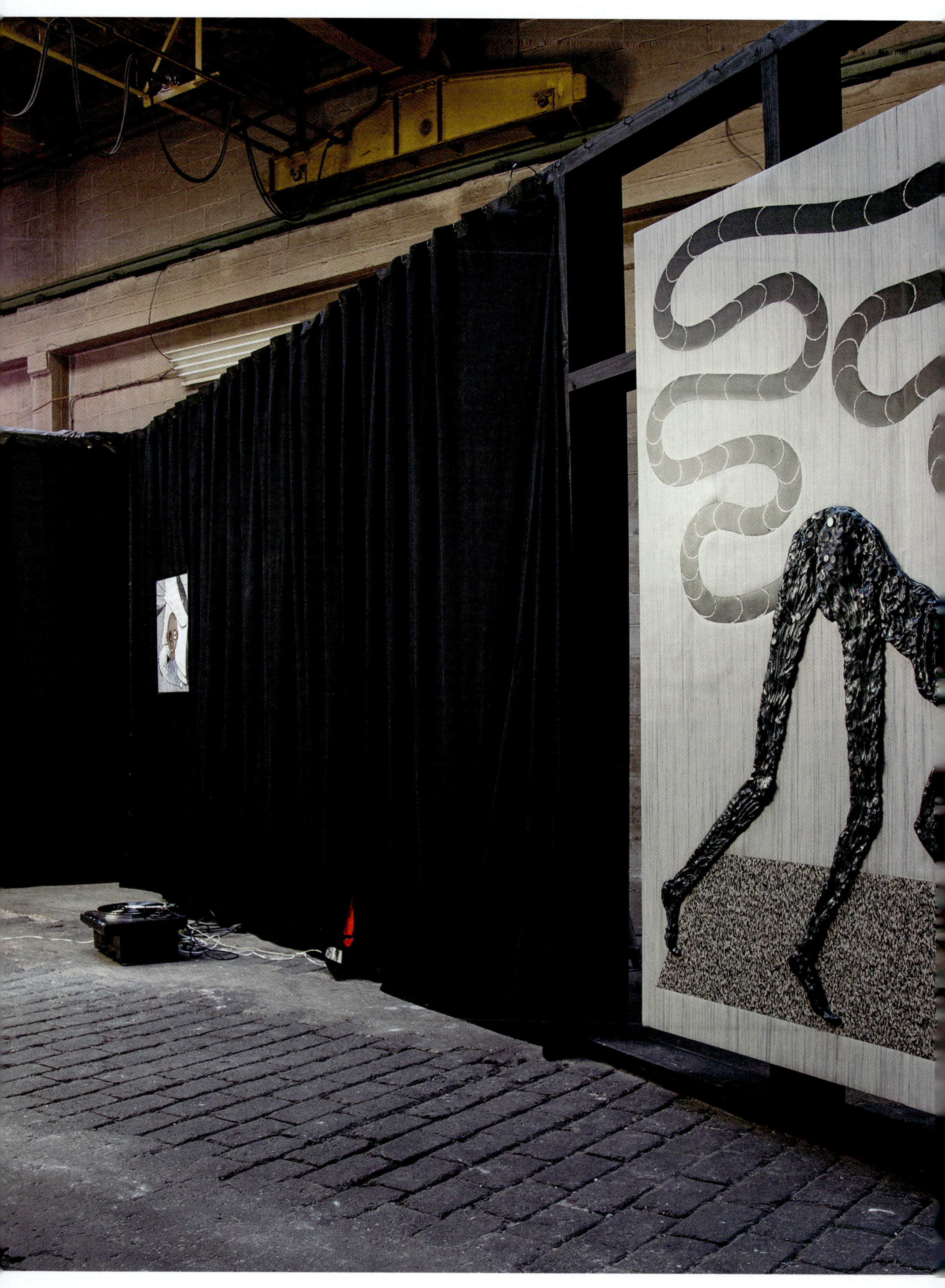

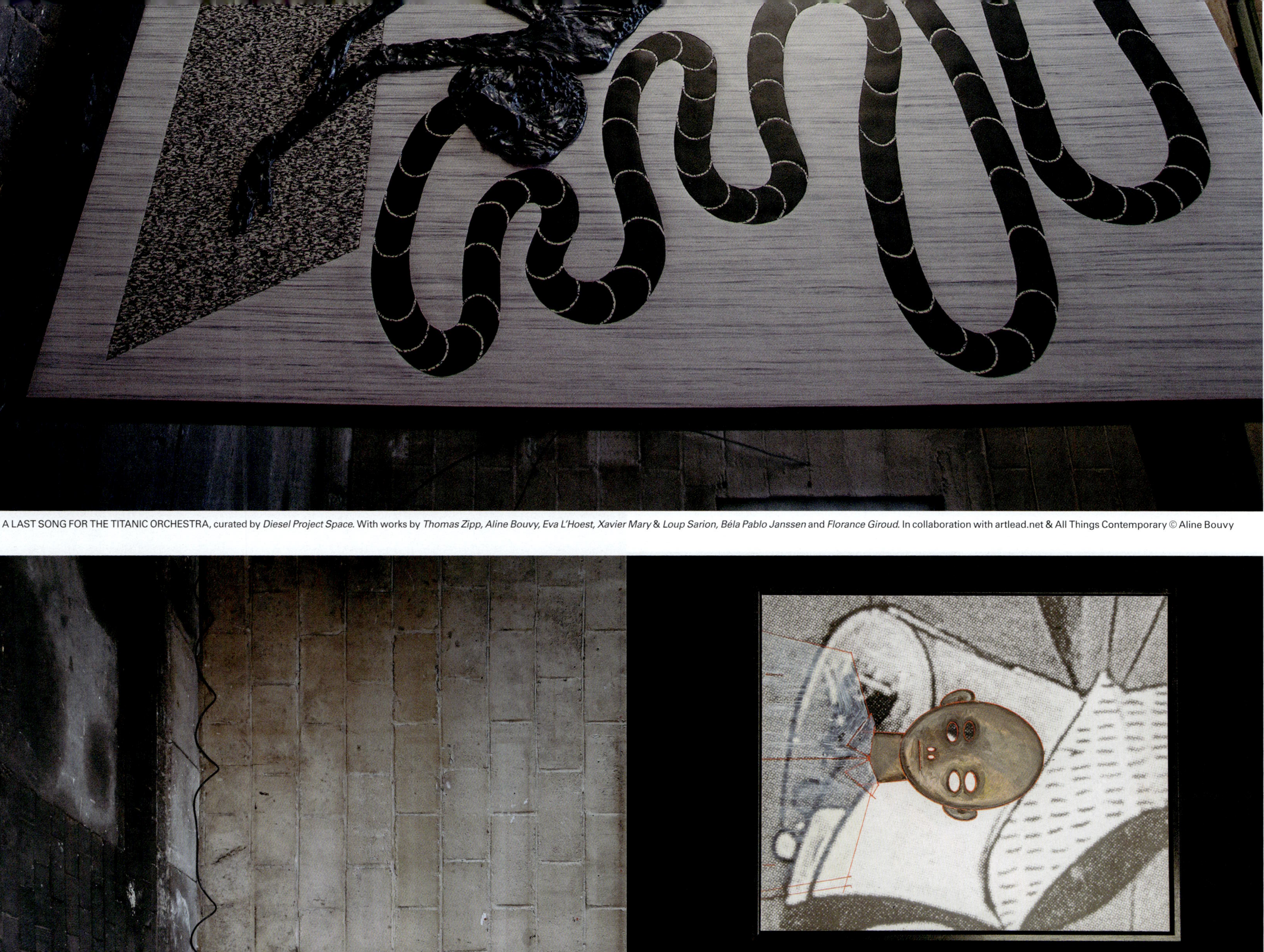

A LAST SONG FOR THE TITANIC ORCHESTRA, curated by *Diesel Project Space*. With works by *Thomas Zipp, Aline Bouvy, Eva L'Hoest, Xavier Mary* & *Loup Sarion, Béla Pablo Janssen* and *Florance Giroud*. In collaboration with artlead.net & All Things Contemporary © Aline Bouvy

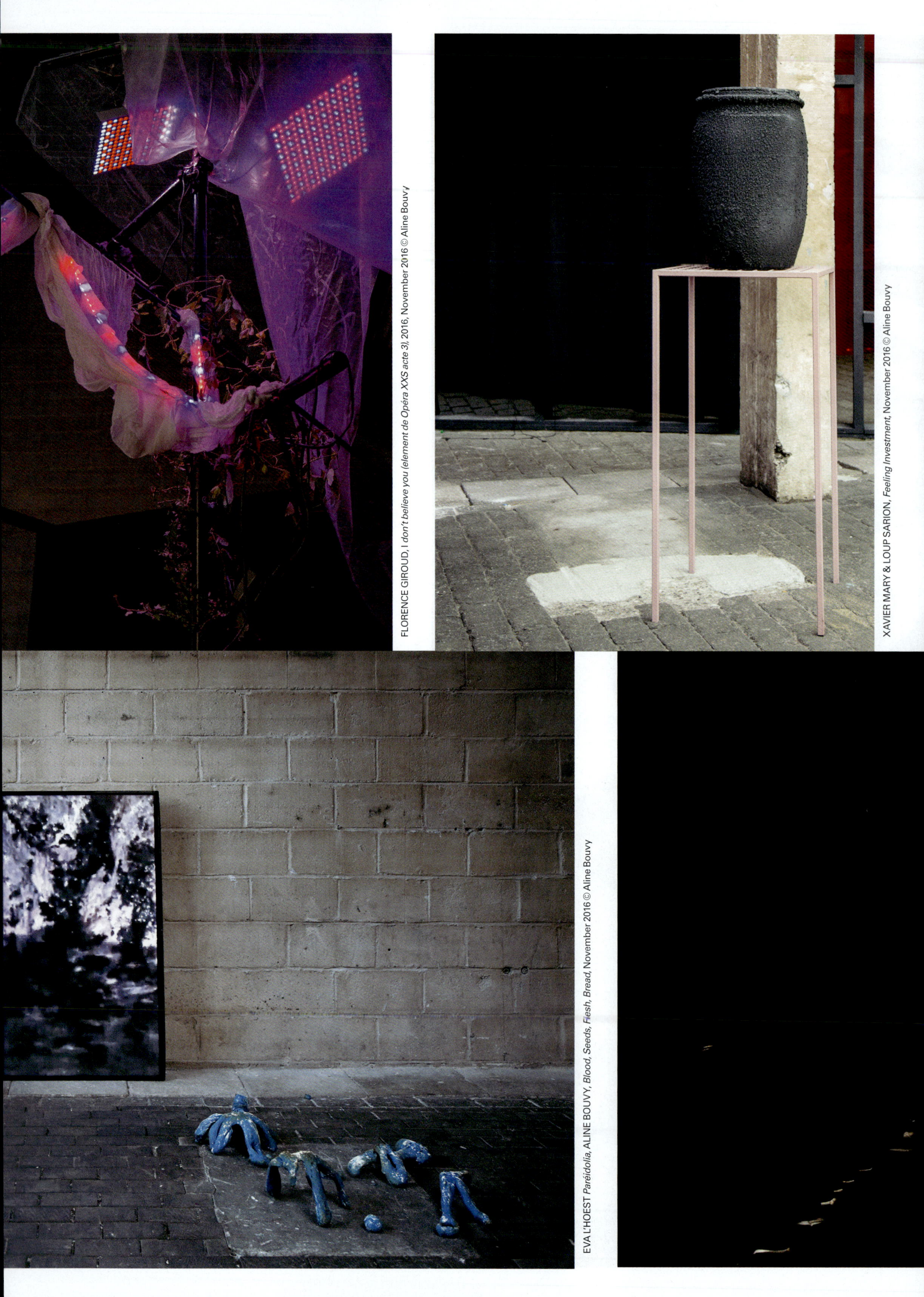

FLORENCE GIROUD, *I don't believe you (element de Opéra XXS acte 3)*, 2016, November 2016 © Aline Bouvy

XAVIER MARY & LOUP SARION, *Feeling Investment*, November 2016 © Aline Bouvy

EVA L'HOEST *Paréidolia*, ALINE BOUVY, *Blood, Seeds, Flesh, Bread*, November 2016 © Aline Bouvy

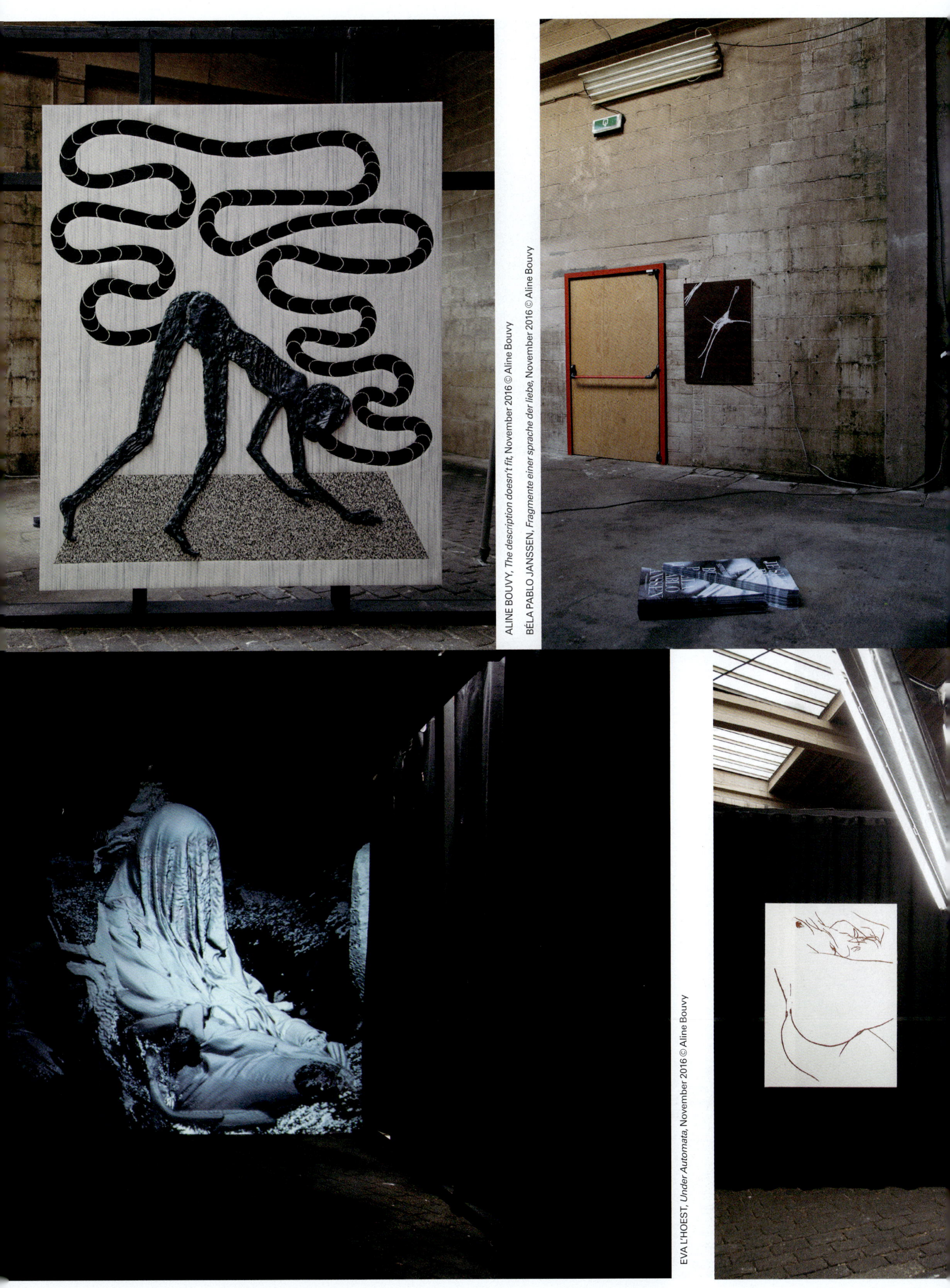

ALINE BOUVY, *The description doesn't fit*, November 2016 © Aline Bouvy

BÉLA PABLO JANSSEN, *Fragmente einer sprache der liebe*, November 2016 © Aline Bouvy

EVA L'HOEST, *Under Automata*, November 2016 © Aline Bouvy

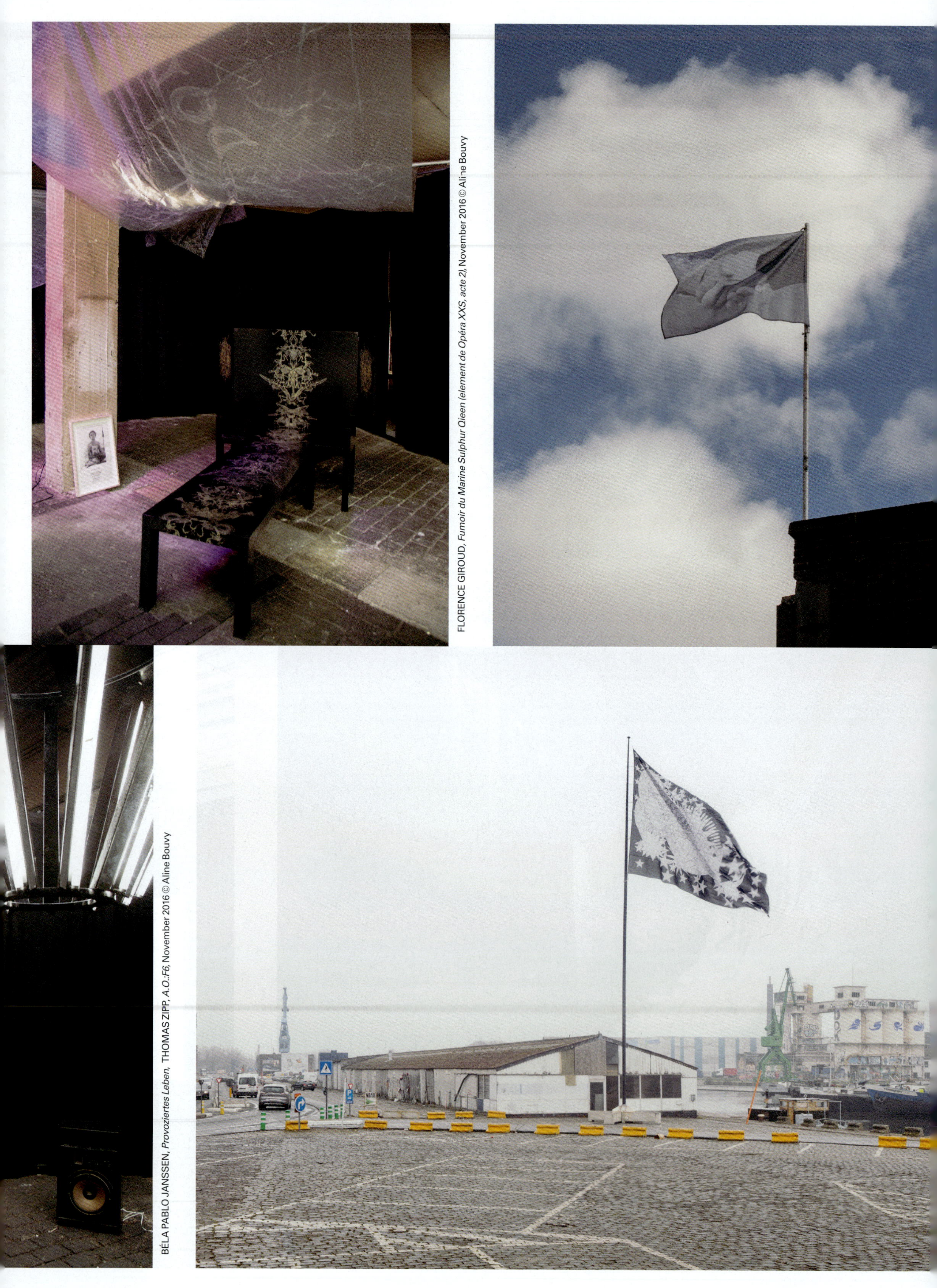

FLORENCE GIROUD, *Fumoir du Marine Sulphur Qieen (element de Opéra XXS, acte 2)*, November 2016 © Aline Bouvy

BÉLA PABLO JANSSEN, *Provoziertes Leben*, THOMAS ZIPP, *A.O.:F6*, November 2016 © Aline Bouvy

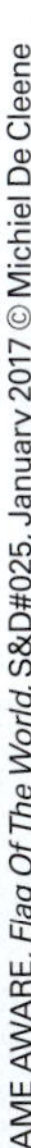

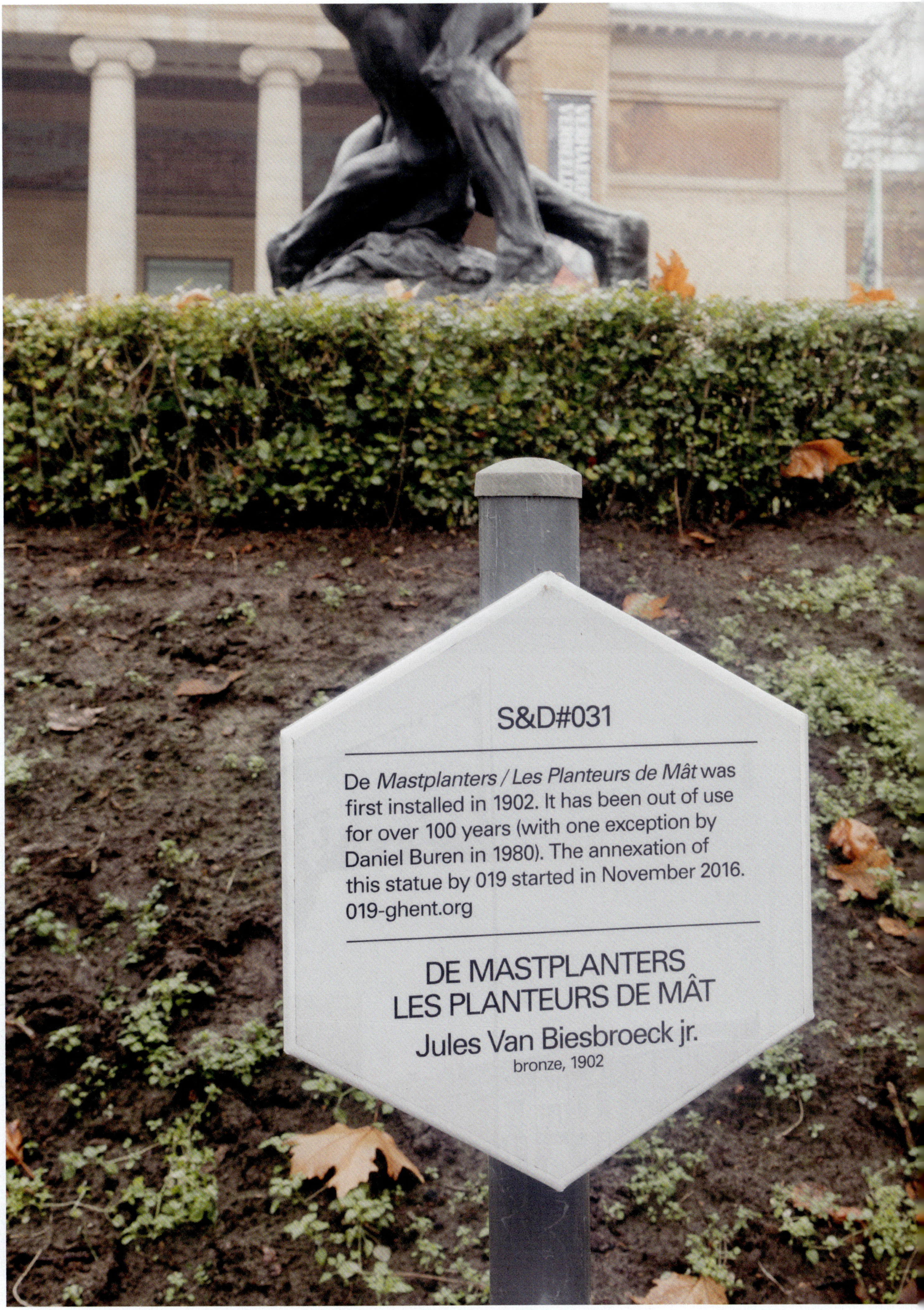

WARD HEIRWEGH, *Meeting with my Banker*, November 2016 © Valentijn Goethals

WE BECAME AWARE, *Flag Of The World*, S&D#025, January 2017 © Michiel De Cleene

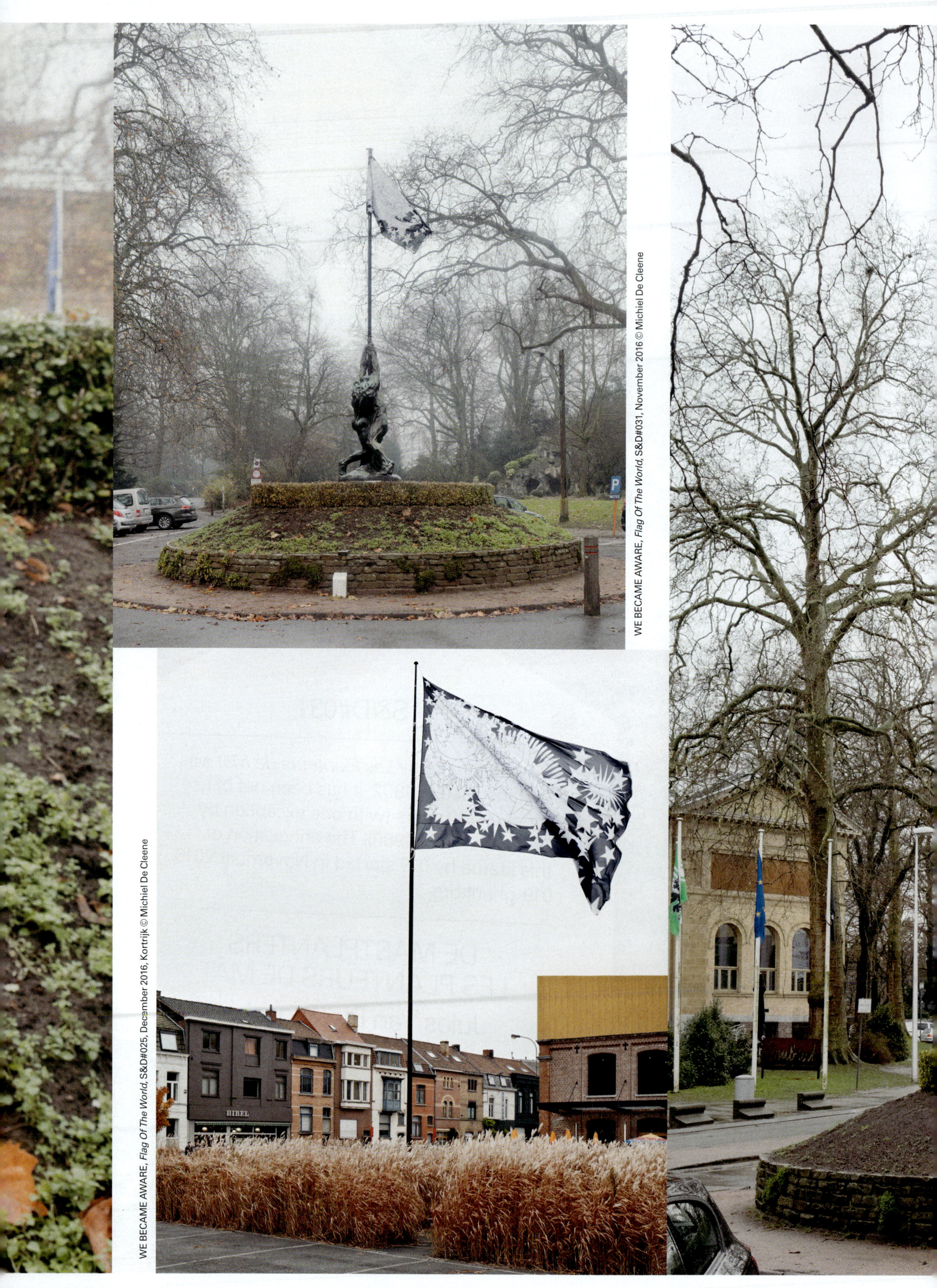

WE BECAME AWARE, *Flag Of The World*, S&D#031, November 2016 © Michiel De Cleene

WE BECAME AWARE, *Flag Of The World*, S&D#025, December 2016, Kortrijk © Michiel De Cleene

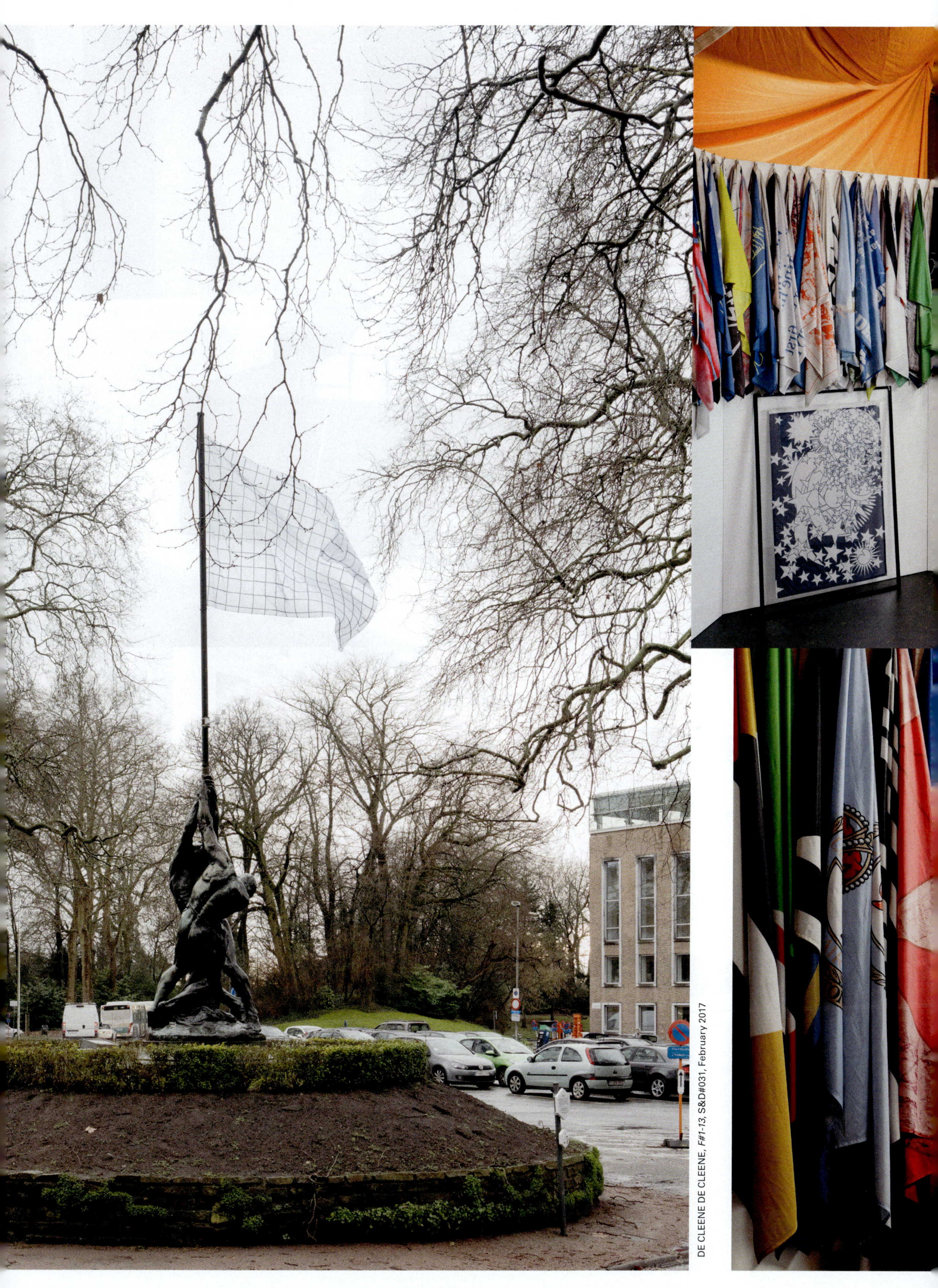

DE CLEENE DE CLEENE, *F#1-13*, S&D#031, February 2017

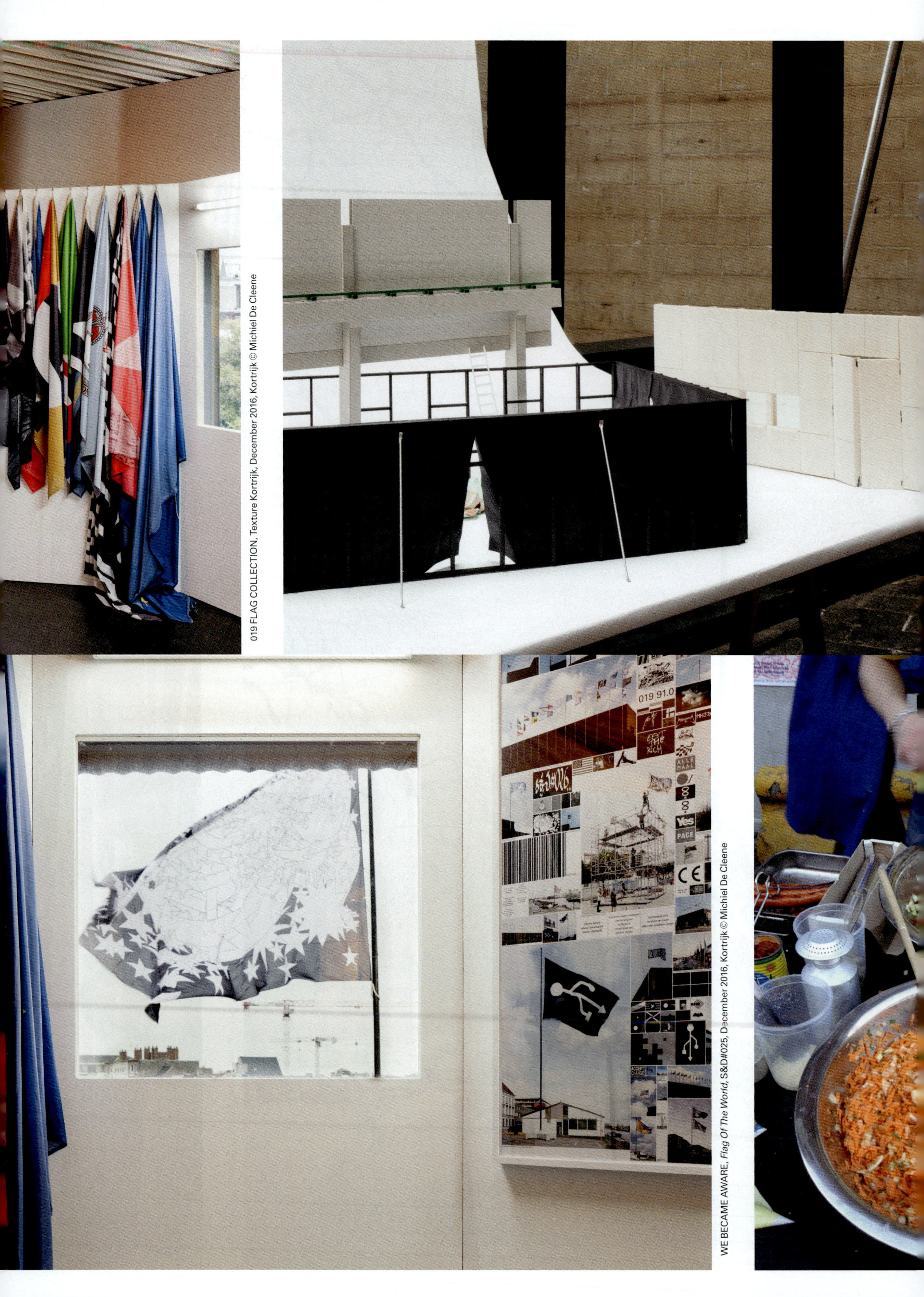

019 FLAG COLLECTION, Texture Kortrijk, December 2016, Kortrijk © Michiel De Cleene

WE BECAME AWARE, *Flag Of The World*, S&D#025, December 2016, Kortrijk © Michiel De Cleene

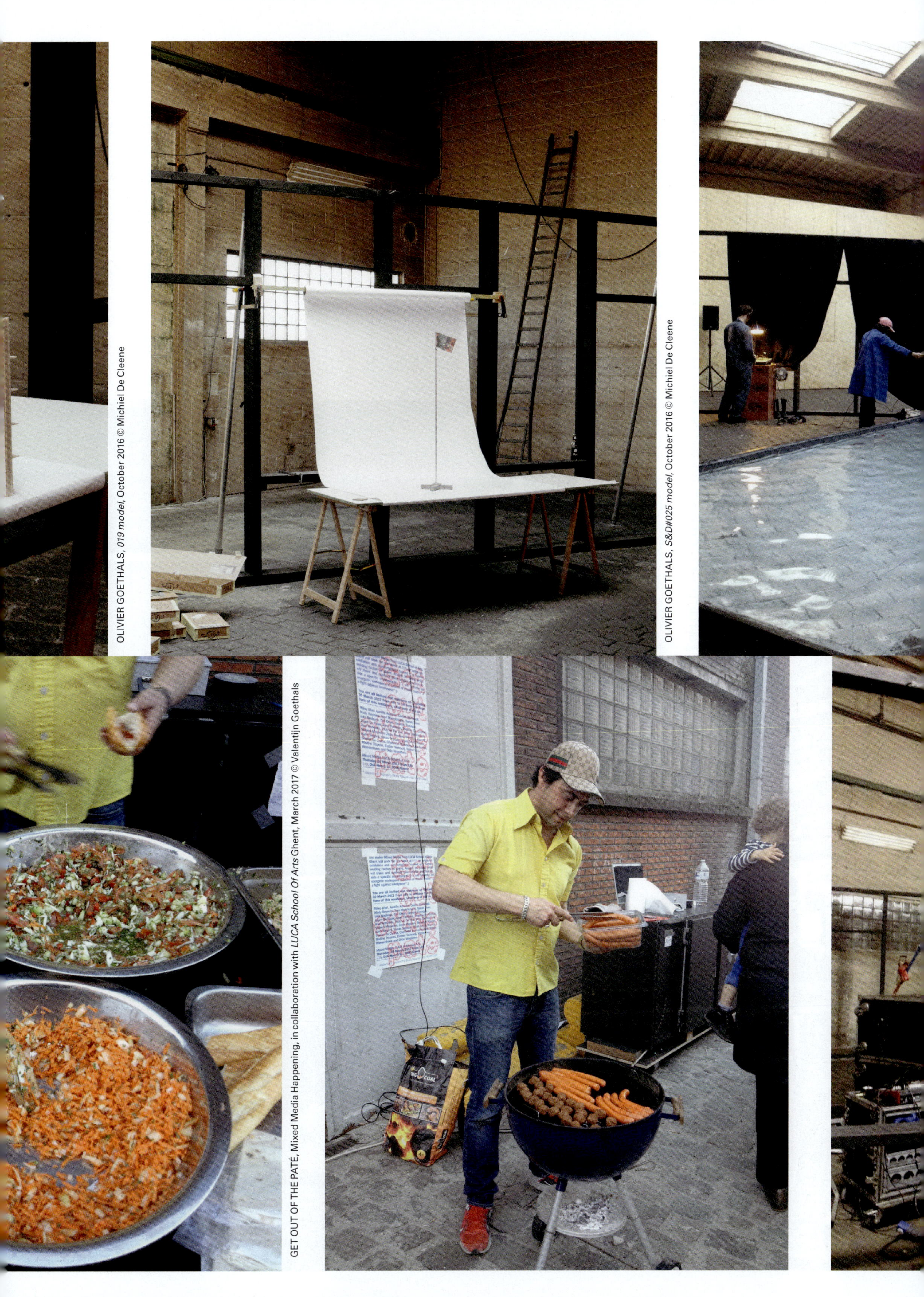

OLIVIER GOETHALS, *019 model*, October 2016 © Michiel De Cleene

OLIVIER GOETHALS, *S&D#025 model*, October 2016 © Michiel De Cleene

GET OUT OF THE PATE, Mixed Media Happening, in collaboration with *LUCA School Of Arts* Ghent, March 2017 © Valentijn Goethals

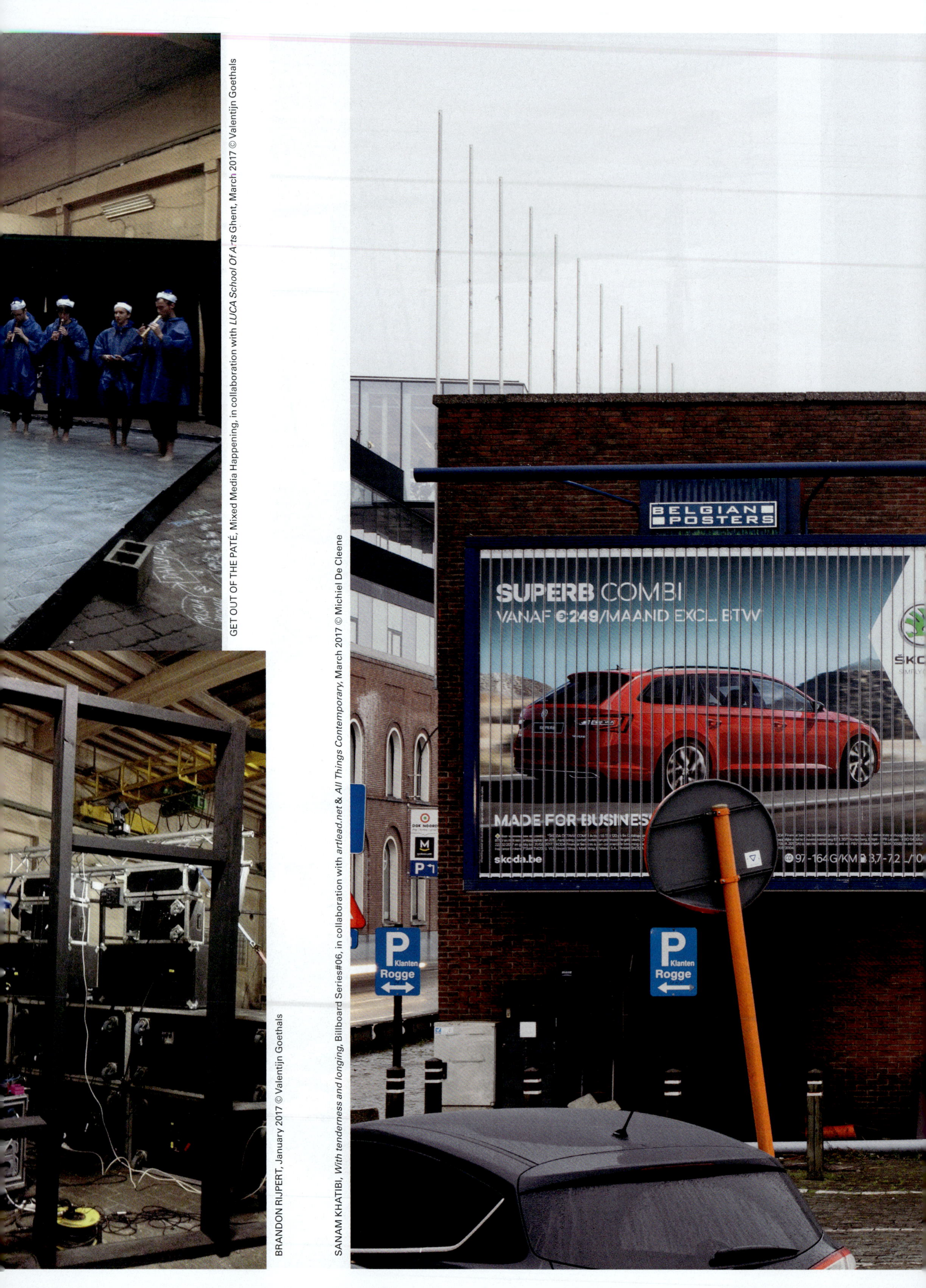

GET OUT OF THE PATÉ, Mixed Media Happening, in collaboration with *LUCA School Of Arts* Ghent, March 2017 © Valentijn Goethals

BRANDON RIJPERT, January 2017 © Valentijn Goethals

SANAM KHATIBI, *With tenderness and longing*, Billboard Series#06, in collaboration with *artlead.net* & *All Things Contemporary*, March 2017 © Michiel De Cleene

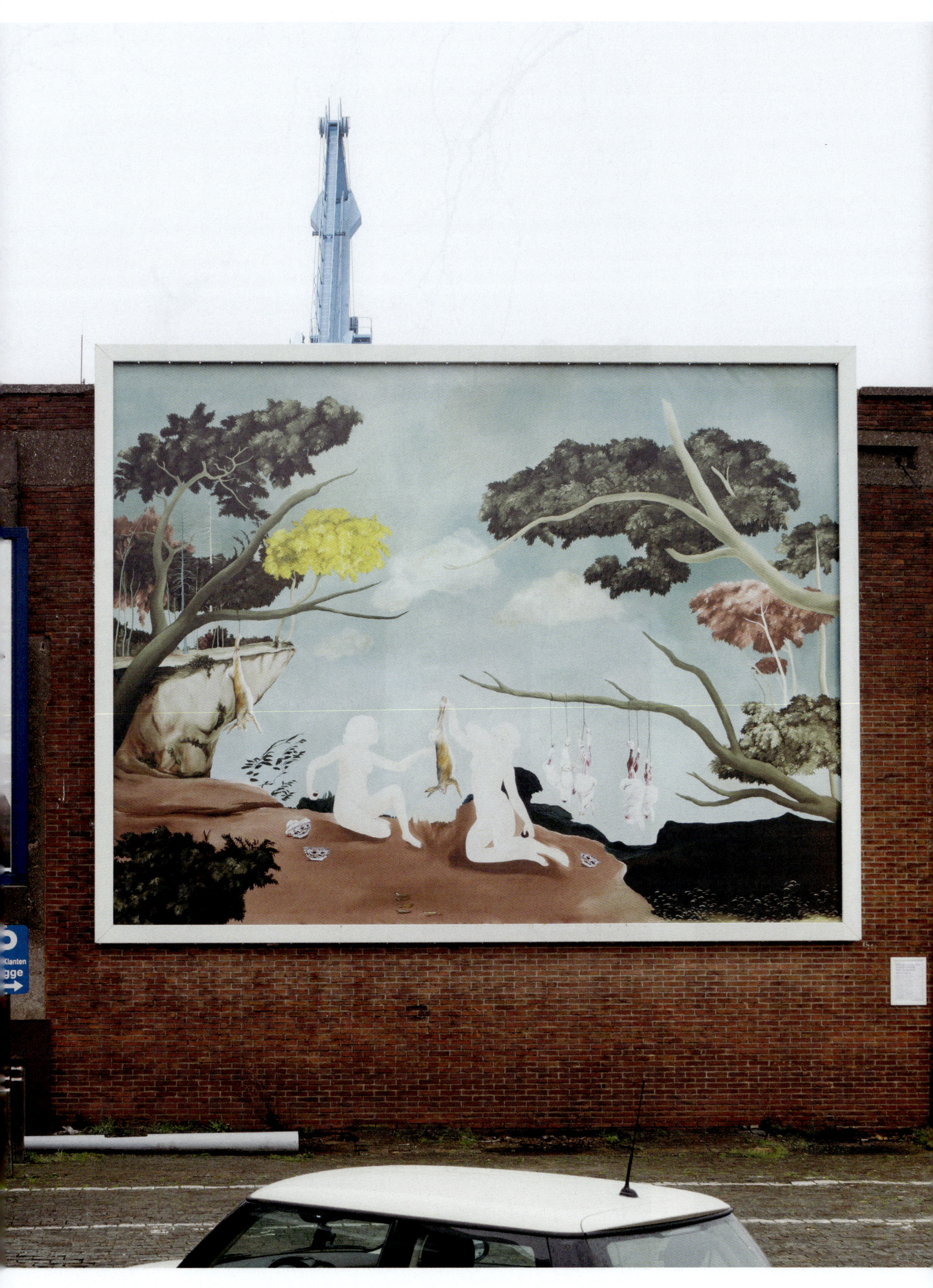
Klanten

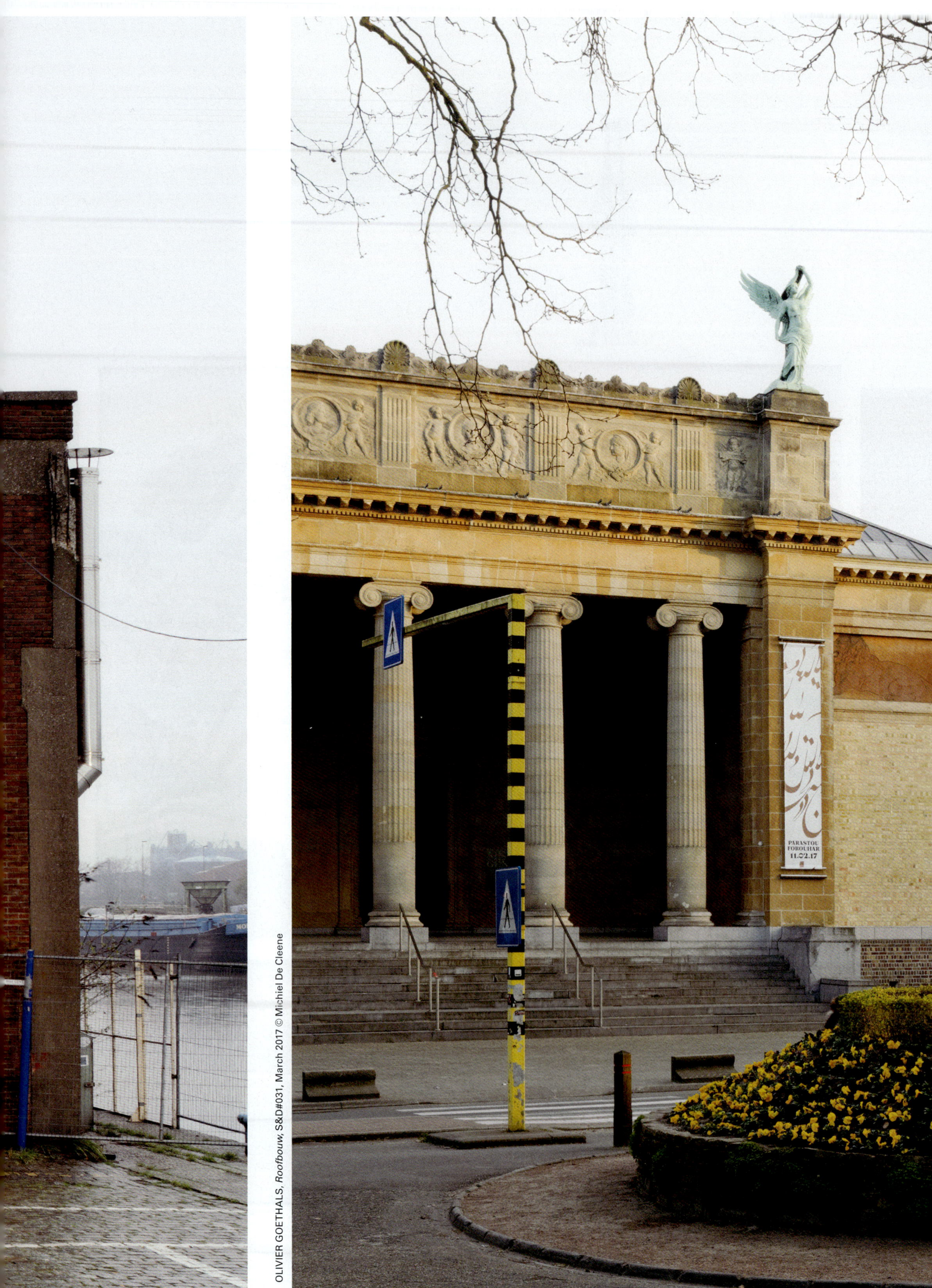

OLIVIER GOETHALS, *Roofbouw*, S&D#031, March 2017 © Michiel De Cleene

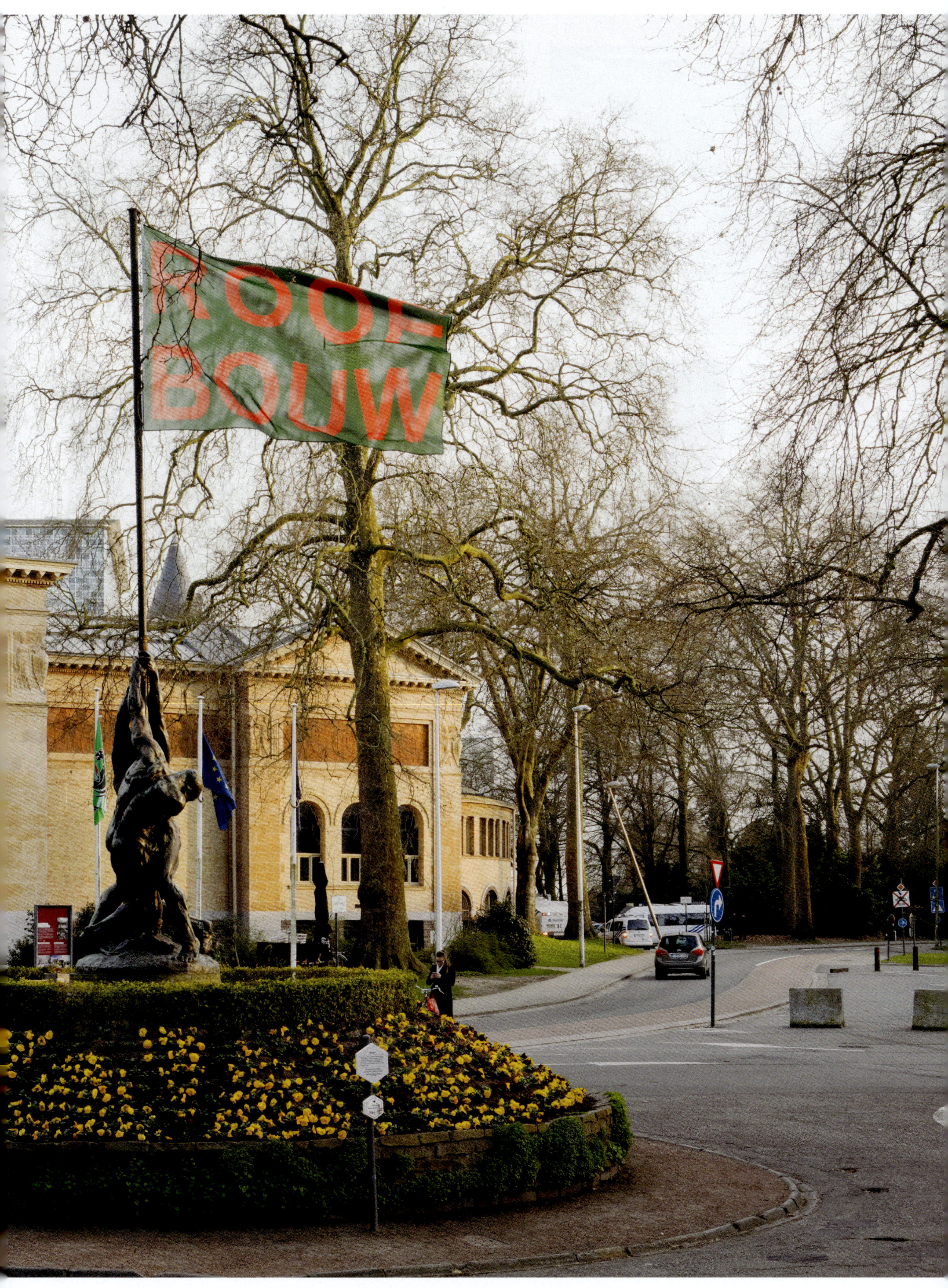
BOUW

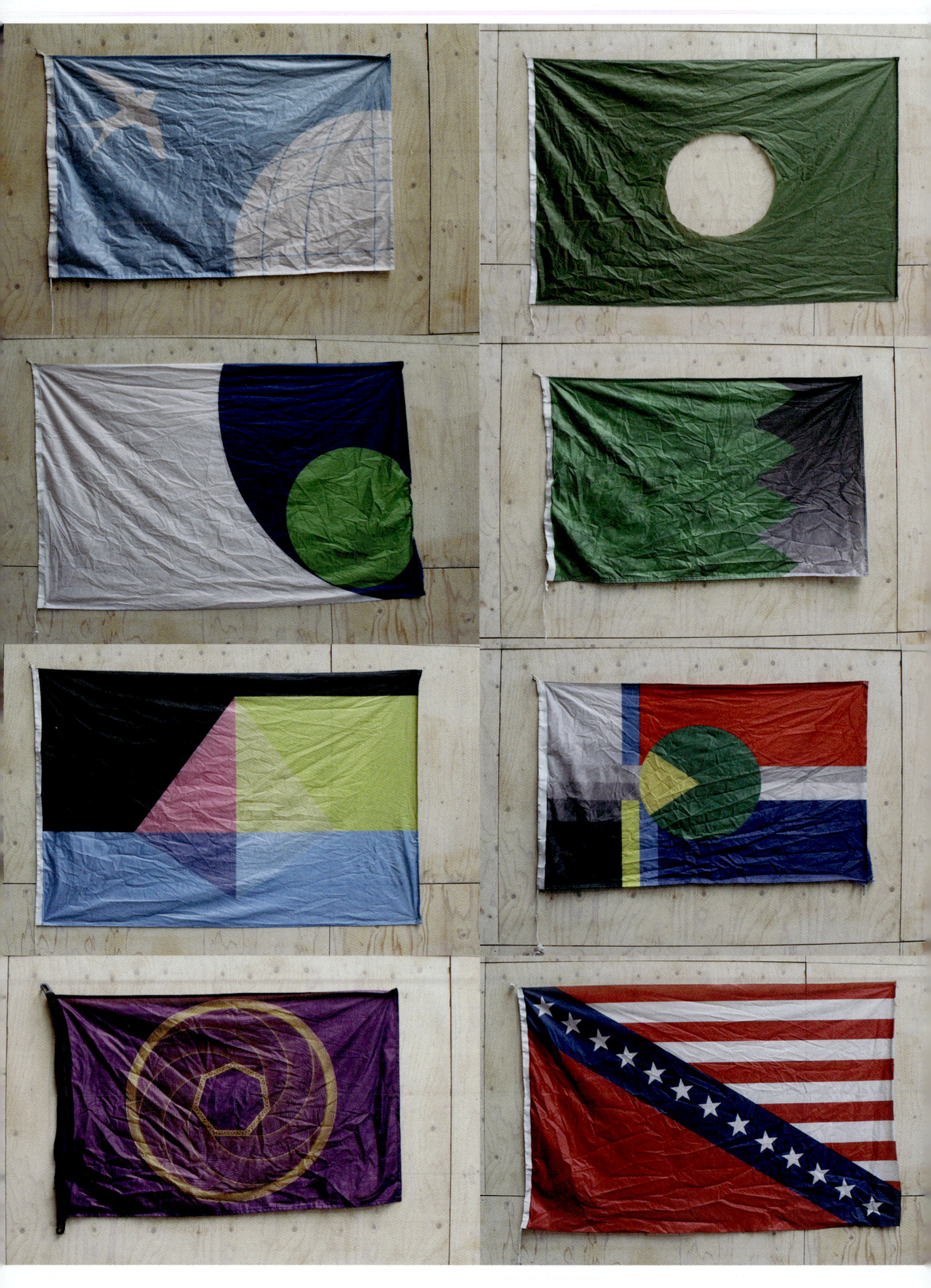

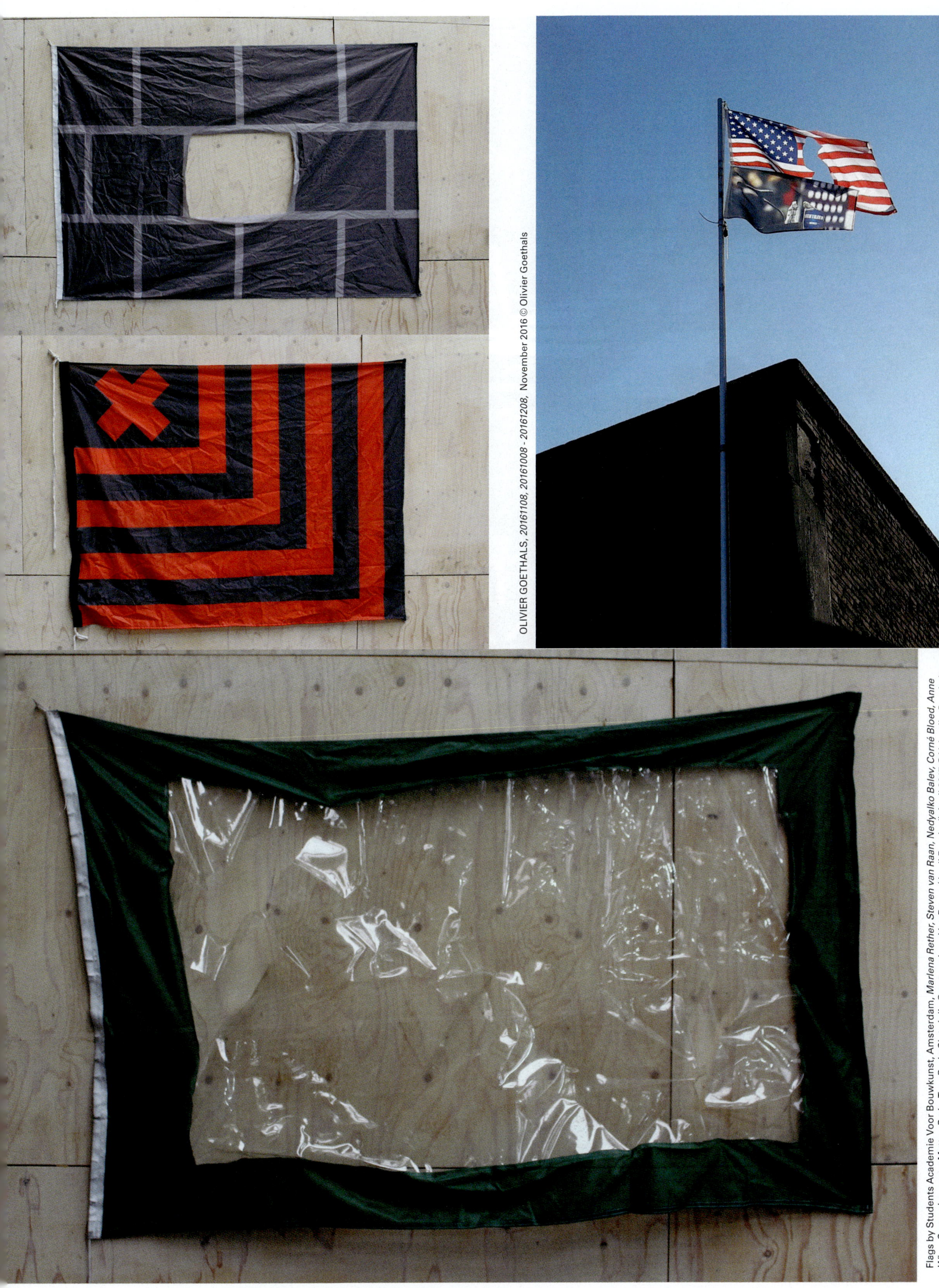

OLIVIER GOETHALS, *20161108, 20161008 - 20161208,* November 2016 © Olivier Goethals

Flags by Students Academie Voor Bouwkunst, Amsterdam, *Marlena Rether, Steven van Raan, Nedyalko Balev, Corné Bloed, Anne Wies, Sanne Janssens, Matteo Paris, Tom Bruin Slot, Julia Gersten, Joep Van Baast, (Jordi Rondeel),* April 2017 © Valentijn Goethals

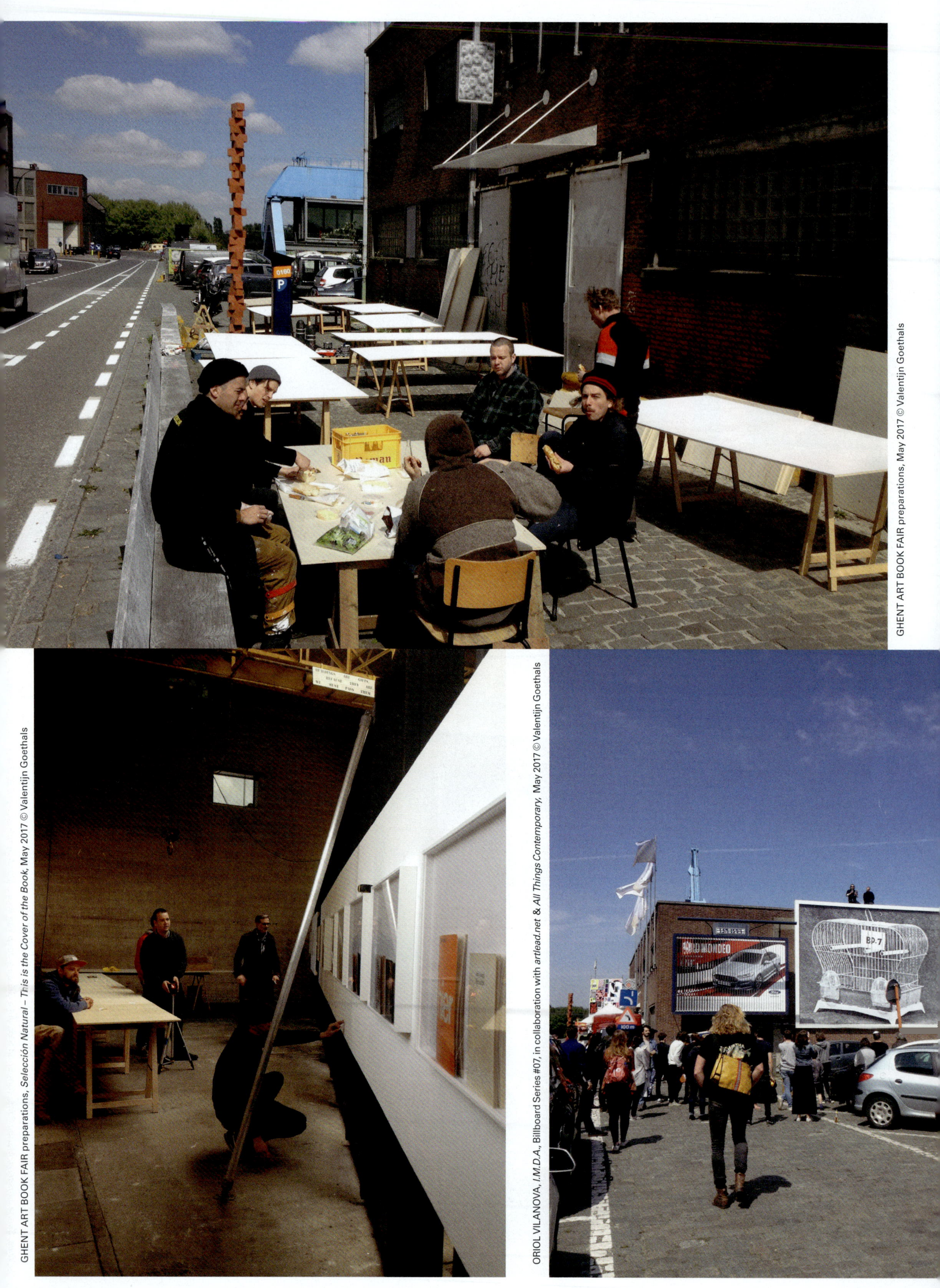

GHENT ART BOOK FAIR preparations, May 2017 © Valentijn Goethals

GHENT ART BOOK FAIR preparations, *Selección Natural – This is the Cover of the Book*, May 2017 © Valentijn Goethals

ORIOL VILANOVA, *I.M.D.A.*, Billboard Series #07, in collaboration with *artlead.net* & *All Things Contemporary*, May 2017 © Valentijn Goethals

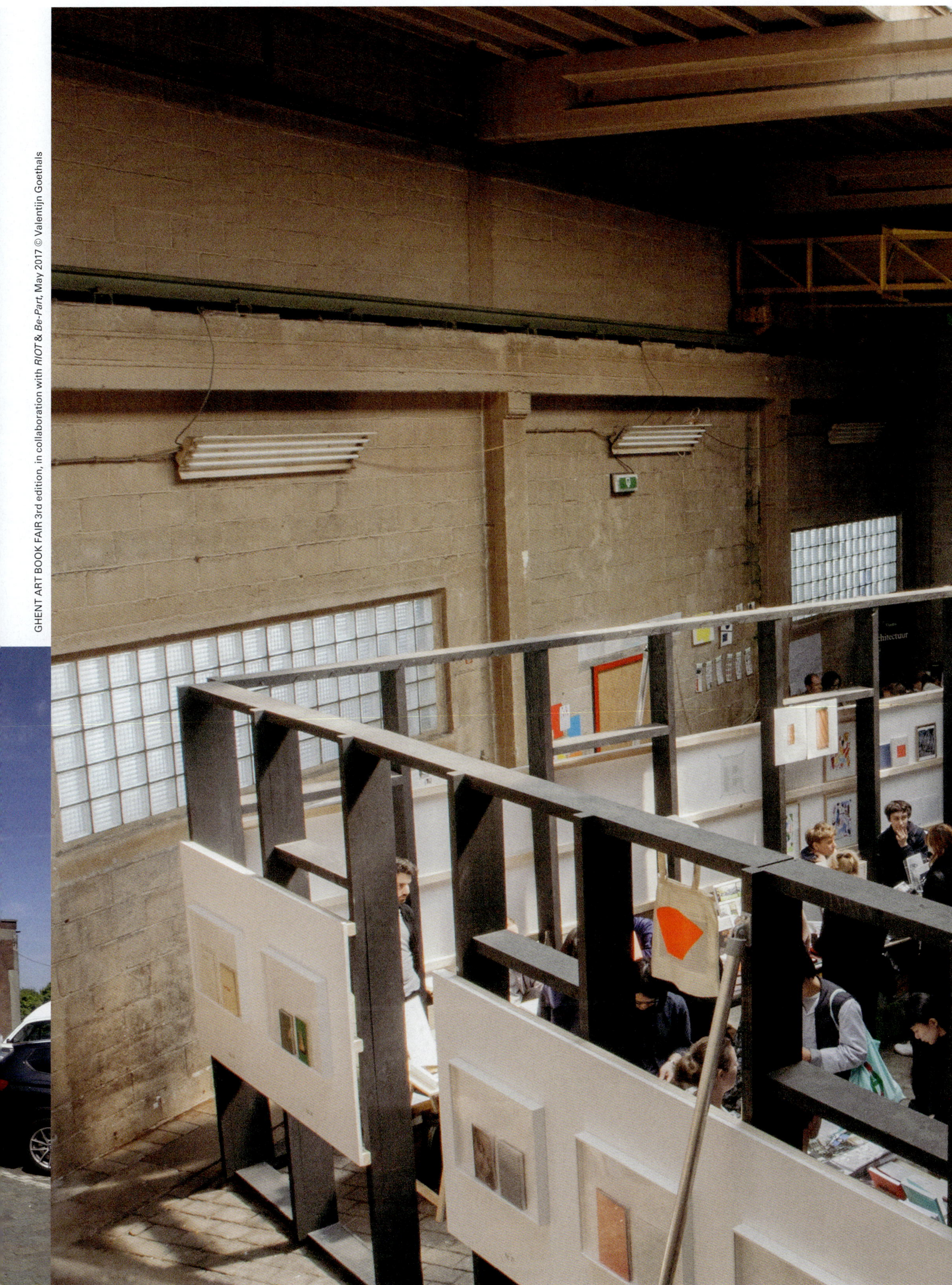

GHENT ART BOOK FAIR 3rd edition, in collaboration with *RIOT* & *Be-Part*, May 2017 © Valentijn Goethals

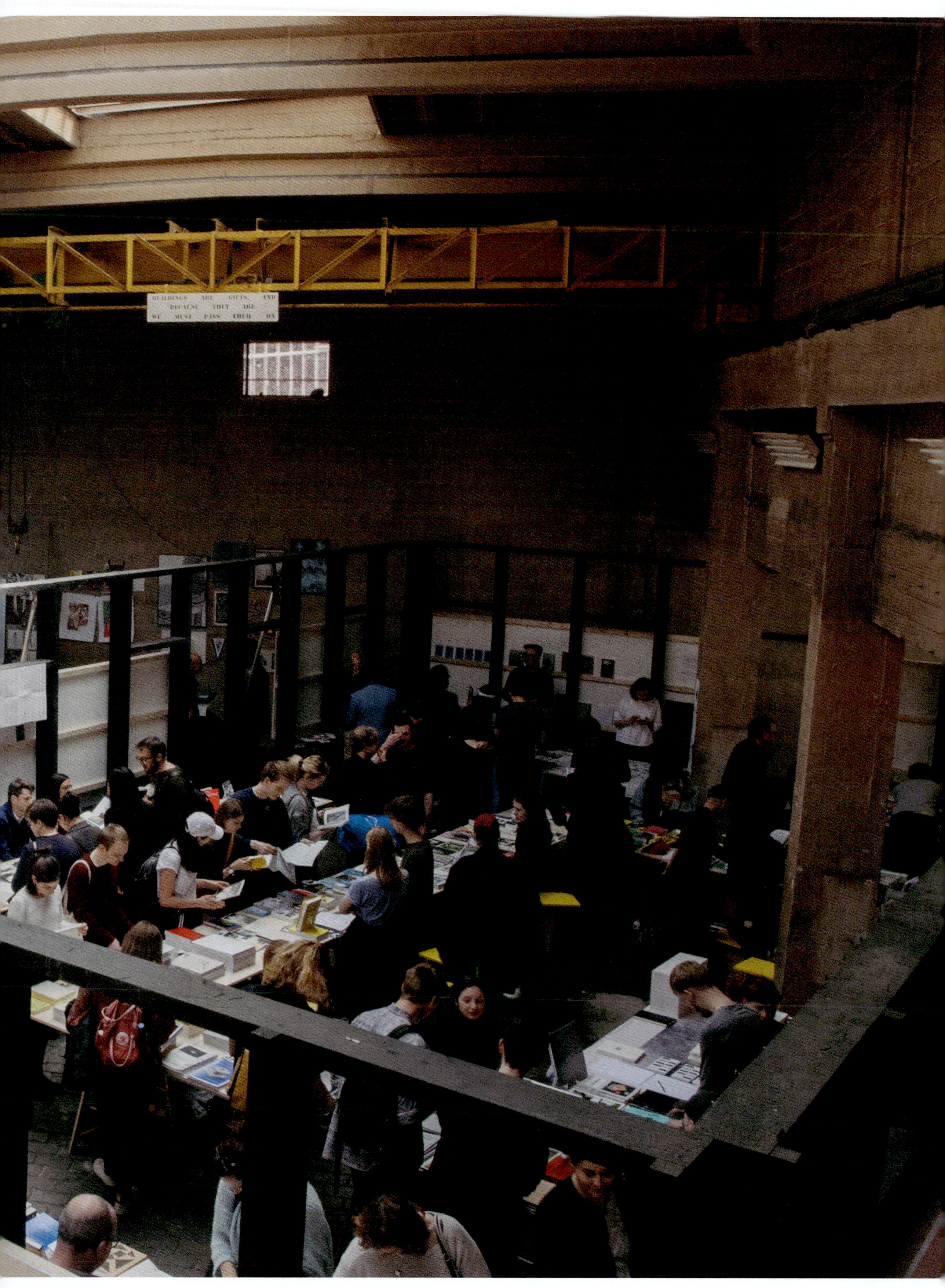
BUILDINGS ARE GIFTS, AND
BECAUSE THEY ARE,
WE MUST PASS THEM ON

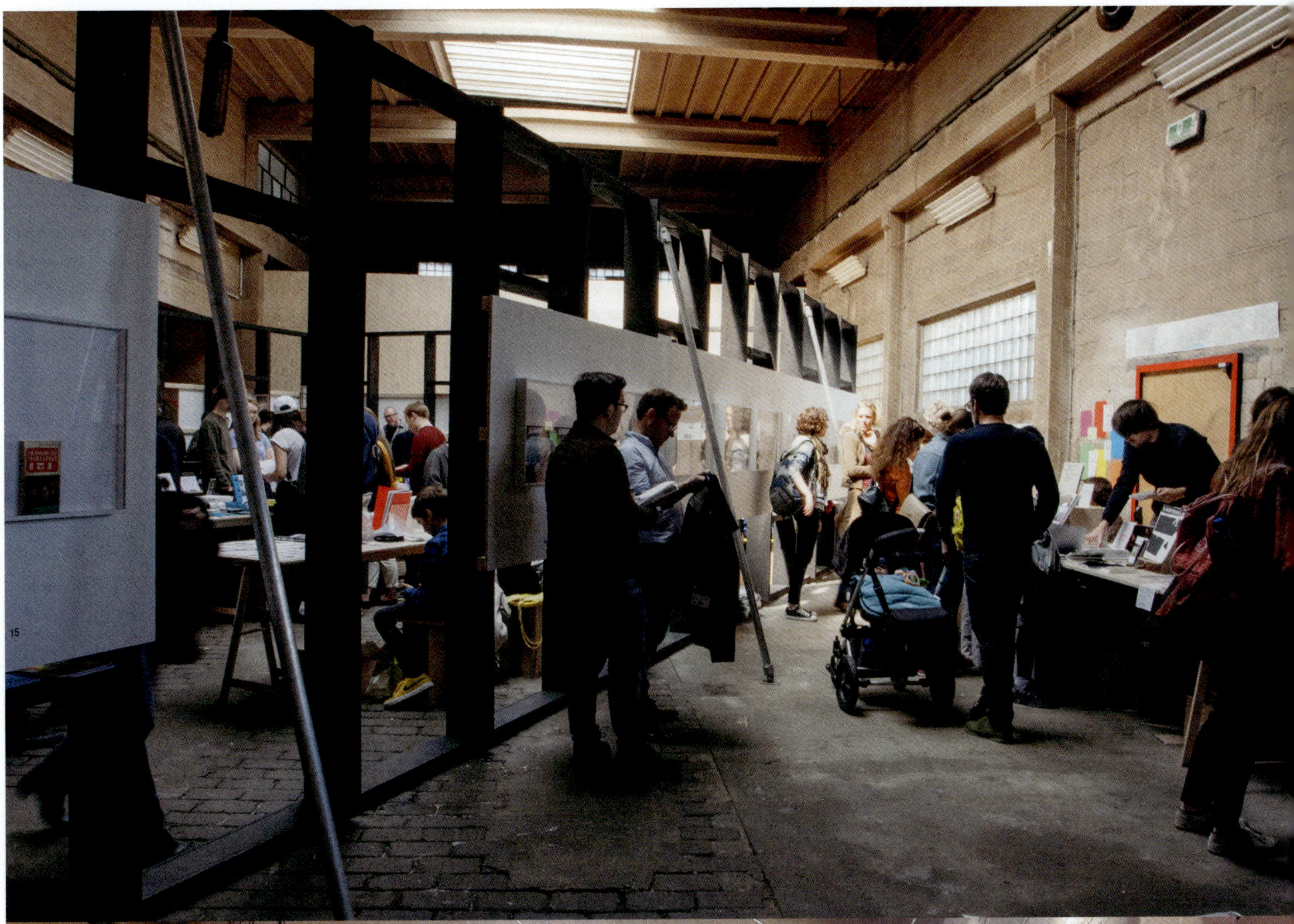

GHENT ART BOOK FAIR 3rd edition, in collaboration with *RIOT* & *Be-Part*, May 2017 © Valentijn Goethals

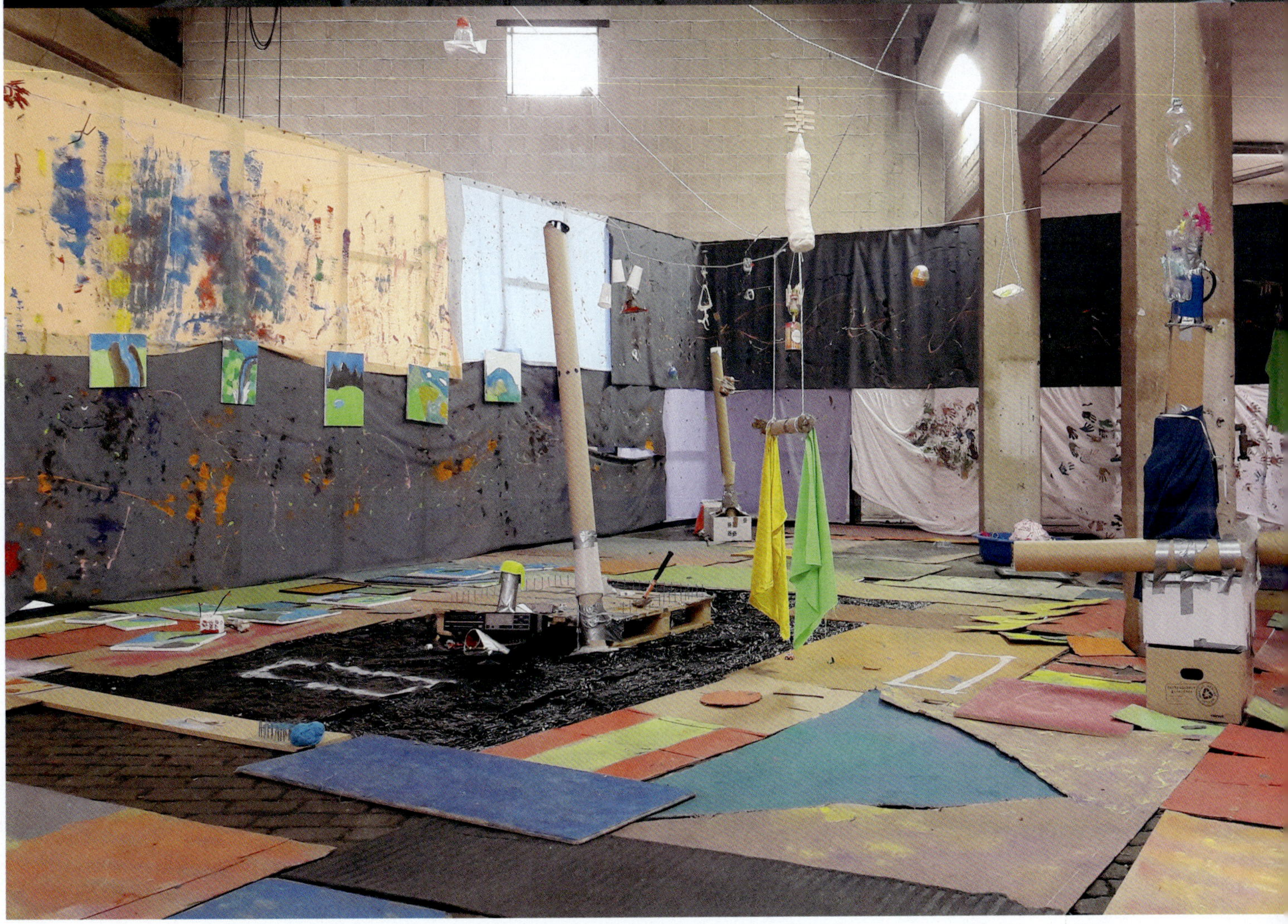

WORKSHOP DAS KUNST, *under guidance of Bert Huyghe*, April 2017 © Olivier Goethals

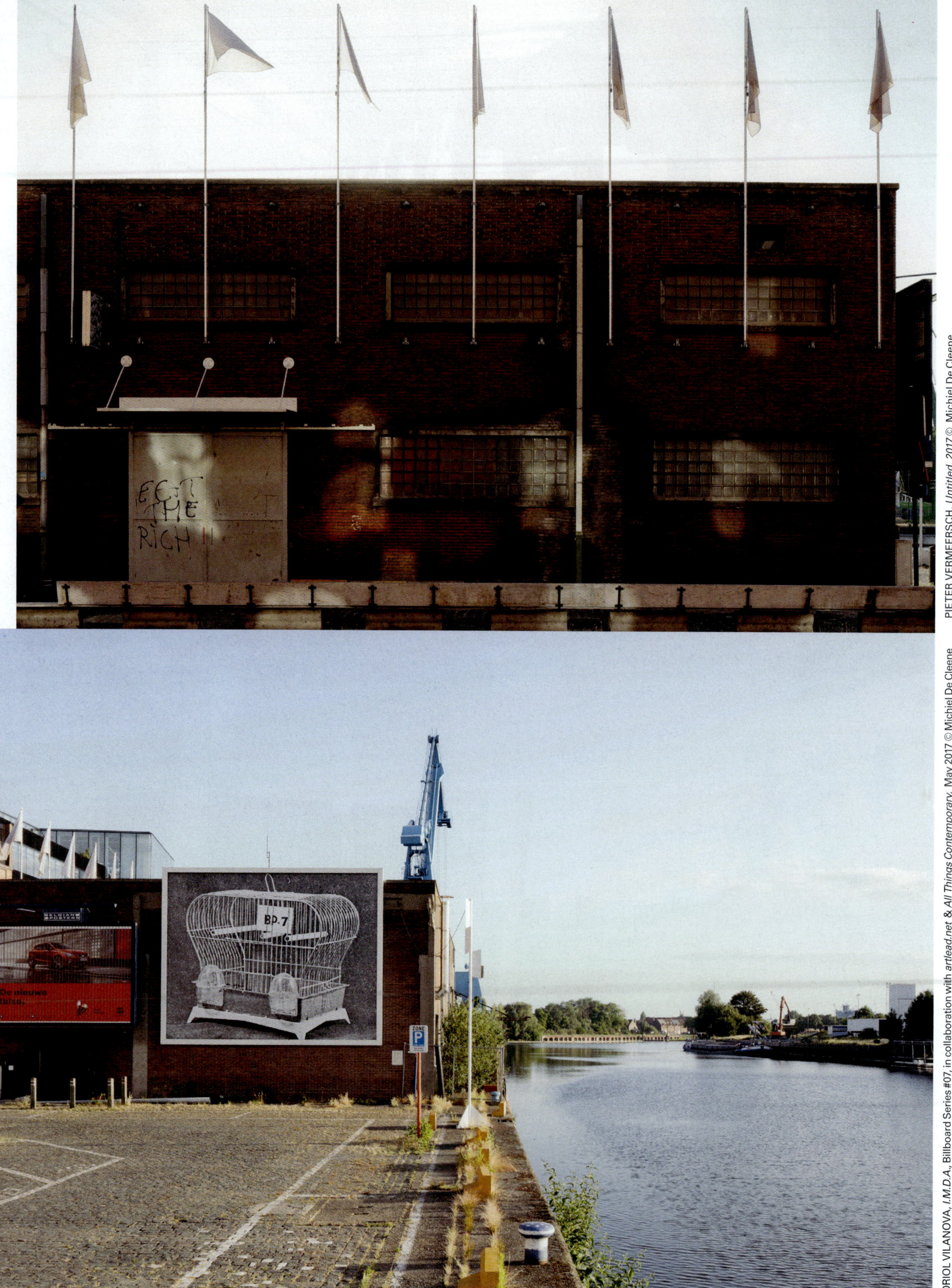

PIETER VERMEERSCH, *Untitled*, 2017 © Michiel De Cleene

ORIOL VILANOVA, *I.M.D.A.*, Billboard Series #07, in collaboration with *artlead.net* & *All Things Contemporary*, May 2017 © Michiel De Cleene

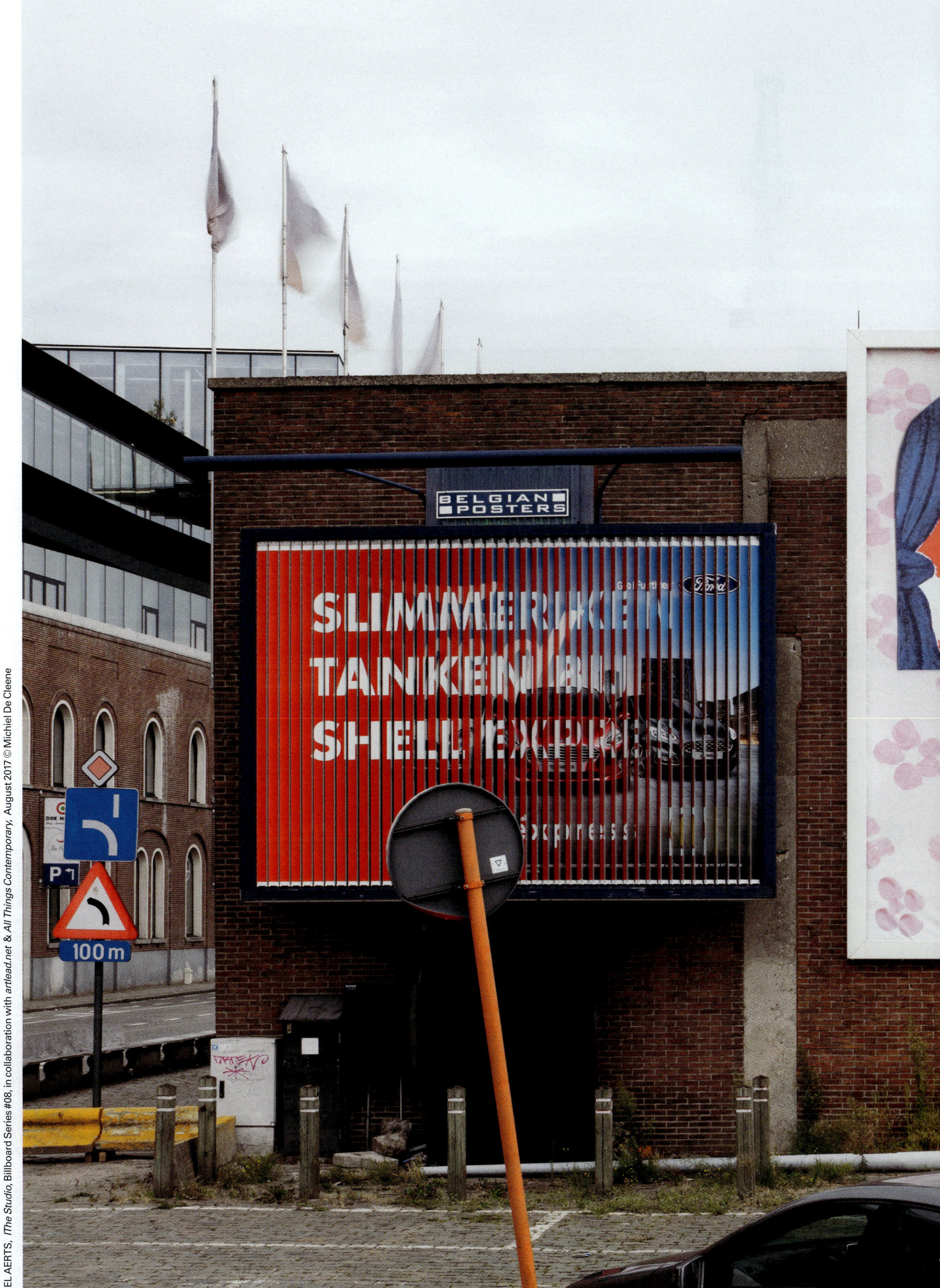

NEL AERTS, *!The Studio*, Billboard Series #08, in collaboration with *artlead.net* & *All Things Contemporary*, August 2017 © Michiel De Cleene

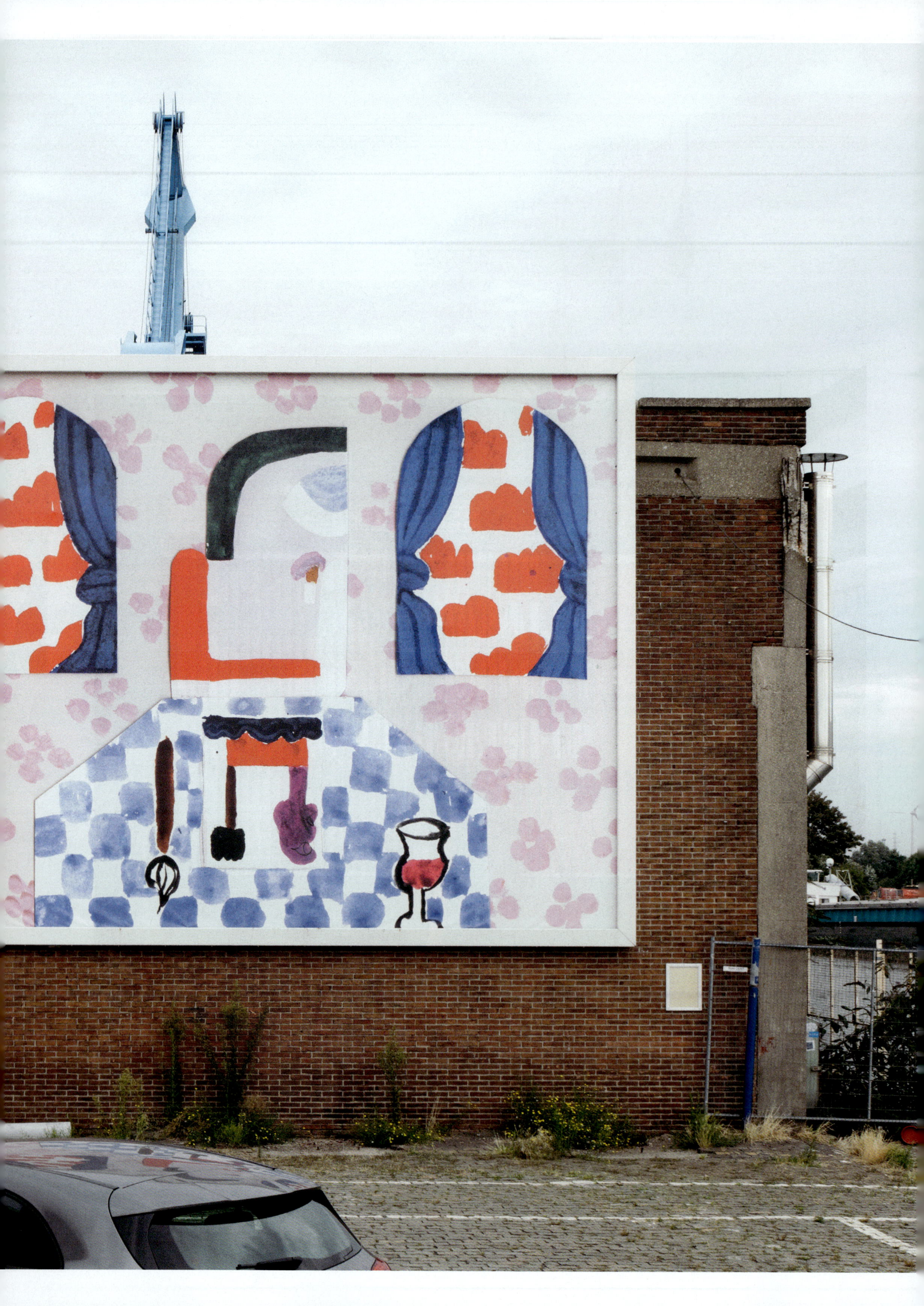

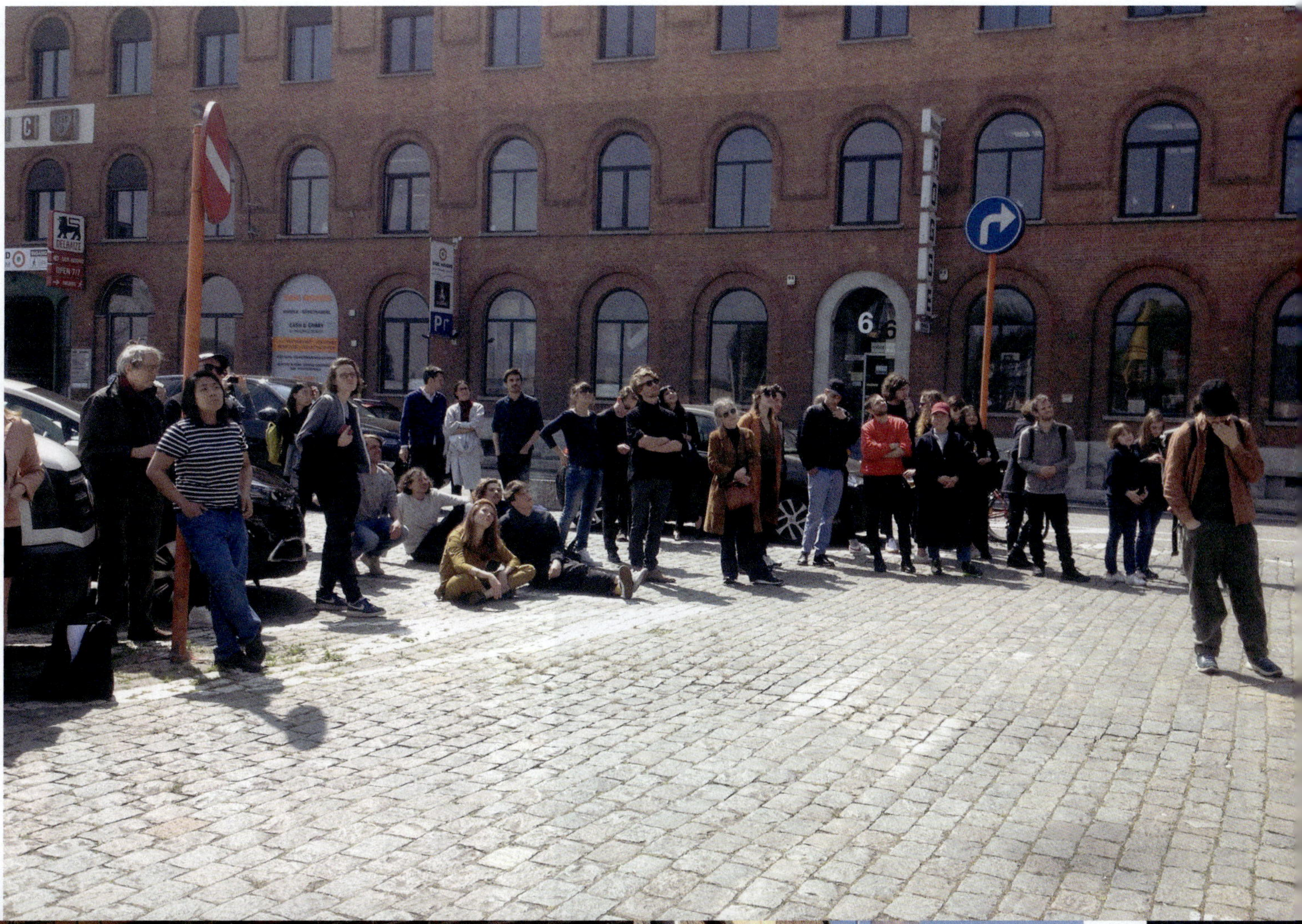

ORIOL VILANOVA, *I.M.D.A*, Billboard Series #07, in collaboration with *artlead.net* & *All Things Contemporary*, May 2017 © Valentijn Goethals

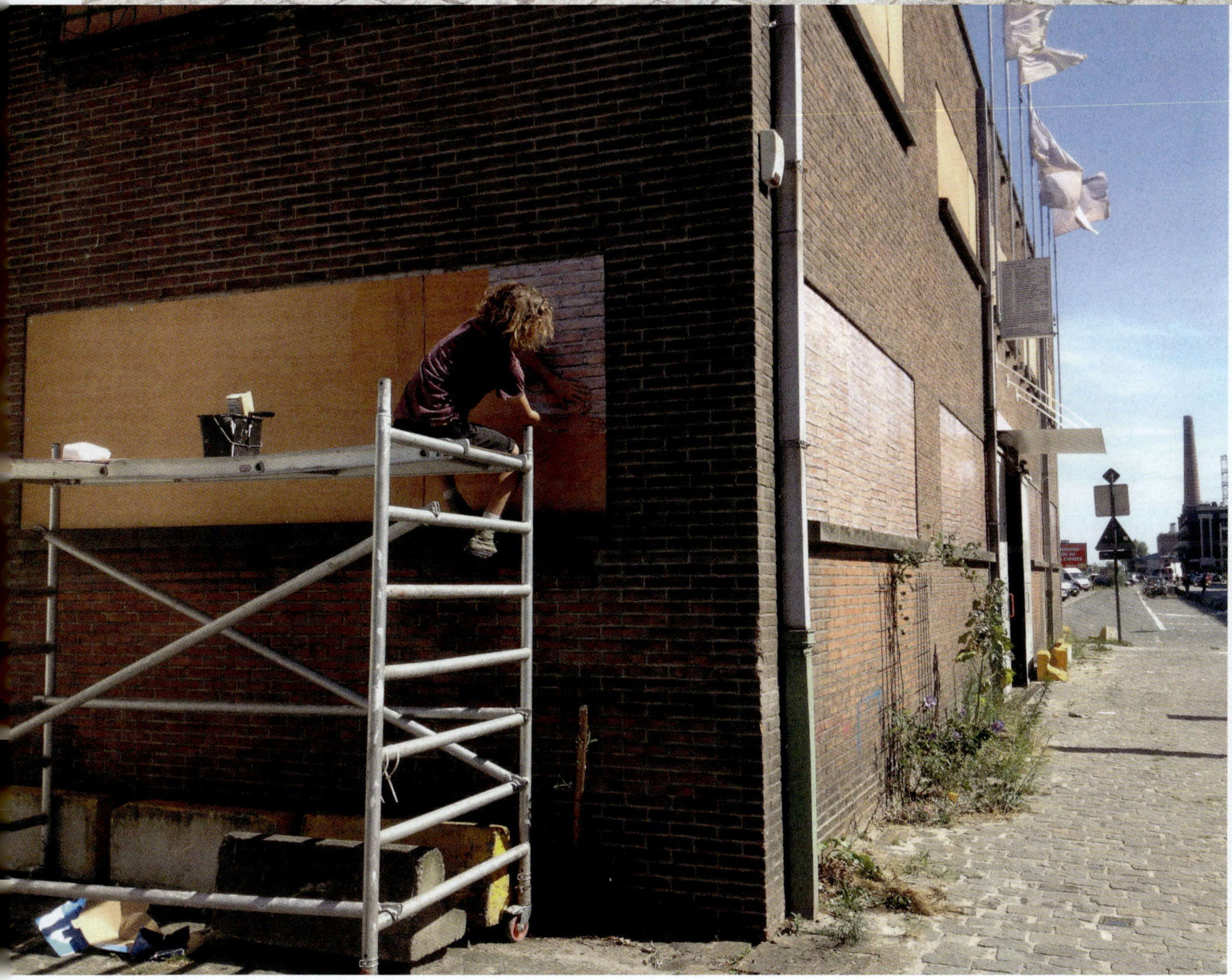

CLOSING EVENT#01: INE MEGANCK, *The Secret Portal*, July 2017 © Valentijn Goethals

DIFFERENT CLASS, in collaboration with Subbacultcha, August 2016 © Lara Gasparotto

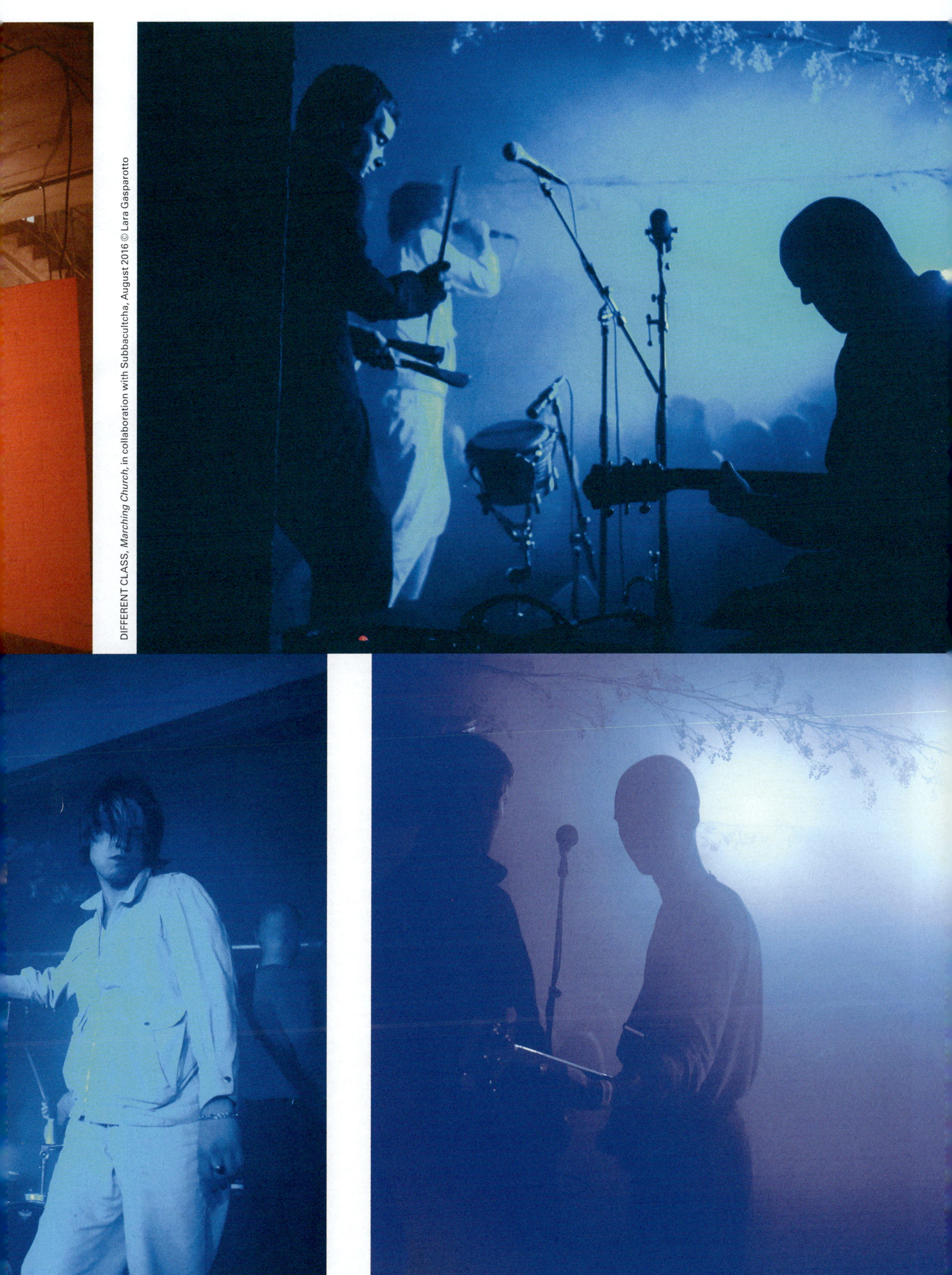

DIFFERENT CLASS, *Marching Church*, in collaboration with Subbacultcha, August 2016 © Lara Gasparotto

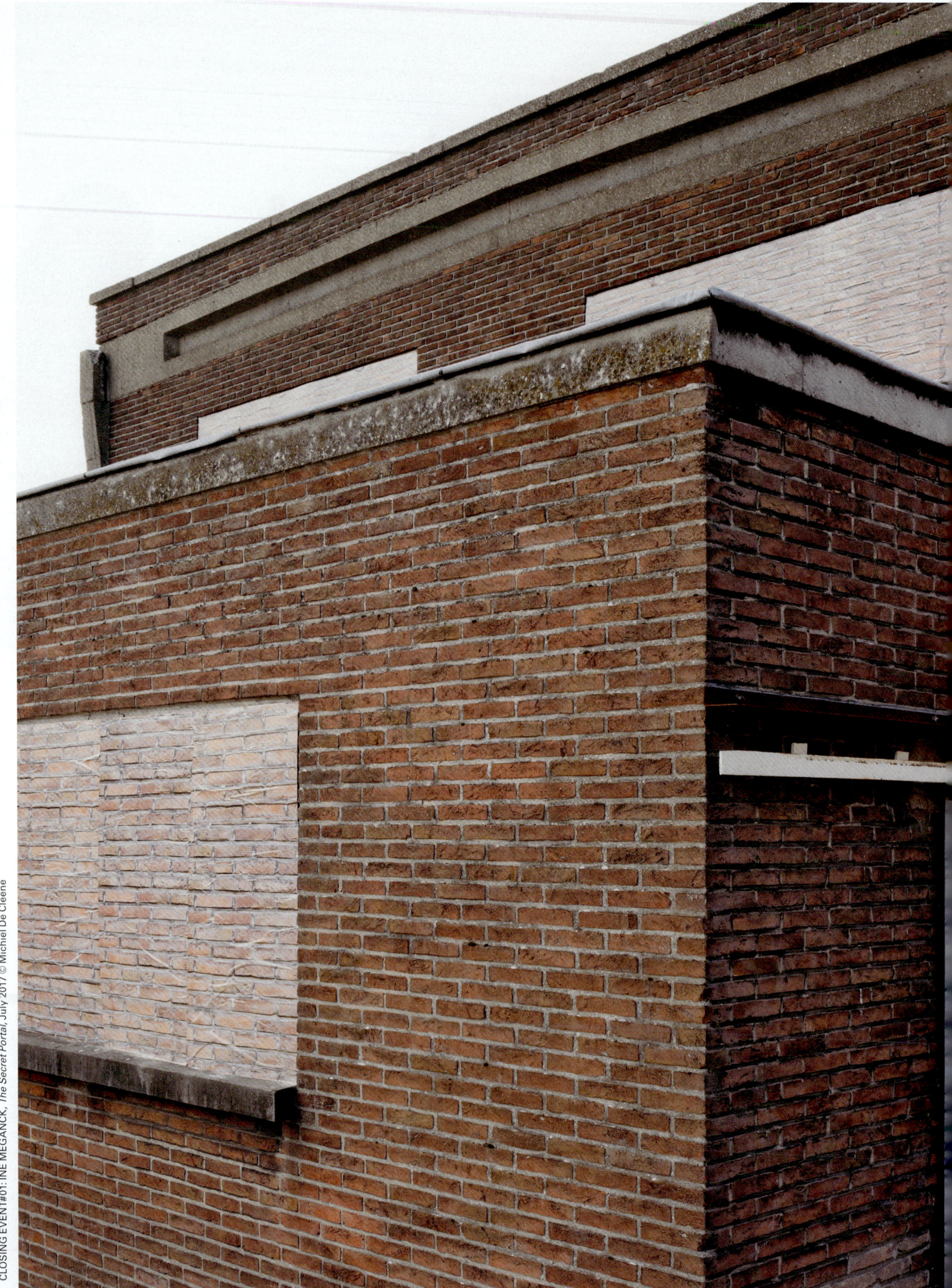

CLOSING EVENT#01: INE MEGANCK, *The Secret Portal*, July 2017 © Michiel De Cleene

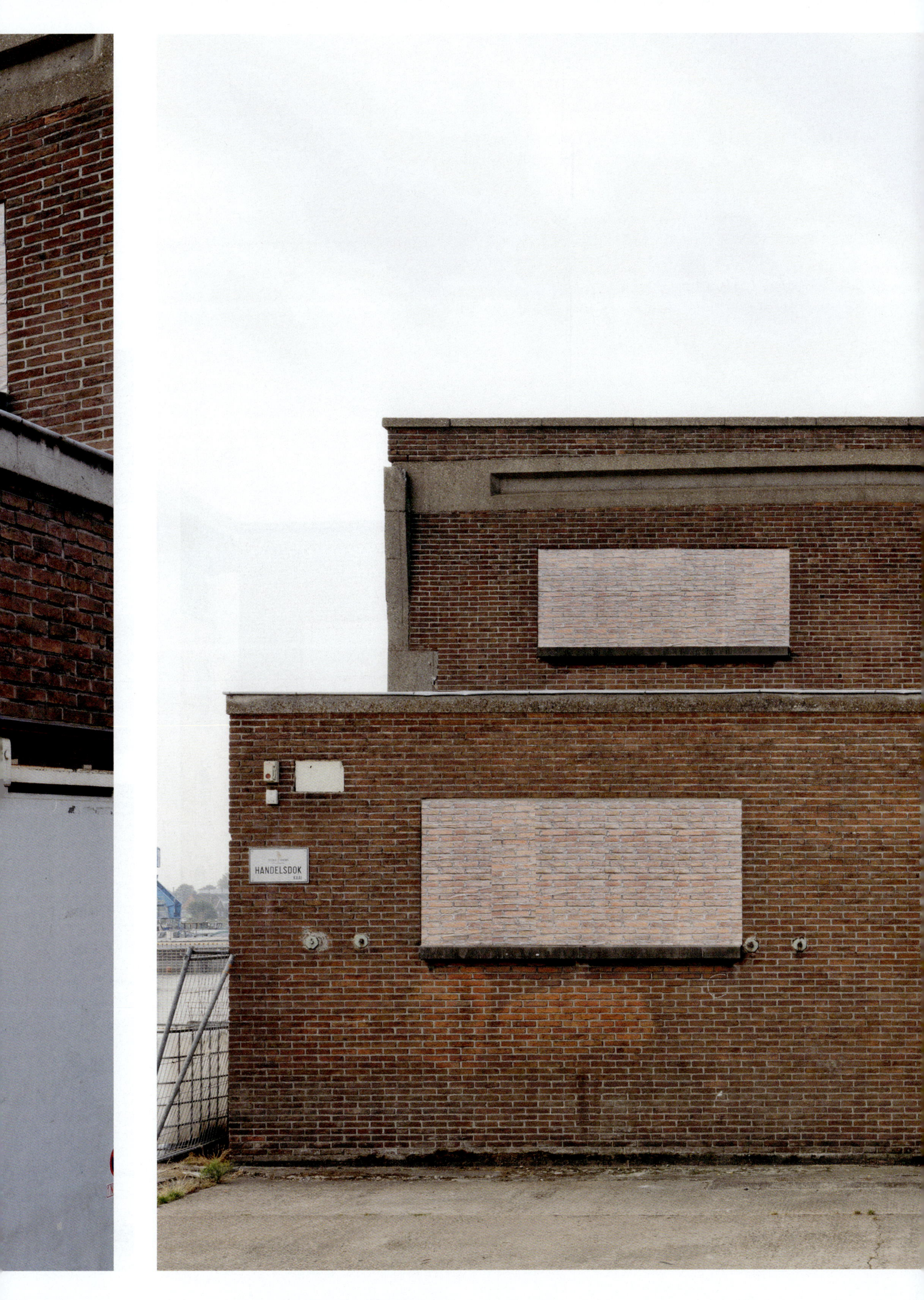
HANDELSDOK
KAAI

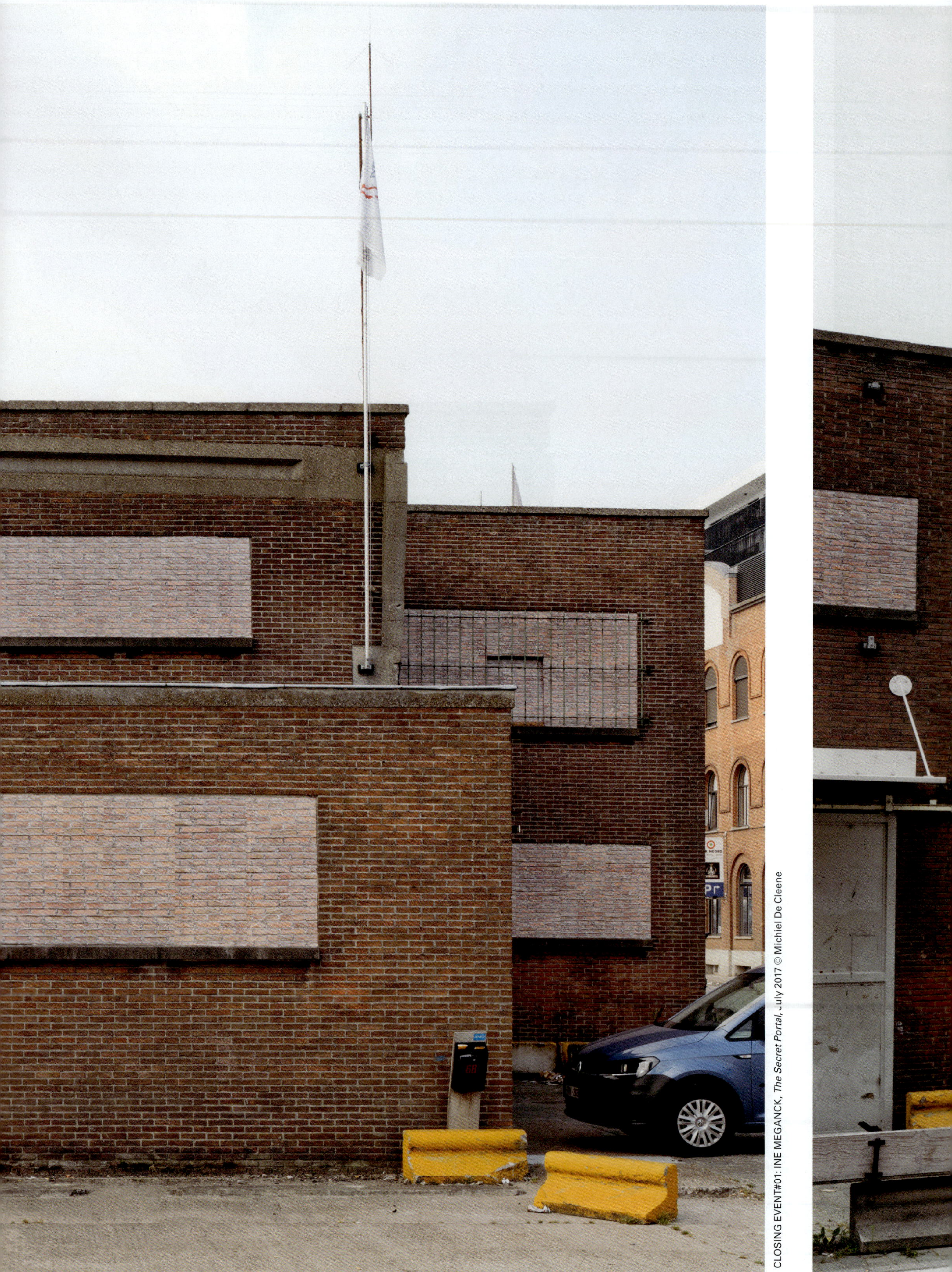

CLOSING EVENT#01: INE MEGANCK, *The Secret Portal*, July 2017 © Michiel De Cleene

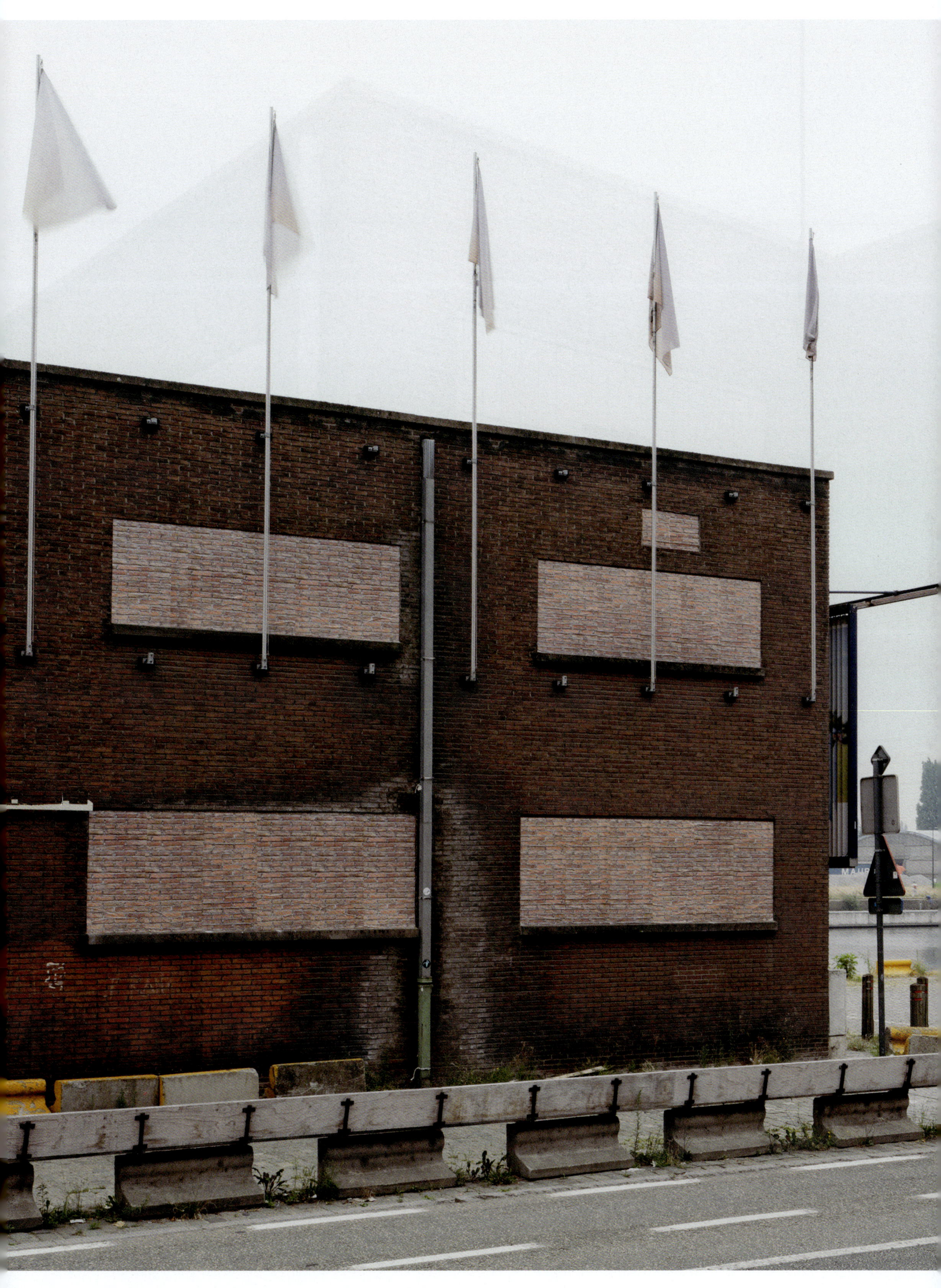

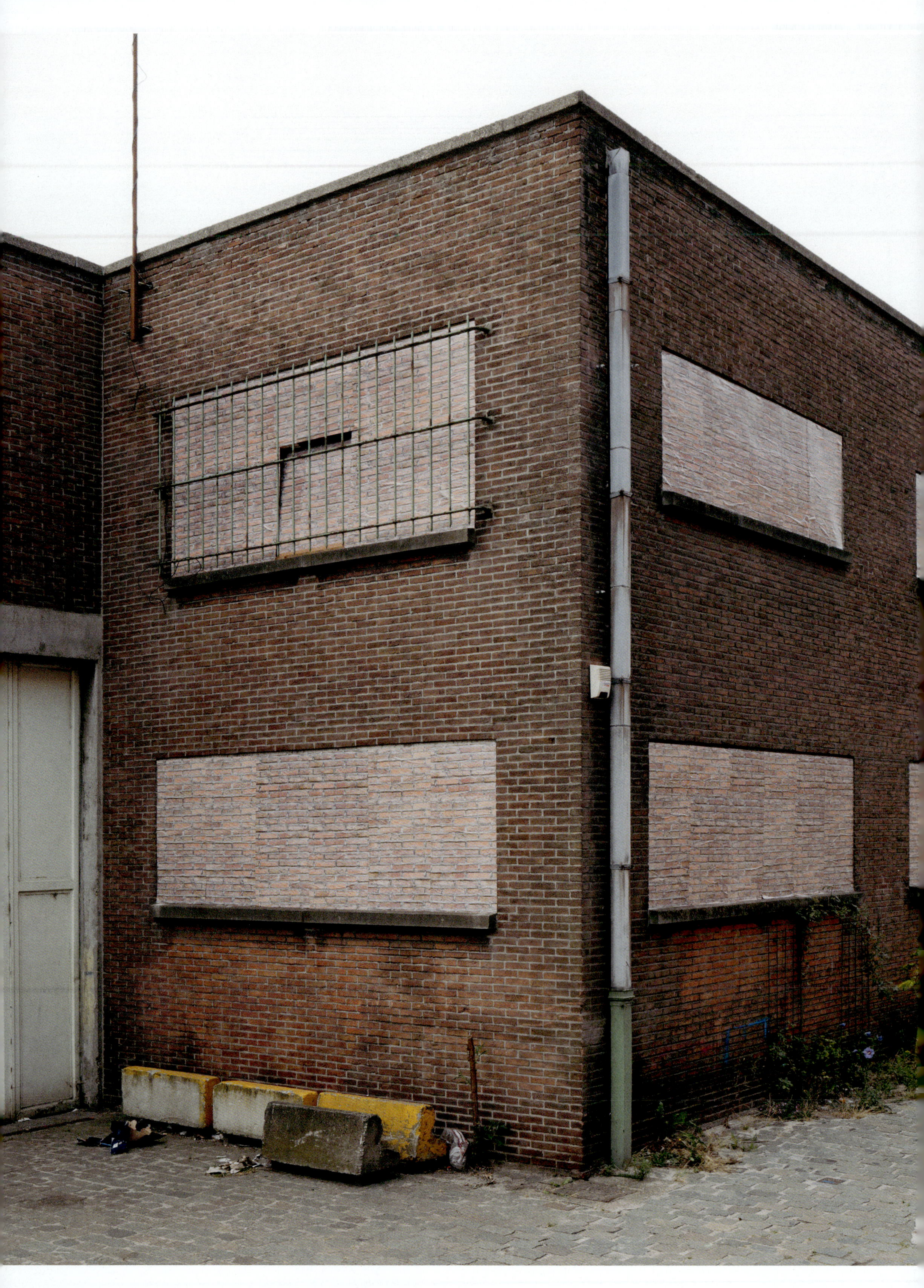

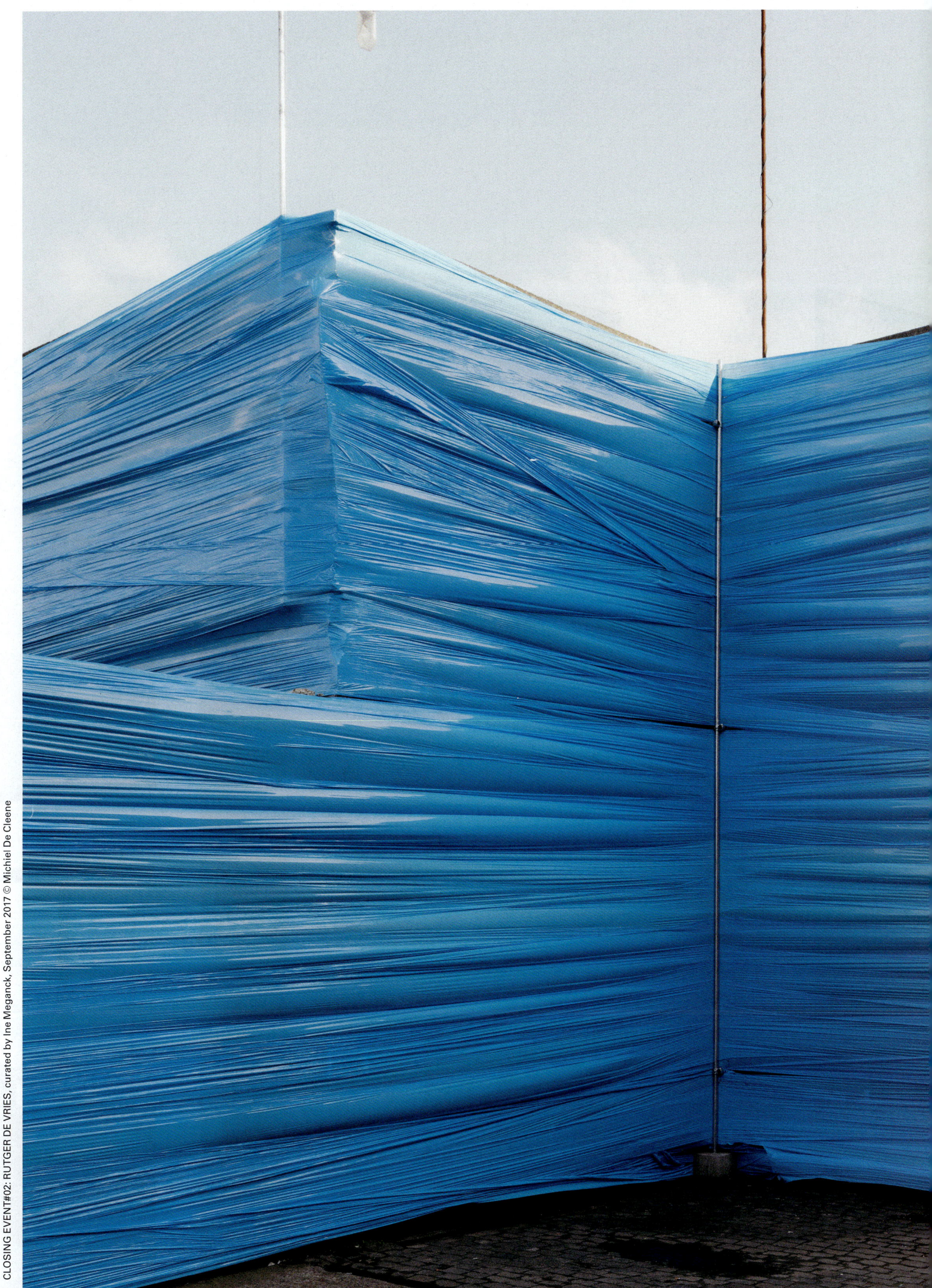

CLOSING EVENT#02: RUTGER DE VRIES, curated by Ine Meganck, September 2017 © Michiel De Cleene

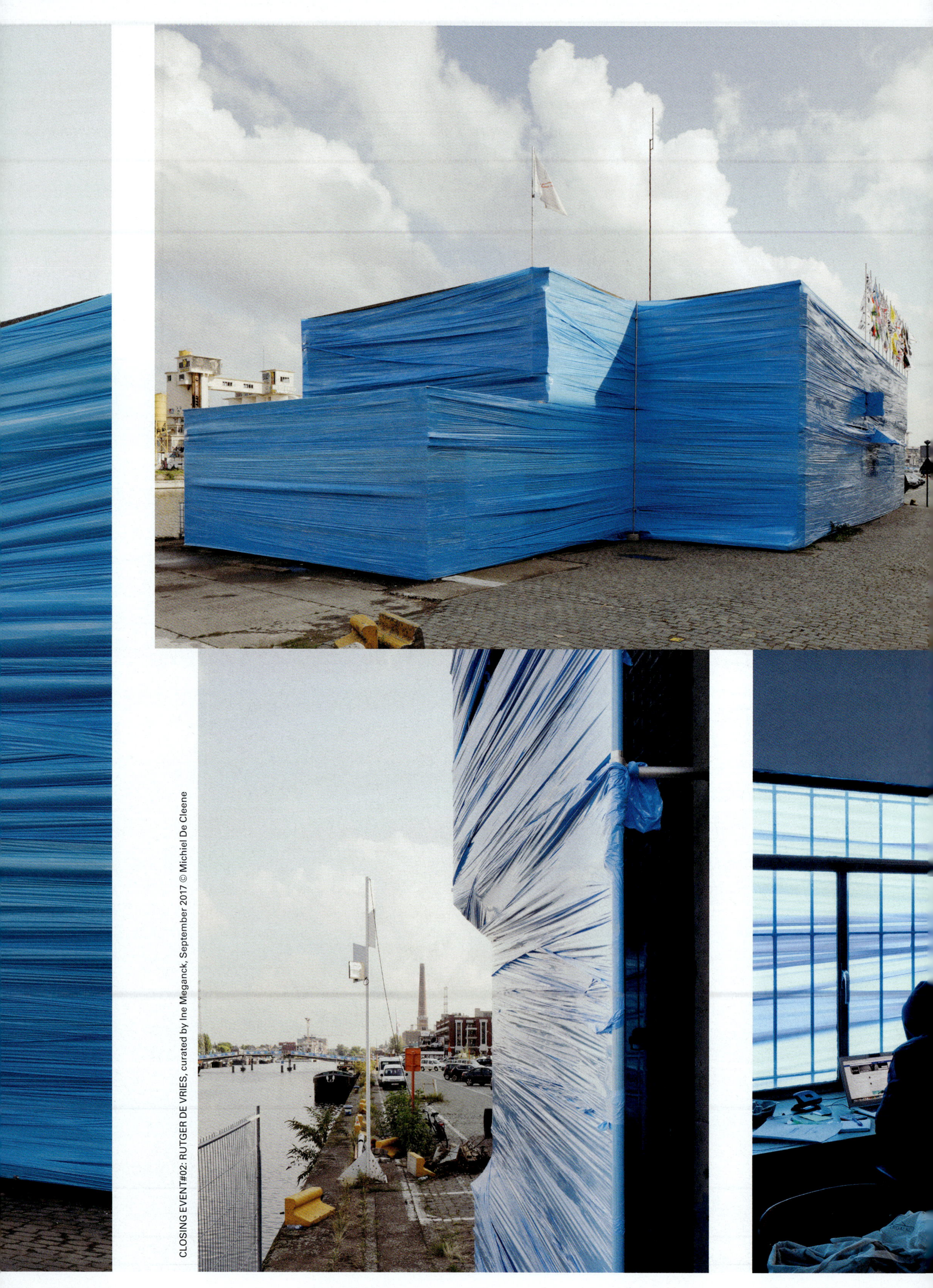

CLOSING EVENT#02: RUTGER DE VRIES, curated by Ine Meganck, September 2017 © Michiel De Cleene

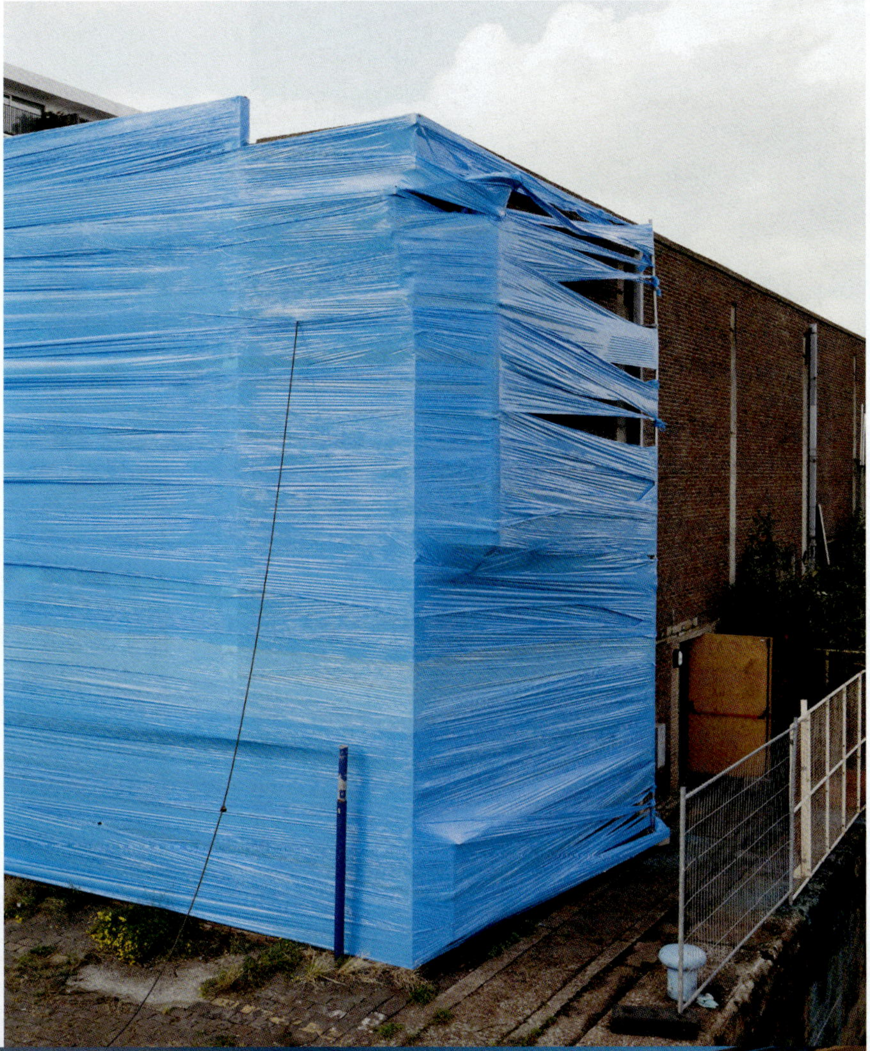

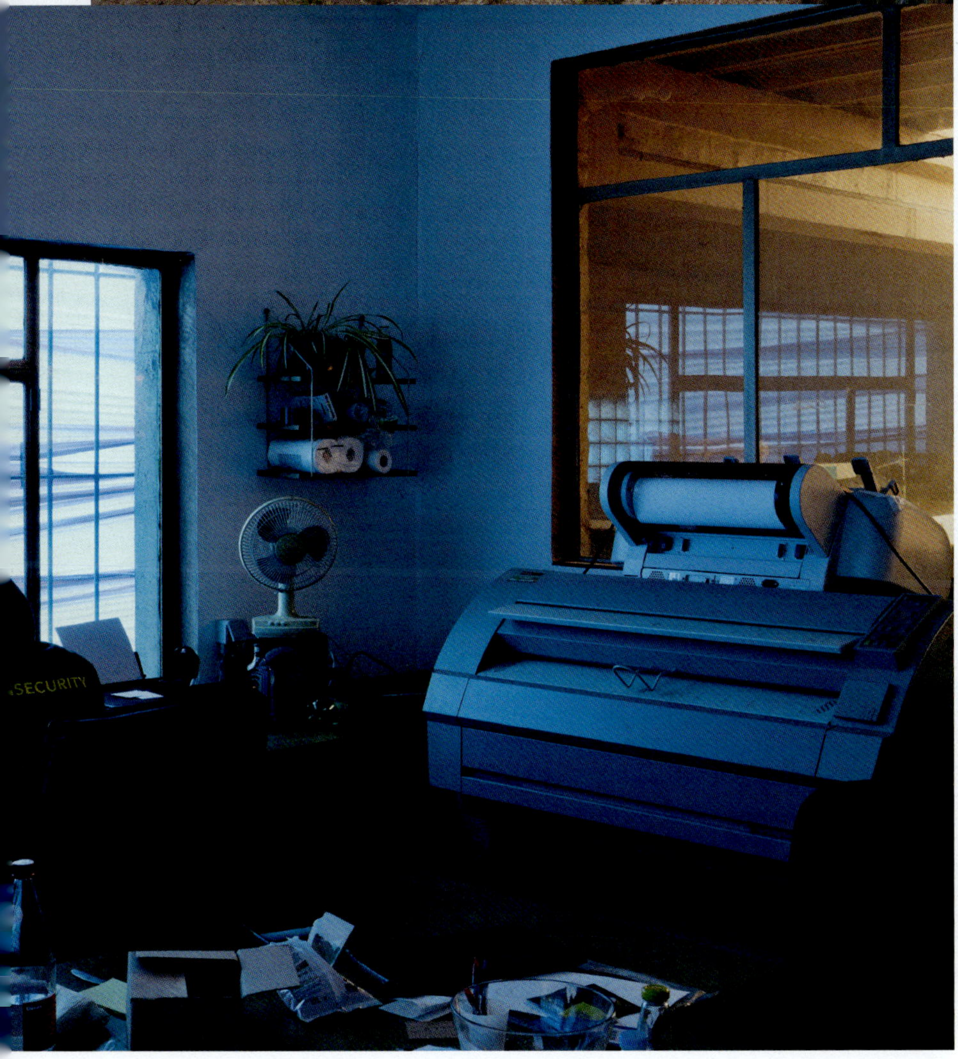

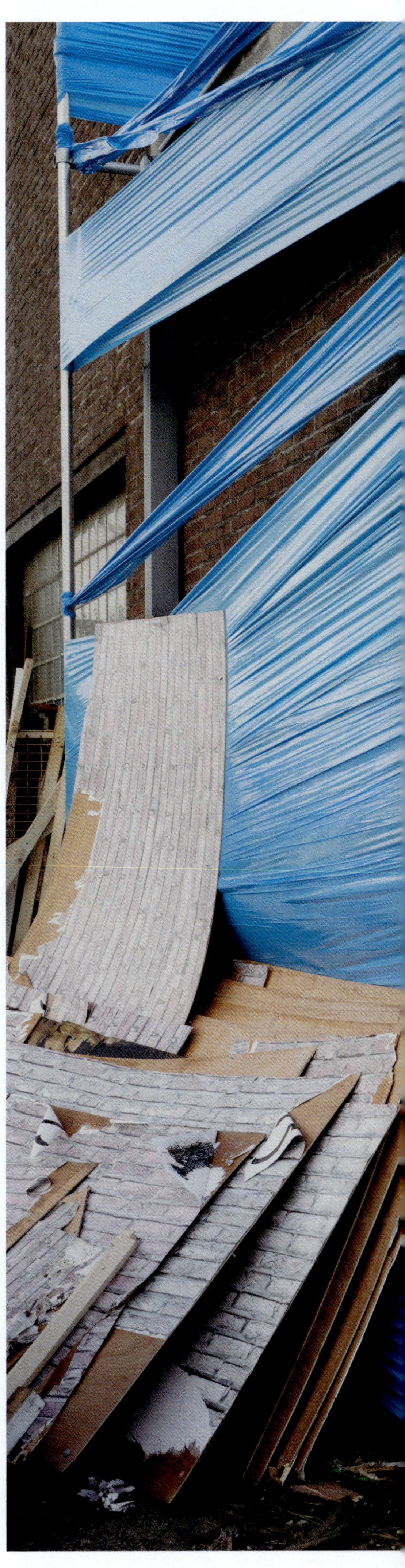

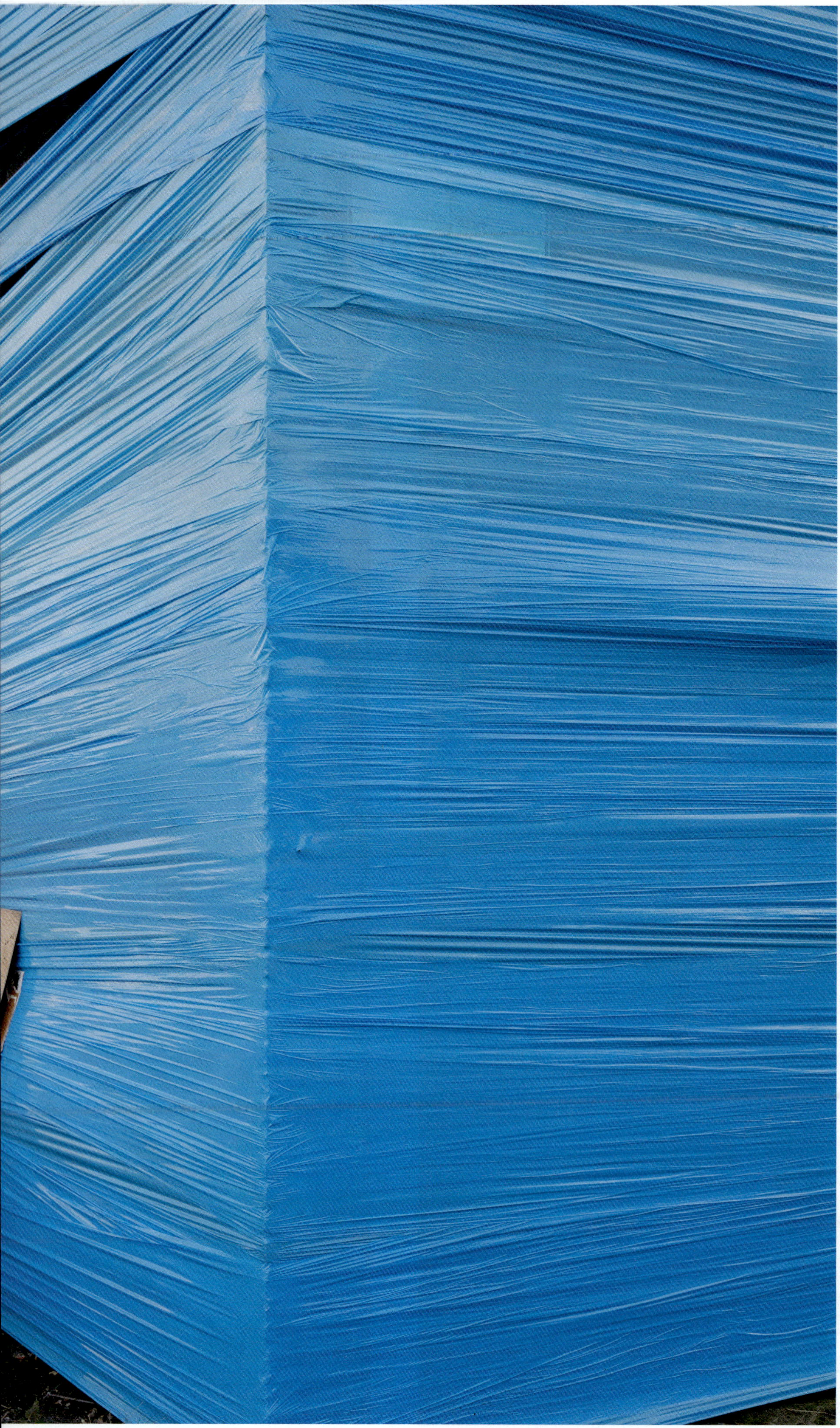

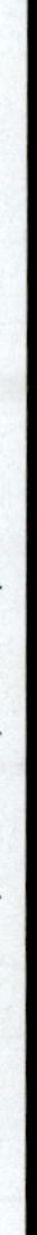

VERENA BUTTMANN, Sorry, Not Sorry 2017, September 2017 © Jonas Von Lenthe

BIEKE CRIEL, *Untitled*, S&D#025, March 2017 © Michiel De Cleene

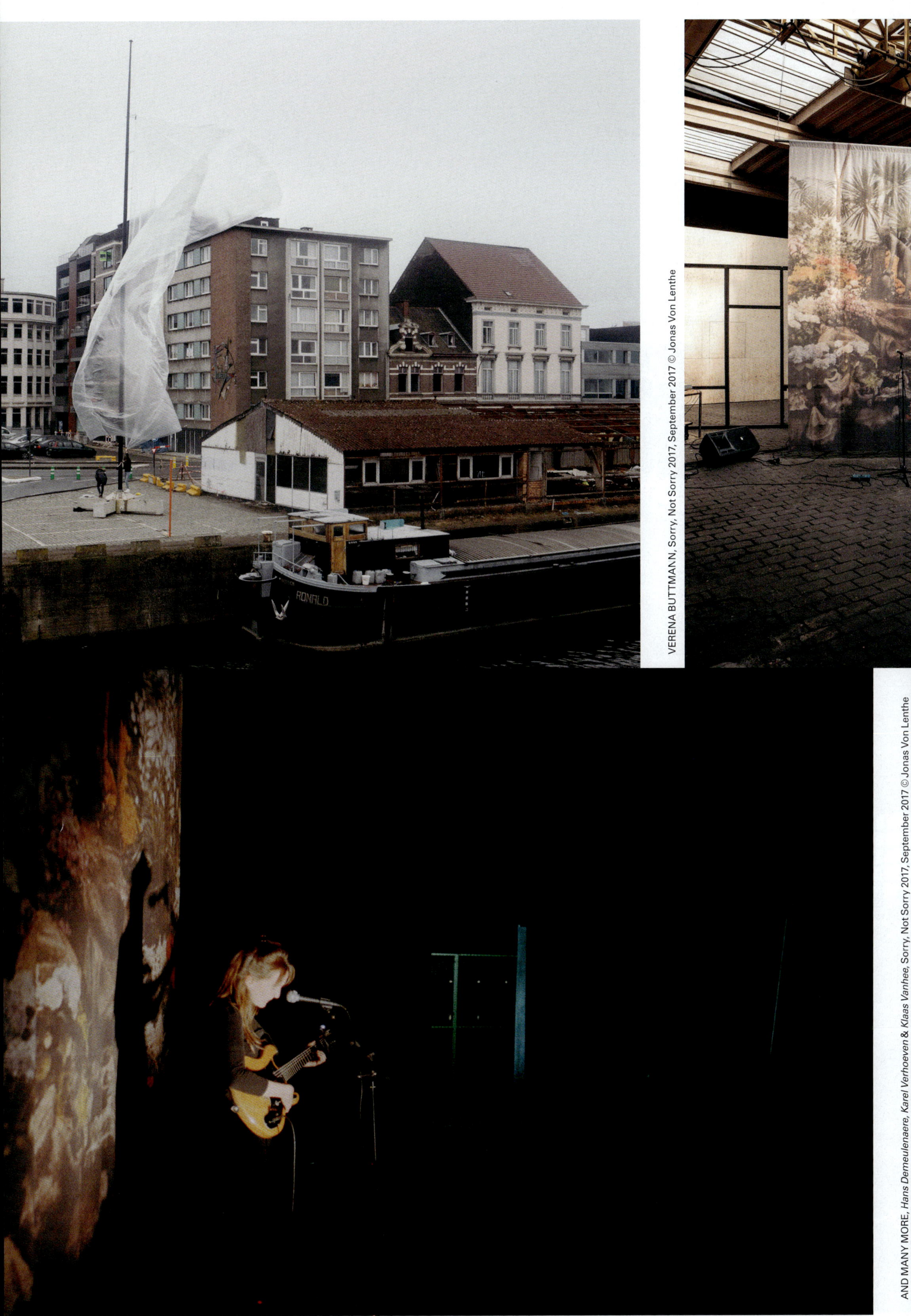

VERENA BUTTMANN, Sorry, Not Sorry 2017, September 2017 © Jonas Von Lenthe

AND MANY MORE, *Hans Demeulenaere, Karel Verhoeven & Klaas Vanhee*, Sorry, Not Sorry 2017, September 2017 © Jonas Von Lenthe

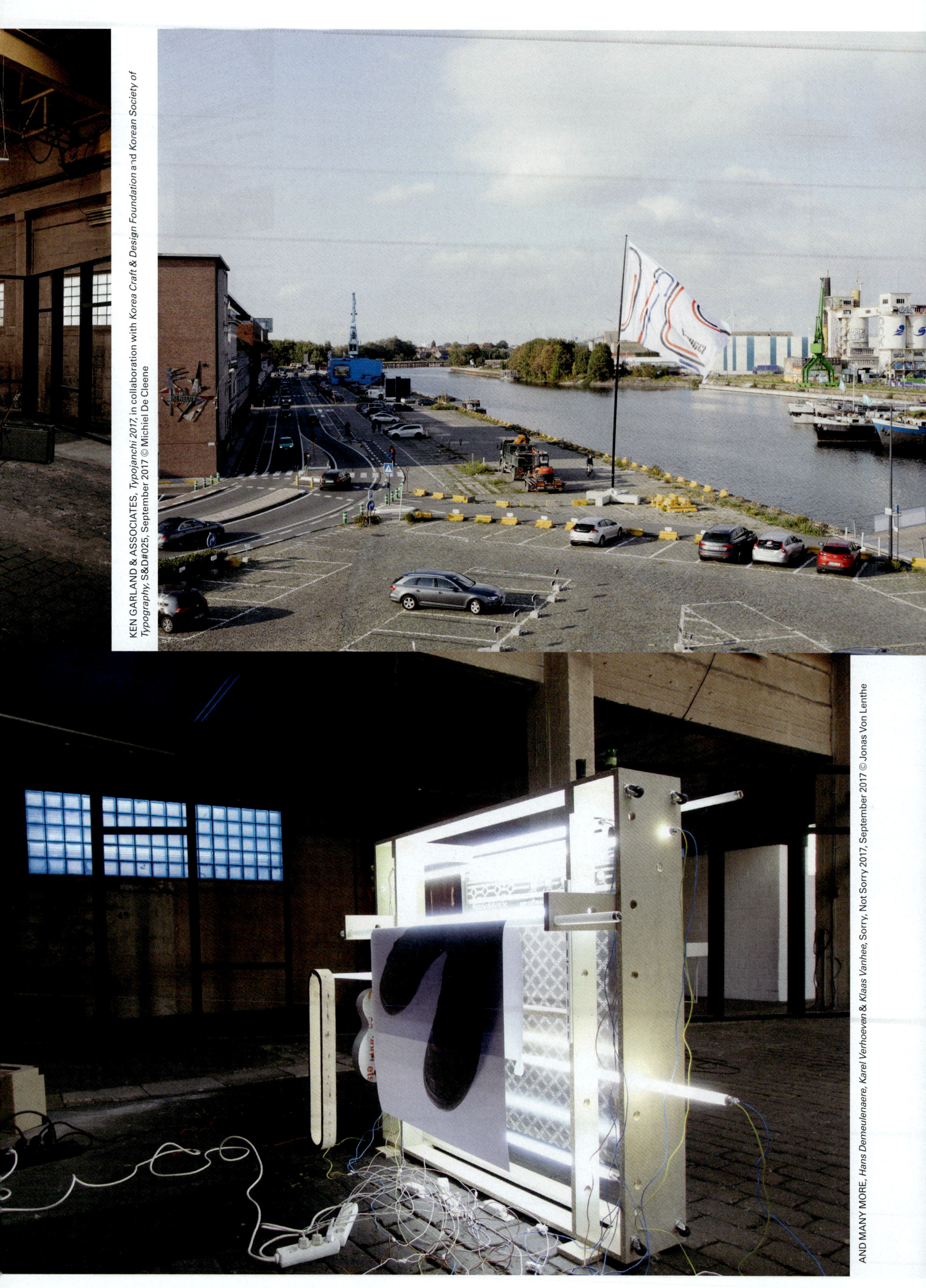

KEN GARLAND & ASSOCIATES, *Typojanchi 2017*, in collaboration with *Korea Craft & Design Foundation* and *Korean Society of Typography*, S&D#025, September 2017 © Michiel De Cleene

AND MANY MORE, *Hans Demeulenaere, Karel Verhoeven & Klaas Vanhee*, Sorry, Not Sorry 2017, September 2017 © Jonas Von Lenthe

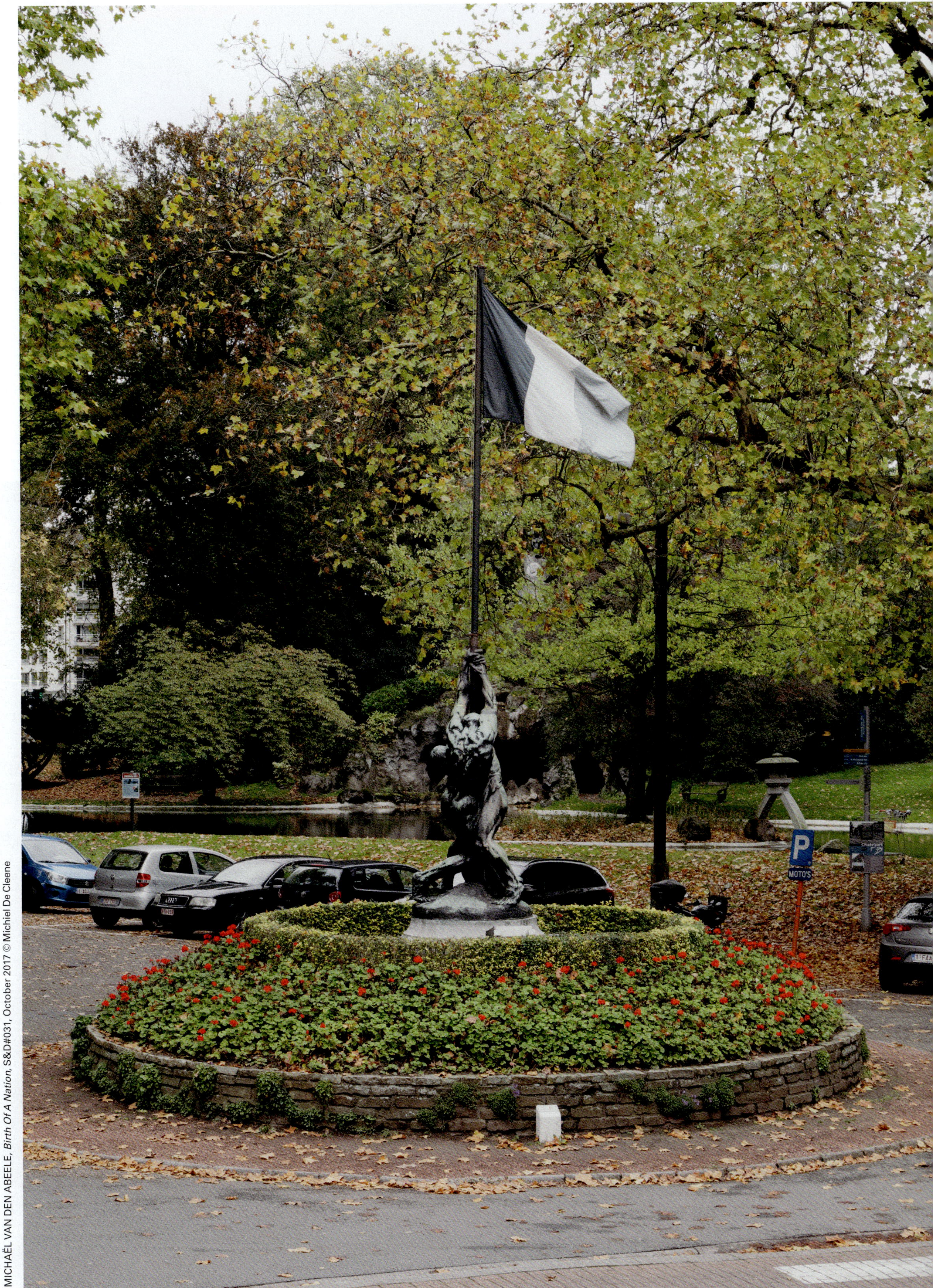

MICHAËL VAN DEN ABEELE, *Birth Of A Nation*, S&D#031, October 2017 © Michiel De Cleene

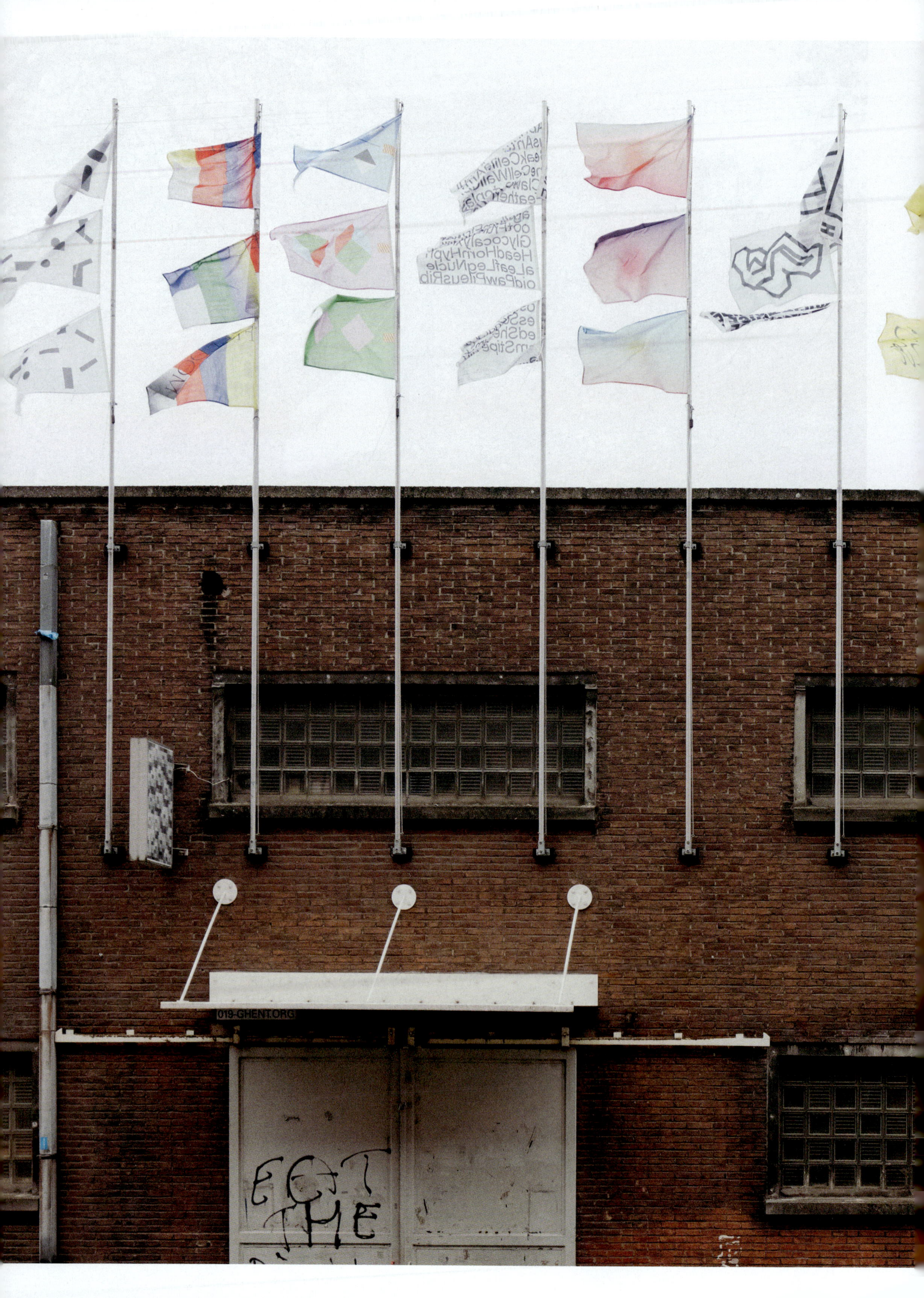
019-GHENT.ORG

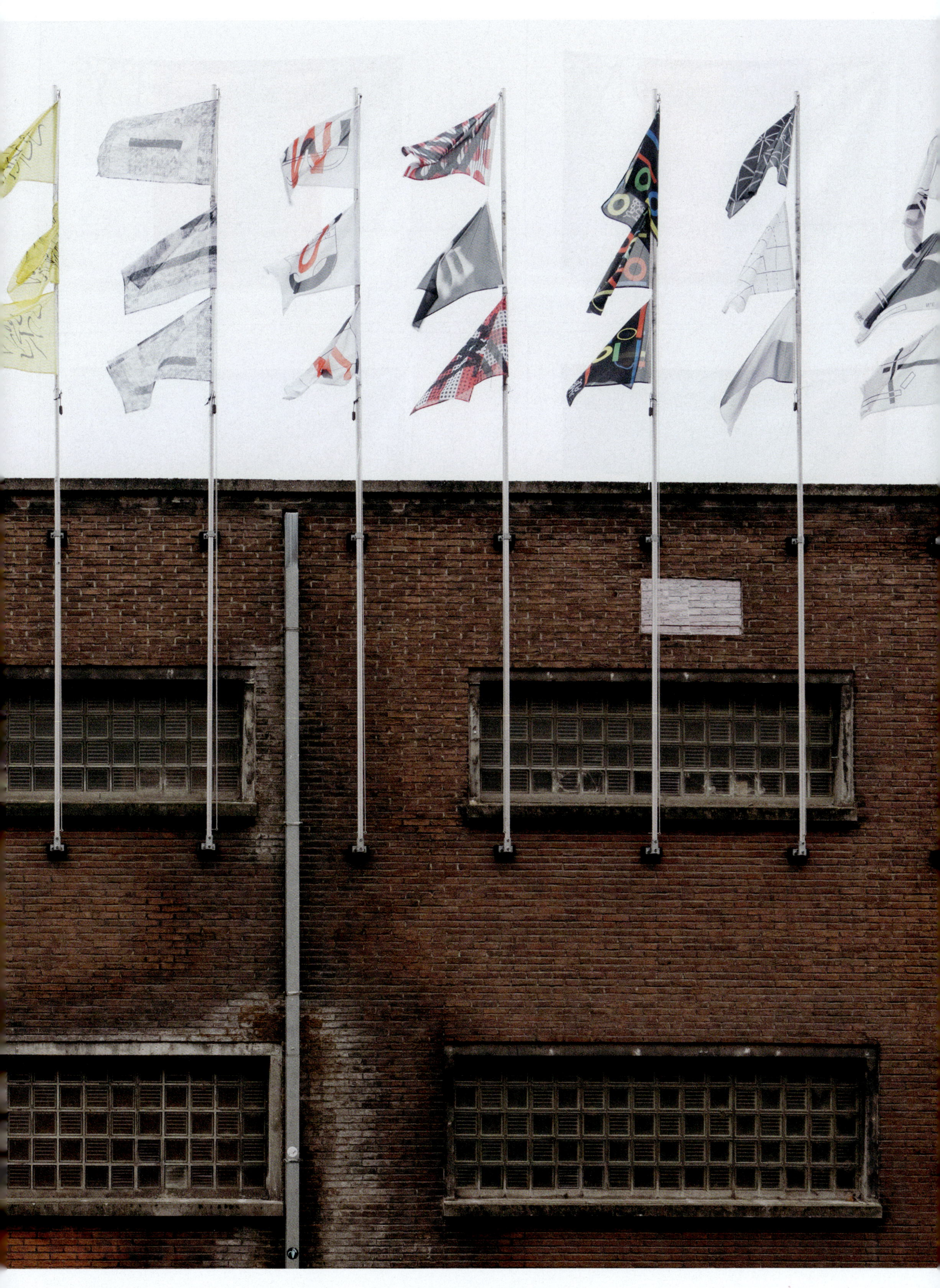

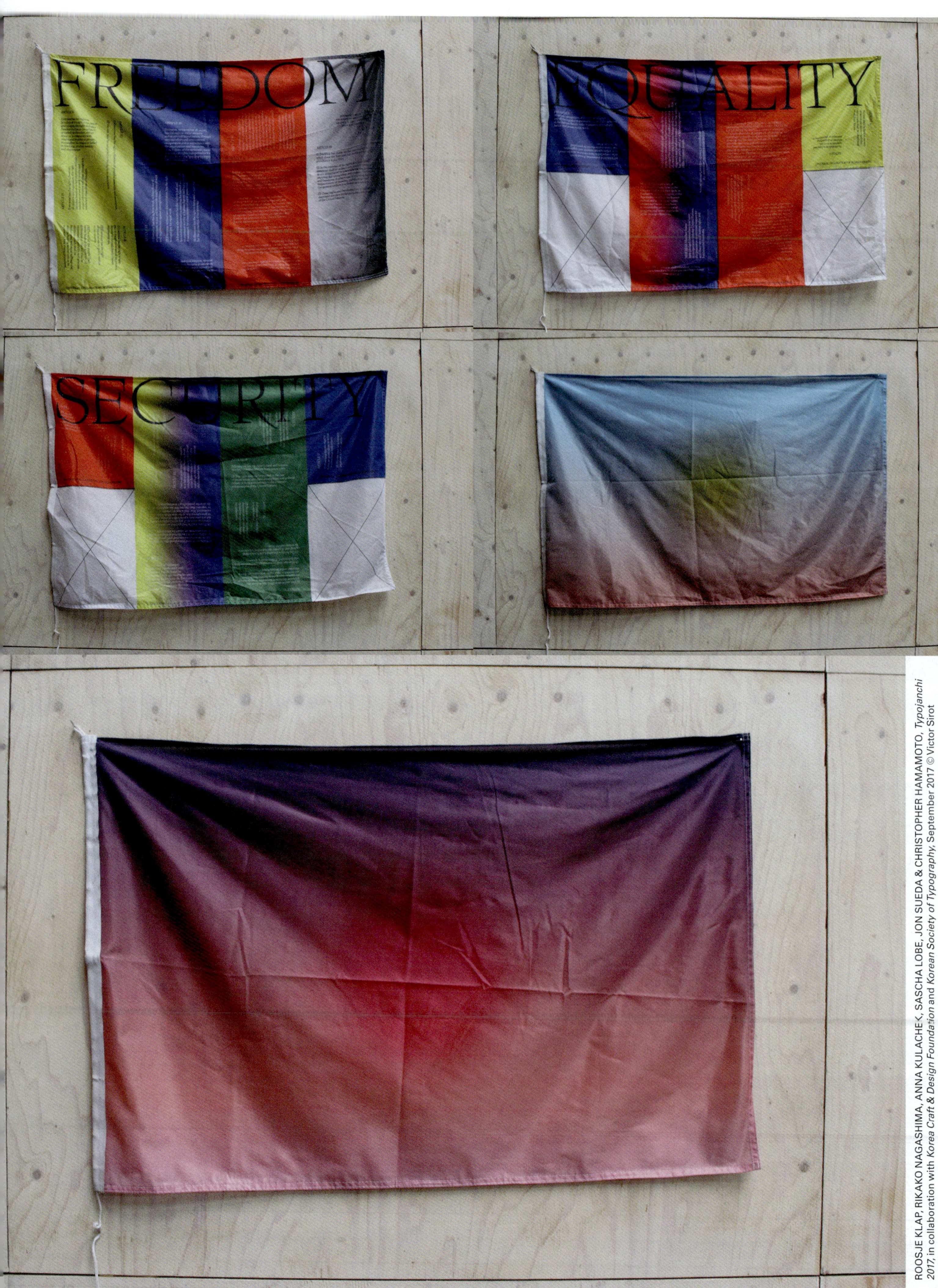

ROOSJE KLAP, RIKAKO NAGASHIMA, ANNA KULACHEK, SASCHA LOBE, JON SUEDA & CHRISTOPHER HAMAMOTO, *Typojanchi 2017*, in collaboration with *Korea Craft & Design Foundation* and *Korean Society of Typography*, September 2017 © Victor Sirot

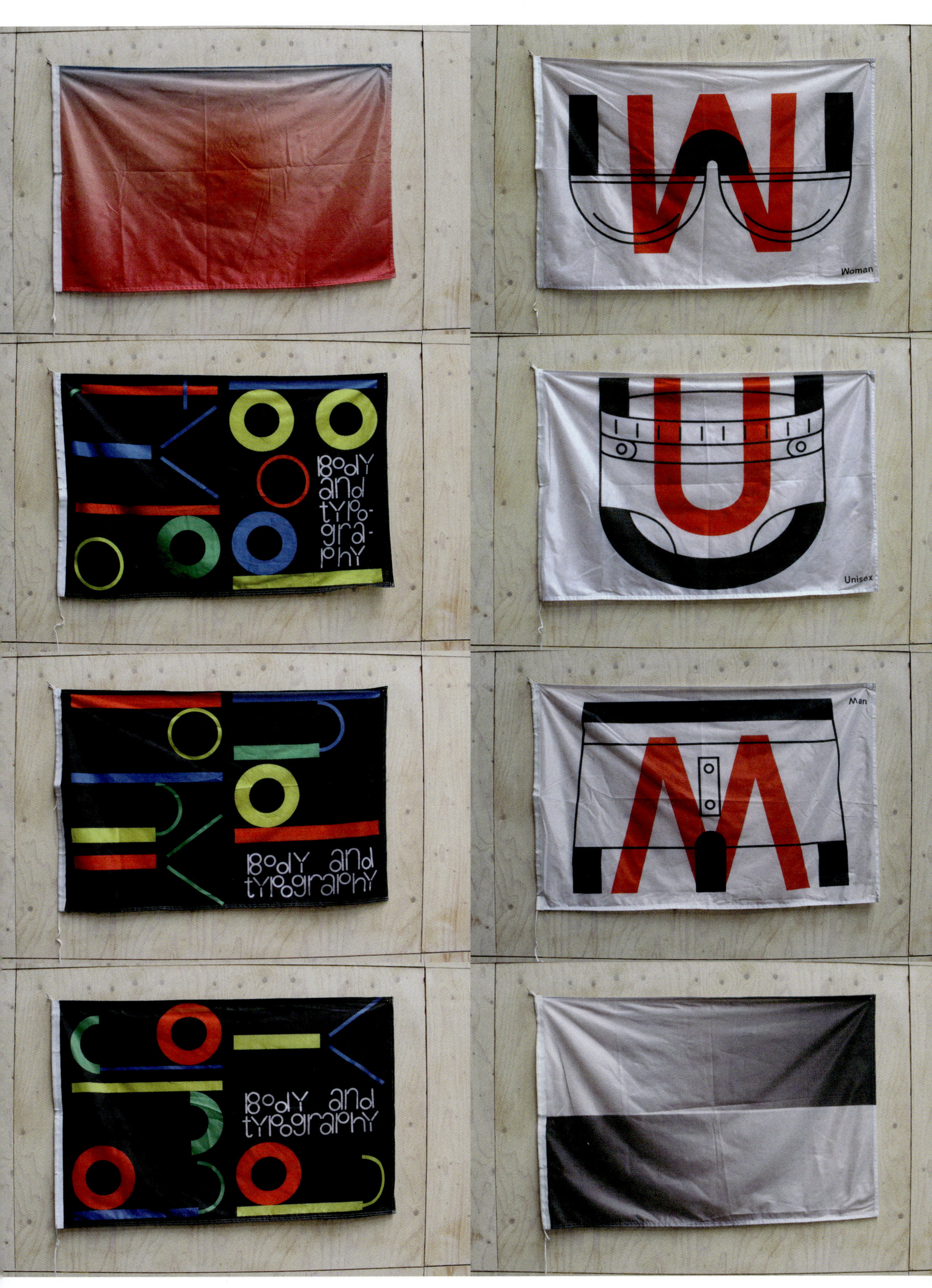
Woman
Body and typography
Unisex
Body and typography
Man
Body and typography

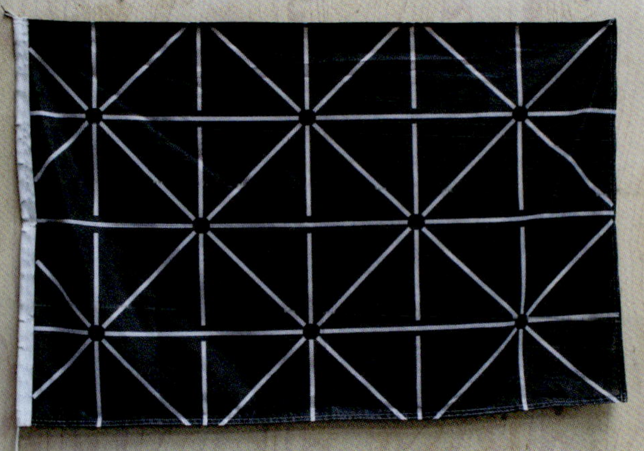
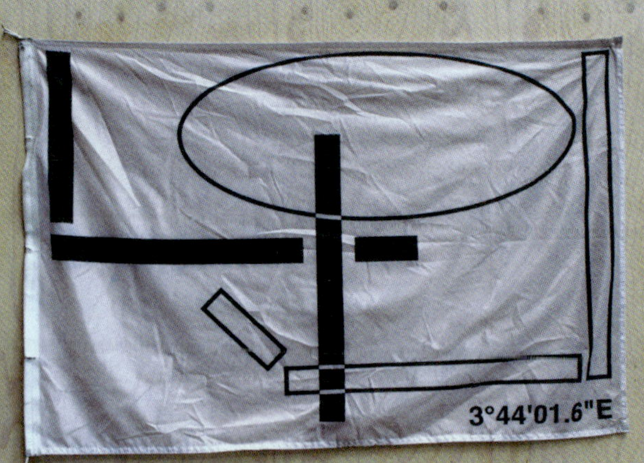
3°44'01.6"E
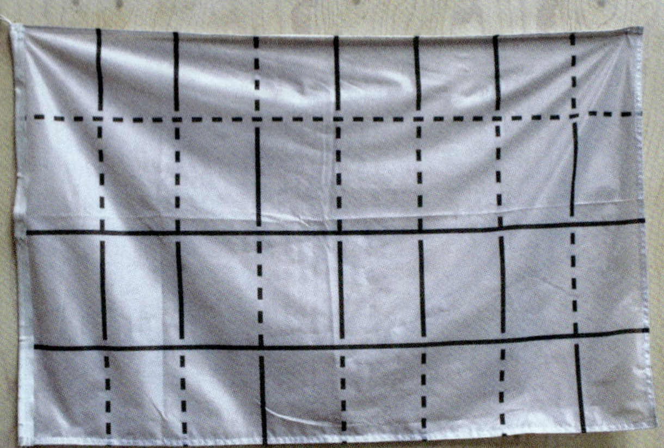
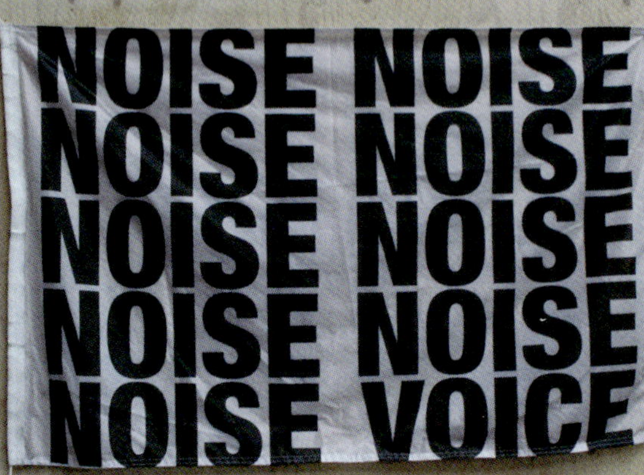
NOISE NOISE
NOISE NOISE
NOISE NOISE
NOISE NOISE
NOISE VOICE
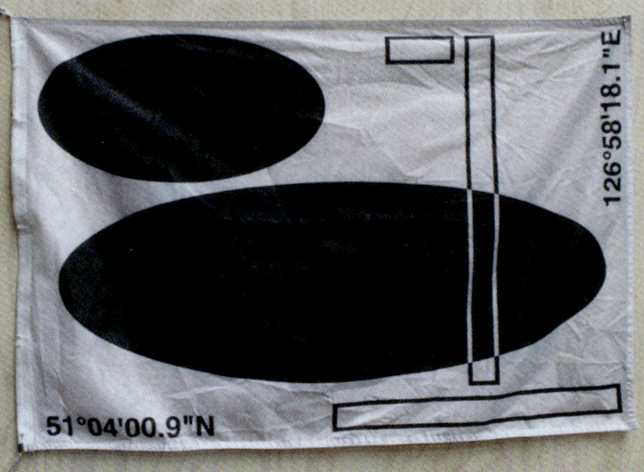
126°58'18.1"E
51°04'00.9"N
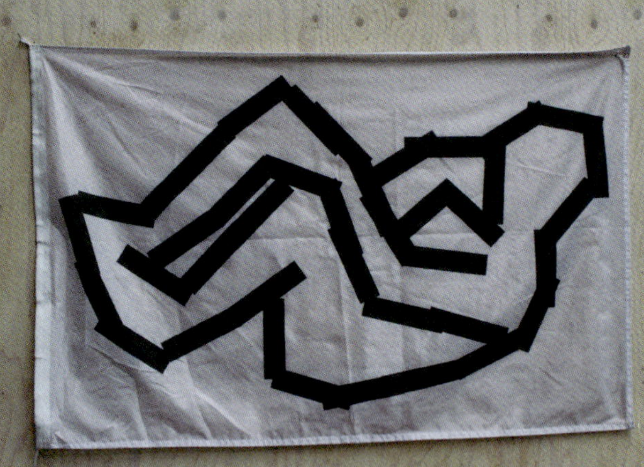
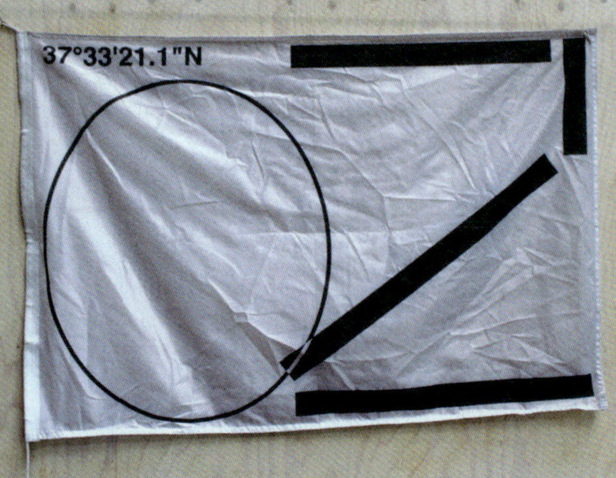
37°33'21.1"N
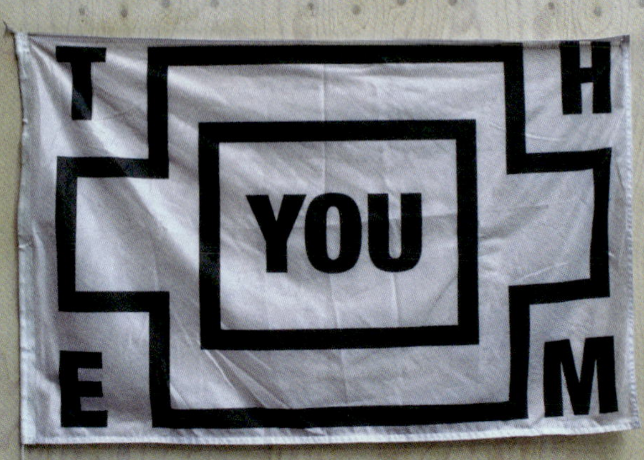
T
H
YOU
E
M

AbdomenAnnul
usAntannaArm
BeakCellMembr
aneCellWallChe
stClawCytoplas
mFeatherFinsFl

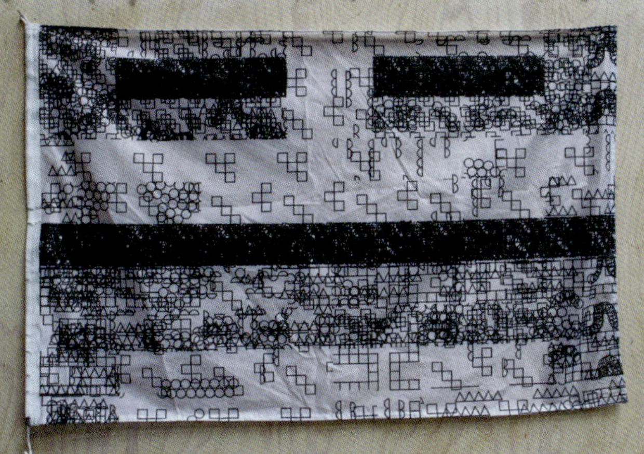

agellumFlowerF
ootFruitFurGills
GlycocalyxHand
HeadHornHyph
aLeafLegNucle
oidPawPileusRib

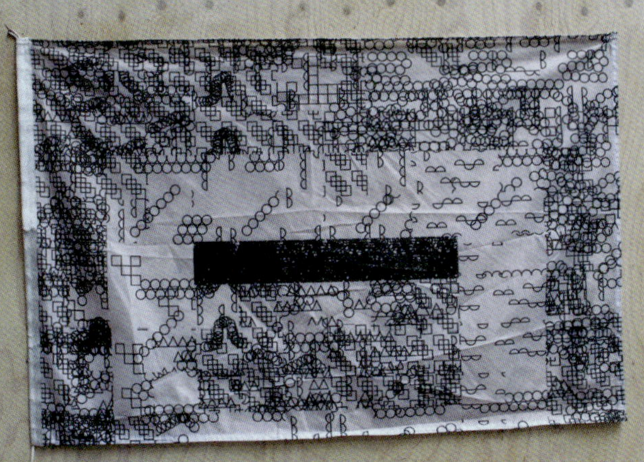

osomeRootScal
esSclerotiumSe
edShellSporeSt
emStipeTailWin
g...

Typojanchi 2017
The 5th International Typography Biennale

Body
September 15 - October 29, 2017

Edit-Grotesk 60
Designed by Guang Yu

JON SUEDA & CHRISTOPHER HAMAMOTO, SHIM DAEKI & SHIM HYOJUN, EIKE KÖNIG, GUANG YU, STUDIO JOOST GROOTENS,
Typojanchi 2017, in collaboration with *Korea Craft & Design Foundation* and *Korean Society of Typography*, September 2017 © Victor Sirot

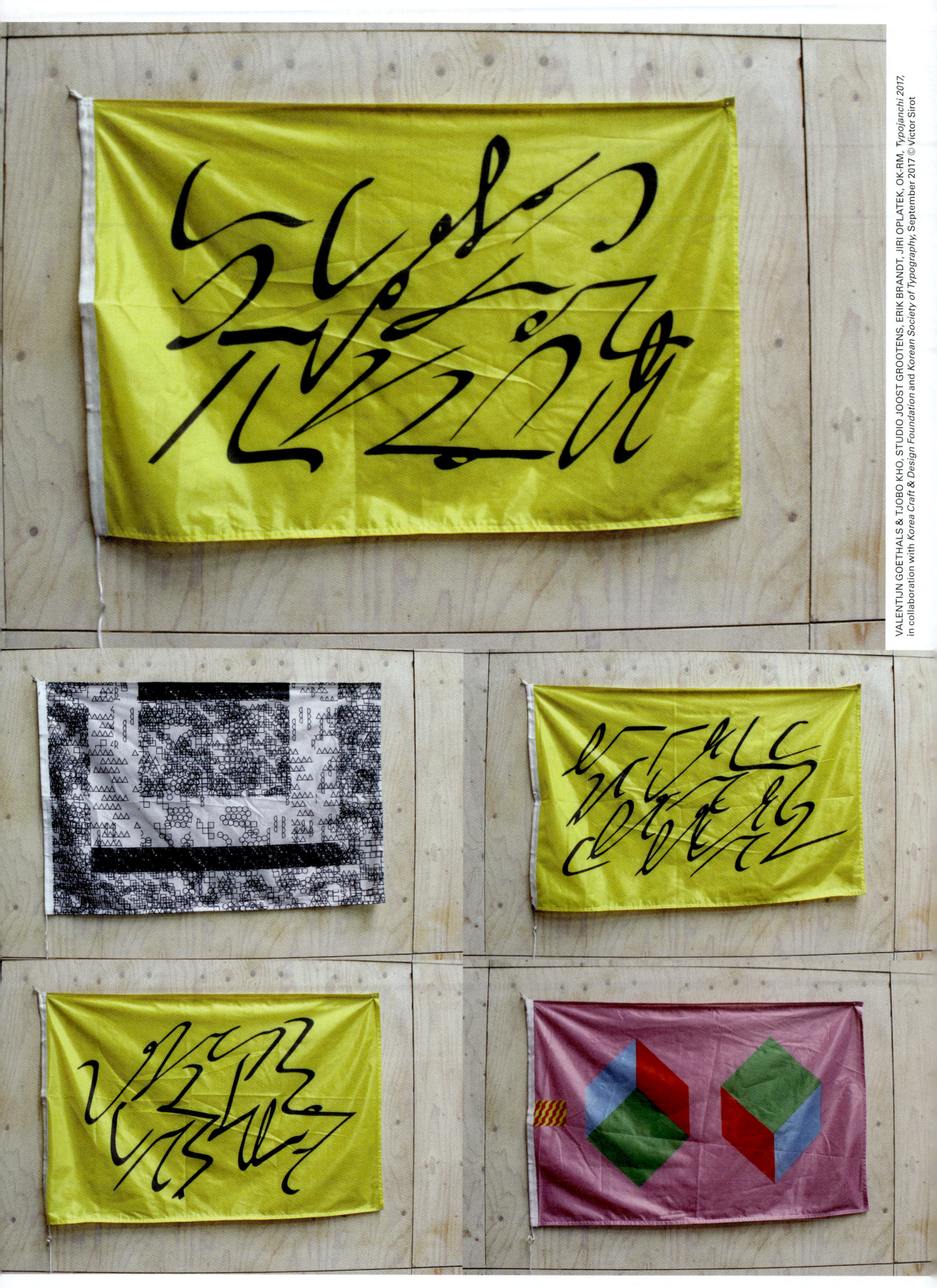

VALENTIJN GOETHALS & TJOBO KHO, STUDIO JOOST GROOTENS, ERIK BRANDT, JIRI OPLATEK, OK-RM, *Typojanchi 2017*, in collaboration with *Korea Craft & Design Foundation* and *Korean Society of Typography*, September 2017 © Victor Sirot

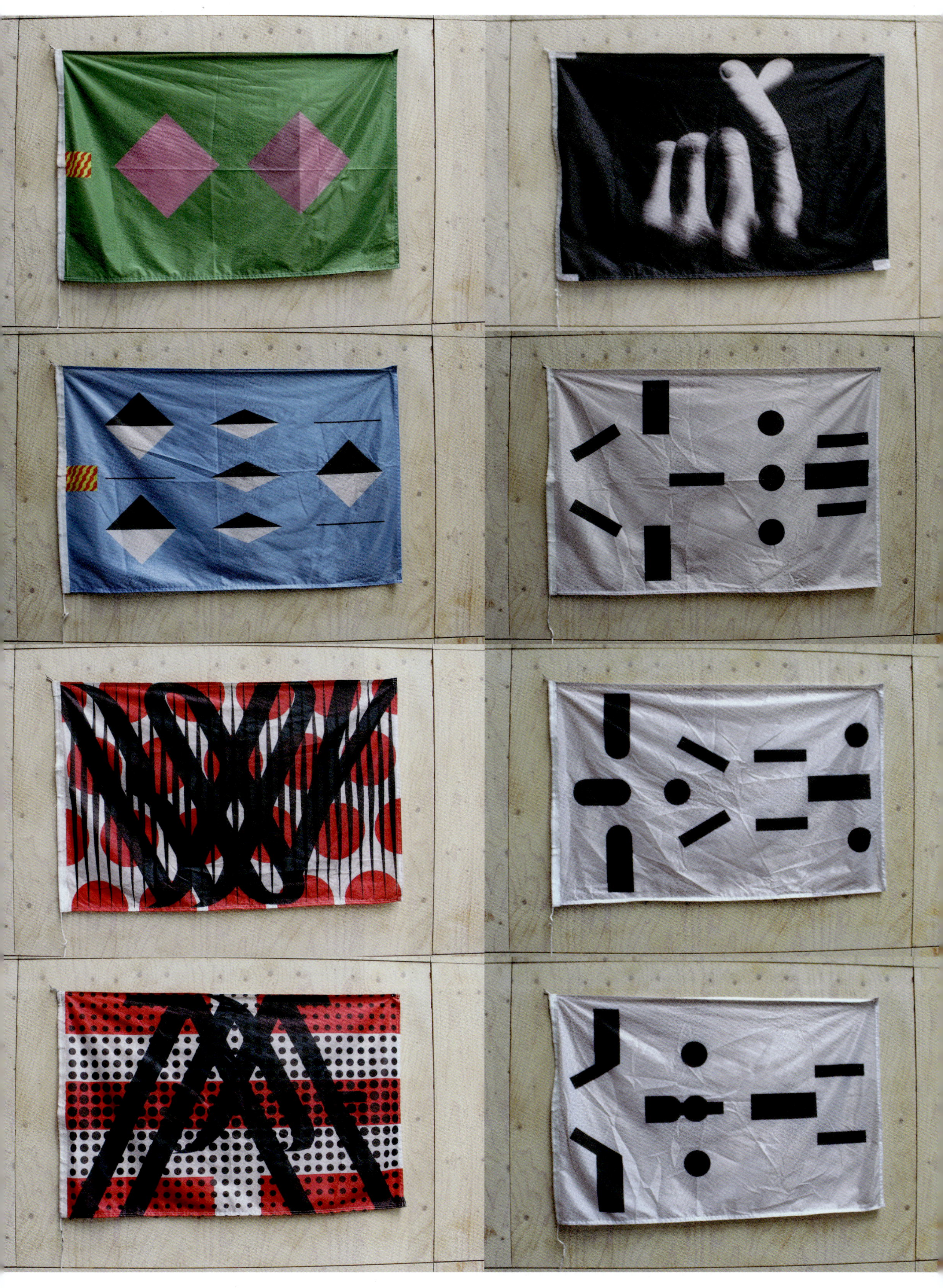

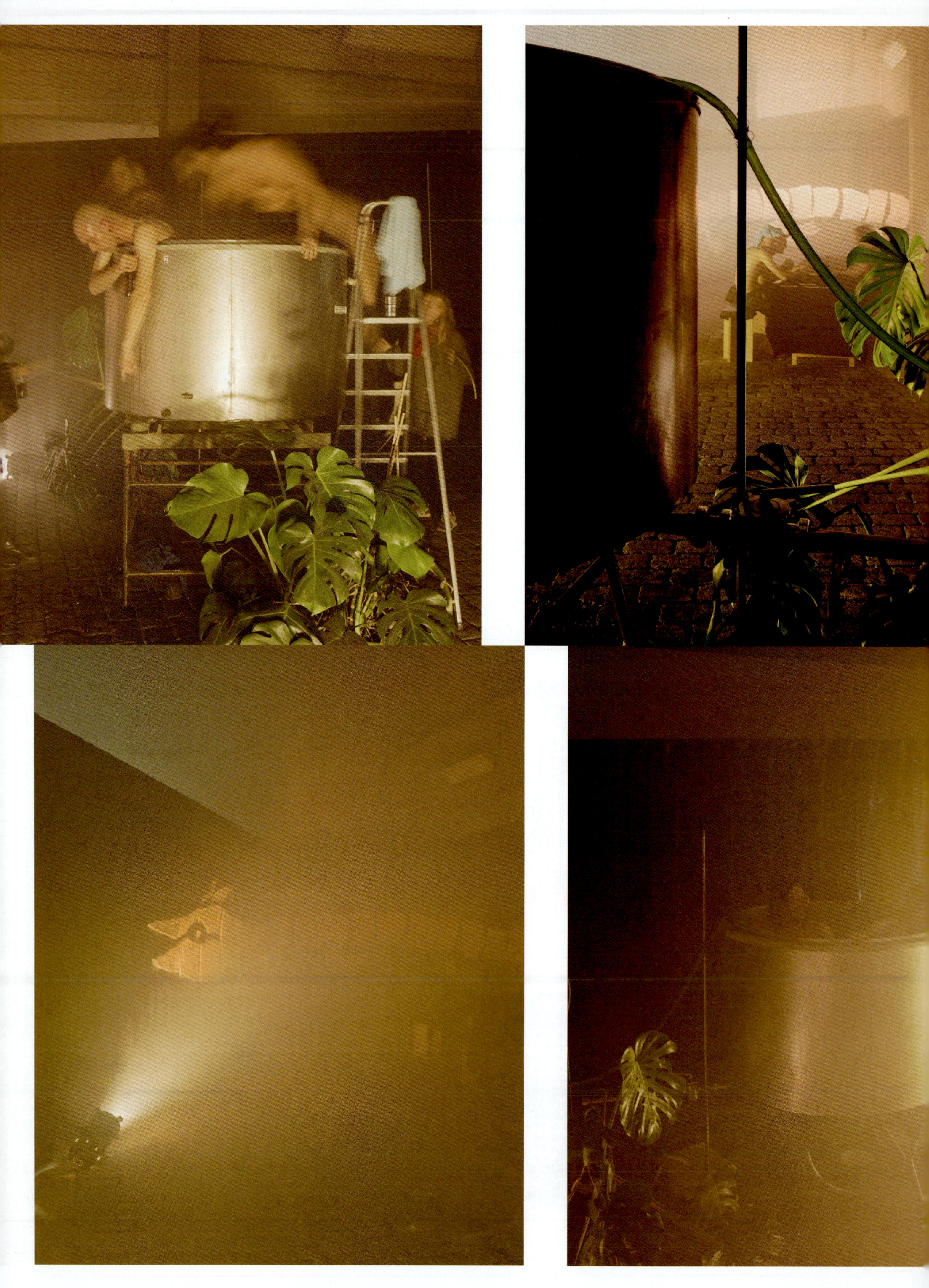

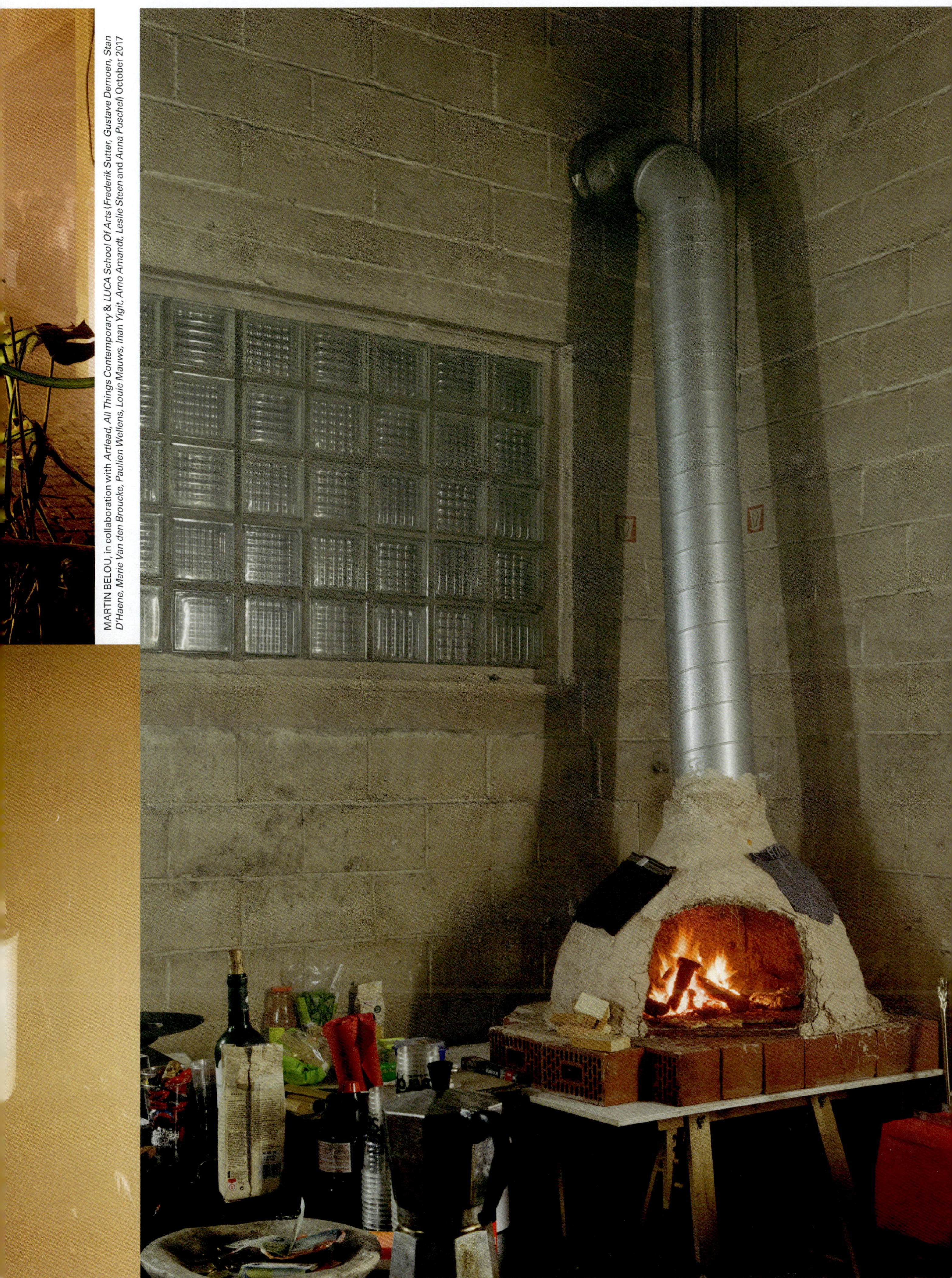

MARTIN BELOU, in collaboration with *Artlead, All Things Contemporary* & *LUCA School Of Arts* (*Frederik Sutter, Gustave Demoen, Stan D'Haene, Marie Van den Broucke, Paulien Wellens, Louie Mauws, Inan Yigit, Arno Amandt, Leslie Steen* and *Anna Puschel*) October 2017

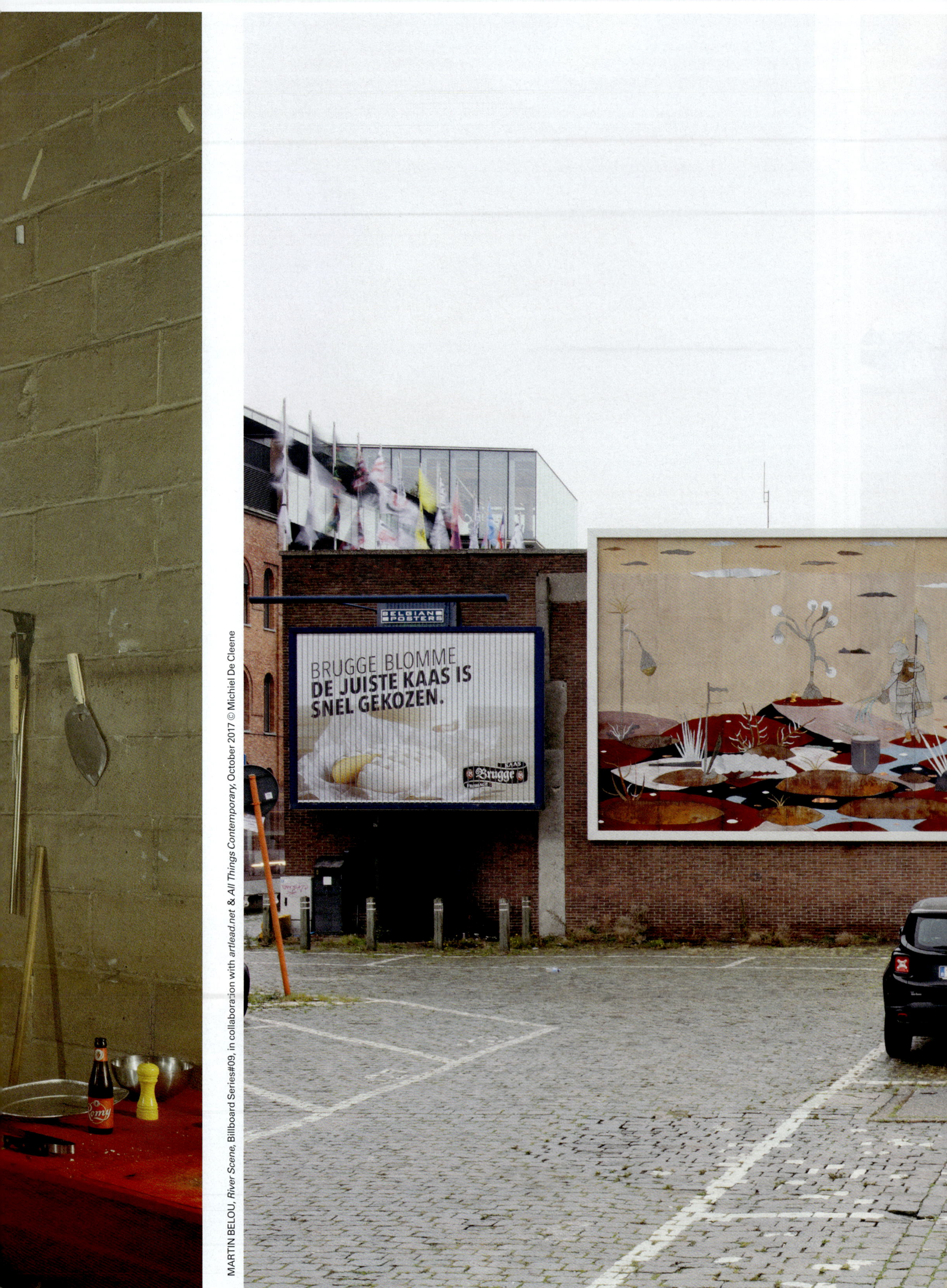

MARTIN BELOU, *River Scene*, Billboard Series#09, in collaboration with *artlead.net* & *All Things Contemporary*, October 2017 © Michiel De Cleene

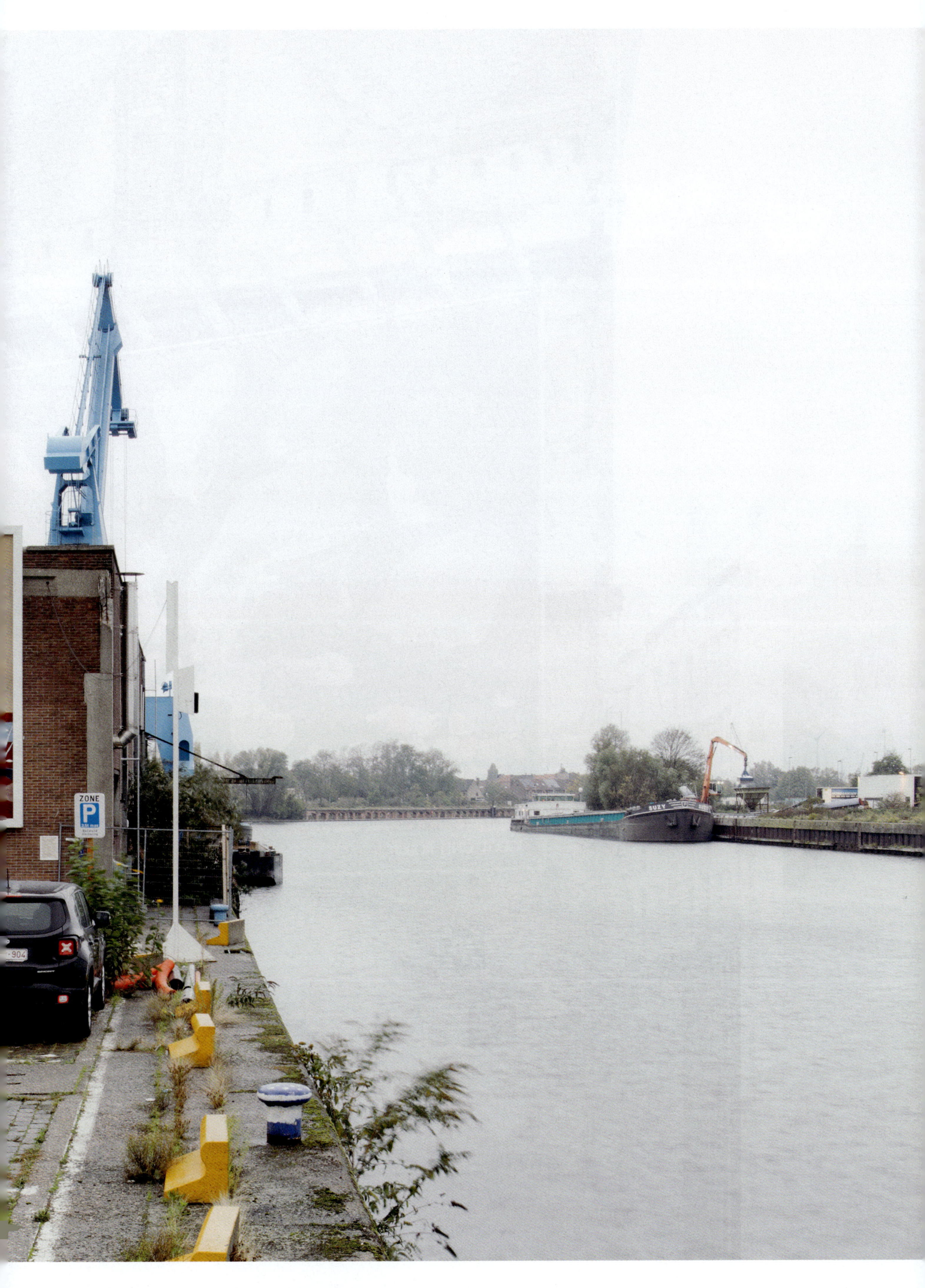
ZONE
P

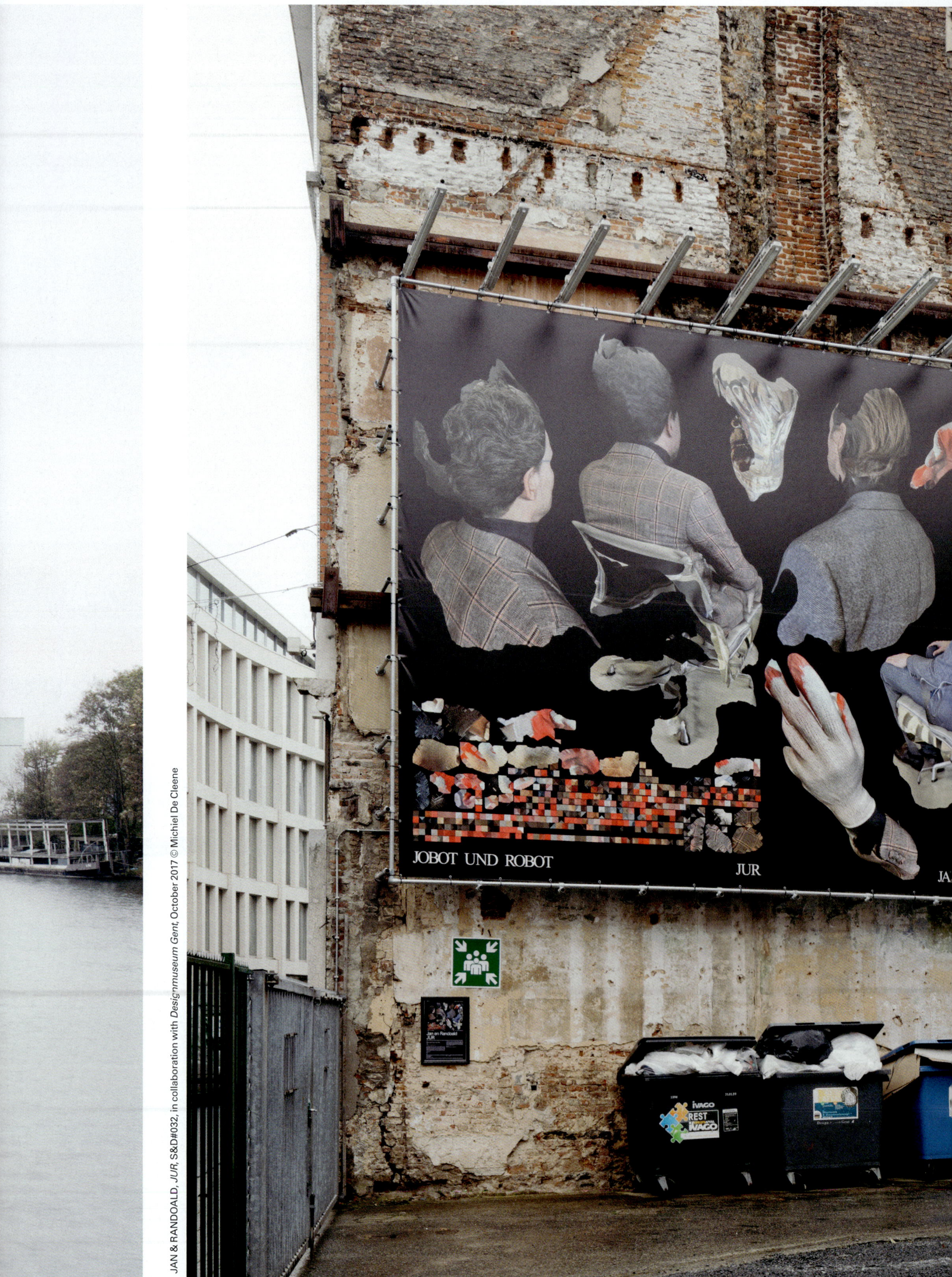

JAN & RANDOALD, *JUR*, S&D#032, in collaboration with *Designmuseum Gent*, October 2017 © Michiel De Cleene

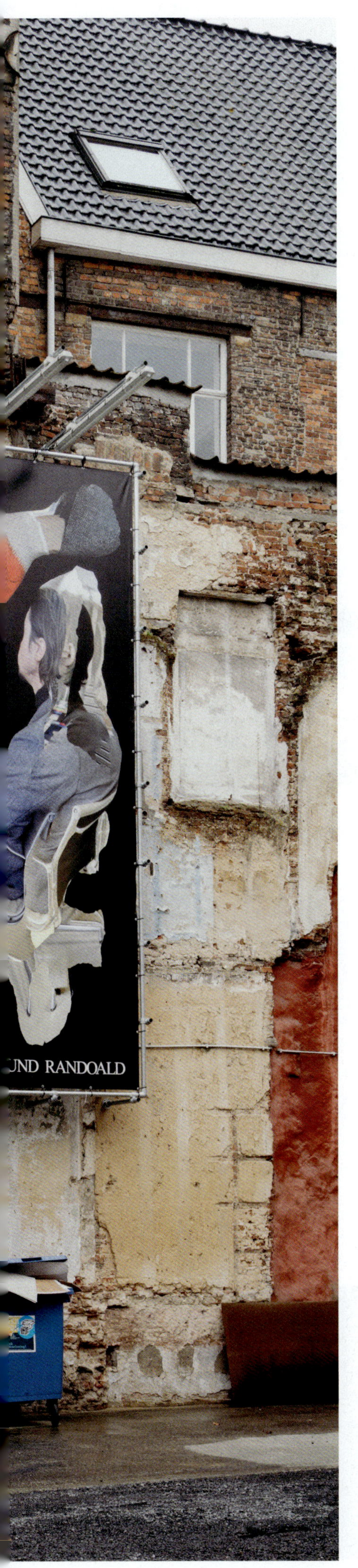

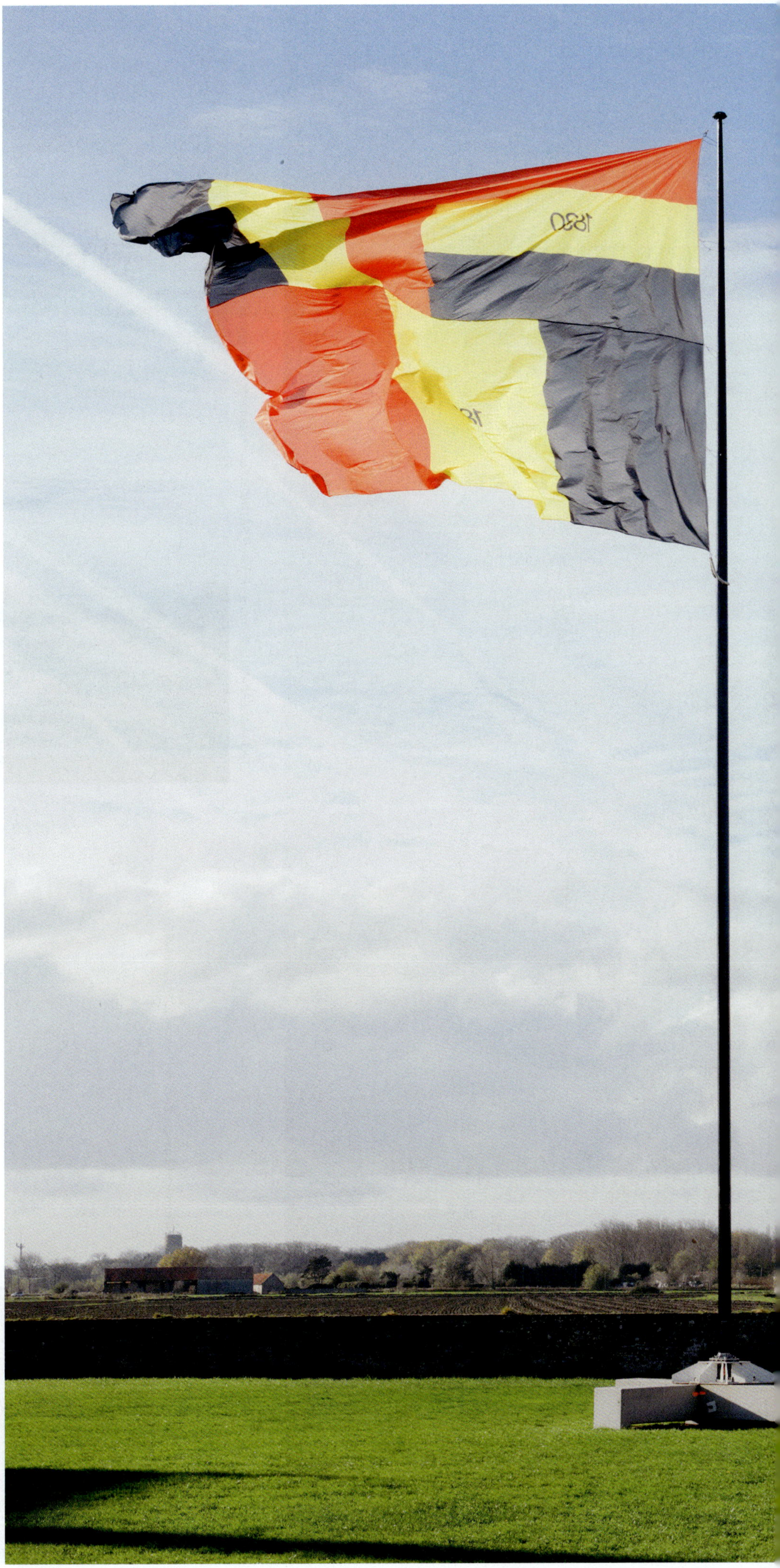

JAN & RANDOALD, *A Brief History of The Belgian Flag*, S&D#025, Kunstencentrum Ten Bogaerde, Koksijde, October 2017 © Michiel De Cleene

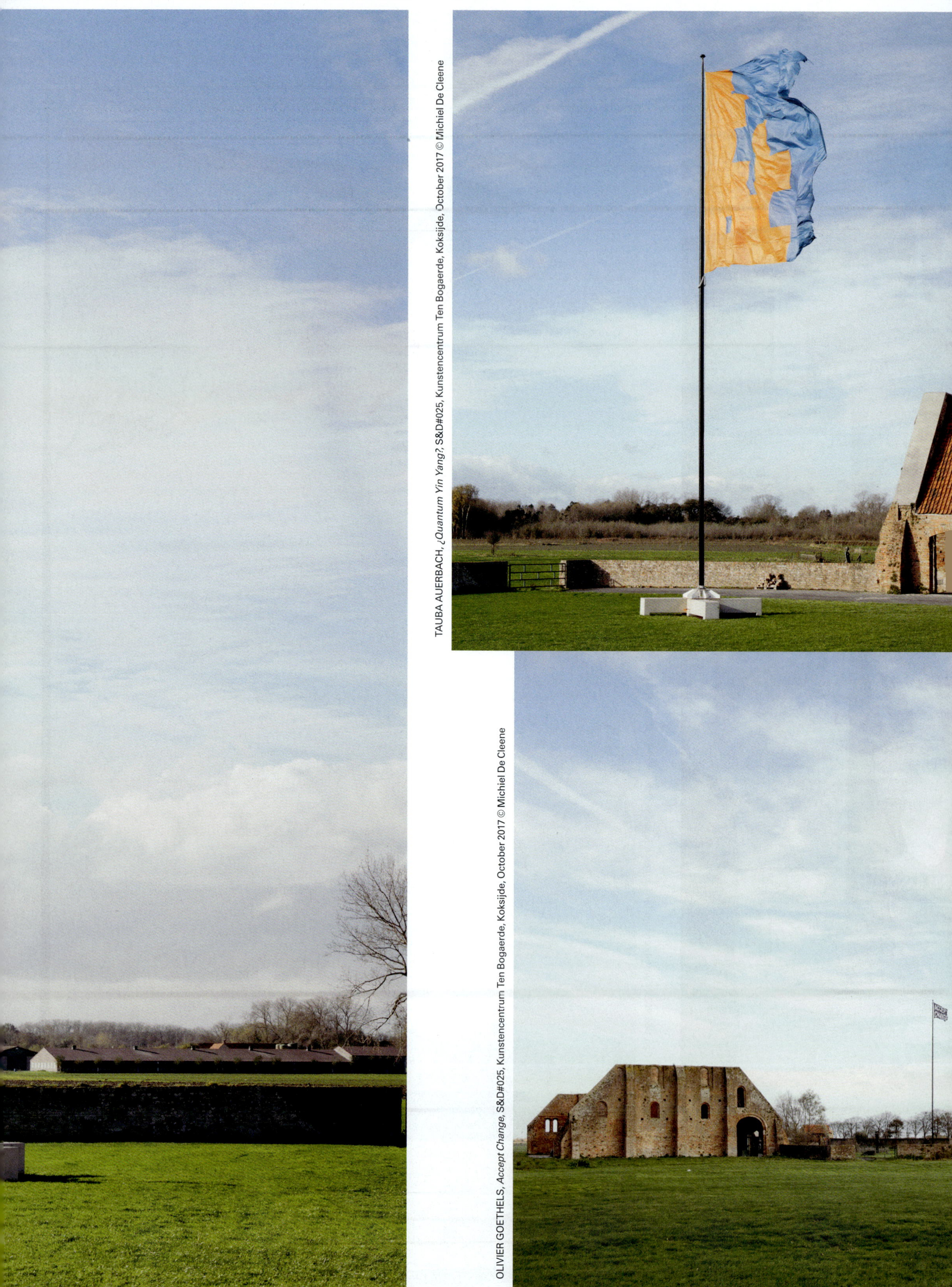

TAUBA AUERBACH, *¿Quantum Yin Yang?*, S&D#025, Kunstencentrum Ten Bogaerde, Koksijde, October 2017 © Michiel De Cleene

OLIVIER GOETHELS, *Accept Change*, S&D#025, Kunstencentrum Ten Bogaerde, Koksijde, October 2017 © Michiel De Cleene

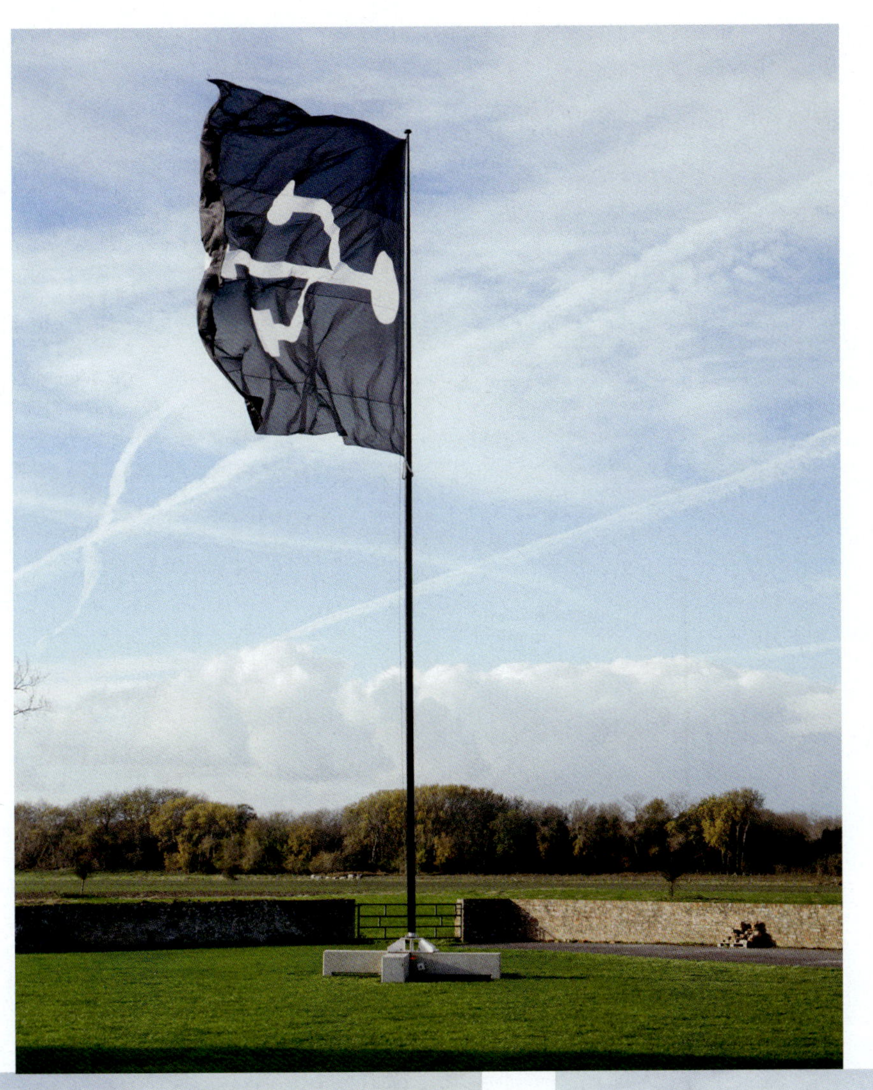

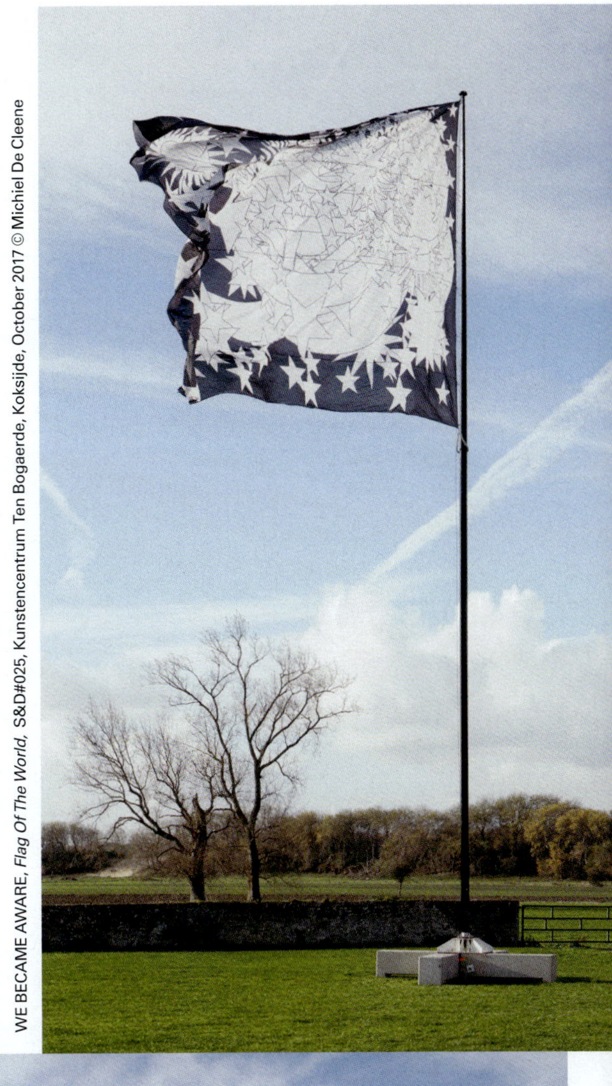

WE BECAME AWARE, *Flag Of The World*, S&D#025, Kunstencentrum Ten Bogaerde, Koksijde, October 2017 © Michiel De Cleene

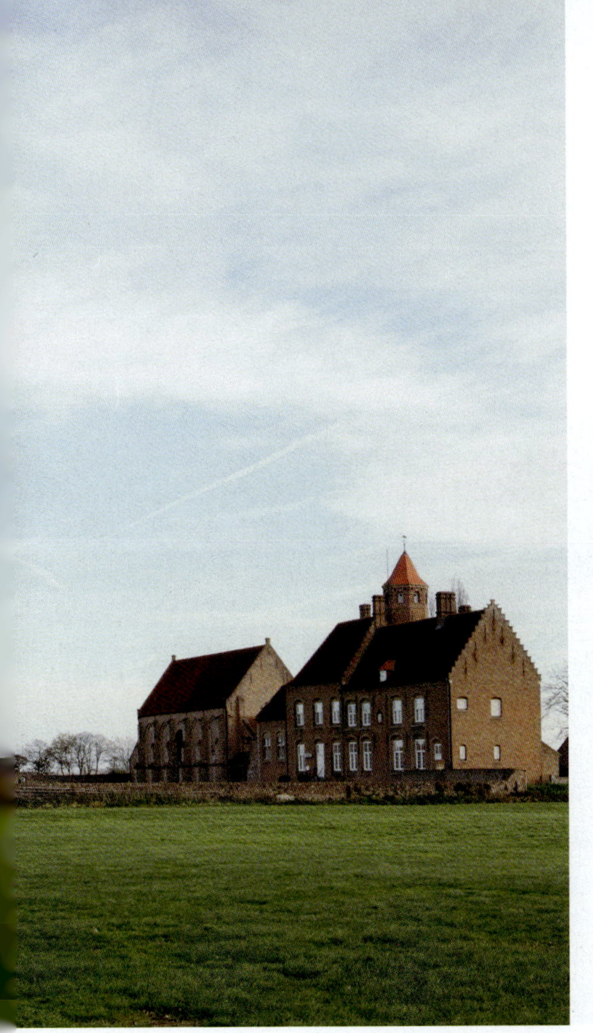

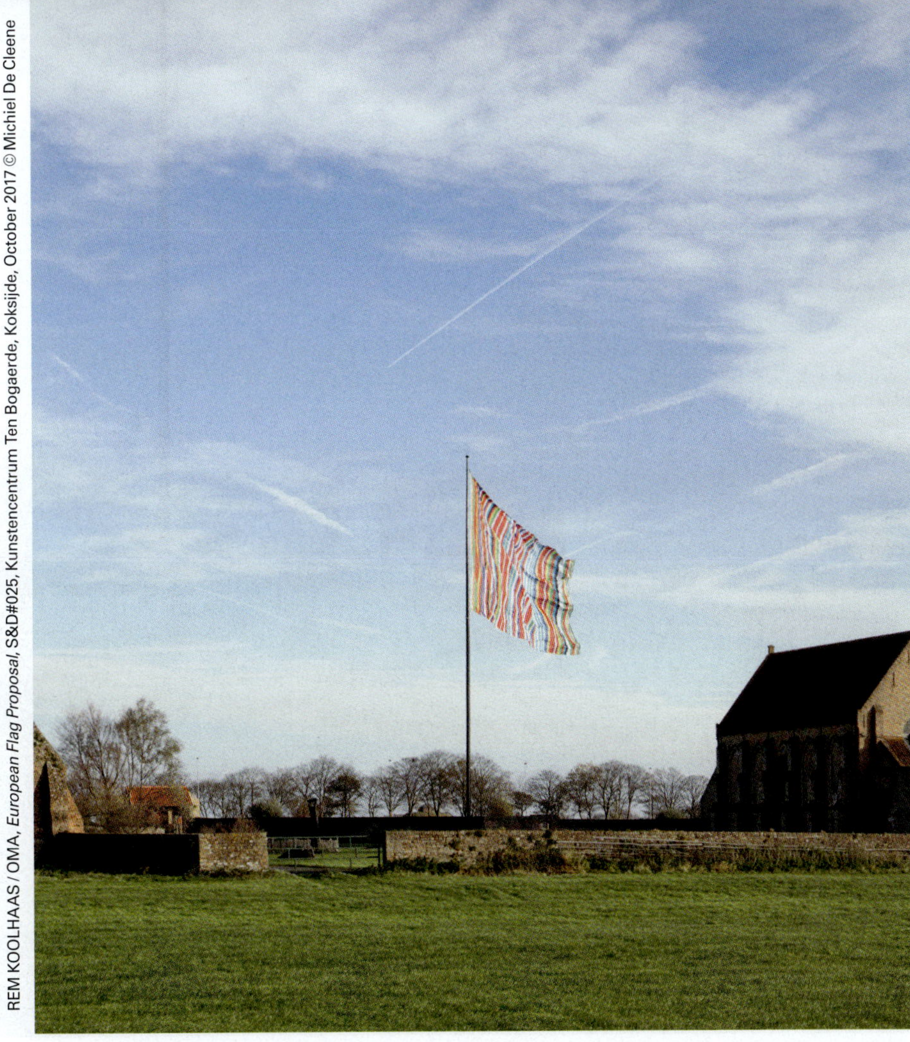

REM KOOLHAAS / OMA, *European Flag Proposal*, S&D#025, Kunstencentrum Ten Bogaerde, Koksijde, October 2017 © Michiel De Cleene

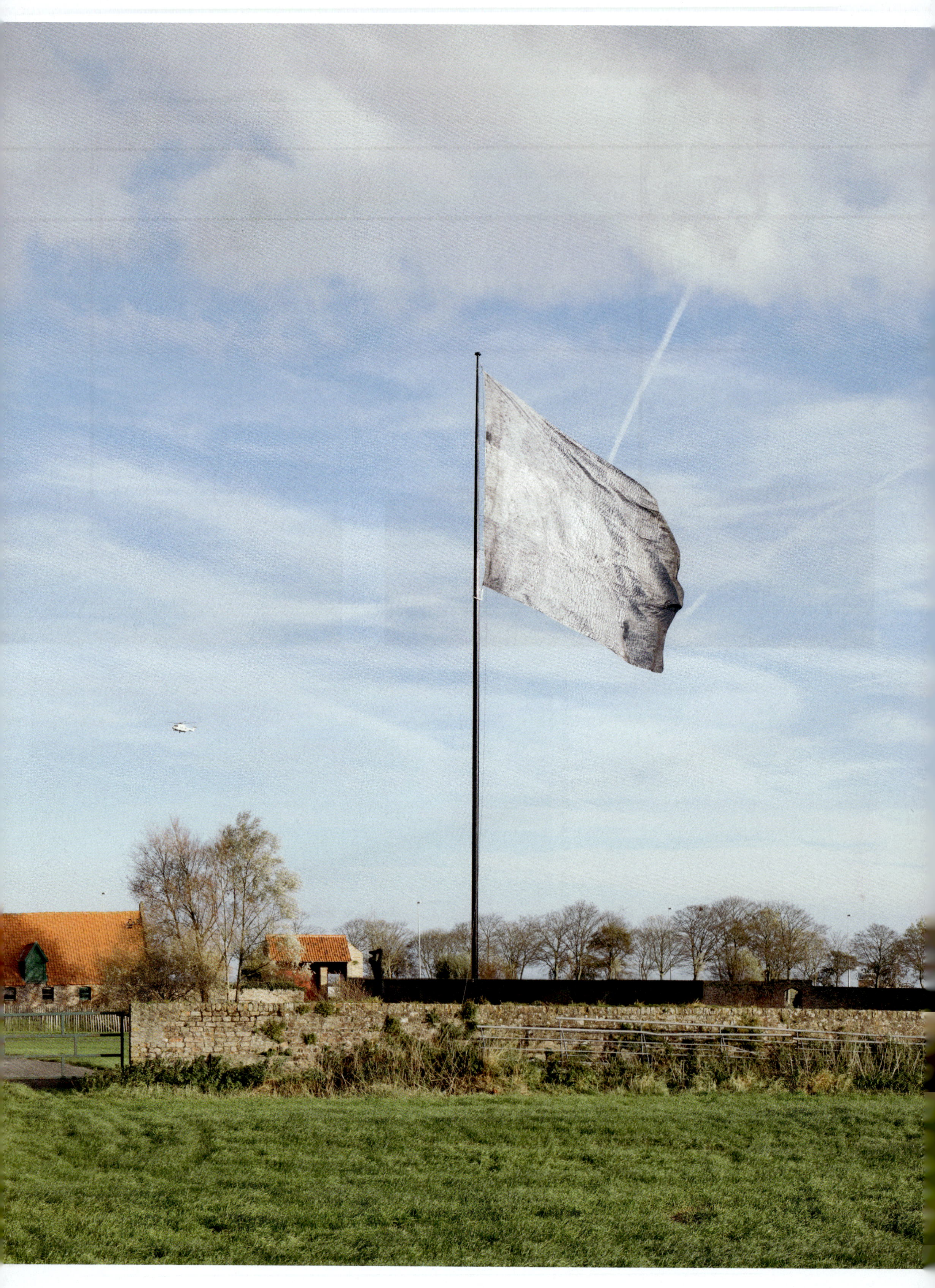

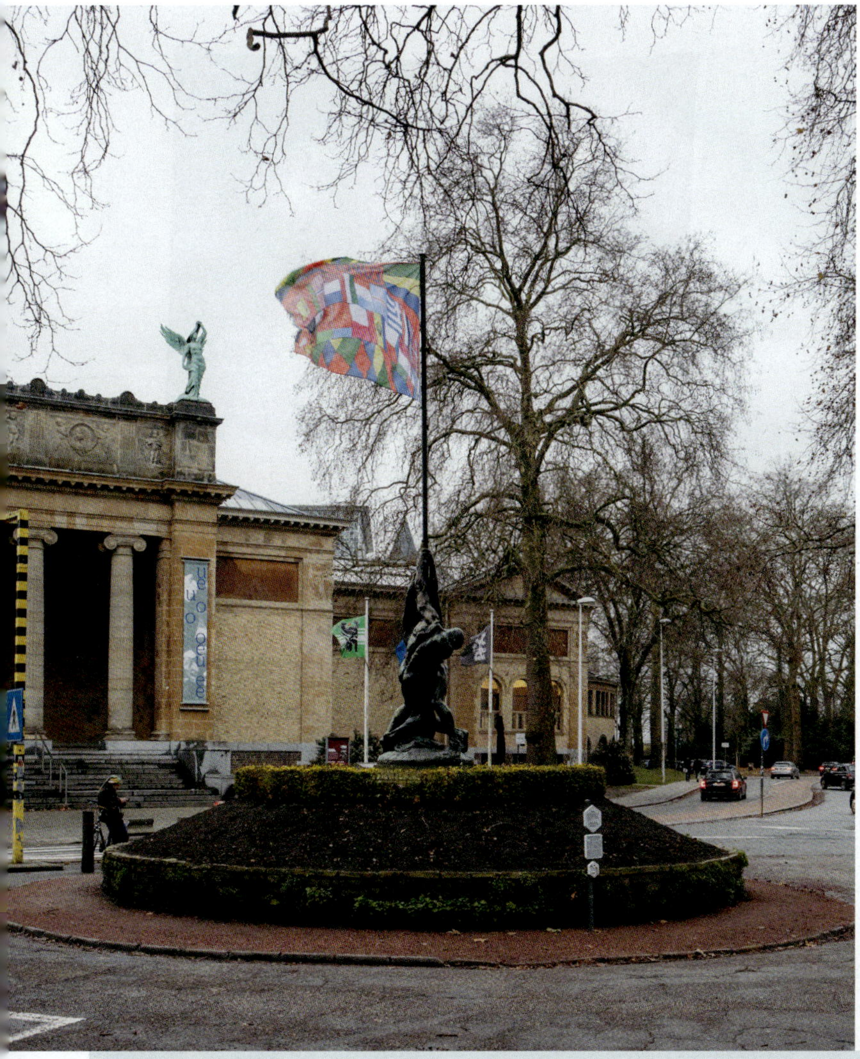

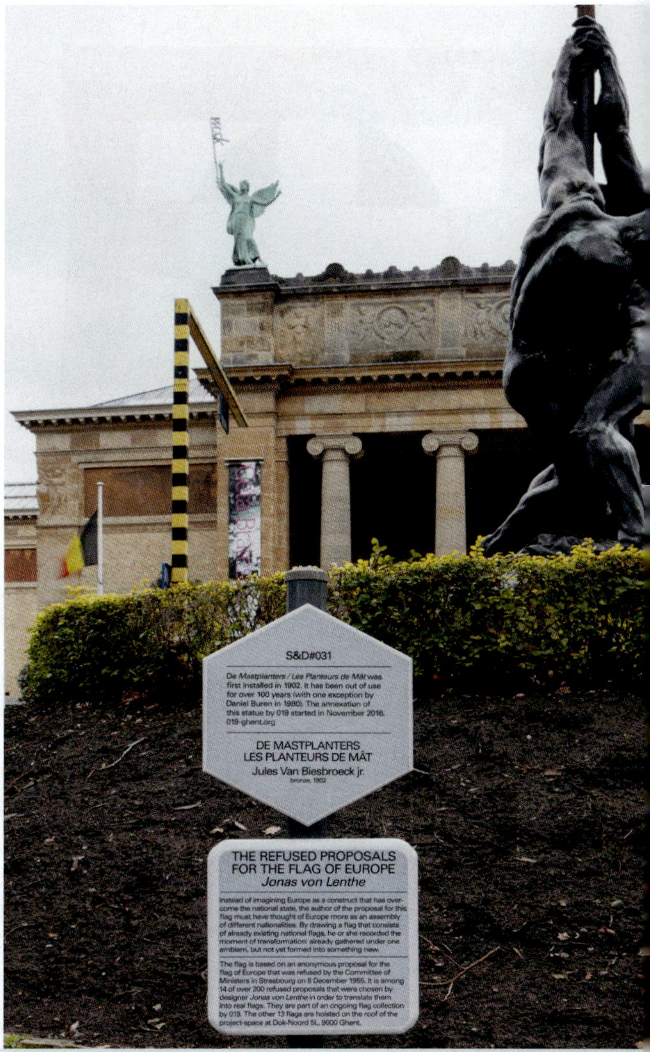

JONAS VON LENTHE, *The Refused Proposals For The Flag Of Europe*, S&D#031, December 2017 © Michiel De Cleene

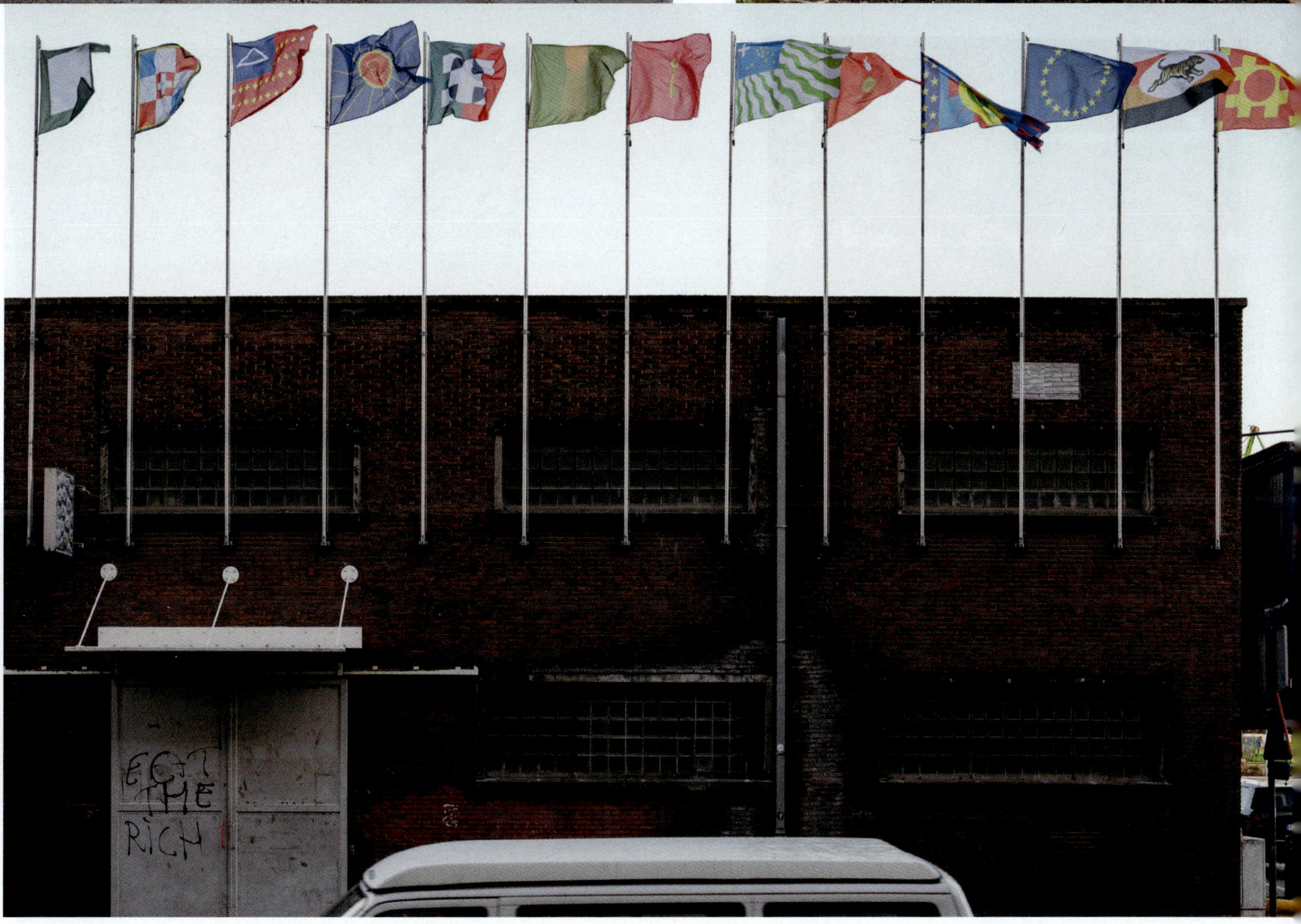

HANNELORE VAN DIJCK, *One Flag*, S&D#025, Kunstencentrum Ten Bogaerde, Koksijde, October 2017 © Michiel De Cleene

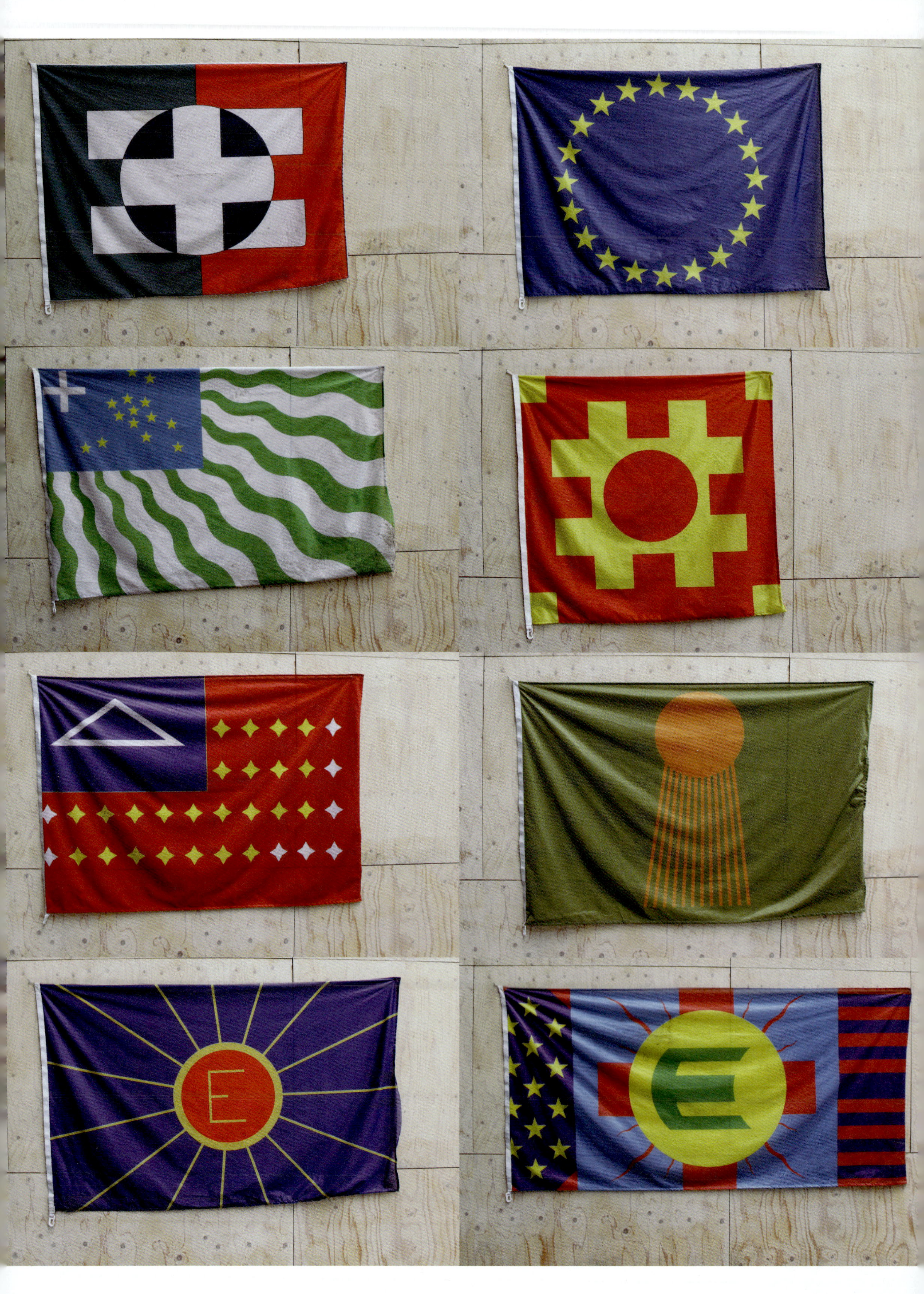
E
E

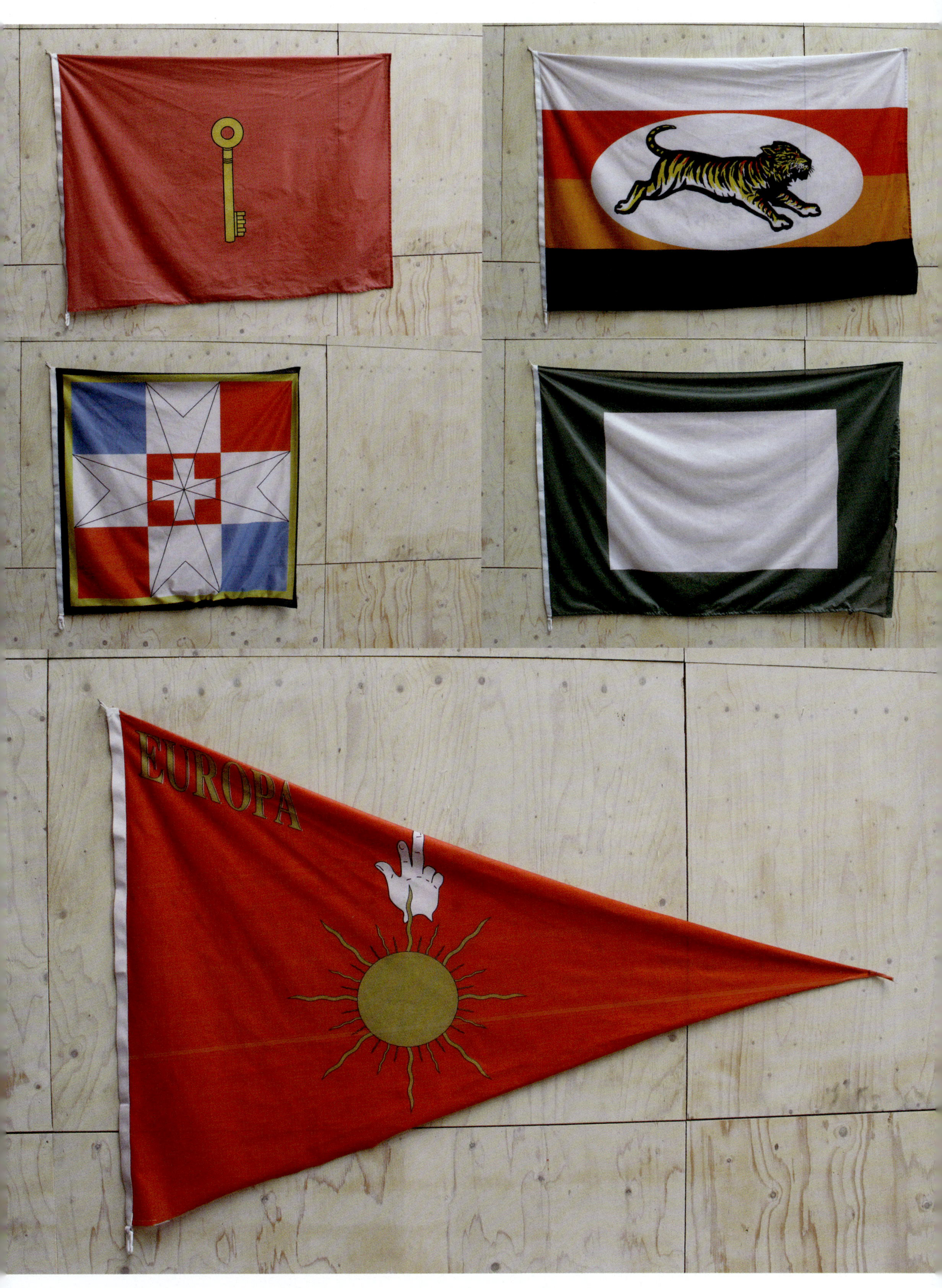
EUROPA

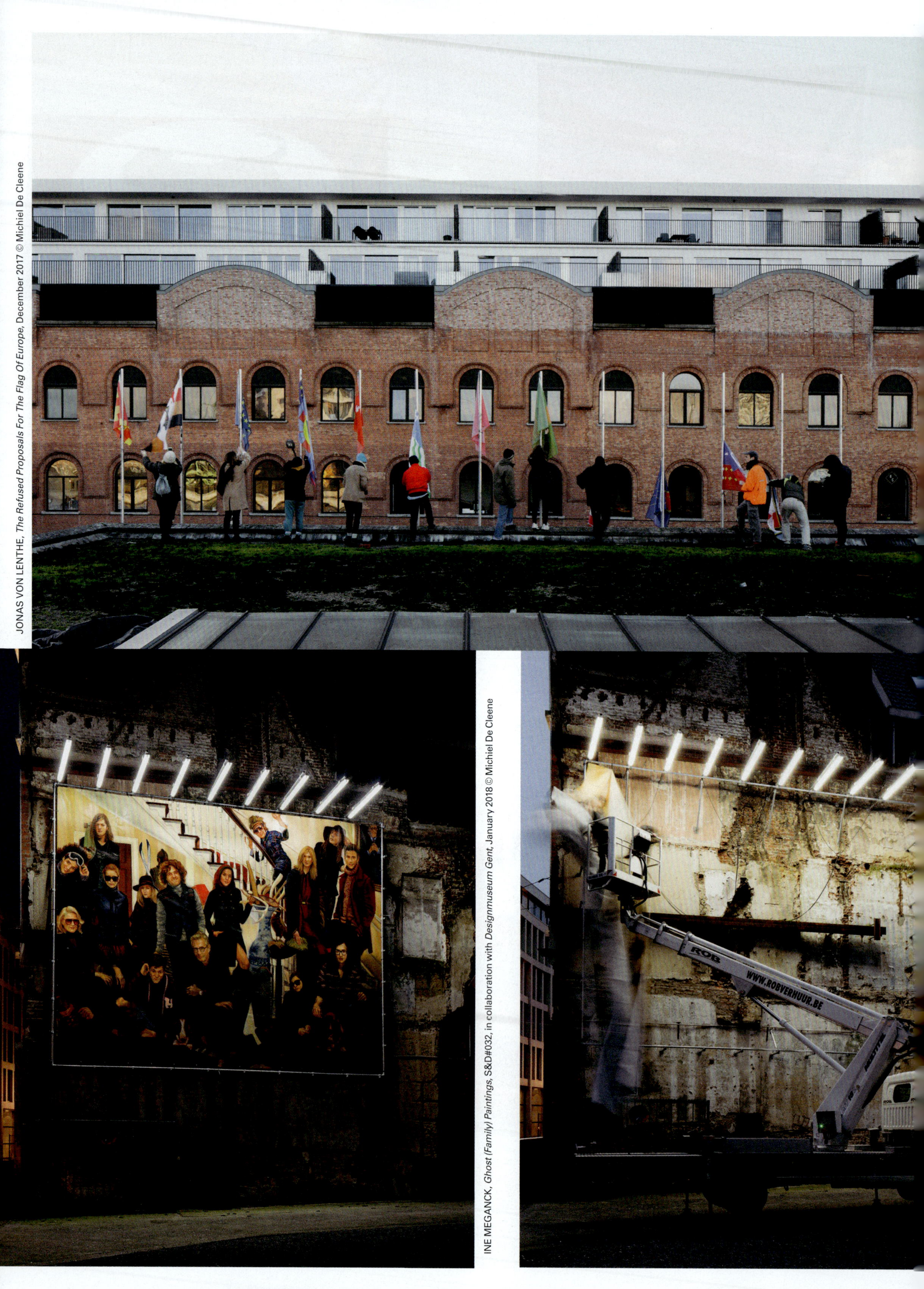

JONAS VON LENTHE, *The Refused Proposals For The Flag Of Europe*, December 2017 © Michiel De Cleene

INE MEGANCK, *Ghost (Family) Paintings*, S&D#032, in collaboration with *Designmuseum Gent*, January 2018 © Michiel De Cleene

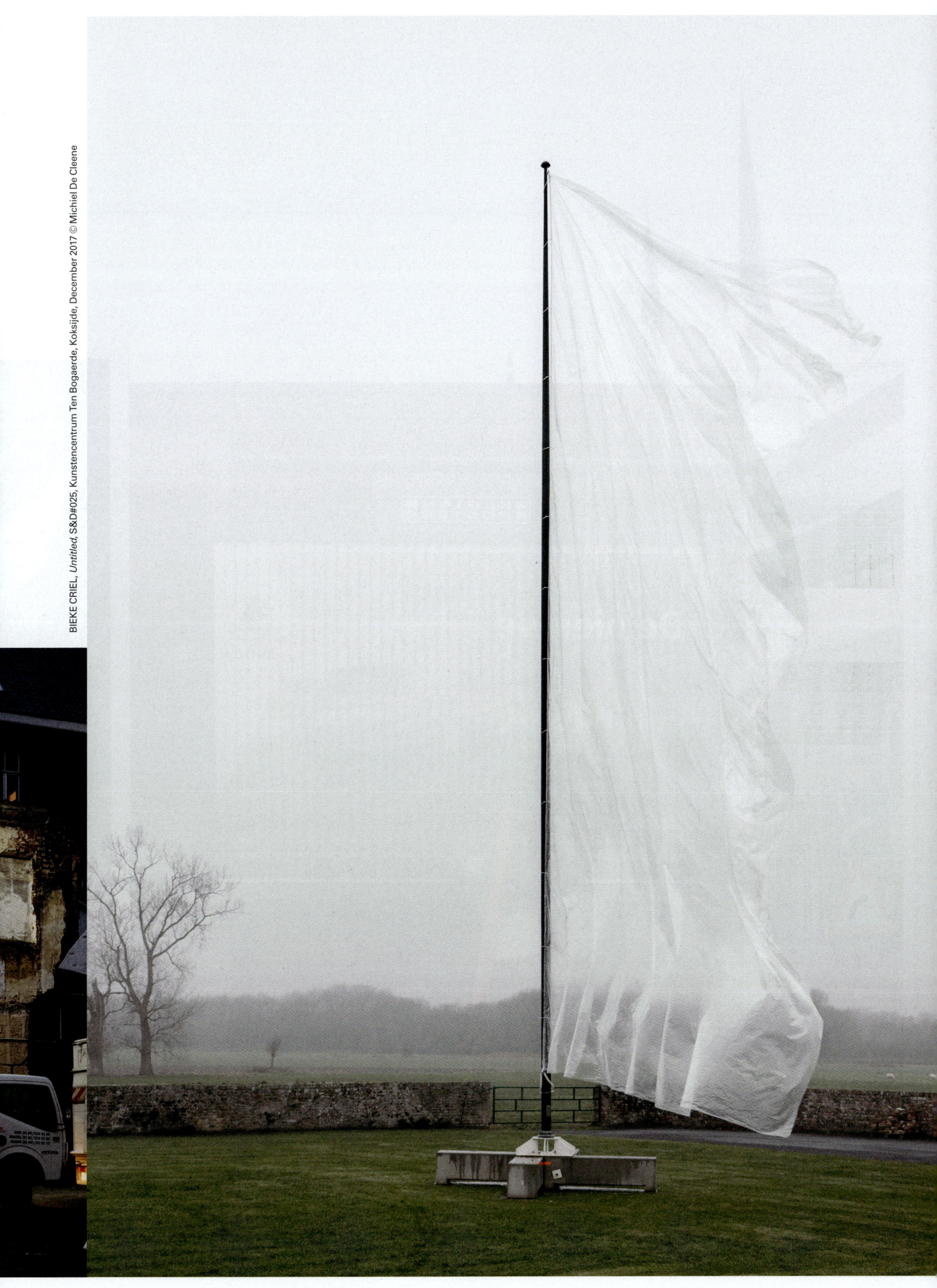

BIEKE CRIEL, *Untitled*, S&D#025, Kunstencentrum Ten Bogaerde, Koksijde, December 2017 © Michiel De Cleene

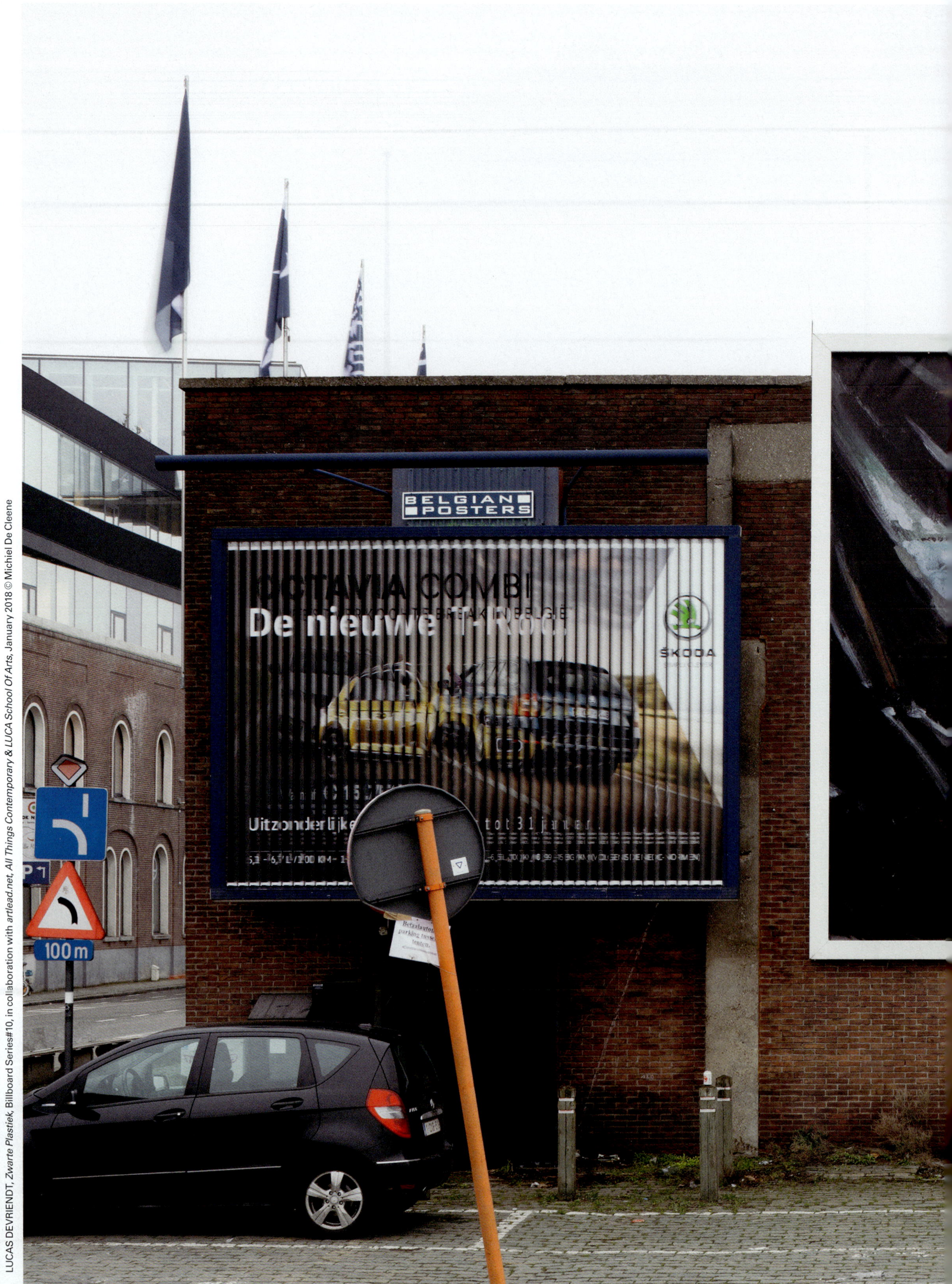

LUCAS DEVRIENDT, *Zwarte Plastiek*, Billboard Series#10, in collaboration with *artlead.net*, *All Things Contemporary* & *LUCA School Of Arts*, January 2018 © Michiel De Cleene

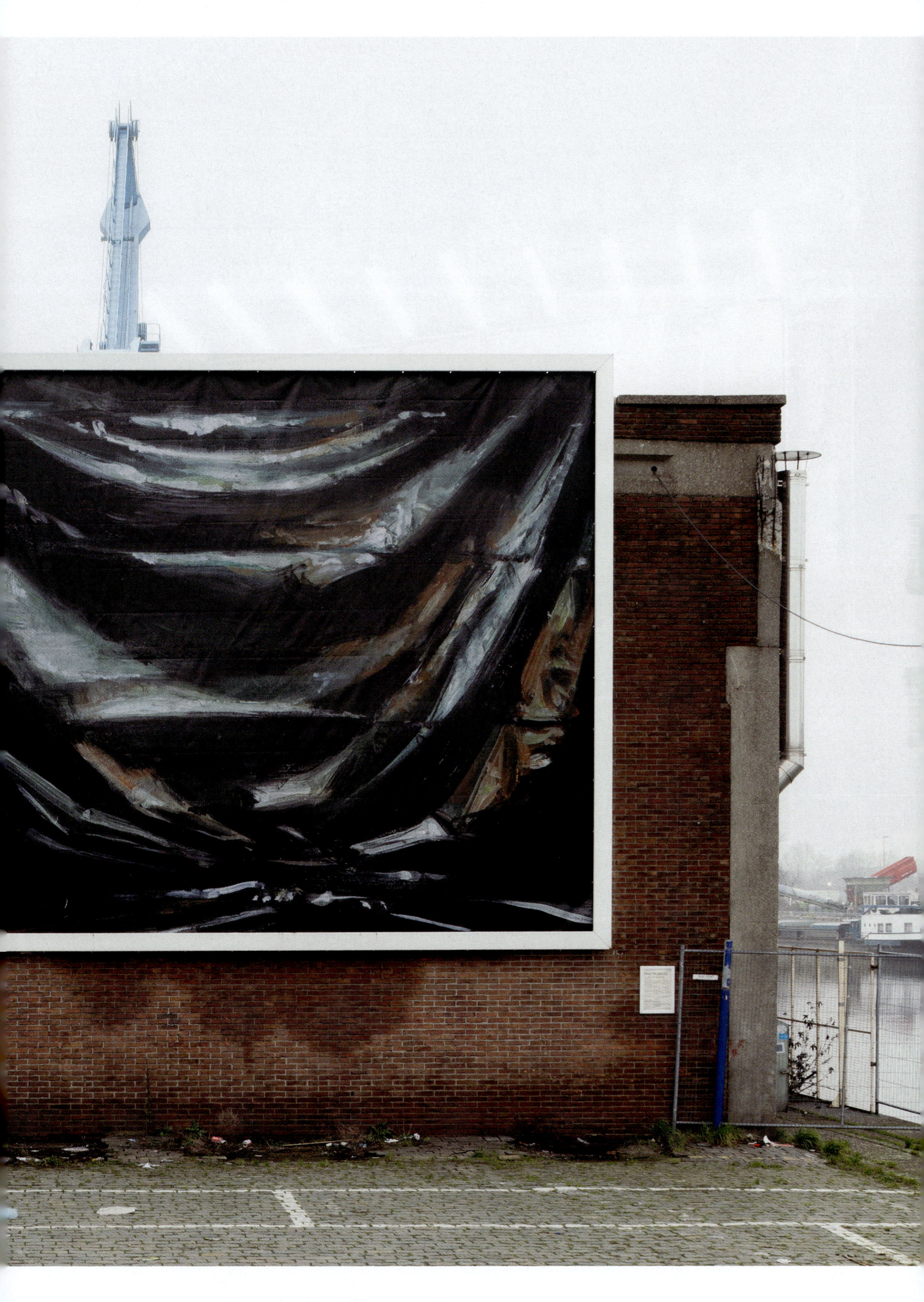

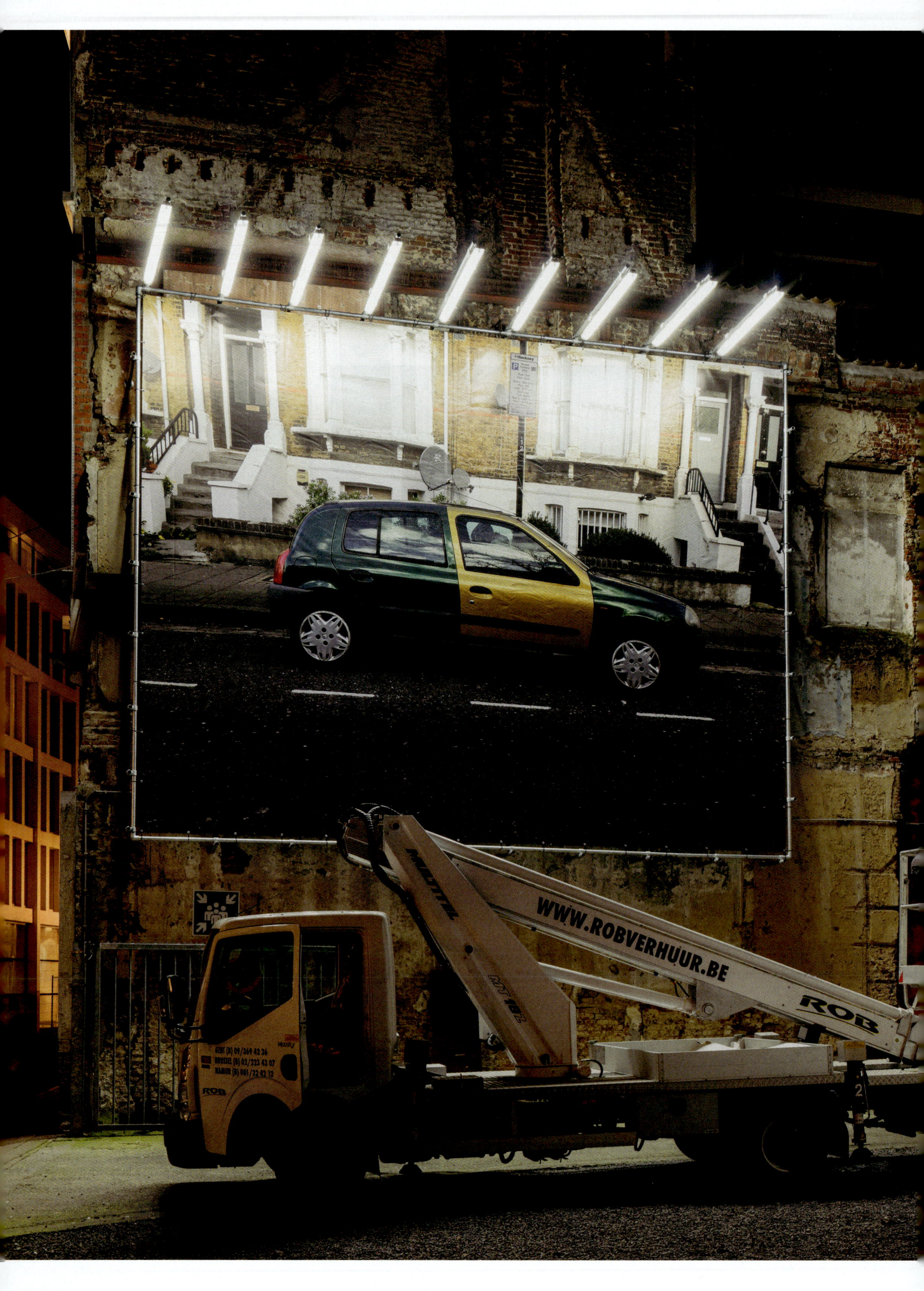
WWW.ROBVERHUUR.BE
ROB

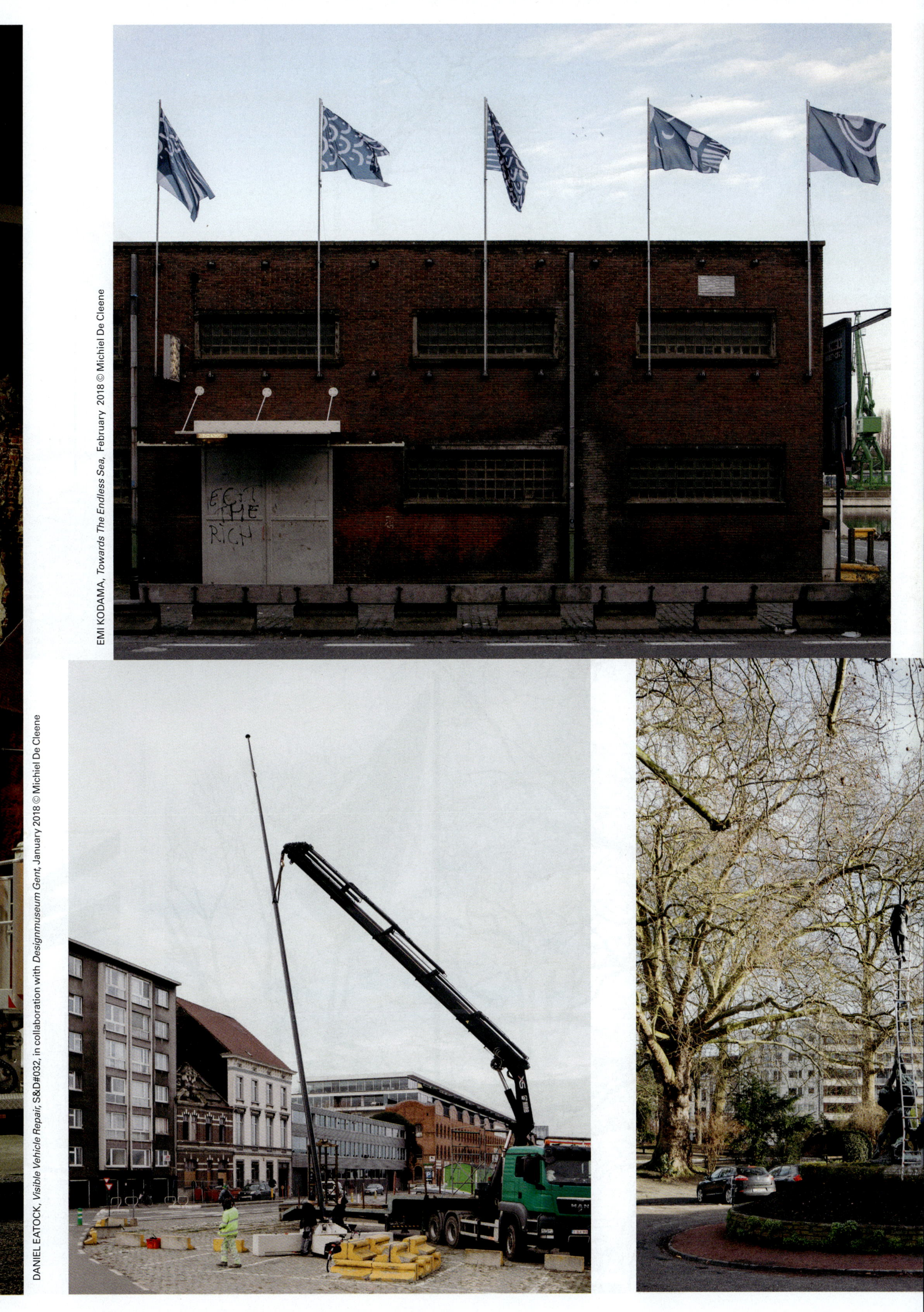

EMI KODAMA, *Towards The Endless Sea,* February 2018 © Michiel De Cleene

DANIEL EATOCK, *Visible Vehicle Repair,* S&D#032, in collaboration with *Designmuseum Gent,* January 2018 © Michiel De Cleene

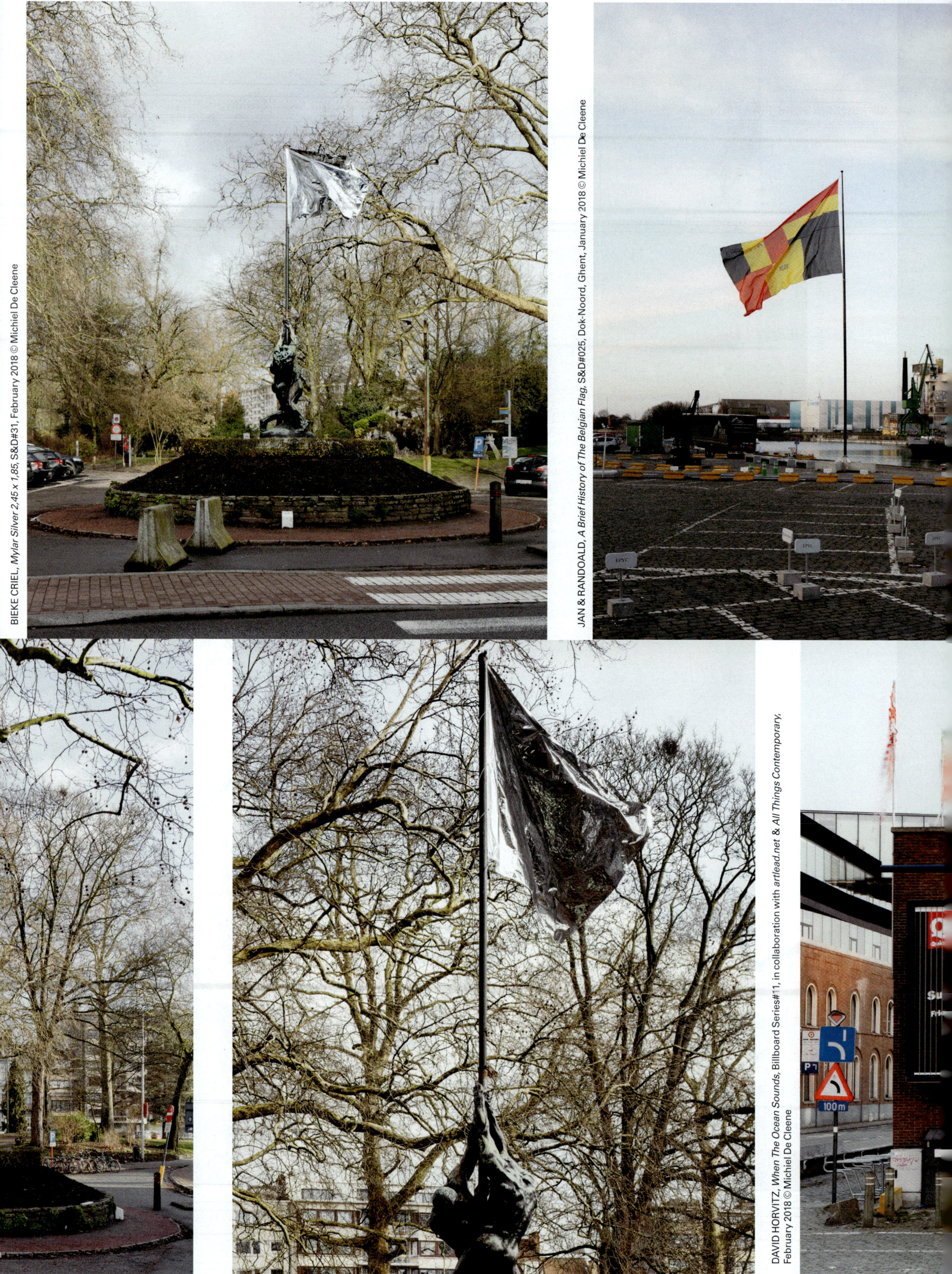

BIEKE CRIEL, *Mylar Silver 2,45 x 1,85*, S&D#31, February 2018 © Michiel De Cleene

JAN & RANDOALD, *A Brief History of The Belgian Flag*, S&D#025, Dok-Noord, Ghent, January 2018 © Michiel De Cleene

DAVID HORVITZ, *When The Ocean Sounds*, Billboard Series#11, in collaboration with *artlead.net* & *All Things Contemporary*, February 2018 © Michiel De Cleene

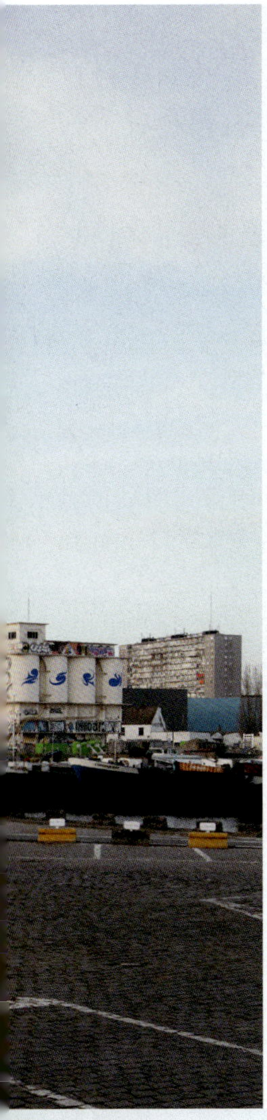

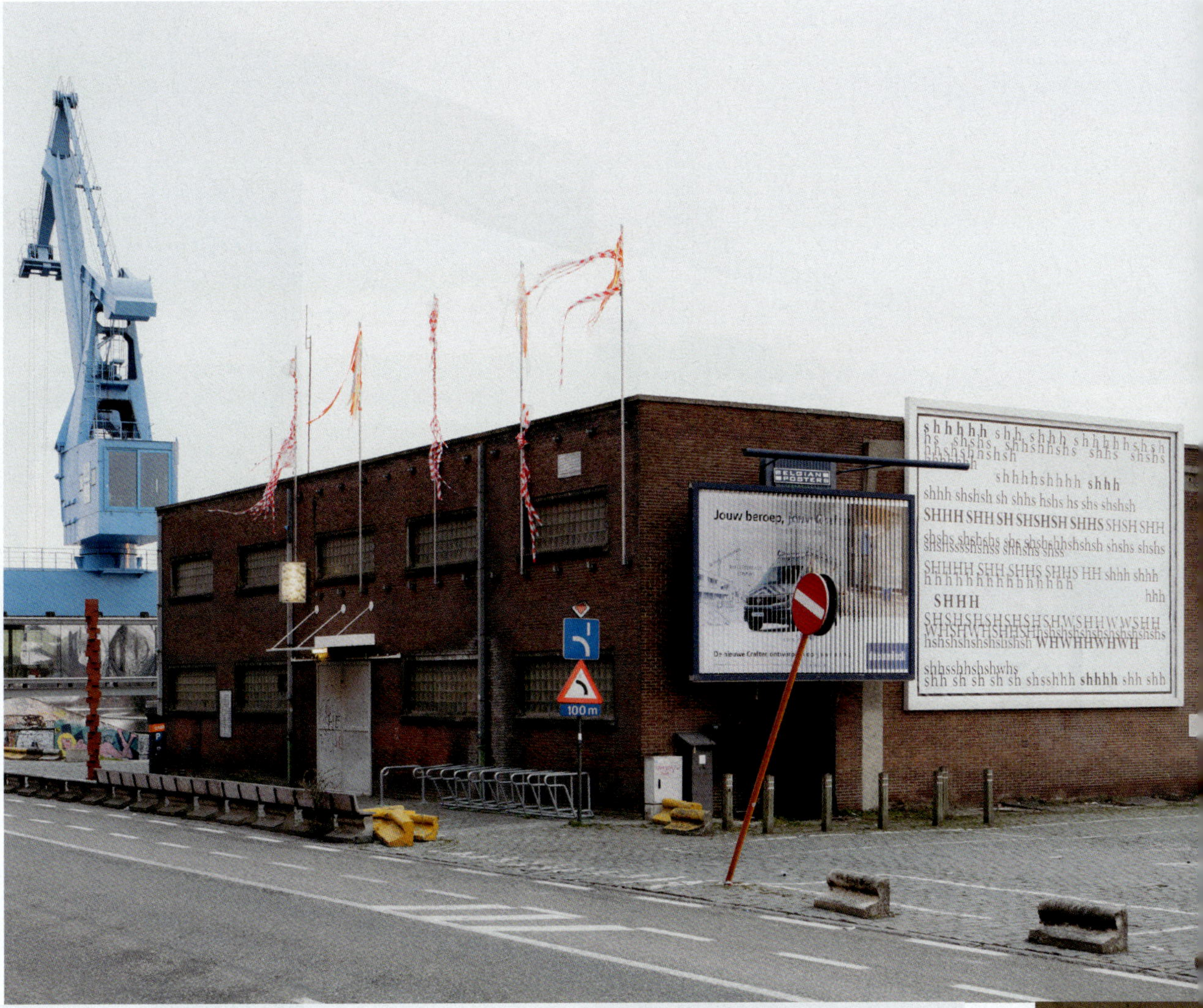

MARIJS KEMPYNCK, *We Act We Glow We Burn We React We Maintain We Persists We*, five flags on the roof of 019, March 2018
© Michiel De Cleene

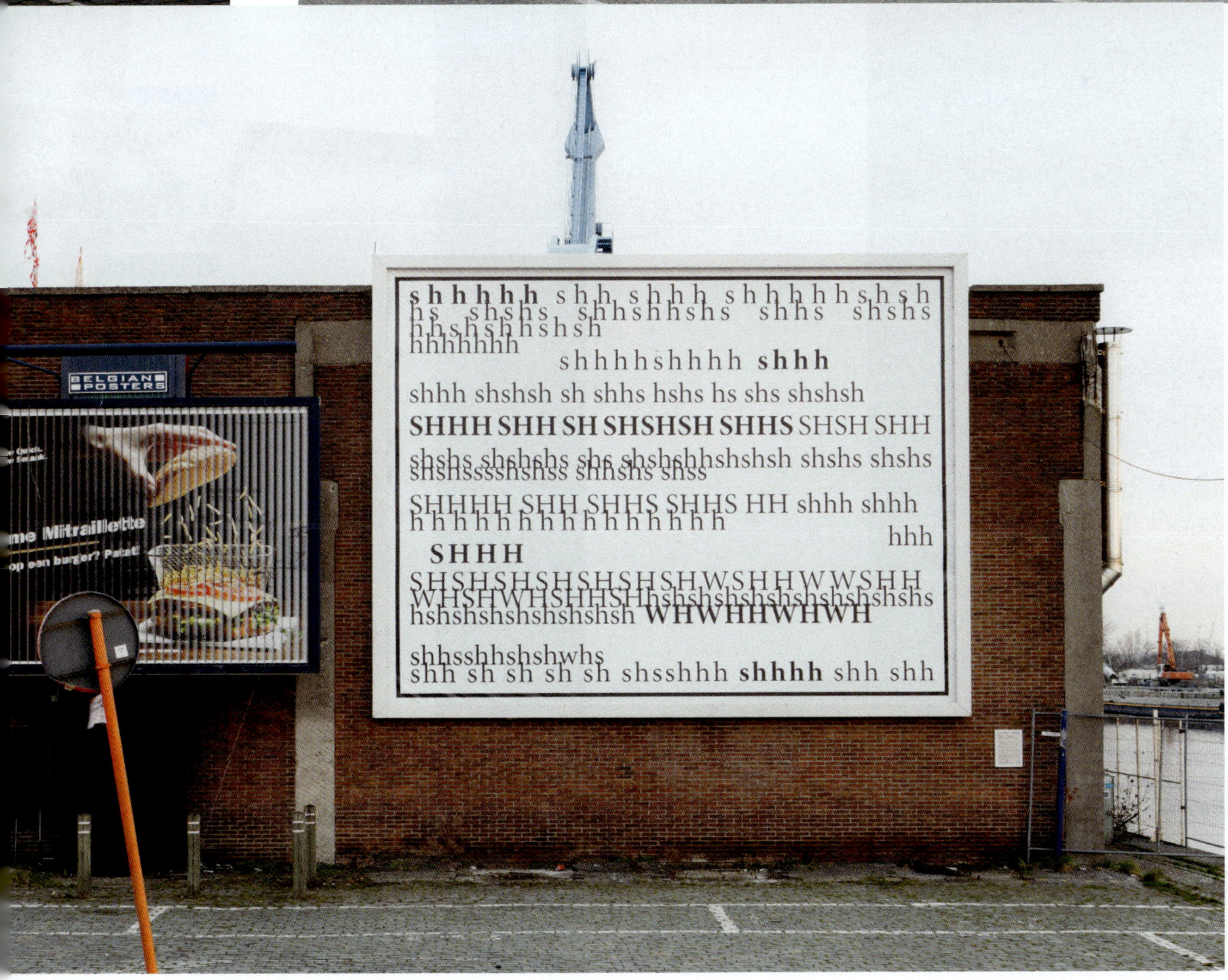

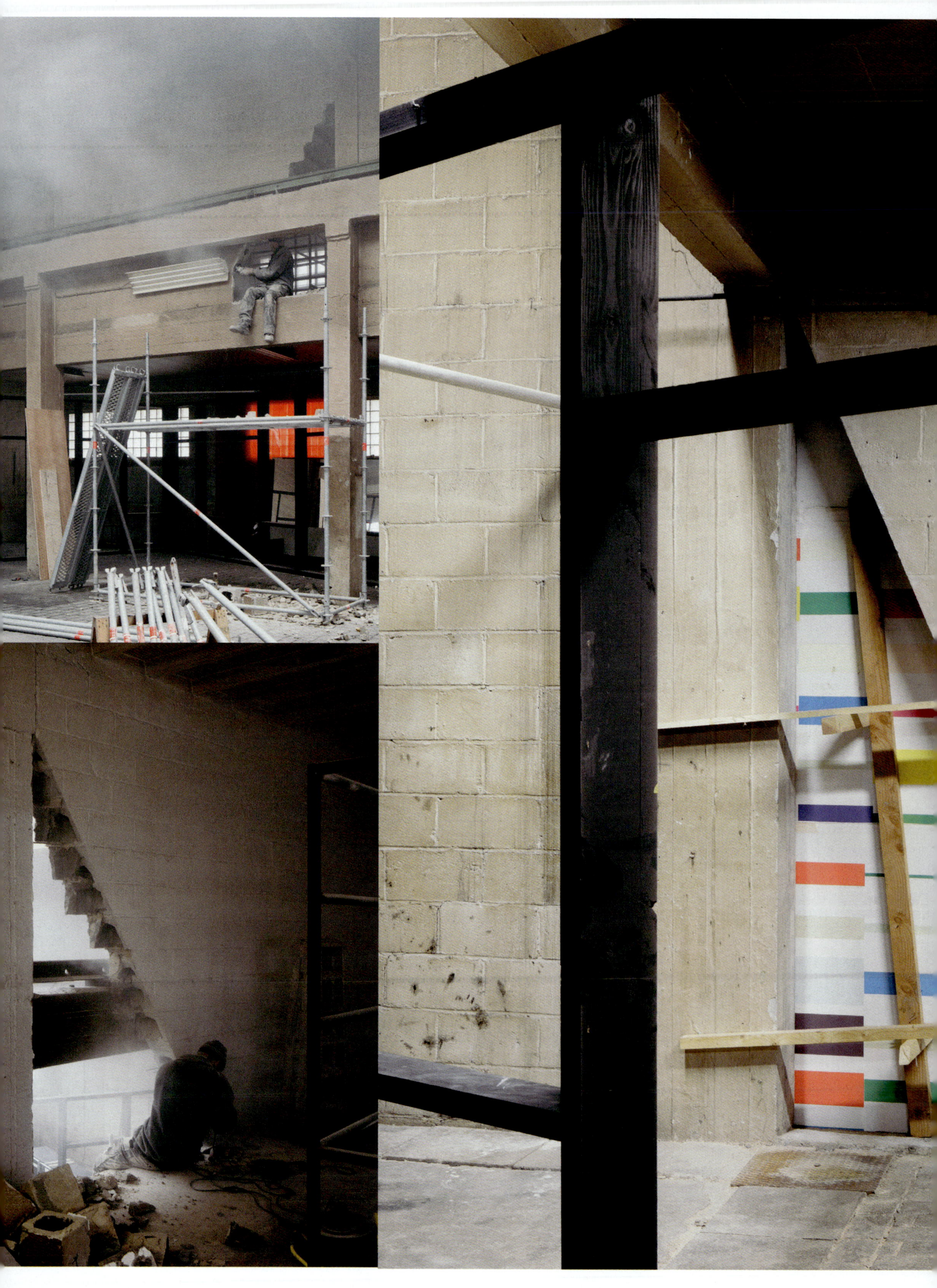

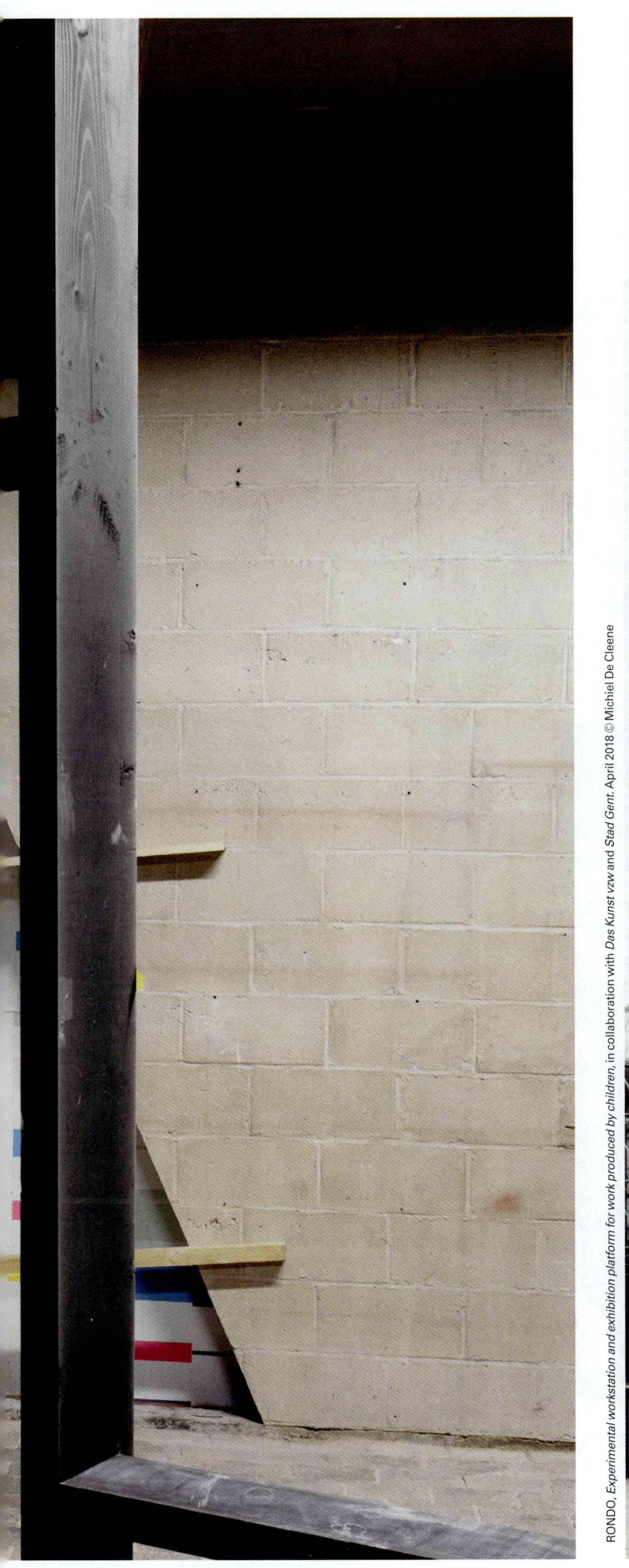

RONDO, *Experimental workstation and exhibition platform for work produced by children*, in collaboration with *Das Kunst vzw* and *Stad Gent*. April 2018 © Michiel De Cleene

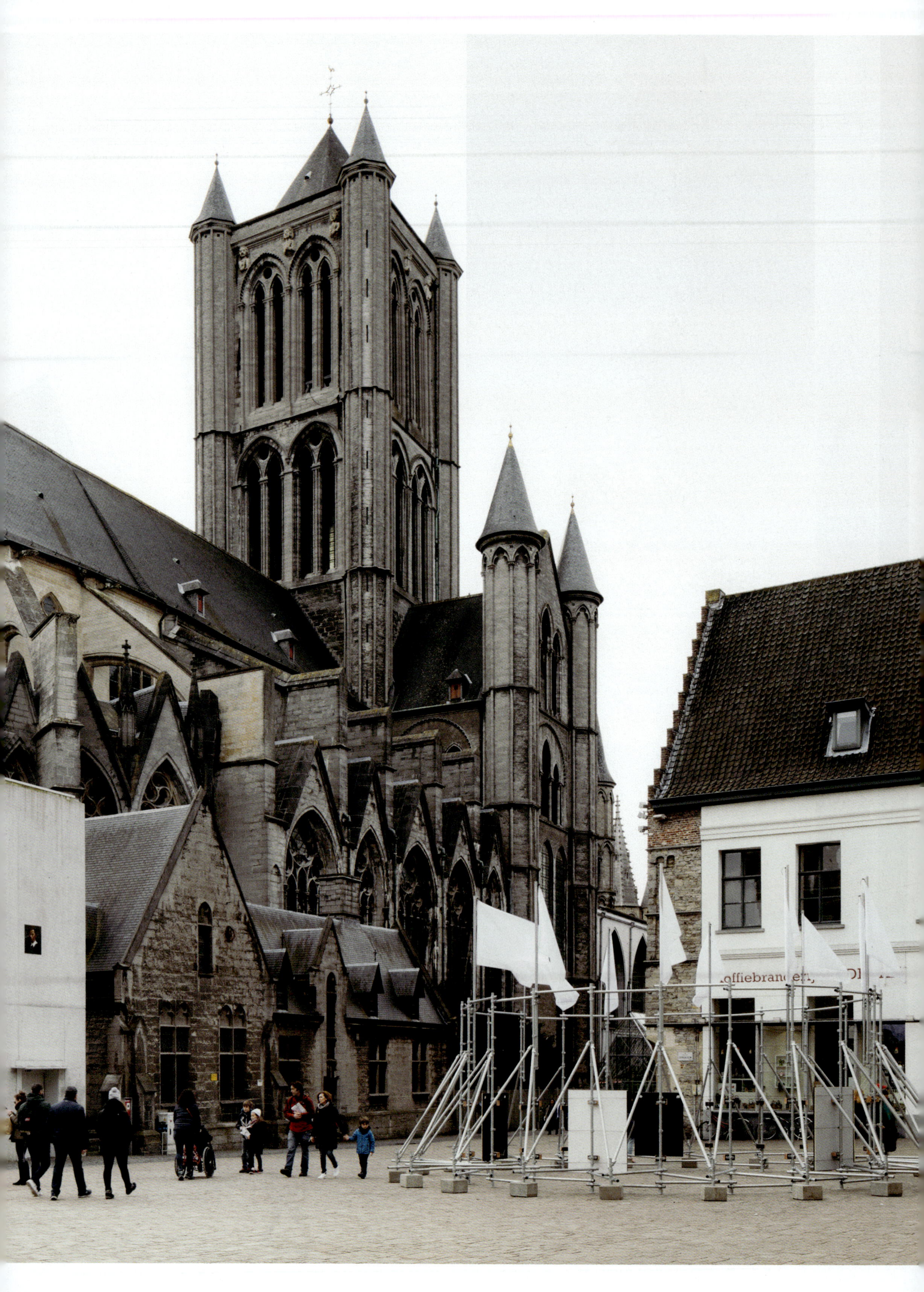

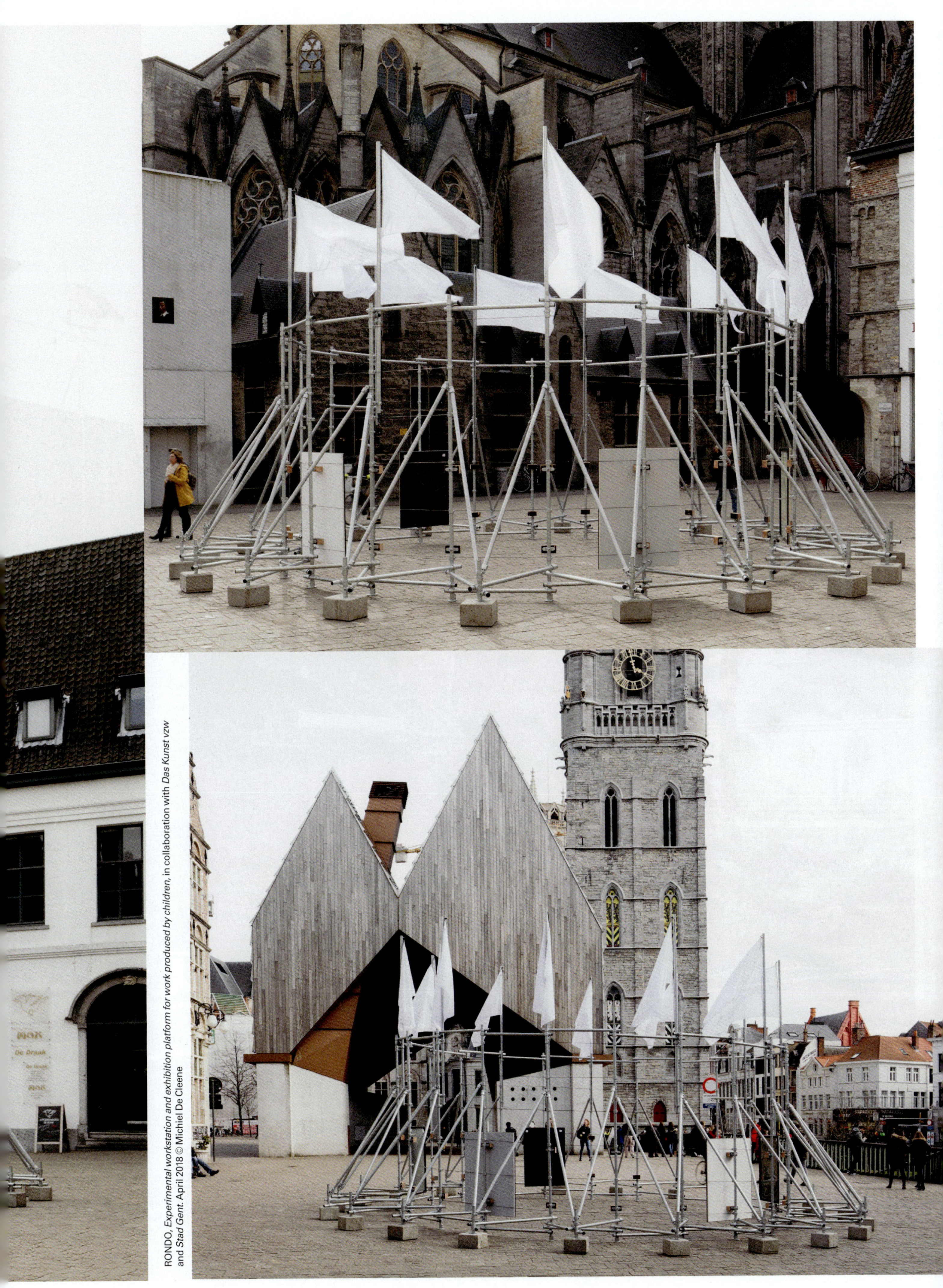

RONDO, *Experimental workstation and exhibition platform for work produced by children*, in collaboration with *Das Kunst vzw* and *Stad Gent*. April 2018 © Michiel De Cleene

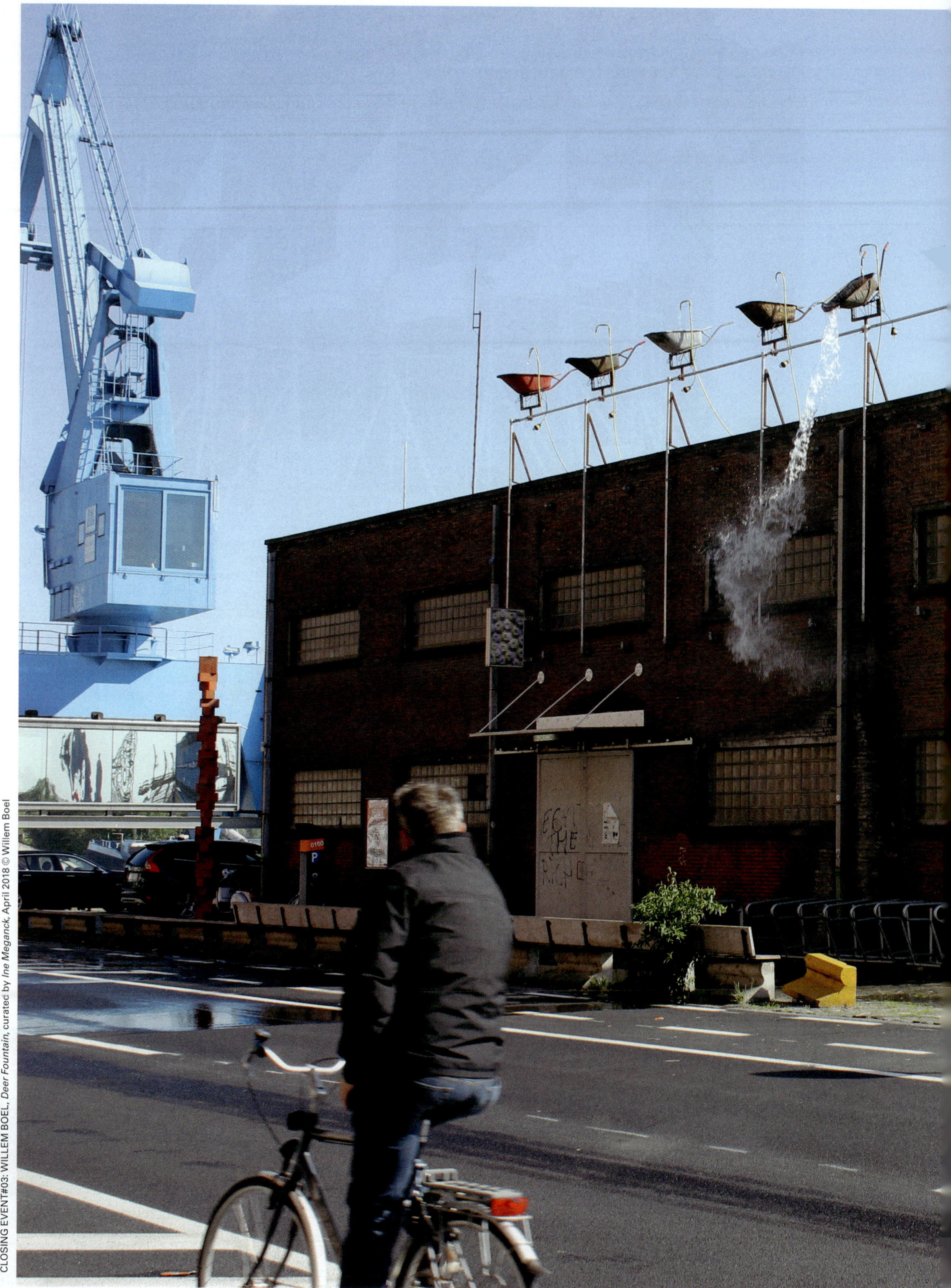

CLOSING EVENT#03: WILLEM BOEL, *Deer Fountain*, curated by *Ine Meganck*, April 2018 © Willem Boel

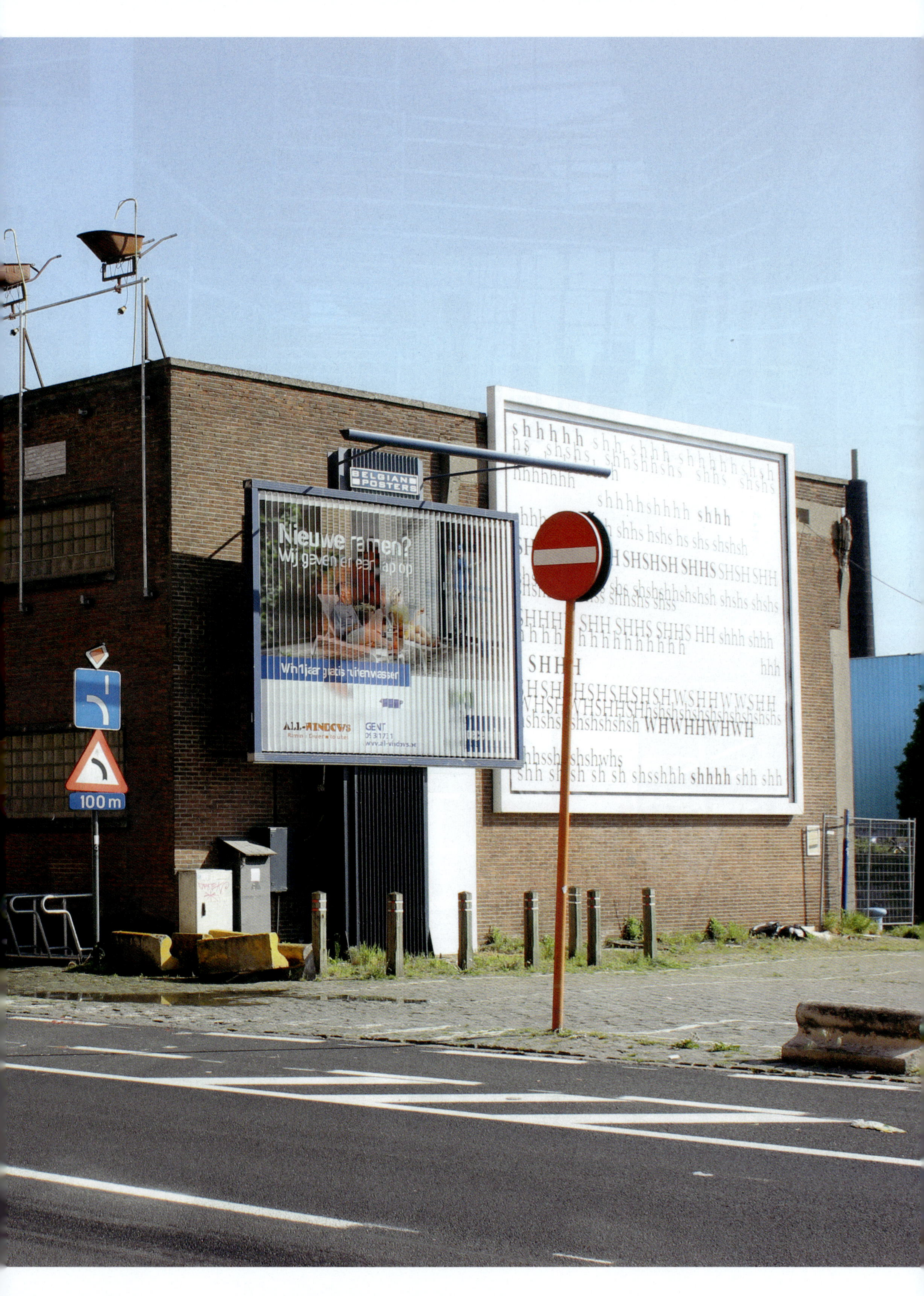
BELGIAN POSTERS
Nieuwe ramen?
GENT
100 m

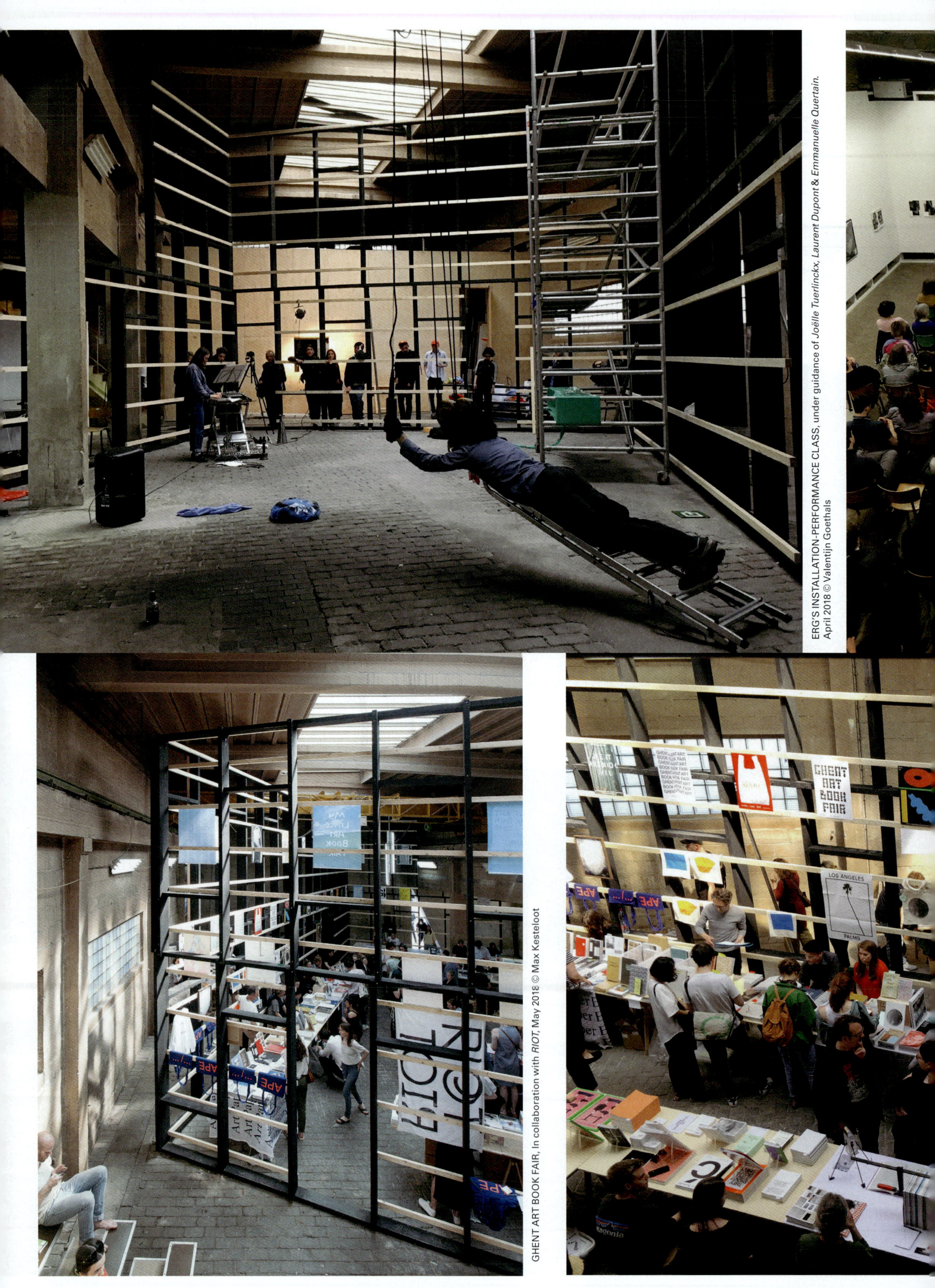

ERG'S INSTALLATION-PERFORMANCE CLASS, under guidance of *Joëlle Tuerlinckx, Laurent Dupont & Emmanuelle Quertain.*
April 2018 © Valentijn Goethals

GHENT ART BOOK FAIR, In collaboration with *RIOT*, May 2018 © Max Kesteloot

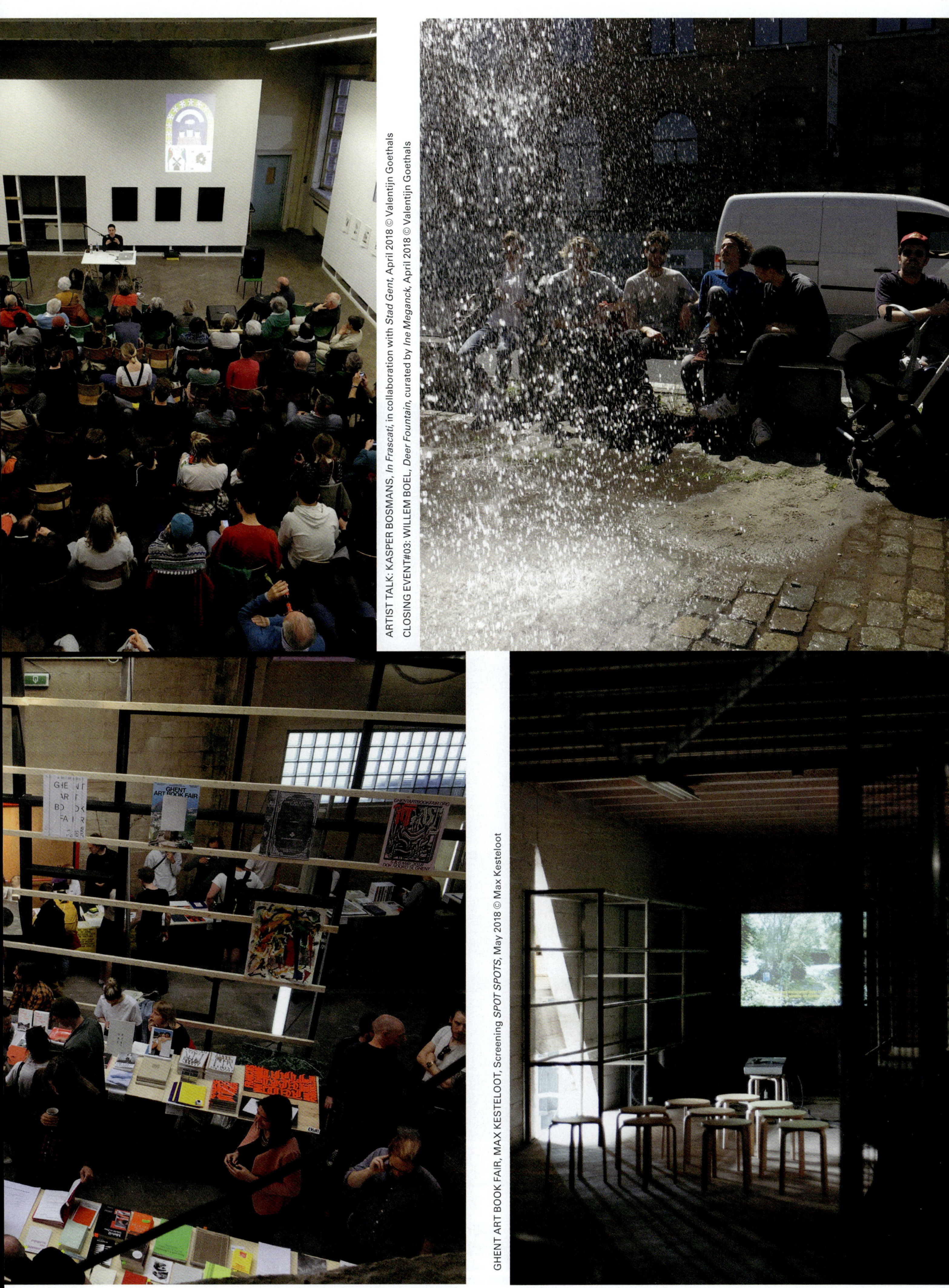

ARTIST TALK: KASPER BOSMANS, *In Frascati*, in collaboration with *Stad Gent*, April 2018 © Valentijn Goethals

CLOSING EVENT#03: WILLEM BOEL, *Deer Fountain*, curated by *Ine Meganck*, April 2018 © Valentijn Goethals

GHENT ART BOOK FAIR, MAX KESTELOOT, Screening *SPOT SPOTS*, May 2018 © Max Kesteloot

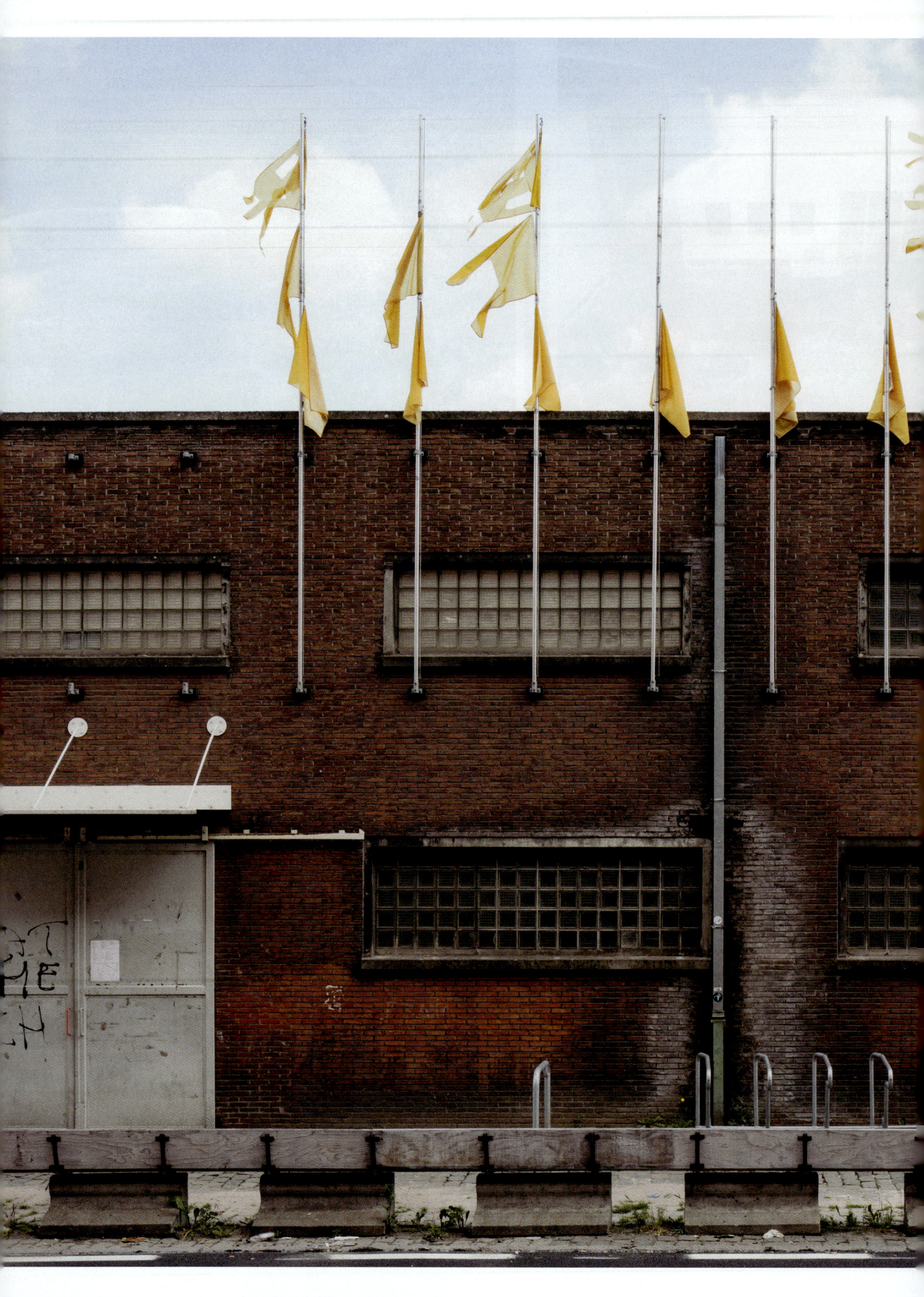

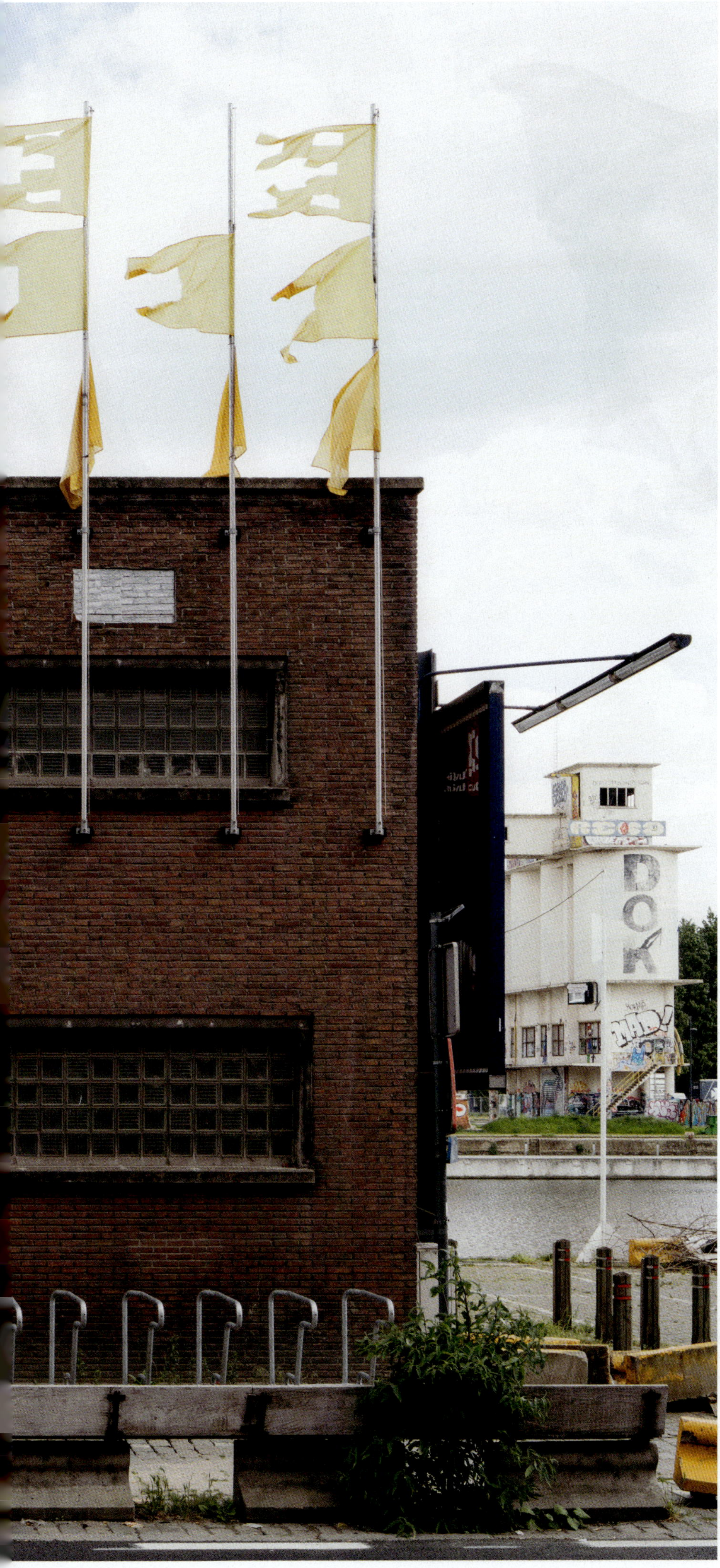

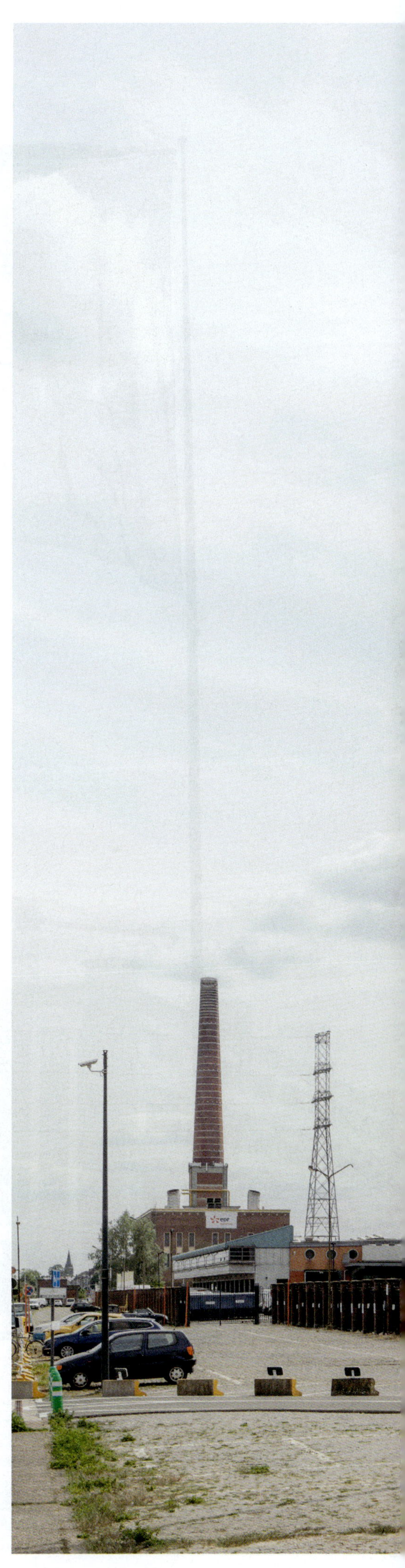

TAUBA AUERBACH, *OoO*, May 2018 © Michiel De Cleene

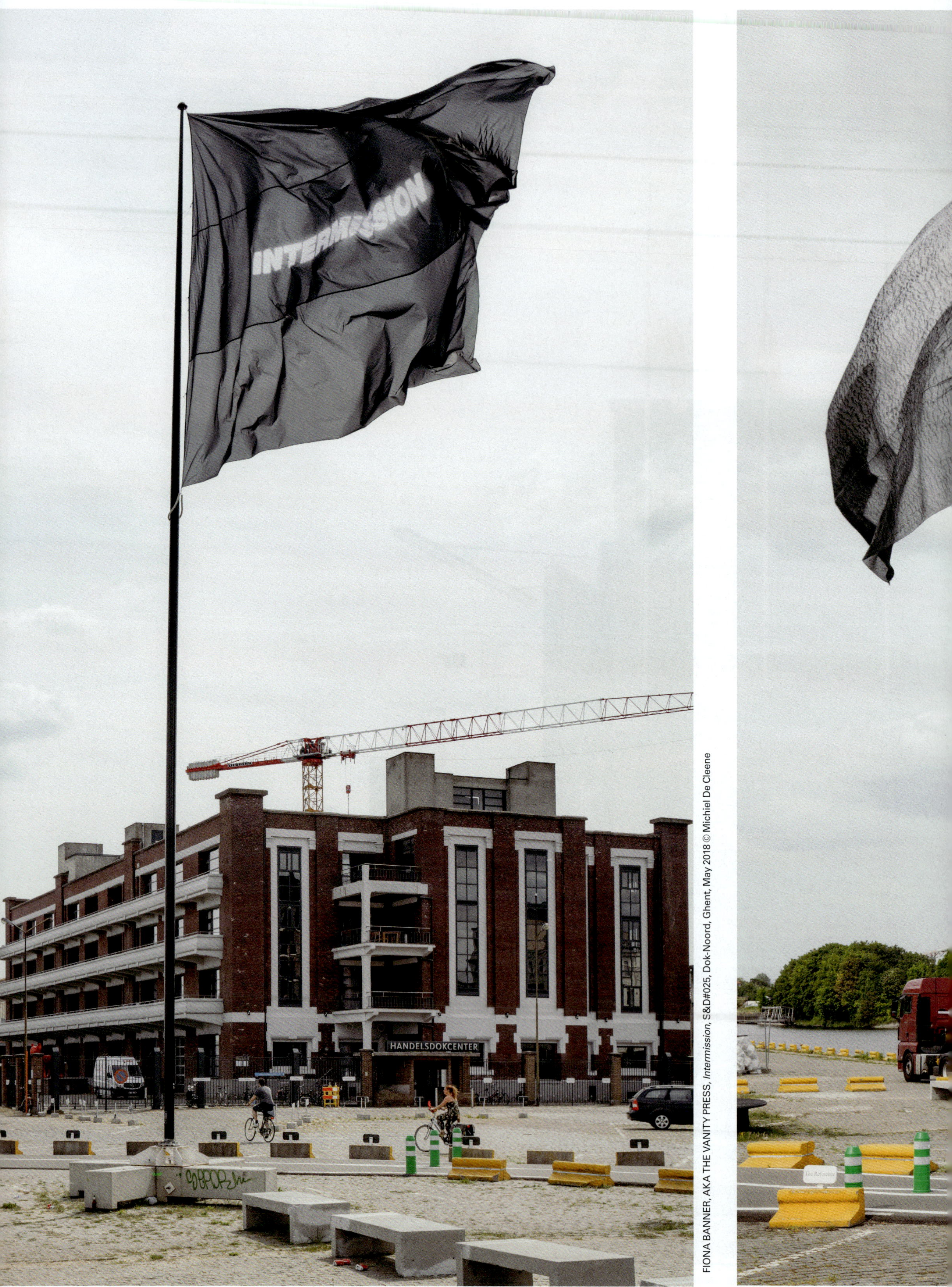

FIONA BANNER, AKA THE VANITY PRESS, *Intermission*, S&D#025, Dok-Noord, Ghent, May 2018 © Michiel De Cleene

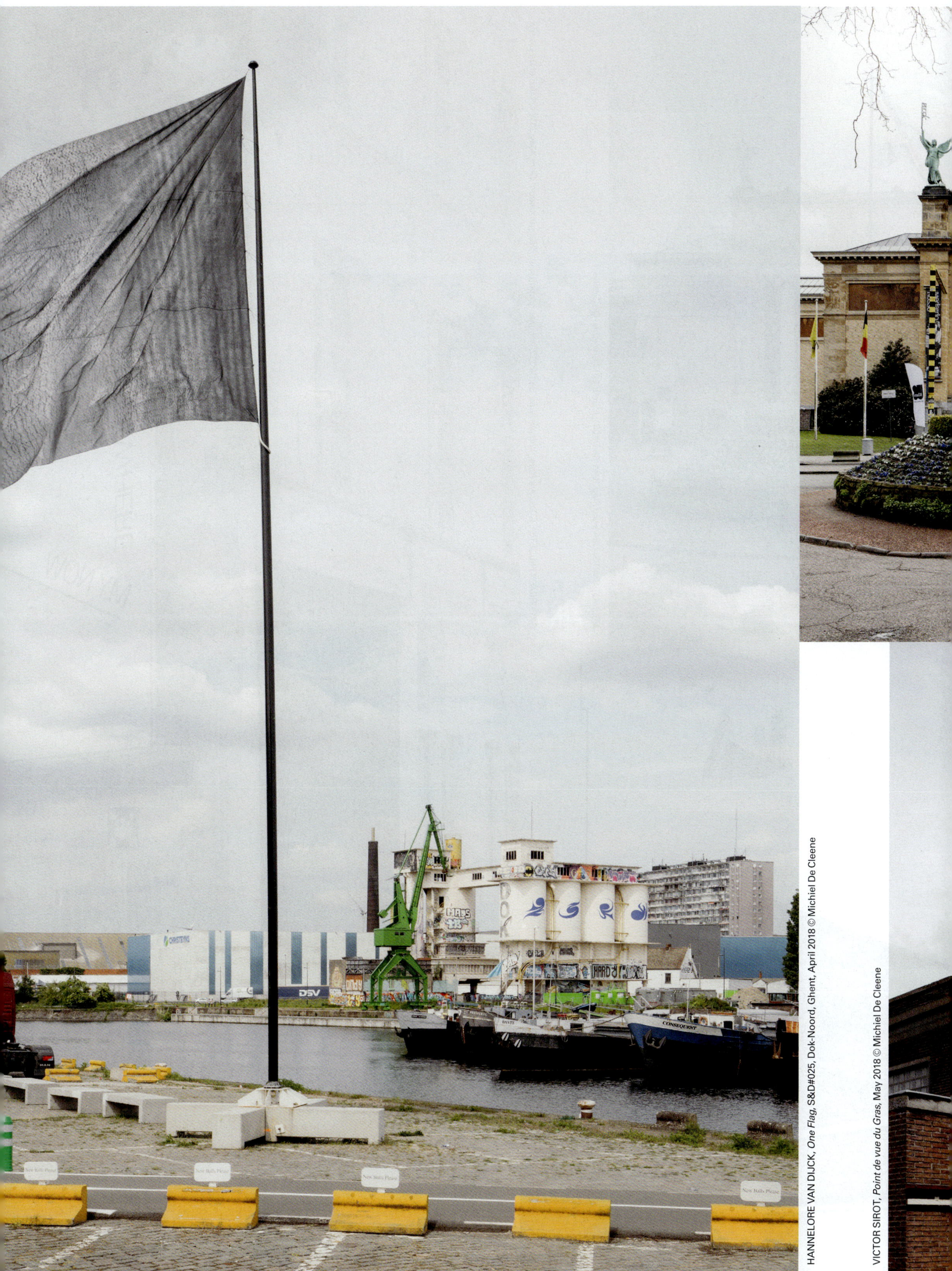

HANNELORE VAN DIJCK, *One Flag*, S&D#025, Dok-Noord, Ghent, April 2018 © Michiel De Cleene

VICTOR SIROT, *Point de vue du Gras*, May 2018 © Michiel De Cleene

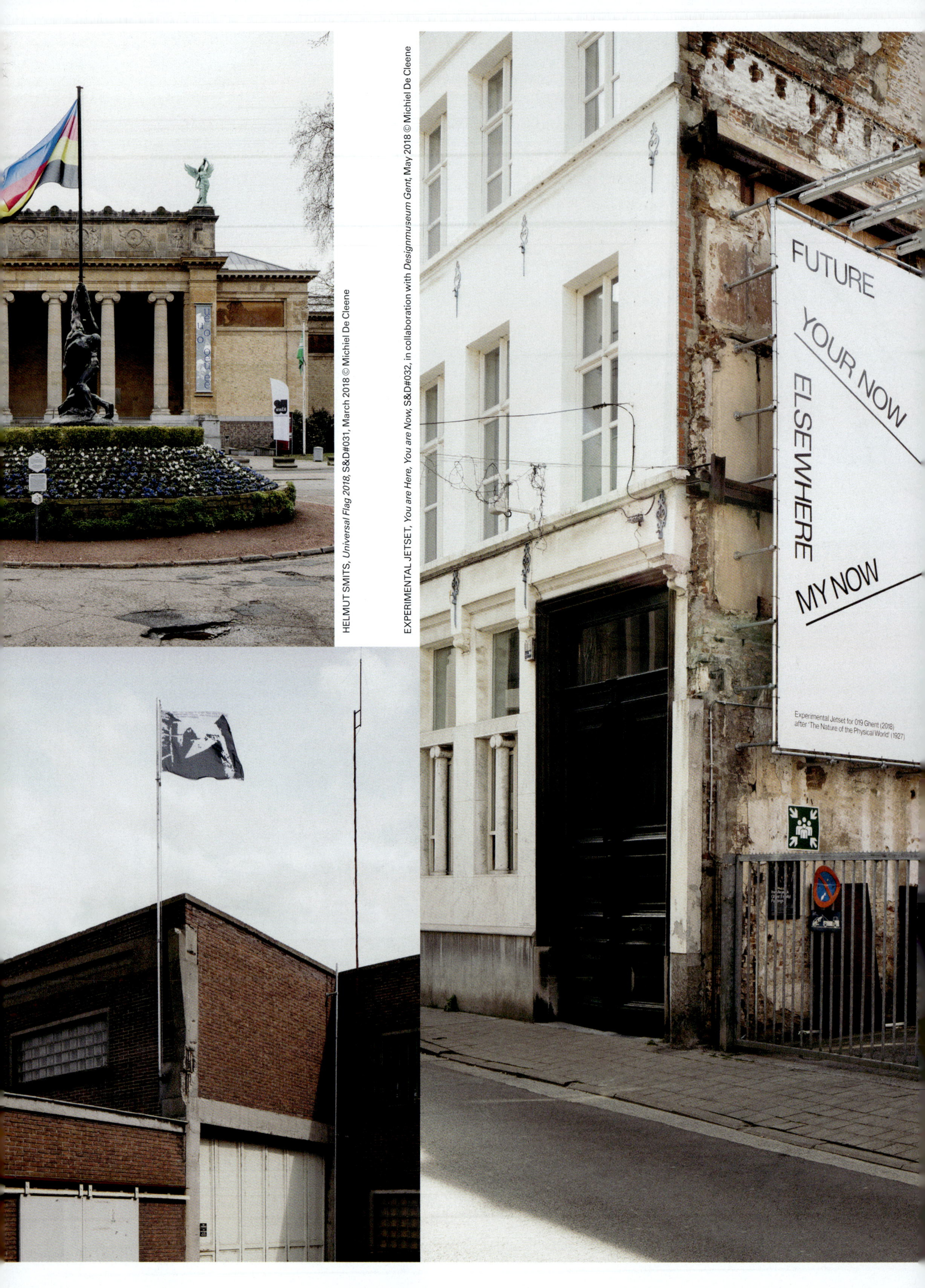

HELMUT SMITS, *Universal Flag 2018*, S&D#031, March 2018 © Michiel De Cleene

EXPERIMENTAL JETSET, *You are Here, You are Now*, S&D#032, in collaboration with *Designmuseum Gent*, May 2018 © Michiel De Cleene

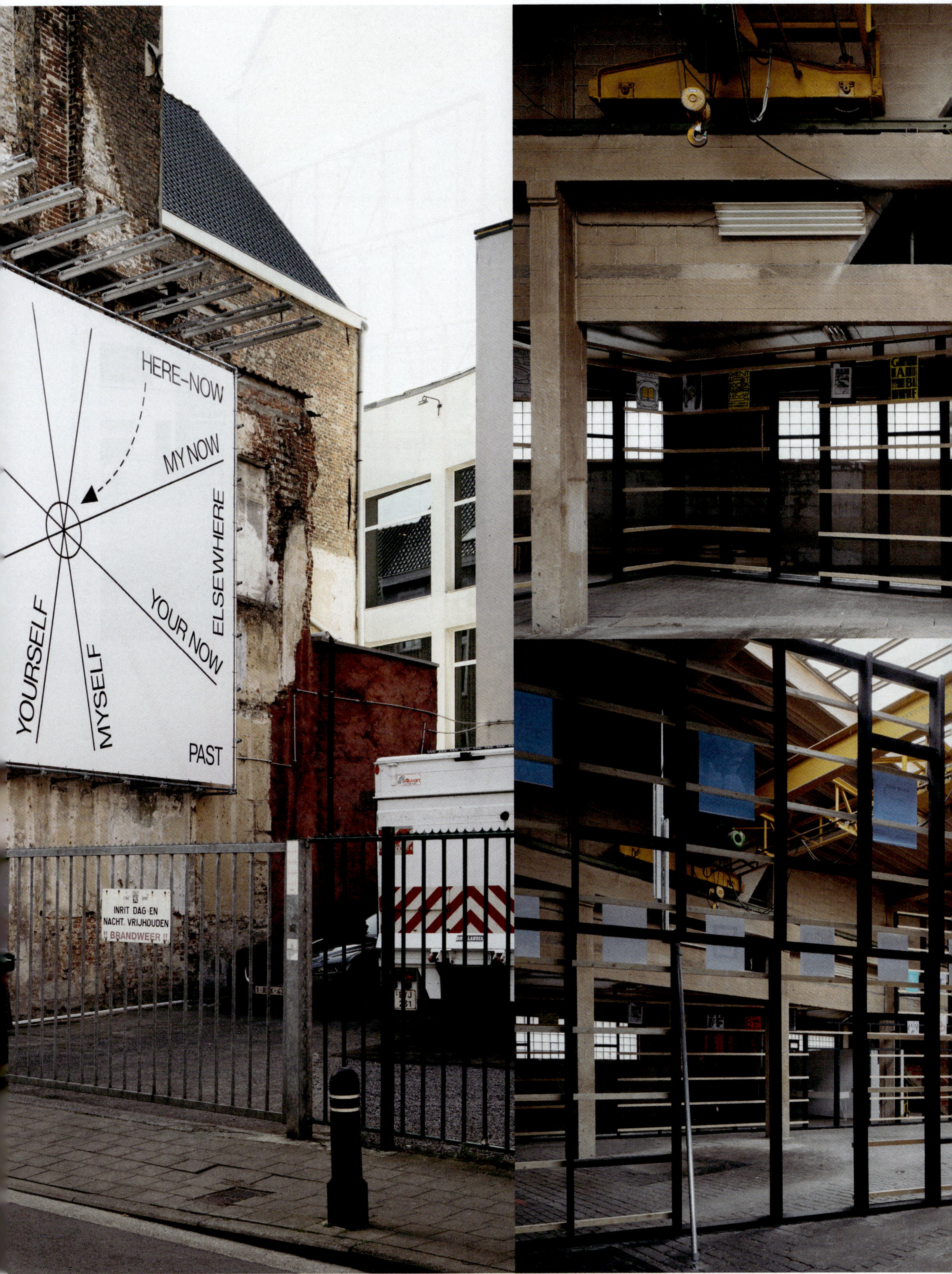
HERE–NOW
MY NOW
ELSEWHERE
YOUR NOW
YOURSELF
MYSELF
PAST
INRIT DAG EN
NACHT VRIJHOUDEN
!! BRANDWEER !!

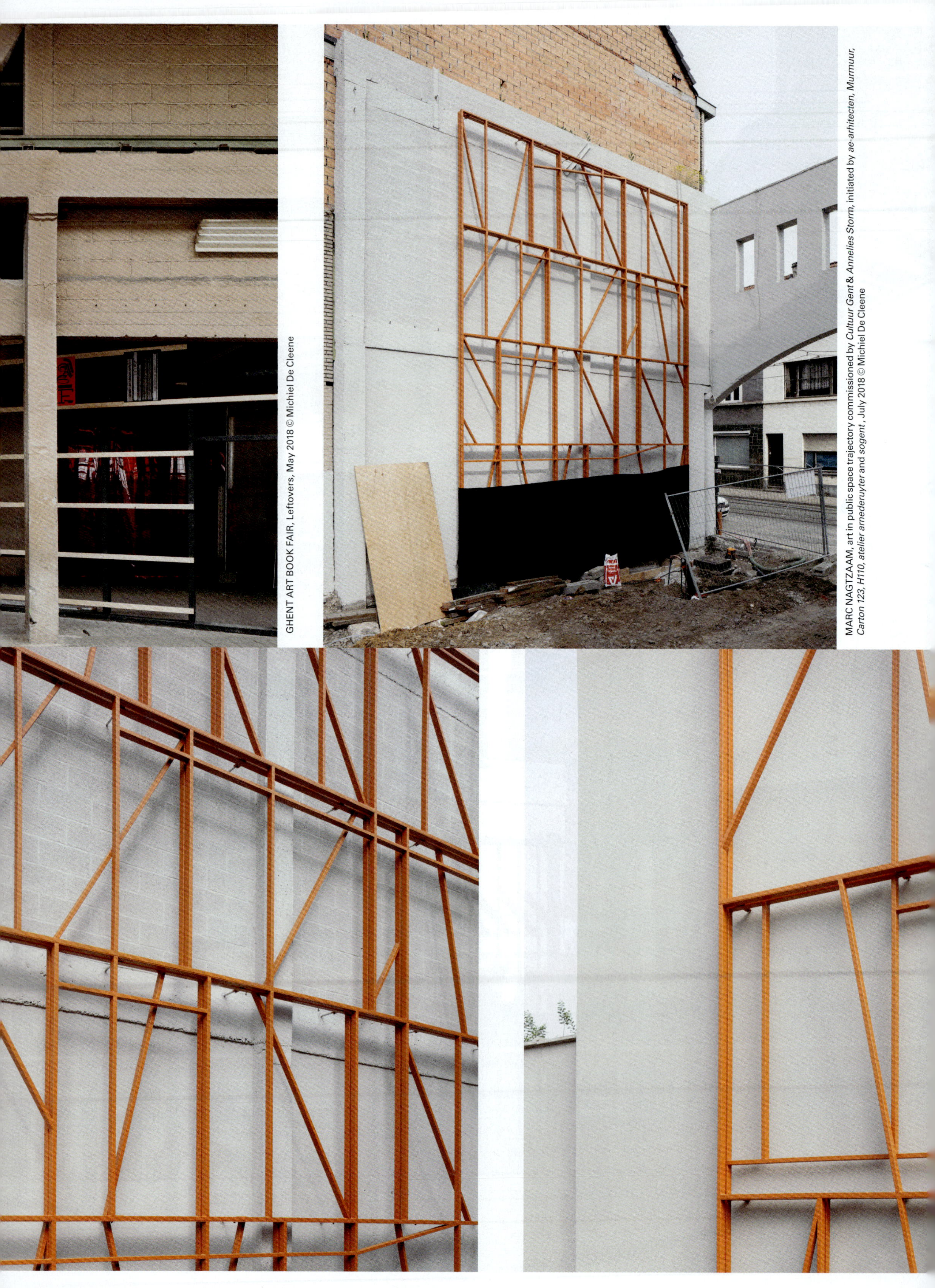

GHENT ART BOOK FAIR, Leftovers, May 2018 © Michiel De Cleene

MARC NAGTZAAM, art in public space trajectory commissioned by *Cultuur Gent* & *Annelies Storm*, initiated by *ae-arhitecten*, *Murmuur*, *Carton 123*, *H110*, *atelier arnederuyter* and *sogent*, July 2018 © Michiel De Cleene

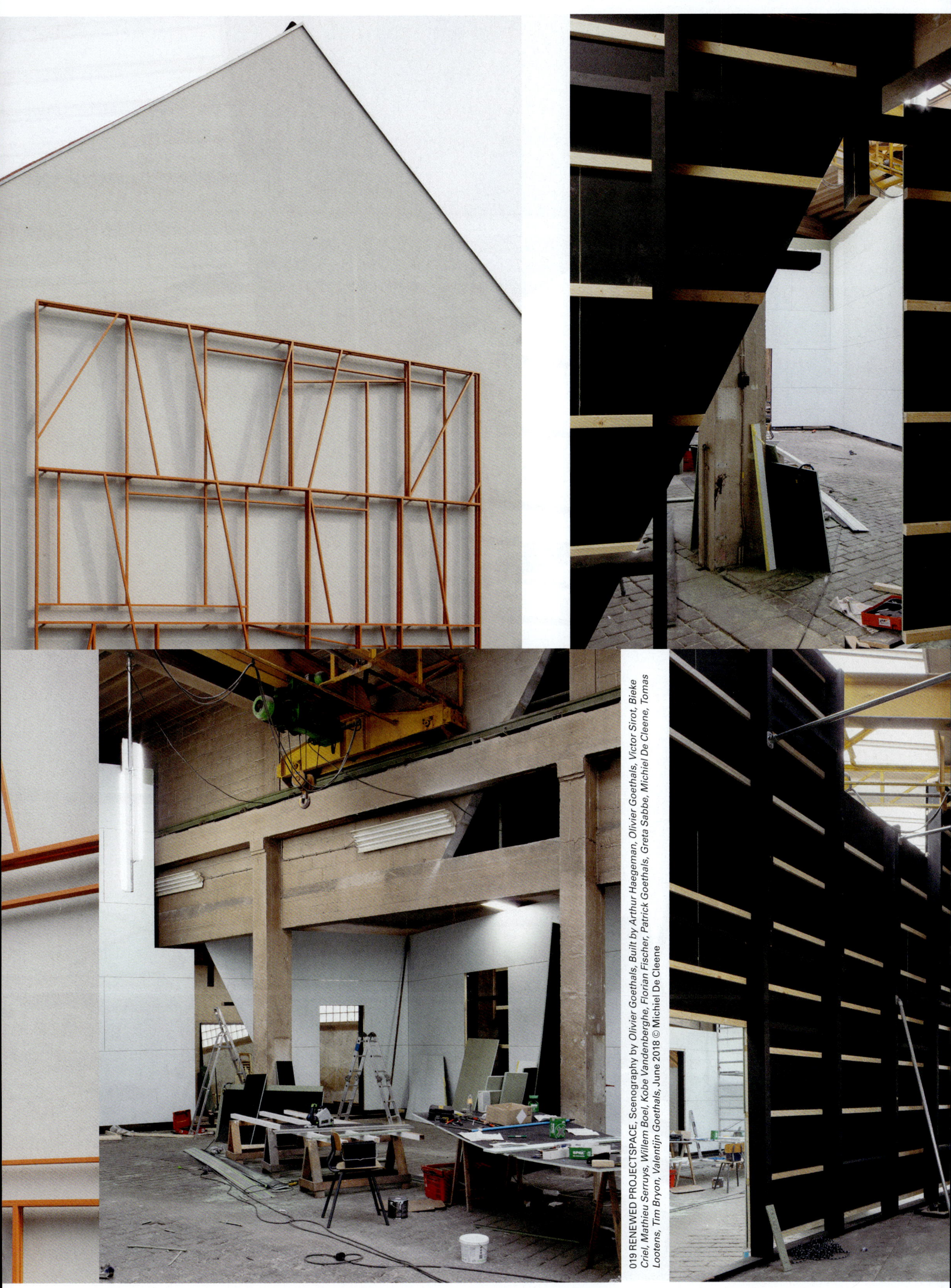

019 RENEWED PROJECTSPACE, *Scenography by Olivier Goethals, Built by Arthur Haegeman, Olivier Goethals, Victor Sirot, Bieke Criel, Mathieu Serruys, Willem Boel, Kobe Vandenberghe, Florian Fischer, Patrick Goethals, Greta Sabbe, Michiel De Cleene, Tomas Lootens, Tim Bryon, Valentijn Goethals,* June 2018 © Michiel De Cleene

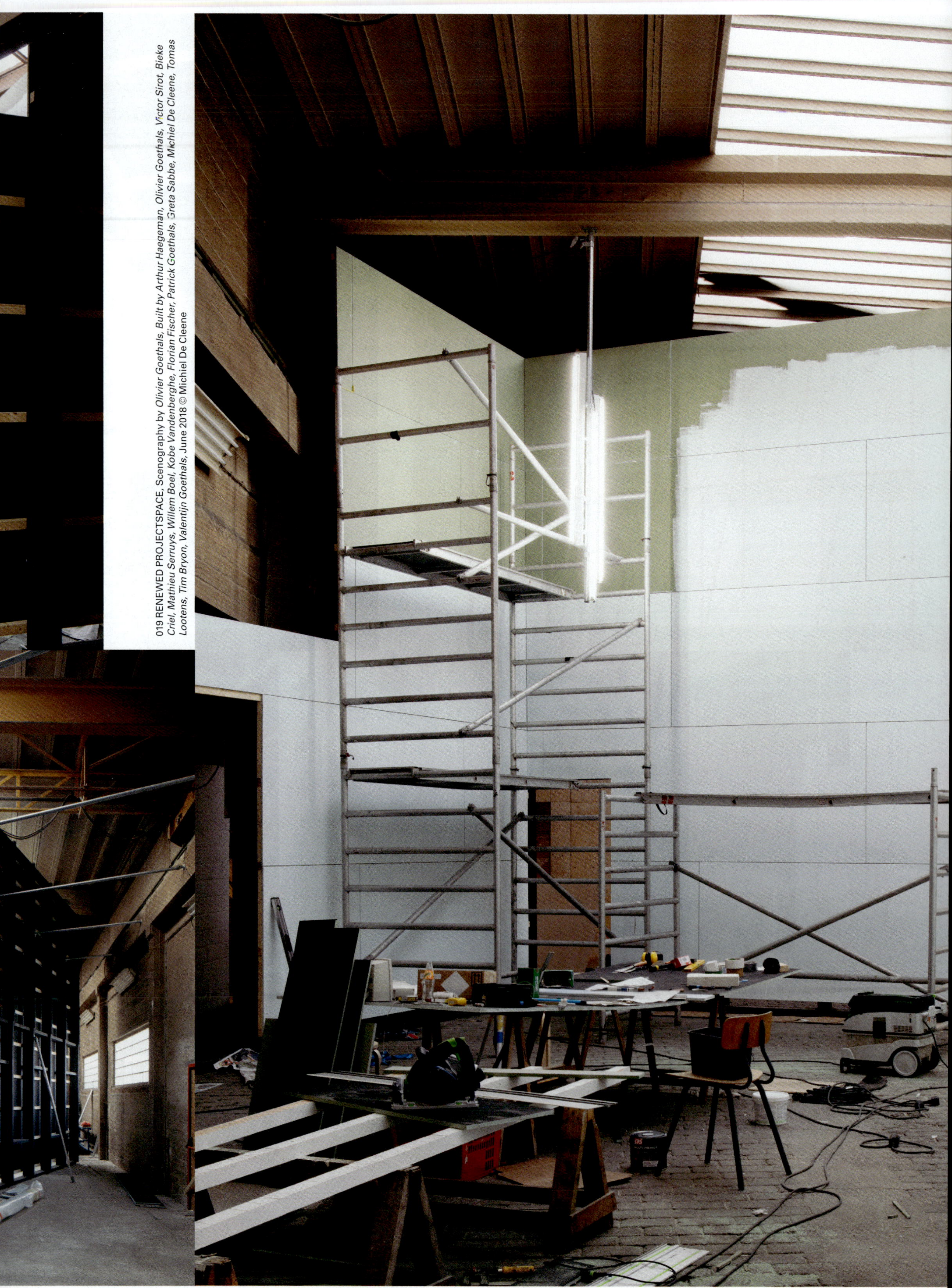

019 RENEWED PROJECTSPACE, Scenography by *Olivier Goethals*, Built by *Arthur Haegeman, Olivier Goethals, Victor Sirot, Bieke Criel, Mathieu Serruys, Willem Boel, Kobe Vandenberghe, Florian Fischer, Patrick Goethals, Greta Sabbe, Michiel De Cleene, Tomas Lootens, Tim Bryon, Valentijn Goethals*, June 2018 © Michiel De Cleene

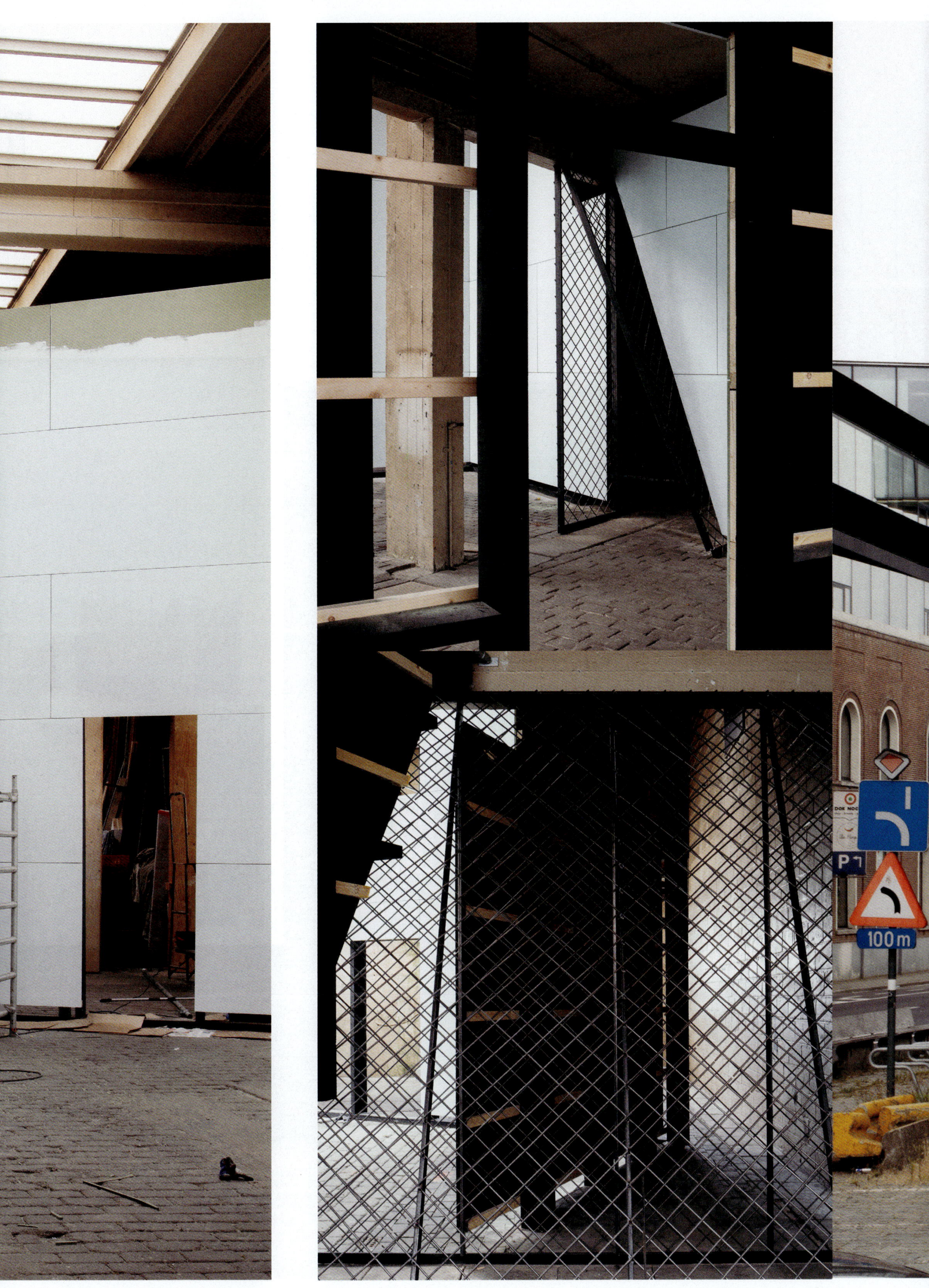
P
100 m

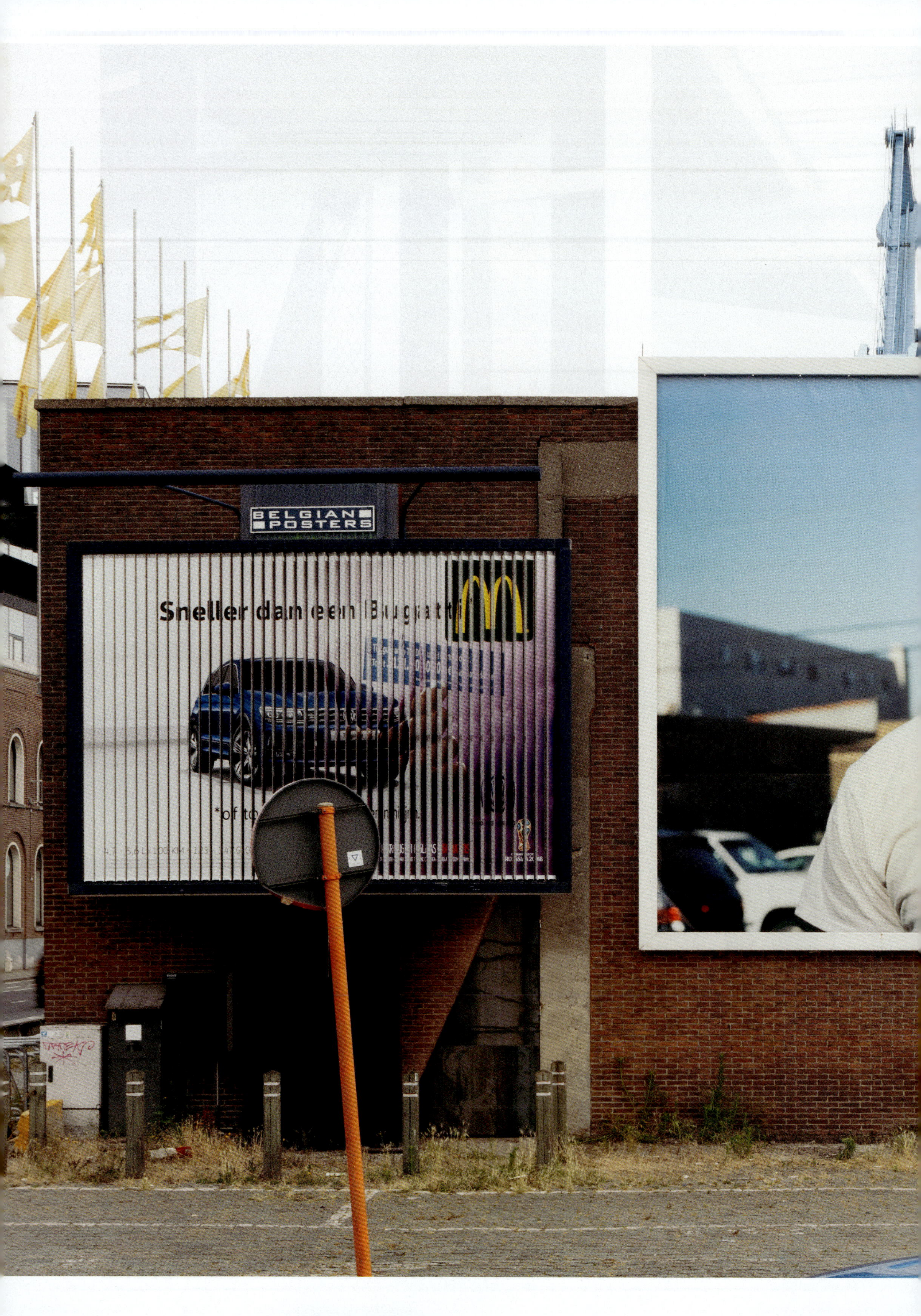
BELGIAN POSTERS
Sneller dan een Bugatti

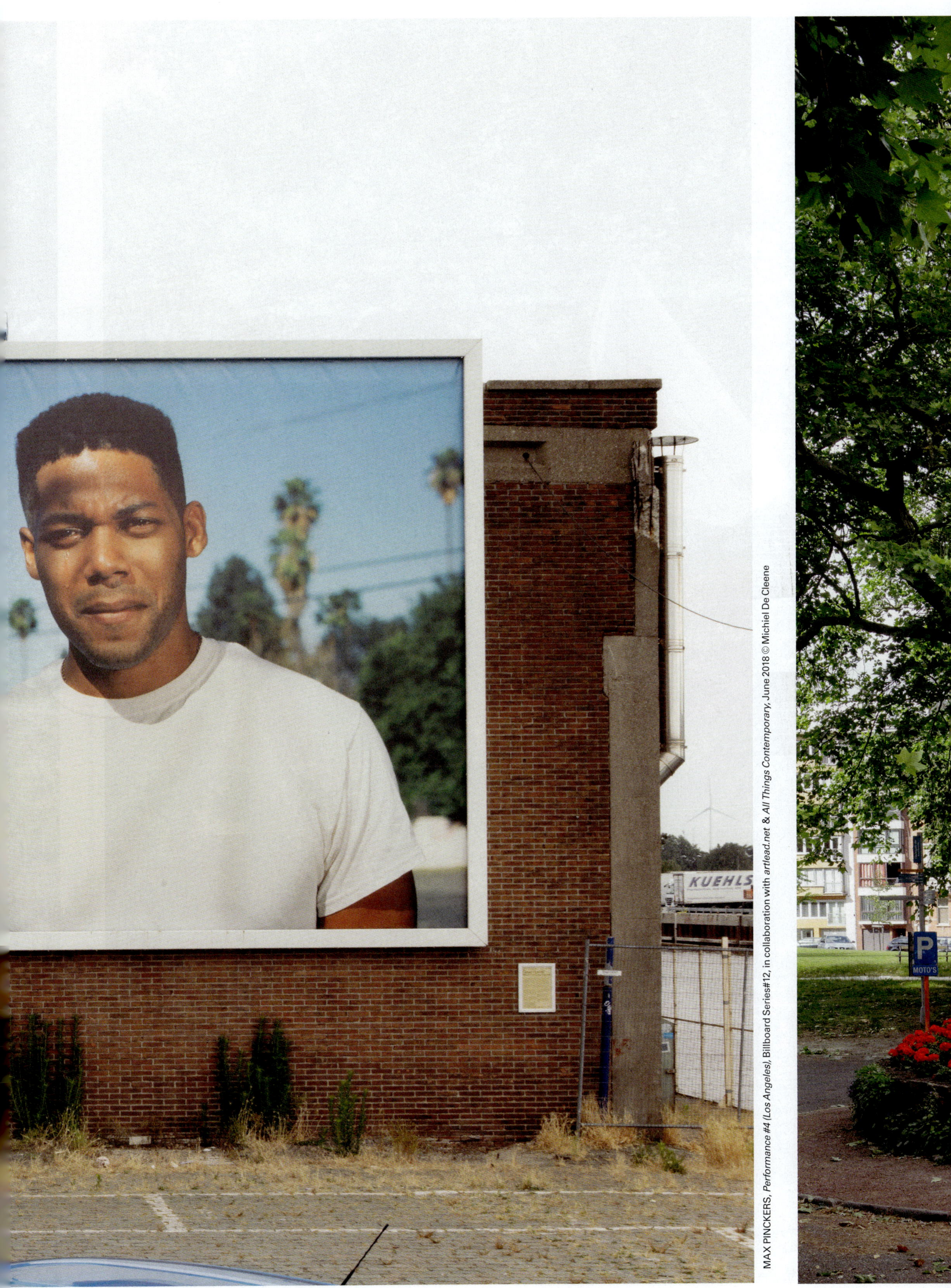

MAX PINCKERS, *Performance #4 (Los Angeles)*, Billboard Series#12, in collaboration with *artlead.net* & *All Things Contemporary*, June 2018 © Michiel De Cleene

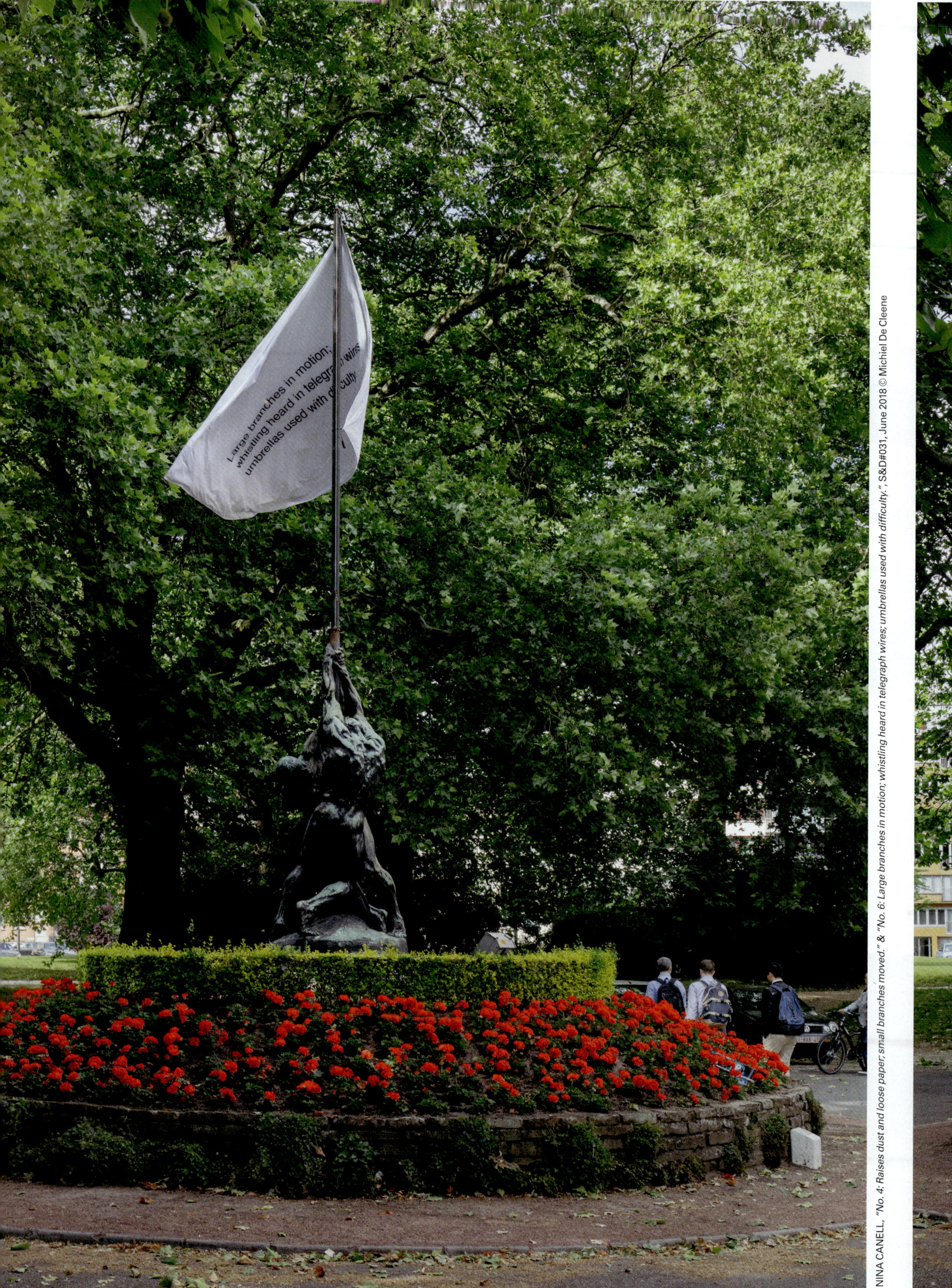

NINA CANELL, *"No. 4: Raises dust and loose paper; small branches moved."* & *"No. 6: Large branches in motion; whistling heard in telegraph wires; umbrellas used with difficulty."*, S&D#031, June 2018 © Michiel De Cleene

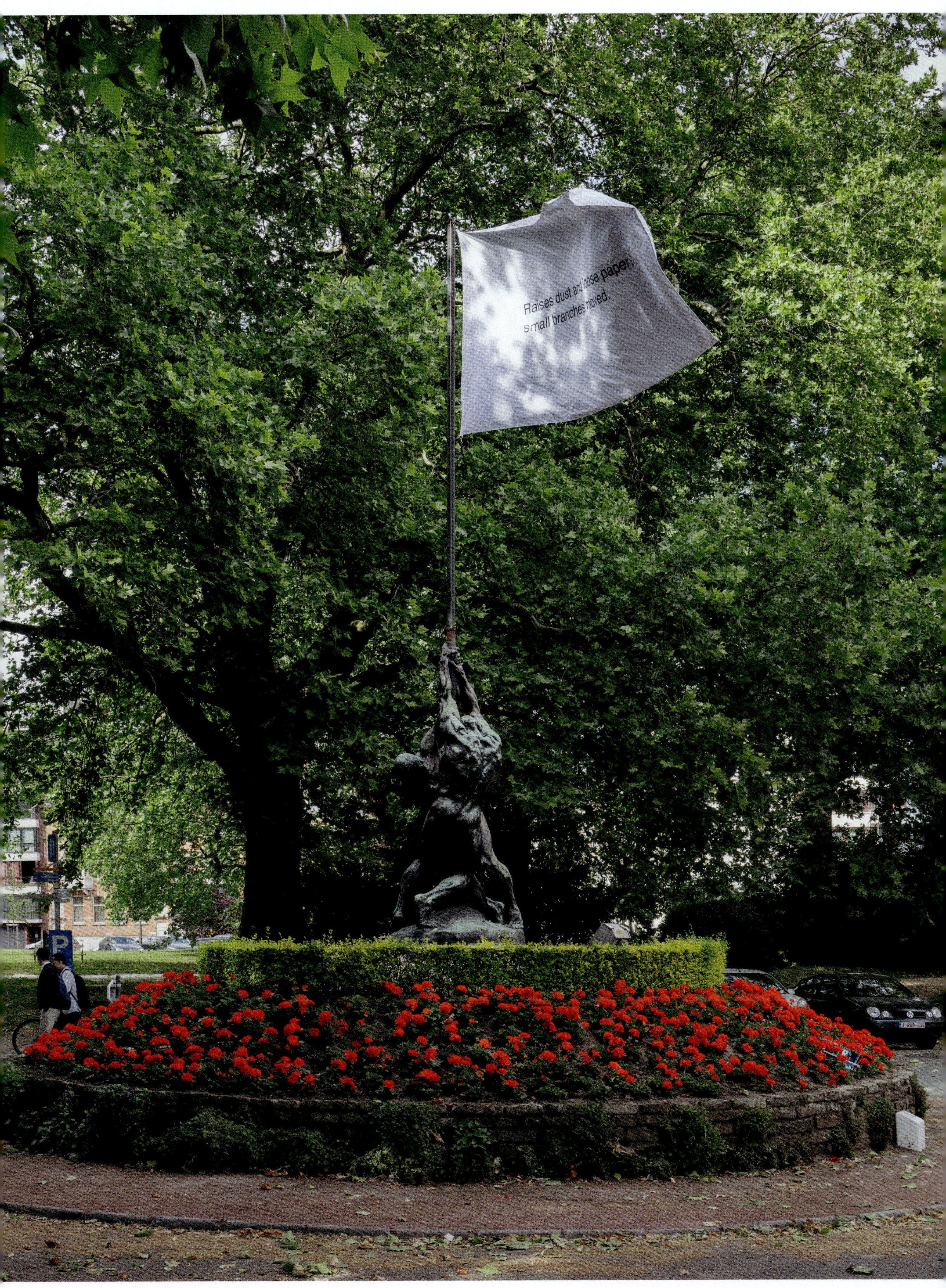
Raises dust and loose paper;
small branches moved.

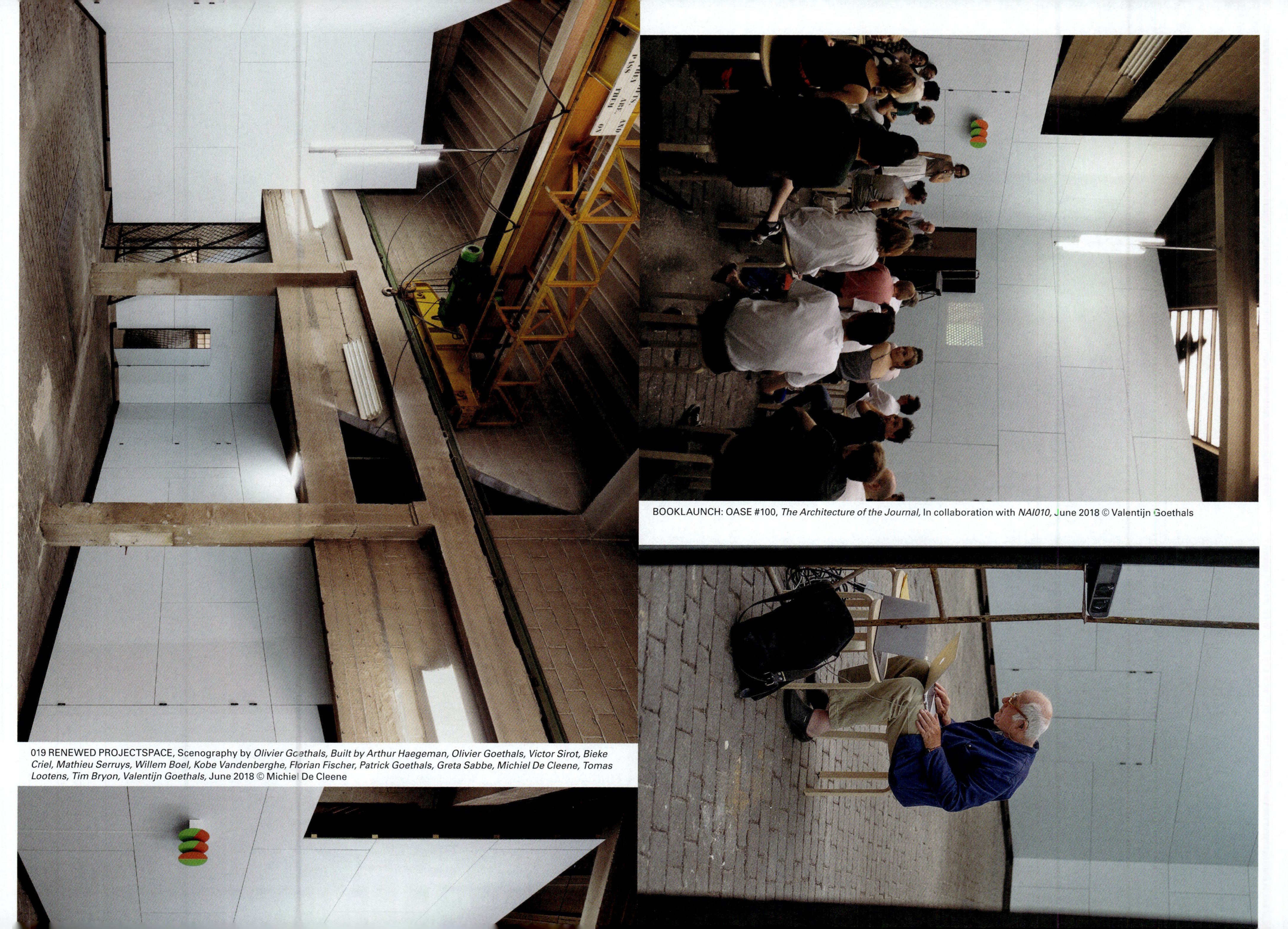

BOOKLAUNCH: OASE #100, *The Architecture of the Journal*, In collaboration with *NAI010*, June 2018 © Valentijn Goethals

019 RENEWED PROJECTSPACE, Scenography by *Olivier Goethals*, *Built by Arthur Haegeman, Olivier Goethals, Victor Sirot, Bieke Criel, Mathieu Serruys, Willem Boel, Kobe Vandenberghe, Florian Fischer, Patrick Goethals, Greta Sabbe, Michiel De Cleene, Tomas Lootens, Tim Bryon, Valentijn Goethals*, June 2018 © Michiel De Cleene

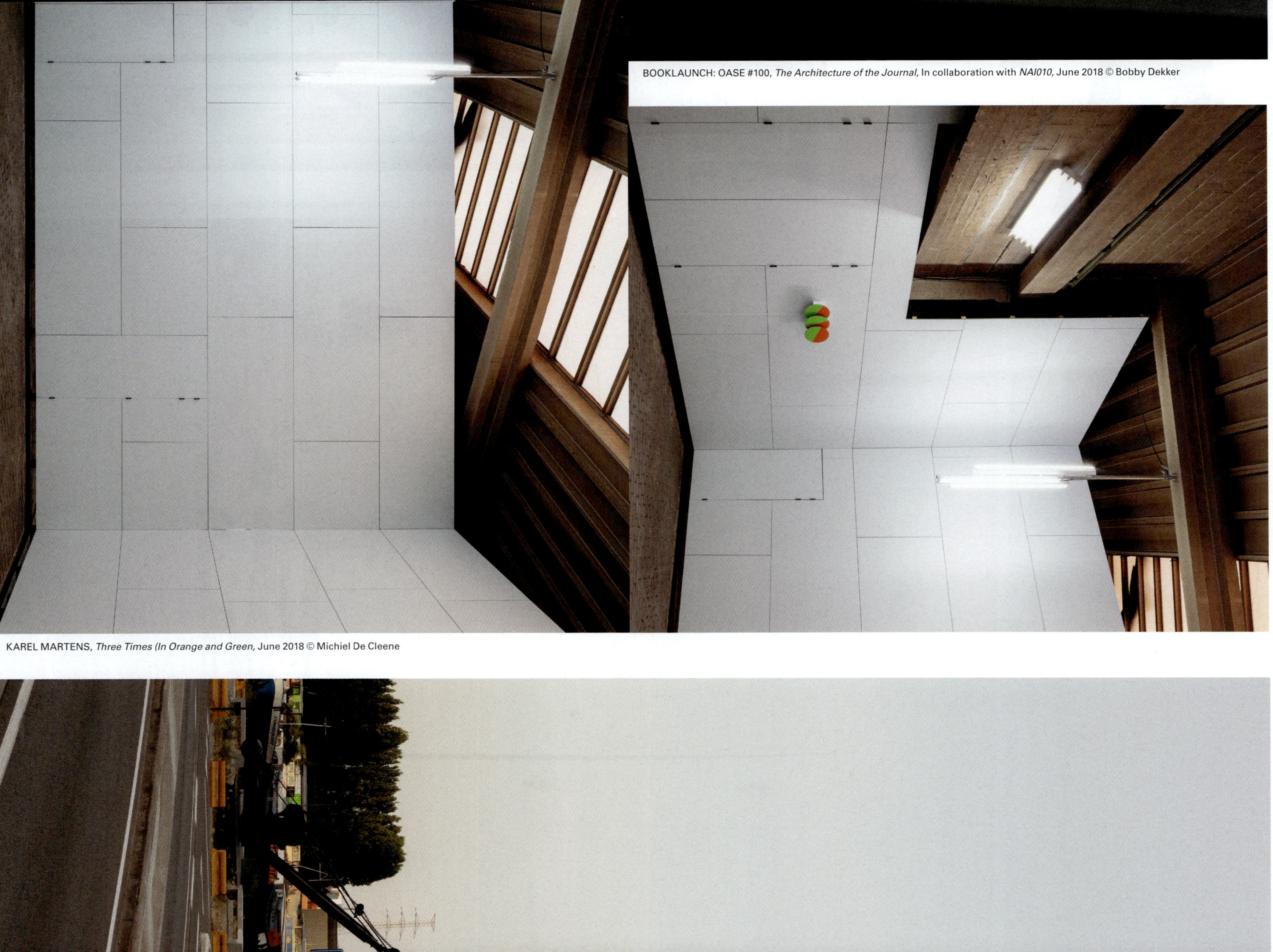

BOOKLAUNCH: OASE #100, *The Architecture of the Journal*, In collaboration with *NAI010*, June 2018 © Bobby Dekker

KAREL MARTENS, *Three Times (In Orange and Green*, June 2018 © Michiel De Cleene

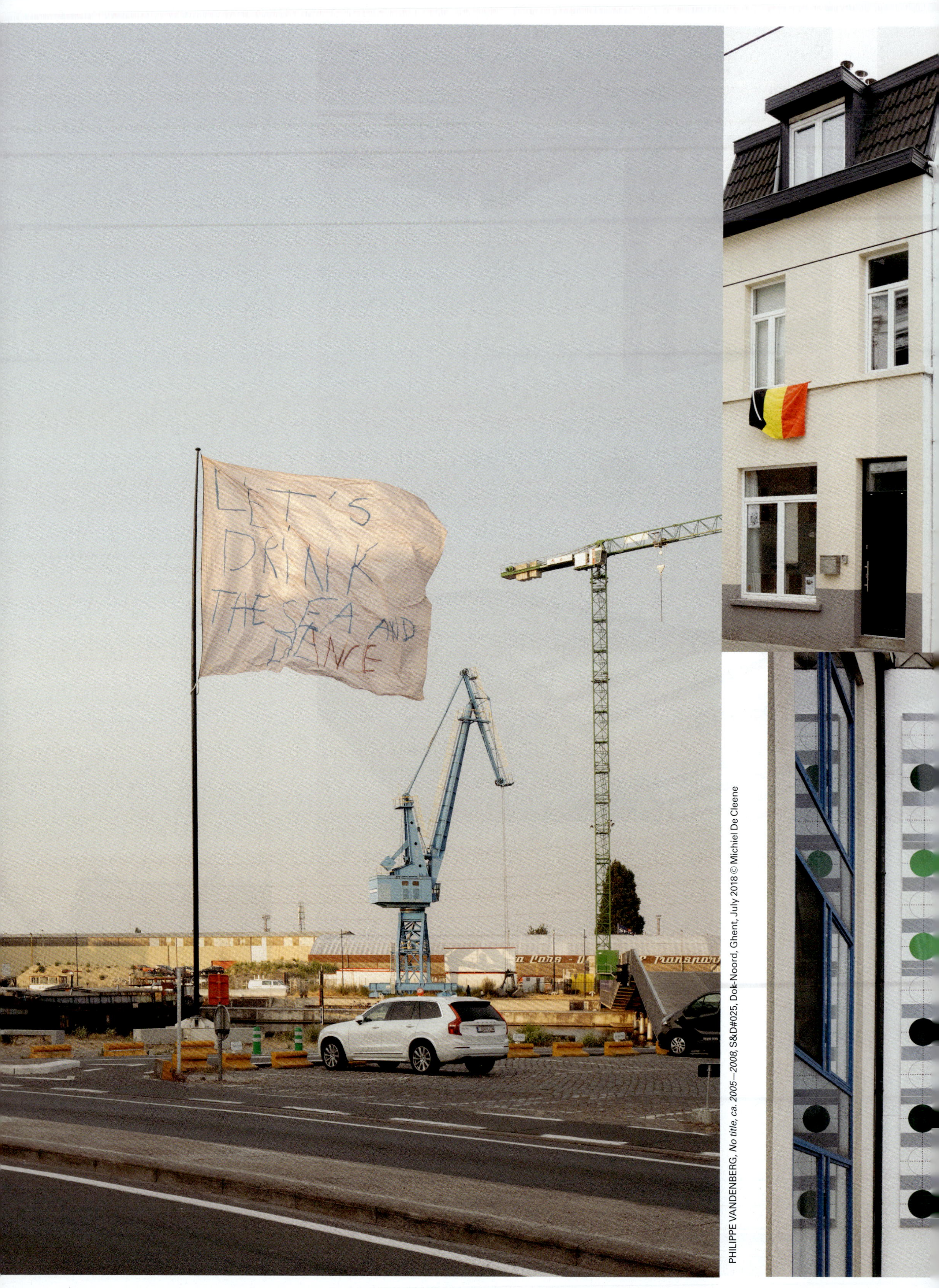

PHILIPPE VANDENBERG, *No title, ca. 2005–2008*, S&D#025, Dok-Noord, Ghent, July 2018 © Michiel De Cleene

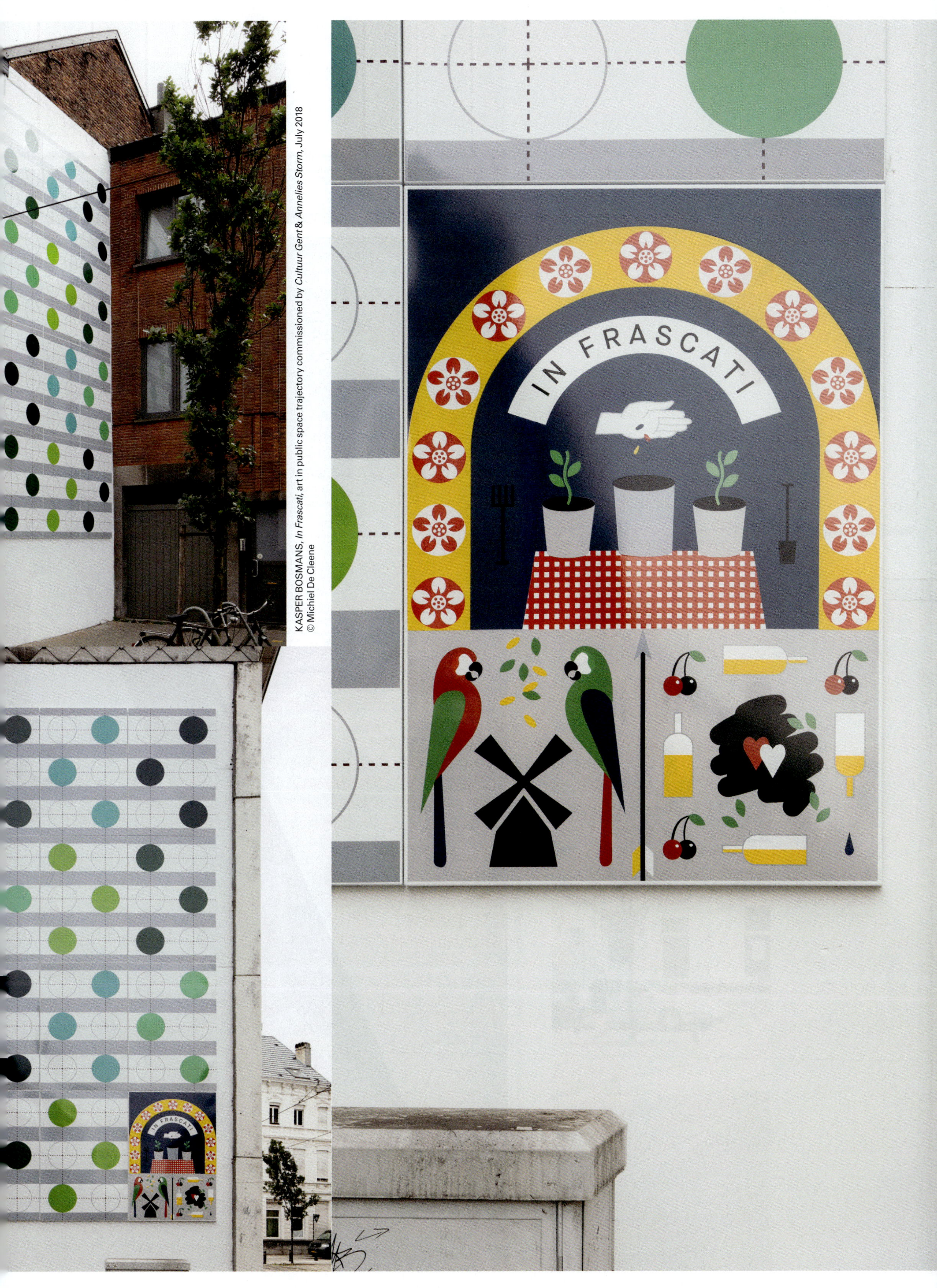

KASPER BOSMANS, *In Frascati*, art in public space trajectory commissioned by *Cultuur Gent* & *Annelies Storm*, July 2018
© Michiel De Cleene

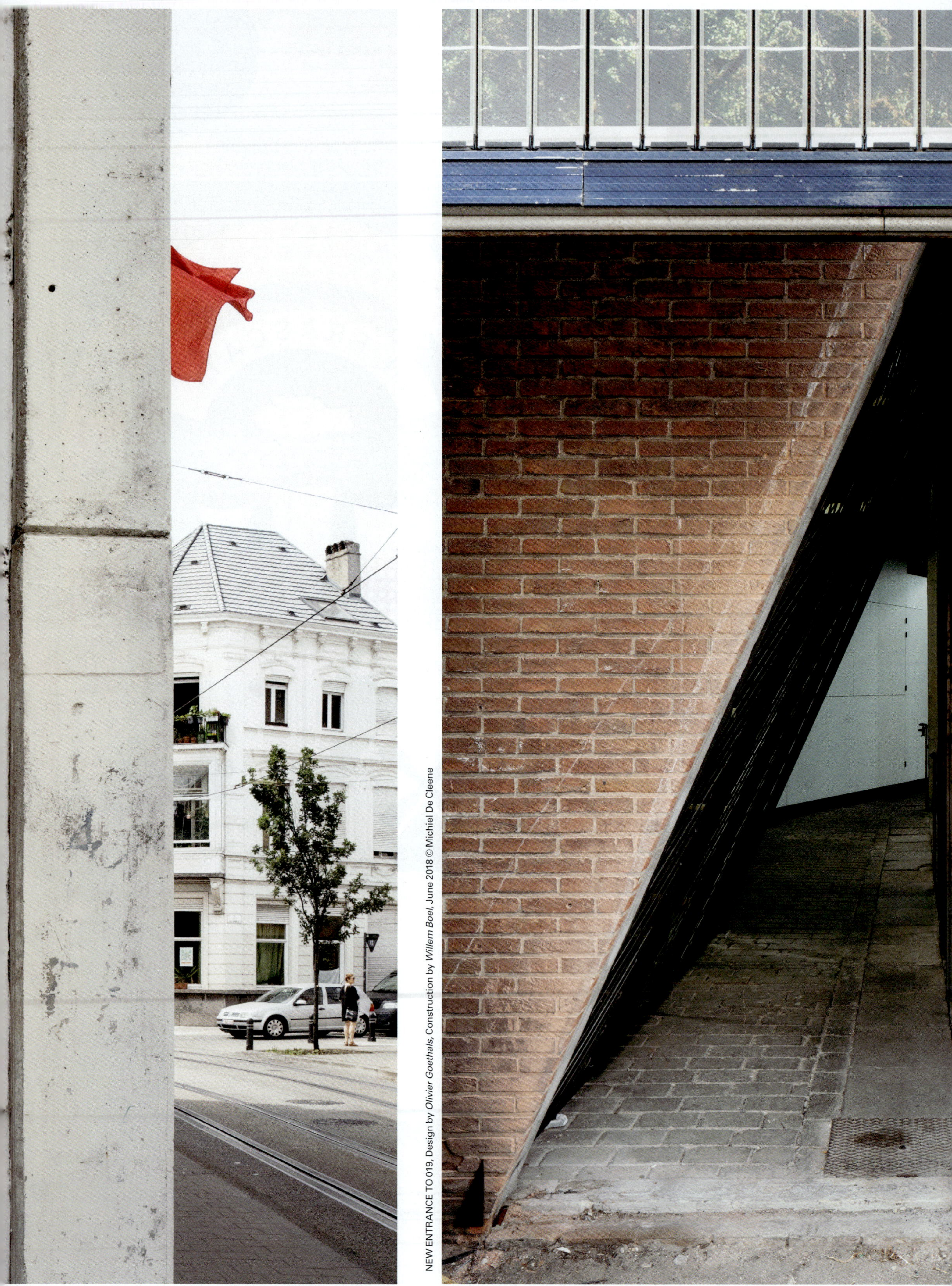

NEW ENTRANCE TO 019, Design by *Olivier Goethals*, Construction by *Willem Boel*, June 2018 © Michiel De Cleene

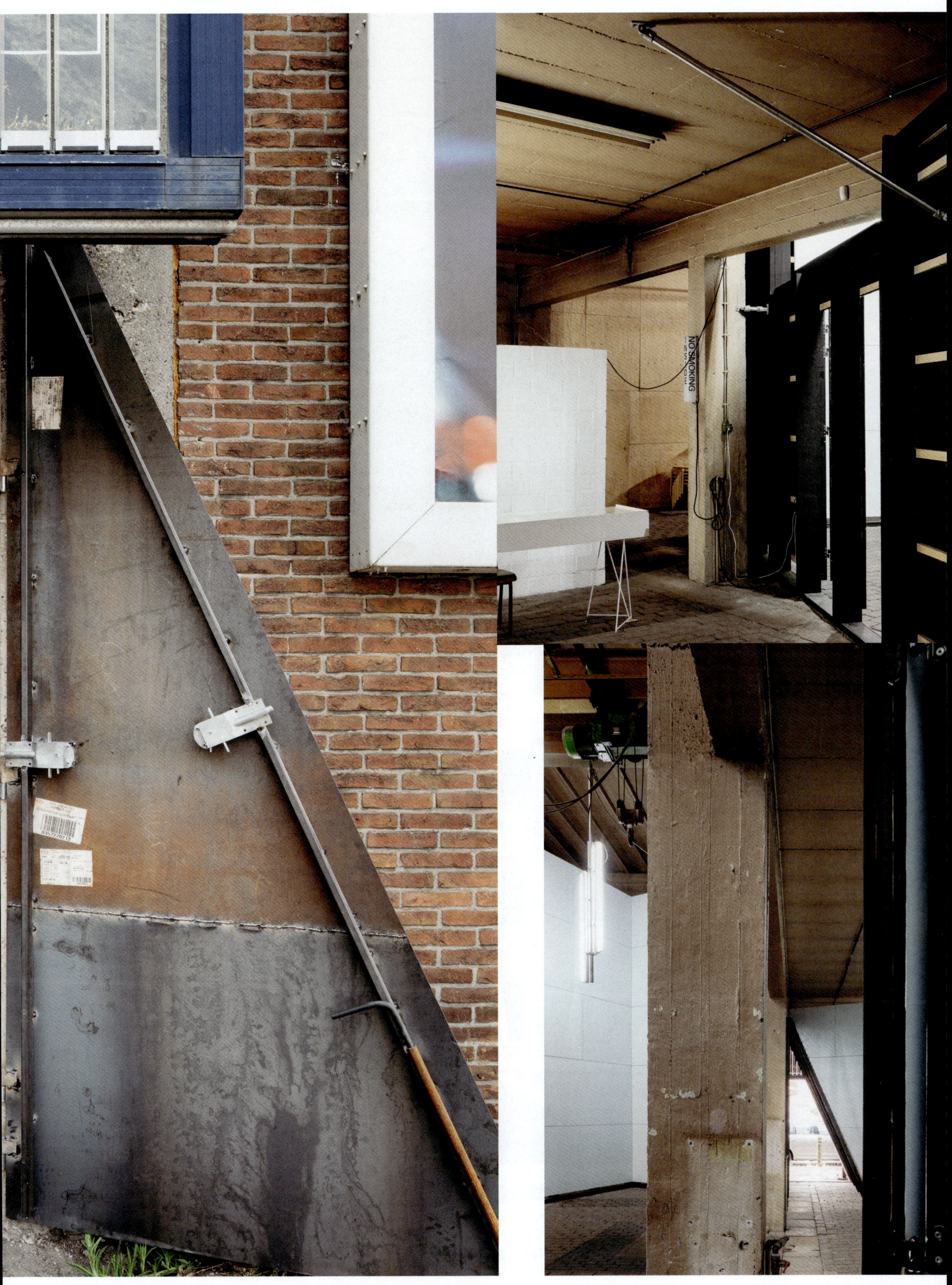
NO SMOKING

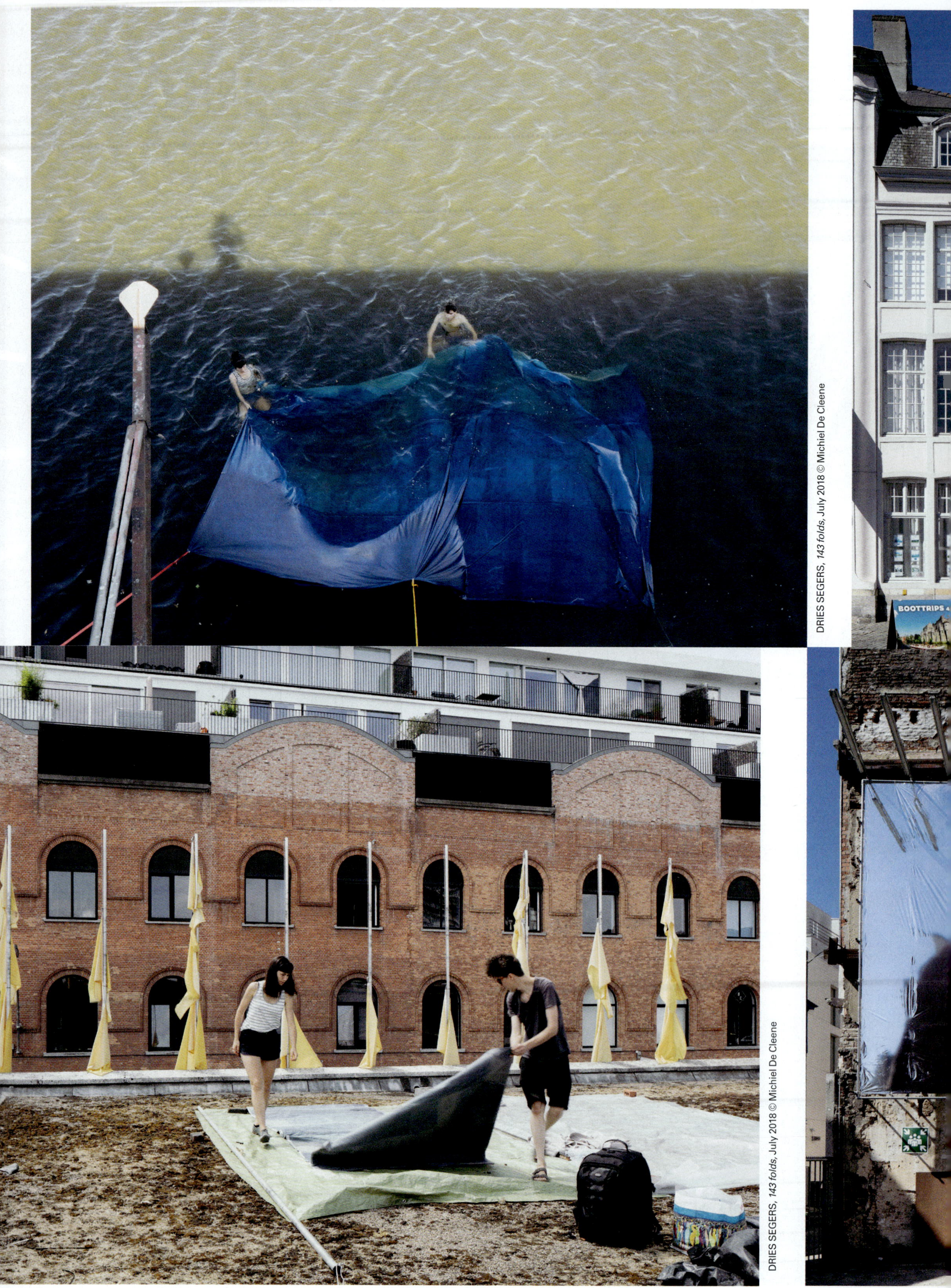

DRIES SEGERS, *143 folds*, July 2018 © Michiel De Cleene

DRIES SEGERS, *143 folds*, July 2018 © Michiel De Cleene

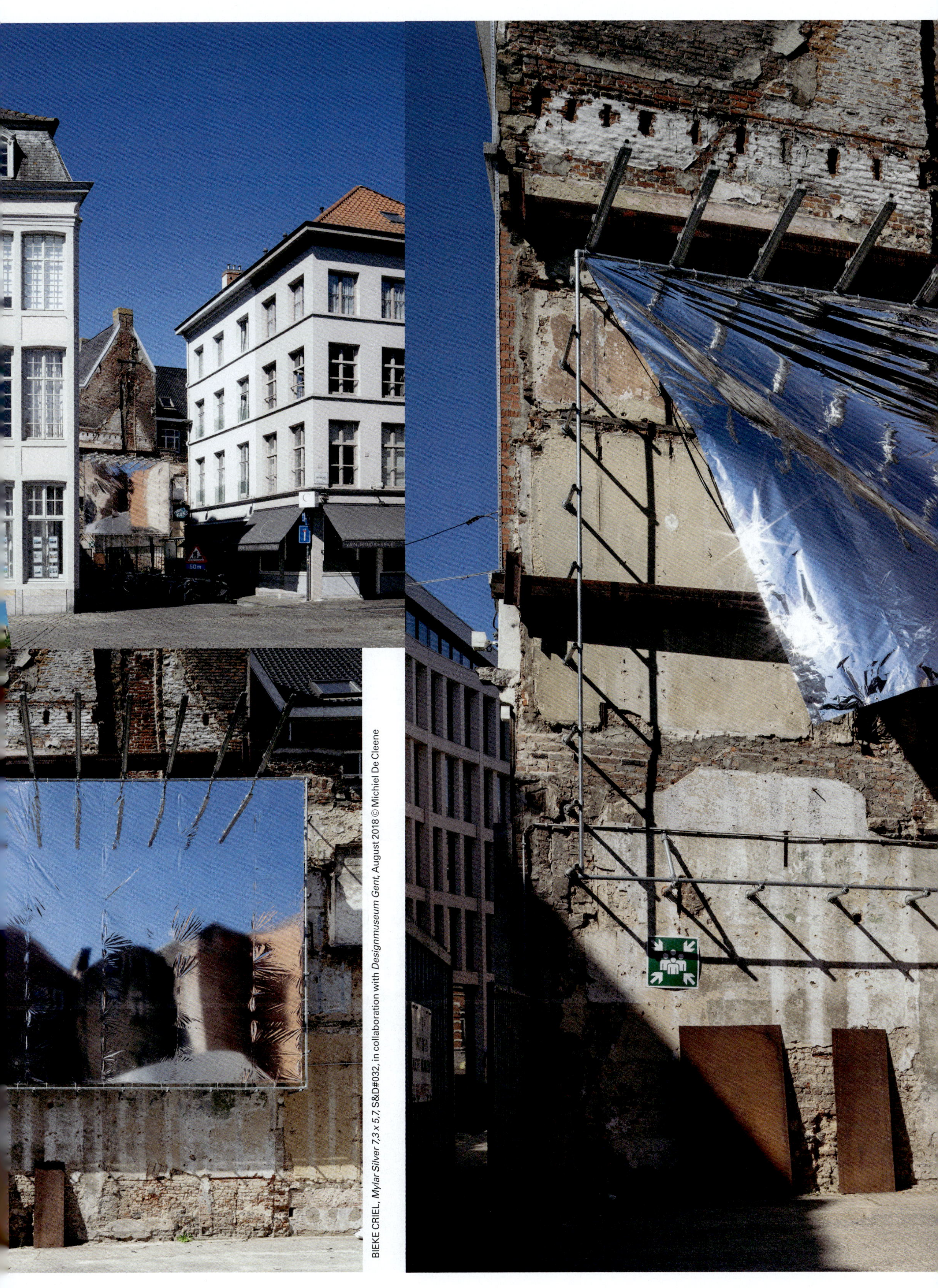

BIEKE CRIEL, *Mylar Silver 7,3 x 5,7*, S&D#032, in collaboration with *Designmuseum Gent*, August 2018 © Michiel De Cleene

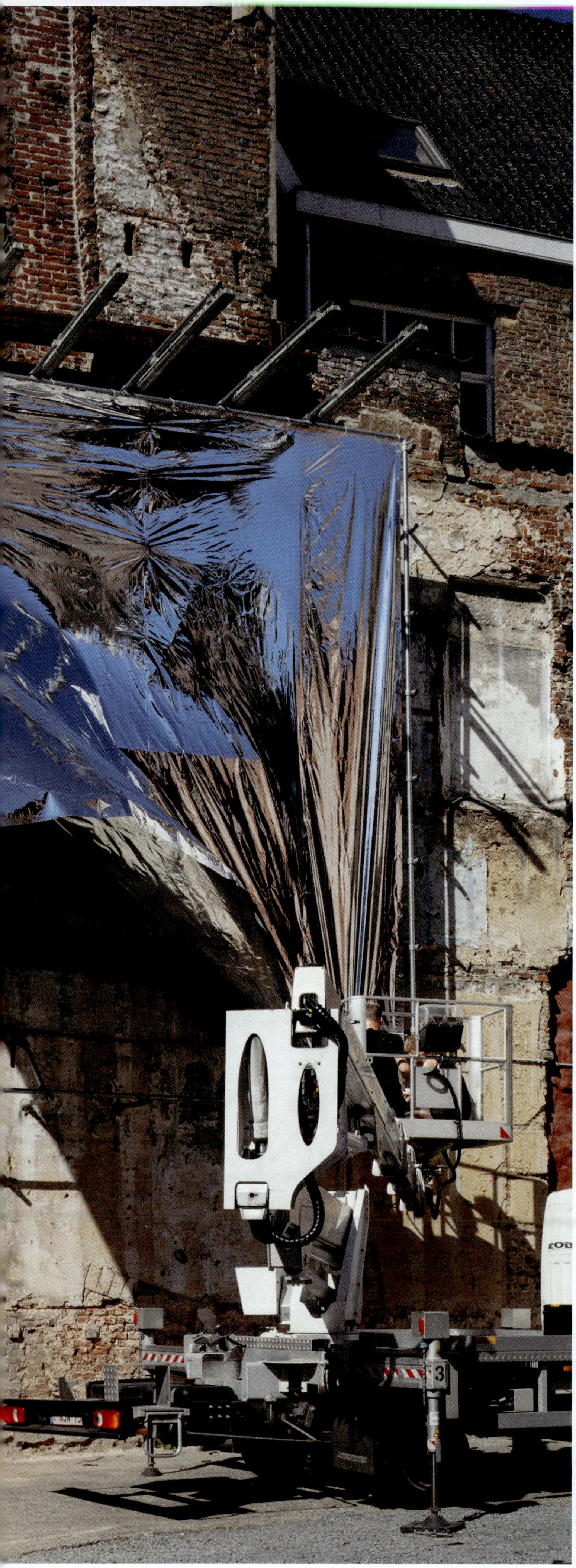

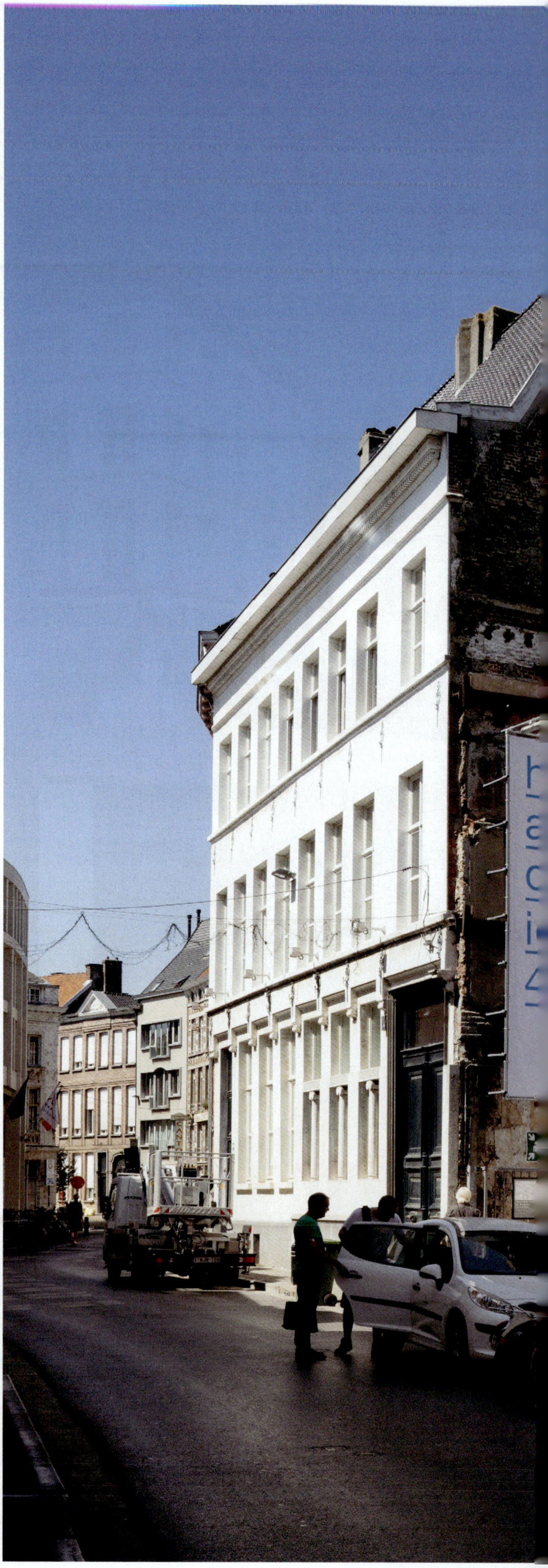

BIEKE CRIEL, *Mylar Silver 7,3 x 5,7*, S&D#032, in collaboration with *Designmuseum Gent*, August 2018 © Michiel De Cleene
BRÁULIO AMADO, *01:05:24*, S&D#032, in collaboration with *Designmuseum Gent*, August 2018 © Michiel De Cleene

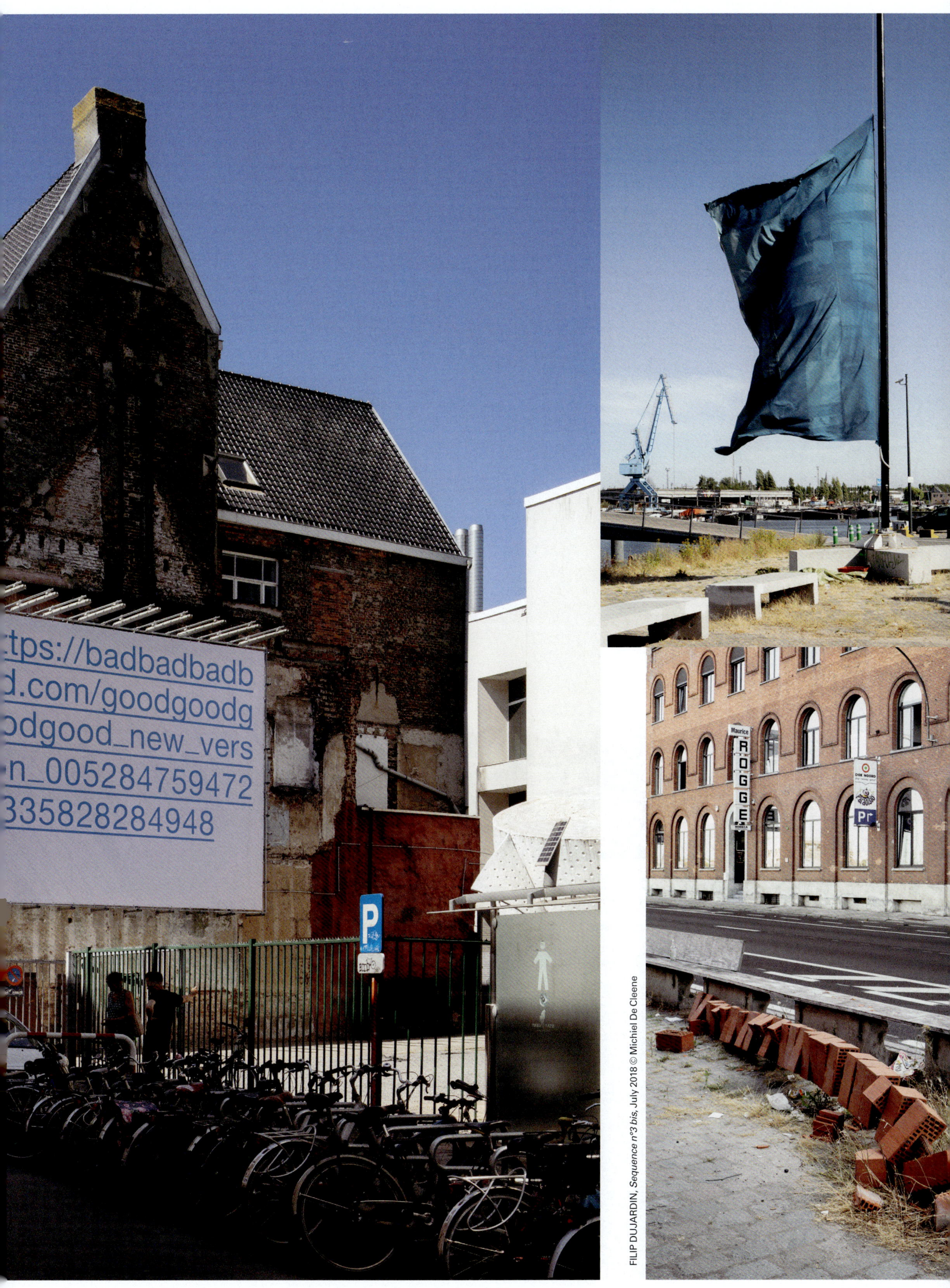

FILIP DUJARDIN, *Sequence n°3 bis*, July 2018 © Michiel De Cleene

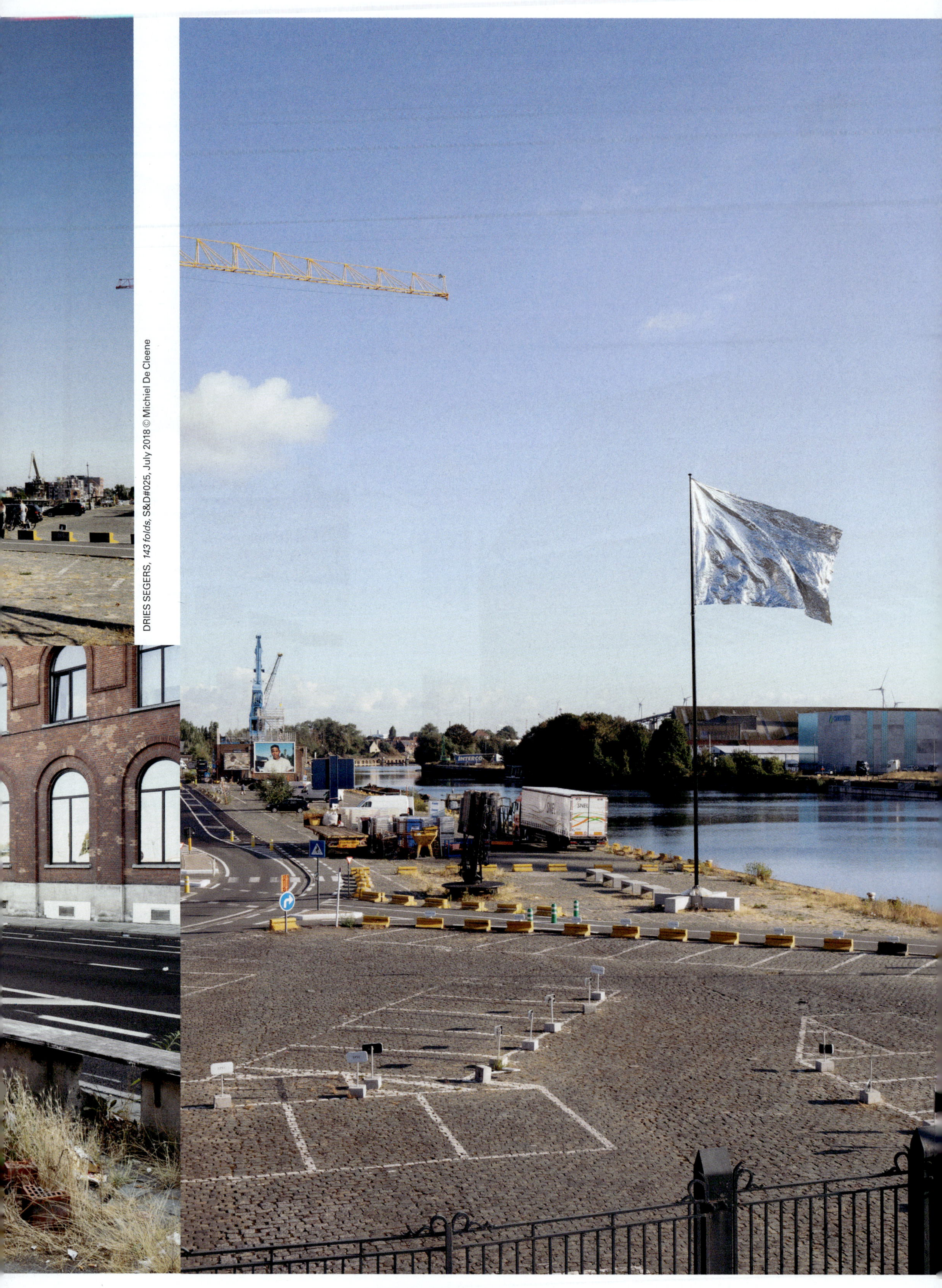

DRIES SEGERS, *143 folds*, S&D#025, July 2018 © Michiel De Cleene

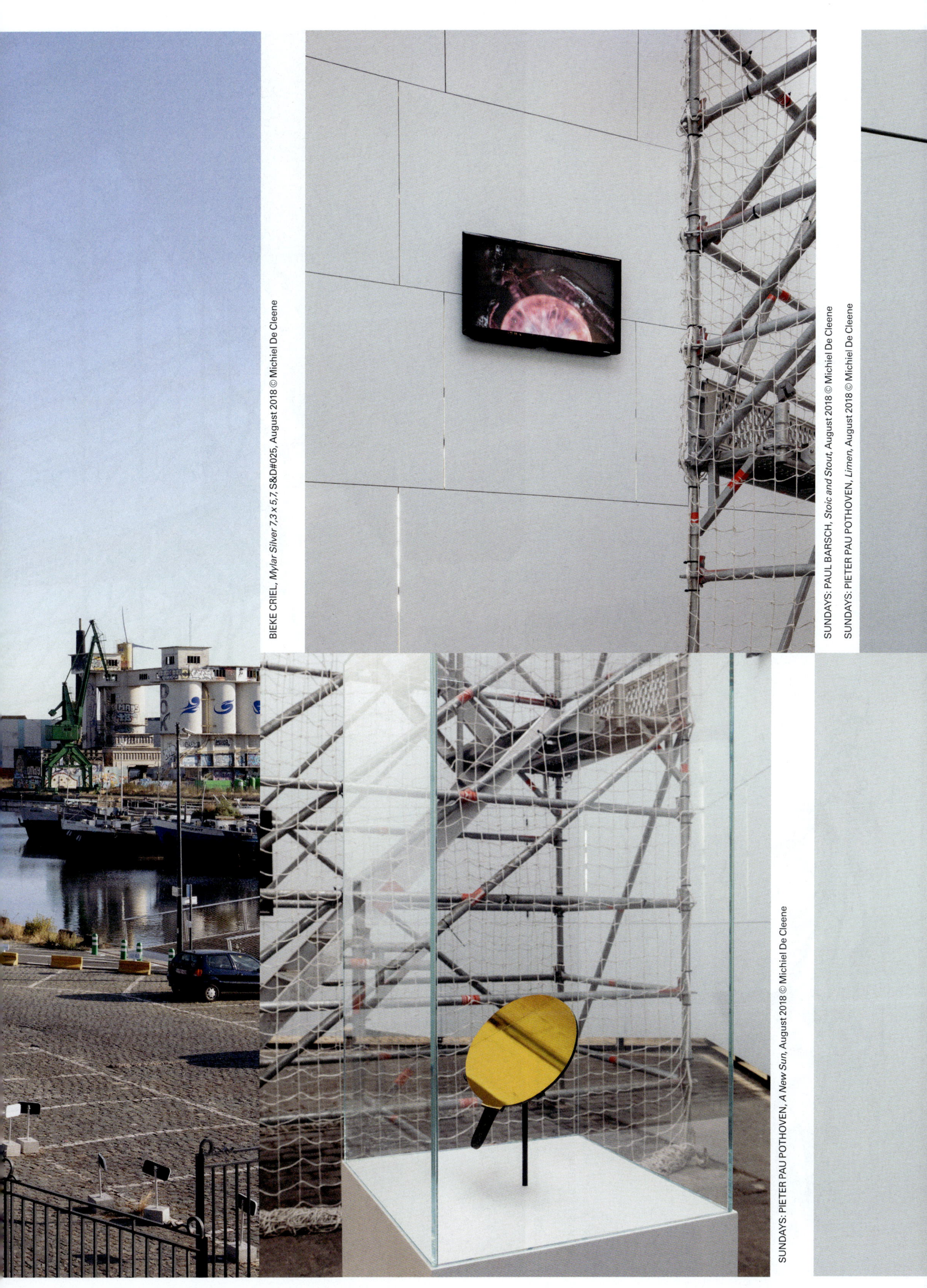

BIEKE CRIEL, *Mylar Silver 7,3 x 5,7*, S&D#025, August 2018 © Michiel De Cleene

SUNDAYS: PAUL BARSCH, *Stoic and Stout*, August 2018 © Michiel De Cleene

SUNDAYS: PIETER PAU POTHOVEN, *Limen*, August 2018 © Michiel De Cleene

SUNDAYS: PIETER PAU POTHOVEN, *A New Sun*, August 2018 © Michiel De Cleene

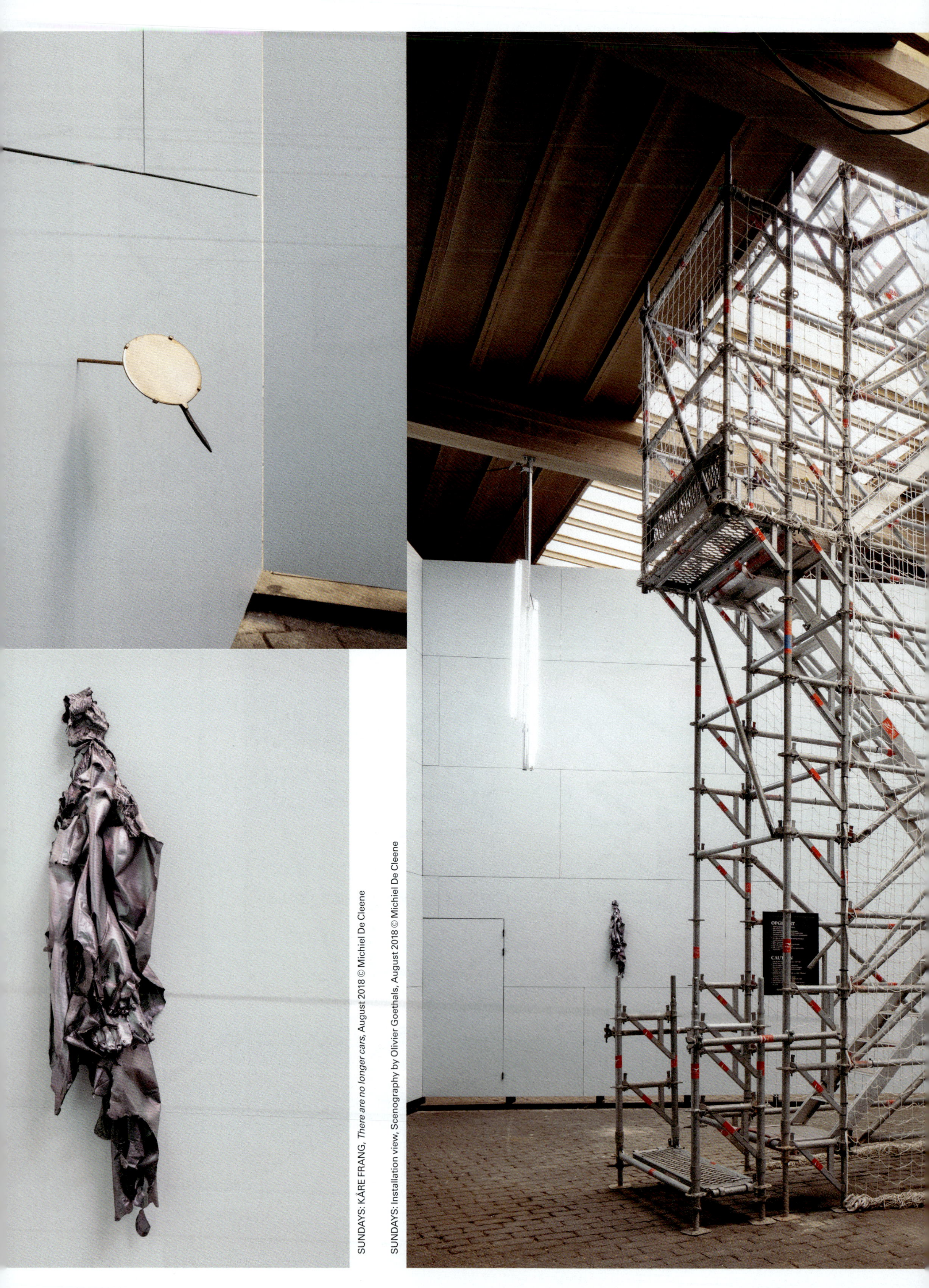

SUNDAYS: KÅRE FRANG, *There are no longer cars*, August 2018 © Michiel De Cleene

SUNDAYS: Installation view, Scenography by Olivier Goethals, August 2018 © Michiel De Cleene

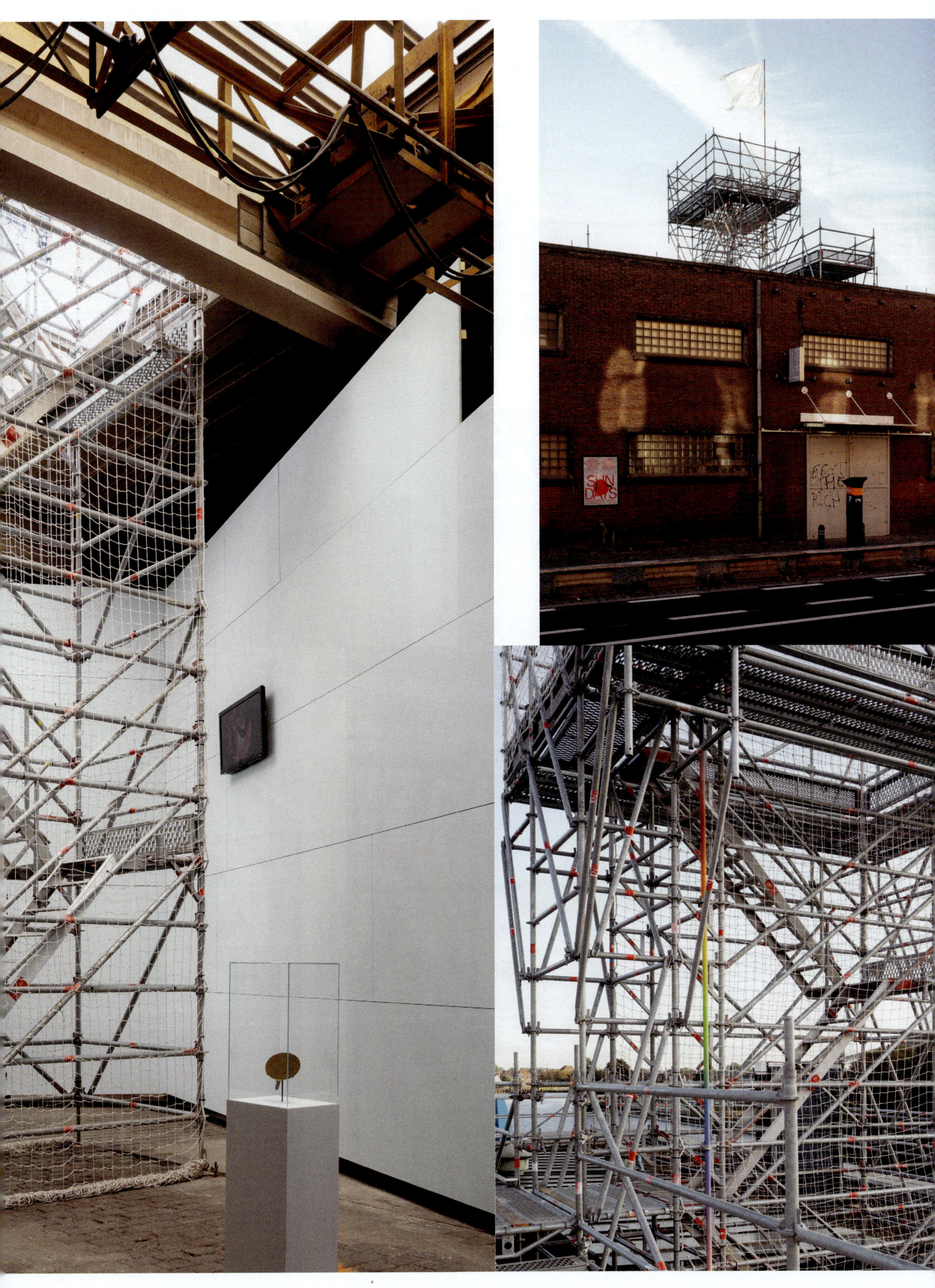

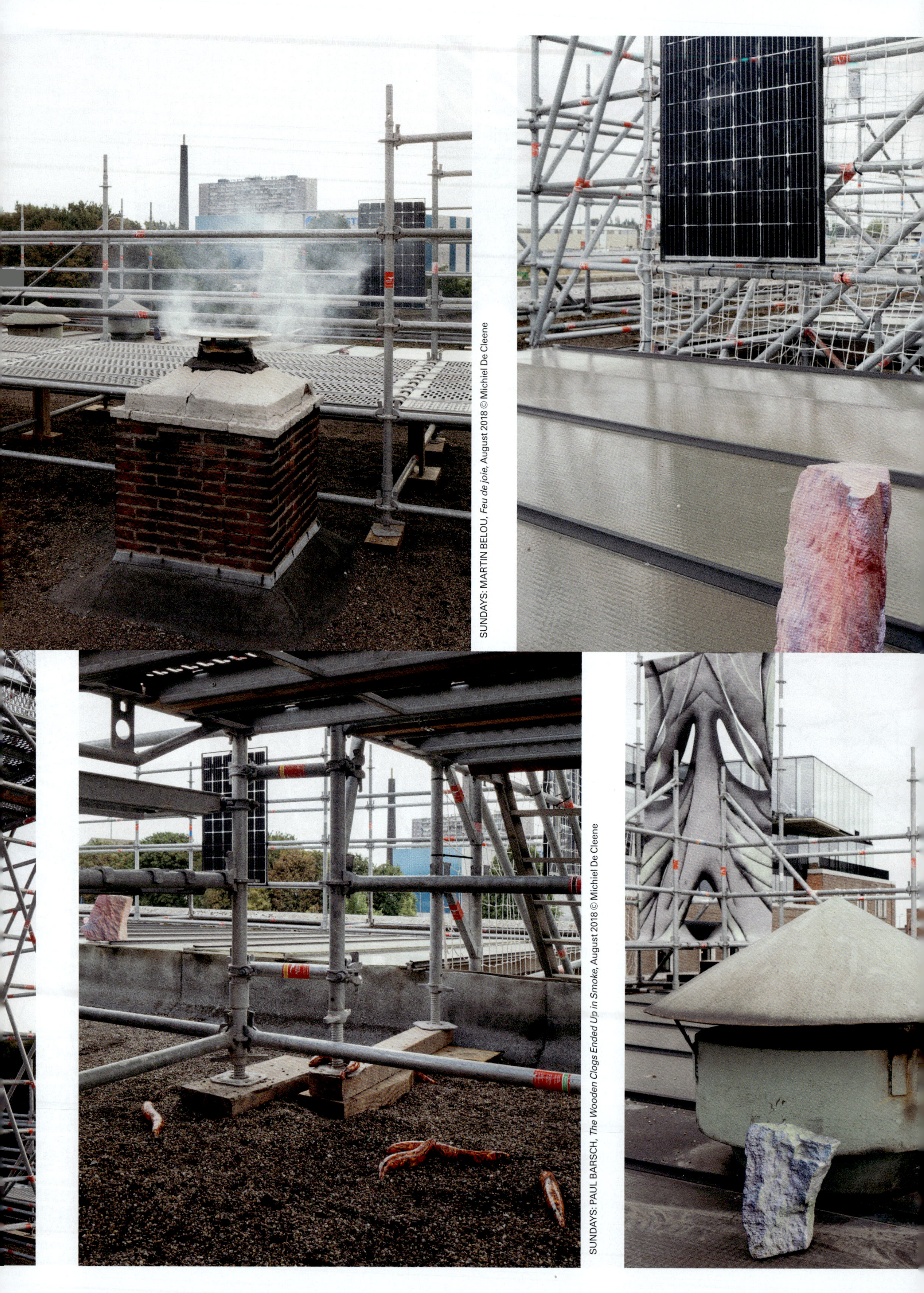

SUNDAYS: MARTIN BELOU, *Feu de joie*, August 2018 © Michiel De Cleene

SUNDAYS: PAUL BARSCH, *The Wooden Clogs Ended Up in Smoke*, August 2018 © Michiel De Cleene

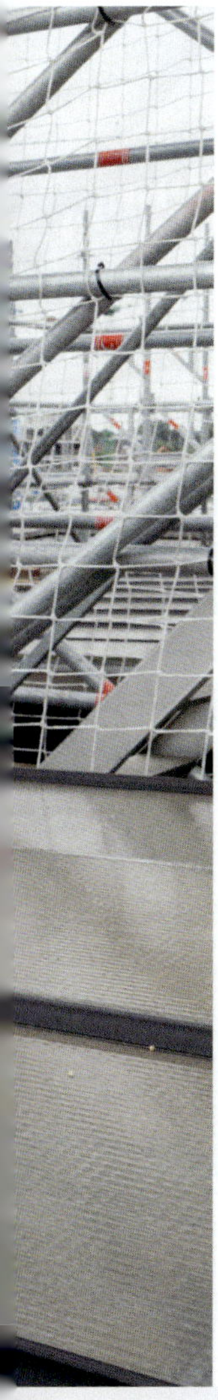

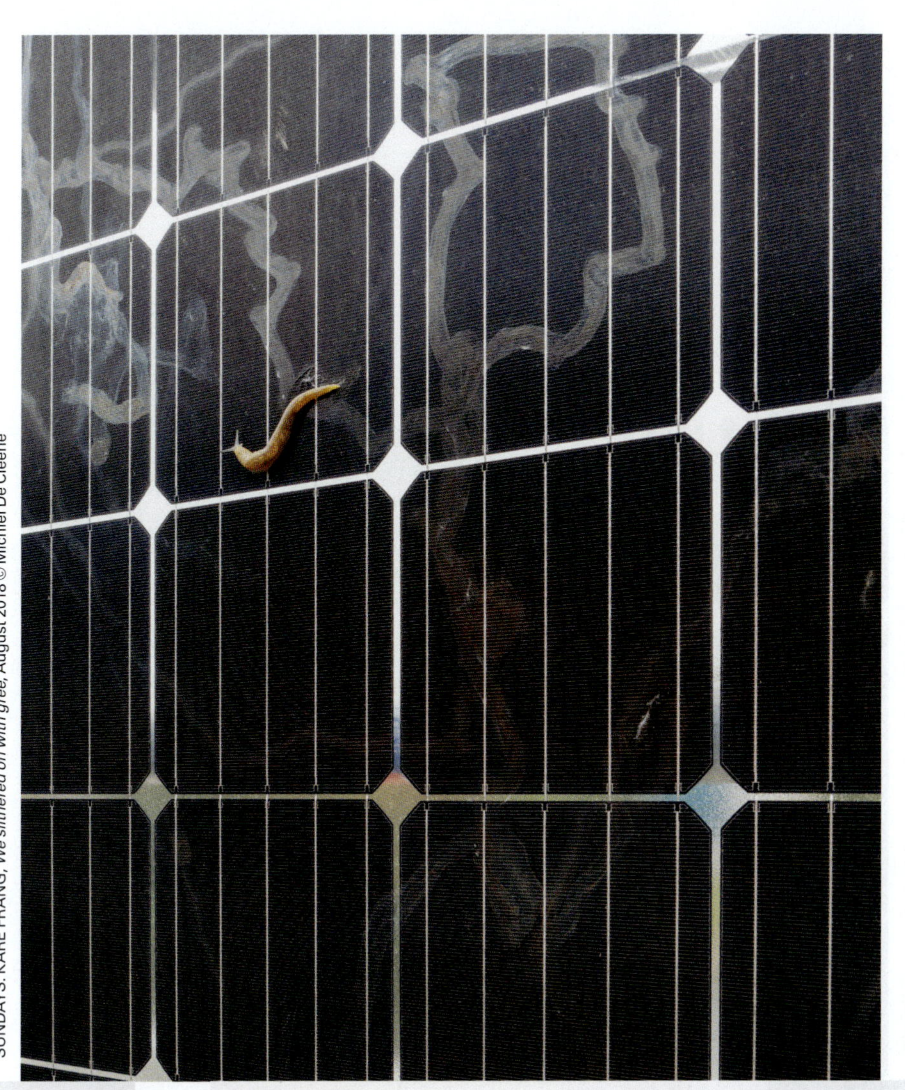

SUNDAYS: SANTIAGO TACCETTI, *Non-Smokers*, August 2018 © Michiel De Cleene
SUNDAYS: KÅRE FRANG, *We slithered on with gree*, August 2018 © Michiel De Cleene

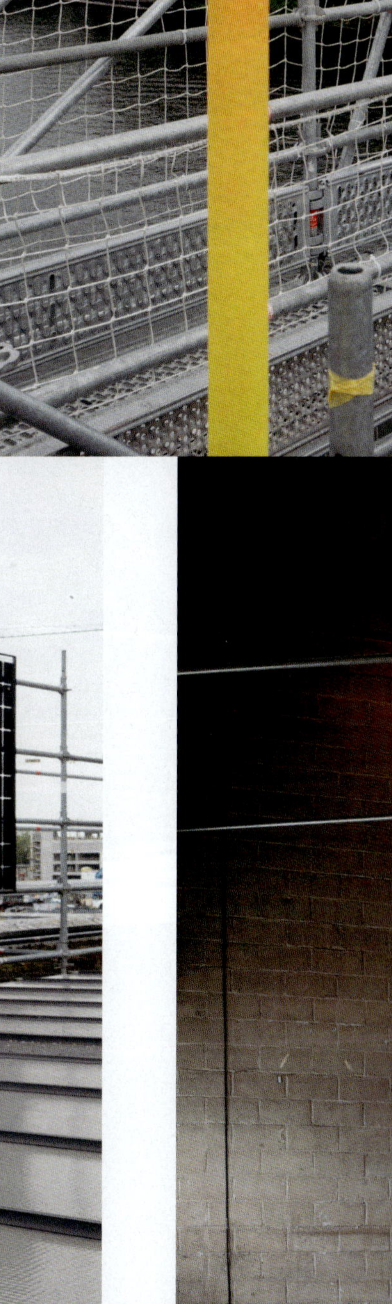

SUNDAYS: OLIVIER GOETHALS, *Visible Phantom*, August 2018 © Michiel De Cleene

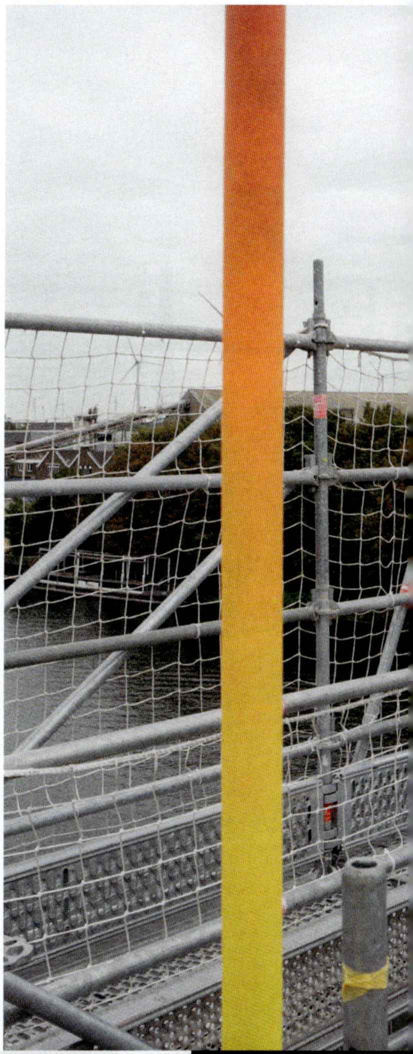

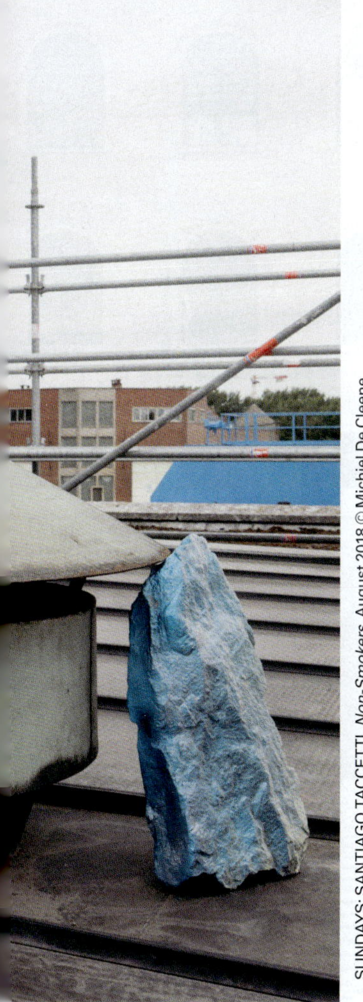

SUNDAYS: SANTIAGO TACCETTI, *Non-Smokers*, August 2018 © Michiel De Cleene

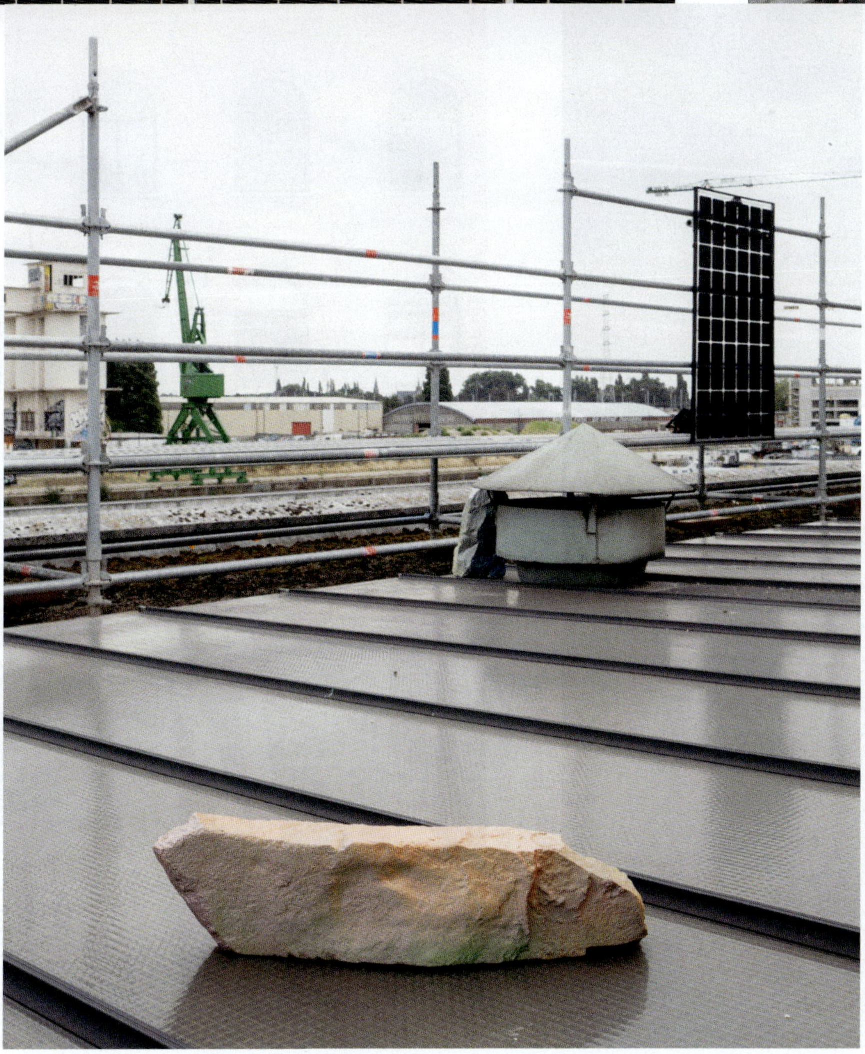

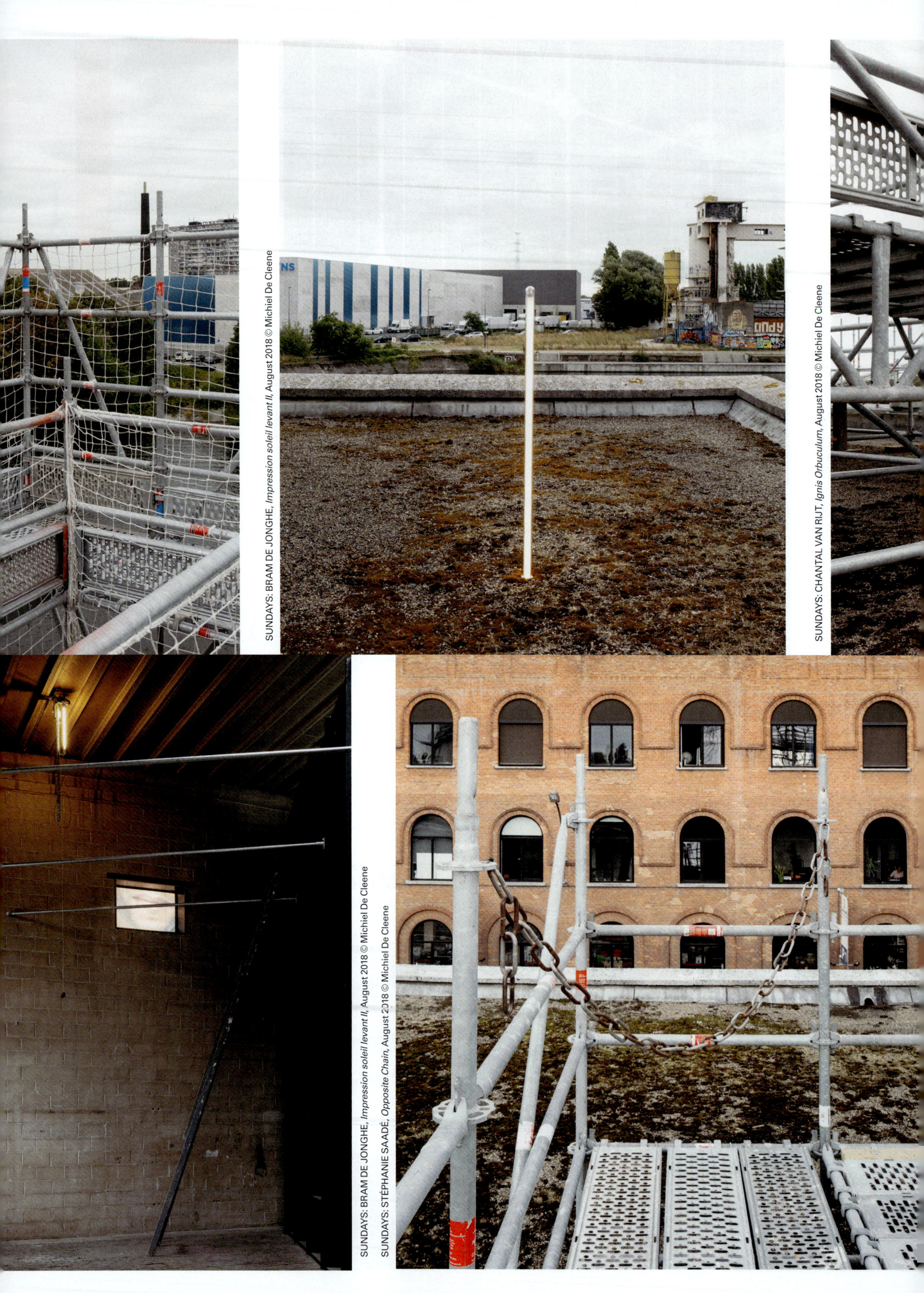

SUNDAYS: BRAM DE JONGHE, *Impression soleil levant II*, August 2018 © Michiel De Cleene

SUNDAYS: CHANTAL VAN RIJT, *Ignis Orbuculum*, August 2018 © Michiel De Cleene

SUNDAYS: BRAM DE JONGHE, *Impression soleil levant II*, August 2018 © Michiel De Cleene

SUNDAYS: STÉPHANIE SAADÉ, *Opposite Chain*, August 2018 © Michiel De Cleene

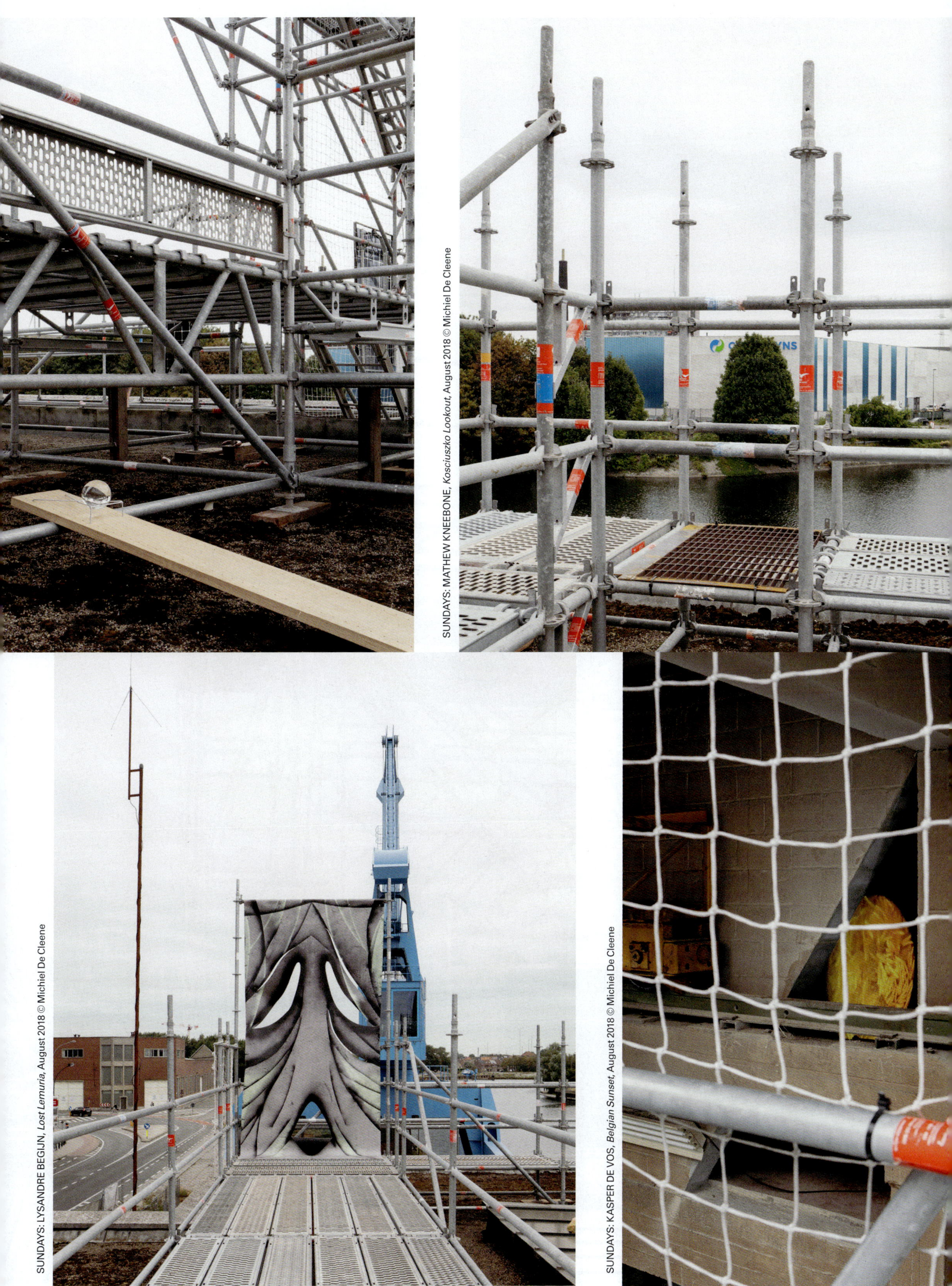

SUNDAYS: MATHEW KNEEBONE, *Kosciuszko Lookout*, August 2018 © Michiel De Cleene

SUNDAYS: LYSANDRE BEGIJN, *Lost Lemuria*, August 2018 © Michiel De Cleene

SUNDAYS: KASPER DE VOS, *Belgian Sunset*, August 2018 © Michiel De Cleene

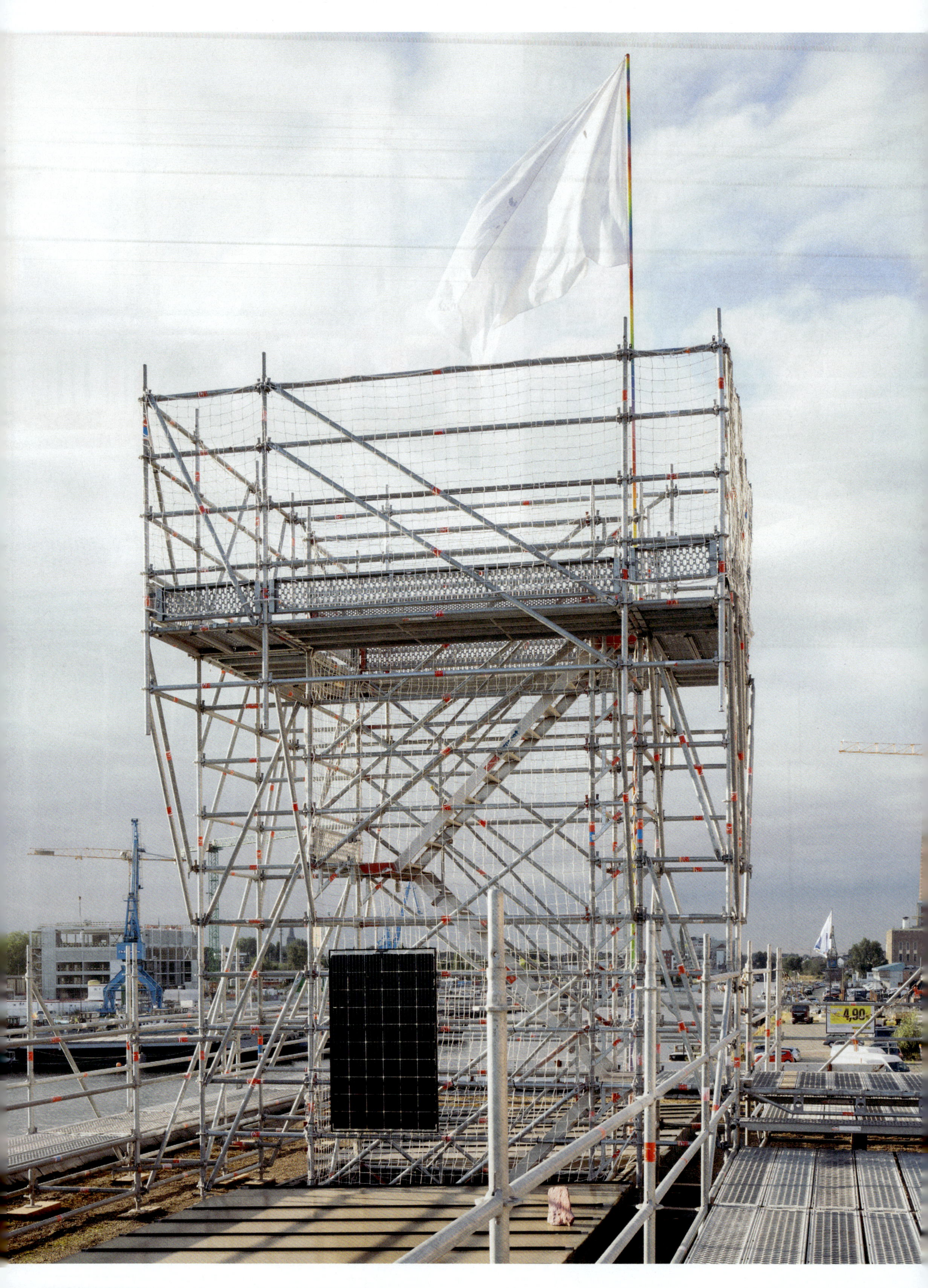
4,90

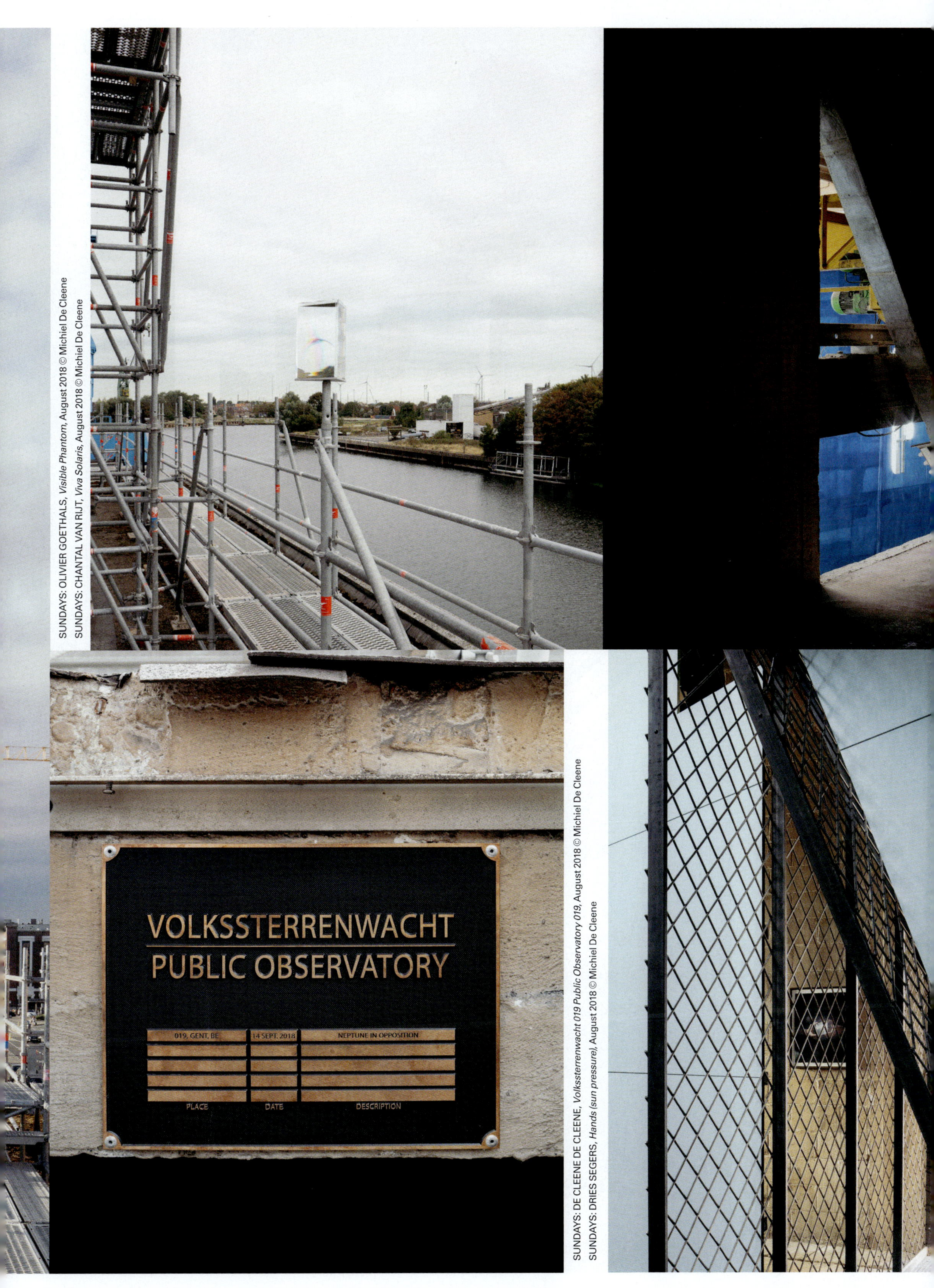

SUNDAYS: OLIVIER GOETHALS, *Visible Phantom*, August 2018 © Michiel De Cleene
SUNDAYS: CHANTAL VAN RIJT, *Viva Solaris*, August 2018 © Michiel De Cleene

SUNDAYS: DE CLEENE DE CLEENE, *Volkssterrenwacht 019 Public Observatory 019*, August 2018 © Michiel De Cleene
SUNDAYS: DRIES SEGERS, *Hands (sun pressure)*, August 2018 © Michiel De Cleene

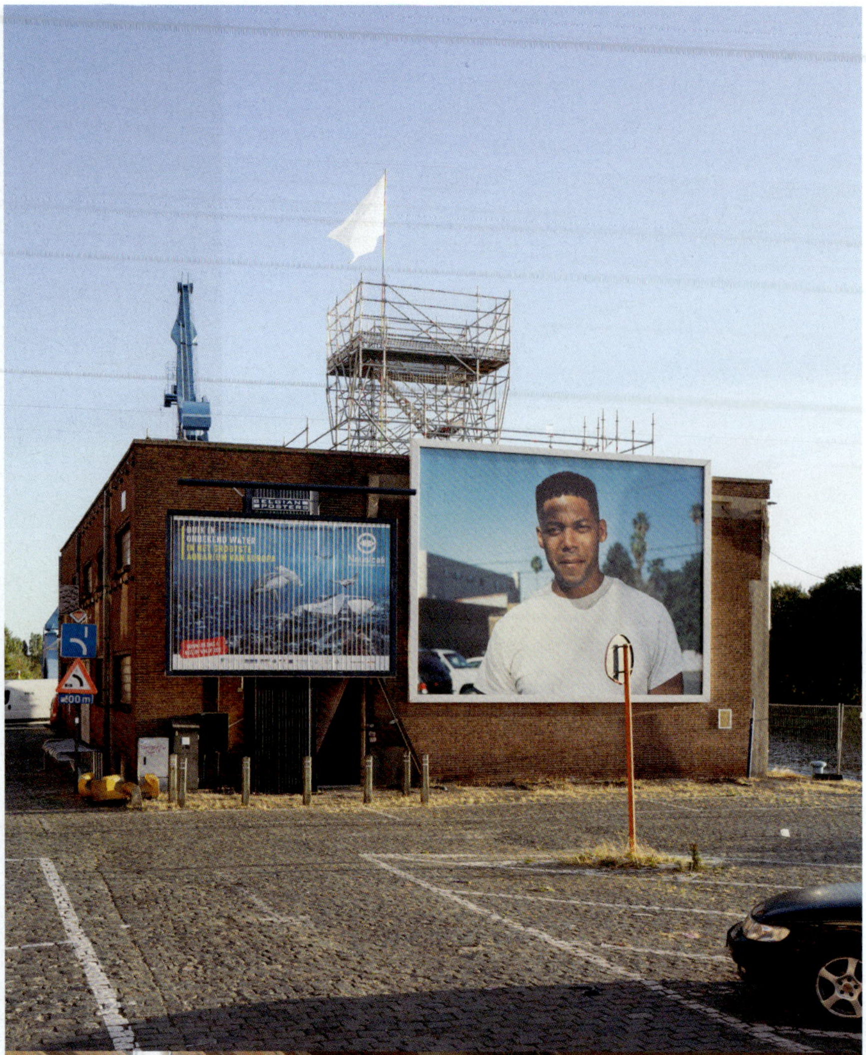

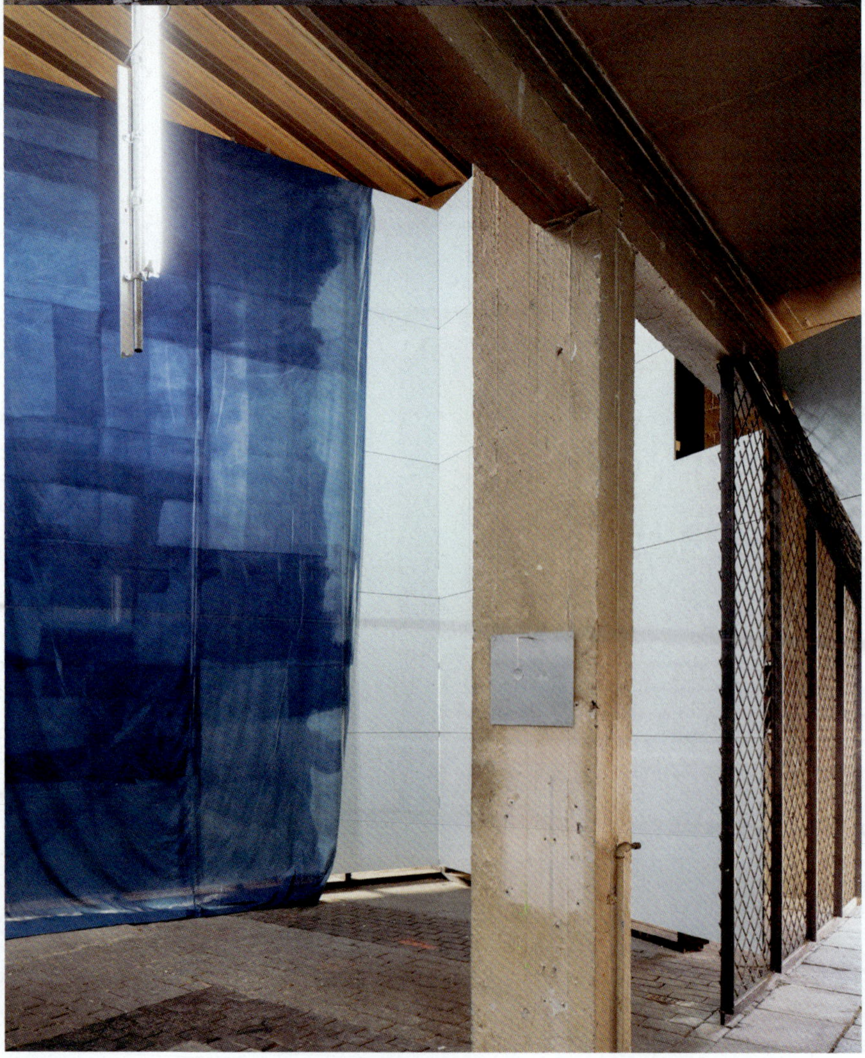

SUNDAYS: DRIES SEGERS, *143 folds*, July 2018 © Michiel De Cleene
CHANTAL VAN RIJT, *Camera Illuminati*, August 2018 © Michiel De Cleene

SUNDAYS: OLIVIER GOETHALS, *Visible Phantom*, August 2018 © Michiel De Cleene
MAX PINCKERS, *Performance #4 (Los Angeles)*, Billboard Series#12, in collaboration with *artlead.net* & *All Things Contemporary*

SUNDAYS: STÉPHANIE SAADÉ, *Faux-Jumeaux*, August 2018 © Michiel De Cleene

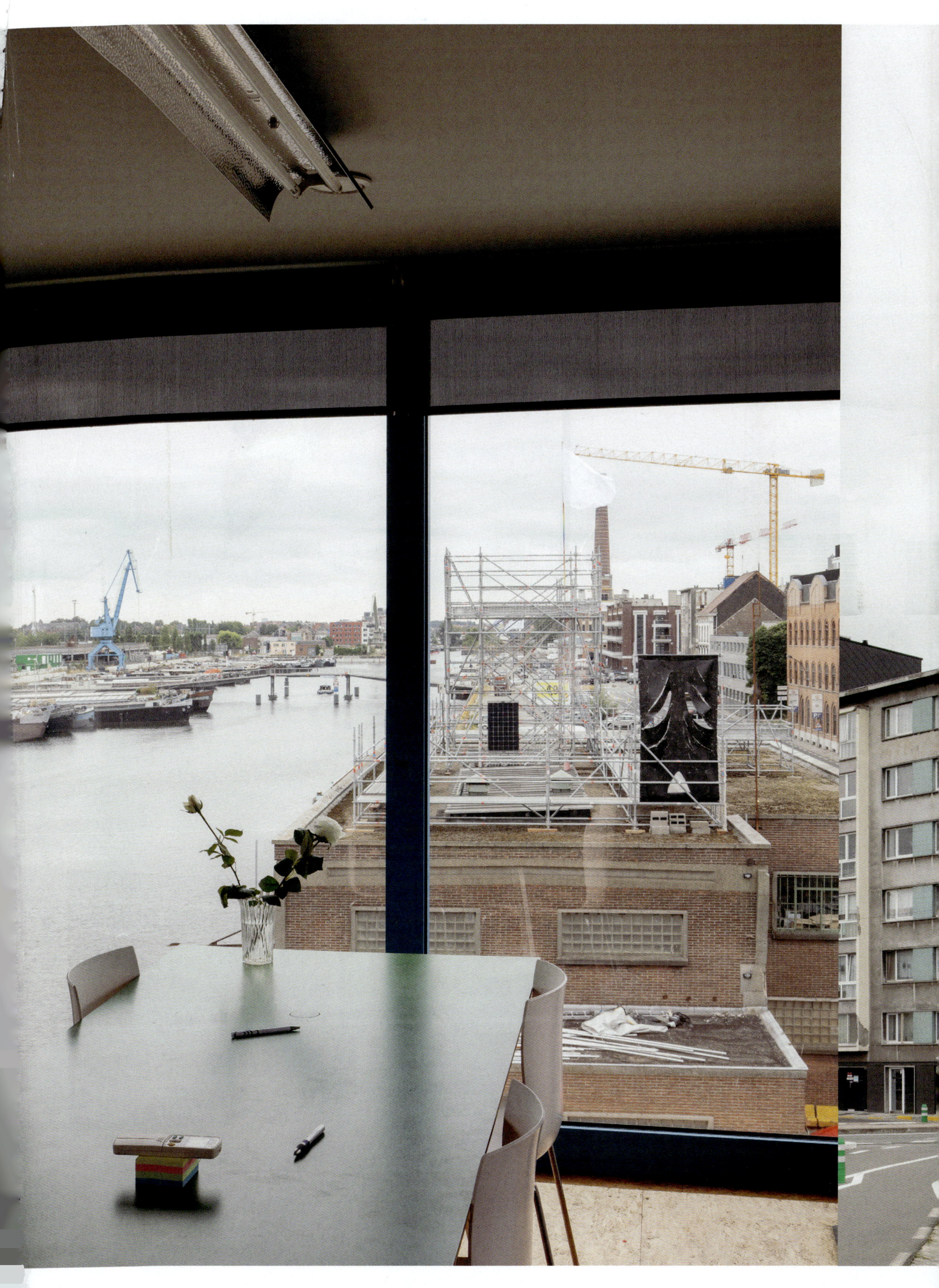

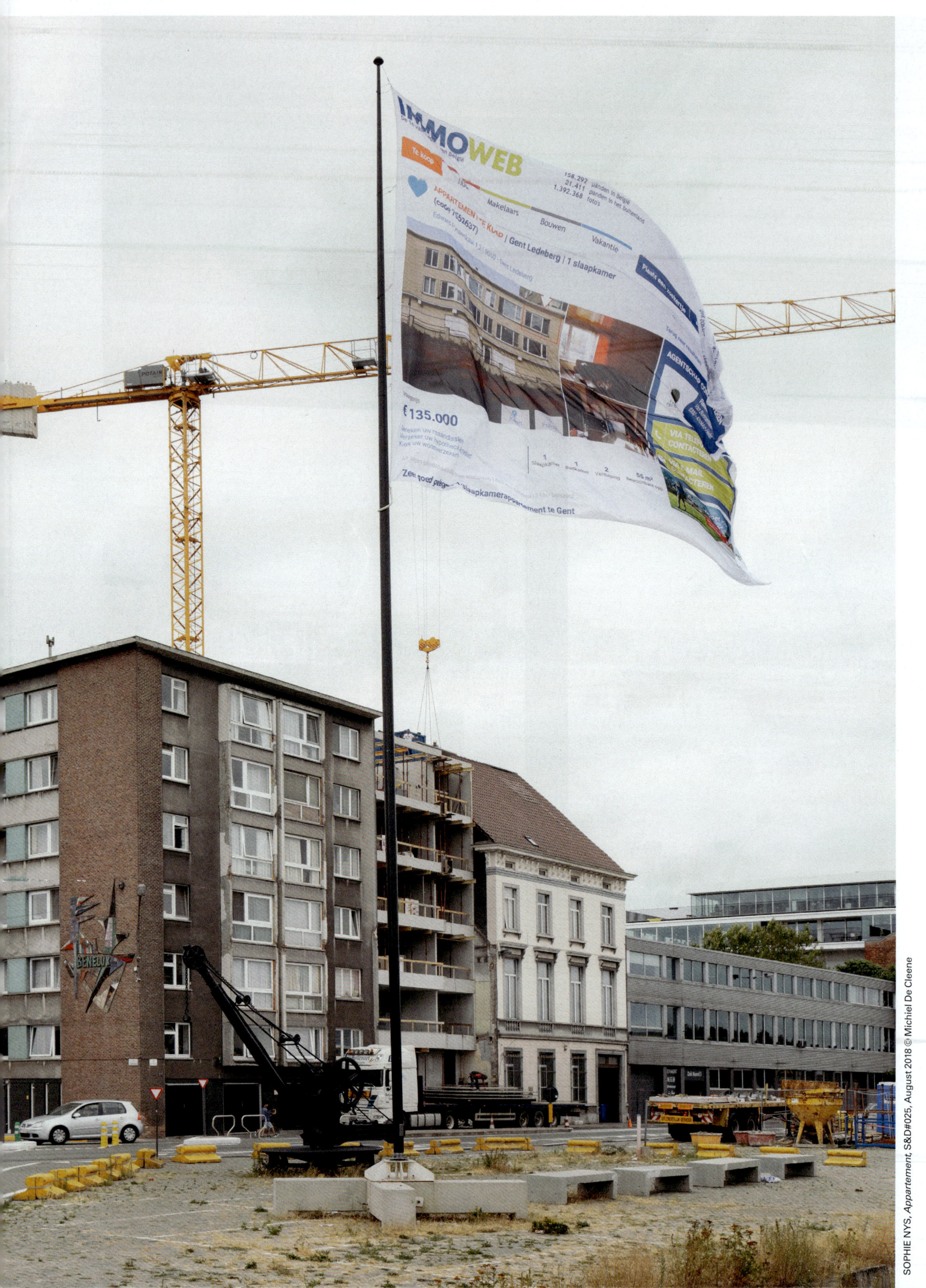

SOPHIE NYS, *Appartement*, S&D#025, August 2018 © Michiel De Cleene